ON THE ALTAR

Published by Princeton University Press
41 William Street, Princeton, New Jersey 08540
99 Banbury Road, Oxford OX2 6JX

press.princeton.edu

GPSR Authorized Representative: Easy Access System Europe - Mustamäe tee 50, 10621 Tallinn, Estonia, gpsr.requests@easproject.com

ISBN 978-0-691-19088-4
ISBN (e-book) 978-0-691-27953-4

British Library Cataloging-in-Publication Data is available

Editorial: Fred Appel and Tara Dugan
Production Editorial: Karen Carter
Jacket/Cover Design: Chris Ferrante
Production: Erin Suydam
Publicity: Maria Whelan and Charlotte Coyne
Copyeditor: Karen Verde

Jacket/Cover Credit: Courtesy of The Metropolitan Museum of Art

This book has been composed in Miller

Printed in the United States of America

10 9 8 7 6 5 4 3 2 1

On the Altar

A HISTORY OF SACRIFICE FROM THE SACRED TO THE SECULAR

Jonathan Sheehan

PRINCETON UNIVERSITY PRESS
PRINCETON & OXFORD

CONTENTS

ILLUSTRATIONS

Color versions of the following figures appear after page 300: Figures 3.1, 3.2, 3.3, 3.4, 3.7, 5.7, 8.1, 11.1.

ON THE ALTAR

INTRODUCTION

Christianity and the Secular Imagination

TOWARD A HISTORY OF SACRIFICE

Complacencies of the peignoir, and late
Coffee and oranges in a sunny chair,
And the green freedom of a cockatoo
Upon a rug mingle to dissipate
The holy hush of ancient sacrifice.
She dreams a little, and she feels the dark
Encroachment of that old catastrophe,
As a calm darkens among water-lights. . . .
The day is like wide water, without sound,
Stilled for the passing of her dreaming feet
Over the seas, to silent Palestine,
Dominion of the blood and sepulchre.

—WALLACE STEVENS, "SUNDAY MORNING" (1915)[1]

IN HER CHAIR she lies, satisfied with sunlight, coffee, and a cockatoo. But more older satisfactions haunt her Sunday dreaming too. Dark offerings prowl around the gentle call of the flesh. The holy hush of ancient sacrifice disturbs drowsy thoughts, which pass "over the seas, to the silent Palestine, dominion of the blood and sepulcher." These dreams are *her* dreams, her sleeping mind swells with ancient blood and death. And yet the dreams—like all dreams—are not hers to master. "What is divinity if it can come only in silent shadow and dream?," Wallace Stevens's 1915 poem asked. One answer surely must be that divinity has *always* also come in silent shadow and dream.

For those of us who live in the long shadow of Latin Christianity, there are no sacrifices untouched by its dreamworld. The death of a God for the salvation of mankind, the redemption from sin, the ransom paid to satisfy God's wrath, the blood He shed to offer the possibility of life: the cross of Christ's atonement accompanies how we think about sacrifice the way that we do. It is an imaginary cross, one that is dreamed anew in every era, entangled in new ways of life, new priorities, new commitments. But if imaginary, it is real enough for thought, real enough to shape the world we live in now and the stories we tell about it.

We are not the first so affected. Sacrifice has always haunted the dreams of those who have lived after. The sacrifice to end all sacrifice, the Christians called their Messiah, the final death that abolished the temple sacrifices of Judaism and paganism. The Lamb of God closed the chapter on the rites of primitive man, or so was the hope, preparing the way for a new gospel of universal salvation. And yet, sacrifice lived its afterlives. The lavish rites of the Hebrew Bible, in tabernacles, temples, and on high places, for sin, trespass, guilt, and thanksgiving; the wild offerings of the ancient Greeks and Romans, the temples of the pagan world ringing with the bleats of dying animals: these sacrifices never really disappeared. They too lived their own afterlives in a dreamworld, haunting Christianity's own intimate Sunday mornings.

This is a book about these afterlives, past and present, sacrifices ancient, Christian, and modern.

It is, above all, a work of history. But a *history* of sacrifice confronts an immediate concern. From where we stand now, steeped in modern ways of knowing, sacrifice seems properly the subject of anthropology, not history. It is one of those apparent constants of human experience—like sex, family, and death—whose nature transcends the vagaries of history. Virtually, or perhaps every human culture has practiced or practices some kind of sacrifice. Jewish temple offerings and circumcision rites, Greek libations, practices of self-mortification and asceticism, Roman military rites of devotion, Carthaginian infant-sacrifice, Vedic burnt offerings, the vegetable offerings of the ancient Pythagoreans, mysterious corpses dropped into northern European bogs, the children killed, wrapped, and deposited in ceremonial shrines across the Inca Empire, the feasts of Muslim *Eid al-Adha*, the human sacrifices of medieval Tibetan Buddhists, the

Christian Eucharist: the variety of actions compassed by the idea of sacrifice is nearly infinite.

No less various are the things offered. Prayers, smoke, wine, bread, salt, flowers, beans, onions, garlic, birds, sheep, pigs, goats, cows, and human beings are just a few of the examples preserved in sacred and other records. Some sacrifices are simple, no more than an offering laid in a special place. Others are among the most complex ritual actions known. The New Year's sacrifices of the precolonial Hawaiians stretched over three months, for example, and involved offerings to the Pleiades, the breaking of ritual coconuts, the feeding of the moon, procession of the god Makahiki across the islands, feasts, drunken revelries, pig sacrifices, and more.[2] Sacrifice has created social hierarchies, elevating the priests dedicated to serving the gods above the common rabble. It has organized political and military imaginaries, whether in hecatombs offered to the gods, or the giving of the self essential to cultures of valor. It has structured economies, animals circulated from fields to temples to markets, farmers and priests and merchants all trafficking in sacrificial flesh. It has organized where people live, human geography organized around special places of sacrifice: altars, temples, shrines, and holy places of all sorts. Indeed, whole cities—ancient Jerusalem or Tenochtitlan in the Aztec Empire, to name two—were designed around performances of sacrifice, and whole cultures were built to sustain them.

Nor have many other human activities attracted so much attention from anthropologists. Already in the nineteenth century, at the very beginnings of the discipline, people sought to explain the universal human desire to offer worldly things to the gods. Sacrifice entails "the whole field of sacred ritual," wrote William Robertson Smith in 1886, "an action within the sphere of things sacred to the gods."[3] Since then, scientific theories of sacrifice have grown thick on the ground. For some, sacrifice is a means of communication with the gods; for others, a way to solemnize human fraternity. For some, the most important aspect of sacrifice is the killing, for others, it is the eating afterward. For some, sacrifice is a way to restrain human violence, for others, a way to assuage human guilt. For all, sacrifice opens a window into the durable structures of human religion, politics, society, and culture. Writing a *history* of sacrifice may thus seem to miss what is essential, exploring superficial change rather than deep continuity.

There are unusual aspects of sacrifice, however, that invite an historian's curiosity. It is not quite clear, for example, why such diverse activities have fallen under one conceptual umbrella. Ancient cultures had a rich vocabulary that *distinguished* among these practices, after all. In classical Greece, this included *thusia* (things burned for the Olympian gods), *sphagia* (things offered to the infernal gods), *aparchai* (offerings of first fruits), *spondai* (pouring out of libations), and *askesis* (giving something up). The Hebrew Bible included words like *korban* (draw near), *olah* (burnt offering), *zebah* (slain offering), and *minha* (gift), and distinguished sharply between their various purposes: burnt offerings, cereal offerings, peace offerings, sin offerings, and votive offerings, as a standard translation has it.[4] The mass interment of live sheep in the Egyptian temple of Tebtunis, the mummification of dogs in veneration of Osiris, the apotropaic burning of donkeys in Thebes: does the concept of sacrifice have *any* "descriptive utility," one Egyptologist has recently asked, if it is supposed to explain such different things?[5] The historian wonders how and why we came to think that it did.

To the historian, however, there is something even more puzzling about sacrifice. Compare it with sex, that pillar of anthropological inquiry. Virtually everyone has sex, or wants to have sex. Neuroses aside, at the social level, behavior and biology are reasonably well synced. A sexless life is perfectly fine as an idiosyncratic choice—ascetics of various sorts have been around forever—but a sexless society is a short-lived oxymoron. And because of this, every society also has a culture of sex, various ways of imagining, controlling, and celebrating human sexual relations. Or compare it with kinship. Everyone has a family, like it or not, but every culture also organizes kinship, often in various ways. Roman emperors expanded kinship through adoption, medieval Christians counted godparents as kin, some Native Americans treated animal as kin, and so on.[6] No human society has *no* conventions of kinship, however, no conventions for which people are counted as kin and which are not. Anthropology traffics in constants like these.

It is hard to say the same thing about sacrifice. In the so-called Abrahamic traditions, the scholar Guy Stroumsa has observed, sacrifice *ended* in the late antique world. Sometime between the fall of the Second Temple in 70 CE and the rise of Islam in the seventh century, blood gave way to *text* as the heart of religious life.[7] For those who have inherited this history, sacrifice is not something that we do anymore, except perhaps in some metaphorical way. Few in the so-called West leave gifts to the gods, burn victims in hopes that the scent might please the gods, bring fruits, vegetables, animals, or people to the altar. "First fruits" does not mean much, and the "sacrifice of praise" of the Psalms rings oddly in the ear. We don't burden goats with our collective guilt and send them from our cities.

In some sense, then, sacrifice is *only* historical for us. It is something that used to happen. If it happens still, it happens elsewhere, among other people who have not yet left it behind.

Yet there is more to it than that. To all appearances, modern Western society is not just unsacrificial. It is actively *anti*-sacrificial. We are encouraged to take, not to give. Maximize your profit, not your pain, economic rationality commands. Altruism is not an ideal, but a problem to be solved. The so-called selfish gene—popularized by the biologist and "new atheist" Richard Dawkins—explains why we only appear to sacrifice for others. An ethics of renunciation struggles to be heard in a culture where self-interest is the highest good. Politics is the realm of competing interests and factions, not a world of self-denial. The exception that proves the rule is the military: a culture of sacrifice that we acknowledge with the feeble gratitude of "thank you for your service."

So there are puzzles here. If sacrifice is as foundational to the deep structure of human experience as sex or kinship, then we must be doing it too. But it does not seem that we are. Perhaps we live in a post-anthropological age now. Or perhaps we just *think* that we've left sacrifice behind, but in reality it is present in some hidden fashion. Or perhaps we're just asking the question in the wrong way (my suspicion). But no matter what, something has changed. Here then we are on the terrain of the historian, who asks: what is peculiar about the history of sacrifice in the West?

The answer is, in a word, Christianity. And not just Christianity in the abstract, but the specific *history* of Christianity in the Latin lands from the later Middle Ages to the present.

Christianity has never quite known what to do with sacrifice. In the New Testament, for example, the Gospels barely mention sacrifice. Matthew uses the Greek word for sacrifice twice, both times to reject it: "I desire mercy, and not sacrifice," Christ says, quoting the prophet Hosea (Matt. 9.13; Hos. 6.6). The Gospel of John describes the Passion in moving detail, but mentions sacrifice not once. Later New Testament writings were more open to things sacrificial. The apostle Paul—and especially the author of *Hebrews*, long presumed to be Paul—connected the death of Christ to older temple sacrifices, both pagan and Jewish. Even this connection was a complicated one, though. Christ was the *last* sacrifice, Paul insisted, and the only real one. The bulls and sheep of the temple were mere "shadows" of the true sacrifice on the Cross. The death of Christ thus both ended, the story goes, and *perfected* a prior world of Jewish and pagan sacrifice.

From early on then, we might say, Christianity both abolished and absorbed sacrifice. It abandoned the sacrifices of its rivals, the "new" covenant superseding the old. In that sense, sacrifice represented a past that Christianity left behind. But sacrifice was also alive *inside* the Christian imagination. It was alive textually. The fateful decision to retain the Hebrew Bible, what Christians called the Old Testament, as part of Christian scripture meant that the sacrifices of Leviticus were never forgotten. It was, for the same reason, alive liturgically. From early on, the celebration of the death of Christ in the Eucharist was intimately bound to the more ancient sacrifices of Cain, Abel, Abraham, and Isaac. Sacrifice was alive theologically. The doctrine of Christ's atonement—very slow to develop but well established by the Middle Ages—was unimaginable without the "shadows" that prefigured it, that established the Crucifixion as an eternal truth of the world, there in Genesis as in John. And it was alive practically, as ordinary Christians only slowly relinquished the world of gifts and offerings, especially to the martyrs that populated the early centuries of the Church, and to the saints who came later.

Put another way, for Christianity, sacrifice is a name for *history*. Sacrifice is the past that Christianity left behind on its journey to becoming a universal religion. But sacrifice is also the past that makes Christianity what it is, the religion that does not sacrifice, yet continues to do so. The sacrifice of Christ, Sigmund Freud remarked in his 1939 *Moses and Monotheism*, energized the new religion because it recalled an "historical truth": the murder of historical Moses, the true Father-God of ancient Israel, the original crime that monotheism was designed to conceal.[8] We do not have to accept his analytic framework to recognize a deeper truth: "nothing that has once come into existence ever goes away."[9] A history of Christian sacrifice—as we will see—is a history of history itself.

History can feel like home, comforting and familiar. And for long centuries after the Christian conquest of the Roman Empire, and the expansion of Latin Christianity in the West, it did. The peculiar history that sacrifice carried, abandoned yet persisting, worked well for a church that controlled its own story without much fear of contradiction. The growth of an ever-more sacrificial Christianity from the tenth century onward showed just how comfortable Latin Christians had grown with their own past.

History can also feel alien, however, a land of truths you would prefer not to know. The collapse of the medieval Latin Church into competing heirs of the Christian past turned sacrifice—and its history—inside out. "Reformation," as it came to be called, gazed back to go forward, looked to Scripture and the earliest Christians for a new, better Christianity. In so doing, Christian sacrifice became strange again. Not only was the sacrificial church of the later Middle Ages—with its Eucharistic devotion, its dedication to the Man of Sorrows, its sacrificing priesthood, and its cult of saints—discovered (by its opponents) to be a secret preserve of pagan and Jewish sacrificial rites. But even that ancient structure of "abolition+absorption" came under suspicion. Perhaps Christianity *never was* as Christian as all that.

"Autonomy is the sole principle of morals," wrote the German philosopher Immanuel Kant in 1785. To the extent that we can legislate our own inner moral life, we are free. Anytime we seek the moral truths in an outer world—in history or nature or God or society—we are unfree, subjected to the will of another. Then, he remarked, "heteronomy always results."[10] Heteronomy is subordination to forces that we do not control. Autonomy releases us from these, from the world and history.

Adapted for our story, I have found these an historically useful semantics. The Christian doctrine of revelation might well be understood as a claim for autonomy, for example, at least from *human* truths and histories, the "city of God" declaring its independence thereby from the world. We detect a similar bid for autonomy in the Christian notion of "orthodoxy," the "right teaching" that points toward the eternal beyond the mundane, and beyond history. Since the early centuries of Christianity, the drive to orthodoxy sought a self-legislating religion, a once-and-for-all right teaching free of worldly contingency. In the Latin west, the Church became the guardian of this dream of autonomy, Christ's bride on earth, subordinate to heaven alone. The fall away from the eternal, back into the merely human, was given new names: heterodoxy and, especially, heresy.

Orthodoxy was not just a hope, but also a politics. It "worked" as long as the church believed it was legislating its own inner life, as long as it felt confident that it had the power to determine what belonged essentially to Christianity and what did not. In the Latin church, the Reformation ended this power once and for all. It ended it practically, for now there were many who claimed the title of orthodox. And it ended it theoretically, for the new contest over the eternal was waged on the terrain of

Christianity's own history. The Reformation insisted that much of what the Latin church called "Christianity" was no such thing at all, that Christianity had never legislated its own life, that it was as much a creature of history as any other human thing. It revealed, in short, the stubborn fact of Christian heteronomy.

Even before the fracture of Reformation, in fact, the Christian past had begun to seem less familiar. The fourteenth and fifteenth centuries were difficult years for the Roman church, plagued by schisms and competition over authority between Pope and councils. At the same time, learned writers began to pay new attention to the past, the classical revival that eventually encompassed the ancient Christian world as well. By the 1450s, and coinciding with the rise of print, a new Christian antiquity began to emerge, an "archive"—as I will call it—of writings from the first centuries of Christian life. For the first time, the varieties of ancient Christianity became public and visible.

The theological revolutions of the sixteenth century expanded and weaponized this archive. When did the church lose its way? And how can we find a path back to the world we have lost? Reformers tirelessly asked these questions as they groped toward new forms of Christian life and thought. In so doing, they repeatedly demystified the eternal verities of their Catholic opponents as merely time bound, the product of human concerns, not the mandate of heaven.

They also suggested another possibility, however, one whose likelihood grew as the prospects of Christian unity receded: perhaps Christianity has *never* been unshackled from the world. The early church seemed to promise a Christianity pure and homogeneous, a model for Christian life. But as reformers quickly discovered, no church was more variable than the ancient one, no church more indebted to the religious and intellectual environments where it thrived. The story of Christianity is not one of autonomy—they discovered—but heteronomy, past and present.

Sacrifice lay at the heart of this uncomfortable thought. And no wonder, since it had marked the controversial frontier between Christianity and its religious opponents since the earliest days of the church. Can we eat the meat from the temple sacrifices? Should we conform to the state's demand to participate in a public cult? Can we build altars to the martyrs and worship there? Can we use bread and wine—traditional elements in Roman sacrifices—in our Eucharistic rites? Is the Hebrew Bible and its complex sacrificial law part of the Christian canon? Different communities had different answers at different times.

By the fifth century, most of these issues were settled, if not by agreement then by political fiat. The ancient controversies were suppressed, and sacrifice normalized in the Christian imagination. By the dawn of the Reformation, sacrifice supported three pillars of the Latin Christian church: the Eucharist with its sacrificing priesthood; the cult of the martyrs and saints; and the Atonement, the belief that Christ's crucifixion was a sacrifice for the sins of mankind. Liturgy, politics, and doctrine, to put it schematically.

Each had a separate history. The cult of the martyrs was the most continuous, dating to the first centuries of Christianity and growing over time to sustain a broader medieval culture of sainthood. The eucharistic devotions of the later Middle Ages had a more recent provenance, though eucharistic piety—typically if not always accompanied by some aspects of sacrifice—is already present in the earliest liturgical documents of the church. A specific doctrine of the Atonement was almost entirely new from the eleventh century, though again, we find traces of Christ's saving sacrifice already in the New Testament. Three different and overlapping histories of sacrifice, each with different roots in the early church.

Each of these would have to be rewritten, in the minds of reformers, so that we might create a new, less earthly faith. This was no easy business, however. It was simple enough to reject the Catholic cult of images, to destroy the icons of impious worship, as so many people did in the early years of the Reformation. Sacrifice was different. It was delicately threaded through Christianity, always both central to the faith and potentially alien to it as well. Iconoclasm was too crude for sacrifice. What was required instead was a new kind of theology, one attuned to the past and capable of sorting the Christian archive for piety and profanity alike.

Sacrifice was thus the catalyst for new, mostly Protestant theologies, new methods of assessing and establishing Christian claims that advanced new kinds of evidence for Christian truths. These theologies were experimental. They combined reflections on expected doctrinal matters—the nature of God, Christ, salvation, and so on—with historical materials drawn from a rapidly growing Christian archive. At first, the church fathers were most important, but later pagan and Jewish writers were consulted. Antiquarianism, histories, chronologies, law codes, anthropologies: from the mid-sixteenth century onward, all were recruited to the cause. Theology itself became an ever-more syncretic intellectual project, bulging with claims about the nature and history of sacrifice, the origins and varieties of religious worship, the forms of ancient religion, the history of law, the nature of politics, the history of mankind, and more.

In the seventeenth century, this syncretic project began to fall apart. Or better put, the original purpose that it served—the management of doctrinal, liturgical, and ecclesiastical disputes between Protestants and Catholics—began to lose its relevance. How and why this happened will be taken up in later parts of the book. But the consequence was the emergence of a new sacrificial imagination, an imagination turned *ad saeculum*, energized not by Christian doctrinal disputes, but by human history, anthropology, law, and politics.

Imagination is a key word in this book. Broader than doctrines or theories or ideologies, I use it to indicate the ideational furnishings that create and make sense of the world around us. It is both the deep background that lends a tacit sense of fitness to things, as well as the common fund of arguments used to make such commitments explicit. It compasses both the carefully reasoned propositions found in the works of philosophers and theologians, and the stories and images that circulate in poetry, literature, painting, and the other arts. It lives in language, but is no less embodied in practical actions, rituals, architecture, clothing, and so on. It is a collective idiom for orienting ourselves in the world, in short, cohesive without necessarily being coherent, a "common repertory," in the words of Charles Taylor.[11]

Most importantly, to me, the imagination is a way of making. "This world of nations has been made by men," wrote the Neapolitan philosopher Giambattista Vico in 1744, forged from "the modifications of the mind."[12] These worlds are products of what he called "imaginative metaphysics," and we make them, even as they make us. Man "makes the things out of himself, and becomes them by transforming himself into them."[13] The imagination is not just a passive storehouse, but an active agent that creates and constrains the horizons of the possible.

As such, it is a distinctively *human* way of making. For limited mortals like us, for better and worse, *ex nihilo nihil fit*, nothing comes from nothing. "Worldmaking . . . always starts with worlds already on hand," the philosopher Nelson Goodman tells us, "the making is a remaking."[14] To put it another way, nothing is ever only itself. Rather, we create our imaginative worlds from the new things we discover, and from the jumbled inheritances stored in our collective culture.

Whatever else it is, Christianity is a stupendous way of making, a 1,500-year-old experiment in what Vico called "poetic wisdom."[15] Sacrifice has always been at the heart of this. It was essential to Christian doctrine, to the teaching that God became man and died for our sins, Christ crucified the *salvator mundi*. But it inspired far more than dogma. Relics from ancient martyrs flowed through the Latin church, required by canon law for all consecrations. Veneration of these relics was among the most popular forms of Christian devotion, connecting modern worshippers with the sacrificial dead. Every Mass was accompanied by a "litany" in remembrance of these special dead, and the feast days that organized the calendar celebrated their "birthdays" into heaven. Ancient mosaics from Ravenna already populated churches with the sacrifices of the priest-king, Melchizedek, Cain and Abel, and Abraham (fig. 0.1). Altars were decorated with similar motifs, a circulating set of images that connected the celebration of the Eucharist with the world of the ancient patriarchs. Sermons and homilies regularly explored the sacrifices of the Hebrew Bible to shed light on the Crucifix. What Christians called typology—that is, the connection of Old and New Testaments through a logic of type/anti-type, shadow/reality, prophecy/fulfillment—meant exegetes could discover the death of Christ already in the early chapters of Genesis, and across the entire corpus of Hebrew scripture. The Christian sacrificial imagination formed hopes for salvation, habits of reading, ways of worship, and the politics of community.

This making was, however, also a remaking. Take the Christian political imagination, for example, whose intimacy with sacrifice dates to the ancient world and extends into the early modern period and beyond. This intimacy was hardly unique to Christianity. "Make sacrifice," cried the doomed Iphigenia to the Greek armies, "and sack Troy! That shall be my long-lived memorial . . . my marriage, my good name!"[16] Ancients had always knit sacrifice into practices of politics, both through the giving of the self, and the giving of another. Warfare was a rich site for this, conquered enemies slain, treaties ratified, cities purified, battles begun, rituals of devotion declared, all accompanied by blood and altars. No less important were the more routinized forms, the public administration of Rome depending on regular civic rituals of sacrifice, its college of priests made into functionaries of empire. So when Christ died on the Cross, King of the Jews, as the inscription often reads, it echoed the ancient intimacies of kingship, priesthood, and sacrifice. No less for the Christian martyrs, who sacrificed themselves that they might *not* sacrifice at Roman altars, the early political imagination of Christianity suffused with twinned images of sacrifice and

FIGURE 0.1. *The Sacrifice of Abel, Melchizedek, and Abraham.* Mosaic, Basilica Sant'Apollinaire in Classe, Ravenna (ca. 533–549 CE). Cameraphoto Arte, Venice / Art Resource, NY.

self-sacrifice. All of these were re-energized in the sixteenth century, when a new and bloody world of Christian martyrs emerged, and reshaped the politics of Europe.

This book follows these makings and remakings of the Christian imagination. It also discovers the makings and remakings of a *secular* imagination of sacrifice, from its early modern roots to our own age. Like Christianity, this too was a motley affair. It incorporated much from the Christian world of its birth, as we will see. But it was no less populated by the sacrifices of ancient Rome, which antiquarians, historians, sculptors, and painters began exploring already in the fifteenth century. Roman law too was drawn into this archive, both the sacrificial laws of the ancient Roman kings and the later compilation known as the *Corpus iuris civilis*. It too developed new ways of reading, typology giving way to history. Those Hebrew sacrifices that had once pointed toward Christ now became evidence of broadly human ways of negotiating with the divine. This was only aided by the encounters in the New World, an empire of sacrifice that assisted new imaginative projects in the broader history and anthropology of religion. A secular political imagination took shape too, efforts to think beyond the politics of Christian martyrdom and holy war. From seventeenth-century treatises on political theory, to the revival of Stoic tragic drama, to Enlightenment conjectural and comparative anthropologies of religion, to the republicanism of the eighteenth-century Age of Revolutions, this secular imagination shaped both horizons of thought and action. We bring this book to a close in a world near to our own, with the human sciences of the nineteenth century, which discovered in sacrifice a key to unlock the riddles of our very human worlds.

I call this latter epoch in the sacrificial imagination "secular" partly as a provocation. Over the past three decades, the very idea of "secular"—meaning colloquially either non-religious or anti-religious—has suffered withering criticism. So too have its various conceptual analogues: *the secular*, denoting roughly a social or political space free of religion; *secularism*, in the nineteenth century, a normative ideology of "free thought," but now typically used to designate forms of political control over religious life; and *secularization*, the social-scientific name for the process by which either societies lose their religion altogether, or religion is demoted into just one value sphere among many.[17] It would be tedious to rehearse all the recent objections (theological, ethical, philosophical, political, historical, postcolonial, anthropological, sociological, to name just some) to this constellation of concepts.[18] But at their collective heart rests a simple observation: the secular is simply not as secular as all that.

Empirically, for example, it is undeniable that religious commitments persist even in an ostensibly secular age.[19] More significantly, critics argue that the very notion of the secular has a religious provenance. Already in the 1950s, there were spirited debates about whether vaunted secular ideals like progress and history were not in fact *sub-rosa* versions of earlier theological descriptions of the world.[20] Recent work has continued in this vein, seeking to demonstrate the genealogical dependence of the secular on a Christian past. Thus, for example, the separation of church and state, it is argued, was the product of a specifically Protestant milieu.[21] As such, it should not be surprising that Protestantism should thrive reasonably well under its terms, while other, differently organized religions (e.g., Catholicism, Judaism, Islam) find it much more difficult. The organization of secular disciplines, and more specifically the academic study of religion, suffers similar criticism, that it reflects specifically Christian ways of describing religious belief, religious practice, the church, orthodoxy, and so on.[22] State sovereignty, rule of law, toleration, religious freedom, women's equality: these are just a few of the supposedly universal secular values indebted, it is argued, to Christian history and power.[23] Some go so far as to argue that secularism *is* Christianity, full stop.[24]

I am partly sympathetic to these views. Even if the "green freedom of a cockatoo" dissipates the holy hush of sacrifice, in Wallace Stevens's terms, Christianity still doubtless lives on in the imagination of the modern.

This book wants to show *how* it lives on, however. It offers less a critique of the secular, than a history of Christianity and its secular afterlives. And this history indeed shows that the secular is heteronomous, that our age depends on previous ones, that the concerns, commitments, and conflicts of Christianity profoundly shape the modern imagination. This surely deflates the ideological hope that we might be (thank heaven!) finally over and done with Christianity.

But what is this "Christianity" that we might be done with? Theorists of the secular often assume that, once upon a time, there *was* an autonomous Christian realm with a consistent worldview supplied by a theology of its own making. In his 1985 *Disenchantment of the World*, for example, the political philosopher Marcel Gauchet discovered the "decisive originality of Christianity" in its "dogma of the Incarnation." This theological innovation inaugurated an "irretrievable split" between terrestrial and divine, from which the secular world emerged. Christianity was "a religion for departing from religion," he memorably wrote, and the secular a child of Christian metaphysics.[25]

This is simply to take Christianity at its own word, however, to assume that there is or was a decisive metaphysics that defines the Christian. But why should we assume this? If history teaches us anything, after all, it is that the most allegedly foundational Christian views have been subject to violent dispute even (especially) *among the theologians*. Almost nothing has vexed theologians more, for example, than that very dogma of the Incarnation! It seems peculiar, to say the least, for historians or philosophers to adjudicate among the varieties of views that have called themselves Christian, as if to speak from the throne of orthodoxy itself.

The view that theology (or Christianity) had a conceptual estate, in other words, that was either partitioned out to, or requisitioned by, ungrateful heirs assumes far too much.[26] It assumes that Christianity "had no immanent preconditions," in the words of philosopher Hans Blumenberg. It assumes that its "*final* historical formation" was already there at the beginning, and thus that any other or later ways of imagining the world are dependent on a "truth that belongs to Christianity" from the outset.[27] It assumes that Christianity owns, legislates, and controls its own concepts, in short, and that there is a final way to determine what is, and what is not, a Christian form of thought.

But this seems unlikely. What this book shows, above all, is that Christianity *too* is a motley thing, that its concepts often have dubious provenance, that its archive is filled with stories, values, and concepts poached from other peoples, religions, and times. The heteronomy of the secular mirrors, in short, the heteronomy of Christianity.

If we acknowledge this, perhaps we can reclaim the language of the secular. Once we set aside the ideal of autonomy, for *both* the secular and Christianity, we can start paying attention, for example, to the subtler dynamics of historical change. We can speak of a Christian sacrificial imagination populated with figures from the Hebrew, Roman, and Greek past. *And* one populated with suffering Christs, bleeding Eucharists, sacrificing priests, and cults of martyrs, one in which the devout feel largely at home, and where controversy is manageable. We can speak of a Christian sacrificial imagination native to the age of confessional conflict, where sacrifice becomes the flashpoint for intractable liturgical, political, and doctrinal disputes. And we can speak of a secular imagination when, these particular disputes receding in time, the imaginative archive they helped create was translated and refashioned for new intellectual and cultural projects.

What is meant by secular here is thus simple: oriented toward the world, temporal, in the original sense of "*saeculum*." What has sacrifice meant in this human world that we find ourselves living in? What kind of work has it done, and what kind of work does it do *in the world*? The secular imagination of sacrifice is filled with efforts to answer questions like these.

So the book explores how—starting already in the late sixteenth century, but accelerating through the age of Enlightenment—the Christian sacrificial archive was repurposed, materials first gathered for doctrinal deliberation now translated into new imaginative projects. The result was a period of extraordinary syncretism of what we now regard as distinct domains of theology, history, law, politics, and anthropology. It was also period of extraordinary creativity, as authors with a variety of agendas found sacrifice useful to think with. Sometimes they were interested in sacrifice per se, that is, they tried to explain where it came from, why and how it worked, why all people seemed to do it. Sometimes they used sacrifice to think about more abstract issues, like the nature of ritual, ceremony, or religion in a universal sense. Sacrifice also found a home in histories of human institutions, and in political discussions of sovereignty, the relations of kings and priests, the nature of political solidarity, and later what Jean-Jacques Rousseau would call "civil religion." These were just some of the work, writers discovered, that sacrifice might do *ad saeculum*.

These experiments in the secular imagination took disciplinary form in the secular human sciences of the nineteenth century. Anthropology, psychology, sociology, the higher criticism of the Bible, even philosophy: all made sacrifice foundational to the stories they told about human religion, politics, and the institutions of social life. The murder of Moses hidden behind the sacrifice of Christ, the original violence that religion aims to conceal: Freud's was just one of many secular stories of sacrifice that shaped and organized the modern sciences of man.

These stories were innovative. But they were also familiar, bearing witness to the afterlives of Christianity in the sacrificial imagination. For Freud and others struggled to understand what Christians too had always struggled to understand: was sacrifice something alien and better left behind? Or is it something essential to the worlds that we inhabit? As it had been in the Christian imagination, sacrifice thus became a fault line in the secular imagination too. For some, it came to stand for the primitive world of religious violence that we moderns are happily exiting, now free of the burdens of religion. For others, sacrifice showed precisely the *failures* of secular autonomy, the dream of freedom belied by the survival of sacrifice, the "dark encroachment of that old catastrophe," in the words of Wallace Stevens, still haunting those who dream of a world beyond religion.

The secular is no less heteronomous than Christianity, in short, and no less original for all that.

Some final words about the scope of the book.

Part I supplies a deep background, partly because it is my conviction that Christianity's troubles with sacrifice began at the outset of the tradition, but more importantly because the archive of materials created by these early troubles played such an enduring role in the long history of the Christian sacrificial imagination. For scholars of the ancient world, much of this material will feel familiar. That early Christianity was composite and very slow to assume anything like an authoritative form is by now a learned commonplace.[28] The field of late antiquity has grown immensely over the past fifty years, moreover, as scholars have used new languages, and new discoveries in archaeology and epigraphy, to rewrite the history of the ancient Mediterranean. Our understanding of ancient Christianity is changing fast, probably too fast for a nonspecialist truly to appreciate. I have done my best in this regard, but at the end of the day, the picture of the ancient world in *this* book is oriented principally toward its reception, the creation of that archive that proved so essential to the sacrificial imagination of the early modern and modern worlds.

The challenges posed by the scope of our story do not end here. This book was written in the hope that a deep history of sacrifice could supply new stories about Christianity, politics, the human sciences, and the secular. But to write across nearly two millennia—even if limited "just" to Europe's Latin Christian world—is an historian's nightmare. Extraordinary scholarship exists for every moment of this, and the sheer variety of languages, circumstances, and contexts puts paid to any fantasy of complete or even coverage.[29] To the extent that I managed this problem of scale, I did so by treating the material episodically and recursively.

Part II of the book, "Sacrifice and the Deep Time of Christianity," consists of three chapters (2 through 4) that each reach back from the European sixteenth century into the Middle Ages, before moving forward into the conflicts that transformed Latin Christianity in the early modern era. This structure has its costs and benefits. The reader is spared a thousand-year march from ca. 400 to 1400 CE, but is also deprived of a careful treatment of the Latin church during the period of its greatest confidence. The luxurious growth of sacrifice in the bosom of the medieval Church—the sacrificial priesthood, the sacrificial Eucharist, the cult of the holy blood, the cult of the saints, the development of sophisticated doctrines of Atonement—will be taken up as necessary to understanding the *later* story. Because we will focus more on the reception than the internal structure of this imaginative terrain, readers will miss, then, many of the important nuances that a study of medieval Christian sacrifice per se would offer. Yet I hope those interested readers should find a sufficient sketch of its geography to pursue further study on their own.

Readers will find similar recurrences throughout the book. In part III, "The Heteronomy of Christianity," four chapters (5 through 8) explore the ways that the archives of Christianity expanded between the late sixteenth and late seventeenth centuries. There again particular problems faced in the later period summon the histories that framed and shaped them. From the late sixteenth century, for example, we turn back to the early Renaissance and its symbiosis of Christian and pagan worlds. The early seventeenth-century appearance of *global* histories of religion recalls us back to the first reports of New World sacrifices and their curious fate in the European public imagination. The politics of sovereignty and civil war invites consideration of ancient Stoicism and its political and literary revival. And the rise of new, anti-Trinitiarian heresies brings us back to the medieval discovery of the Atonement and the Man of Sorrows.

Part IV, "Sacrifice *ad saeculum*," brings the story up to the early twentieth century. Here, as the religious conflicts of the Reformation recede into the past, three chapters (9 through 11) explore the new sacrificial imagination of the post-confessional age. Here too histories are remembered and remade. Archives of sacrifice collected for Christian polemic are reappropriated by freethinkers and skeptics, for example. Anthropological speculations forged in scriptural idioms are refashioned into new theories of human culture and religion. The politics of the martyrs and the kings are abandoned but also reimagined for a new age of sentiment and citizenship. And finally, the new human sciences of the nineteenth century fold all of these into stories of human culture, religion, and politics that continue to shape our own modern imagination.

The book resembles more the Ptolemaic than the Copernican cosmos, in short, complex epicycles rotating around a chronological trajectory from the deep time of Christianity to the dawn of our present. This organization is certainly a concession to the limits of my knowledge. But it also serves a methodological purpose. For it allows us to see how various pasts are recovered and reanimated in the long history of the imagination. History does not imitate the smooth orbits of the planets, after all, but is filled with complex whorls, unpredictable disappearances and returns. Any given present discovers the past that it finds exciting or disturbing, oppressive or inspiring. The past remains buried, until it emerges, for whatever reason, snagging the attention, nails poking from the worn floor of time. Most of the chapters in this book are built around such moments of rediscovery, moments when something familiar became alien and strange. This is a book of history, but it is also a book *about* history.

"What you inherited from your fathers/acquire it, to make it yours": so spoke Goethe's Faust, an epigram of life and history alike.[30] When we seize this inheritance, in active acts of imagination, so the poet wrote, we make the past our own. And yet much of the time we hardly realize what we have inherited, what belongs to us and what not. History-making *is* this process of realization, a process no less exhilarating for the liberation that it promises than it is sobering about the debts we owe to the dead.

PART I

In the Beginning

CHAPTER ONE

In the Archives of Ancient Sacrifice

PAGANS, HEBREWS, AND CHRISTIANS

Christianity is neither a form of Hellenism, nor of Judaism, but . . . a religion with its own characteristic stamp.

—EUSEBIUS OF CAESAREA, *DEMONSTRATIO EVANGELICA*, CA. 315 CE[1]

CHRISTIANITY WAS a *new* religion. From the beginning, Christians insisted that their religion was unlike any of the others found in the ancient near East. It burst into a pluralistic religious environment—one filled with competing polytheisms, pagan monotheisms, Judaism, and a stunning variety of local cults—and it claimed for itself not just recognition as one among many, but a singular authority. Its truth was a truth never seen before, a new truth that stood apart from all the complex traditions that wended throughout the near East. It had a *new* testament and a *new* revelation, paths that led away from the worlds of paganism and Judaism to a new truth.[2] This truth was free from the barnacles of time and custom. It appeared at a certain moment in human history, revealed by the birth, the ministry, the death, and the resurrection of Jesus Christ. Before this death, the fullness of the Christian message was absent; afterward, the possibility of redemption under the sign of the Cross.[3]

At the same time, Christianity was an *old* religion. "Is God the God of Jews only? Is he not the God of Gentiles also?" the apostle Paul asked, and answered: "yes, of Gentiles also, since God is one" (Rom. 3.29–30). When Paul spoke to the men of Athens, and told them that the "unknown God" inscribed on their altars was the Christian god, he reassured them that

Christianity had been there all along. What Christians came to call the Old Testament, and prefixed to their new revelation, likewise declared that Jews were Christians too, at least those with eyes to see the prophetic message hidden in their own texts.[4] The very universalism of Christianity required these sorts of religious and cultural translations. If Christianity is a *universal* truth, a truth that should subdue Jew and Gentile alike, then the terms of its truth had to be made in a common idiom. Indeed, the project of conversion virtually demanded this. And these demands for cultural translation never failed to muddle that ideology of Christian uniqueness. You do it like this, we do it like that: even the terms of contrast contain something in common, that thing that we are all doing, that thing that Christians and pagans and Jews called (in one idiom or another) religion.[5]

From the beginning, then, the Christian urge to reject everything that surrounded it vied with its urge to consume it. "I have come not to abolish" the law and the prophets, Christ said, but "to fulfill them," and the logic of fulfillment meant that Christians integrated as much as they abandoned (Matt. 5:17). For this reason, *the* Christian genre of its earliest centuries was apologetics, that effort to define the new religion for outsiders and (more often) for insiders, building it through a series of contrasts and distinctions. What came to be called orthodoxy, "right teaching," was not constructed *ex novo*. It was, instead, built through an iterated series of confrontations between those who appointed themselves speakers for a normative Christianity and the variety of "errors" they detected in their opponents, even in their sympathizers. As a result, Christianity's incorporations were never naive. They were made suspiciously and agonistically, alert for improper slippages from pious into impious cult.

Incorporations were nonetheless made. "Here are my mother and my brothers!" Christ called to his apostles and bade them to leave their natural families and take up a new family under the Cross (Matt. 12:49). But if radical separation were the litmus test for Christianity, then Christianity has never been as Christian as all that. Heterodoxy and heteropraxis—practices and beliefs ostensibly foreign to the spirit of normative Christianity—were instead integral to its earliest constitution, a fact that shaped Christianity in its earliest centuries, and that would shape it again in the great religious upheavals of the early modern period. Christianity was heteronomous, in a word, never quite in control of its own contents.

No practice shows this vexatious process more clearly than sacrifice. Sacrifice was, for Christians and pagans alike, at the center of the traditional religious systems of the ancient Near East. Greeks did it; Romans did it; Jews did it; even barbarians did it. Christian autonomy demanded nothing less, in consequence, than the destruction of this religious foundation. And yet Christians—Romans themselves after all—were no less wedded to the world of sacrifice than those whom they hoped to supersede. Incorporation and rejection: Christianity was built in the rocking between these two urges, always differentiating, always absorbing. Orthodoxy and heterodoxy, hand in hand.[6]

This chapter explores these dynamics in the ancient world. It has two somewhat different goals. On the one hand, it lays out the perplexing challenges of sacrifice for an early Christianity seeking autonomy but always indebted to the world of its birth. Even its *critiques* of sacrifice were common among learned pagans, for example, who were also quick to point out the ways that Christians failed to meet their own critical standards. Various communities of Christians—some later condemned as heretics—repeatedly tried to square this circle throughout the first centuries of the Church, not least in the wake of the persecutions that created such a rich culture of martyrdom in places like North Africa. On the other hand, and perhaps more importantly, the chapter explores the *archive*—of texts, authors, questions, and problems—that was later reanimated in the early modern era. The chapter offers something slightly different, in other words, than "the history of late antique Christianity." In recent decades, this field has been completely revolutionized by the exploration of new texts, new languages, and new material objects.[7] But none of this was known, of course, to the writers who, starting in the fifteenth century, created their own revolution in Christianity, and an equally revolutionary picture of the ancient Church. Insofar as it is *their* story and its aftermath that centrally preoccupies this book, it is the archive that they reinvented that coordinates our concerns.

A Piety Beyond Atheism, Superstition, and Sacrifice

Sometime in the early second century CE, the Greek historian and biographer Plutarch ruminated about the nature of religion and its errors. Around the rock of true piety, "two streams" flow, "of which the one produces in hardened characters, as it were in stubborn soils, atheism [ἀθεότητα], and the other in tender characters, as in moist soils, produces superstition."[8] Plutarch thought he knew which one was worse. That atheists "do not see the gods at all" is certainly an affliction, but that the superstitious man thinks "that they do exist and are evil" is far worse.[9] The superstitious man worships the gods, but because in his heart he hates them, his worship is terrible to behold.[10] Better, Plutarch wrote, if the

"Gauls and Scythians . . . had absolutely no conception, no vision, no tradition, regarding the gods, than to believe in the existence of gods who take delight in the blood of human sacrifice and hold this to be the most perfect offering and holy rite."[11]

We will never know how this Greek would have classified the Christians, since his huge corpus of extant writings betrays not the least awareness of the new religion. But we can certainly make an educated guess. Plutarch would, in all likelihood, have seen it as a bizarre congeries of *both* errors: atheists insofar as Christians denied the existence of the gods; superstitious insofar as the God they did venerate was a bloodthirsty one.

If he had seen it this way, he would not have been alone, since charges of atheism and superstition dogged Christianity from the outset. "How can men not be in every way impious and atheistic who have become estranged from ancestral customs through which every nation and state is nurtured?" asked the author of the most notorious anti-Christian book of the period.[12] The neo-Platonic philosopher Porphyry was no defender of traditional Greek religion, but he was a thorn in the side of early Christians, so much so that his writings were banned by the Roman emperor Constantine on penalty of death, according to the ancient church historian, Eusebius.[13] Porphyry saw Christians as fundamentally impious, "heretics and perverts" whose so-called gospel was filled with "scandals" against the very notion of the divine.[14] In the eyes of another disgusted critic—whose attacks have long been associated with Porphyry—nothing was more scandalous than the Eucharist.[15] Nothing is more "bestial and absurd" than that "a man should taste human flesh and drink the blood of the same tribe's members and race—and by doing so he should partake of eternal life."[16] Better atheism than the Christian blood rite, we might hear Plutarch saying.

Whatever Plutarch might have said about them, early Christians agreed that true religion lay in the high place between atheism and superstition. This place of true piety was not big enough for two, however, and few were as aggressive in defending it as were the early Christians. These defenses typically began with simple inversions. Among the oldest martyrologies in the Church—the first after the murder of Stephen in the *Acts of the Apostles*—tells of the death of Polycarp, the bishop of Smyrna, in the first half of the second century.[17] In the stadium, Polycarp confronted the Roman proconsul. "Swear by the Fortune of Caesar," the Roman is supposed to have demanded, "and say, 'Away with the atheists.'" But, the story goes on, "Polycarp looked with a stern face at the entire crowd of lawless Gentiles in the stadium; and gesturing to them with his hand, he sighed, looked up to heaven, and said, 'Away with the atheists.'"[18] Early apologetics would gesture just as Polycarp did, throwing the charge of atheism right back upon their pagan accusers. "We confess that we are atheists with reference to gods such as these, but not with reference to the most true God," Justin Martyr wrote in his *First Apology*, and by "gods such as these," he meant those "lifeless and dead" objects that "people have named gods."[19] Clement of Alexandria agreed. Pagans were the true atheists, both "ignorant of God" and credulous in "calling by the name of gods those who are not really gods."[20]

This rhetoric of inversion characterized the Christian approach to their pagan opponents. If Christian records can be trusted, no charge was more common in ancient attacks on the new religion than that of cannibalism and child-murder. Thyestean banquets was the term of art, after the king Thyestes, tricked by his brother into eating his own children. Slaves, the acts of the martyrs record, accused their Christian masters of "dinners in the manner of Thyestes," a charge that the martyrs, needless to say, denied.[21] The late second century apologist Minucius Felix was more explicit. Christians kill a child, his pagan interlocutor reports, and then:

> It is the blood of this infant . . . that they lick with thirsty lips; these are the limbs they distribute eagerly; this is the victim by which they seal their covenant; it is by complicity in this crime that they are pledged to mutual silence; these are their rites, more foul than all sacrileges combined.[22]

Whether or not there was any truth to this accusation, Christians were quick to rebound it on their pagan accusers. It is not *us* who kill children, but you pagans. "In fact, it is a practice of *yours*," Minucius retorts, "to expose your very own children to birds and wild beasts, or at times to smother and strangle them."[23]

Christian polemics did not stop at such "gotcha" moments. No one in the ancient world doubted that cannibalism was deviant, after all. Turning this accusation back on pagans did little to accomplish the much larger objective of the early church fathers, namely, the destruction of their entire pagan surround. Their real charge was the one that we saw already in Plutarch, namely that what pagans thought was religion was, *in its very essence*, a monstrous blend of atheism and superstition. The most basic institutions of paganism, even the entire concept of what religion can and should be, were impious.

Sacrifice epitomized this impiety. The horrors of the Gauls and the Scythians were neither aberrations, nor exceptions to pagan piety, the church fathers insisted. They were the inevitable expression of pagan religion. The apologetic literature of early Christianity, therefore, ruthlessly charted the slippage from "ordinary" sacrifice to its extraordinary application to human beings. The early church father Tertullian (ca. 160–225 CE) cataloged the barbaric pagan sacrifices of the ancient world: the Africans who sacrifice infants to Saturn; the Gauls who kill children; the Taurians who sacrifice foreigner visitors. These barbarisms did not stop at the borders of civilization. Even in Rome itself, he comments, "in that most religious of all cities, the city of the pious race of Aeneas, is a certain Jupiter, whom they drench with human blood at his own games."[24] These accusations continued well into the post–Constantinian era. In the fourth century, the historian Eusebius celebrated the thirtieth year of the reign of Constantine, for example, with a list of pagan sacrificial crimes. He spoke of how the Phoenicians devoted their children to Saturn; how in Salamis at the temple of Minerva, a man was "compelled to run thrice round the altar, afterwards pierced by a lance by the priest, and consumed as a burnt offering on the blazing pile." He spoke of the murderous appetites of the Egyptians, the Spartans, the Rhodians, the Cretans, the Libyans, and the Carthaginians.[25] The sacrificial system of paganism always ended at an altar stained with human blood.

The problem was the pagan gods themselves. "Your gods are inhuman and man-hating daemons," Clement of Alexandria wrote in ca. 200 CE, "who not only exult over the insanity of men, but go so far as to enjoy human slaughter."[26] Clement here echoed Paul's letter to the Corinthians, which already made clear the close association of pagan sacrifice and the demons. "What pagans sacrifice they offer to demons and not to God," the apostle wrote (1 Cor. 10:20). Clement went further, assigning a demonic origin to the very institution of pagan sacrifice. Since the very beginning, these daemons have misled men, even "the well-known Phoroneus . . . who set up temples and altars to the daemons, and [is] also said in legend to have been the first to offer sacrifices."[27] Later fathers followed suit. When the Greek philosopher Celsus antagonized Christians for their unwillingness to admit comparison between Christ and Zeus, the Alexandrian father Origen replied that, for Christians, Zeus and the other gods are nothing more than "gluttonous daemons, who wander around sacrifices and blood and the portion taken from the sacrifices."[28] These god-daemons haunt the altars of pagan worship, drinking the smoke and the reek of corpses. From animals to humans was only a shift in kind, not in nature.

More generally, then, a vast literature of Christian apology made sacrifice *the* marker of the difference between true and false religion. "You cannot drink the cup of the Lord and the cup of demons," Paul wrote, and later fathers agreed (1 Cor. 10:21). Christians were Christians, in a sense, because, unlike all of the religions that they confronted, they did not sacrifice. To mount the rock of piety required the rejection of sacrifice and all it entailed. And what it entailed was enormous. As Tertullian recognized, sacrifice was a system, one that ramified out from the temples, where builders laid their foundations and artists carved the idols, to farmers who supplied the animals, to butchers who sold the sacrificed remains in the market.[29] To reject sacrifice was, in effect, to reject the entire culture of paganism. Sacrifice was not just one impious practice among many. It was the very operating system of impiety itself.

There were practical reasons why early Christians seized on sacrifice as their chosen mark of difference. In fact, it's not altogether clear whether they chose sacrifice, or sacrifice chose them. Already in the letters of the Roman provincial governor Pliny the Younger to the emperor Trajan (ca. 112 CE), Christians were distinguished from adherents of traditional religion by a test of sacrifice.[30] Versions of this test can be documented as early as 67 CE, when, according to the Jewish historian Josephus, it was used in Antioch to distinguish Jews from non-Jews.[31] Pliny not only applied the test to Christians, but also set it into a specifically legal context. Those who denied the name of Christian, in Pliny's court, had to prove it by sacrifice. Those who were willing to "offer adoration with wine and frankincense, to your image . . . together with those of the Gods" were deemed free of the Christian stain, and thus exempt from execution. This call for sacrifice doubtless had pragmatic as well as religious intentions. Sacrifice was a big business in the ancient world, requiring substantial investments from elites to keep the temples supplied with necessary materials.[32] By quelling Christianity, Pliny hoped to restore the "established religious rites" and the market in sacrificial animals that the new cult threatened.[33]

Christianity's refusal of the Greco-Roman sacrificial system may well have suggested the sacrifice test. Or the sacrifice test may have consolidated this refusal in the first place. In either case, in subsequent years and in the absence of any established imperial law against Christianity, the sacrifice test seems to have become a regular if de facto legal institution in the Empire.[34] The early acts of the martyrs, for example, repeatedly staged the confrontation between authorities commanding (or pleading with) Christians to sacrifice, and the latter refusing.[35] No doubt the uses of the sacrifice test were more complicated than the drama of the *passiones* allows us to see. Roman governors seem to have viewed the test less as a way of flushing out Christians than as an invitation to Roman citizens to return to their senses.[36] But as Christians understood it, martyrs became martyrs, by and large, because of their refusal to join in *any* sacrificial rite, however minimal.

During the second century, the Christian apologetic project seized on sacrifice as *the* way of emphasizing "the different character of the Christian God" and Christians' "distinct way of perceiving the divine."[37] In blunt terms, sacrifice became negatively fundamental to the constitution of Christian community. To be part of the Christian world required that one "pass" the sacrifice test by rejecting its demands. Until 249, opportunities to take the test were rare. This changed in the reign of the Emperor Decius, however, who was the first to impose a uniform mandated sacrifice test on all inhabitants of the Empire, Christian and pagan, male and female. From the Roman perspective, this was a revolutionary shift, establishing *one* rite as the common foundation of the diverse religious culture of the Empire. To whom you sacrificed did not matter, it mattered only that you did it. As J. B. Rives puts it, "Decius' decree on universal sacrifice . . . summarized the huge range of local cults in a single religious act that signalled membership in the Roman Empire."[38] Until this point, no imperial legal requirement to sacrifice; afterward, to live in the Empire was to sacrifice.

To enforce this edict, Decius created a system of bureaucratic oversight. Central to it were the "certificates" that proved membership in this new community of the sacrificing. Some of these certificates still exist, papyri found in the late nineteenth century in Oxyrhynchus and the Faiyum oasis (Egypt). They are generic documents, all of which contain sentences like this, from 72-year-old Aurelius Diogenes: "I have always and without interruption sacrificed to the gods, and now in your presence in accordance with the edict's decree I have made sacrifice, and poured a libation, and partaken of the sacred victims."[39] The certificates were then signed—first by a witness to the sacrifices, and second by a Roman official—and deposited in a local archive. For the first time in the history of Rome, not only was an imperial policy of cultic uniformity imposed, but adherence was documented and subject to legal scrutiny.

The "persecution"—as Christians called it—of Decius did not last longer than the Emperor, who died in 251. But it lasted long enough to cause huge headaches for the Christian community. One of the biggest was what to do with those whom Cyprian, the bishop of Carthage, called the "lapsed," those who failed to resist legal authorities. These were, if Cyprian is any witness, a substantial number. Some broke under torture; some (*sacrificati*), in Cyprian's words, "did not wait to be questioned before they denied their faith" and performed the required sacrifices.[40] Some colluded with authorities, pretending to be tortured so that they could more easily justify their apostasy. And some (*libellatici*) simply procured certificates for themselves, whether buying them outright, or sending pagan neighbors or slaves to impersonate them at the sacrificial rites.[41] However they lapsed, all violated the Christian prohibition on sacrifice.

Once the persecution ran its course, the obvious question arose: whether and how to reconcile with those who failed the sacrifice test? Already in 251, bishops like Cyprian confronted two opposite positions. In Carthage, the priest Felicissimus began readmitting the lapsed to the Christian church unconditionally and without penance, while in Rome, the bishop Novatian declared the lapsed eternally irredeemable.[42] For his part, Cyprian hewed to a middle course, readmitting the lapsed only under strict penance. But the controversy, and indeed the entire trauma of the persecution, only amplified the incompatibility of pagan sacrifice and Christian community.

A story from Cyprian could not make the point more clearly:

> Listen to what happened to my presence, before my very eyes. There was a baby girl, whose parents had fled and had, in their fear, rather improvidently left her behind in the care of a nurse. The nurse took the orphaned child to the magistrates before the idol . . . Because it was too young to eat the flesh, they gave it some bread dipped in . . . the wine offered by those who had already doomed themselves. Later, the mother recovered her child . . . [and] brought her in with her while we were offering the Sacrifice . . . [but] when the sacred rites were completed and the deacon began ministering to those present, when its turn came to receive, it turned its little head away . . . , it closed its mouth, held its lips tight, and refused to drink from the chalice. The deacon persisted and . . . poured in some of the consecrated chalice. There followed choking and vomiting. The Eucharist could not remain in a body or mouth that was defiled; the drink which had been sanctified by the Lord's blood returned from the polluted stomach.[43]

It is not just that Christians should not sacrifice, the story shows. It is that a true Christian *cannot* sacrifice, that the very suggestion of sacrifice—however mild in form, mere wine on bread in this case—vomits a Christian out of the church. The innocent baby who has taken sacrifice is so polluted that even the Eucharist cannot cleanse it. "Not like that!" in the words of John Milbank, was the Christian response to the pagan culture of sacrifice.[44]

The General Rules of Incorporation

Yet expulsion was hardly the only game in town. How could it be otherwise for early Christians who, if educated, were educated in the imaginative world of their pagan opponents? Indeed, the very weapons that Christians applied to the polytheistic tree were invented, not by Christians, but by pagans themselves. The pagan world was not a naive religious environment, after all. Robust philosophical, anthropological, and historical critiques of religious institutions were widespread, and sacrifice was no exception.

Take, for example, Christian stories of human sacrifice. These were well known to pagan authors. Already in the fifth century BCE, Herodotus offered detailed descriptions of Scythian horrors, how they "sacrifice one man in every hundred" of their captured enemies, how they cut their throats and sever their arms and hands.[45] This anthropological sensibility was given a more critical edge by Herodotus' near contemporary, Euripides, who made infamous those customs of Taurians accustomed to sacrifice visiting Greeks to Artemis. In his play, Iphigenia was rescued from the knife of Agamemnon, only to be made a reluctant priestess at the Taurian temple. She was not amused by the irony of this. "Just as I find it incredible that the gods at Tantalus' feast enjoyed the flesh of his son," she wryly commented, "so I believe that the people here, themselves murderous, ascribe their own fault to the goddess. None of the gods, I think, is wicked."[46]

No one in the Greek world doubted that human sacrifice was very wicked indeed, since the practice of human sacrifice often marked the very borders of what Greeks regarded as civilization. Scythians, Taurians, Carthaginians: their bloodthirsty rites established a cultural geography that put them beyond the pale for Greek, and later Roman civilizations.[47] And so when Plutarch commented that no religion at all would be better than the religion of the Carthaginians, who "buy little [children] from poor people and cut their throats as if they were so many lambs or young birds," he merely restated in different terms a basic cultural assumption of educated pagans.[48]

This skepticism extended beyond human sacrifice. Sacrifice *itself* was subjected to a fair amount of scrutiny from within the pagan traditions. In *The Republic*, for example, Plato associated zealous sacrifice with the insincerity of the unjust man, anxious to "pay court" to the gods "that he may reasonably expect the favor of heaven."[49] Not only could sacrifice mask injustice under the guise of piety, it was also a staple of just those immoral poetic fables that Plato was eager to exclude from his ideal city. "We cannot allow our men to be acceptors of bribes or greedy for gain," Socrates commented, apropos of that *do ut des* economy that was supposed to have driven the sacrificial system.[50] Later on, Lucretius mocked that falsely pious urge to "sprinkle the altars with much blood of beasts."[51] And in Virgil's *Aeneid*, the "fraud of Sinon" that got the wooden horse into the city of Troy entirely turned on the credulity of men about sacrifice.[52]

By the early Christian era, these critiques were quite elaborate. The satirist Lucian scoffed at priests and their sacrifices: "They sell men their blessings, and one can buy from them health, it may be, for a calf . . . a safe return from Troy to Pylos for nine bulls, and a fair voyage from Aulis to Troy for a king's daughter!" Such fools demand *both* a Heraclitus and a Democritus, "the one to laugh at their ignorance, the other to bewail their folly."[53] But by far the most sustained internal attack on pagan sacrifice came from that enemy of Christianity, the neo-Platonic philosopher Porphyry. Like Christians, Porphyry too saw barbarism as integral to the system of sacrifice. In the beginning, Porphyry argued in his *On Abstinence from Killing Animals*, the "most learned of all people" began to "sacrifice firstfruits to the gods of heaven." But over time, this innocent offering grew corrupt, as people themselves grew corrupt. From the seed of the firstfruits grew, Porphyry went on, the most awful crimes:

> The use of the most terrible sacrifices was introduced, full of savagery, so that the curses once pronounced against us seemed now to have reached their fulfillment: people slaughtered, and stained the altars with blood, from the time when, having experienced famine and war, they had blood on their hands. So the divine power . . . in retaliation for both of these, imposed upon us, it seems, a fitting penalty.[54]

Porphyry's attack was powerful enough to incite his younger contemporary, Iamblichus, to attempt what may be the only sustained philosophical defense of sacrifice in the ancient world, an effort to show how the very "relation that binds together creators with their creations and generators with their offspring" makes sacrifice an indispensable tool of pious worship.[55]

The larger point is that a tradition of auto-critique was alive and well in the pagan world. Christians were thus quick to incorporate this tradition, turning pagan against pagan as a way of distinguishing their own project. Any religion as vulnerable to *its own* philosophical criticism, they argued, could not possibly be a true one. So, for example, Cicero's *De natura deorum* had famously distinguished between religion and superstition this way:

> Religion has been distinguished from superstition not only by philosophers but by our ancestors. Persons who spent whole days in prayer and sacrifice to ensure that their children should outlive [*superstites*] them were termed "superstitious" . . . Those on the other hand who carefully reviewed and so to speak retraced all the lore of ritual were called "religious" from *relegere*.[56]

For Cicero, then, sacrifice, or at least its overabundance, marked the superstitious soul; sober reflection the religious soul. The Bishop of Hippo Augustine—a man steeped in pagan classics—picked up on exactly this passage in his *City of God*. "Who does not understand," Augustine sharply asked, "that, because [Cicero] is afraid of showing disrespect for the customs of the city, he is trying to praise the religion of the ancestors while at the same time disentangling that religion from superstition?" Cicero cannot possibly succeed, he went on, since the very ancestors that Cicero wants to save are exactly those who "spent whole days in prayer and sacrifice."[57] Cicero was right in his diagnosis of the problem, but without Christian revelation, he could never free himself from its snares.

Like other church fathers, then, Augustine made ample use of this pagan archive, raiding Herodotus, Seneca, Varro, even Porphyry for weapons against the religious world they inhabited. This could make for unusual sympathies. Pagan atheists were treated with particular affection, for example. Diagoras, who "chop[ped] up the wooden image of Heracles to cook his turnips," was well loved by Christian apologists like Athenagoras.[58] Clement of Alexandria defended a pack of now obscure atheists—including Diagoras, Hippo of Melos, Nicanor of Cyprus, and Euherus of Acragas—as men "who lived sensible lives and discerned more acutely . . . than the rest of mankind the error connected with these gods." Even if these atheists didn't know the truth, "they at least suspected the error," and from this suspicion grew a "living spark of wisdom."[59]

The most suspicious, and so the most important, of these atheists was Socrates. It was Socrates who tried to "deliver people from the demons," Justin Martyr wrote, and was rewarded for his troubles with accusations of "atheism and impiety," and ultimately death.[60] It was Socrates who defended himself, in his apology, against this charge of atheism, asking his prosecutors whether the crime for which he was accused was being *godless*, or just subscribing to *different* gods than those supported by the state. And it was Socrates, most of all, who insisted that his heterodoxy could not be hidden, but must be proclaimed to the world. To remain silent about his beliefs would be "disobedience to the god."[61] Better to die, he insisted, and let his death serve as a reproach to the men of Athens. A martyr before his time, "Socrates was condemned, because he was destroying the gods," Tertullian commented. As then, so now, "truth is hated."[62]

Socrates served Christians as an early skeptic, as a proto-martyr, and as a model apologist. But most of all, he served Christians as a cornerstone of their great revisionist project, the discovery of a stipulated monotheism among the wisest of the pagan philosophers. Just as Socrates looked to his own pagan archive for his apologetic project, so too did Christians discover the traces of its most fundamental teachings scattered among the books of their antagonists.[63] Plato, Justin Martyr argued, accepted "the doctrine of Moses, and the other prophets regarding one only God," but hid his knowledge lest he "raise up some Anytus or Meletus against himself, who should accuse him before the Athenians."[64] But Plato was not the only one. Many, Justin believed, were Christians *avant la lettre*: "among the Greeks, Socrates and Heraclitus, and people like them; and among the barbarians, Abraham, and Ananias, and Asarias, and Misae, and Elias, and many others."[65] The Latin apologist Minucius Felix recruited an even larger stable of pagan authors, including Thales, Anaxagoras, Pythagoras, and Xenophanes. Even Democritus and Epicurus, notorious materialists and later heresiarchs for the Christian tradition, were folded into the Christian canon of primitive monotheists. "[E] ither present-day Christians are philosophers, or philosophers of the past were already Christians," he went on, in a line that ran throughout the writings of the early church fathers, from Clement of Alexandria to Eusebius and Lactantius.[66]

These were amazing sentiments for a religion that put a new revelation at its very center, but they were of a piece with the wider Christian absorption of the pagan world. These absorptions were never planned in advance. Instead, they served particular needs in the larger project of Christian definition via apology. The novelty of Christianity was, after all, as much a *liability* as a virtue. In a world where religious truth was evaluated largely (if not entirely) by its age and provenance, the innovativeness of a religion had little to recommend it. Early and skeptical Romans looked at Christians as charlatans preying on the credulous. The historian Tacitus talked ca. 105 CE of how "Christus" founded a "pernicious superstition" that was checked briefly by his crucifixion, "only to break out once more, not merely in Judaea, the home of the disease, but in the capital itself, where all things horrible and shameful in the world collect."[67]

Christ's appearance in time—so central to much Christian theology—was here proof of Christianity's essential error.

Other pagans were more direct. "Who is this unique god of theirs . . . so solitary, so totally forlorn that no free nation has knowledge of him, nor any empire," asked the pagan critic in Minucius Felix's *Octavius*.[68] Porphyry found "impious and atheistic" anyone who was as "estranged from ancestral customs" as Christians.[69] Christianity's most self-aware (or at least well-documented) opponent—the emperor Julian, the so-called Apostate, who tried to dechristianize the Empire in the early 360s—scoffed at the novelty and narrowness of Christianity. How can a religion claim universality, let alone truth, if its God "looked on for myriads, or if you prefer, for thousands of years, while men in extreme ignorance served idols, as you call them, from where the sun rises to where he sets"? "If he is God of us all alike," Julian asked with some justification, "why did he neglect us?" Truth cannot just appear at one time and in one place, for the benefit of what Julian called that "little tribe" from Judaea.[70] Truth must compass all human history and geography.

Paul had tried to answer the objection already in his letter to the Romans. Three hundred years later, it had not lost its edge. And so Christians continued to seek Christ in what Ignatius of Antioch called, as early as the late first century, the "ancient records." For pagans unlikely to be convinced that the "ancient records are [Christ's] cross and death, and his resurrection, and the faith that comes through him," church fathers looked into the pagan archive itself.[71] And there they found Christ, announced under a veil, but present enough to ensure a living connection between the oldest traditions of the ancient world and the newest member of its religious pantheon.

We have no way of knowing how Christians would have framed their enterprise had they not found their environment already populated with skeptical pagans (and Jews). But the counterfactual helps illuminate what is an essential fact about early Christianity, namely, that it dialectically assimilated its cultural matrix, laying the heteronomous foundations of its own tradition. In short, incorporation was as much a part of the Christian project as rejection.

Jews, Christians, and the Types of Sacrifice

How did these general rules of incorporation bear on sacrifice, the one thing supposedly indigestible to Christianity? Answering this question is tricky. Since the Reformation (as we will soon see), few topics have been as theologically charged as Christian sacrifice. The following discussion is thus fraught with controversies that divide and aggravate theologians even today. I will do my best to step lightly through this, and to lay out what will become the *archive*—of texts, questions, and problems—that so powerfully shape the later Christian sacrificial imagination.

First of all, it can hardly be denied that, from the very earliest of times, Christian theology and liturgy were inundated in sacrifice. Already in his first letter to the Corinthians, Paul established a line of sacrificial continuity running through pagan, Jewish, and Christian worlds:

> The cup of blessing which we bless, is it not a participation [κοινωνία] in the blood of Christ? The bread which we break, is it not a participation [κοινωνία] in the body of Christ? . . . Consider the people of Israel; are not those who eat the sacrifices partners [κοινωνοὶ] in the altar? What do I imply then? That food offered to idols is anything, or that an idol is anything? No, I imply that what pagans sacrifice they offer to demons and not to God. I do not want you to be partners [κοινωνοὺς] with demons. You cannot drink the cup of the Lord and the cup of demons. You cannot partake of the table of the Lord and the table of demons. (1 Cor. 10.16–21)

To be sure, Christian, Jew, and pagan were oriented in different directions, but they rotate around the axis of *koinonia*, that participation in the sacrificial meal that can be documented all the way back to Homer.[72] Early Christianity was suffused with a language and practice of sacred eating shared across the Greco-Roman world. Banquets came in many forms, but they were, as Dennis E. Smith remarks, "almost always" connected with sacrifice in some way.[73] When Christians broke their bread, when they blessed their cup, they also participated in a wider culture that entwined sacrifice and meals intimately together.

Such meals complemented a semantics of sacrifice that surrounded Christ's death on the Cross. The hints of this that run through the Gospels have provided fodder for scholars and controversialists for millennia. But suffice it to say that Mark and Matthew both call Christ a ransom (λύτρον), the one who gave "his life as a ransom for many" (Mark 10:45; Matt. 20.28). As a term, the *lutron* does not quite fall into a sacrificial vocabulary. In Hellenistic Greek and in the Greek of the Septuagint, it denotes quite literally the ransom owed to free captives or slaves.[74] Paul, however, set this concept (via its root verb λύω) explicitly into dialogue with a sacrificial economy. Sinful men, he wrote to the Romans, are "justified by his grace as a gift, through the redemption [ἀπολυτρώσεως] which is in Christ Jesus, whom God put forward as an expiation [ἱλαστήριον] by his blood, to be received by faith" (Rom. 3.24–25). *Hilasterion* is a curious word. In the Septuagint it refers to the mercy seat, the covering of the ark of the Covenant where the sacrificial blood is poured (Exod. 25.16). Outside the biblical context, it also had the simpler, if equally sacrificial, significance of "propitiation."[75] However the passage is interpreted, Paul connected the ransom offered by Christ for our sins, and the offerings made at altars and in temples.[76]

Within just a few years, or perhaps already in Paul's time, this connection became equivalence. *Hilasterion* is used just twice in the New Testament. Its second appearance is in that most sacrificial book of the canon, the anonymous *Letter to the Hebrews*. Above all, *Hebrews* is the foundation of what later will be called Christian supersessionism, the view that Jewish rites and rituals were made obsolete when perfected by the person and teachings of Jesus Christ. Where *before* the Levitical high priest sprinkled atoning blood on the mercy seat (*hilasterion*) in the Holy of Holies—the innermost sanctuary of the Temple—*now* Christ has become that priest, and offered his own blood for us (Heb. 9:5). This sets the stage for the ultimate supersession:

> Without the shedding of blood there is no forgiveness of sin. Thus it was necessary for the copies of the heavenly things to be purified with these rites [blood sacrifice], but the heavenly things themselves with better sacrifices than these. For Christ has entered, not into a sanctuary made with hands, a copy of a real one, but into heaven itself . . . Nor was it to offer himself repeatedly, as the high priest enters the Holy Place yearly with blood . . . [but] he has appeared once for all at the end of the age to put away sin by the sacrifice of himself. (Heb. 9:22–26)

As a perfection of Jewish sacrifice, Christ's death achieved what the death of a bull intended but could never accomplish, a full purification of sinful man. It did so by its own perfection, and by the perfection of Him to whom it is offered, God Himself. In the perfection of the gift, the giver, and the receiver, mankind finds its final salvation.

For the *Hebrews* author, Christ's death was the sacrifice that ended sacrifice. But for early Christians, this final sacrifice was extended beyond the Cross by that central liturgical element of early Christianity, the thanksgiving ceremony of the Eucharist. The earliest liturgical documents in the church testify that Christians almost immediately conceived of this ceremony in sacrificial terms. The collection of apostolic writings called the *Didache*—dating from the late first century, it is virtually as old as the New

Testament itself—speaks of the Eucharist in the language of sacrifice. "On the Lord's own day," its author writes, "when you gather together, break bread and give thanks [i.e., celebrate the eucharist] after you have confessed your unlawful deeds, that your sacrifice [θυσία] might be pure."[77] "The Master [e.g., Christ] has commanded," the early church father Clement of Rome declared at virtually the same time, "that the sacrificial offerings [προσφορὰς] and liturgical rites be performed not in a random or haphazard way, but according to set times and hours."[78] This vocabulary of offering—as well as the practice of bringing offerings to the thanksgiving meal—became standard by the third century.[79] As in theology, then, so too in liturgy did sacrifice provide fundamental structures of the early Church.

Why not purge this new religion entirely of all things sacrificial, given the repugnance Christians evidently felt about the institution of sacrifice more generally? Again, the particular history of Christianity made this very unlikely. For whatever forces pushed Christians *away* from gentile sacrifice also pulled them *toward* the sacrifices of Jews.

In the *Didache*, for example, we read about the Eucharist that it is: "the sacrifice mentioned by the Lord: 'In every place and time, bring me a pure sacrifice. For I am a great King, says the Lord, and my name is considered marvelous among the Gentiles.'"[80] The citation is from the Hebrew Bible, from the prophet Malachi (1.11,14). And it points us toward another fundamental procedure by which Christians assimilated the world from which they emerged, that interpretive method called "typology," by which the Hebrew Bible was read with an eye to its fulfillment on the Cross.

Jesus, the evangelists, Paul, and most early Christians were themselves Jewish, so it is not terribly surprising that the new teachings were woven with older fibers. But typology as it developed in the early Church was a far more ambitious enterprise. It was the most stunning act of absorption, all the more remarkable by how *mundane* it came to seem in the history of Christianity. And it answered in full (at least to Christian satisfaction) that charge of religious innovation that was such the staple of ancient skepticism about the new cult. Christians were not new, typology affirmed; they were, rather, the oldest religion of all. Tertullian put it perfectly in his *Apology*, when he wrote:

> All the subject matter, all the material, all the origins, chronologies, sources, of every ancient pen you know . . . your very gods, temples, oracles, rituals and all—the book of a single prophet [Moses] . . . beats them all, with centuries to spare,—that book in which is seen summed up the treasure of the whole Jewish religion.[81]

Christian typology effectively stole this treasure for itself, and used it both to refute skeptical pagans and to persuade skeptical Jews that the fingers of their prophets pointed toward the coming of Jesus Christ.

The discovery of Christ's sacrifice hiding in the words of Malachi was just one example of a project audacious in scope. The aim was to find, from the beginning of time, signs of the coming of Christ and, critically, his death and resurrection at Calvary. This death was the great scandal of Christianity after all. What kind of god, any thoughtful pagan or Jew would ask, would let himself be crucified like a slave or a thief? Christians knew the problem. As Justin Martyr put it, "with what reason should we believe of a crucified man that He is the First-begotten of the Unbegotten God . . . unless we had found testimonies proclaimed about Him before He came?"[82] To find these testimonies, Christians pored over the Hebrew Bible, and found there, in its rich sacrificial idiom, the means to convince the world that the Crucifixion was no mere execution, but a death foretold.

Sacrifice was thus a cornerstone of the entire typological project. "The antiquity of the practice of worshipping God by sacrifice is sufficiently shown by the two brothers Cain and Abel," Augustine remarked in the *City of God*.[83] The first sons of Adam already knew that sacrifice is due to God. And God confirmed it, rejecting Cain and his offerings of firstfruits, and embracing Abel and his plump sheep. Genesis 4 already showed to Augustine's satisfaction that "though performed or offered by man," sacrifice, or at least the right sort of sacrifice, "is a divine thing."[84] Sacrifice thus had two histories, one righteous and one impious. From the sacrifice of Cain grew the story of human error, as when, after Israel's departure from Egypt, "rites were instituted by the kings of Greece in honour of false gods."[85] Abel's sacrifice had a legacy too, one that led through the patriarchs to the Messiah on the Cross.

Typology is thus a temporal Möbius strip, in which beginnings and endings double back on themselves. Genesis 14 supplied one such set of doublings. There Christians as early as the *Hebrews* author discovered another type of Christ. In the text, Abraham meets Melchizedek, the "priest of God Most High," who blesses the Jewish patriarch and offers him bread and wine (Gen. 14.18). In return, in some versions, Abraham pays obeisance and tithes to the mysterious priest-king. Melchizedek reappears in the Psalms, where God assures David that he is "a priest forever after the order of Melchizedek," and it was this reference that *Hebrews* author applied to Jesus Christ, the new "high priest" who perfects and replaces the Levitical order (Ps. 110:4; Heb. 5). Augustine took the typology one step further, speaking in reference to Abraham's tithes:

> Here, indeed, is the first appearance of that sacrifice which is now offered to God by Christians all over the world, in which is fulfilled what was long afterwards said in prophesy to Christ . . . "Thou art a priest forever after the order of Melchizedek."[86]

Melchizedek was not only a priest of God who *predated* the Jewish patriarchs, but also one whose authority these patriarchs immediately recognized. Much to the shame, of course, of those stubborn Jews who rejected the hermeneutics of Christianity.

One could go on from here, of course. The sacrifice of Isaac in Genesis 22 was explicitly compared with Jesus's sacrifice on the Cross, so much so that some church fathers argued for an identity between Abraham's mountain in Moriah and the hill of Calvary itself.[87] Abraham's altar and Christ's Cross were, by this argument, connected by a transtemporal link. "Time," as Tertullian put it, "which seems to us to be two-fold (past and present), in those books is one."[88] Already in the fourth century, the primitive canons of the Mass, such as that of Ambrose in Milan, included the three sacrifices of Abel, Melchizedek, and Isaac as "prefigurations of the Eucharist," and the story of Abraham's sacrifice was read aloud in the Easter vigil.[89] Just as important, too, to the later typology of Christ's sacrifice was the story of the suffering servant in Isaiah 53:

> It was the will of the LORD to bruise him;
> he has put him to grief;
> when he makes himself an offering for sin,
> he shall see his offspring, he shall prolong his days;
> the will of the LORD shall prosper in his hand. (53.10)

From very early in the history of the Church, its fathers associated Christ with this "offering for sin." By "his bruising we are healed," wrote the author of the early *Epistle of Barnabas*, citing Isaiah 53.5, and associating Him as well with the scapegoat in Leviticus 16, the "cursed" who is ultimately "crowned" by God.[90] Later fathers like Augustine regularly took the Isaiah song to be a prophecy of Christ's life and death.[91]

The larger point is that even as early Christians set themselves outside the world of sacrifice, they also reincorporated it. The end of Jewish sacrifice itself with the destruction of the Temple in 70 CE seemed a providential sign to Christians that the era of Hebrew ritual had yielded to a new era of Christian sacrifice. As Augustine wrote: "the old things have passed away and new ones have come to be in Christ . . . altar yields to altar . . . bread to bread, animal to animal, blood to blood."[92] And so the language of sacrifice was reinhabited by early Christians. Even Cyprian of Carthage, so revolted by the pagan temples, confidently spoke of the Eucharist as "the sacrifice offered by the bishop [*sacrificio a sacerdote celebrato*]."[93] Needless to say, Christians were very careful to distinguish their sacrifices from those of Jews and gentiles. The sacrifices of the gentiles are nothing, Augustine insisted. But Christian sacrifice is *not* nothing. It is, rather, "the visible sacrament of an invisible sacrifice."[94] It is something present in the world, even if its real significance is elsewhere. And its presence is fundamental to that whole thing called Christianity:

> The whole of the redeemed City—that is, the congregation and fellowship of the saints—is offered to God as a universal sacrifice for us though the great High Priest Who, in his Passion, offered even Himself for us in the form of a servant, so that we might be the body of so great a Head. For it was this form that He offered, and in it that He was offered, because it is according to it that He is our Mediator. In this form He is our Priest; in it, He is our sacrifice. . . . this also, as the faithful know, is the sacrifice which the Church continually celebrates in the sacrament of the altar, by which she demonstrates that she herself is offered in the offering that she makes to God.[95]

It is the church; it is the city of God; it is Christ; it is the service of the Mass: in all of these, the servant offers himself in making offerings to God. Without sacrifice, in Augustine's mind, there is not much left of Christianity.

The Perils of Absorption

This project of absorption—whether from pagan or Jewish sources—was a risky one. Christians effectively said "no" to the sacrifice of others, and "yes" to a sacrifice of their own making. This new sacrifice would be once-and-for-all rather than regular, spiritual rather than carnal. Our altars, wrote Origen, are "the mind of each righteous man."[96] And yet, of course, these translations retained something of their original. Christian sacrifice was, for Augustine, offered "continually" at the altar. It was not purely spiritual, but *sacramental*, that is, incarnated in the world in some concrete fashion. The logic of incorporation thus left Christians open to the charge that they *too* were a sacrificial cult.

This charge could come from a variety of directions. "Why do you not sacrifice," asked the Roman emperor Julian of a sect he regarded as Jewish heretics, "since you have invented your new kind of sacrifice and do not need Jerusalem at all?"[97] From the other side came the accusation that Christians sacrificed too much. Augustine confronted one such, someone who saw the appropriation of the Hebrew Bible as poisonous to real Christianity. "Those who sacrifice, sacrifice to demons," this critic purportedly said, in paraphrase of Paul. Augustine's reply was indignant: "as if all who sacrifice, sacrifice only to demons"! Christians, he argued from typological principles, offer their sacrifice "not according to the order of Aaron, but according to the order of Melchizedek."[98]

This critique did not come from *outside* the Christian tradition, importantly, but from *inside* it, from one of its many offsprings and crossbreeds that circulated in the ancient world. Later "orthodox" Christians would call these varieties by the epithet of "heresy," and give them names like Gnostics, Marcionists, Manichees, Montanists, Novatianists, Donatists, Arians, and many more. This labeling project has proved extraordinarily effective—even now, we tend to describe ancient Christian variety in the terms proposed by those determined to root it out. Small wonder, in fact, since much of our knowledge of these so-called heresies, and their devotees, comes directly from the critical pens of church fathers aimed to eliminate them as competitors for the title of "Christianity." These accounts are thus hardly the most reliable source of information about these various forms of ancient Christianity. They nonetheless reveal much about the controversies that split Christian communities.

Among the first of the heresiologists was Irenaeus of Lyon, whose *Adversus haereses*, written ca.180–85, served as a sourcebook for later Christians trying to chart a course between the bewildering varieties of their age. The book was aimed first and foremost against the Christian "gnostic" Valentinus, who (among other crimes) seems to have denied the relevance of the Hebrew Bible to the Christian dispensation and to have accused Christians of impious attachment to Jewish sacrificial norms. In effect, Valentinus argued, Christianity was *not nearly Christian* enough. It had not adequately freed itself of its cultural and historical matrix, had not become the religion of innovation that was promised from the beginning. In effect, it still took sacrifice too seriously—eat the meat of sacrifice, insisted Valentinus, for then you show indeed you are pure, and that sacrifice is nothing whatsoever. Given this impious attachment to ancestral ways, in Valentinus's view, only radical exclusion could truly pioneer a new form of religious devotion.

What Valentinus was actually after is a bit hard to say, again since we know about him largely from his opponents. Nevertheless, these were charges that Irenaeus felt compelled to address. Irenaeus argued that

Christians cannot simply make up new mythologies, and furthermore, they do not need to, since they have to hand an authoritative source of their own tradition. "The books of Moses are the words of Christ," Irenaeus declared in a pithy restatement of typological reason.[99] Sacrificing patriarchs like Abraham are therefore as much a part of the Christian tradition as the apostles.[100] And when prophets like Malachi speak of the "pure offering" made to the Lord of hosts, they are speaking of Christ.[101] These defenses of a normative Hebrew Bible culminated, finally, in a defense of Christian sacrifice:

> The sacrifice of the church, which the Lord instructed should be offered to the whole world, is reckoned a pure sacrifice by God, and accepted by him, not because he needs a sacrifice from us, but because he who offers glorifies himself through which he offers . . . sacrifice in general is not to be condemned.[102]

The weakness of the final clause, "not to be condemned," perhaps signals some insecurity about this institution of sacrifice. If so, this would not be much of a surprise, since the very idea of Christian sacrifice was, as should be clear by now, a fragile and delicate one.

Opponents were not shy to prod this sensitive spot. The Manichean Faustus, for example, ridiculed the new cult for fetishizing the body of a dead man, embracing the obvious lies of the Hebrew Bible, and for doing just what Christians always spurned—sacrificing. When he defended Christianity against Faustus, therefore, Augustine (the former Manichean) offered yet another defense of its sacrifices. Faustus, the Bishop of Hippo reported, "dare[d] to deplore the sacrifices of the Old Testament and call them idolatry and also to link us to such a sacrilege." Augustine redeemed the sacrifices, by turning them into typological "symbols." The sacrifices "were removed from being actively celebrated, but they remained in the authority of their meaning."[103] You and the Jews, Faustus argued, are just "schisms of the gentiles," and it was Augustine's never-ceasing job to show why this was not true.[104]

"Orthodox" Christians signaled their concern about the stability of Christian sacrifice in their attacks on the dissident Christianities that filled their age. One of the great fourth-century heresiologies, Epiphanius of Salamis's *Panarion,* spent much time on the false sacrifices of those who deviate from the Christian "consensus" he was bent on creating. Thus, for all their anti-sacrificial rhetoric, those same gnostics (he reported) ejaculate on their hands, and then "eat it . . . , and they say, 'This is the body of Christ; and this is the Pasca, because of which our bodies suffer and are made to acknowledge the passion of Christ.'"[105] This scandalous Eucharist only gets worse, because the gnostics (according to Epiphanius) commit in fact the crime of which Christians were falsely accused. These deviant believers "take . . . [an] aborted infant, and cut it up . . . And they mix honey, petter, and certain other perfumes and spices . . . and each eats a piece of the child with his fingers."[106] Augustine repeated a similar libel against the so-called Cataphrygians—rigorist followers of the Christian prophet Montanus, who concentrated in Asia minor and north Africa—who, he reported:

> confect their eucharist from the blood of a year-old infant which they squeeze from tiny punctures all over its body; they mix it with wheat and make bread from it. If the child dies, he is regarded by them as a martyr, but if he lives, he is regarded as a great saint.[107]

Some arguments never die, I suppose. But the irony of these Christian accusations—the most common pagan libel of the early Church—aside, the more important point is that Christian sacrifice was constantly slipping, in the eyes of these fathers, into deviance and heterodoxy. Balancing on the knife-edge of piety was hard work.

It was that much harder because even "reasonable" Christians were unsure how to make the translation successfully between gentile/Jewish sacrifice and its proper Christian form. We can see this in the sheer variety of eucharistic practices in the early Church, as Andrew McGowan has shown. The use of wine, for example, in the early Eucharist was an exact parallel of the wine offered at pagan sacrifices—should the Christians not, perhaps, drink water instead? As it turns out, some indeed did. The apocryphal *Acts of Peter*, for example, describes how Christians "brought bread and water to Paul for the sacrifice that he might offer prayer and distribute it among them."[108] Other things were given at the altar as well: one early breviary describes how milk and honey should be left there, not as a eucharistic offering, but with "appropriate blessings."[109] Christian sects like the Marcionites took this to another level, rejecting bread and wine altogether and substituting milk and honey for their offerings. Other Christians attacked this practice as insufficiently sacrificial—"Honey is not brought as an offering/nor is milk used for sprinkling and libation"—but this was exactly the point for the Marcionites.[110] Christianity, they said, had not yet fully purged itself of pagan error. What McGowan calls the "intimidation of the orthodox by the radical rejecters of the cuisine of sacrifice," came from both outside and inside the new sect.[111] Vegetarianism, for example, was not a practice associated solely with pagans like Porphyry;

it was also a reality in the early Church, when the devout sought to break the connection to a sacrificial economy in which meat from the temples often appeared in the marketplace.[112] And so when Cyprian of Carthage tries to reassure those who "feel apprehensive at our morning sacrifices that if they taste the wine they may exhale the smell of the blood of Christ," we can see, behind this reassurance, a wider concern even among Christians at how easily their religion might slip back into gentile ways.[113]

In short, the project of defining a Christian orthodoxy against enemies both inside and outside the faith—that is, apologetics—could never leave sacrifice alone. Incorporation was agonistic; it was a process of constant struggle. And the process left early Christians with an enduring suspicion about the success of their new altars and new blood.

An Exemplary and Final Case: Martyrdom and Sacrifice

This torture was all the more exquisite because early Christianity came so to depend on an institution rooted in the sacrificial imagination, that of the martyr. The world of early martyrs not only offers an astonishing example of how challenging it was for early Christians to harness and restrain the sacrificial imagination. It also points us forward to the great crisis in the Latin church, when, a millennium later, a world of martyrdom *returned* to Christianity, with all of its promise and peril (see chapter 4). In both cases, martyrdom lived in an uneasy borderland between the sacred and the profane, the pious and the scandalous.

From the beginning, the acts of Christian martyrs were haloed by sacrifice. Thus in the early second century, Ignatius of Antioch, on his way to meet his demise in Rome, wrote to the Ephesians: "I am your lowly scapegoat [περίψημα]; I give myself as a sacrificial offering [ἁγνίζομαι] for you Ephesians, a church of eternal renown."[114] To the Romans he asked only that he be granted "nothing more than to be poured out as a libation to God while there is still an altar at hand." Let me be "a sacrifice [θυσία] through these instruments of God," he continued.[115] A few decades later, the *Acts of the Martyrs of Lyon* (ca. 177–78 CE) described how the faithful were collectively "sacrificed [ἐτύθησαν], after being made all the day long a spectacle to the world to replace the varied entertainment of the gladiatorial combat," even the "sacrificial savour" that rises from the burnt flesh of Attulus.[116]

This language of sacrifice was fundamental to that absorptive work that martyrs performed for the early Church. When Augustine praised how martyrs "extinguished . . . smoking altars with the blood of the dying," for example, he indicated the strategy by which Christian martyrs conquered and incorporated the sacrifices of their pagan opponents.[117] Instead of the blood of beasts, the blood of men is laid on the altar as a sacrifice that ends sacrifice, and replaces it with . . . sacrifice. Even such a common (in after-times) Christian image as the martyr's crown was repurposed from the scene of sacrifice. The *passio* of Pionius (late third century) described how the martyr tore apart and threw away the crowns laid on his heads in the sacrificial ceremony. "After his victory in the great combat," however, "his crown was made manifest through his body."[118] Tertullian wrote an entire treatise on this crown, arguing that Christians cannot accept the pagan crown of victory. "If, perhaps, you object that Christ Himself was crowned," he commented with his usual bitter irony, "I will have a very simple answer for you: 'By all means, you may wear *that* kind of crown.'"[119]

In short, Christian martyrs—typically executed for their *failure* to sacrifice themselves—took over the institution of sacrifice. By doing so, they became essential foundations of the sacrificial imagination of the early Church. This was true in (at least) three ways, broadly construed as liturgical, theological, and political.

I. First, liturgy. For the first centuries of the Christian church, absent official support for its institutions and facing often hostile resistance, Christians developed their worship around the physical remains of their special dead. The acts of the martyrs were not just accounts of Christian heroism. They were also, in effect, liturgical texts for early Christians, making the martyrs and their bodies into physical sites of the Christian sacred. Many martyrologies end not with the death of the victim, but the disposition of their bodies by the faithful. We find an eloquent version in the *passio* of the Bishop Fructuosos and his deacons in 259 CE:

> the Christians were sad, . . . [and] they missed him and recalled the memory of the faith and the contest of each of the martyrs. When night fell, they hastened to the amphitheater with wine in order to quench the smoldering bodies. This done, each one collected the ashes of the martyrs, so far as he could, and claimed them for his own. And here too the miracles of our Lord . . . were not wanting to increase the faith of believers . . . And so, after his death, [Fructuosus] appeared to his brethren and urged them that what each had taken of his ashes out of love for him should be restored without delay.[120]

Christians gathering the ashes for comfort made sense, to the ghost of Fructuosus, but it also divided what needed to remain whole. In another later version of the story, the ghost is more specific, and asks his unhappy faithful to bury the "gathered remains . . . in the holy church under the holy altar."[121]

These gathered remains became the polestars of later Christian worship. In Prudentius's *Peristephanon liber*—hymns to the Diocletian martyrs written in the late fourth century—each poem began with the martyr's call to sacrifice, and ended with scenes of worship and veneration by those left behind. The hymn to eighteen martyrs killed in Sargossa, for example, ended with the company "laid under the everlasting altar." "Come," Prudentius exhorted, "let us with pious tears wash the letters cut on the marble slabs under which lies my hope of unloosing the bonds which hold me fast. Cast thyself down along with me, noble city, on the holy graves."[122] The most graphic of these martyrdoms was that of of Hippolytus, whose foes dragged his dead body across the countryside, scattering its bones and flesh. Afterward, the devout carefully collected all the parts, and hid them under a secret tomb where they come to worship:

> That table both gives the sacrament and is set there as faithful guardian of its martyr; it keeps his bones in the tomb for the hope of their everlasting deliverer and feeds the dwellers on Tiber's banks with the holy food. Wonderful is the grace that attaches to the spot, and the altar, ever ready to receive its suppliants, fosters the hopes of men with kindly favour.[123]

Prudentius's descriptions of careful collection, burial, and then celebration at the tomb-altar of the dead were written at the end of the age of martyrs. But he repeated motifs common already in the early Church. The "Martyrdom of Polycarp," likely from the early third century, described how the faithful "removed his bones, which were more valuable than expensive gems and more precious than gold," how they put them in a "suitable place," and then "gather[ed] together" there to commemorate his martyrdom.[124] From these earliest deaths onward, then, the bones of the martyrs were magnets for Christian worship.

Martyrs, in other words, organized the early geography of Christian worship. "Tomb and altar were joined," as Peter Brown puts it, in the early cult of the saints.[125] Martyrologies record this, but so does archaeology. Christians gathered, for example, in cemeteries to venerate their sacred dead and beginning in the second century, they began (slowly) to build their own cemeteries to house them.[126] Early imperial edicts specifically targeted gathering in cemeteries, as a way of hampering Christian practices of worship.[127] Later, when Christians were allowed formal structures for their gatherings, they built *martyria*, structures founded on or near the bones of the martyrs. Over time, cemeteries and martyria were enclosed, some of them becoming churches—that is, buildings where Mass was celebrated and overseen by regular clergy—and others remained informal sites for Christian veneration of the dead martyrs.[128] Ancient churches therefore record Prudentius's "letters cut in marble," inscriptions to the dead: "Here within are contained the bones of the martyr Trophismos," reads one inscription in Suhut, in western Turkey, "if anyone, at any time, should throw out these bones, that person shall be answerable to God."[129] Under ancient churches in North Africa, among other places, archaeologists regularly find tombs and ossuary urns. Thus began too that long Christian tradition of burial *ad sanctos*, that is, the deposit of the Christian dead as near as possible to the altar.[130]

In essence, the martyr's bones were a crucial nucleus of Christian community. living and dead. In 1906–7, the French archaeologist A. L. Delattre excavated the basilica majorum outside the walls of Byzantine Carthage—where St. Perpetua, one of the most famous of Christian martyrs, died—and discovered tablets commemorating her death, a tomb epigraph to "*Perpetue filie dulcetissimae*," and a number of ancient graves. Whether the graves really contained her bones (as Delattre argued) or not, there is no doubt that early Christianity built many of its sites of worship atop the consecrated graves of the martyrs.[131]

These graves were not just places for silent contemplation. They were also places for celebration. Early Christians took over the Roman and Etruscan practice of the *refrigerium*—the banquets given in honor of the dead, with offerings of food and wine made at the tombs—and made them a part of regular worship.[132] They built tables and altars over the martyr's graves and gathered there to observe the anniversaries of their special dead. Some, as in Salona in Dalmatia, had inset bowls for food and drink offerings.[133] These can be found as well in the Roman catacombs (another, physical reoccupation of a pagan practice), in addition to cups, benches, chairs, and artistic renditions of these celebrations, as seen here carved into the side of a sarcophagus (fig. 1.1).[134]

These celebrations were not necessarily intimate affairs. While *refrigeria* in the catacombs would have been limited in size, later structures built to celebrate these Christian *refrigeria* could be enormous, housing huge groups. They also became institutionalized: the *dies natalis*—the day of the martyr's birth into a new life with Christ—was over time established as a day for a special commemorative Mass. By the early fifth century, some

FIGURE 1.1. Relief of a Christian banquet scene on a sarcophagus. Via Tiburtina, Rome. 3rd century CE. Museo Nazionale Romano (Palazzo Massimo alle Terme). Scala/Art Resource, NY.

150 of these feast days are recorded.[135] Augustine, for his part, offered many celebratory sermons for the martyrs. "A table was erected to God" in the place where he died, Augustine declared in one, "and yet it's called Cyprian's table, not because Cyprian ever dined there, but because he was sacrificed there, and because by this very sacrifice of himself he prepared this table."[136] These tables of the martyrs—the deaths they commemorated, the sepulchres they covered, and the celebrations they invited—were a heart of Christian ceremony in its first centuries.

It hardly seems accidental, in this light, that Constantine's Christian reign coincided with the discovery of the sepulchre of the man-god Himself.[137] Although Christ's corpse was only around for a few days, they were eventful ones. In the synoptic Gospels, Joseph of Arimathea donated his own tomb for the body (Matt. 27.57; Mark 15.42; Luke 23.50), where it was laid and wrapped in linen, before it disappeared in the mystery of the Resurrection. The Gospel of John was more specific. The tomb, it reported, was in a garden "in the place where he was crucified,"—Golgotha, the place of skulls—which was convenient because the Sabbath was near at hand and the body could not be moved far (19.41–42). Assuming it ever existed, the exact location of this tomb was quickly lost, forgotten, or destroyed in the reconstructions of Rome by the Emperor Hadrian in the early second century. Hardly had the great unifying council of the early church in

Nicaea concluded in 325 CE, however, than the tomb was rediscovered under a pagan shrine built on a quarry on the western edge of Jerusalem.

The church historian Eusebius of Caesarea described the discovery thus:

> Once upon a time wicked men—or rather the whole tribe of demons through them—had striven to consign to darkness and oblivion that divine monument to immortality. . . . above the ground they constructed a terrible and truly genuine tomb, one for souls, for dead idols, and built a gloomy sanctuary to the impure demon of Aphrodite; then they offered foul sacrifices there upon polluted and defiled altars . . . [after this was destroyed and removed by Constantine] the underground site was exposed, at last against all expectation the revered and all-hallowed Testimony (*martyrion*) of the Saviour's resurrection was itself revealed, and the cave, the holy of holies, took on the appearance of a representation of the Saviour's return to life.[138]

The logic of Eusebius's apologetics is by now familiar, the terrible tomb of the gentiles overcome by the *martyrion* of the resurrected Christ. Apologetics aside, what Eusebius called the "tomb of divine presence" came to undergird Christianity's holiest church.[139] The pagan site was cleared, the tomb exposed, and a grand basilica erected around it, and for the next 700 years, this church sat at the symbolic heart of Christianity.[140]

After the emperor Constantine made Christianity the official religion of Rome, more holy sepulchres were built across the Christian world. On a prosaic level, Constantine's christianization program effectively ceded to the Church the places where martyrs had been buried. From then on, this land would belong to Christians, who converted their cemeteries and tombs into the most basic buildings of faith.[141] With the legalization of Christianity, too, the martyr's table and the communion altar gradually converged. Those tombs in the catacombs, for example, were expanded into basilicas "*ad corpus*," that is, basilicas built atop or right next to the body of the special dead.[142] Spaces carved out of rock—like the Roman basilica of SS. *Nereo e Achilleo* raised atop the catacomb of Domitilla, or, more dramatically, that of San *Lorenzo fuori le mura* built in the late sixth century—were opened up, and eventually raised above ground.[143] And more generally, altars themselves became depository sites for martyrs' remains both in the Greek east and the Latin west. Already in the fifth century, some North African churches called for the destruction of churches *not* sanctified by the remains of the sainted. The 401 Council of

Carthage similarly declared that "altars . . . erected as martyr's *memoriae*, in which no body or relic of martyrs has been shown to have been placed" should be destroyed by the local bishop.[144] By the early Middle Ages, altar and martyr were firm companions in the world of Christian worship.

II. Martyrs also played an important, if smaller, role in the world of theology. There they took their value from their proximity to the Crucifixion, their sacrifices given a value analogous to the sacrifice that ended sacrifice. Indeed, the early Church made the sacrifices of the martyrs central to Christian soteriology. Taken immediately into heaven and standing at the side of Christ, the martyrs were active agents of redemption in the world. Already in the *passio* of Perpetua, the martyr dreamt of her own intercessory power, seeing her brother "delivered from his suffering" by the prayers of this woman preparing for her execution.[145] Origen was more explicit. "The souls of believers that are beheaded for the testimony of Jesus," he wrote, "do not assist in vain at the altar of heaven, but procure for them that pray the remission of sins."[146] The soteriological power of the martyrs was not always uncontroversial. After the Decian persecutions, Cyprian was skeptical that the Christian heroic dead had bought full redemption for their weaker lapsed brethren, as some laxer Christians apparently argued.[147] But on the whole, early Christians agreed with Prudentius, that the martyrs "listen to our prayer and straightaway carry it to the ear of the everlasting King," and by doing so, propitiate Christ and temper his relations with ordinary sinners.[148] This intercessory power made the martyr's tombs efficacious places for interacting with the divine. Miracles were especially common around the relics of martyrs, Augustine documented, since God "sometimes acts through the spirits of martyrs."[149]

III. The theological and liturgical importance of the martyrs amplified, thirdly, their communal and political value. From the outset, willingness to die was constitutive of an early Christian ideal of community. Those who successfully resisted pagan sacrifice, and paid the terrible penalty, were exemplary; those who did not, those "too tenacious of life or too weak in the face of suffering," as Origen put it, were rejected.[150] The lapsed, as Cyprian saw it, excluded themselves from Christian communion. Reincorporation was by no means given, and further apostasy was usually punished by permanent exclusion. Politically, then, martyrdom helped demarcate the edges of early Christian community.

When Christianity became the religion of empire, martyrdom continued to play this political role, and with no less urgency. The fierceness of the Decian, Valentinian, and Diocletian persecutions concealed, after all, what was a really crucial question for early Christians: who is a martyr? If martyrs were the seeds of the Church, Christians had to be sure that there were no weeds hidden in their midst. The special dead were only special if their numbers were heretic-free.

Cyprian foresaw the problem as early as 250. Facing the schism occasioned by the problem of the lapsed, he was clear. Novatian and his rigorist followers—those who admitted no lapsed Christians back to the fold—could not be reckoned Christians at all: "Nay, though they should suffer death for the confession of the Name, the guilt of such men is not removed even by their blood; the grievous irremissible sin of schism is not purged even by a violent death. *No martyr can he be who is not in the Church.*"[151] Someone who "profane[s] the true victim in the Lord's sacrifice by pseudo-sacrifices [*falsa sacrificia*]" is, he went on, an "enemy of the altar, a rebel against the sacrifice of Christ."[152]

The problem was deep. Dying in the name of Christ was a necessary but not sufficient condition for martyrdom. How then to separate the sheep from the goats, Abel from Cain, true from false sacrifice? For Cyprian the bishop, the answer was conceptually simple. Anyone who "acts in opposition to the bishops of Christ" can, by definition, never attain the blessed state of martyrdom, no matter how much they suffered.[153] Practically, this was no solution at all, however, since it required more unity than the Church ever knew in its first centuries. The number of early Christian "heterodoxies"—what were later called by the epithets of Sabellianism, Monophysitism, Nestorianism, and many more—testifies to the incredible intellectual diversity of its early champions. Tertullian became a Montanist; Eusebius was an Arian; Origen's works were anathematized in the early fifth century and his followers purged from monasteries.[154] Cyprian's enemy Novatian was himself made a bishop, and there was no shortage of the so-called heterodox among the senior ranks of the early Christian clergy.

Cyprian's later successor to the bishopric of Carthage was one of these. Donatus was a rigorist like Novatian, anxious to create a Christian community free of backsliders. Donatus's backsliders were the so-called *traditores*. Rather than die for the faith, they handed the holy scripture over to Diocletian's persecuting authorities in the Great Persecution of 303–5. From these early seeds, Donatism, as it came to be known by its Catholic opponents, grew into a sizable fraction of the North African church. Communities of dissident Christians, with their own bishops and ecclesiastical property, formed, as they saw it, a better and purer Church on earth.[155]

Throughout the fourth century, therefore, two roughly equal Christian groups laid claim to the martyrological past in North Africa. Their conflicts were not just theoretical. Violence between Catholic and dissident Christians was common, and the victims included both clerical buildings and clerics themselves. At the heart of these conflicts was a "perfect hatred," as Brent Shaw puts it, both Christian groups contrasting their sacred martyrs with the "traitors" who had betrayed the faith to pagan Rome.[156]

By mid-fourth century—and by now Christianity was the favored religion of the Empire—this hatred was boiling hot. It was then that we hear the first mention of holy fighters (*agonistici*) warring on behalf of the dissident church even, as their Catholic enemies reported, against Rome itself. Here the bishop Optatus of Milevis reports on these groups:

> In the present day, there are also men . . . who, driven by a desire for false martyrdom, hire assassins to strike them to death. Also of this same type of men are those who hurl themselves headlong from the peaks of high mountains, so discarding their already cheap lives. You should consider from what sort of men your bishop [Donatus] . . . created these armed bands.[157]

The violence of these so-called circumcellions, as they came to be known, justified the imperial repression of the Donatist church, Catholics like Optatus argued. It also scored the line between the false sacrifices of the impious and the holy sacrifices of Christ's martyrs.

This was not lost on Augustine, the most tireless critic of the dissidents. In 410, he preached a sermon on the birthday of St. Cyprian, that great apologist for episcopal unity. Satan, he recalled, dared Christ to throw himself from the "pinnacle of the temple" (Matt. 4:5). Christ refused, but the Donatists succumb to these very blandishments, in Augustine's sermon, casting themselves down not for piety but for glory. Even worse than those who submit to Satan's temptations, however, are those who honor their memory. The "greater murderers" are "the people who take up the bodies of the cliff jumpers with honor, who collect the blood of the cliff jumpers, who honor their graves, who get drunk at their tombs."[158] These circumcellions die and call it martyrdom; they venerate their dead with Christian honors; they weave their stories into the Christian tapestry of suffering, recruiting even martyrs like Cyprian to their diabolical cause. If Christ's resistance to Satan defined Christian virtue, for Augustine, the Donatist way of death showed clearly that they are not even "false Christians." They are "simply not Christians at all."[159]

In the end, then, he agreed with Cyprian. If you "separate from the structure of unity and the bond of love," Augustine wrote to a Donatist priest, "you will suffer eternal punishment even if you are burned alive for the name of Christ."[160] That famous Augustinian tag line—that it is not the punishment, but the cause that makes a martyr—has to be amended somewhat.[161] Dying for Christ is not enough; sincerity of faith is not enough. Only *right* faith, backed by the authority of a unified church, makes the martyr.

These distinctions made a difference. Even as Augustine wrote his anti-Donatist works, Christian emperors were beginning a process of legal and political sorting to enforce religious uniformity across the Empire. It is not an accident that, in this letter to the Donatist, Augustine turned to Christ's parable of the feast in Luke 14—where the master "compel[s] people to come in, that my house may be filled"—to make the case that unbelievers should be forced into the church.[162] Edicts requiring legal conformity were appearing already in the rulership of Constantine. These began by threatening those who force Christians to sacrifice.[163] In the 380s, imperial laws began to target "forbidden sacrifices"; a decade later, the courts in Milan prohibited *all* sacrifices, and it wasn't long before authorities started closing pagan temples.[164] And then finally, edicts took aim at *Christian* heterodoxies, punishing those who "assume, with studied deceit, the alien name of true religion," those, in other words, who call themselves bishops when they are not, priests when they are not, and by implication, martyrs when they are not.[165] By the late fourth century, heretics were thus explicitly subject to coercive measures to "compel them to come in." Put another way, protecting the category of the Christian martyr had real political stakes.

This was all the more important since the *very idea* of a martyr was—like Christian sacrifice more generally—so vulnerable to critique. From the beginning, this worship of the dead smacked, to pagans, of a dreadful error, a terrible superstition. The fourth century sophist Eunapius, for example, was particularly disgusted. The oracles had prophesied that "temples would become tombs," he recounted, and now it was so. Christians collected "the bones and skulls of criminals who had been put to death for numerous crimes"; they "made them out to be gods, [and] haunted their sepulchres." "'Martyrs' the dead men were called," he went on, with horror.[166] The Emperor Julian was no less scornful of a cult that "filled the whole world with tombs and sepulchers," especially when, as he rightly pointed out, there is no scriptural warrant for "grovel[ling] among tombs."[167] And Celsus—Origen's great pagan opponent—evidently made the same critique, accusing Christians of both hypocrisy and tomb veneration. They "ridicule those who worship Zeus because his tomb is shown in Crete," he is supposed to have written, yet they "worship one who rose from his tomb."[168]

Celsus hit a nerve with Origen because he was onto something. It was, after all, early *Christians* who had accused pagans of worshipping the dead. Origen's teacher, Clement of Alexandria, had already railed against pagan tomb worship:

> Temples . . . are called by a fair sounding name, but in reality they are tombs. In the temple of Athena in the Acropolis at Larissa there is the tomb of Acrisius; and in the Acropolis at Athens the tomb of Cecrops . . . if I were to go through all the tombs held sacred in your eyes, the whole of time would not suffice my need.[169]

As we saw above, the entire Christian apologetic apparatus assumed that the pagan gods were dead things. As Prudentius said to the pagan defender Symmachos, you may "count as many temples of gods at Rome as tombs of heroes in all the world."[170] When the idols were torn down, Eusebius reported, disgusted pagans found only the "bones and dry skulls from dead bodies," and so left their superstitious ways.[171] And they particularly liked Celsus's example. How could Zeus be a god, Athenagoras asked, if he was buried in a grave in Crete?[172]

Pagans obviously could and did ask the same question. So Christians had to be careful about their relationship to the self-sacrificing dead and the tombs built to house their bones and dry skulls. Augustine was aware of the risk. Those who are "hostile to us and perverse in mind . . . suppose that, whereas gods were worshipped in temples by pagans, we worship the dead in tombs," so he tried hard to inoculate Christianity against the charge of necrolatria.[173] Indeed, the *City of God* ended on just this note, where Augustine delicately disentangled (or at least tried to disentangle) Christianity from the paganism to which it bore such a resemblance. *They* "have built temples for their gods, established altars, instituted priesthoods and offered sacrifices," but *we* do not. Appearances to the contrary, we "do not make temples . . . but memorial shrines"; we do not "erect altars on these shrines" to make sacrifices to the martyrs, but "to the one God of the martyrs"; the priest is "God's priest, not theirs"; and so on.[174]

To the skeptics, such careful distinctions looked like sophistry. Among his other accusations, Faustus the Manichean charged Christians with making "idols into martyrs." Your new religion has "changed nothing," he declared, hiding the worst bits of Judaism and paganism under a cloak of novelty.[175] Altar does *not* yield to altar, nor blood to blood, he might have said, for by keeping altars and blood and bones and sacrifices, you keep the very architecture of the religion you reject.

Augustine's response—that "what is offered is offered *to* God, who crowned the martyrs, but *at* the memorials of those martyrs he crowned"—would hardly have been convincing.[176] Not least because, as his own sermons show, so many Christians were themselves confused by all of these substitutions and incorporations. Augustine felt compelled to remind even a Christian audience that "God has bestowed the bodies of the saints on the Churches for memorials to pray at and as reminders to pray, not for monuments to the martyrs to give them glory."[177] These sober distinctions were apparently lost on more ordinary Christians, as Faustus and other skeptics may well have known. Gatherings at the tombs of the martyrs could get boisterous, for example, an uncomfortable reminder to the fathers of how close Christian and pagan *refrigeria* actually were. In the late fourth century, Ambrose set out to abolish the feasts at the martyr's graves in Milan. Augustine's own mother, in fact, was turned away from the tombs when bringing offerings of wine, cakes, and bread.[178] When Augustine speaks of Cyprian's table as "not as one on which to feed or be fed," he is clearly making reference to overenthusiastic Christian practices.[179] In 405, Augustine preached specifically against the "aggressive rowdiness of dancers" at Cyprian's grave, a practice that he had already started condemning some ten years earlier.[180] And his letter to Alypius, bishop of Thagaste, inveighed against those basilicas filled "crowds of banqueting drunks." Even St. Peter's, he wrote, was subject to the same plague.[181] And so, in final response to Faustus, he commented that "what we teach is one thing; what we put up with is another. . . . [it is] a far lesser sin to return drunk from the memorials of the martyrs than to offer sacrifice to the martyrs while fasting."[182] Perhaps, Faustus might have said, but why do either? Why not leave behind the tombs of the pagans and their bloody gods, cut Christianity loose from the past, and create something new?

Conclusion: The Legacy of Sacrifice

As we have seen, this did not, and probably could not, happen. The structure of early Christianity; its project of typology and the absorption of the Hebrew Bible into its sacred canon; its disavowed dependencies on the gentile imagination of its opponents; the sociology, history, and politics of Christian conversion: all of these factors, and doubtless more, made Christianity a peculiarly heteronomous beast. It was a religion virtually at war with itself, constantly scouring itself for imperfections. And it could not help but find them, since it was aided in the effort by legions of skeptics, inside and outside the Church, who asked, again and again, are you *really* Christian? Are you Christian enough? Have you really left your ancestral homeland for a new and better place?

Sacrifice offered us an itinerary through this complex territory. This token of ancient error, firmly rejected as antithetical to the Christian thing, yet folded into itself, made foundational to the theology and practices of the early Christian church. Heterodoxy—literally, the teachings of another—and orthodoxy joined together in the Christian world of sacrifice. Sacrifice was a thing incorporated, yet with struggle, even agonized struggle, over the terms of its incorporation.

Three points, then, in summary. First, Christianity was, from the beginning, a comparative religion. Its logic was powerful and consistent. It was integration with a difference: you do this, we do this too, but differently. Everything distinctive about Christianity was dynamically positioned against its competitors, both internal and external. Apologetics was the enterprise of Christian comparison, paradoxically performed in the name of Christian liberation from its cultural and religious surround.

Second, Christianity's archive was (and is) constitutively heteronomous. By that, I mean two things. One, that the agonistic incorporation that was so characteristic of early Christianity, and that gave Christianity its particular form as it moved from a religion of opposition to one of near hegemony, built an archive inherited by later Christians. In this archive, Christians preserved the words of their detractors, and often, indeed, are our *only* source of these words. Two, that the apologetic *form* made heteronomy a structural feature of the Christian archive. Apologetics repeatedly demonstrated, above all, how much Christians struggled with the contents of their own theologies, and the unstable dependence of Christian orthodoxy on *other teachings* in the making of its own constitution.

Finally, Christianity was a religion of demystification. It not only demystified the religion of its opponents, showing its gods to be bones, skulls, or nothing at all, but it also demystified *itself*. That is, the contentious form of early Christianity, the fights between and among those who laid claim to the legacy of Christ's teachings, produced a constitutive instability in the religion that lasted for nearly four centuries. At the center of this instability were those perilous incorporations. Or better, the agony of these incorporations, the work of keeping them present in both theology and praxis, without falling into the obvious errors that they constantly invited. Christianity constantly discovered it was something that it had no intention of being and, as a result, the entire theological enterprise was fragile, involuted, and contentious. These fragilities and instabilities were not, in my view, resolved by a conceptual breakthrough. Instead, they were resolved by the slow decline of Christianity's competitors, and the emergence of a church better able to regulate the borders and boundaries of the Christian imagination. Such regulations did not erase the older archives of heteronomy, however, and, in the early modern period, they would come powerfully back to life.

PART II

Sacrifice and the Deep Time of Christianity, ca. 1450–1580

AS THE WORLD of late antiquity faded, new challenges and opportunities confronted a Church whose fortunes had been so intimately tied to Rome. With the fragmentation of that Empire, Christianity gradually divided into eastern Orthodox and western Latin churches, a separation formalized in 1054, but begun much earlier. For its part, the Latin church grew up in tandem with the Merovingians, the Carolingians, the Ottonians, and all of the powerful European dynasties that, from the early Middle Ages, created the Holy Roman Empire. These centuries of expansion saw a Church spreading ever more widely over Europe and developing its own robust institutions: the European monasteries, with their great landholdings; a coordinated hierarchy of secular clergy, from parish priests to popes; the administrative territories that this hierarchy oversaw; the schools and bureaucracies that these institutions required; the legal institutions and codes that regulated broad areas of European life. This expansion was no easy process. From the conversion of the Franks in the eighth and ninth centuries, to the appearance of new heresies within Christendom, to the internecine struggles among Europe's noble houses, to the challenge of Islam, and later the felt compulsion to reconquer the Holy Land: the tasks of growth and consolidation consumed a Church whose connections to the conflicts of late antiquity grew ever more attenuated.

As this Church changed, so too did its liturgies and theologies. Christian sacrifice in the later Middle Ages shows the distance the Church had traveled from its earlier concerns. Beginning well before the millennium, but then accelerating afterward, the Latin church became unabashedly sacrificial. In Carolingian times, Christ's principal roles were as king and judge.[1] By the year 1000, however, he had become a suffering victim, and his bloody death on the Cross moved to the center of the religious imagination. With it came the discovery that the real body and blood of Christ could be found in the bread and wine of the Mass, the doctrine of transubstantiation, as it became known in the eleventh century, ratified as formal orthodoxy at the Fourth Lateran Council of 1215. The result was a flood of Eucharistic piety that cascaded throughout the Church and western Christendom. It affected the built enviroment of churches, for example, as Eucharistic veneration was given substance through the erection of Holy Sepulchres in European churches, in which the host was "buried" during Easter celebrations.[2] The Eucharistic pyx—the special box used to separate the consecrated host from the profane world—also dates to this period. This new piety affected the office of the priest as well, whose ritual actions were increasingly standardized around the Eucharist. A "Christo-mimetic" priesthood liturgically re-enacted the passion of Christ at every Mass, the priest offering in the bread and wine the self-same sacrifice that Christ had suffered on the Cross.[3] The custom of elevating the host, and later the ringing of the bell to announce the transformation of the Eucharistic elements into the real body and blood of Christ, in turn became standard elements in the ritual repertoire of the Mass. Eucharistic piety affected the festival calendar of the Church too, as when, in 1264, Pope Urban IV sanctioned the feast of Corpus Christi for the second Thursday after Pentacost. This celebration of the Eucharist generated a huge variety of new popular devotional forms. Processions, pageants, and passion plays grew up around the feast, celebrating the body, blood, and sacrifice of Christ.[4] Around the same time, but intensifying in the fourteenth and fifteenth centuries, England and northern Europe saw the development of popular cults that featured mass pilgrimages to view the wonder of hosts, statues, and images that spontaneously shed Christ's redemptive blood.[5] Veneration of the wounds of Christ spread from monastic to lay Christian circles. Masses dedicated to the wounds appeared in the early fourteenth century, proclaiming both the humanity of Christ and the salvific effect of his holy blood. Christian art followed suit. The Man of Sorrows—the suffering and bleeding Christ surrounded by the instruments of his torments—emerged as a major theme of visual culture in Germany and the Low Countries in the thirteenth century.[6] Rivers of blood poured from Christ's wounds in late medieval crucifixes, sculptures, drawings, and paintings. By 1500, no Christian could have failed to know that, at the heart of their faith, lay the sacrifice of Christ, accomplished once on the cross in ancient Palestine, and again, daily, in every church in Christendom.

Fifty years later, however, what had energized the everyday life of the Church had become the source of division and despair. From the earliest days of the Reformation, in fact, the entire structure of medieval sacrifice began to collapse. In Wittenberg, Zürich, Geneva, London, Amsterdam—the capital cities of the new forms of Christianity that we call Protestantism—passionate cries rang against the Eucharistic piety of the medieval Church. The elevation and adoration of the Eucharist, the Roman Canon of the Mass, the priesthood offering in sacrifice the body of Christ to God the Father: the heart of medieval piety was, reformers argued, no better than pagan superstition. No less anathema were the cult of the saints and martyrs, whose sculptures adorned the medieval church and whose litanies were read at every Mass. Eventually even the atonement itself, the Crucifixion offered in salvation of all mankind, fell prey to the same suspicion, that what we have inherited as Christianity is no such thing. Over the course of the sixteenth century, then, the problem of sacrifice splintered whatever unity there was in the Latin church, spinning out new communities of faith and practice. Evangelical Lutherans, reformed Calvinists, Anabaptists, and many other smaller confessions became intrinsic features of the religious geography of western Europe.

Along the way, Christianity was remade. Already in the fifteenth century, for example, the Christian *past* began to matter in ways it never had before. When Renaissance humanists rediscovered the power of classical antiquity, they also rediscovered the hidden worlds of the ancient Church. Humanists—and later Protestant reformers in their wake—began to construct the Christian *archive*, the historically sedimented set of authors, texts, theologies, and traditions that compose what is called Christianity. This archive was intended to show how the present Church had departed from Christianity's historical origins, and to map a return back to a time of unity and purity. Growing ever larger throughout the early modern period, first with the collection and publication of the earliest church fathers, and later with materials exogenous to Christianity itself, what this archive revealed instead was the deep and intractable *variety* of historical Christianity.

Nothing witnessed this as powerfully as sacrifice. In the first place, as we have seen, sacrifice was *already* a site of deep uncertainty in the ancient church. Christians marked themselves as Christians, in part, by their rejection of their sacrificial surround, whether Jewish or pagan. At the same time, they had integrated this sacrificial surround, sometimes with great difficulty, into the matrix of their own religious imagination. These ancient struggles were long forgotten by the later Middle Ages, when sacrifice became such a dynamic source of Christian piety. But they were quickly rediscovered by humanists and reformers, who plumbed the archive in the name of a Christianity lost to time and history. To answer the question "what *is* Christian sacrifice," in other words, they asked another question: what *was* Christian sacrifice?

What they discovered, and the intellectual transformations that these discoveries unleashed, are the subject of the next three chapters. Chapter 2 focuses on the early formation of the Christian archive, paying particular attention to its great architect, the Dutch humanist scholar and theologian Desiderius Erasmus. The events of the Reformation play a background role here. Foregrounded instead are the new kinds of humanist theology, and the new forms of the sacrificial imagination, that emerged with the rediscovery of the patristic heritage of Christianity. Chapter 3 turns to the Reformation itself. It explores the damage it did to, and the innovations in liturgy and theology it invented to replace, the sacrificial piety of the medieval church. In both Protestant practice and theory, Christian sacrifice was given a new history and anthropology, one rooted in the patristic world and put in the service of reform. Chapter 4 moves from theology to the violence of the Reformation era, when a new world of martyrdom emerged from the crucible of religious war. These new sacrifices prompted a renewed engagement with the ancient world of Christian martyrdom, a world where heretics and saints sat uncomfortably close together. Each chapter circles back into the later Middle Ages, tracing how elements of an earlier sacrificial piety were remade by the religious transformations of the early modern period. By the 1570s, we will observe, the sacrificial crisis of the Reformation created an entirely new picture of the Christian past, one characterized by heterogeny and variety rather than concord and unity.

CHAPTER TWO

From the Thesaurus to the Archive

SACRIFICE AND THE PRACTICE OF THEOLOGY

All I do is restore the old; I put forward nothing new.

—ERASMUS, LETTER TO GODSCHALK ROSEMONDT, 1520[1]

And Christ died once and for all (semel)*, that is on the cross . . . neverthless everyday* (quotidie) *he is immolated in the sacrament, because it is recalled in the sacrament that which was done once.*[2]

—PETER OF LOMBARD, *SENTENCES* (CA. 1150)

TOO MUCH OF human life is lost or unknown, the German historian Leopold von Ranke once wrote. We bury the dead, their traces grow faint, and memories fail. For one remembered, thousands disappear forever. Only the special endure, conserved by labor and creativity, their memories institutionalized, preserved in words, ceremonies, and objects that insist on the possibility of survival. That we remember the death of Socrates, Moses, or Christ at all is an astonishing testament to the labor of commemoration.

Walk into a medieval church, and observe how this labor is built into its bones. In the Latin world, you are likely to enter from the west side and to look east toward the altar. Inside the altar you should imagine a fragment of Christianity's special dead, remnants of saints consecrating a site that, in ancient times, might have been built directly atop the cemeteries that housed them. The statues and mosaics adorning the interior trace a history from the Passion, to the apostles who preserved it in writing, to the later saints who labored to keep these Gospels alive in the world. These palaces of memory light up for every saint's day in the ritual calendar, each festal occasion recalling those who died in His name.

At the center of Christian memory work stands the Eucharist. "Do this in memory of me," Jesus told his apostles at his final supper. Communion celebrates not only the union of a Christian community, but also the union of past and present. Throughout the Middle Ages, this union was forged in sacrifice. Christ died once and for all, perfecting and completing the sacrifices of the ancient world. And then his sacrifice was repeated and commemorated in every Eucharistic celebration across the Christian world. Sacrifice—that rite both left behind and renewed in the making of Christianity—gave liturgical form to the temporal unity of medieval Christianity, keeping the past alive even as the Church moved forward in human time.

In the early modern period, this temporal unity began to collapse. That great change in historical consciousness called the Renaissance announced that the past was *different* from the present, that time was discontinuous, and that the learned must dedicate themselves to understanding and mapping historical difference in service of cultural, political, and religious renovation. Whether collecting manuscripts or developing new philological tools or purging Latin of alleged medieval solecisms, the humanist intellectuals of the fifteenth and sixteenth centuries tirelessly pried apart past and present.

Christian time did not survive this challenge unscathed. Medieval theology was energetic and creative, incorporating new philosophical authorities and developing new traditions of exegesis and commentary. Yet it typically treated the Christian past as homogeneous, as a stable repository of truths useful for the development of doctrine. The new forms of theological reasoning that developed in the Renaissance, by contrast, did not. The theology of humanism rejected the scholasticism of its ancestors, the philosophical quiddities that had tantalized thinkers like Aquinas and Scotus. It also rejected the formal commentary tradition that wove together ancient and modern authorities into vast citational tapestries, the tradition that created the *Glossa ordinaria* on the Bible, for example, or the canon law commentary known as the *Decretals*. Humanist theology pulled past from present, ancient from medieval from modern. In doing so, it discovered in antiquity (and in the present) a heterogeneity that disaggregated the Christian temporal horizon, indeed began to disaggregate Christianity itself. In its wake, sacrifice—that rite that bonded the past and present of the medieval Church—became something far more uncertain, an at-times disconcerting, even alien remnant of a world left behind.

This process began with the formation of what I call a Christian archive—that is, a host of competing and often disagreeing traditions and authorities—out of the patristic world of early Christianity. The great pioneer in this was the irenic Dutch humanist and theologian Desiderius Erasmus (1466–1536), by far the most consequential figure in the history of early modern study of patristics. From early in his learned life, Erasmus worked to build a new archive of Christianity, assembling a revolutionary collection of writings from Greek and Latin fathers that gave new texture and depth to the Christian past. When the religious revolution of the 1520s began to destroy that integrative sacrificial economy of medieval Christianity, Erasmus looked to this archive in hopes of refounding Christian fellowship and unity. What he revealed in this archive was not a comforting vision of consensus, however, but rather plurality and conflict. The once-and-for-all sacrifice of Christ on the Cross, and the daily sacrifice of the Eucharist, became ever stranger as the time of Christianity splintered into pieces.

Sacrifice Once and Everyday: Time and the Form of Medieval Theology

In the greatest theological textbook of its age, Peter of Lombard's *Sentences* (ca. 1150), it was asked whether "Christ is immolated at the altar every day, and whether what the priest does should be called a sacrifice." The answer was short:

> That which is offered and consecrated by the priest, is to be called a sacrifice and an offering, because it is a memorial and representation of that true sacrifice and holy immolation made on the altar of the cross. And Christ died once and for all (*semel*), that is on the cross . . . nevertheless everyday (*quotidie*) he is immolated in the sacrament, because it is recalled in the sacrament that which was done once.[3]

At the altar, every day (*quotidie*) in churches across Christendom, something mysterious occurs. An event that happened one time (*semel*), Christ's death on the Cross, happens again, when the priest consecrates and offers the Eucharist to God in the liturgy of the Mass. A sacrifice was made, a sacrifice is made. Christ's death, once and for all, *ephapax* in the words of the *Letter to the Hebrews* (10.10), yet now present in the immolation of the sacrament, every day, everywhere. Peter did not pretend to explain this mystery, made no less mysterious by its ubiquity.[4] Rather, he laid it out in bare form, affirming that at the center of Christianity's holiest ceremony lay the temporal mystery of sacrifice. For the next three hundred years, the sentence commentary tradition confidently repeated more or less the same thing.[5]

The remarkable durability of this tradition depended both on the original form of the *Sentences* and the later commentaries that it inspired. The *Sentences* were organized topically in the form of "distinctions," each of which Peter broke down into a set of questions. Thus the final book on the sacraments began with general questions on the nature of sacraments, before proceeding to more systematic exploration of each sacrament. Each *quaestio* was short and confident, and each supported its teaching with authoritative patristic citations. In book IV, distinction 12, chapter V—"whether Christ is sacrificed (*immolatur*) at the altar every day, and whether what is done by the priest, is a sacrifice"—for example, Peter called on the authority of the fourth century Bishop of Milan, St. Ambrose:

> In Christ, the saving victim is offered one time. What then of us? Do we not offer every day? Although we do offer every day (*quotidie*), it is done in memory of his death; and there is one victim, not many. In what way one and not many? Because Christ is immolated one time (*semel*). This sacrifice however is an exemplar of his; the same thing, always the same, is offered, hence it is that sacrifice. Otherwise, seeing that it is offered in many places, are there many Christs? No, but there is one Christ in all places, and fully existing here, and fully existing there; just as the same body is offered everywhere, so too is the sacrifice the same. Christ offered a victim, we offer that victim now; but what we do is a memorial (*recordatio*) of his sacrifice.[6]

The sacrifice of Christ, as the church father described it, was a fundamental figure in the Christian theology of time. In Him, the victim was offered "one time," and that time was in the past. But *we* offer Him "every day," now, in our present and as long as the Church abides. The father's call-and-response exploration of this temporal mystery did not seek to resolve it in some final way, but rather to elaborate the miracle of Christ and the mystery of the church militant, the community of Christians that bear the body of Christ forward in time and space. Christ's sacrifice thus collapsed temporal distinctions. What "we do is a memorial," a *recordatio*. It is neither a mere memory of an event long past nor the actual repetition of his singular Passion, but the coexistence of past and present in drama of the liturgy. Sacrifice and sacrament combine past and present intimately together.

When we read Peter of Lombard, then, we can observe how his exploration of the Eucharist not only preserved the *content* of the church father, but also the method. Peter did not seek to dissolve the conflict between *semel* and *quotidie*, but set these times of sacrifice into proximity, confirmation of the mystery of the Passion. To modern readers accustomed to looking for innovations in the history of ideas, this approach can make Peter look like a "mere rehash of patristic theology, a *florilegium* of no originality."[7] Such a criticism would completely misunderstand how someone like the Lombard related to the world of the ancient church, however. He was almost by definition uninterested in "originality," after all, since the larger project was to recreate in a new idiom the unity of past and present. By letting his own views simply stand in conversational proximity to the ancient church, Peter confirmed that same collective, transtemporal continuity figured by our *recordatio* of Christ's death.

Sacrifice-once/sacrifice-everyday had an analogue, in other words, in the formal structure of Peter's work. This helps put into perspective the (from a modern point of view) startling discovery that even an immensely learned churchman like Peter of Lombard had relatively little first-hand knowledge of the patristic corpus that featured so prominently in the *Sentences*. He had direct knowledge, for example, of only four works of Augustine, the most important of fathers for the medievals. Even what we now take to be the Bishop of Hippo's greatest work, the *City of God*, was only familiar to Peter through other collections.[8] Nor was the Lombard unusual in this respect. The theologians of the twelfth century were eager students of the Fathers, but knowledge of them was typically indirect. Extracts, quotations, and summaries were gathered in massive, topically arranged compilations that provided handy reference works for theologians exploring specific topics. Patristic authorities were also refracted through long chains of interconnected commentary. The early church father Origen, for example, was commonly received through multiple interpretive screens: Origen's third-century views of Ezekiel, seen through Jerome's fourth-century commentaries and translations, seen in turn through the compilations of the ninth-century Carolingian abbot Hrabanus Maurus, and then collected together in the middle of the twelfth century.[9]

From a formal perspective, however, none of this mattered. The ancient fathers with whom Peter felt in communion were nodes in a web of authorities whose connections united the past into a continuous theological present. He would have been unimpressed, one suspects, by the observation that his "Ambrose" was actually the Greek father John Chrysostom, from whose homily on the *Letter to the Hebrews* the quotation derives. This misattribution was altogether conventional at this time. He would have found the same "author" and quotation in the *Decretum* of Ivo of Chartres, for example, a canon law collection from ca. 1100. There, in a section relating to the Mass and the Eucharist, Ivo cites "Ambrosius" on the *Letter to the Hebrews* as his patristic witness to Christ's sacrifice both once-and-for-all, and every day.[10] The same citation also entered the great collection of canon law, the *Decretum* attributed to Gratian, around the same time that the Lombard compiled his *Sentences*.[11] And it can be found in the *Glossa ordinaria*, that gargantuan collection of patristic and medieval biblical commentaries assembled in the twelfth century.[12] An ambitious medieval reader might have been able to track down the original source of the quotation—Thomas Aquinas had considerable firsthand knowledge of the patristic corpus, for example—but for even the learned it is not clear why one should bother.[13]

Not only was the misattribution common, after all, it was also irrelevant given the role the fathers were asked to play in works like the *Sentences*. There they supplied an integrated but temporally flat system of theological referents. This reference structure was analogous to a *thesaurus*, a treasury of patristic authors and citations that collectively formed a common language of inquiry. It would make no more sense to say that Ambrose's views on the sacrament are better or more authentic than Chrysostom's than it would be to argue that the word "book" is better or more authentic than "codex." One word might suit a particular occasion better, but both share equal status in the horizon of reference. The art of the commentator, like that of a writer, lay in choosing the most suitable. At the end of the day, this patristic treasury offered a coherent ideational semantics that distributed authority more or less equally across its terms.

This horizontal distribution of patristic authority was particularly important given the wider theological context of the *Sentences*. This context was characterized by deep diversity, on the one hand, and efforts to pull this diversity into systematic shape, on the other. Medieval theology encompassed a vibrant range of literary forms from scholastic philosophy to exegesis to homilies to mysticism and more. The vocabulary used to describe this heterogeneous intellectual terrain was equally diverse: *sacrum studium, sacra eruditio, sacra doctrina, sacra pagina, divina pagina*, and *divinitas*. The study of these also took place in a highly differentiated environment, with individual cathedral schools and the *studia* of the various orders offering distinct approaches to theological matters.[14]

As a canon at Notre Dame in Paris, and teacher in the cathedral school there, Peter tried to pull this diversity into unity, to create "systematic theology," in Marcia Colish's language, a theology seen as a formal discipline with a coherent curriculum.[15] Over the long term, this effort was successful, especially as the professionalization of theological elites accelerated with the emergence of the university in the early thirteenth century. A minor player in this new institution—most university-educated priests matriculated in law, far and away the most important faculty in the early university—theology needed both its own specific content, apart from (and above) the other faculties, but also a definite pedagogical form.[16] The *Sentences* became this form. Its teachings were affirmed by the Fourth Lateran church council in 1215, then taken up in university faculties in Paris and later Oxford, and by the 1240s, they became the foundation of theological instruction and inquiry.[17]

What recommended the *Sentences* was not only its ingenious organization of theological topics, but also a method that systematically created a "harmony from dissonance."[18] Lombard was not naïve. He was well aware that patristic authorities often disagreed with one another, not least from the contemporary work of the controversial theologian Peter Abelard. "The very prophets and apostles were not altogether strangers to error," wrote Abelard, who collected the dissents and contradictions of the church fathers in his early twelfth century *Sic et non*.[19] Nor was the Lombard unaware of dissonant voices in the medieval church. Indeed, the prologue to the *Sentences* vigorously attacked the "mendacious hypocricy" [*hypocrisis mendax*], the "feigned piety" [*simulatam pietatem*], and the "false doctrine" [*falsae doctrinae*] of those he called the "students of contention" [*studentes contentioni*].[20] As Spencer Young, G. R. Evans, and Jaroslav Pelikan have argued, the formation of the new theological disciplines in the medieval university drew much energy from the determination to refute perceived heresies, not least the Cathars in the south of France.[21]

The genius of the *Sentences* was its ability to clarify and stabilize, however, to proceed *as if* there was a consensus on matters doctrinal, if only to allow one to better judge where heresy lay. Indeed, the Lombard concluded his exploration of the Eucharist with the curt statement that, regarding the mystery of the Lord's body and blood, "we have summarized some things which are to be held by Catholics; whoever contradicts these is adjudged a heretic."[22]

Time and form, in conclusion, converged in the *Sentences*. "Sacrifice once, sacrifice everyday," married the Passion, the patristic fathers who adored it, and its present sacramental repetition in a timescape whose unity Christ guaranteed with His gift of an abiding Church. The form of theological inquiry preserved this timescape with a careful arrangement of doctrine, scripture, and patristic commentary. The *semel* and the *quotidie* were joined in a common mystical horizon, protected by a canopy of theological consensus rooted in the thesaurus of the Fathers.

Building the Patristic Archive

The patristic thesaurus, however, did not long survive the Middle Ages. Already in the time of Peter of Lombard, conflicts between Byzantine and Roman churches—the formal schism between east and west in 1054, but especially the sack of Constantinople by Norman crusaders in 1204—put pressure on the patristic heritage to which both sides laid claim. The 1252 treatise *Contra graecos*, written in the Dominican monastery in Constantinople, used patristic sources to criticize the Byzantine church, for example.[23] Ten years later, Thomas Aquinas echoed this approach, exploring the tensions both between ancient Greek and Latin patristic writers and between Greek and Latin churches. These centrifugal forces might well have been contained by the flexible interpretive structures of medieval theology, however, had not the past and its witnesses become such forces of estrangement at the dawn of the modern era.[24]

On the face of it, the whole idea was startling. Medievals like the Lombard had mislaid the truths of their own history, and it was the obligation of the learned to restore them. The quest "to awaken the true Aristotle" and all the ancient authors believed corrupted or forgotten by the medieval church, the desire to rupture the present by restoring to the past its own dignity, has become such an iconic story in Western intellectual history that it often fails to surprise as much as it should. We live in the shadow of this history, after all, and all-too-easily feel the past as distant and unsettling, all-too-readily assume the moral obligation to curate this past that we inherited from this period called the Renaissance. It takes some effort to recall just how bizarre the idea was, and how disorienting in matters religious.

The Renaissance did not only awaken Aristotle, rediscover Plato and Cicero, unearth Lucretius and Livy. It also produced massive new libraries of patristic learning largely unknown to medieval readers. Already in the first decades of the fifteenth century, the Florentine chancellor and humanist Coluccio Salutati collected manuscripts of most of the known Latin fathers.[25] In the same decades, the translation of the Greek fathers began in earnest through the work of the self-taught Camaldolese monk Ambrogio Traversari, aided by Florence's chief bibliophile, Niccolo Niccoli.[26] These efforts were redoubled in the context of the Council of

Florence (1439), an effort to heal the east-west schism during which patristics became the terrain of disputations about the *filioque*, the Latin addition to the Nicene Creed that had caused such trinitarian troubles in the Christian churches. In this case, paradoxically, an axiomatic commitment to the unity of the patristic thesaurus, that "the saints of the ancient church were in unquestioned communion," became the source of controversy, as each church presented examples of *different* patristic views of the same matter.[27] The very quest for unity began to pull the patristic thesaurus apart, encouraging ever more scrupulous interest in the varieties of patristic opinion about matters doctrinal.

Take, as a brief example, the case of the humanist George of Trebizond (1395–1474?). Born in Crete, but living in Italy from the 1430s, he was called upon at the Council to translate Basil of Caesarea's *Contra Eunomium* specifically to shed light on the controversial question of the procession of the Holy Spirit.[28] After the failure of the Council, Trebizond continued as a patristics translator in Rome, working for the humanist pope Nicholas V. A colorful and often outrageous scholar—jailed for a knife fight with the Renaissance book collector Poggio Bracciolini and then again for supposedly pledging fealty to the Ottoman king Mehmed, among other misadventures—he was also crucial transmitter of such texts as the fourth-century father Eusebius's *Praeparatio evangelica*, one of the great apologetic texts of the ancient world. Even more interesting than the 1448 translation itself—a poor one by all accounts—was Trebizond's surprising and novel attitude toward patristic authority.[29] "Ignorance of history" will not be overcome, Trebizond argued, "*unless the differences in times are known* . . . unless you know when things happened." Eusebius gives us the tools for such analysis, letting us see "as in a mirror, the variety and multiplicity of doctrines" of the ancient world. Moreover, Eusebius himself *exemplified* this multiplicity. We know, Trebizond argued, that the *Praeparatio* was written before the Council of Nicaea because it contains doctrines later condemned by this council that surely no father as holy as Eusebius would keep in the face of conciliar disapproval.[30]

Already before the coming of print, then, the patristic world had dramatically expanded, as the learned grew the available corpus through collection, compilation, and translation.[31] Afterward, easily accessible works of the fathers—including, among others, Athanasius, Athenagoras, Augustine, Chrysostom, Cyprian, Gregory Nazianzenus, Hilary, Irenaeus, Jerome, Lactantius, Origen, and Tertullian—wildly multiplied. These new currents of patristics fed new kinds of piety, especially in the so-called *devotio moderna* of northern Europe, which, with its emphasis on education and lay piety, built major patristic libraries in Dutch spiritual centers like Deventer and Windesheim.[32]

The transformation was not merely quantitative. For many humanists, it entailed as well a new *attitude* toward this patristic world. The *devotio moderna* still stressed the continuity between the patristic authors and the writers of the Middle Ages. But for George Trebizond, it was the *discontinuity*, among the fathers and between the fathers and ourselves, that was a given. This discontinuity made the church fathers useful weapons in the battles between eastern and western churches. And it also made them useful weapons against those, like Peter of Lombard, who imagined the ancient writers within the singular temporal horizon of Christianity.

Few so ruthlessly disrupted this temporal horizon as did Trebizond's contemporary, the Italian humanist Lorenzo Valla. Since the 1440s, when he exposed the Donation of Constantine as a forgery and came into open conflict with ecclesiastical authorities in Naples, Valla had been a thorn in the side of the scholastic theologians.[33] Shortly before his death in 1457, he offered a mighty oration at Rome's *S. Maria sopra Minerva* church. The *Encomium of St. Thomas* simultaneously praised the Angelic Doctor for his learning, and attacked the "timelessness and perennity" of his theological system.[34] Valla prosecuted his critique by insisting on the essential difference between the ancients (*veteres* or *antiqui*) and the moderns (*recentes* or *novi*).[35] The latter are "barbarians," overly committed to philosophy, ignorant of the true purposes of theology.[36] The church fathers, by contrast—and Valla singled out Cyprian, Lactantius, Hilary, Ambrose, Jerome, Augustine, Basil, Gregory Nazianzenus, and John Chrysostom—followed the example of Paul. Together they offered the "true method of theologizing (*germanus theologandi modus*)."[37] The precise nature of this "method" Valla left vague. What was more important, however, was the source of the divergence. It was the *recentes*, the medievals, who had libeled and abused these fathers. It was thus in *defense* of patristic holiness, learning, and eloquence that Valla made his stand. The gulf between past and present that Valla exploited to such great effect in his *Encomium*, in other words, he blamed on the scholastics themselves.

By the later fifteenth century, then, not only could a learned humanist reader have identified Peter of Lombard's quotation exactly—for example, in the 1483 printing of Chrysostom's complete homilies on the *Letter to the Hebrews*—but it would have been his duty to do so.[38] Correct authorial attributions, the sorting of spurious from true works, the correction of works to a presumed original: these were among the highest ethical goods for the Renaissance culture of reading. Moreover, in the context of a humanist theology eager to distinguish itself from the labors of its (newly denominated) medieval competitors, this obligation took on sharply polemical force. It was the lever that people like Valla used to pry apart the *recentes* from the *antiqui* and to elevate the differences discovered between past and present into matters of high theological urgency.

This process rearranged the Lombard's patristic thesaurus. It disaggregated its unified temporal field, pulled its flat ideational structure into three dimensions, vertically arranging the fathers and assigning each a niche defined by a body of authentic works written at particular times and places. Not only might an early modern reader discover conflicts and disagreements among the fathers; he might well (and often did) discover them even within an authorial corpus. This disaggregation of the patristic horizon first enabled and then demanded that modern readers approach the patristic world as a complex and sometimes contested stratigraphy of authorities and ideas.

This reconfigured patristic world—a new Christian archive—supported and required a theological practice different from the Lombard's. This archive was not a repository of presumed consensus but one from which consensus had to be extracted. Consensus became the *endpoint* of theology, rather than its stipulated beginning. Put differently, this new patristic archive coordinated with new practices of theology in ways that reshaped European religious and intellectual history.

Sacrifice and The Godly Feast

In the wake of this transformation, the mystery of the "sacrifice once, sacrifice everyday" became something altogether more puzzling for early modern Christians. We begin exploring this change in 1522, when nine friends gathered in a country garden for a convivial feast. The fountains and herbs recalled the godly delights of heaven, while the coming meal brought Christ to mind. An institution once "holy to pagans"—the *convivium*—now imitated the sacred supper that Jesus shared with his disciples in his last hours.[39] As they sat down to eat, the friends began a Christian conversation with a reading from Proverbs 21. Initially unsure whether laymen like themselves should speak on biblical topics absent a learned theologian, they quickly lost their inhibitions and began to discuss. When they got to the final verse—which reads "to do righteousness and justice is more acceptable to the Lord than sacrifice" (21.3)—the host, Eusebius, asked the following: how can God both reject sacrifice and so often command that sacrifice be done in His honor?

When Desiderius Erasmus—schoolboy in Deventer, epicenter of the *devotio moderna*, and later prince of northern humanism—wrote *The Godly Feast*, the question had grown suddenly difficult. For centuries, as we saw above, Christianity's own holy feast of the Eucharist had offered a ritual answer to Eusebius, declaring sacrifice complete in the crucifixion, and yet mysteriously extended in perpetual repetition. By 1522, however, the Eucharist was no longer uncontroversial. In an April 1520 sermon, the German monk Martin Luther—first Erasmus's ally, later his bitter enemy—declared that the reconciliation of *semel* and *quotidie* was over. The story of the Bible, Luther insisted, was the *overcoming* of sacrifice, not its preservation. "Before the old law of Moses the ancient patriarchs had no other way to observe the law of God than sacrifice," he remarked. But beginning with the Mosaic law, sacrifice grew increasingly constrained in function. Moses instituted sacrificial laws in order to show the Jews, Luther put it, "that human nature might recognize how *little* help the law is, in making people pious." It was through an understanding of sacrifice as a primary "work," that is, something that humans do for God, that Luther developed what became the foundational distinction for the Reformer and his followers, that between word and work. The *word*—the New Testament, Christ as the Word, the words of scripture—should be present in the Mass. The work must be cast out. And above all, for Luther, this meant the casting out of sacrifice (for a fuller discussion, see chapter 3).[40]

When Eusebius and his friends unfolded the puzzles of biblical sacrifice, then, they did so under the shadow of Luther and the controversies over the Mass already roiling the German lands.[41] Their approach was deliberative, not didactic. One of the guests, Theophilus, recollected the passage from the prophet Hosea (repeated in the Gospel of Matthew): "I desire mercy and not sacrifice" (Hos. 6.6; Matt. 9.13). The line might be interpreted as the stark rejection of sacrifice. Recall the prophet Isaiah—"bring no more vain offerings" (1.13)—Theophilus pointed out, and the condemnation of Jews who "embraced the shadows and neglected the substance." In this interpretive tradition, Jews elevated sacrifice over God, substituting (as Luther would later put it) the work for the word. And yet, Theophilus continued, perhaps the passage was not as clear as all that, for, he supposed, "this is the Hebrew idiom for 'I desire mercy *more than sacrifice*.'"[42] Softening his stance, he suggested that sacrifices (and by analogy, human rituals generally) are "not to be omitted entirely," but that these become "displeasing to God" if, in pursuing them, we neglect works of mercy.

For Eulalius, a third guest, this called to mind Paul's first letter to the Corinthians: "All things are lawful for me, but not all things are helpful" (6.12). This issue of law and expedience again raised the question of sacrifice. What should Christians hold about "the eating of food offered to idols" (8.4)? Since sacrificial meats were sold for food in public markets, the Corinthian community needed to know whether they could partake. Following Paul, Eulalius suggested that, although the meat itself is always the same and that "gospel liberty" should allow Christians to eat, nonetheless they ought to refrain lest they tempt weaker brethren to slip back to gentilism.[43] The discussion continued, demanding exegetical scaffolding from St. Ambrose; a clever distinction between the views of the "false apostles" who argued that some food is naturally unclean and Paul's insight that in Christ, all food may be eaten; and a final interpretive aside to the medieval commentator Theophylact, who suggested that eating too much makes you shameless.[44]

As regards sacrifice, then, Erasmus defended a cautious approach. Just as the gospel abolished law, the Crucifixion abolished the need for the elaborate sacrifices so powerfully featured in the Old Testament. Although the prophets had seen this, it was left to Christ to free humanity from its sacrificial obligations. Sacrifice was not *intrinsically* wrong, however. Just as "an idol has no real existence," sacrifice was neutral, a human thing that God neither requires nor needs (1 Cor. 8.4). The pious recognize this, but the weak may not. They may be seduced into thinking that the ceremony has a value of its own. They may thus set its performance above those works of charity and mercy that should occupy a good Christian. Sacrifice, meaning "whatever pertains to corporeal rites," posed the question: what should humans do for God? In Erasmus's 1522 answer—some things, but always with charity—we can already detect the fault lines that will shape not only his relationship to Luther and the reformers, but generations of Christian engagement with the sacrificial.[45]

Even more interesting (for the moment) is the *way* Erasmus made his argument. Exegesis proceeded in dialogue with a dense network of authorities. Old and New Testament texts; a patristic reference to Ambrose; a medieval Greek commentator; and the illustrative contrast of some unsourced false apostles: by Erasmian standards, this is not an extraordinarily learned list. Closer inspection, however, shows the complexity of Erasmus's intepretive project. Take the Byzantine author Theophylact, bishop of Achrida in the eleventh century. A Latin edition of his commentaries was published 1477 and attributed to the ancient church father Athanasius. Erasmus dug up the Greek edition ca. 1514, gave the collection its correct author, and incorporated it into his 1519 edition of the New Testament.[46] The reference to "false apostles" was obscure, but Erasmus would have found many examples of ancient vegetarianism—the so-called Encratites, for example, supposed followers of one Saturninus—in the second century heresiologist Irenaeus of Lyon, whose works he edited in 1526. Behind his reference, in other words, was the work of archival rearrangement, moving an important author from the Latin to the Greek canon, and setting his works forward some eight centuries.

A new archive was thus at work in this literary colloquy. Indeed, Erasmus pioneered its creation. Even as he wrote *The Godly Feast*, for example, he was editing Arnobius the Younger's *Commentary on the Psalms* (late fifth century CE). Addressed to Pope Adrian VI, its preface witnessed a new complexity of the patristic world. Readers had to know, for example, whether Arnobius the Younger was the author of another work attributed to "Arnobius," the then still-lost *Against the Gentiles*. Erasmus thought he was (incorrectly, as it turned out), and to show this, mobilized a host of other patristic authors who helped locate Arnobius in time and place. Using Augustine, he was able to argue that the crude Latin of the *Commentary* was designed for a crude audience and, using Jerome, he placed Arnobius as a rhetoric teacher in Sicca before his conversion.[47] Further temporal precision could be gained, Erasmus argued, by the absence of certain heresies in the text, especially those of the fourth- and fifth-century Donatists and Pelagians. And, finally, Erasmus compared Arnobius with a differentiated set of patrisic authorities, arguing that while "in the works of Tertullian and Origen and almost all the early Fathers there are elements either of manifest error or dubious doctrine," Arnobius was well-balanced and orthodox.[48]

Arnobius was only one element of Erasmus's grand patristic project. This project began with a 1516 edition of the letters of St. Jerome, a father whose reputation for piety and learning had exercised Erasmus's imagination since his early school days. Jerome was "learning at its best," and Erasmus attentively read and copied his letters well before he began the monumental task of editing them. In 1514, at the urging of the humanist publisher Johann Froben, Erasmus joined a team in Basel and worked with them for the next two years to publish the collected works of the "chief among the theologians of the Latin world."[49] For Erasmus, Jerome was the exemplar and summit of a pious Christian theology. "Who ever so successfully united every part of the sum of knowledge in such perfection," he wrote in a letter to Archbishop William Warham, as Jerome?[50]

The Jerome edition only whetted Erasmus's enthusiasm for things patristic. He played a major part in editions of Cyprian (1520), Hilary (1523), John Chrysostom (1525), Irenaeus (1526), Athanasius (1527), Ambrose (1527), Augustine (1529), Gregory Nazianzenus (1531), Basil (1532), and Origen (1536).[51] More than anyone else in his age, Erasmus *created* the patristic archive in its printed form, an archive that grew ever more challenging to navigate as it grew in scope and scale.[52]

Finally, *The Godly Feast* showed how this archive might be *used*. The gentlemen at dinner were laymen (*idiotis*), as they put it, not professional theologians (*theologi*).[53] The learned sentence commentary—with its systematic ambitions and firm conclusions—was foreign to them. Their discussion proceeded dialogically, with apologies for interpretive wagers, and invitations to the others for correction. This open structure allowed the guests to *do* theology—that is, to answer the questions that someone like the Lombard had once addressed—in a new key. What *The Godly Feast* rewarded was the ability to mobilize a certain kind of learning in combination with an ethic of communal investigation in which final authority rested somewhere else. The *theologus* is absent, but *theology* is present.

Erasmus knew how radical this departure was from the university theology of the Lombard. "All can be Christian, all can be devout, and I shall boldly add, all can be theologians [*nulli non licet esse theologum*]," he wrote in a preface to his learned 1516 Greek edition of the New Testament.[54] Two years later, Erasmus expanded and published this preface as a comprehensive treatise on his new vision of theological practice.[55] In his *Method of True Theology*, Erasmus offered a set of contrasts between the virtues of "those ancient theologians Origen, Basil, Chrysostom, [and] Jerome" and the vices of modern ones who "dispute about divine things."[56] Those ancient fathers remind us, Erasmus argued, that "above all the goal [*scopus*] of theologians is to explain wisely the holy letters. . . . to sow belief and piety deeply and effectively, to incite tears, to inflame souls toward the heavens."[57]

The theory was simple: less dialectic, more piety. But the practice entailed a comprehensive act of sorting within the Christian archive to discover when and where the true *scopus* of theology had been achieved. As Erasmus put it, "attention to the variety of periods disperses the obscurity in the holy books."[58] Not only must we know the difference between the ages of law and gospel, but also between the ages of Christianity, between gospel and mission, mission and church, church and empire. It would not be absurd "to arrange a certain order of authority in the holy books themselves," Erasmus pointed out, distinguishing between the gospel of Matthew, and Revelation, between the letters to the Romans and to the Hebrews, not to mention the early creeds.[59] This interest in variety extended even to Christ himself: "Truly nothing is more simple than our Christ, nevertheless in a certain mysterious sense, he represents with the variety of his lives and his doctrines a kind of Proteus," playing different roles at different times for different people, in an effort to bring to His side a world filled with heterogeneity.[60] What seems like the simplest message of all, "belief and love [*fidem et caritatem*]," turned out to be the most complicated thing of all.[61]

Uses of the Patristic Archive: An Excursus

In 1530, Erasmus published the third edition of the collected works of St. Cyprian, the third-century bishop of Carthage. The first two editions (1520, 1525) were nearly identical, but the later version expanded its table of contents to include a new treatise entitled *A Book to Fortunatus on Two Kinds of Martyrs*. Read carefully, it was a subversive little work. A martyr means a witness, a *testis*, but at some point after the Gospel age, it noted, the term had come to refer to those who lost their lives professing the name of Christ.[62] No wonder, since "no testimony is clearer among men than blood, that is, disregarding ones life, and boldly suffering death, on account of God."[63] And yet, it hesitated, blood is not enough. Pirates and murderers bleed too when they are killed. Applying the Augustinian dictum that the cause, not the death, makes a martyr, the author pivoted to a form of martyrdom "common to all times," namely living in obedience to Christ's teachings.[64] Indeed, it became clear by the end of the treatise, this was not just one kind of martyrdom, but the essence of martyrdom itself. "[I]n itself neither the touch of the idols, nor the entry into the temples . . . stains the soul"—here the two main reasons for Christian death in the Roman era—but avarice, rape, hypocrisy, and other crimes of conscience cannot but leave their marks.[65] At the end of the day, every true Christian "has his cross."[66] Who needs blood?

The work was not written by Cyprian, however. In 1978, an Italian scholar showed what had long been suspected, that Erasmus himself had written the work and inserted it into the patristic archive.[67] It is startling to imagine Erasmus, the great textual purist, forging anything of such gravity. Exactly why he might have done so is unclear, although it is suggestive that, by the late 1520s, the violence that had so marked the early Church had returned. The bloody suppression of the largest peasant's revolt in European history was followed quickly by the first major wave of violence directed against those religious heretics called Anabaptists. The survivors were quick to respond, collecting new martyrologies that sacralized Anabapist suffering. These circulated in manuscript in, among other places, Erasmus's home town of Basel.[68] That *life* was martyrdom enough was, for an Erasmus bent on church unity, a barely concealed rebuke of those new martyrs so eager to die for the faith.

The point was all the more striking when fathered on *Cyprian*. This particular bishop had fled during the first persecutions of Emperor Decius (ca. 250 CE), and then exorcised his guilty conscience by showing merciless rigor toward those who refused the martyr's crown. Fortunatus had been the addressee of Cyprian's (genuine) *Exhortation to Martyrdom*, which had declared death:

> a baptism greater in grace, more lofty in power, more precious in honour [than the first] . . . a baptism which, as we withdraw from the world, immediately associates us with God. In the baptism of water is received the remission of sins, in the baptism of blood the crown of virtues.[69]

What Christians "knew" about Cyprian—his fierce hatred for the "pestilence which masquerades as compassion," that is, for the policy of easily readmitting lapsed Christians to the communion of the Church, and his fierce love for those who, in refusing sacrifice, received their bloody end—turned out to be wrong.[70] Instead, a new Cyprian emerged from the "most ancient library" where Erasmus purported to find this manuscript.[71] This Cyprian was not someone entirely comfortable with the culture of ancient martyrdom, or at least was someone who offered the resources for its critique.

Forgery was one way to get the patristic archive to speak differently. Another approach was to revive works and writers long overlooked. Circa 211 CE, for example, the Latin church father Tertullian wrote a polemical work against the Roman "military garland," the *corona militis* bestowed for valor in battle. At stake were big issues in the early Church, among them the norms for Christian life in a still largely pagan world. How, he asked, can a pious Christian don the laurels "invented and . . . dedicated to the honor of those the world calls 'gods'"?[72] In their simple nature, laurels were "fit for common use," but for the Romans, they were an integral element of the "dress ceremony, and pomp connected to sacrifices to the idols."[73] Scripture forbids such pagan adoptions, Tertullian insisted, though he admitted that there were many things about which Scripture seemed to say nothing. Even the holiest mysteries of the Christian faith, this ancient father reported, seemed to have no warrant in sacred text, as when, after baptism, "we are given a taste of milk and honey." As for the Eucharist, "we . . . receive the sacrament . . . which the Lord entrusted to all at the hour for *supper*, at our early morning meetings, and then from the hand of none but the bishop."[74] Already in the earliest Church, Tertullian showed, it took a fine sensibility to discern just how Christian a Christian custom actually was.

Tertullian was known neither for fine nor his orthodox sensibilities, however. His unconventional trinitarianism, his startling emphasis on the body over the soul, and above all his slide into the early "heresy" of Montanism, would put him beyond the pale for later orthodoxy. By the sixth century, his name was enrolled in a catalog of apocryphal, schismatic, and heretical authors unfit for reception into the Christian canon.[75] By the Middle Ages, he and his works were enigmatic elements of the early Christian archive, known more by hazy reputation rather than substantive presences in commentary and theology.[76]

Until 1521, that is, when the German humanist Beatus Rhenanus (1485–1547)—student, friend, editor, and biographer of Erasmus—published, after nearly twenty years of work, the first full collection of Tertullian's major works.[77] As one of the "first theologians" of the Church, Rhenanus argued, Tertullian offered powerful resources for humanists seeking to escape the "little summaries" of the medieval scholastics.[78] Yet there was no denying the peculiarity, even heresy, of some of Tertullian's teachings. By collecting everything in an *Opera omnia*, Rhenanus invited readers to explore the difference themselves. Along the way, he also introduced readers to a *new* Tertullian: an author with a distinctive intellectual personality, whose historical trajectory carried him from the center to the margins of ancient Christian consensus.

The preface to the first edition (1521) made this introduction—with a *Life of Tertullian*—and defended the larger archival project on just these historical grounds. We must read Tertullian, Rhenanus argued, because he is an "ancient author," the "first of the Latins," someone who "preceded all of the councils."[79] Surely there must be more value in Tertullian than in those pagan writers so carefully collected during the Renaissance. "Since there is nothing in the literature of the gentiles, no matter how profane or obscene, which is not proudly gathered into an edition by Christians," Rhenanus wrote, "I cannot see why then our ancient author, who first among the Latins put his hand to explaining sacred matters, . . . should be suppressed."[80] The ancient fathers themselves knew how to manage these kinds of issues, he pointed out. "We should likewise apply to Tertullian the advice of Jerome on the reading Origin"—another patristic author whose reputation was complicated by his various heterodoxies—namely, "having accepted the good parts, we should reject the bad."[81]

This final point—that the archival project itself had ancient Christian roots—was a characteristic piece of humanist reasoning. The reconstruction of Christianity's heterogeneous early voices was no innovation, it argued. Instead it was a return to practices that had been abandoned or denied in the age of the medieval patristic thesaurus. The temporal horizon that medievals imagined they shared with the earliest Church in fact broke faith with that Church. Only by insisting on temporal *discontinuity*, in other words, might a real continuity be forged. When it came to the actual Tertullian texts, then, their revelation of a heterogeneous Christian past was nothing to fear. Read against Nicene orthodoxy, Tertullian certainly posed a challenge. But Tertullian lived before the Council of Nicaea, so we cannot expect him to know what orthodoxy would become. "It is hardly astonishing that he should have at times followed the opinions of his age," Rhenanus commented, and these opinions were various in the early days of the Church.[82] To better understand this Church, to bring it back to life again, meant embracing, not rejecting this variety.

To showcase this variety, Rhenanus focused on *De Corona*, exploring in rich annotations the heteronomous world of ancient Christianity. Tertullian's minor aside on eucharistic milk and honey, for example, invited a lengthy reflection on the history of Christianity's most sacred rite:

> It is remarkable what is said here about the Eucharist, but we may recall that he was ancient and lived near the times of the apostles . . . Saint Jerome points out that the ancients were in fact accustomed to receiving the Eucharist in their own homes . . . Nevertheless, it is likely that Christians feasted together in the temple on the day of the Lord's supper, vestiges of which practices still exist among us. . . . Pliny wrote to Trajan that it was the custom among Christians to gather to partake of food, but common and ordinary food.[83]

The issues were many: where and when did early Christians take the Eucharist? What was the relationship between Christian feasting and the Lord's Supper? What did Christians eat at these meals and what did it mean? Answering these, however tentatively, invited a series of commentators to the table, from Tertullian, to Jerome, to the Roman persecutor of Christians, Pliny the Younger. This inspired Rhenanus to explore the early history of the liturgy, and to describe some unusual varieties of liturgical practice still existing among Christian communities, like those "accustomed to suck the Lord's blood from the chalice through a straw" described to Rhenanus by his friend, the Benedictine abbot Paul Volzius.[84]

We are clearly in a different world from that of the Lombard. The Eucharist and the *recordatio* of Christ's sacrifice were not, for Rhenanus, liturgical elements that bound past and present. Instead, they were dispersive in their effects—not only is "our" practice different from those in the days of Tertullian, but this practice is *always* different. Different in the age of the Apostles, different in the age of Jerome, different in the age of Gregory, and different again now. The patristic archive contained these differences, provided a structure for understanding and organizing them, and invited readers "to be piously curious about Christianity."[85]

Theology in the Age of the Archive I: Semel

In 1521, Rhenanus was still sympathetic to Luther and his reformers. By 1539, however, he had amended the sentence to invite readers "to be piously and *prudently* curious about Christianity." A minor change, but it marked deep shifts not only in Rhenanus's allegiances—like Erasmus, his sympathies for the Reformation project waned quickly during the 1520s—but also in the religious landscape he inhabited.[86] Even as Rhenanus published his Tertullian, theological disagreements within the Church became explicitly political. In 1521, Luther was excommunicated and the conflict between the Emperor and Luther's patron, the Elector of Saxony, became an open one. The first acts of iconoclasm, the efforts to cleanse churches of their "idols" and the confrontations these provoked, started in the German lands and elsewhere. By the summer of 1525, local conflicts became general. During that summer, the largest peasant revolt that Europe had ever confronted swept through central Europe, leaving hundreds of thousands dead and displaced. Persecution of the new and radical critics of the existing Christian order, later called Anabaptists and Spiritualists, followed quickly, and violence over religious matters broke communities both large and small. Differences in the archive now echoed differences in Christianity itself, as variety was violently institutionalized in the different principalities of central Europe.

How should a humanist do theology in this new age? Christian variety was not a problem in 1518, when Erasmus first wrote his *Method of True Theology*. Later, when he wrote his *Pious Explanation of the Apostle's Creed* (1533), everything had changed. Creeds like this—supposedly gathered from the sayings of the apostles and handed down to the great church council of Nicaea—had once represented for Erasmus the primitive simplicity and unity of the early church. But by the 1530s, creeds, and creed-like documents called confessions, had multiplied beyond imagination. Anabaptists wrote manifestos; peasants and their supporters published new doctrinal formulae; new church orders and liturgical texts appeared across central Europe; a wild assortment of abbreviated vernacular creed-like documents found a home in elite and common circles alike.[87]

This extraordinary outburst of creedal creativity was epitomized in the 1530 *Confession of Augsburg*, delivered to the Holy Roman Emperor Charles V by Luther's princely patrons. Composed of doctrinal first principles and critiques of the Catholic sacramental system, the *Confession* formally defined the teachings of a new Protestant church.[88] Much as the Nicene Creed determined the content of early Christian orthodoxy, the *Confession* did the same for the Lutherans. Others would follow suit: the Helvetic Confession (1536), the Ten Articles (1536), and so on.[89] By 1533, then, Erasmus's earlier remark that "when faith began to decline among Christians, then creeds grew in kind and number," must have felt prophetic.[90]

When Erasmus sent his *Explanation of the Apostle's Creed* to Thomas Boleyn, father of the new Queen of England, it was in the shadow of this collapse of Christian unity into intractable variety. "I believe in God the Father almighty, creator of Heaven and Earth," the Apostles' Creed began, and reciting it was (and is) a foundation of Christian community. Erasmus subtitled his exploration of this creed a "*catechism*" and staged it as a dialogue between a catechist and a catechumen exploring this "rule of faith," this "unvarying measure of truth" by which human opinion is judged.[91]

For a catechism on a creed—a simplification of a simplification—Erasmus's work was startlingly complex. After initial praise for the creed's modesty (featuring Tertullian as witness to early versions), Erasmus hesitated, noting how the "impious inquisitiveness of philosophers and the perversity of heretics gave rise to a multitude of words and creeds." Even among the faithful, he noted, variety reigned. Tertullian and the church father Athanasius testify that the earliest versions of the Apostles' Creed "differ[ed] in many words both from ours, and from the one sung at the mass." The phrases "he descended into hell," "creator of heaven and earth," and "who was conceived," were absent in some ancient versions; "he suffered" sometimes appeared as "he was crucified," "he died" as "he was buried." Words were added, subtracted, and substituted "to deal with contentious and stupid people," Erasmus wrote.[92]

Credo in deum, the creed began, a statement typically taken as a public sign of Christian unity and community. Not for Erasmus. "I believe in God" offered him an occasion to reflect not on the consensus of the faithful, but on the host of heresies and heretics that this simple statement has spawned. The "senseless Noetus and the impious Sabellius," the "heresy of Patripassianism," the mad "doctrines of Basilides and Marin," Arius, Macedonius, Eunomius, the Manichees, the Gnostics: all "believed in God" but in ways aberrant and disgusting, as the patristic archives amply demonstrated. These same archives—Irenaeus, Tertullian, and Augustine—also revealed the ancient heresies attending the doctrine of Christ. Gnostics denied him a human birth; Manichees denied him a human body; Arius denied him a human soul. There is "scarcely an ancient writer who does not deviate in some points from the rule of Catholic faith," exclaimed the understandably frustrated catechumen.[93]

What might this archival sensibility mean for the "once and for all" of Christ's sacrifice? At the heart of the creed was the crucifixion: "I believe . . . in Jesus Christ . . . [who] suffered under Pontius Pilate, was crucified, died, and was buried." Perhaps understandably, Erasmus's catechumen wondered why God "redeem[ed] the world by the death of his Son." Instead of a doctrinal answer, he got a long and unusual story from the archives:

> Among certain peoples it was a public custom to support diligently for a whole year a man who had offered himself voluntarily for death; in the meantime, they venerated him as a sacred victim dedicated to God. When the year was over, they threw him into the sea, thinking that by the death of one whatever evils threatened the city could be averted. Codrus, Quintus Curtius, and the Decii, who devoted themselves to the infernal deities for the safety of the state, are honoured with great enthusiasm. When the salvation not of one city or people but of the whole world was in question, it was fitting (*congruebat*) that a true and efficacious victim be sacrificed, who would invalidate all other sacrificial victims as superstitious or ineffective. So great was Christ's love, so great was his purity, that when he had been sacrificed once (*semel*), he was able to wipe out all the crimes of the human race.[94]

Veneration of a sacred victim whose death wards off divine vengeance, the catechumen learned, was not unique to Christians. Other ancient peoples had subjected themselves voluntarily to sacrificial death too. The archives of ancient religions proved that Greeks, Romans, indeed much of the ancient world, acted on similar impulses, committing violent acts of devotion to preserve themselves from divine threat. The Crucifixion was unique neither in form nor in the underlying conviction that "the sins of men are wiped out by death and blood."[95] It was unique because Christ's singular death *worked*, not just one time or for one people, but always and for everyone.

However orthodox his Christology, in Erasmus's archival creed, the *semel* was intimately tied to the deep history of human depravity. Some of this history was doubtless known to medievals like the Lombard. But it is inconceivable that it would have featured in a text purporting to teach the basics of the faith. For Erasmus, this history elevated the tremendous accomplishment of the Crucifixion. At the same time, however, the Crucifixion was now an *instance* rather than a *rejection* of those terrible pagan convictions that underwrote ancient systems of human sacrifice. The heterogeneous materials that this archival theology demanded, in other words, made even the most foundational Christian event into a site of dissonance.

Theology in the Age of the Archive II: Quotidie

Although the *Explanatio* said little about the daily sacrifice of the Eucharist, in 1533 the sacraments were on Erasmus's mind. For in that year, he also wrote a major work on church unity, one that reveals just how much strain the changing practices of religious life were putting on the fabric of Christianity. Framed as a commentary on Psalm 84, *The Restoration of Church Concord*—popular enough to enjoy six editions in 1533, the year of its publication, and three more reprints before 1540—marked a transformation for Erasmus.[96] The Erasmus of 1517 seemed to think that mercy and charity alone were enough for Christian life. Sixteen years later, it seemed clear that the sacrifice of the Mass was more important than he first thought, not least to the durability of a fractured Christian community.[97]

Quam dilecta tabernacula tua, Domine virtutum, "how lovely your tabernacles, Lord of hosts," the Psalm opens.[98] In the late medieval church, the *tabernaculum* had a specific liturgical referent, namely the locked box near the altar where the consecrated host was stored before and after the Mass.[99] Examples of special boxes and niches built to protect and venerate the Eucharist date back to Carolingian times. In the centuries after 1215, however, when the Fourth Lateran church council commanded their use, these boxes grew more physically and symbolically elaborate.[100] Also known as "sacrament houses," imposing tabernacles like the one in the St. Peter's Church in Leuven, where Erasmus spent a great deal of time, were majestic pieces of architecture found in major churches across northern Europe (fig. 2.1). In the early sixteenth-century northern Europe, indeed, few Christian would have been unfamiliar with them.

The sacrament house was more, however, than just ecclesiastical furniture. According to the thirteenth-century Frenchman William Durandus, the liturgical tabernacle "serves as a figure of the Church militant," a figure of the Church serving and struggling in the world.[101] In his Psalm commentary, Erasmus discovered the same thing in the Jewish feast of the tabernacles. "Seven days you shall present offerings by fire to the Lord . . . you shall dwell in the tabernacle for seven days," was how the Leviticus author prescribed this great sacrificial festival (23.36, 42). Zechariah turned the feast into prophecy: "I will gather all the nations against Jerusalem to battle . . . every one that survives of all the nations that have come against Jerusalem shall go up year after year to worship the King, the LORD of hosts, and to keep the feast of tabernacles" (Zech. 14.2, 16). For his part, Erasmus took this prophetic feast as a figure of "the assembly of the Catholic Church" gathered on earth in advance of judgment.[102]

The gathering of the Christian faithful demanded labor, however. Early Christians were not born fully formed, but rather entered Christianity from diverse and alien worlds. Jews and gentiles from North Africa, Greece, Rome, and Asia had to be remade into something new. "No one suddenly becomes fully Christian," Erasmus had commented in 1519, "just as nature has its stages of development, so also does religion."[103] What he called *synkatabasis*—accommodation and condescension to human frailty—was fundamental to the constitution of Christian life. In the Hebrew Bible, this creation of unity from diversity found a perfect model in the feast of the tabernacles. There Moses "substituted for popular merrymaking, religious thanksgiving . . . for obscene verses, spiritual psalms, thus converting the impure worship offered to false spirits . . . into worship of the true God."[104]

Sacrifice under the canopy of the tabernacle, in short, made sacred what had once been profane. In the Psalm, David "shows us the altars of the Lord, a holier and more beautiful part of the Temple," a "tabernacle not made by hands." These are not the "sort of altars which are spattered with the blood of calves, goats and rams," but a different sort of sacrifice, the spiritual one prophesied in Isaiah, and fulfilled in Christ:

> If through love of Christ you have slaughtered in yourself the desire for money, and have given away to the members of Christ what previously you kept hidden and worshipped as God, you have offered up to

FIG. 2.1. Tabernacle for the Eucharist in St. Peter's Church, Leuven. 1450. Photo by Paul Vanden Bossche. Wikimedia Commons.

> God a victim most pleasing in his sight. If your faith is strong and your heart warm with love . . . if you are prepared even to suffer death and hell should he so decide, then you have performed a burnt sacrifice . . . This is the "rational" or spiritual worship, the living sacrifice, holy and acceptable to God . . . the sacrifice of praise . . . is the truly pure offering, made continually throughout the world upon the church's altars.

The victim we now offer God is a living one, in Erasmus's view, a self-slaughter for the love of Christ, a continuous offering made in praise and love. But this living sacrifice was more than just an interior act of conscience. Given the "tabernacles of wickedness" growing thick on the ground in the 1520s—Lutherans, Anabaptists, sacramentarians, all of the new sects of reformed Christianity—Christians must discover this living sacrifice in the *concordia ecclesiae*, the "fellowship of the church."[105]

Happily, this living sacrifice was *already* offered daily in every Catholic church in Europe. "Made continually throughout the world upon the church's altars," the Mass preserved sacred sacrifice—"the same thing, always the same . . . offered in many places," in the words of Chrysostom—from the earliest times of Church fellowship to the present. Various aspects of the Mass might be optional (e.g., singing, chants for good harvests, private Masses, special Masses), but this did not require Christians to "reject the mass itself, accepted for so many centuries, as though it were something abhorrent and impious":

> The Doctors of the church in former times expressed no horror at this [sacrifice]. Christ having died once (*semel*) dies no more, I agree; but that one sacrifice is as it were daily (*quotidie*) renewed in mystic rites as we continue to draw fresh grace from that perennial spring. Our appeal for the living and the dead made to the Father by his Son's death is our sacrifice of the victim on their behalf. Moreover, the word "sacrifice" properly applies to all prayer, praise, and thanksgiving, so that it is particularly appropriate for the Mass.

In this daily sacrifice performed in the Roman rite of the Mass, and in the sanctifying tabernacle of the universal church, Christians might find peace and unity. "With one voice, rejoicing with each other, we shall all together say: 'How lovely are the tabernacles, O Lord of hosts,'" Erasmus ended his 1533 *Explanation of the Apostle's Creed*, hoping that he had created a Christianity inside which all might dwell.[106]

Three years later—at the very end of his life and with no end of religious conflict in sight—Erasmus returned to the Psalms and their tabernacles in a final plea for unity. *The Purity of the Tabernacle*, the aged Dutch scholar titled his 1536 commentary on a Psalm that opened with the cry, "Lord, who shall sojourn in thy tabernacle? Who shall dwell on thy holy hill?" (Psalm 15.1). The questions were more pressing than ever, and it was with a certain air of desperation that Erasmus again exhorted Christians to put aside differences under the figure of the tabernacle. No more exclusive tents, the tabernacle stood ready to host all Christians willing to offer "a sacrifice of praise by which God loves to be honoured; a sacrifice of justice which he demands from us; and a sacrifice of mercy by which we appeal to the Lord's mercy." "Let us offer ourselves everyday (*quotidie*) as pleasing offerings to him who offered himself for us," "let us continually offer sacrifices to the Lord" that "we may be conveyed from this tabernacle to the heavenly tabernacle to reign with Christ," he concluded his plea.[107]

Nec est in corde veritas, ubi est opinionum varietas. Truth in the age of variety was a difficult thing. Gone was the sense that Christians shared the same temporal horizon of those "doctors of the church" that Erasmus mentioned. Gone, in fact, was the "we" that this shared temporal horizon presupposed. If Erasmus's tabernacle imagined a Christianity within which all might dwell, it also violently expelled those who refused to take shelter beneath it:

> Anyone who wishes to walk without blemish *must* walk inside the tabernacle, because outside the church even the things which appear impressive are defiled. Heretics and schismatics also fast, pray, sing hymns, give alms, live chastely, preach the word of God, and perform other deeds that have the appearance of virtue. But all these things are but faults because they are performed outside the tabernacle.[108]

The "impious . . . have no common tabernacle," Erasmus wrote of the Greeks, Romans, Egyptians, Sadducees, and Herodians. Likewise early Christianity saw a "whole multitude of abominable heretical tabernacles pitched against the tabernacle of God." To make matters worse, ancient and modern heretics always imagine that *their* tabernacle is the true one, accuse their rivals of tyranny, and cry out "Christ is with us, not with you." The consequences of this—the desire to claim Christ, yet stand outside the church—are terrible: perversion, violence, even (or especially) in the most sacred matters, as in those sects:

> where mothers willingly handed over their own children to be killed and watched the horrendous deed quite cheerfully, believing that those killed in this way would be numbered among the greatest saints. . . .

> The adherents of this sect used to make the eucharistic host from flour moistened with the blood of a small child. For this purpose they made tiny pinpricks in the child's body, and if he happened to die, he was venerated as a martyr.[109]

This story is by now familiar (see chapter 1), and was was one of the most durable libels in the pantheon of religious polemic. Already in the late second century, the apologist Minucius Felix reported the libel, not directed at heretics, but at *Christians* themselves. In his *Octavius*, his pagan interlocutor described the Eucharist in particularly disgusting terms, remarking how the Christians kill a child, and then:

> It is the blood of this infant . . . that they lick with thirsty lips; these are the limbs they distribute eagerly; this is the victim by which they seal their covenant; it is by complicity in this crime that they are pledged to mutual silence; these are their rites, more foul than all sacrileges combined.[110]

Erasmus likely didn't know the story from Minucius Felix directly, but the libel can be found throughout the early Christian archive. Justin Martyr, Athenagoras, Tertullian, Origen, and others repeated, and rejected, this pagan accusation.[111] Later apologists like Irenaeus and Epiphanius leveled it against their own opponents within the broader Christian canopy. It then enjoyed a terrible afterlife in Christian antisemitism from the Middle Ages right through the Jewish blood libels in Erasmus's day.[112] In short, this was an example carefully chosen from the Christian archive to demonstrate the demonic danger of disunity. Erasmus's moral was simple: "You see what horrific practices people slide into when once they leave the tabernacle of God."[113]

Conclusion: A New Time of Christianity

"All I do is restore the old; I put forward nothing new," Erasmus wrote in a 1520 letter.[114] But restoring the old *was* something new. Excavating the Christian past, and making the past serve contemporary needs, demanded extraordinary work. The doctrinal content found in works of earlier writers could be replicated, to be sure, the *semel* and the *quotidie* of Christ's sacrifice embraced as much in one as the other. But the ways of investigating and defending the truth of this content could not have been more different. Humanists like Erasmus were powerfully drawn to a vision of a Christianity united, but this consensus was the *destination* rather than the beginning of inquiry. To get there, the sources of Christian authority were differentiated, false works separated from the true, the patristic authors assigned theological personalities, and their works organized in temporal sequences. The new *theologus* sifted these authorities, paying attention to similarity and difference alike.

As it was archived, Christianity's smooth temporal horizon fell apart. Time was punctuated. The early history of Christianity was distinguished from its supposedly debased medieval afterlife, for example. Yet even the timescape of the first church fathers took on jagged and heterogeneous qualities. It began to *matter* whether it was the Milanese Bishop Ambrose or the Constantinopolitan Archbishop Chrysostom who wrote: "Christ offered a victim, we offer that victim now." The early Church was populated with both saints and heretics, and discerning the difference was hard work. Tertullian was not an authority until he was; the Latin fathers pointed in slightly different directions than the Greek; the creeds of the ancient Church were disputed and misunderstood; and so on. The new humanist *theologus* had to be practiced in the arts of distinction, of defending particular (historical and contemporary) versions of Christian unity against those who leave the tabernacle of God. Erasmus prayed for Christian amity, but wrote polemical works that covered 1,400 close-printed pages in his collected works.

As for sacrifice, the dynamics were clear. An integrative element in the age of the Lombard—a rite and a doctrine not only tightly bound together but also serving to hold past and present in intimate proximity—sacrifice had become altogether stranger and harder to fathom. In Erasmus's telling, the *semel* of Christ's crucifixion was haunted by the terrible errors of ancient human sacrifice, the *quotidie* of the Mass by the errors of modern schismatics. But stepping back from Erasmus, the challenges were fundamental. How *should* we understand the relationship between the once-and-for-all, and the everyday? Can Christ's singular atonement become present in the daily lives of Christians? Or is it gone, far in the past? The felt force of these was muted in Erasmus, at least in comparison to their overwhelming urgency to the world of Protestant Reformers. For Reformers, the sacrificial Christianity of the Middle Ages was everything they detested. And yet sacrifice *itself* could hardly be abandoned. The dilemma, as we will see, will cut across the entire Reformation.

CHAPTER THREE

Sacrifice Abandoned, Sacrifice Redeemed

POLEMICS IN THE CHRISTIAN ARCHIVES

Est autem Reformare, formam pristinam reducere.
Oportet itaque Reformationem per omnia
similem ac parem esse antiquae formae.

—HEINRICH BULLINGER, *ON THE ORIGIN OF ERRORS* (1539)

WHEN ERASMUS DIED, he left behind a fractured Christianity. Late medieval Christianity was hardly uniform. The first decades of the sixteenth century, however, pulled Christian communities, indeed Christianity itself, in directions wholly unknown a century earlier. Differences between doctrines, liturgies, and church organizations widened from cracks into fissures, defining by century's end a new religious geography of Europe.

At the beginning of these enormous transformations—call it Reformation—was sacrifice. Years ago, when the great historian John Bossy wrote about this period, he remarked on the irony that the very symbol of Christian unity, the Eucharist celebrating Christ's sacrifice on the cross, split the sixteenth-century Church asunder.[1] But this was not an irony. It was rather the expression of a gene lodged deep in the Christian sacrificial imagination. Sacrifice was present from the beginning of Christianity's celebrations of solidarity and community. But it was there under a shadow, a figure whose original, whether Jewish or pagan, could easily be antithetical to the Christian thing. That the European churches of the sixteenth century would split along sacrificial lines then can hardly be seen as an accident. The return of the repressed, Freud might have called it, at the risk of psychologizing a complex historical conjunction. What was repressed was not sacrifice itself, however, as much as the distinctive history of its absorption. When this history came out, and when its peculiarities were energized in the heat of religious conflict, sacrifice quickly transformed from something utterly mundane to something dark and threatening.

This chapter traces aspects of this history from the late Middle Ages into the sixteenth century, with particular focus on the continental reformers who together built the Lutheran and Reformed (Calvinist) churches. In particular, it follows the fortunes of the sacrificial Eucharist, beginning with the figure of Gregory the Great, the first monk pope and perceived mastermind of church consolidation as the Roman Empire slowly slid into disarray. Gregory—or better, his afterlives in the later Middle Ages—help us to capture the imaginative power of the sacrificial Mass in the years leading up to the Reformation, years characterized by richly elaborated festivals, rituals, and theological writings that together made Christ's sacrifice on the Cross both present and active in the lives of medieval Latin Christians. The afterlife of Gregory—as a figure of disgust and disdain in the early years of the Reformation—also help us to understand what happened when the sacrificial culture of the later Middle Ages came to be seen not as the pinnacle of piety, but its diabolical corruption.

Cleansing the Church of the scent of blood was no easy matter, however. The challenge was twofold. First, and already familiar from our discussions of early Christianity, how can we abolish the wrong sacrifice but keep the right sacrifice? After all, virtually no one thought that sacrifice *itself* should disappear from Christian life, not least because that would banish Christ and his Passion altogether. Second, and intimately connected to this one, how can we discover this right sacrifice inside historical Christianity? As we saw in the last chapter, the early sixteenth century created a robust and theologically energized archive of things sacrificial. The project for reformers, then, was to mobilize this archive behind a sacrifice both new and as old as Christianity itself, to prove that *their* sacrifice was the sacrifice that Christianity somehow forgot in the long centuries of its decline. A project of conceptual clarification—what *is* Christian sacrifice?—and a project of historical explanation—what *was* Christian sacrifice?—converged already in the first decades of the Reformation.

This complex weave of the historical and the normative became characteristic of the Reformation approach to sacrifice. We will call this weave "apologetics," not only because of its formal similarity to ancient apologia, but also because of the polemical context inside of which it developed.

Ancient apologetic developed and advanced its theological claims through means agonistic; it defended Christianity through complex strategies of appropriation and assimilation; it was aimed as much at its own communities as at perceived critics. The apologetics of the Reformation shared these features, but added a powerful recursive element, reanimating these ancient Christian apologia for its own urgent ends. The Reformation sacrificial imagination thus developed with a very particular framework of inquiry, developed in the first decades of the sixteenth century but lasting for years to come.

Afterlives of Gregory: The Canon and the Mass

Gregory the Great looms large in the Christian archive. This classically trained son of a Roman senatorial family was bishop of Rome from 590–604, after a political career and at least fifteen years of monastic life. He was a talented writer, a poet, a Bible commentator, interested in music, a great activist in expanding the Christian church, a man who reinforced the institutions of the Roman Church as the center of imperial power gradually moved east to Constantinople. He is also indelibly associated with the central liturgical drama of the Latin Church, the Mass.

The link between Gregory and the Mass is an ancient one. Already in the eighth century, Gregory's biographer, Paul the Deacon, made the link concrete. A Benedictine monk in the service of Charlemagne, the story goes, Paul was sent by the Emperor from Aachen to Rome to search for the most authentic Roman liturgical texts. It was Paul who supposedly began the negotiations that brought what was called the Gregorian sacramentary into the Carolingian court, and thereby into the imperial Christianity of the Franks.[2] The sacramentary is one of the oldest comprehensive liturgical forms in Christianity. It contains all of the materials needed for a priest to perform the Mass, the words of the rite, the instructions for special Masses, the calendar of feasts and celebrations, and so on. The Benedictine biographer John the Deacon reported in the ninth century that the Gregorian sacramentary was, in turn, a revision of an earlier one, allegedly written by Pope Gelasius (d. 496). Gregory, John tells us, "shortened the Gelasian codex of the holy mass into a single volume, removing much, changing a few things, adding some others for the exposition of the gospel readings."[3] From this point onward, the work of abbreviation and formalization bound the Roman rite with the name of Gregory.

At the heart of the Gregorian sacramentary was the Roman Canon of the Mass, the "core of the celebration" of the Eucharist, the *oratio oblationis* spoken over the body and blood of Christ as the priest prepares himself and the parish for communion.[4] We come to You (*Te igitur*), Father, says the priest at the beginning of the Canon, and implore You to "accept and bless these gifts, these offerings, these sacred sacrifices that we give to you."[5] After this, the Mass intensifies. The priest asks for God's benevolence to the community and the Church, and offers their praise and thanksgiving in return. He beseeches God that the eucharistic elements might be transformed into the very body and blood of Christ and repeats the holy words of institution, "take this, all of you, and eat, for this is my body . . . take this, all of you, and drink, for this is the very cup of my blood."[6] Consecrated host and chalice are laid on the altar, the holy elements are adored by the priest and congregation, and then together they:

> offer up to your most excellent majesty from those gifts that you have given us, a pure victim, a holy victim, an immaculate victim, the holy bread of eternal life and the cup of everlasting salvation. Upon which might you deign to look with a propitious and serene face, and to accept them just as you deigned to accept the gifts of your just servant Abel, and the sacrifice of our patriarch Abraham, and that which your high priest Melchizedek offered to you, a holy sacrifice, and immaculate victim.[7]

The Canon of the Mass thus imagined and enacted a complex set of sacrificial exchanges: the offering from priest to the Father of the Father's gift of the son (namely, the bread and the wine), which, the priest hopes, the Father will accept as a gift from the Christian community just as He accepted the gifts of Abel and Abraham, and which, on acceptance, will convey to the assembled Christians the benefits of these self-same gifts.

The Canon was by no means the first time that Christ's sacrificial death was set into transtemporal dialogue with the founding sacrifices of Genesis. The early church fathers, early Christian sepulchre art, the Milanese rite often attributed to St. Ambrose, early Greek liturgies: a huge range of sources explicitly mention the sacrifices of Melchizedek and Abraham in connection to Christ. In a sixth-century treatise on the Holy Land, for example, the author placed the Crucifixion and the *Akedah* at the same place, the hill at Calvary where "Abraham offered his son as a sacrifice (*holocaustum*)," and other contemporaneous authors claimed to have seen Abraham's altar itself there.[8] The seventh-century mosaic from the Basilica of Sant'Apollinare in Classe in Ravenna—roughly contemporary with Gregorian sacramentary—linked Abraham, Melchizedek, and Abel in an intense visual form (see fig. 0.1), a linkage that would be present on medieval altarpieces, stained glass windows, chalices, reliquaries, and more. This rich sacrificial surround carried the tradition of Christian absorption forward, setting the death of Christ into a history both continuous with, and distinct from, the Judaism that had given it birth.

At the liturgical heart of this interpretive system lay Gregory's sacrificial Canon, which, after the eighth century or so, developed from one-prayer-among-many into the holiest part of the Mass. In that century, for example, the Canon began to be spoken quietly, if not silently, by the priest.[9] The Carolingian and post-Carolingian churches also began to expand a comparison already made in the book of Hebrews between the ancient Hebrew High Priest, who entered the *tabernaculum* once a year with his blood sacrifice, and Christ, who entered it "once and for all" and offered his own blood to secure "an eternal redemption" (Heb. 9.12). Later the comparison came to include ordinary priests as they daily performed the holiest part of the liturgy. After 1215, recall, the consecrated host dwelled in the *tabernaculum*, the sacrament house that conserved the holy element from profanation. The subsequent elaboration of the liturgy—the elevation of the host, the kissing of the altar, the ritualization of the signs of the Cross—all explored the parallels between the priest's approach to the altar, the offering of the Eucharist, and the structured actions of the Hebrew high priest entering the presence of God and making his oblations.[10]

As the sacrificial Canon grew in imaginative power in the later Middle Ages, Gregory too loomed larger in the imaginative world of sacrifice. There was a story already circulating in the eighth century, for example, about a miraculous Mass celebrated by Gregory. Standing at the altar and offering the body of Christ, he noticed one of his communicants laughing. When he asked why she laughed, she replied that she had to smile at the notion that bread she had made herself (*ego manibus meis feci*) might become the body of Christ. Gregory exhorted her to look at the sacrament with the eyes of faith, and when the Mass concluded, discovered a miracle. He lifted the corporal, the square of linen cloth used to protect the sacred elements, and on it he discovered a piece of a little finger, smeared with blood [*partem digiti auricularis sanguine cruentatam invenit*]. Turning to the woman, Gregory declared, "now learn to believe the truth shown to you" [*Disce, inquam, veritati vel modo iam credere contestanti*]. And she did, ever after zealous in matters of faith and religion.[11]

In the later Middle Ages, this miraculous Mass came back to life. The doubting matron dropped out, and the bloody incarnation on the altar took center stage.[12] One of the earliest examples of the Mass of St. Gregory, as it came to be known, came from Weingarten, the south German home to the relic of the Holy Blood that became a powerful cult center in the thirteenth and fourteenth centuries.[13] Over time, images of the Mass of St. Gregory became common in prayer books, altarpieces, engravings, and fine art, even serving to illustrate to the *Te igitur*, the first words of the Canon of the Mass.[14]

Circa 1400, the image was "indulgenced," meaning that prayer in front of it provided relief from sin and purgatory.[15] In these images, what had been a little finger grew in scope, an economy of scarcity now become one of plenitude as Christ's body appeared in its fullness to both Gregory and the viewers of his Mass.[16] Gregory confronted not the Eucharist or a relic, but the very Man of Sorrows himself, stepping down from the Cross and offering himself as a substitute for the Eucharistic elements. The Gregory Mass was a moment of divine materialization, the blood of Christ pouring into the chalice, the viewers invited into a moment of "sacramental vision" of the body of Christ.[17]

Historians often use this image of the Mass to illustrate the importance of the doctrine of real presence—the teaching that Christ's body miraculously replaces the accidents of bread and wine with its own substance at the moment of consecration—in the later Middle Ages. As Caroline Walker Bynum has argued, however, the Mass of Gregory did more than just illustrate this doctrine of presence.[18] It also offered a powerful meditation on Christian sacrifice. The Christ that appeared on the altar of Hans Baldung Grien's 1511 *Mass of St. Gregory*, for example, was caught just after his self-sacrifice on the Cross (see fig. 3.1 and color plate 1). The inclusion of the *arma Christi*, the instruments of Christ's humiliation and punishment that appear behind the empty sepulchre and are common on nearly all such images, suggested that this is Christ just after his death, as does the crucifixion on Gregory's vestments in the foreground.[19] In contrast to the fixed image on Gregory's robes, however, Christ's position on the altar was unsettlingly alive. His hands lifted to show his stigmata, and His blood flowed onto the corporal. This was less the Eucharistic wine than it is the very life of Christ, bleeding onto the linen cloth understood as a token and sign of the shroud with which Joseph of Arimathea tenderly wrapped the body of Christ before burial. Life touched death here, flowing blood liquifying, as Beate Fricke puts it, the "temporal gap" between Christ's death and its continued activity in service of our salvation.[20] And yet it also served as a reproach, his wounds in hands and side reminding us of culpability in His death, and His blood staining the very instruments the Church used to protect the Eucharistic elements. As a meditation on

FIGURE 3.1. Hans Baldung Grien, *The Mass of Saint Gregory*, 1511. Courtesy of the Cleveland Museum of Art.

sacrifice, then, it restaged the agony of Christ's offering, and in doing so, it made present the infinite benefit of this death for a sinful humanity.

Exploration of this circulation between life and death, past and present, was common in the Gregory Mass tradition. We can find it, for example, on the outer surface of Hieronymus Bosch's *Epiphany Altarpiece*, where Christ stood in his sepulchre in front of the praying Gregory, both painted in the grey tones common on the closed faces of Netherlandish altarpieces (see fig. 3.2 and color plate 2). Both Christ and Gregory are spectral in contrast to the two lively figures, also praying, at right and left.[21] The image offers, in a sense, a meditation on time, with Christ and Gregory part of a more ghostly past, attended by those who come after. The ghostliness of this image stands out, in particular, against the *inside* of the altarpiece, where Bosch has painted a brilliant and colorful depiction of the Adoration of the Magi (see fig. 3.3 and color plate 3).

What connects inside to outside—the birth of Christ and his Resurrection—is that double temporality of sacrifice itself, again, simultaneously past and present. Thus we discover, looking closely, the miniature rendering of the *Akedah*—Abraham's near sacrifice of his own son—sitting

FIGURE 3.2. The Mass of St. Gregory. Hieronymus Bosch, *Epiphany Altarpiece*, outer wings. 1510. Museo del Prado, Madrid. The Yorck Project (2002) 10.000 Meisterwerke der Malerei (DVD-ROM), distributed by DIRECTMEDIA Publishing GmbH. Wikimedia Commons.

FIGURE 3.3. The Adoration of the Magi. Hieronymus Bosch, *Epiphany Altarpiece*, retable. 1510. Copyright of the image Museo Nacional del Prado / Art Resource, NY.

at Mary's feet (see fig. 3.4 and color plate 4). The tiny demonic toads that support this tableau, and that lend it such an unsettling feel, remind viewers that the sacrifice of Abraham was an imperfect type of the real sacrifice to come. But the image also used both sides of the altarpiece to bind past (Abraham and Isaac), present (the baby Christ), and future (Christ's Crucifixion) into one sacrificial drama.

As it grew in popularity, the Gregory Mass image explored the Christian sacrificial imagination.[22] There is a fifteenth-century French book of hours found in the Bodleian library, for example, in which an angel lifts an obviously dead Christ from the Cross and offers it to Gregory, who in turn offers the Eucharist back to God.[23] Even more than the Grien painting, where the Eucharistic host is either absent or hidden by Gregory, this anonymous work kept its focus on the sacrificial circles at play in the

FIGURE 3.4. The Sacrifice of Abraham. Hieronymus Bosch, *Epiphany Altarpiece*, details. Copyright of the image Museo Nacional del Prado / Art Resource, NY.

liturgy, giving and receiving, life and death. Small wonder that the Gregory Mass would be linked in nearly all of the fifteenth-century prayer books with the prayer "*adoro te in cruce pendente*," a meditation on the Passion and the sacrifice of Christ.[24]

On the other end of the visual spectrum, meanwhile, Grien's contemporary Albrecht Dürer created a majestic Mass of Gregory in woodcut, in which Christ again rises in company of the instruments of his torture. But in this one, Christ seems fully alive, well formed and powerful, the wounds in the hand already stanched (fig. 3.5). In Dürer's version, the kneeling Gregory is almost alone with his vision of the Man of Sorrows. With his con-celebrant attending to the eucharistic elements and the other ecclesiastics distracted by chatter or incense, only Gregory and the angels

FIGURE 3.5. Albrecht Dürer, *Mass of St. Gregory*, 1511. Minneapolis Museum of Art. Gift of Herschel V. Jones, 1927. Public Domain (CC-PDM).

see the living Christ. What one might see as the "spiritualization" of the Gregory Mass—the evident regeneration of Christ's body, and the transformation of Paul the Deacon's public miracle into a private instance of spiritual seeing—did not evacuate the scene of sacrificial content, however. Rather it preserved one aspect of eucharistic mystery, the sense that, as Chrysostom wrote about the sacrifice, "there is one Christ in all places, and fully existing here, and fully existing there." The "blood of Jesus" is the "new and living way" into the sanctuary, the *Hebrews* author reminded his readers (*Heb.* 10.19–20), the life standing in death, Christ rising from his tomb before Gregory.

The Mass of St. Gregory, then, offered a powerful visual meditation on the sacrificial mystery that "Christ offered a victim, we offer that victim now"—in the language of Peter of Lombard—that he died once but dies again, that he died in Jerusalem, but dies again here and everywhere, that he is gone but everywhere, that he offered himself and we offer him.[25] Christ cycled between activity and passivity, active in his self-sacrifice, passive in his victimhood. He also cycled between past and present, dead on the Cross, alive in glory, the once and for all atonement still active in the lives of Christians today.

Luther and the End (?) of Sacrifice

In 1519, Martin Luther's *Sermon on Indulgences and Grace*, one of the most successful pamphlets of the early Reformation, appeared with a by-now familiar frontispiece (fig. 3.6). In the first year after publication, the *Sermon* went through approximately twenty editions in cities ranging from Wittenberg to Basel.[26] But this edition, printed in Leipzig by Martin Landsperg, was adorned with a woodcut version of Dürer's *Mass of St. Gregory*. It was a curious idea, to put an indulgenced image on the cover of the first vernacular "translation" of Luther's *95 Theses on Indulgences*, the 1517 work typically used to date the beginning of the Reformation. After all, this was a ferocious *attack* on the practice of indulgence, an attack on the idea that the Church possesses any power over the ultimate fate of the dead, or the living.[27]

It is unlikely that Luther knew about this frontispiece. If he had, doubtless he would have been ambivalent, and not just because of the indulgence issue. To a young friar like him, Gregory could still stand for the dynamic piety of the early Church: "one can still feel that [he] believed as we do, what the church believed since the beginning, and what we still believe," Luther later commented.[28] But most often, Gregory teetered on

Eyn Sermon
von dem Ablas vñ gna
de durch den wirdigē do
ctorū Martinū Lutther
Augustiner tzu Wittē
bergk gemacht.

FIGURE 3.6. Frontispiece. Martin Luther, *Sermon on Indulgences and Grace* (1517). Courtesy of the Bayerische Staatsbibliothek. PDM 1.0.

the precipice between real Christianity and the diabolical servitude into which the medieval church had definitively slipped. Indeed, "leprous with ceremonies," it was *Gregorius fabulosus* who shoved the Church into the world of superstition that Luther's earliest writings aimed to expose.[29]

Chief among these superstitions was the sacrificial Mass, which Luther linked definitively to Gregory and his fables. The sacrificial Mass, Luther had already declared in 1520, was the "most wicked abuse of all" in the contemporary Church. His great pamphlet of that year, the *Babylonian Captivity of the Church*, railed against the foundations of this abuse, which it found in the Canon of the Mass so closely associated with Gregory:

> Even the words of the Canon seem to imply [that the Mass is a sacrifice], when they speak of "these gifts, these presents, these holy sacrifices," and further on "this offering." Prayer is also made, in so many words, "that the sacrifice may be accepted even as the sacrifice of Abel." Hence Christ is termed "the sacrifice of the altar." Added to these are the sayings of the holy fathers, the great number of examples, and the widespread practice uniformly observed throughout the world [*per orbem constanter observatum*].[30]

The Roman Canon, Luther wrote in reference to Gregory, was "cobbled together from lies." The Eastern Church did not use it, nor did the heirs of Ambrose's church in Milan. In fact, Luther recounted, it was said that God himself prevented the Milanese from falling under the spell of Gregory. Wondering whether to use their native Ambrosian liturgy or the Roman one, they asked for a sign: "having left both books overnight in their church, when they returned in the morning they found the book of Ambrosius on the altar, and that of Gregory torn apart and scattered."[31] The story, Luther went on, had long explained why Gregory's Mass was everywhere, "*durch die gantze welt zerstrewet werden.*" It was indeed everywhere, he conceded, but as a result, everywhere were lies, superstition, and the sacrifice of the Mass.

Long before anyone could reasonably speak of a "Reformation" in the larger historical sense, then, we already see in sharp relief Luther's antipathy for the sacrificial Eucharists of the Middle Ages. "Your sacrifice is nothing else than the crucifying of Christ again and again," a sin "against the gifts promised in the sacrament," the behavior of "a heathen and a Jew," the "most abominable idolatry on earth," he wrote in the 1521 *Misuse of the Mass*.[32] From the doctrinal point of view, sacrifice was what Luther called a work. It was a thing—perhaps the most basic thing—that human beings do to affect God's opinion, to assuage his anger or please his desire. All these things not only misunderstand, but also corrupt, the relationship of man and God. God does not need anything from us; we cannot affect his views of us; he alone can make us just in his eyes, in a free act of mercy. The Mass cannot be a sacrifice therefore because "the former is something that we receive and the latter is something that we give."[33] Christ has *already* given his blood for our salvation: he did that on the Cross, once and for all, "his Cross was his altar, on which he was offered for us, when he offered us in his very self."[34] That sacrifice made, we receive God's gifts, his mercy and the faith that he freely gives us that we might be made just in his sight.

Once we forget this truth, all manner of corruption ensues. From Gregory's first superstitious lapses grew errors that, over time, obscured the body of Christ from our sight. Once the Eucharist became a sacrifice, a priest was needed to do the sacrificing. Once the priest began to sacrifice, then you must draw a sharp line between those who sacrifice and those who don't. The sharper the line between priesthood and laity, in turn, the more sacrificial the rituals become: the priest turned his back on the laity, he tended secretly to the consecration of the host, he held the host up for communal adoration, he reserved the right to drink from the chalice for himself, and then he and the entire Church came to believe that they were repeating the act that Christ himself performed on the Cross. With that came repeated crucifixions of Christ, the sins of the Jews and heathens repeated every day in every church across Christendom.

Eliminating sacrifice from the Mass would, in short, require remaking the whole liturgical order of medieval Christianity. From the offertory chants and prayers that open the Mass—they "sound and smell like sacrifice"—to the reception of communion that ends it, God's services needed a complete renewal, the divine altar moved out of "the temple of idols" and given a new home.[35] With that, a new home for the Mass, a new church, with new priests, new teachings, new parishes.

From an initial doctrinal objection—sacrifice is a work—Luther was driven into more and more foundational problems. If Eucharistic sacrifice was a cancer consuming the body of the Church, then the basic logic of the Reformation demanded that the surgeon trace an historical line in his search for healthy tissue. "The closer our mass is to the first mass of Christ, doubtless the better it is," Luther wrote already in his 1520 *Sermon on the New Testament, that is, On the Holy Mass*.[36] The project of renovation required tracing back the declension in precise terms. As far back as the earliest church, Luther's 1523 *Order of the Mass* argued, we can find elaborations of the Lord's Supper described in Scripture. The first church fathers added songs in celebration of Christ, for example, readings from the Gospels, recitation of the creeds, and so on. By the time of Gregory, however, the transformation in the liturgy, and indeed the entire Church, had become so breathtaking that Luther struggled to explain how it happened. One possible source was a simple accident of semantic drift. The early father did use "words [like] 'sacrifice' and 'offering,'" but these referred only to the collections of food made by early Christians on behalf of the poor. Only later were these words transferred to the sacrament, he concluded. Another source might have come from practices that carried over from pre-Christian communities. Thus, he thought, the elevation of the eucharistic elements seemed to be a "survival [*reliquum*] of that Hebrew rite of lifting up what was received with thanksgiving and returned to God" (Lev. 8.27). At the end, Luther left the precise historical causes open. Whatever the crucial tipping point, it would "be safer to reject them all [these authorities] than admit that the mass is a work or a sacrifice."[37]

Sacrifice with a Difference

And yet . . . if it was such an abomination, why not just *abandon* everything that "smelled of sacrifice," everything that smelled of Jerusalem and Rome? Once again, as in chapter 1, the counterfactual is illuminating. In his letter to the Corinthians, recall the fine line that Paul was forced to walk, when he confronted a flock uncertain of how best to worship in a Christian way. The absorptive capacity of early Christianity—its ability to fold its competitors, Jewish and pagan, into itself—made this uncertainty especially sharp. Paul did not *reject* sacrifice, in this moment, but rather insisted on a set of translations: the table of the Lord, but not the table of demons; the bread of the Lord, but not the bread of demons; the cup of Christ's blood, but not the cup of demons. The *Letter to the Hebrews* was a long exercise in such translations, Christ the *real* high priest, the *real* sacrifice, that completed the religion of the Jews. The fundamental Christian interpretive framework of typology, moreover, gave the things left behind "once for all," like sacrifice, a powerful afterlife. Christ "enter[s] once for all [*ephapax*] into the Holy Place, taking not the blood of goats and calves but his own blood, thus securing an eternal redemption," the Hebrews author wrote, letting us see Christ as abolition, repetition, extension, and perfection of the sacrifices found in Israel (9.12). No wonder that sacrifice would come to play such an important role in the theological and liturgical life of Christianity, even as Christians insisted that they, in their view uniquely among the religions of the world, were not the sacrificing sort.

No less than Paul and the *Hebrews* author, Luther was unwilling to abandon sacrifice. Sacrifice was simply too important—theologically but also now *historically* as well—to hand over to his opponents. So he instead pursued the same path as his ancestors: sacrifice . . . but not like that. In his 1513–16 commentary on Psalm 84 ("even the sparrow finds a home . . .

where she may lay her young at thy altars, O Lord of Hosts" (84.3)), Luther wrote passionately about the sort of sacrifice that *he* wanted to preserve:

> Our first altar is Christ, he himself is the priest, the offering, and our altar, on which we will be laid and offered to God the Father . . . His cross however was his altar, on which he offered himself for us, as he offered us in himself . . . debasement, disgrace, filth, defect . . . those are our crosses, our Passion, and our altars, on which we present our bodies as living offerings. If Christ is the priest, that is, then he is also the altars, then he [also] slaughters the victim. The altars are the crosses, the sacrificial knives, with which he slaughters, are the word of God.[38]

For young Luther, Christ's sacrifice and our sacrifice are different kinds of things: his altar was the Cross, our altar is Christ. But the formal symmetry between these two sacrifices let him capture the sacrificial imagination for his own purposes. Indeed, it might be said that Luther *expanded* the domain of sacrifice. It is no longer something to be done at distinct places and times, but to be done all the time, every waking moment a sacrifice to God.

We can find this same urge to re-assimilate sacrifice along new lines also in the 1530 *Admonition Concerning the Sacrament of the Body and Blood of Our Lord*. There Luther described a "sacrament rich in grace," reminding his readers to find in the Eucharist a "glorious remembrance of Christ," a sounding out of praise and worship so beautiful as to silence the rest of creation.[39] With this remembrance and praise comes sacrifice, "the most beautiful sacrifice, the supreme worship of God, and the most glorious work, namely, a thank offering."[40] This sacrifice is not bloody; it is not restricted to the priestly caste. Instead it is open to all Christians, a sacrifice universally accessible to anyone who can receive the Eucharist and offer their thanks-offering for its blessings.[41] The sin offering of the Catholics, like the temple offerings of the Jews, reserved sacrifice for the priests alone. What is needed was thus not less, but more sacrifice, albeit of the right sort.

From an analytical point of view, this expansion of the sacrificial operated on two levels. On the first level, the distinction between sin- and thanks-offerings opened the latter to all Christians. On the second level, this same distinction also subjected sacrifice to a *critical* project of sorting between the sheep and the goats, the sacrifices that belonged in Christianity, and those that did not.

This was well-trodden interpretive ground. Already in the Psalms, we find something similar: "Shall I drink the flesh of your bulls or drink the blood of he-goats? / Offer to God the sacrifice of thanksgiving" (Ps. 50. 13–14) or "thou has no delight in sacrifice . . . My sacrifice, O God, is a broken spirit" (Ps. 51.16–17). Augustine took up this last passage in his *City of God*, where the psalmist "said that God does not desire sacrifice" but "also made it clear that God does desire sacrifice," as the Reformation's favorite Church Father put it. "Sacrifice is the visible sacrament of an invisible sacrifice, that is, it is a sacred symbol [*signum*]," Augustine wrote in response to the pagan Porphyry (see chapter 1).[42] This insight allowed him to do two things at once. First, offer a general (if still vague) definition of sacrifice that extended even to the pagans: "even though sacrifice is made or offered by man, sacrifice is a divine thing (*res divina*)—and so the ancient Latins also called it by that name." And then discern a specifically true sacrifice:

> every act whose purpose is that we may cling to God in a holy fellowship . . . and this sacrifice the Church continually celebrates in the rite [*sacramento*] of the altar well known to the faithful, in which it is made clear to her that in her offering she herself is offered to God.[43]

Like both the Psalmist and Augustine, Luther too refused to concede the sacrificial imagination altogether. Instead, he walked that same tightrope, agonistically assimilating sacrifice for a new reformed sacrificial imagination.

Beyond Luther: The Reoccupation of Sacrifice

It did not take long for Luther's vision of a church freed of the *wrong* kind of sacrifice, but renewed by the *right* kind, to take concrete form. Even as his visibility grew dramatically between 1517 and 1521—from professor at a small university town in Saxony to the object of interest of Popes and Emperors—so too did the excitement for liturgical innovation. In those four years, dozens of published treatises attacking the regular order of the Mass appeared in German cities from north to south.[44] Practical measures quickly accompanied them. Already in 1521, when Luther was in hiding and busily translating the New Testament, his allies in Wittenberg began to enact new forms of worship. Communion "in both kinds" was offered—the laity given the chalice of Christ's blood long reserved for the clergy. Clerical robes were simplified or removed entirely. And on Christmas Day 1521, Andreas Bodenstein of Karlstadt celebrated the first new reformed worship, clothed as an ordinary man, distributing the bread and the wine to everyone, and eliminating all references to sacrifice in both the spoken and the performed liturgy.[45]

Karlstadt's service was only the first of many new reformed worships invented in the 1520s. Luther described a "formula" for the Mass in 1523—a set of general guidelines—and then wrote a vernacular German Mass in 1526. Others were quicker. In the Saxon town of Allstedt, Luther's early follower and later archenemy, Thomas Müntzer, wrote and celebrated a vernacular liturgy in 1523.[46] In the same year, in Zürich, Huldrych Zwingli—the spearhead of the Swiss reformers and later opponent of Luther—also published a new order of the Mass.[47] The next year, in Strassburg, German Mass began to be celebrated in the Cathedral Chapel of St. John.

Many of these liturgies still bore family resemblances to the older Catholic service. At the beginning, for example, the Strassburg rite dispensed with the offertory prayers that Luther had condemned, but kept the elevation of the host.[48] Despite its association with sacrificial oblation, Luther also kept the elevation in both of his 1523 and 1526 formularies. Others were impatient for faster change. In Zürich, some began to celebrate their eucharistic rituals in secret, eliminating the priest altogether.[49] In Silesia in 1526, the nobleman Caspar Schwenckfeld urged his followers to stop holding Mass altogether, calling for an inner devotion to the Eucharist rather than "cast that which is holy unto the dogs."[50] In 1527, the Anabaptist Balthasar Hubmaier wrote a wholly innovative liturgy that featured lengthy pledges of mutual affection and discipline before taking communion as a sign and seal of this communal bond.[51]

All of these new liturgies eliminated the sacrificial center of the Mass, the Roman Canon. For some, this elimination involved an effort to root sacrifice out of Christian worship entirely. Zwingli was adamant that Christ's one-time death on the Cross was the last sacrifice admissible in a Christian framework, for example. The very word sacrifice, he insisted, whether in Hebrew, or Greek, or Latin, means "to kill," so all sacrifice must involve a dead victim. Since Christ was the last dead victim—the death that ended death—so too did Christian sacrifice come to an end 1,500 years ago.[52] Since all sacrifice involves destruction, *Christian* sacrifice happened only one time, long ago on the Cross at Calvary.

Zwingli defended this inflexibly philological approach of sacrifice in the first public debate about the sacrificial Eucharist in the Reformation in January 1523. His Catholic opponent Johann Fabri was merciless in his response. This enormously learned humanist and vicar-general of Constance had already spent years laboring in the Christian archives. Long before his friend Erasmus published the collected works of Irenaeus, Fabri had read the manuscript of *Adversus haereses* in Roman libraries.[53] This work was reported lost in the early Middle Ages, but in Faber's hands, the ancient heresiologist came to life as a weapon against the latest heresies, Irenaeus who wrote how "the offering (*oblatio*) of the church . . . is reckoned a pure sacrifice by God, and accepted by him" and even that "sacrifice in general is not to be condemned."[54] As a disciple of Polycarp—apostolic father, martyr, and bishop of Smyrna—Irenaeus bridged the age of the apostles and that of the more well-known church fathers like Cyprian, Ambrose, Chrysostom, and later Augustine. Together they witnessed how "the oriental and the occidental church, indeed the whole world and all priests, from the morning until night" have always held that this "sacrament is a sacrifice."[55] The cost of Zwingli's philological absolutism was *any* claim on the whole history of Christianity, a cost that later Catholic critics were happy to inflict at every opportunity.[56] And at a moment when the critique of the Roman Church depended on historical argument, this was a very high price to pay.

In his 1521 *Misuse of the Mass*, Luther waved away history, declaring that "we are not baptized in the name of Augustine, Bernard, Gregory, Peter or Paul . . . but in the name of Jesus Christ," as if even Scripture were a secondary source.[57] But his intellectual comrades, above all that great synthesist of Lutheran theology Philip Melanchthon, quickly rushed to rescue this history from the hands of Catholics like Faber. As Peter Fraenkel has beautifully shown, the humanist-educated Melanchthon buried himself in the patristic archive, seeking to understand and weigh the various fathers in ways familiar from the previous chapter.[58] Greek fathers like Cyprian and Gregory Nazianzenus were useful, and he was especially delighted to discover Epiphanius's *Panarion*, which he summarized and excerpted in the effort to document the heresies of his day.[59]

It was Melanchthon, for example, who insisted that the *entire* Reformation depended on its historical character. "*Semper ecclesia coetus est exiguus*," the true church is always a remnant, he wrote; the *real* church had always been weak, small, but continuous across time.[60] This continuity had a particular historical shape, however, as the Church declined from its most authentic early period, to the corruptions of the age of Gregory. To write this history, Melanchthon differentiated among the fathers, all of whom might err, but some of whom erred grievously. Against Faber's "the whole world and all priests," Melanchthon opposed a broken and interrupted past. A wholesome apostolic and post-apostolic age ending with Irenaeus, a middle period with much virtue lasting through and beyond Augustine, a long period of decay, and finally the rediscovery of a truth long buried under heretical innovation. "Any movement from the false to the true faith will necessarily be a movement back to origins and thus back in time," a movement only successfully accomplished by careful differentiation within the Christian archive.[61]

This fundamental sensibility underwrote many evangelical enterprises, not least the later histories of the Church that told and retold narratives of revelation, decline, and rebirth: the *Chronicles* of Johann Carion (1521, with many later editions in the sixteenth century); the *Catalogus testium veritatis* (1553) and the titanic *Magdeburg Centuries* (1559–1574), both products of the tireless energies of the later Lutheran Matthias Flacius Illyricus. These ecclesiastical histories took inspiration from patristic writings, not least the *Ecclesiastical History* of Eusebius. Eusebius was one of the fathers recalled from obscurity in the wake of the 1420 Council of Constance, and became a crucial model for Reformation-era sacred histories.[62] These new histories mirrored not only the ambition and creativity of this fourth-century church father, but also his apologetic and controversial method. As with Eusebius, defending Christianity against external critics, so for the reformers, defending it against other Christians: it was *apology* that drove the creative project.[63]

With respect to sacrifice, it was quite literally in an apology—Melanchthon's *Apology for the Confession of Augsburg* (1531)—that we can see how important it became to reclaim the right sacrifice on historical grounds. The previous year, the princes defending the reformers—including Philip of Hesse, and John of Saxony—had presented an account of the evangelical project to Emperor Charles V in a meeting of the imperial diet in Augsburg. Attached to the confession was a list of "abuses" they intended to correct, and chief among them was the Mass and its "abominable error" of sacramental sacrifice.[64] The confession was read aloud in both Latin and German before the Emperor, who immediately commissioned an official examination and confutation by a committee of theologians, including the well-known enemy of Luther, Johann Eck. Even before the confutation was received, however, Melanchthon and other reformers were already at work on a defense of the confession. When the *Apology* came out, it was under Melanchthon's name.[65]

The chief apology was for the new unsacrificial Mass. We know, the draft to the *Apology* insisted, that "the mass was called a sacrifice by the ancient writers, because it was to be a memorial of Christ's sacrifice, as Irenaeus said." It is a calumny "that we would destroy sacrifice," then, since "we preserve the custom of the ancient church."[66] Sacrifice itself was not the problem; the problem is what sacrifice has become. This difficult thought Melanchthon developed in the published edition of the *Apology* as follows:

> Sacrifice is a ceremony, or a work that we offer to God in order to move him with this honor. There are, however, only two kinds of sacrifice, and no more. The first is the propitiatory sacrifice, that is, a work of satisfaction for guilt, and punishment, that is, for reconciling God, or placating his anger, or that earns the remission of the sins of others. The other type is eucharistic sacrifice, which does not earn the remission of sins, or reconciliation, but is performed by those already reconciled, in order to give thanks for the gift of sin's remission, and for other benefits received.[67]

We already know from Luther how to map these sacrificial distinctions. Propitiatory sacrifice—the blood sacrifice of the Jews perfected by the *ephapax* oblation of Christ—belongs in the past; eucharistic or thanksgiving sacrifices to the present. Catholics are guilty of both innovation *and* regression, then, reviving ceremonies belonging to a past abolished by Christianity.

Over the next decades, Melanchthon developed an ever more robust historical framework for exploring the decline of the Church. The *Apology* insisted that the eucharistic-propitiatory distinction, and the reformed Lord's Supper, was "consistent with the fathers and scripture."[68] Later texts added some detail, but more important to Melanchthon was how this distinction, so clearly made (in his mind) in Scripture, began to fall apart over time. His 1539 *De ecclesia et auctoritate verbi dei*, for example, systematically scrutinized the patristic archive for its many errors: Cyprian was condemned for his rigorism; Origen for thinking that even the Devil might be saved; Tertullian for attacking second marriage.[69] When it came to the sacrifice, Melanchthon described how early semantic slips—fathers conforming to "the customs of the people" and calling the Lord's Supper an oblation—the "sprinkled seeds" of impiety grew into major error.[70] "Great is the power of custom, and the men who follow this often speak improperly," he remarked, and "thus the ancients kept the language of oblation and sacrifice, in no way attending to its etymology or proper significance."[71] Even though Irenaeus and the other fathers clearly *meant* eucharistic sacrifice, Melanchthon concluded, the power of their "metonyms" refashioned the Mass into the very propitiatory sacrifice that it was meant to abolish.[72]

Among the earliest evangelicals, then, the sacrificial world of the later Middle Ages was not abolished so much as transformed. The eucharistic sacrifice taken for granted by Peter of Lombard, and put into such rich liturgical practice in the late medieval Church, was the object of unrelenting scorn. But the response was, among magisterial reformers like Luther and Melanchthon, less rejection than *reoccupation* of the language of sacrifice. This was a delicate business. After all, the original problem was the early fathers' loose language, and their unwitting absorption of a sacrificial vocabulary into Christianity's holiest rituals. Lutheran reformers hoped to manage this threat by clarification—the sacrifice that *we* mean (and that the ancient fathers meant) is neither a bloody sacrifice for guilt, nor a sacramental offering for sin. It is instead the sacrifice of praise that Christians offer in grateful acknowledgment of the offering that Jesus made, once and for all, on his Cross.

Sacrifice and the Origin of Error

The Lutherans were alone neither in their renewed practices of agonistic incorporation, nor in their efforts to reorganize the patristic archive in service of new liturgies and theologies of sacrifice.[73] By the time that the Zürich reformer Zwingli died in 1531, multiple claims on the history of the Church, and multiple claims about sacrifice, were competing in the reformed republic of letters. Disagreements were visible already at the 1529 Colloquy of Marburg, which foundered on the rocks of the Lord's Supper: Luther insisting on the ubiquitous presence of Christ in the eucharistic elements, Zwingli on the commemorative nature of the ritual. This parting of the ways proved final, culminating in the formation of mutually loathing "evangelical" (e.g., Lutheran) and "Reformed" (e.g., Calvinist) Protestant camps for centuries to come.[74]

On the eve of this colloquy, a very young Heinrich Bullinger (1504–1575)—future leader of the Swiss church in Zürich—published a short work entitled *On the Origin of Error in the Matter of the Eucharist and the Mass* (1528). Already in ways far more detailed than anything found in Wittenberg, Bullinger adapted patristic apologetics for a new era.[75] "What did the ancients think Christian sacrifice was, and why did they think the eucharist was a sacrifice and offering?" Bullinger began the work anticipating the need to appropriate the fathers for reforming ends.[76] What followed was a list of early patristic authorities—including Irenaeus, Cyprian, Tertullian, Lactantius, Ambrosius, and Augustine—and their views on Christian sacrifice. From the outset, the argument was clear. From Lactantius's *Divine Institutes*, for example, Bullinger selected this: "there are two things that should be offered, a gift [*donum*] and sacrifice: the gift always, the sacrifice at the right time [*ad tempus*] . . . the gift is the integrity of the soul, the sacrifice praise and hymns."[77] "Proving" that the early Christians would not sacrifice by citing pagan testimony—Pliny the Younger's letter to Trajan complaining of Christian refusal to sacrifice—Bullinger insisted, "you see . . . what things should be sacred to Christians, not to devour and sacrifice the flesh of god, but to offer thanks, to pray, to unite [*confoederare*], to develop discipline."[78]

Again, then, the question was an historical one: if the ancient church had supplied a Reformed Eucharist *avant la lettre*, then where and how did things go so terribly wrong? Bullinger gave this an exact date: the year 407, when Alaric and his Visigoths invaded Rome, there began a "first stage of error" when knowledge of languages declined, books were trampled, erudition neglected, and brutality venerated.[79] It was this social and political disaster that set the stage for the monk-pope *Gregorius fabulosus*, "born in an unhappy age, he was the master of the most unhappy ceremonies," introducing "not only an infinity of superstitions, but also the chief . . . of all superstitions, the mass."[80]

In the early Church, Bullinger reported, "no one was compelled to adhere to prescribed words . . . the Jews were addicted to ceremonies, from which Christ wanted us to be free." The result was a diversity of rites, "each church had its own rite, and yet in substance they were together as one."[81] Rome remained in communion with the rest until in the age of Gregory, when she was severed from this unity by the fixing of superstitions in ritual form and their mandatory prescription for the Church. Thus, for example, already in the late third century, Bullinger wrote, a sacrificial element had crept into the liturgy, when, as a concession to the many gentiles who had converted to Christianity, Pope Eutychianus (as the *Liber pontificalis* reported later) allowed for the blessing of beans and grapes on Christian altars.[82] Gregory grew these beans and grapes into something altogether more pernicious, however, when he consolidated a local practice into a universal requirement. And thus "a man who loved novelty, who, although desirous of remedying abuse, was nonetheless lacking in judgement, and filled with Gothic ideas, thus the very man that wanted to abolish abuse, established the worst abuse of all."[83]

This worst abuse was the Roman Canon. It was "most customary" among the ancients to preach to their assemblies, Bullinger argued, and to offer prayers to God on behalf of the people. From this innocent practice came the *Te igitur*, the opening prayer of the Canon. It was equally common, as Augustine tells us, to honor the martyrs (see chapter 1) in formal Christian ceremonies.[84] This could, and should, have been an innocent ritual. Admittedly, when fathers like Augustine, Tertullian, and Cyprian talked about martyr veneration, they often used the language of sacrifice. But this was just cultural shorthand for the praise, hymns, and other acts of thanksgiving proper to ancient Christian worship, Bullinger believed.[85] At some point—and Bullinger blamed Gregory's predecessor, Pope Pelagius I (556–561)—the Roman Church again formalized these behaviors, celebrating the "memory of the dead" after the consecration of the host.[86] With this formalization of an early informal practice, the language of sacrifice began to be taken more literally, "offerings" now more than just praise. This error reached its zenith with Gregory's oblations:

> Gifts are brought, but to the altars by a sacrificing priest [*sacrificulo*]. Where in fact is the assembly? Where are the people's acts of gratitude? Where are the covenants [*foedera*]? Everything was transferred once and for all [*semel*] to one sacrificer [*sacrificulum*], who more plays the role of actor at the altar than priest [*qui verius ad aram histrionem gestibus exprimit, quam sacerdotem*] . . . Now you see how everything ancient was abolished in the rule of Gregory, and the worst superstition brought in.[87]

In this clever piece of critique, the "once and for all (*semel*)" of Christ's sacrifice became the once and for all of Roman superstitions. The pious office of a priest, offering prayers to God, was now usurped by an actor (*histrionem*), a sacrificer pantomiming piety with his actions at the altar.

Over time, Bullinger's early pamphlet on the Mass grew. In 1529, he wrote a companion piece on idolatry; in 1539, he expanded both essays and compiled them into one long treatise entitled simply *Two Books on the Origin of Errors*, a volume later translated into French, German, and Dutch. This latter work proved of signal importance to the Reformed sacrificial imagination, providing the first *general* history of sacrifice from its origins in the world of Adam and his children.

Once upon a time, there was a "true religion" untrammeled by false rites, a religion already found in the Garden. Corruption waited no longer than sin, however. God desired "innocence alone," the church father Lactantius taught and Bullinger repeated, but humans "think they are religious if they go smearing temples and altars with the blood of victims and drenching hearths with a profusion of fragrant old wine."[88] Already in Cain and Abel, then, the "first servants of god" fell prey to the impious. Abel declared his piety with "fat victims offered to God and with his own blood spilled in the name of God," while Cain began a "cult of impiety" whose long afterlife Christians still endure.[89] Piety was always haunted by impiety, so *Two Books* argued, a dynamic that Bullinger traced through the Hebrew Bible, into the early Christian era, and beyond.

Bullinger thus restaged normative theological controversies in his theory of history. Abel's piety suggested that there has always been a true religion, a pristine *ur*-Christianity easy to discern and define. "True religion does not move around externals, but is centered in the pious soul," Bullinger wrote in the *Two Books*.[90] But for every pious Abel, there is an impious Cain, attached to externals. The warfare between these supplied the basic drama of Christian history. From the age of the martyrs, for example, Bullinger seized on Polycarp, the bishop of Smyrna who died in the late second century, charging his persecutor with the very crime of atheism for which he was burned and stabbed in the Roman stadium. After his death, the faithful "removed his bones, which were more valuable than expensive gems and more precious than gold," and gathered around them to commemorate his martyrdom.[91] This was, in one sense, pious. The early Christian community did not *worship* the martyrs or their remains, Bullinger observed, but merely honored their passion for Christ.[92] But, in another sense, it also augured a darker future for the Christian church. Is it not the case, the Jew Nicetas asked the Christians gathering the pearly bones, that they had "abandoned he who was crucified, and begun to worship Polycarp?"[93]

Like Abel and Cain, the story of Polycarp shows the twinned history of piety and error. "Calamity erupted from a pure religion," Bullinger observed, when the pious cult of Polycarp became the demonic cult of the saints, early Christians starting to "exhume and move the bones, and gather them in golden urns and sepulchres, and place them in the oratory."[94] Even the much venerated church father Jerome found himself on the wrong side of history in this regard, in Bullinger's view, Jerome who, in the early fifth century, vehemently defended the piety of relic cults against the ascetic priest Vigilantius.[95] From this relic cult came the swarm of errors that beset the church as it entered its sixth century, when Christians "erected temples, built altars, consecrated statues, instituted priesthoods" such that over time, "there was no difference from the impiety of the Gentiles."[96]

Harmonizing the normative and the descriptive—doctrinal credo and historical narrative—was a major intellectual challenge. The doctrinal difference between true piety and mere ceremony was clear enough. What was much harder to understand was how it applied to particular cases. Sacrifice was, in this respect, the hardest case of all. On the one hand, it could be construed as paradigmatic of the merely external: what does God need sacrifice for, anyway? Such a view would have abandoned the entire history of Christian sacrifice to Catholic opponents, however. Moreover, it was impossible to comprehend even in the reformer's own historical terms. Why, after all, did *Abel*, son of Adam, and prototypical pious patriarch, offer "firstlings of his flock" to God (Gen. 4.4)? And why did God accept these gifts? And why not the gifts of Cain? Augustine had already used this story to argue that there was *something* essentially sacred about sacrifice: "though performed or offered by man," sacrifice, or at least the right sort of sacrifice, "is a divine thing."[97] What that might be was hard to establish, however, as reformers endlessly discovered.

Redeeming Sacrifice

The idealized contrast between (false) ceremony and (true) piety was hardest to sustain when reformers shifted from critique to their own constructive reforms. Critique could freely abandon ceremony for an idealized piety. But because reformers felt compelled to preserve the distinctive holiness of Eucharistic ceremony—and the sacrifice that it celebrated *semel* and *quotidie*—the creation of a properly reformed means of worship had to redeem sacrifice in *some* form.

Take, for example, the early ally of Bullinger, Martin Bucer. Bucer's home was Strassburg, where he became involved as early as 1523 in that city's reformation of Christian worship.[98] Already by 1524, Strassburg had leapt beyond the Wittenberg reformers, banishing the Mass and instituting the "Lord's Supper" instead, forbidding the elevation of the host, and replacing stone altars with communion tables.[99] Bucer was at the forefront of these reforms, deeply engaged in debates with Catholic opponents about these novel liturgical forms. As so often in the Reformation, however, the novelty was the problem. The great Augustine himself, wrote the Catholic controversialist Johann Eck, confirmed that sacrificial masses, and masses for the dead, had been the "custom of the whole church" for at least eleven hundred years.[100] Indeed, he and others once again noted just how ubiquitous the language of sacrifice was among the earliest church fathers like Irenaeus, Cyprian, Ignatius of Antioch, and Ambrose.[101] In response, Bucer pressed these same fathers into the service of reform:

> Just as the pagans honoured the gods in their sacrifices, ate with one another and joyfully revived their friendship, so it was that . . . on the basis that Christians renew their spiritual and everlasting covenant and testament in the Lord with holy food and drink, [ancient Christians]

were able to say, "the pagans have their sacrifices and offerings in which they assemble to honour their gods. Our Sacrifice will be the Supper of Christ."[102]

In other words, yes, the ancient fathers had set their own liturgical practices into a sacrificial framework familiar from the pagan world. *But* they had done so for pragmatic reasons, to accommodate—as Erasmus would have said—the supper of Christ to the sensibilities of those they hoped to evangelize. This same framework could be applied to the two Testaments as well, the sacrifices of the Jews not just types of the perfected sacrifice to come, but also pedagogical instruments preparing people to abandon their legalistic ways.[103] Nature and law prepare for grace, and so early Christian appropriation of sacrificial ceremony was a form of divine fulfillment, a natural extension of the missionary project.

Within *this* framework, a new and robust sacrificial imagination flourished, especially after 1530, when the Reformation splintered Christianity into ever more diverse groups. In those years, Bucer began to meet both publicly and in secret with learned Catholics in an effort to build a broad consensus on eucharistic sacrifice. Although these meetings ultimately failed, in them, Bucer expanded his sense of what was sacrificial about the divine ceremony of the Lord's Supper. By 1546, Bucer had identified five different sacrifices proper to the Eucharist: the offering of Christ's Passion; the offering of bread and wine; the offering of thanksgiving; the self-offering of the Church; and the offering of gifts. He traced these sacrifices across an archive that included the writings of Irenaeus, Tertullian, Chrysostom, Epiphanius, and many other early texts, developing a *Florilegium patristicum* (1539), a collection of patristic citations for reformed theologians. In doing this, he showed how tightly sacrifice was woven into the liturgical matrix of the early Church, and in what manner this matrix might still be pious and useful. Provided it is understood as both "outward sign of inward grace *and* . . . outward expression of inward worship," in other words, sacrifice could belong to the liturgical imagination of even reformed churches.[104]

Reformers, in short, reoccupied the sacrificial imagination for their own projects. In place of the sacrificial priesthood, they created the new liturgy of the Lord's Supper, which, with no less intensity, placed the sacrifice of Christ at the center of worship. We can see this clearly in Geneva, whose reforms were pioneered by that French refugee theologian, John Calvin. Like all the earlier reformers, Calvin was ferocious in his criticism of the Mass, the "foulest sacrilege," that makes churches into "schools of idolatry and ungodliness."[105] The "cross of Christ is overthrown as soon as the altar is set up," he wrote, the "sacrifice of the Mass dissolves and tears apart the community."[106] Calvin's *Form of Prayer*, a handbook introduced in Geneva in 1542, rejected all of this in favor of a liturgy rooted in, Calvin claimed, that very liturgy that "Jesus Christ commanded, that his Apostles preserved and pursued, whose uses the primitive church retained."[107] This new Genevan liturgy discarded much of the traditional Mass. No elevations, no breaking of the host, no commemoration of the dead, and certainly not that Canon that epitomized, for Calvin and others, the sacrificial heart of the medieval church. In their place the Genevans introduced a communion rite centered on the reading of St. Paul: "This is my body which is for you. Do this in remembrance of me . . . this cup is the new covenant in my blood. Do this, as often as you drink it, in remembrance of me" (1 Cor. 11.24–25).

Simplification did not mean a reduction in intensity, however. Standards for participation in the communion rite often grew *stricter* among the Reformed. In local parishes, communion was typically delayed until the age of 12 or even 16, that the young might receive proper instruction in the faith. They also maintained lists of "worthy communicants"—in some cases, even issuing paper and metal identity tokens to prove eligibility—and excommunication was essential to the process of consistorial discipline for the unworthy.[108] Once eligible, communicants were expected to prepare for the rite a week in advance, so that, during the rite, they might "truly participate in his body and his blood . . . possess them entirely."[109] The event itself also shifted its focus from the traditional priest to the communicants. Sacrifice was no longer performed on behalf of the sinner, but by the sinner. "When you eat the bread, and drink from the chalice, you will announce the death of the Lord," read the *Form of Prayer*.[110] This new Lord's Supper re-enacted the sacrifice in the minds of its participants, indeed re-enacted it so powerfully as to transform the pious Christian into a living sacrifice to God. "The eucharistic prayer," comments the historian Christian Grosse, "inscribes the celebration of the supper into the perspective of a Christian life entirely marked by its sacrificial character."[111]

With the demise of a sacrificing priesthood came, then, an *expansion* in the scope of the sacrificial imagination. What Calvin called the "chief exercise of faith"—prayer—turned everyday worship, for example, into a continuous sacrifice of praise. "Words fail to explain how necessary prayer is," for it both offers God a continuous recognition of his blessings, and returns the "profit of this sacrifice" to us.[112] The "sacrifice acceptable to God is a broken spirit," proclaimed Psalm 51, thus prayer must acknowledge man's vitiation and dependence on God's mercy.[113] Even what we might imagine to be the archetypes of propitiatory sacrifice, the temple sacrifices of ancient Israel, were actually forms of prayer:

> God had taught in the law that the priest alone entering the sanctuary should bear the names of the tribes of Israel upon his shoulders . . . but the people should stand afar off in the court, and there join their petitions with the priest. Nay, the sacrifice even had value in ratifying and strengthening the prayers. Therefore that foreshadowing ceremony of the law taught us that . . . we need a Mediator . . . [and] that our prayers are cleansed by sprinkled blood.[114]

Like the Eucharist, prayer covered daily Christian life with the blood of Christ, not only recalling his sacrifice to memory, but activating it as well. Prayer "worked," in this sense, insofar as it opened a connection between the petitioner and the Cross. Prayer and the sacrifice of thanksgiving are thus two names for the same thing, Calvin remarks, two ways of offering ourselves to Christ just as He offered Himself for us.[115]

Like other reformers, Calvin rooted these innovations in the deep time of the faith.[116] Cast out of the garden, the only "hope of salvation" that remained for Cain and Abel, Calvin argued, lay in the "signs of sacrifice" [*tesseras sacrificiis*] they had inherited from their father, Adam.[117] Sacrifice was not merely a human invention, then, but a ceremony "divinely delivered." The sacrifices of this first age of mankind were acceptable to God, a ceremony "sublime and secret" that hinted at the promise of salvation. Even the "adulterated imitations" of these first sacrifices discovered among the gentiles were a reminder of this promise, "making the exercise of piety common to all" even if in a manner obscure.[118] What distinguished the rejected Cain from the beloved Abel was not *what* they sacrificed, but *who* did the sacrificing. As Calvin wrote, "the strong scent of burning fat could not conciliate the divine favour to the sacrifices of Abel; but, being pervaded by the good odour of faith, they had a sweet-smelling savour."[119] As for the sacrifices of Abel, so for the sacrifices of Christians: sanctity depends not on the gift, but the giver.

As for the Eucharist, there too Calvin incorporated, in new terms, older aspects of the sacrificial imagination. Like Zwingli, Calvin denied the real presence of Christ in the eucharistic elements. But he was never content to imagine the Eucharist as *merely* symbolic, a mnemonic device with no special value of its own. The Eucharist was a sacrament, after all, a divinely mandated ceremony with the awesome power to conduce us to God. It was, Calvin liked to say, a "seal" of God's promises, more than a sign, a physical ratification of a promise made:

> What can the slaughter of a sow accomplish unless words accompany the act, indeed, unless they precede it? For sows are often slain apart from any inner or loftier mystery. . . . Yet when words precede, the laws of covenants are by such signs ratified . . . The sacraments, therefore, are exercises which make us more certain of the trustworthiness of God's Word. And because we are of flesh, they are shown to us under things of flesh.[120]

The analogy between sows and the Christian host was not an accident. In both, act and word were bound together by sacrifice. "The mystery of Christ's secret union with the devout is by nature incomprehensible," Calvin wrote: although "the Lord's body was once and for all so sacrificed . . . by feeding [we] feel in ourselves the workings of that unique sacrifice."[121] The "bread is given as a symbol of Christ's body," but when it does so, "it causes us to feel the power of that bread."[122] "His flesh is truly food, and his blood truly drink," so that "Christ's flesh, separated from us by such great distance, penetrates to us."[123] "By truly partaking of him, his life passes into us and is made ours," a mystery so deep, he confessed, that his "mind is conquered and overwhelmed by the greatness of the thing."[124] The Lord's Supper does not repeat the Crucifixion. Yet still there *is* a sacrifice conveyed by the eucharistic elements, a sacrifice that infuses the believing recipient with the very "workings" of the Cross.

Even as he lamented the sacrificial Mass, then, he defended the importance of sacrifice to a Christian life. Sacrifice generally means, he tells us, "every sort of thing offered to God." But the Hebrew Bible distinguishes between offerings for sin, and those "symbol[s] of divine worship and . . . attestation of religion." These latter include all those pious acts—"burnt offerings, libations, oblations, first fruits, and peace offerings"—through which the Jews showed their love of God. As for Jews, so for Christians. One kind of sacrifice was made by Christ on the Cross, once and for all expiating the sins of humanity and propitiating an angry God.[125] The other kind of sacrifice is never-ending.

> all the duties of love . . . all our prayers, praises, thanksgivings, and whatever we do in the worship of God. All these things finally depend upon the greater sacrifice, by which we are consecrated in soul and body

to be a holy temple to the Lord . . . this is so necessary for the church that it cannot be absent from it . . . it will continue forever as long as God's people shall abide.[126]

Virtually everything pious thus depends on that first sacrifice, conveyed mysteriously under the workings of the eucharistic host, a sacrifice made once but now multiplying throughout the Church, in all of its activities. Of the reformers, as Lee Palmer Wandel has noted, there is a curious way in which Calvin turned out to be the most sacrificial of all.[127]

Conclusion: Sacrificial Collectives

When historians of theology write about the first decades of the Reformation, there is a natural urge to explore the differences, both among reformers and between reformers and Catholics. The urge is natural not only because we know that very different religious communities emerged from this crucible, but also because theological inquiry in this era lived and breathed polemics. Tracing these polemics doubtless invites us to overvalue the distinctions that our historical characters took to be crucial. Thus we are invited to stress the different views of Christ's presence inside the eucharistic elements and to map them onto different confessional communities, because the reformers themselves made these into such bones of contention.

And yet when we step back from the theological particulars, what seems remarkable is the durability of the Christian sacrificial imagination. Yes, altars were replaced by communion tables, pulpits loomed newly large in reformed churches, and church interiors were rebuilt in accord with current theological norms. But every magisterial reforming community, Lutheran or Reformed, whether in Geneva or Wittenberg or London, retained what they called the Lord's Supper as its main organizational rite. In the Lutheran world, majestic altarpieces reappeared that concentrated attention on the Crucifixion, no longer set—as in the Gregory Mass—into a dynamic liturgical framework, but exquisitely elevated as the *only* sacrifice worthy of attention. In the remarkable Weimar altarpiece (1555), begun by Lucas Cranach and completed after his death, the redemptive blood streams first onto the head of the deceased painter, and then, beyond, toward the Bible opened to 1 John 1.7: "the blood of Jesus his Son cleanses us from all sins" (see fig. 3.7 and color plate 5). Here is the "miraculous and immediate reception of the thing shows," as Joseph Leo Koerner remarks, "the blood shed at the crucifixion and now present in the altar rite," in word and deed alike.[128]

FIGURE 3.7. Weimar Altarpiece. Lucas Cranach and workshop. Church of Saint Peter and Paul, Weimar (1552–1555). bpk Bildagentur /St. Peter und Paul, Weimar / Photograph by Roland Dreßler/ Art Resource, NY.

This sacrifice assumed its own special intensity in reformed lands. The institution of church inspections developed in the Lutheran lands, for instance, aimed to ascertain who among the community was ready to participate in the Lord's Supper. The Lutheran requirement of confession before communion tightened bonds between parish and pastor, and scripts were developed by church governors to manage these confessions.[129] Elaborate ceremonies of princely communion confirmed the connection between sovereign and parish.[130] Reformed churches did things somewhat differently—inventing the consistory as a disciplinary wing of the church and threatening excommunication for sins—but they too organized the social life of liturgy around the Lord's Supper and its celebration of the *ephapax* of the Cross. The Eucharist may have pulled communities apart, but it also helped to reinstitute them.

Sacrifice thus endured, a deep structure of continuity in a pluralizing religious environment. But this was no longer Gregory's sacrifice. For the sacrifices of the reformers were no longer "naive," but rather developed in a self-critical dialogue with Christianity's own history. The Christian archive shaped the survival of sacrifice, not least by offering itself as a model for how new churches might be imagined. That the Strassburg church ordinances of 1534 required every parish library keep on hand a copy of Eusebius's *Historica ecclesiastica* is only one token of the felt power of this history over theological and liturgical experiment.[131] Ecclesiological innovation happened in a curious timescape, the needs of the present always coordinated with origins buried deep in the Christian past.

Fealty to this Christian past was demanding. It required vast research on the early fathers, a field of knowledge that grew exponentially over the sixteenth century. Some eighty patristic anthologies were collected and printed in the sixteenth century, mostly in order to defend one or another disputed doctrinal position.[132] Here are a few that explored what this patristic archive had to say about the Eucharist: Peter Martyr, *Tractatio de sacramento eucharistiae* (1549), John Veron, *The Godly Saiyings of the Old Auncient Faithful Fathers Upon the Sacrament of the Body and Blood of Chryste* (1550), Andreas Musculus, *Enchiridium sententiarum ac dictorum insignium . . . scripturae sacrae, doctorumque Ecclesiae sanctae . . . ad consensum purae doctrinae Evangelii* (1552), Christoph Herdesianus, *Consensus orthodoxus sacrae scripturae et veteris ecclesiae, de . . . coenae Domenicae* (Zürich, 1578), and so on. Works like these demanded carefully sorting the fathers, whose diversity in time, space, and opinion called for careful discernment. All of this, finally, forced reformers to come to terms with the enormous power that sacrifice had held in the early Christian imagination, a recognition that, for better or worse, the religion that abandoned sacrifice was also the religion that redeemed it.

The very historico-theological project that supplied reformers with weapons *against* their Catholic opponents, therefore, made their own reintegration of sacrifice an inevitability. But in the face of their opponents, reformers did what the ancient apologists had done, namely engage the machinery of agonistic incorporation. Sacrifice, yes, but *not like that,* was the shorthand version. And just as in the ancient Church, sacrifice could serve as both a rite of inclusion and exclusion, creating kinship between groups in the very moment that it declared them utterly distinct.

To what sacrifices, in the end, did the reformers say yes? Most obviously, they said yes to the once-and-for-all sacrifice of Christ on the Cross. And they said yes to the sacrifice of praise and thanksgiving, the grateful acknowledgment of His sacrifice and the benefits that it brings to us. Less obviously, they said yes to a *communal* sacrifice, the *communion* of their sacrifices. The Lord's Supper, Calvin wrote, is "distributed in the public assembly of the church to teach us of the communion by which we all cleave together in Christ Jesus."[133] When Christ's flesh becomes ours, we are not only confirmed in our relationship to him, but also to each other. No more priests devouring their victims, mumbling their silent consecrations, and insisting on their unique relationship to God. Now instead what Luther called a "priesthood of believers," whose members are bound to one another by the sacrifice of collective worship. We have what Bullinger called the "assembly," the *foedera*, the covenanted community. True sacrifice is religious and social at the same time, in other words. It binds together collectivities, and seals them with the body and blood of Christ. It gives these collectivities a history, a city of God *peregrinans*, as Augustine put it, conserved in time from the apostles until now.

No wonder, then, that the Lord's Supper would continue to play such a crucial role in the ecclesiastical structure of sixteenth-century confessions, since as much as ever, sacrifice was seen as both the activity and sinews of a church. What happens when these sacrificial communities were put to the test—when the ancient cult of the martyrs comes back to life in the new martyrological world of the sixteenth century—is the subject of our next chapter.

CHAPTER FOUR

Polycarp's Bones

PROVING THE MARTYRS OF THE SIXTEENTH CENTURY

And [Saul] said, "Divine for me by a spirit, and bring up for me whomever I shall name for you."

—1 SAMUEL 28.8

How did this pious horror of the Mass become the morbid fascination for the death of the martyrs, this eloquent and spectacular death that has all the external appearance of a sacrifice?

—FRANK LESTRINGANT, *LUMIÈRE DES MARTYRS*[1]

When the fire doth his appointed office, thou shalt be received, as a sweet burnt sacrifice, into heaven.

—JOHN CARELESS TO JOHN BRADFORD, 1555[2]

IT IS DANGEROUS TO raise the dead. What comes back is often a surprise, and rarely pleasant. Saul raised the ghost of Samuel for advice and instead learned of his doom, to die with his sons and deliver Israel to the vengeance of the Philistines. Like Samuel's ghost, ancient Christianity was raised up in the sixteenth century to service urgent contemporary needs. At a moment when the churches of Europe were in danger, when Christian communities were under the rack of confessional violence, the ancient martyrs seemed an archive of authentic Christian living. Everyone knew, or thought they knew, just how essential the ancient martyrs had been to the formation and vigor of early Christianity. The blood of Christians was what the early church father Tertullian had called the seed of the church.

By bringing it back, people hoped not only to understand their experiences of violence and death, but also to rejuvenate the new Christianities of early modern Europe. But the ghosts of ancient martyrs were more unsettling than anyone might have imagined.

Martyrs offer a final witness to a truth that they can no longer defend. The violence done to them immediately puts into question the meaning of their death, with both sides—the sufferer and the aggressor—set into necessary struggle over causes, justifications, and significance. The ancient church had turned the suffering of its followers into a witness for the truth of the Gospel in the face of strenuous opposition, not least from the Roman authorities who saw these deaths as the just outcomes of legal and political punishment. Once the ancient church succeeded, moreover, it immediately faced competition from *other* groups—those dissident Christianities that we met in chapter 1—for the same palms of glory that had crowned the first martyrs. A sacrificial death is never something given or taken easily.

These same dynamics re-emerged in the sixteenth century. No less than in Roman times, the martyrs of the sixteenth century strove to convert judicial and political spectacles into religious ones, execution into sublime sacrifice. No less than in Roman times, too, this conversion of the profane into the sacred hardly went unchallenged. Every death became a site of struggle over the very meaning of sacrifice, indeed of sacrality itself. But the Reformation collapse of Christian unity introduced a crucial difference. Now that there were *multiple* Christianities on offer, the older ways of delimiting sacrificial sanctity no longer obtained. And so the same dynamic played out that we saw in chapter 3—to determine what Christianity *is*, we need to determine what it *was*. The meaning of early modern martyrs came to be adjudicated in historical terms, every claim for a sacrifice refracted through the archives of the ancient church. The maelstrom of confessional conflict drew thus the archives of ancient sacrifice into every corner of the political and theological landscape, forcing deliberation on Christianity past and present. If new theological and liturgical approaches to sacrifice formed the thin edge of a wedge between "Christianity as it is" and "Christianity as it was," the martyrs hammered the wedge home.

Proving martyrs thus became a serious project in the later sixteenth century. From an older and more generous world of sanctity—the shared cloud of witnesses that surrounded the medieval church—Protestants and Catholics undertook new projects of discernment, reflexive efforts to demonstrate *which* Christian dead (past and present) indeed deserved the name. In the reformed martyrologies of the mid-sixteenth century; in the reformed critique of the cult of the saints; in the new and radically revised Roman martyrology; in new histories of the ancient church; in the catacombs of Rome itself: Catholics and Protestants turned the martyrs and their sacrifices into a battlefield over Christianity itself. Once seen as the very cement of the Christian polity, the martyrs instead began to trace fractures between competing polities, each battling for the truth of Christianity, ancient and modern. The sacrifice of the martyrs amplified the importance of the deep past for the Christian present, remaking the Christian sacrificial imagination along historical lines. Even as they did, however, they also honed the tools of Christian suspicion, pursuing *critiques* of sacrality that made Christian sacrifice ever more challenging to understand.

The Itinerary of Polycarp: Bones and Texts in the Medieval Church

When the second-century Bishop of Smyrna Polycarp died, the earliest account of this Christian martyr tells us, the faithful who witnessed his martyrdom at the hands of Roman authorities:

> removed his bones, which were more valuable than expensive gems and more precious than gold, and put them in a suitable place. There, whenever we can gather together . . . the Lord will allow us to commemorate the birthday of his martyrdom, both in memory of those who have already engaged in the struggle and as a training and preparation for those who are about to do so.[3]

From our distant horizon, the Christian intimacy of tomb and altar seems ordinary. But as we saw already in chapter 1, the gathering of remains, their burial, and their reclamation as things of veneration and memory were all startling innovations in the religious world of the early Mediterranean. Christianity became public around these "very special dead," their tombs gathering the faithful together for the celebration of a common Christian life.[4] The flourishing of Christian churches in the soil of earlier martyria witnessed this, the cemetery often providing the literal sacred ground upon which basilica were built to house the meeting of the faithful. From their roots in the dead, churches and their altars in turn drew the dead nearer to themselves. Cemeteries long consigned outside city walls moved into the center of public space, and with this, the rise of the church yard. Burial *ad sanctos*—burial as close as possible to holy remains and to the altar itself, something seen in every church in Europe—offers a glimpse of just how extraordinarily intimate Christianity became with the precious remains of its martyrs and saints.[5]

In the beginning, remains stayed in place and people came to them. As Latin poet Prudentius wrote, the altar "keeps [the martyr's] bones in the tomb . . . [and] ever ready to receive its suppliants, fosters the hopes of men with kindly favour."[6] When Christianity was a local and regional religion, this worked fine. But when the age of Christian empire dawned, things changed. The supply of new martyrs dried up at the very moment that demand surged. The new Christian churches of the Roman Empire needed new altars to gather the faithful, and new altars needed new relics to "foster the hopes of men." Already in the fourth century, emperors began to support the "translation" of sacred remains, the disinterment and relocation of bones, as well as other things in intimate contact with the sacred dead, to new sites for the gathering of the faithful. Places that had few or no martyrs or their own, like Milan, Constantinople, and Gaul, happily received bodies from elsewhere to establish their new Christian communities.[7] In fact, they had to do this, especially after the Council of Carthage (401) demanded that all altars *without* relics be destroyed.

The imbalance of supply and demand created problems. Very quickly, for example, there was concern that sacred bodies might become objects of commerce or theft. Imperial laws were enacted to regulate this issue. "Let no one divide a martyr's body: no one is to be sold," proclaimed the *Theodosian Code* in 386, a prohibition repeated by the later *Code of Justinian*.[8] Both were clear efforts to manage not only tomb desecration, but also the movement of relics around the Christian world. These rules were restated many times, especially in Rome, which had huge numbers of prestige remains and where the prohibitions against disturbing them were especially strong. In the late sixth century, for example, Pope Gregory the Great steadfastly rejected requests from the Empress Constantina for the head of St. Paul to consecrate a new church in Constantinople, arguing that Roman customs demanded the bones remain undisturbed.[9]

As Christianity grew, however, the supply of remains had to grow too, either by finding new relics, or or by dividing up the bodies that remained, or by expanding the category of relic to include things besides precious bones. All three of these approaches were taken in the first centuries of Christianity. Finding new holy remains was the simplest approach. The other two demanded more creativity. The holiness of the saints was extended, for example, beyond the limits of their own mortal remains. Things that had touched the living body of the martyr became holy in their own right, so-called contact relics like clothing, the instruments used to punish the martyr, and so on. This power did not cease with death, either. Items placed near the sepulchres of holy men and women became sacred enough themselves to serve as devotional objects. The result was the rapid diversification of relics, the expansion of the class of things that could be used to support the expansion of Christianity. Gregory did not want to send the head of St. Paul to the Empress, but he suggested that he would be willing to send some filings from the apostle's chains.[10]

Despite these efforts, the gold standard remained the bodies of the holiest saints, preferably in their entirety, but in parts as needs must. Pressure to move the remains was therefore huge. In the Latin west, the Popes eventually relented and allowed for their dispersal. In the mid-eighth century, Pope Paul I (757–767) responded to urgent demands from the newly powerful Frankish kings and allowed Roman relics to flow over the Alps. This flow began a robust "gift economy of spiritual exchange" between Rome and the Franks, with relics binding Christian communities in networks of obligation.[11] The Carolingians were especially enthusiastic about the uses to which relics might be put. By the later eighth century, it became common to swear all important oaths on relics; laws requiring relics in altars were re-instituted by the Carolingians; relics were used in the Christianization of the Saxons; relics could receive their own gifts and own property; and so on.[12] Given how desirable a powerful relic was, it is not surprising that bones circulated into the Carolingian Empire, still less surprising that this circulation created a black market. The *Translation of the Relics of Sts. Marcellinus and Peter*—written by the eighth-century aristocrat and abbot Einhard—described arranging to have bodies spirited from the cemetery of the Via Labricanna in Rome, the "holy remains of the blessed martyrs" put into a silken bag, and brought north to Frankish churches.[13] Nor was the story unique. By the ninth century, professional relic thieves were peddling their wares in markets, to bishops, to monasteries, and to noblemen. Competition for the best relics was fierce.[14]

Christian sacrality, in short, expanded in tandem with the body of the saints. Every church in Christendom collected relics, and the larger ones accumulated hoards of these, ensuring a continuous connection between the altar and the body of the saint. Long lists of relics held at important churches and monasteries can be found from the early Middle Ages onward. Indeed, the idea of "relic" was so strong that it also enveloped the Eucharist, which by the central Middle Ages, itself became a relic of uncommon power and devotional attachment. The ritual burial of the Eucharist on Good Friday; the deposit of eucharistic crumbs in the sepulcrum of the altar, alongside, together with, or instead of relics; the development of eucharistic processions: all these witnessed a church for which relic and Eucharist lived in the same imaginative space.[15]

For such an important saint, Polycarp's physical relics were rare: a fragment in the Sant'Ambrogio della Massima church in Rome, an entire arm in the Monastery of Panagia Ambelakiotissa in Greece (stolen in 2013, testament to the ongoing lure of *furta sacra*!). Instead his body circulated across Christendom in that other conduit of saintly sacrality, the *story*. This too had ancient pedigree. The so-called *Acta martyrum* were an eclectic congeries of first- and second-hand descriptions of exemplary Christian deaths, for example, which were then taken up, repeated, and expanded by later, more authoritative patristic authors.[16] The acts of Polycarp were written down in a letter from the mid-second century, but then elaborated by the early father Irenaeus. In the fourth century, the church historian Eusebius compiled these different versions together in his *Ecclesiastical History*, a book that served as a repository of martyrs' lives for many later readers in the Latin west.

Alongide the *Acta* came the hagiographies, the saints' lives (*hagios, sanctus*). This textual form was also ancient, pioneered in the fourth century, just as the first great age of martyrs drew to a close, by Athanasius (*Life of Antony*) and Sulpicius Severus (*Life of Martin*).[17] These *vitae* were an enormously resilient form, not least because they allowed for unfolding of a continuous history of saintliness from the earliest church onward. New saints were enrolled in an expanding lineage of holiness, an inclusive textual tradition flexible enough to accommodate Latin Christianity's spread over the whole of Europe. Soon hagiographies were collected into "legendaries," anthologies of saint's lives like *The Glory of the Martyrs* or *The Glory of the Confessors*, both by the sixth-century Gregory of Tour.[18] As the corpus grew, so did the legendaries. Over time, too, different ecclesiastical orders produced their own legendaries, effectively mapping their history onto that of the church more generally.

These trends crescendoed in the thirteenth-century Dominican collection known as the *Golden Legend*, whose author, the Italian Dominican Jacobus de Voragine, compiled a continuous history of Christian saintliness. Near its beginning was the *vita* of Polycarp, which offered a condensed version of the materials found in Eusebius's *Ecclesiastical History*. There readers would discover that Polycarp preached the Gospel in Smyrna; that he was renowned for his defense of the church against pagans and heretics; that when the fourth age of Christian persecution dawned, he went to Rome and prepared himself to suffer the fate of the pious. Readers learned how imperial authorities tried to force him to call Caesar "lord" and "do sacrifice to the gods," and about his stout refusal to participate in the pagan sacrifices. They would learn how the tyrants bound him to a stake, and lit the fire, while the crowd roared for blood. They would learn that Polycarp was no ordinary victim; that the fire vanished when it touched his flesh; that his body was not "as flesh burnt in the flame but as fair as if it had been purified in the furnace"; and that the sweet odor of precious ointment filled the arena. And finally, they would learn how the tyrants pierced him with a spear, how his "glorious blood" gushed out of his body, and how the people departed, chastened, marveling that the Romans "did so much cruelty to the friends of god."[19] Like others in the collection, the legend of Polycarp was a poignant story of Christian forbearance, suffering, and redemption.

Finally, the martyrs expanded across Latin Christendom in liturgical texts. Indeed, early liturgy included the hagiographies, especially in places like Spain and Gaul, where readings from the *vitae* became part of feast day celebrations.[20] By the eighth century, the saints migrated into the Canon of the Mass itself, which came to include the litanies, the reading out of the names of saints and martyrs during regular services.[21] In the Frankish kingdoms, relic veneration was translated into name veneration with the development of "festivals of the saints' names." These in turn generated new textual forms for itinerant martyrs, the most striking of which was the *Martyrology of Jerome*, a comprehensive list of the sacred dead organized around a yearly calendar. Developed in the early 700s, and expanded throughout the century, this list represented a radical departure from the brief and largely local compilations of sacred names that preceded it. In turn, it would become the foundation for a long-lasting liturgical tradition that associated dates, feasts, and names throughout the year.

In its original form, then, the "martyrology" was a calendar. Already in the *Martyrology of Jerome*, Polycarp's feast day was set for January 26, which remained largely consistent in the tradition.[22] The calendar offered a flexible framework to grow the rolls of Christianity's special dead. By the eighth century, it began to be filled out by people like the Venerable Bede, whose addition of historical materials to the saint's feast days became a model for later martyrologies, including the Roman one.[23] As an Anglo-Saxon, Bede naturally included saints relevant to the community to whom he ministered, like St. Aethelthryth (June 23), whose virgin body was found uncorrupted after burial. Other martyrologists enrolled other local saints. The result was generic stability coupled with local diversity. The first martyrology in the age of print—the Latin

Viola sanctorum, printed in Basel in 1475—recounted Polycarp's story in detail, for example, importing substantial hagiographic materials into its calendrical form.[24] The German version of the same book, printed in Strassburg in 1484, radically shortened the story, reporting only that "he was thrown into a big fire, and it did not hurt him; finally he was stabbed."[25] As it developed throughout the Middle Ages, the calendrical form of the martyrology offered a flexible structure whose contents depended on the community, language, and traditions of the authors.

The bones and texts of the martyrs, in short, permeated the medieval church. They were present in physical form: bones, hair, teeth, instruments of saintly passion, scraps of clothing, many of these deposited in altars or preserved in elaborate reliquaries integral to the daily practice of Christian devotion. They were also present in textual form: church histories, ancient acts, saints' lives, litanies, calendars, and martyrologies, in short an enormous literature of sanctity that grew ever more diverse as the centuries passed. Saints varied: their stories were told in many different ways, and different churches had different relics, different devotional practices, and different liturgies. There were also various *kinds* of saints. Some, like Polycarp, were killed in the early Roman persecutions. John the Evangelist, St. Silvester, and St. Ambrose died at venerable ages, the *Golden Legend* recounted, never suffering the violence of Roman persecution. The Holy Innocents, those infants slaughtered by Herod, were killed well before witnessing the Gospel was an option. St. Peter of Verona was a Dominican missionary murdered on the road between Como and Milan. All were, however, equally enrolled in a catalogue of sanctity. What coordinated it was the shared sense that the special dead of the Church offered a coherent model of Christian living, saint imitating saint through the centuries. Coordinating it too were the shared institutions of ecclesiastical life, and the procedures of canonization that guaranteed the harmonious coexistence of Christianity's many saints and martyrs.[26]

New Blood: Writing about the Dead

Rarely in the Middle Ages, did the Church sort saints from saints, sacrifice from sacrifice. And those exclusions from the rolls of sanctity—the Jews martyred by Christians in the First Crusade (1096–1099) or the various "heretics" murdered by the medieval church—were well concealed by the unifying aspirations of legendaries, martyrology, and hagiographies.[27] All of this changed in the sixteenth century, when the dead came back to life, reanimated by the blood of some 5,000 people executed for heterodoxy and heresy. These new candidates for the litanies of Christian sanctity were killed by authorities in cities and territories across Europe. They came from all of Europe's religious confessions: Lutherans, Anabaptists, Reformed, and Catholic. The executions waxed and waned over the century, but never disappeared. In central Europe, Lutheran sympathizers and Anabaptists were the victims of the 1520s and 1530s. The extraordinary French court for heresy, the *chambre ardente*, began its main work in the late 1540s, targeting mainly Calvinist Huguenots. Queen Mary's short rule in England (1553–1558) witnessed some of the most spectacular heresy trials of the period, claiming some three hundred Protestant victims. Her sister Queen Elizabeth killed nearly the same number of Catholics during her long (1558–1603) reign, but preferred to sentence them under treason statutes. No matter what the context, these executions were typically well-organized legal and penal performances. Official inquiries were made into the alleged crimes, often documented with records and notes. The victims were interrogated, tortured, and usually asked to recant their heretical views. If they refused, they were sentenced in accordance with the relevant penal codes. And finally, the punishment was fierce: the convicted were drowned, beheaded, burned, strangled, or stabbed in the public display of state violence typical of early modern justice.[28]

In a period of pervasive communal violence, it should be noted, these numbers were actually small. They were tiny compared to the tens of thousands killed by the Reformation's first spasm of religious warfare, the 1524–25 peasant's rebellion in Germany. The Schmalkaldic Wars of the 1540s, the French wars of religion that spanned nearly forty years of the late century, the extraordinary violence of conversion and conquest in the New World: death and religion were close companions in the sixteenth century. Nearly as many people died in one week in August 1572, for example—during the bloody St. Bartholomew's Day massacres in France—as in all these judicial executions combined.[29] Yet we know very little about these other victims. Angry mobs killed them, or the armies of territorial princes, or the swords of conquistadors. But their blood was sowed in rocky places and bore little literary fruit.

About the martyrs, those special dead of early modern Christianity, by contrast, we know an awful lot. Tertullian's seeds were broadcast far and wide in the print public sphere of the sixteenth century. In German, French, English, Dutch, and Latin, authors from across Europe's confessional spectrum compiled the stories of the dead. These spectacular witnesses told stories that ranged from the inspiring to the heartwrenching, from the grotesque to the transcendent. They began to appear already in the 1520s, in floods of pamphlets that described the spectacle of Protestant executions. Songs and poems circulated orally, in manuscript, and in print, celebrating the deaths of venerated Christians. Letters of the men and women who died were collected and earnestly republished, offering personal and poignant testimony of their sufferings. Images were engraved and circulated, in large and small formats, to compel the imagination with the torments of the innocent. And by mid-century, these smaller works were compiled into monumental ledgers of new Christian sanctity. Jean Crespin's *Livre de Martyrs* (1554), Ludwig Rabus's *Historien der Martyrer* (1555), Adrian van Haemstede's *De geschiedenisse ende den doodt der vromer Martelaren* (1559), and John Foxe's *Acts and Monuments* (1563) collected the special dead in gigantic editions, whose printing and reprinting ensured the martyrs a long afterlife in newly divided European Christianity.[30]

These stories of sanctity represent something new in the religious and intellectual culture of early modern Europe. As Brad Gregory has written, "martyrs and martyrdom coursed through the veins and strengthened the sinews of late medieval Christianity."[31] Yet the forms these new martyrologies took hint at how discontinuous the history of Christian self-sacrifice was. These works resembled neither hagiographies, nor the calendrical martyrologies of the Middle Ages. Their closest relative in size, scope, and organization was the legendary. Even so, their contents were altogether different. Sacrificial sanctity remained the norm, but the forms of its display were completely different.

Take the most well-known English martyrology of the period, John Foxe's 1563 *Acts and Monuments*. Foxe was an important voice in the Protestant world of Edward VI, with connections to reformed leaders like Nicholas Ridley, Hugh Latimer, William Cecil, and John Bale. It was with the latter—a former Carmelite friar turned evangelical—that Foxe began working on things martyrological. His first effort, the Latin *Commentarii in ecclesia gestarum rerum*, was started in 1552 and published in 1554. This early work became an important source for other martyrologies, including those of the Dutch Haemstede, the German Rabus, and the French Crespin. After its publication—and with Catholic Queen Mary ascendent—Foxe went into continental exile, joining his reformed colleagues in Frankfurt. When that community split over liturgical differences, Foxe joined Bale and others in Basel. There he continued martyrological research, weaving himself into wider networks of continental religious scholarship. He forged ties with the Lutheran scholar Matthias Flacius Illyricus, for example, whose *Catalogus testium veritatis* (1556) offered rich materials on medieval critics of the Catholic Church. In 1557, the powerful English reformer and later archbishop Edmund Grindal recruited Foxe to write a Latin history of the Marian martyrs, which was published as the *Rerum ecclesia gestarum* in 1559. This work too was recycled by other continental martyrologists—Crespin incorporated large portions into his Latin martyrology, the *Actiones et monumenta martyrum* (1560), and the Swiss Reformer Heinrich Pantaleon did the same with his *Martyrum historia* (1563). And Foxe returned the favor later on, using these continental materials to fill out his own. All along, he continued to collect information from friends and correspondents to build the research archive for his magnum opus, the *Acts and Monuments*.[32]

This complex intellectual milieu produced complex stories about the sacred dead. Beginning with the first edition of the *Acts*, for example, Foxe paid special attention to John Hooper, an English evangelical close with Swiss Protestants like Heinrich Bullinger. Hooper's career spanned the great religious upheavals of sixteenth-century England—first, a religious refugee in the early 1540s, after his path crossed that of Henry VIII's prickly persecuting bishop Stephen Gardiner, Hooper lived briefly in Paris, and later in Zürich. With the ascent of Edward VI, Hooper returned to England, and following bitter controversies with other leading evangelicals about clerical vestments, was made bishop of Gloucester. When Hooper's fortunes reversed, as they did for many after Edward's death, he was first imprisoned for debt in 1553 and then burned as a heretic in 1555.

Hooper's life and death filled fifteen folio pages of Foxe's first edition. The entry was not long by the standards of the work, but it included many of the *Acts and Monuments'* most distinctive elements. It opened with an abbreviated biography of Hooper, and then a description of his character, whose piety Foxe attested personally. It then reprinted a copy of the King's grant for Hooper's consecration to the bishopric of Gloucester, and recounted his divisive role in the vestment controversy, about which Foxe charitably remarked that "nothing is more occasion of war, than overmuch peace."[33] It included a letter of reconciliation from Nicholas Ridley to Hooper concerning the vestment matter, a description of Hooper's ministry during the last years of Edward's reign, a first-hand account of his humiliations at the hands of the Marian bishops, Hooper's own account of his imprisonment in the Fleet prison, extracts from official papers elaborately detailing his degradation and condemnation, and a letter where Hooper denied rumors of his recantation.

Only after many asides, then, did the story climax with its elegiac account of Hooper's last moments:

> even as at the first flame he prayed, saying mildly and not very loud (but as one without pains): O Jesus the son of David have mercy upon me, and receive my soul. After the second was spent he did wipe both

> his eyes with his hands, and beholding the people he said with an indifferent loud voice: For gods love (good people) let me have more fire: and all this while his nether parts did burn. . . . The third fire was kindled within a while after, which was more extreme than the other two: and then the bladders of gunpowder broke, which did him small good, they were so put, and the wind had such power. In the which fire he prayed, with somewhat a loud voice: Lord Jesu have mercy upon me: Lorde Jesu have mercy upon me. Lord Jesus receive my spirit. And they were the last words he was heard to sound.[34]

Even then, Foxe did not rest in admiration of Hooper's prayerful fortitude in the face of repeated efforts to burn him alive. Instead he continued his editorial work, printing a letter from prison in which Hooper consoled his readers: "he is blessed that looseth this life. . . . It is a payne and griefe to depart from goods aud frendes: but yet not so muche, as to depart from grace and heauen it selfe."[35] After yet another editorial addition (see below), Foxe finally concluded his story with a woodcut depicting the burning of Hooper, and a celebratory poem by the Swiss humanist and botanist Conrad Gessner.

Medieval saints' lives sought immediacy. The *Golden Legend* told short and powerful stories, tracing clean narratives from birth to ministry to death. The *Acts and Monuments* had none of this narrative punch. Between the announcement of the subject—the martyrdom of John Hooper—and the accomplishment of his death, stood an archive of side notes, documents, and data. Elsewhere Foxe layered his stories with eyewitness accounts, letters, church and trial registers, and other primary materials. The life and death of the evangelical preacher John Bradford ran to nearly forty-five folio pages, the bulk of which Foxe dedicated to his letters and prison disputations. As Foxe expanded the *Acts and Monuments* over four editions—growing it from five books to twelve between 1563 and 1580—its archives of sanctity grew ever more heterogeneous and dense.

This was not unique to Foxe, Over the century, Protestant writers wove their stories of the special dead into ever-more complex texts. Jean Crespin's 1554 *Livre des Martyrs* went through more than a dozen editions in the two decades after its publication.[36] Already in the first edition, Crespin included a hundred-page history of Jan Hus, the Bohemian heretic executed in 1415 and embraced by many Reformers as a spiritual ancestor, supplemented with thirteen letters showing Hus's constancy and fidelity. By 1570, thick historical contextualization filled out the originally scant stories. The book more than doubled in size, including letters, court records, royal proclamations, becoming a thick archive of the sacred dead. The same expansion was apparent in the Lutheran Ludwig Rabus's *Historien der Martyrer*, whose bare-bones entries in the first edition (1555) sprouted thickets of annotations, excerpts, and commentary from patristic, medieval, and modern authors in the second (1571). The first entry on "Abel" in fact grew into its own book, the 1568 *Historia de S. Abele, Ecclesiae militantis in veteri testamento protomartyre.*[37]

Proving the New Christian Saint

Protestant martyrologies drew documents into their textual archives, filed them under different martyrs, and organized these files into complex theo-historical arguments for the significance of their sacrificial dead. Nothing could have been more unlike—formally speaking—those Christian writings that had documented the lives and deaths of saints since the early Middle Ages. These innovations relied on the revolution in historical scholarship that attended Reformation controversies. Those same scholarly circles that produced the martyrologies in the middle of the sixteenth century, for example, also wrote monumental church histories.[38] The Lutheran Flacius Illyricus not only authored the *Catalogus testium veritatis* but was also a prime mover in one of the great historical projects of the age, the *Magdeburg Centuries*. Under Flacius's direction, a team of collectors, copyists, excerpters, source critics, and writers compiled this first Protestant universal history between 1559 and 1574 in the Basel printing workshop of Johann Oporinus.[39] Its critical techniques and organizational creativity set the standard for other major historical projects throughout the period and indeed for the writing of history more generally in the early modern period.[40]

One would suppose that memory, not history, ought to be the main concern for a martyrologist. What made martyrology so difficult, however, was that memory itself was under siege. No one achieved the status of martyr easily in the sixteenth century. Death was only the beginning. Afterward came the posthumous gauntlet of doubt. Miles Huggarde, Catholic controversialist and enthusiastic critic of the Protestants, had nothing but contempt for

> the deaths of our cranky Hereticks, [who] lie dead and are buried in the grave of cankred oblivion, covered with perpetual infamy, except they be enrolled in a few threehalfpenny books, which steal out of Germany

replete as well with treason against the King & Queens majesties, as with other abominable lies.[41]

Similarly charitable were the judgments of Nicholas Harpsfield, the archdeacon of Canterbury during the Marian years and a fierce antagonist of Foxe. Written from Fleet Prison in 1566, his Latin dialogues against the "pseudo-martyrs" cursed "them more strongly than brigands themselves because, for the sake of defending heresies, which surpass all other sins through the gravity of the offense, they prefer to suffer death rather than denounce them."[42] Huggarde, Harpsfield, and other Catholic controversialists did not deny that Protestants died. Rather, they doubted whether these deaths were anything special. To venerate a Protestant martyr was to venerate a heretic, a criminal, a traitor, or, most likely, all three.

The early modern martyrology assumed a burden that no saint's life had to shoulder, therefore. It had to *prove*, rather than praise, the virtues of a Christian saint.

For Protestants, this was no easy task. By the 1550s, after all, they had become expert at *destroying* claims to Christian sanctity. Already in the early Reformation, Luther ruthlessly mocked the veneration offered to the older saints and the miracles that their relics were supposed to accomplish. Just as the Jews abandoned "the parishes and the ministry of the Word and ran to groves and the relics of saints," so too did later Christians, wrote Luther in his *Lectures on Genesis*.[43] Calvin was no less fierce. Like the pagans, Catholics placed "the bones of the dead . . . over the principal altars in the high and lofty place to be adored," he wrote in 1543.[44] Iconoclastic violence directed against the institutions of sainthood—the destruction of relics, statues, images, and altars—was not limited to things physical either. It also extended to the written forms in which saintly memory had been historically conserved, to that entire apparatus of life-writing that we explored above. What Foxe called the "freakish monstrosities of lies (*prodigiosis mendaciorum portentis*)" like the *Golden Legend* were the textual equivalents of St. Anthony's arm or the prepuce of Jesus, idolatrous fantasies and superstitions.[45] The "duty of Christians was to leave the bodies of saints in their tombs," Calvin remarked.[46]

In reformed martyrologies, then, criticism was integral to the project of commemoration. What the historian Brad Gregory has called "anti-martyrology" was not merely "parallel," it was *foundational* to the new cult of the special dead.[47] Foxe visualized this in his frontispiece, a rumination, as fierce as any piece of Reformation polemic, on the nature of true and false sacrifice (fig. 4.1). On the face of it, the message was simple: on the

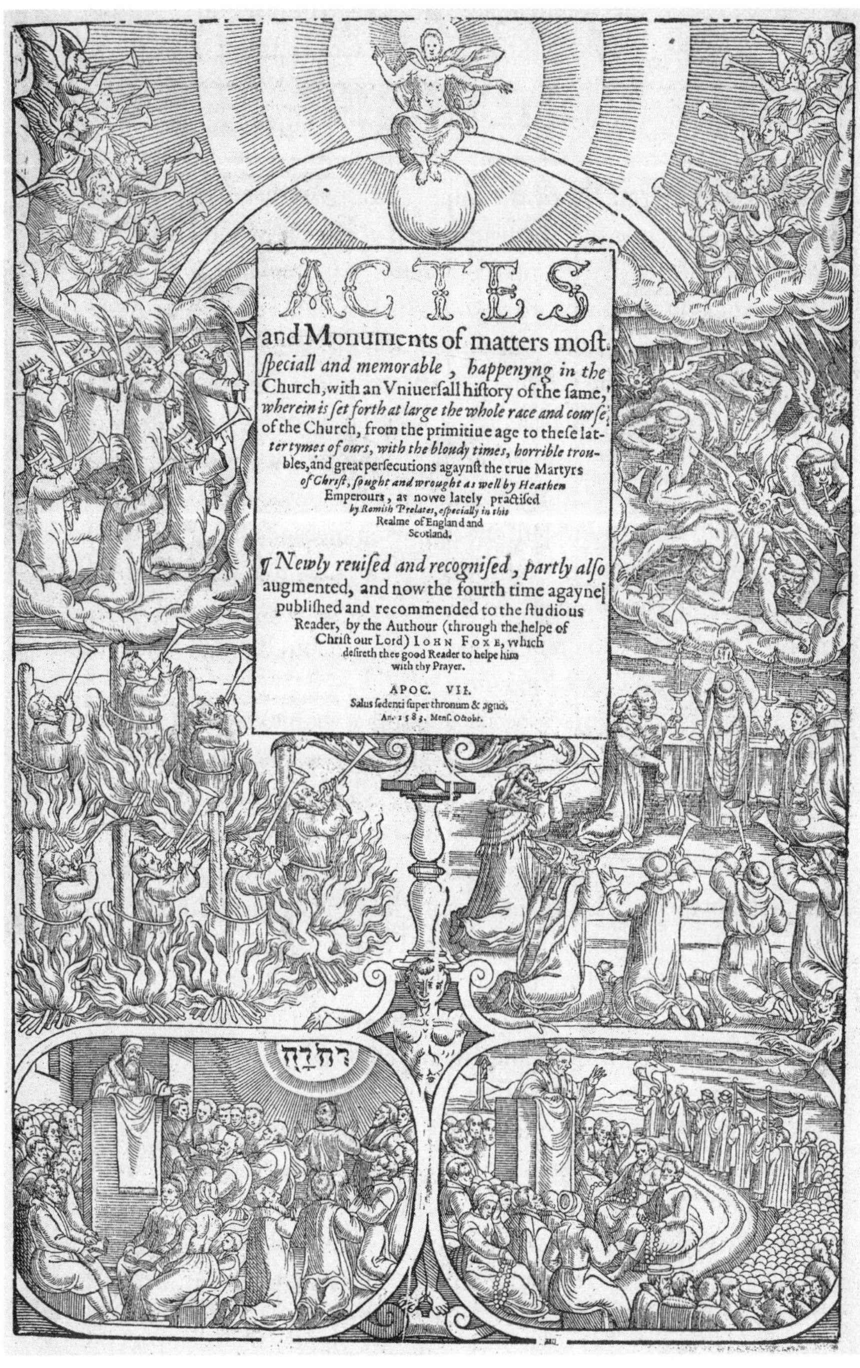

ACTES

and Monuments of matters moſt ſpeciall and memorable, happenyng in the Church, with an Vniuerſall hiſtory of the ſame, wherein is ſet forth at large the whole race and courſe of the Church, from the primitiue age to theſe latter tymes of ours, with the bloudy times, horrible troubles, and great perſecutions agaynſt the true Martyrs of Chriſt, ſought and wrought as well by Heathen Emperours, as nowe lately practiſed by Romish Prelates, eſpecially in this Realme of England and Scotland.

¶ Newly reuiſed and recogniſed, partly alſo augmented, and now the fourth time agayne publiſhed and recommended to the ſtudious Reader, by the Authour (through the helpe of Chriſt our Lord) IOHN FOXE, which deſireth thee good Reader to helpe him with thy Prayer.

APOC. VII.

Salus ſedenti ſuper thronum & agno.

An. 1583. Menſ. Octobr.

FIGURE 4.1. Frontispiece. John Foxe, *Acts and Monuments* ([London], 1583). Courtesy of the Folger Shakespeare Library.

one side, the holy martyrs in a sacred lineage to heaven; on the other side, the Mass. As the preface to the final and by far lengthiest book of the *Acts* explained, however, the message went far deeper. Not only was the Mass the *cause* of the martyrdoms—"we are now come to the time of Quene Mary, when . . . so many were put to death for the cause especially of the Masse, & the sacrament of the altar," Foxe remarked—but the martyrs were also key to cleansing the true church of this pernicious error.[48] These errors Foxe laid out in a learned commentary on the Mass, which included a long disquistion on the word *Missa*, a history of liturgical practices of the early church, a description of errors of the sacrificial priesthood, a complete translation of the Canon of the Mass, and a millennia-long history of objectionable liturgical practices (the elevation of the host, the rituals of eucharistic conservation, the covering of the altars, the use of incense, and more). In sum, concluded the preface, here were the dirty secrets of "the masse, with the canon and all the appurtenances of the same, which . . . was so longe a getheryng, that the temple of Salomon was not so long in building, as the popes masse was in making."[49] Only now was the reader prepared to discover the real Gospel witnesses and the real pious wafers: the holy martyrs of Foxe's England.

It turned out to be much easier to critique than to *prove* sanctity, however, to prove that one's own special dead deserves the title of martyr. Such proof was typically offered in both narrative and documentary terms. Over the decades that Foxe worked on the *Acts and Monuments*, he generated a huge library of documents that witnessed the stoicism of the victims, the confidence in their salvation, the doctrine for which he or she died, the integrity of the ecclesiastical community, and the injustice of the perpetrators. Hooper's letters testified to the state of his conscience and his patience in the face of suffering; the examination accounts showed his humility in the face of injustice; the degradation documents confirmed his likeness to Christ; the letters from other Protestants confirmed ecclesiastical unity; and so on. The same drive to document the dead can be found across the martyrological landscape. When the French martyrologist Jean Crespin recounted the history of the "four martyrs of Lille," just to pick one example, he reproduced supposedly verbatim their interrogations at the hands of the magistrates as well as the letters of consolation the imprisoned martyrs wrote to the faithful.[50] What resulted were intimate firsthand accounts of the martyr's passion, on the one hand, and, on the other, lavishly documented proofs that these accounts were accurate.

However compelling, these stories were still not *proof* to the skeptic. A person might suffer stoically, die heroically, speak passionately, Huggarde and Harpsfield would say, and still fail to achieve the martyr's palm. *Non poena, sed causa facit martyrum* went the Augustinian dictum—"not the punishment but the cause makes the martyr"—suggesting that only the doctrine defended guaranteed the sanctity of the death. According to this criterion, only those who died witnessing authentic doctrine might be considered martyrs, which helps explain why the martyrologists so compulsively restaged complex doctrinal disputes between their suffering lambs and inquisitorial magistrates. The learned and the ignorant, men and women, adults and children, the poor and the rich: sophisticated theologians, according to Foxe and others, could be found in every corner of the reformed world.

But doctrinal criteria only worked for internal audiences. When Augustine wielded his dictum against the heretical Donatists, he hardly expected to persuade *them* of his "cause." Nor could Foxe expect his Catholic opponents either to embrace the doctrine or the sanctity of his Protestant martyrs. At the same time, however, no one was ready (yet) to give up on the notion that *their* martyrs were part of a universal community of Christian suffering. Every man is a hero to his valet, the saying goes, but a martyr had to be a hero for all. From the perfected sacrifice of Christ on the Cross, to the early community of Christian martyrs who died refusing the sacrifices of the pagans, to the early moderns who died refusing the sacrifice of the Catholic Mass: if this *ecclesia triumphans* did not together share in the blessings of heaven, then what was the point of the suffering and death?

Doctrine—the very bone of contention between Christian confessions—could therefore do little to prove the universality of this suffering community. Where doctrine fell short, however, *history* stepped in. Protestant martyrs were martyrs, Foxe's frontispiece argued, because they restaged one of the ancient dramas in the Church, namely sacrificing the self to destroy the sacrifice of the idols. And so Protestants mapped their martyrs onto a longer history of Christian sanctity, uniting their special dead with those of the ancient Church, even with Christ himself.[51] "In the primitive church," wrote martyrologist John Bale in 1547, "many diligent writers collected the . . . triumphant sufferings of the martyrs . . . no less necessary is that office now . . . for now are persecutions all Christendom over, so well as were then."[52] For his part, Foxe followed the footsteps of the ancient church historian Eusebius, tasked by the Emperor Constantine to "search out the names, sufferings and actes, of all such as suffered in all that time of persecution before, for the testimonie and faith of Christ Jesus."[53] The Protestant martyrs joined the ranks of the earliest heroes of the Christian faith, witnesses eternal to the truth of their cause.

Returning to Hooper, then, we now understand the significance of Foxe's final editorial insertions to the *vita*. A life "so pure and good" was matched by a death so tender and terrifying that, Foxe wrote at length, none could doubt that "he now reigns as . . . a blessed martyr in the joyes of heaven prepared for the faithful in Christ, before the foundations of the world."[54] As he took his place at the side of Christ, Hooper joined himself, in Foxe's view, to the ancient community of Christianity's special dead:

> When I see and behold the great patience of these blessed Martyrs in our days. . . . me thinks I may well and worthily compare them unto the old Martyrs of the primitive Church: in the number of whom, if comparison be to be made between Saint and Saint, Martyr and martyr, with whom might I match this blessed martyr, master J. Hooper better through the whole catalogue of the old martyrs, then with Polycarp the ancient bishop of Smyrna, of whom Eusebius makes mention in the Ecclesiasticall story?[55]

The similarities, in Foxe's eyes, were astonishing. Hooper felt "little more then did Polycarp in the fire flaming round him." Like Polycarp, Hooper insisted on standing untied. In teaching they were alike; in their zeal they were fervent; in their lives, unspotted; in their manners and conversation they were inculpable. Even their *names*, Foxe remarked, were alike, "*polykarpus*" = "much fruitful" and Hooper, "ὀπώρη or ὀπώρα" = "tree fruit." In all things, they were "Bishops and also martyrs both," "joyned together in one spirit," just as all members of the true church share a spirit that survives time's corruption.[56]

This claim on Christian history was no simple matter, however. Certainly no Catholic would concede title to a martyr as important as Polycarp, long the foundation of reliquary culture, his bones an ancient prototype of the bones that came to circulate for a thousand years in the Christian world. Too valuable a witness to leave to Catholics, as we saw in chapter 3, the Swiss Protestant Heinrich Bullinger turned the ancient martyr into a star witness *against* the collection and veneration of saint's relics. Why did the first Christians collect his remains, he asked? Solely to bury them, and not for any worship. It was only later that the "sacred rites of Christianity began to be celebrated atop the body or the altar," that "bones began to be exhumed and transferred, and put in golden urns and tumbrils, and stored in the oratory."[57] When Foxe recruited Polycarp to the Protestant cause in the first edition of the *Acts*, then, he operated within an established *critical* context.

In this context, every bid for the authority of history initiated a violently suspicious counter. In his 1566 dialogues against the "pseudomartyrs," for example, the priest Nicholas Harpsfield pulled Polycarp back to the Catholic side—those, like Bullinger, who would attribute relic worship to "pagan superstition" are easily refuted, he argued, by the witness of Polycarp, who testified "that the feast days of the martyrs were celebrated in the primitive church."[58] If Protestants have any analogue in the ancient church, Harpsfield mocked, it was the *heretics* who pretended to the martyr's crowns. Trawling through ancient heresiological literature, Harpsfield found the Marcionites, the Messalians, the Montanists, the Arians, the Donatists, the Circumcellions, the Novatians, the Priscillianists, all ancient sects who vied for the "honored name of martyr."[59] All of these claimants were rejected by the same fathers that the Protestants wanted on their side: Irenaeus, Epiphanius, Augustine, Eusebius, Sozomen, Severus Sulpicius, and others. And this ancient church also provided the right response to these false martyrs:

> They were slain, but not by gentiles and criminals, but by the most Christian princes . . . lest their contagion spread unto the final destruction of the Christian republic . . . they were slain, but with that zeal with which Phineas killed the adulterer and adultress with one dagger . . . they were slain, but according to the law by which the prophet Elias slayed the priests of Baal.[60]

Those who falsely aspire to the name of martyr deserve the same mercy that Elias had for the priests of Baal—none at all. Indeed, the *lex zelotarum*, the sword "that God gave for the vindication of evil," demanded the very thing that Foxe protested, the swift execution of those he called martyrs.[61]

Answering the question—what is a Christian sacrifice?—on historical grounds thus accelerated the growth of the Christian archive. Because the ancient church offered the most authentic forms of Christian witness in the face of violence, it had to be converted to the Protestant cause if Protestants wanted to secure their title to a universal and apostolic Christianity. No martyrologist could resist recruiting this church in defense of their besieged communities. This effort brought ever more historical materials to bear on the question of sanctity, each historical apologia expanding the materials in contention.

This dynamic helps explain ever-thickening comparisons between ancient and modern. In the second (1570) edition of the *Acts and Monuments*, for example, Foxe added some hundred pages of church history, digging into the lives of martyrs like Polycarp. The sources were tangled and difficult. In Polycarp's case, the most important was the *Ecclesiastical History* of Eusebius, whose story of Polycarp began with the ancient heresiologist Irenaeus.[62] In the *Adversus haereses*, Irenaeus provided the biographical frame for Eusebius's extensive paraphrases and quotations of the earliest *Acta* in the Christian tradition, the *Martyrdom of Polycarp*. This latter had its roots in a letter from the church of Smyrna to a neighboring congregation, though in Foxe's time, it was known almost exclusively through Eusebius.[63] In his history, Eusebius cobbled different authorities together, and in the *Acts*, Foxe did the same. He blended Eusebius and the history recounted in the *Magdeburg Centuries* (see above).[64] And he added his own scholarly details to Polycarp's heroic biography: that the ancient martyr had condemned Marcionites as heretics (Irenaeus, Eusebius), that he wrote a letter to the Philippians (Irenaeus), and that he was "scholar to the Apostles" (Jerome). And finally, that Polycarp had differed with Pope Anicetus about the Eucharist (Nicephorus), yet both "friendly communicated" with each other, "which may be a notable testimonye nowe to us, that the doctrine concerning . . . liberty of ceremonies, was at that time retayned in the church."[65]

This new textual intricacy mirrored the equally intricate sense of Polycarp's historical role in the ancient church. Polycarp's disagreement with Anicetus added a useful parallel with Hooper, well-known for his irascibility with other Protestants. But as historical materials grew in scope, so too did the picture of Polycarp as a complex, indeed often heterodox church father. As Foxe put it, "of men and doctors, be they neuer so famous, ther is none that is voyd of [God's] reprehension." Even a martyr like Polycarp celebrated Easter incorrectly (Foxe tells us) after the fashion of the Jews.[66] And indeed, *most* of the ante-Nicene church, Foxe recounted, were exemplary only up to a point. Of the Latin father Tertullian, as Foxe noted, "certayne errours and blemishes are noted in his doctrine"—in fact, late in his life, Tertullian had gone entirely over to the prophetic spiritualist sect known as Montanism.[67] The "holye Cyprian and other blessed Martyrs were holy men, yet notwithstanding they were men . . . , & had their falles & faultes," Foxe remarked, as when Cyprian "contrary to the doctrine of the church, did hold with rebaptising of such, as was before baptised of hereticks."[68] (Rebaptisim was, recall, an offense punishable by death in the sixteenth century!) The great collector of early heresies Irenaeus was himself a heretic of sorts, believing that "man was not made perfect in the beginning," and Justin Martyr was a chiliast among his other errors.[69]

Foxe reserved his special criticism for Origen, the learned Alexandrian who, Foxe wrote, first made sacrifices to false idols and then was "driuen away with shame and sorow out of Alexandria, [and] went into Iewry."[70] And Eusebius himself, upon whom so much of the *Acts and Monuments* was built, was condemned for Arianism.

Lists like these—archives of ancient heterodoxy—were not unique to Foxe. The Elizabethan cleric James Calfhill, for example, clarified some of the errors of Tertullian, that he found it apostolic to give "milk and honey to Infants at their Christening," and Cyprian, for whom the tradition was to administer the Lord's Supper to babies, and Epiphanius, in whose time Christians prepared for Easter by eating "nothing but bread and drink with a little salt."[71] Even the martyrs themselves, wrote Thomas Cartwright in 1575, were "ignorant off [sic] some principal point commanded by the word of god [sic]," singling out Cyprian for his advocacy of rebaptism, and Justin Martyr for his view that "the faithful should in the general resurrection live with Christ here upon earth 1000 years."[72] The ancient church was littered with those both sanctified and heterodox.

Stepping back, we can see how the dynamics of early modern controversy remade the Christian sacrificial imagination. The world of medieval saints did not interest itself in the tremendous conflicts about the martyrs that wracked the ancient church. It had little interest in Cyprian's terrible judgment on the Novatians, that "though they should suffer death for the confession of the Name, the guilt of such men is not removed even by their blood; the grievous irremissible sin of schism is not purged even by a violent death. No martyr can he be who is not in the Church."[73] It had little interest in Cyprian's successor at Carthage, Donatus, whose followers died at the hands of Catholic powers and were ridiculed for their pains. If you "separate from the structure of unity and the bond of love," Augustine wrote in a famous letter to a Donatist priest, "you will suffer eternal punishment even if you are burned alive for the name of Christ."[74] It had little interest in the tremendous scorn heaped on Christians by their pagan critics like Eunapius, who could not believe that Christians collect "the bones and skulls of criminals who had been put to death for numerous crimes," and make "them out to be gods, [and] haunt their sepulchres." "'Martyrs,' the dead men were called," he wrote in disgust.[75] It had little interest in the terrible charge, leveled by Faustus the Manichean, that Christians make "idols into martyrs" and merely conceal the worst bits of Judaism and paganism under a cloak of novelty.[76] And finally it had little interest in the *self*-criticism found inside the patristic archive: Augustine preaching against the "aggressive rowdiness of dancers" at Cyprian's grave, and the "crowds of banqueting drunks" celebrating the feast days of popular saints.[77]

Because the early modern martyrology operated right at the interface between critique and commemoration, however, it *had* to take an interest in things like these. The "revivification of ancient form of sanctity" did not activate Christian ideals "sustained in late medieval Europe through practices pertaining to martyr-saints, devotion to Christ's passion, and cultivation of the virtue of patient suffering in imitation of Christ."[78] The "ancient form of sanctity," in all of its conflict and competition, had anyway disappeared from view by the Middle Ages. When it *was* revivified—in the context of intra-confessional religious violence—it came back to life with a vengeance. For the first time in a thousand years, Christianity was revealed in all its historical heterogeneity: martyrs standing side-by-side with heretics; Christians overlapping with Jews and pagans; true faith entwined with a superstition and corruption that only a suspicious eye could disentangle.

In short, Christian sacrifice became ever *harder* in the age of early modern martyrology. The more that writers competed for the normative advantage that sacrifice entailed, the more they waged this competition on historical grounds, the more difficult it became to enter the rolls of the sacrificial dead. And the more writers struggled to enroll their special dead in the books of sanctity, the more pressure was put on the relationship between contemporary and ancient churches. The result was an accelerating cycle of theological outbidding that drew ever more attention to the difference between "Christianity as it is" and "Christianity as it was."

Proving the Old Christian Saint I: Martyrologies

Catholics could hardly abandon the patrimony of the church to these new heretics. And so they too threw themselves into the Christian archives, building their own case for ownership, if on different grounds. Protestants emphasized the historical corruption of the Church and so had to re-imagine Christian history absent continuous and reliable institutions. For their part, Catholics had to *defend* the historical institutions of the Church as steadfast repositories of Christian sacrifice since apostolic times. Protestants invented new ways of thinking about their new martyrs; Catholics invented new ways of thinking about their *old* martyrs.

Take, for example, the older genre of the martyrology, rooted in the deep time of the Church. Already in the early sixteenth century, the Church had been entertaining the idea of reforming this liturgical text.[79] At the

Council of Trent (1545–1563), when church leaders met to chart a new course for the Catholic communion in the wake of the Reformation, they got serious about renewing the written forms of liturgical life. This renewal included a revision of the Missal, the liturgical book that prescribes the celebration of the Mass over the course of the year. It included a revision of the breviary—containing the Psalter, the prayer book, and the formularies for saints' days—that reduced the liturgical calendar by approximately 150 saints' days. The saints purged were overwhelmingly of later provenance; in the new calendar, 85 percent of the celebrated saints came from the first four centuries of the church.[80] And the renewal included a revision of the Roman martyrology, a task begun in the early 1580s at the behest of Pope Gregory XIII. Editions began to appear in 1582, and by 1586, these editions were reinforced with a substantive scholarly apparatus authored by Cesare Baronio.[81]

Baronio was a luminary of the Counter-Reformation church and pioneer of Catholic historical scholarship. Already in 1576–77, he had been tasked to defend the Church against Protestant historical critique, and for the next twenty years, he was a tireless soldier of scholarship. The twelve volumes of his most ambitious work—the 1588 *Ecclesiastical Annals*—set the standard for Catholic church history for centuries.[82] The notes he wrote to the martyrology were his first scholarly printed work, and he continued to work on them from 1586 until 1598.[83] They included a range of materials, from the dates of various martyrdoms, to the manner of their deaths, to the textual traditions that preserved this information in the present, and they turned a relatively compact calendar of saints' days into a sprawling work of historical learning.[84]

The new Roman martyrology revised the archive of Christian sanctity, redescribing the collective experience of martyrdom across an imagined *Christianus orbis*.[85] In his *Tractatio de Martyrologio Romano* that prefaced the volume, Baronio reflected on this collective experience, and on the textual forms in which it had been preserved. Protestant martyrology had rejected martyrology in its traditional generic sense, blending poetry, images, biography, court documents, and dialogues in its search for a new way of talking about the special dead. Baronio answered this eclecticism with a turn to history: what *was* a martyrology, he asked, and where did it come from?[86]

For the answers, the cardinal searched the archive for the earliest ways that Christians wrote about their dead. About the Roman martyrology, Baronio wrote, it "took its beginning not from Jerome, not from Eusebius, but from those protonotaries of the Holy Roman Church, already from the times of Pope Clement."[87] In the early sixteenth century, the Venetian humanist Pescennio Francesco Negro had extolled these ancient sacred scribes, "those who ought to write the deeds of the martyrs throughout all the regions of the world."[88] What especially interested Baronio was the distinctiveness of this scribal tradition. The lives of the earliest martyrs, he noted, were not preserved in hagiographies, the *acta martyrum*, or church histories. Rather, they were preserved by the administration of the *church*. It was Clement I, second pope of Rome, who established a chancery of notaries in the year 98, in order to conserve the Christian acts in the face of pagan threat.[89] By simply writing down the names of the martyrs, as well as the dates and manner of their deaths, these protonotaries allowed "a few records (*perpaucas tabulas*)" of the Christian archive to survive the "shipwreck" of the Diocletian persecutions.[90] This archive thereafter served to remedy "the confusion of false things with the true . . . and not just among heretical enemies of the catholic faith, but also among catholics themselves."[91]

The Church was not the credulous institution that Protestants made it out to be, in other words. During the earliest periods of persecution, the Latin father Tertullian was already skeptical of certain *acta martyrum*, in particular the apocryphal *acta* of Paul and Thecla.[92] Even more important to Baronio was the "Gelasian decree," the earliest known effort to regulate the authenticity of the ecclesiastical archive. This decree was (and is) a remarkable document. It offered the earliest canon of Christian scripture, including both the Old and New Testaments and their proper order. It listed the canonical Church fathers, and their works, as well as apocryphal works, forged Gospels, and spurious apostolic accounts. It also listed heresies, and even offered critical commentary on the Fathers themselves. Origen was censured, for example, as was Eusebius, while works of fathers like Tertullian, Arnobius, and Lactantius were, remarkably, included on the list of books "written by heretics or schismatics."[93] In Baronio's day, the decree was attributed to Pope Gelasius (492–496) and thus a product of just the century when Protestants saw the Church slipping into the hands of Satan.[94] From this perspective, the Church had *always* been a critical steward of the Christian archive.

In terms of the martyrs, Baronio noted that Gelasius offered the authoritative "discipline of the Roman church for receiving and promulgating the acts of the martyrs."[95] "The deeds of the sacred martyrs, according to ancient custom, by singular caution are *not to be read* in the Roman church," he quoted from the decree.[96] Other ancient churches, he admitted, were more relaxed about the problem of authenticity. The late fourth century Council of Carthage, for example, declared that the passions of the martyrs could be read, "when their anniversary days are celebrated."[97] But the Gelasian decree addressed a real problem, Baronio thought. The *acta martyrum* were stories recorded by "people ignorant and unfamiliar with the use of letters," and moreover marred by the "malevolence of demons, whose task and enthusiasm is to steal the truth" with "interpolations . . . additions . . . changes and subtractions of words."[98] The early acts were in no shape even to be *read* by the ordinary faithful, let alone incorporated into liturgical life.

A martyrology was thus completely different, so Baronio argued, than an "act" or a hagiography. Ever diligent about conserving only the most accurate materials, the Roman Church developed from the earliest protonotarial tradition the general practice of recording the *natalitia*—the birthdays into salvation—of the Christian martyrs. These recordings were simple, and thus resistent to the fanciful corruptions so common in the *acta*. The injunction to celebrate the martyrs recorded by, among others, Augustine in his *On Holy Virginity*, came by the "authority of the church, in which it is shown to the faithful in what place the martyrs . . . died."[99] From these records, "made that [the sacred martyrs] might be commemorated, came the occasion for writing the martyrologies."[100]

The conclusion was stark: an authoritative martyrology cannot be a *narrative* document, to say nothing of the literary confabulations of the Protestants. It had to be a *liturgical* one, written as "ecclesiastical records" such that the names might be "announced in Church . . . of those whose natalitia are to be recorded . . . and . . . who together should be commemorated with the sacrifice."[101] Baronio found proof of this liturgical origin in the Pope we met in chapter 3, Gregory the Great. In response to a request in 598 from the Alexandrian patriarch Eulogius for authentic accounts of the passions, Gregory was surprised to find almost none:

> Beside what is contained in the books of the same Eusebius, on the acts of the holy martyrs, I have not learnt of any in the archives of this Church of ours, or in the libraries of the city of Rome, except for a few samples collected in a volume of a single manuscript. But we have the names of almost all the martyrs collected in one manuscript, with their passions allotted to special days, and we celebrate solemn Mass in venerating them on each such day. However, in the same volume, there is no mention of who suffered, and how he did so, but simply his name, and the place and day of his passion, are put down.[102]

This letter showed a scholar at work, the first monk-pope scouring archives and libraries in order to understand and conserve more completely the tradition to which he was an heir. The martyr rolls might have varied across the different churches, but the gold standard was in the Vatican libraries, the exemplar against which others were emended that "all might together have praised God . . . with the same communion of the saints, and with one and the same rite, and with one spirit."[103] The authenticity and priority of this commemorative form was, in Baronio's view, amply documented in the archives of Christianity.

Doubtless the Cardinal Baronio was an apologist. The veneration of Gregory; the insistence that a proper martyrology must look like a Catholic calendar; the subtle dig at the veneration of Eusebius: these were partisan bids for Catholic authority over the martyrological tradition.

Partisanship should not blind us to the complex and generative work that Baronio pursued, however. Among other things, his papally approved preface argued: first, that the early church was a heterogeneous and conflicted place; second, that the institutions of the ancient church were not naive, but critical; third, that to understand sanctity, we need to pay attention to the forms in which sanctity has been transmitted in time. And when we recall that these critical insights were part of a *liturgical* text, we get a sense of how deeply the sixteenth-century conflicts about martyrs reshaped basic forms of the Christian imagination.

To return to Polycarp, recall how economical his entry was in the first printed martyrology, the *Viola sanctorum*. The new *Martryologium romanum* retained the basic story, but accompanied it with a robust critical apparatus. The priest who opened it in preparation of Polycarp's feast day would, for example, learn that the Greek church celebrated Polycarp on February 23, not January 26. He would also get a bibliography of patristic writings on Polycarp, including Eusebius, Irenaeus, and the various ancient letters from and about the saint.[104] Other entries were more expansive. Just for the month of January, readers would find learned footnotes on ancient vigils, the word "Pope," the *equuleum* (an ancient torture device), and Trajan's persecution of ancient Christians, among many others.[105] None of these were relevant to the author of the *Viola sanctorum*. Now these were crucial elements of the liturgy itself.

Proving the Old Christian Saint II: The Places of the Dead

Ancient texts were not the only way to answer the question "what was a martyr?" Catholics had an enormous *physical* archive as well, those remains of ancient martyrs preserved in churches, cemeteries, and catacombs across the Catholic world. Above all, these remains were concentrated in Rome, the "seat and dwelling place of religion," as the antiquarian Pompeo Ugonio called it. Already in the 1450s, as the papacy regained the prestige and power it had lost in the schisms and conciliar controversies of the previous century, energetic Popes like Nicholas V and Pius II began to reinvigorate the sacred status of the Eternal City. The injuries Rome encountered in the early sixteenth century—from the disappointments of the Reformation to the sacking of the city by the powerful Habsburg Emperor Charles V—were soothed after the Council of Trent, when Catholic sacrality tilted emphatically toward Rome, completing its transformation "from *urbs profana* to *urbs sacra*."[106]

This new Catholic Rome had many forms. The oldest churches of the city—the seven pilgrimage churches—were powerfully energized, for example, for Catholic devotions in the sixteenth century. Ancient holy sites were reconstructed and their walls painted with scenes of ancient martyrdoms. Crypts were excavated and altars rebuilt.[107] Some of the most dramatic projects involved the Roman catacombs. These had been sites of Christian sacrality in the earliest church, with altars placed near the graves to celebrate the Eucharist.[108] But as relics were translated into churches during the Middle Ages, the catacombs dwindled in importance.[109] Their memory was never lost: pilgrims to the cemetery of S. Pancrazio in the fifteenth century could still receive an indulgence worth two thousand years from their purgatorial sentence.[110] The trend lines over the centuries before the Council of Trent were clear, however. The catacombs receded to a Christian novelty, visited by few and left to fall into disrepair.

In the wake of the Reformation, however, the sepulchre was resacralized. The founder of the new lay Oratorian order Filipo Neri, for example, was supposed to have "lived continuously in the catacombs of S. Sebastiano" for nearly a decade in the 1540s.[111] In the wake of the Council of Trent, the process accelerated. Scholars like the Veronese antiquarian Onofrio Panvinio became interested in these ancient places, for example, publishing a 1568 treatise on the history of Christian burial that included an antiquarian defense of the sacrality of the cemeteries and the ancient cult of the martyrs celebrated there. The "most ancient ecclesiastical witnesses" testify that "the ancients were accustomed to celebrate baptism and mass, to chant vigils, . . . that is, to hold all the sacred ceremonies" in the cemeteries of Rome. "Among the ancient fathers, it was the custom to make offerings and sacrifices on the days celebrating the martyrs," he went on, citing Origen and other patristic witnesses.[112] As if inviting readers to discover these sacred sites for themselves, Panvinio included a comprehensive list of Roman cemeteries and catacombs, along with their most famous residents, as documented in ancient records.[113]

In the spring of 1578, one of these ancient sites was rediscovered. Workers digging on the Via Salaria on the northeast side of Rome found a massive underground graveyard, to all eyes the very same one described by the fourth-century Pope Damasus, the *Coemeterium Priscillae*.[114] The catacombs of Priscilla were a majestic find, filled with early frescos, sarcophagi, and the bones of some of Christianity's most storied dead.[115] As the English Catholic and Bible translator Gregory Martin described it in 1580, "there are altars and the images of Christ and his Apostles, evident tokens of antiquitie, when the Christians in time of persecution assembled into these vaults or Cryptes to divine service, and to burie their dead."[116] What Christians had "read in documents," Baronio commented in his *Ecclesiastical Annals*, they now "observed with great wonder" with their own eyes.[117] This discovery resounded in a world where, as Simon Ditchfield puts it, everyone was on the hunt for "paleo-Christian" norms.[118] As the material world of the early church was "reclaimed for veneration," these new catacombs inspired fevered interest among theologians, antiquarians, and historians.[119]

The young Maltese scholar Antonio Bosio—in the most storied example of Catholic catacomb fever—descended into the vaults of Priscilla in 1593, and began a lifetime of exploration that culminated in the publication of his magnificent *Roma sotterranea* (1632). The work appeared three years after his death, edited and augmented by the Oratorian Giovanni Severano.[120] More than most, this work showed just how expansive the archive of Christian antiquity became in the later sixteenth century, when the cultures of ancient martyrdom were brought to life in pictures, objects, and bones.

Take Bosio's exquisite reproductions of images that he discovered in the catacombs of Priscilla, when he explored them (as he recounts) in October 1594. Here we find, for example, an almost perfect reproduction of the image we saw above, the feast celebrating the special dead etched into the stone of an antique Christian sarcophagus much like the one we saw in chapter 1 (see fig. 4.2).[121] Decorated funerary niches, tomb architecture, carved inscriptions, and sculpted tombstones told the story of an underground Christianity whose sacrality concentrated on the bodies of the martyrs. Common Christian iconography—the lambs and shepherds, chi-rho crosses, Christ resurrecting Lazarus, Daniel with the lions, Jonah and the whale—gave warm decoration to these dark places, depicting

FIGURE 4.2. Catacomb of Priscilla. Antonio Bosio, *Roma sotterranea* (Rome, 1632). Courtesy of the Folger Shakespeare Library.

redemptive hope in the face of suffering and death. Suitably for a place that once hosted celebrations of the Eucharist, catacomb images confirmed the martyrs' place in a sacrificial lineage going back to the patriarchs.

The sacrifice of Abraham was an especially common grave decoration in Priscilla, for example, and indeed in all of the catacombs that Bosio examined (fig. 4.3). For Christians in the primitive church, Bosio explained, the cross and the passion of Christ "was a scandal to the Jews and a sign of folly to the Gentiles." Conversion demanded a pictorial ruse, then, substituting for the Crucifixion "various figures and stories" including that of Isaac "when his father Abraham intended to sacrifice him." From this early substitution, Bosio argued, there developed an independent pictorial tradition that ran through the ancient Church. Ancient writers including Tertullian, Origen, and Epiphanius confirmed the typological elaboration of the figure: the wood that Isaac carried foreshadowing the wood of the Cross, the nations that Abraham fathered foreshadowing

FIGURE 4.3. Abraham in the Catacomb of Priscilla. Antonio Bosio, *Roma sotterranea* (Rome, 1632). Courtesy of the Folger Shakespeare Library.

Christ's conversion of the gentiles, and so forth. By the time it was painted in the catacombs of St. Priscilla, it was no longer a scandal, but a source of comfort for Christians suffering the trials of persecution.[122] Small wonder that this sacrificial scene—like that of Abel and Cain, also found in the catacombs—would become part of the Canon of the Mass and the liturgical architecture of the Church.

The catacombs also showed the emergence of a distinctly Christian culture from the matrix of Roman paganism, Bosio argued. From the beginning, gentiles tried to destroy every trace of this new religion, including and especially the bodies of those who died in its name. They threw bodies to wild beasts, into fires, into the ocean, hid and scattered their remains

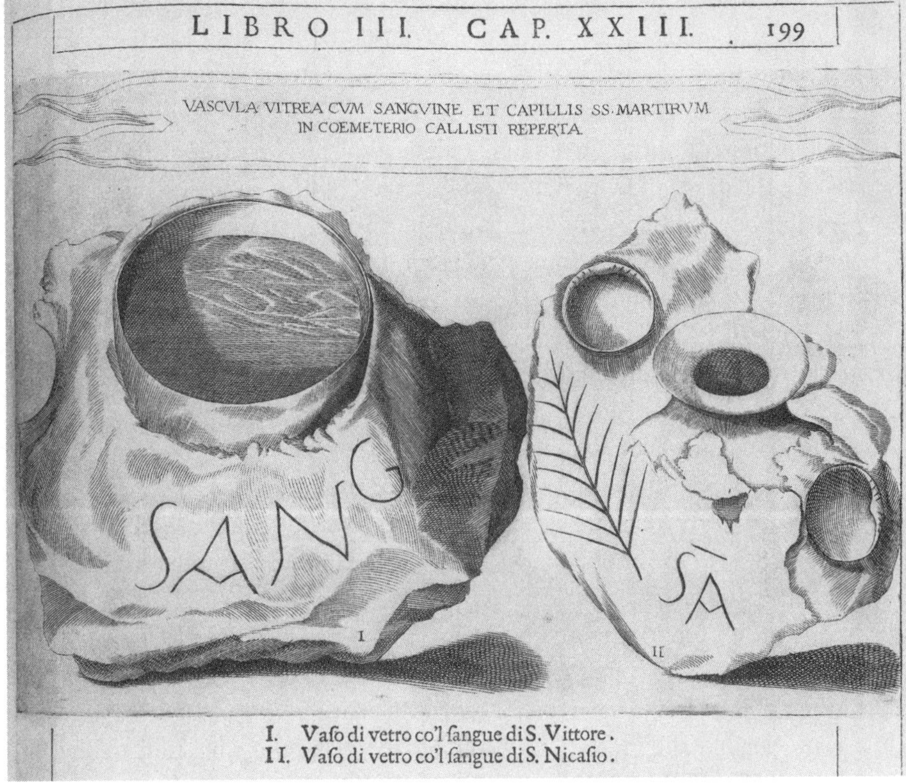

FIGURE 4.4. Glass vases with the blood of the martyrs. Catacomb of Callisto, Rome. Antonio Bosio, *Roma sotterranea* (Rome, 1632). Courtesy of the Folger Shakespeare Library.

to prevent their veneration. Christians, in turn, reverently collected and buried them. The ancients even collected the blood of the sacred martyrs, using "sponges and rags" to gather it from the sands where it spilled. As the Roman poet Prudentius sang:

> With their garments also they wipe
> dry the soaking sand, so that no drop shall remain to
> dye the dust; and wherever blood adheres to the
> spikes on which its warm spray fell, they press
> a sponge on it and carry it all away. (*Peristephanon liber*, 11.141–144)

In fact, Bosio reported that he found vessels for "the pure blood of the martyrs" in catacombs he explored on the Via Appia, vessels that might have looked like this (fig. 4.4).[123] Together, the blood, the bones, and the bodies energized Christianity—the "miracles, virtue, and grace, that the Lord worked in this sacred sepulchres" and "the relics of the saints" resulted in a "marvelous propagation of our faith."[124] To be Christian was, in a sense, to venerate the dead.

The remains of the ancient Roman world thus supplied Catholics like Bosio with material confirmation of a martyrological tradition stretching back to the dawn of Christianity. Vials, vases, bottles, lamps, sepulchres, paintings, inscriptions, and carvings confirmed the vitality of a sacrificial cult whose later incarnations Protestant critics repudiated so violently. Interested readers, moreover, could read the *Roma sotterranea* in conjunction with Baronio's *Ecclesiastical Annals* and the revised Roman martyrology—both are amply cross referenced throughout Bosio's text—to provide a complete historical picture that linked ancient and modern cults of the saints. They could also compare it with the new frescos that sprang up around Rome depicting the suffering of these early Christians, with the many new vernacular lives of the ancient martyrs that rolled off the Roman presses in the sixteenth century, or with more systematic works like the 1591 *Trattato degli Instrumenti di Martirio*, which gave graphic account of the "various manners of martyrdom used by the gentiles against the Christians" (see fig. 4.5).[125] History was as firmly on the side of the Church as it had ever been for the new Protestant martyrologies.

And yet, like the Protestants, Catholics too found this Christian archive an uncomfortable possession. The new Roman martyrology began by expelling scores of would-be saints from its rolls, after all, its new criteria of sanctity too rigorous for many of the special dead. The *Roma sotterranea* too struggled to apply historical criteria to its sacred subjects. One of the strategies pagans used to confound the early Church was to mix bodies together, jumbling the sacred and profane: "sometimes the Gentiles would mix the bodies of the holy martyrs with those of criminal and profane men, and at times with the bones of brutish animals, so that they could not be recognized or distinguished by the Christians." Even Jews, St. Ambrose witnessed, were mixed with the special dead.[126] Although early Christians were diligent about sorting the wheat from the chaff, a shadow of impurity still lay over these ancient places. Hence Bosio's insistence, throughout the book, that "the cemeteries of Rome were never contaminated or used by the pagans."[127] Pagans burned their dead, and Christians buried them, Bosio (incorrectly) insisted. Even if they did bury them, they saw Christians "as plagues on the world" and would certainly have avoided spending eternity in their company.[128] Yet if this was true, then, what to do with images like these? What was Orpheus doing over a *Christian* grave? (See fig. 4.6.)

FIGURE 4.5. Methods of Breaking the Martyrs. Antonio Gallonio, *De sanctorum martyrum cruciatibus Antonii Gallonii Rom. congregationis oratorii Presbyteri liber* (Cologne, 1602). Courtesy of the Zentralbibliothek Zürich.

Modern scholars have no problem with images like this. With our preference for syncretism, we happily discover the blurry boundaries between Christian and pagan in the ancient world, and the long historical connections between Orpheus and Christ.[129] For Bosio, however, the sacred should be apart and distinct. An Orpheus-Christ might show the early Church, or even Christianity itself, as tainted by paganism. To ward this

FIGURE 4.6. Orpheus. Catacomb of St. Calisto. Antonio Bosio, *Roma sotterranea* (Rome, 1632). Courtesy of the Folger Shakespeare Library.

off, then, Bosio offered a remarkable explanation for how the Greek poet and prophet might have ended up in Christian funerary art:

> It may seem strange to many that in the sacred cemeteries of the Christians, the image of Orpheus is found painted . . . Those first Christians, converted from paganism to Christianity, remembering the falsehoods and fictions [of the Gods], introduced mostly by Orpheus, would sometimes paint him in the cemeteries, so that by looking at him, they would also remember that these same falsehoods had been rejected by him, and confessed as false and harmful; and that he himself had repented and written many things in accordance with the doctrine of Christ, who, with the lyre of his Cross, and the merits of his Passion, and with the song of his divine word, has changed the savage hearts of men, . . . [he] has freed our souls from eternal death, pulling them from the jaws of the demon, and has drawn all the world to himself.[130]

It may seem odd that Orpheus the poet and fabulator of the Gods—the man responsible for the impiety of the ancient Greeks—appears in Christian cemeteries. But he is there as an *admonition*, Bosio argued, a reminder of the pagan ways abandoned by this new pious community.

FIGURE 4.7. Funerary Feast. Catacomb of St. Marcellinus and Peter. Antonio Bosio, *Roma sotterranea* (Rome, 1632). Courtesy of the Folger Shakespeare Library.

It was a polemical image, in other words, an image painted on catacomb walls across the Roman underground not to remind Christians who their special dead *were* but who they *were not*.

No easier to manage than Orpheus were images like this one, ubiquitous underground, that showed the communal feasting rites shared by both pagans and Christians (fig. 4.7). From the gentile side, as we discussed in chapter 1, there was a well-attested custom of funerary feasts held at the graves of the recently dead, the so-called *parentalia, vigilia*, or *refrigeria*.[131] From the Christian side, there was both the "love feast" (*agape*) and Christ's last supper with his disciples. These two traditions converged on the walls of the Roman catacombs (and not only there: the Roman Canon of the Mass spoke of the *locum refrigerii* in its *commemoratio pro defunctis*, wishing a "place of refreshment" for the dead). In the catacomb of St. Marcellino, the refreshment was graphically depicted—the two women celebrating, Irene and Agape, with a table of meat, wine, and bread.[132] "Don't believe that this depicts the *silicernium* or the *parentalium* of the gentiles," Bosio insisted, but the comment revealed the problem: how to discern the difference between Christian and pagan practices?[133] Bosio had various suggestions: that early Christians sought to imitate the Last Supper, that this was a representation of the Mass held underground, that this was the love feast, an essentially Christian festival held to celebrate the day when the martyrs finally exited this vale of tears. But he acknowledged that early fathers like Ambrose and Augustine had worried about the "abuses" committed by Christians in their celebrations at the graves of the martyrs, that they tried to eradicate "all similarities that the *agape* had with the superstitious *parentali* of the gentiles," and that early Church councils came to prohibit these underground vigils.[134] By the time of Gregory the Great, the feasts came full circle, according to Bosio, permissible now only as convenient tools to wean gentiles from "their demonic celebrations, with the sacrifices of many oxen" by substituting for them the new Christian sacrificial order most similar to these pagan ways.[135]

For Catholics too, then, Christian sacrifice thus became ever more challenging as the sixteenth century waned. On the one hand, they insisted that the historical Church had been a reliable custodian of martyrological sanctity, whether in liturgies, churches, or cemeteries. On the other hand, the sanctity of the catacombs was no longer something that might be taken for granted. Instead it had to be *proven*, proven that the bodies buried there, the ceremonies held there, the art painted on its walls, the material remains found there belonged to the Christian, not the pagan, past. Such proofs took labor, and were haunted by the specter of critique. The holy altars and relics of Rome, the Jesuit Gregory Martin remarked, must "pearse the hart of every well disposed person, . . . al such as are not profane Atheists or Eunonian and Vigilantian Heretikes."[136] But Vigilantian heretics—those who argued "under pretence of piety" that the cult of the martyrs "made second Gods" of the dead, as Saint Jerome had it—were everywhere in the late sixteenth century, skeptics and doubters in churches from Wittenberg to Geneva to London.[137] Even as the Christian archive grew in scope, in short, it was differentiated, its materials subjected to critical scrutiny, the sacred set apart from the profane in new and sharper ways.

Conclusion: A Theo-Political Coda

The Catholic writer Antonius Paulus commented in 1606, "the sacred and profane [are] all mixed up and confused."[138] In few places were they more confused than in the world of martyrs. For Catholics and Protestants alike, the blood of the dead sealed communities together in mourning and admiration for those who died. But the same violence that spilled the blood left its meaning open to endless contention. Confessional opponents disdained each other's claims to sacrality, and even defenders felt obligated to *prove* sacrality in ways unprecedented since the dawn of the Christian era. To judge the value and nature of Christian sacrifice now required scholars and theologians able to sort between the pious and the heretics who looked just like them. The new martyrologists did so with every tool they could imagine—they praised the stoicism and steadfastness of their special dead, they emphasized their sincerity and commitment to the faith, they insisted on the rightness of their beliefs, and they lined them up as best they could with the world of ancient martyrdom out of which Christianity was born. Along the way, however, they revealed a long history in which Christian sacrality had *always* been uncomfortably intimate with pagan and heretical simulacra. Christianity became, or began to become, alienated from its own history.

For the long history of sacrifice this book wants to tell, this would prove momentous. Sacrifice had been, in the long centuries of Christian hegemony in the Latin West, an integrative concept and practice. Neither local variations in liturgy nor theological dispute threatened the fundamental consensus that the celebration of Christ's death and resurrection, and honor due to those who had died in His name, bonded the Christian community with the blood of sacrifice. In the fifteenth century, with the recovery of a patristic deep time, and then accelerating in the sixteenth century, with the emergence of competing confessional communities and then the violent conflicts that reignited a new martyrological imagination, sacrifice became far less comforting. In an important way, the conflicts of the Reformation age pulled into view what was already apparent in the ancient church, namely that sacrifice was *hard* for Christians to embrace, that it took tremendous work to incorporate a sacrificial order into a Christianity always struggling to distinguish itself from its Jewish and pagan surrounds.

The energies unleashed in the sixteenth century, finally, strained the very ideals that sustained the culture and cult of the martyrs. Whatever the difference between a true and a false martyr, *all* martyrs require a commitment to fundamental ideas like: truth should be defended at all cost, people can and should hold firm to principle in the face of ruthless violence, the willingness to die is (or can be) a rebuke to the secular order, there is a justice that trumps all worldly claims of political right, and so on. The writers of our sixteenth-century martyrologies, however violently they disagreed with one another, all agreed that *there was such a thing as a martyr*. That is, they all agreed that martyrdom was a desirable religious and ethical act, a truthful way to witness for Christ against the powers of the world. But by the later sixteenth century, this martyrological norm itself began to fail. The religious and historical questions posed in the age of the martyrologies were, within short decades, reframed as *political* ones: does the martyr *ever* have the right to challenge the legal and political order? Is there ever anything politically just about the act of self-sacrifice, and if so, in what can it possibly consist?

PART III

The Heteronomy of Christianity, ca. 1580–1685

OVER THE SIXTEENTH century, a thousand-year consensus about Christian sacrifice came undone. A sacrificial liturgy, a sacrificial priesthood, a sacrificial Eucharist, an ancient cult of the saints: these pillars of medieval Christianity trembled and, in many places, collapsed. For Protestants, the hope was to disincarnate the theological and liturgical center of Christian worship, to purge what they took to be the unconverted remnants of older sacrificial orders still clinging to the Christian faith. Catholics were no less energetic in their defenses, no less eager to show the piety, of long received sacrificial traditions. In the heat of controversy, things taken for granted now had to be *proven*, and for their proofs, both sides plumbed the early church for authoritative answers. What they found there were not stable foundations for Christian orthodoxy, however, but wilder worlds of ancient Christian heteronomy, worlds yet ungoverned by the enforced standards of creedal Christianity. The archives of Christianity, swollen with new patristic texts, revealed these worlds in all their messy particulars but afforded few stable conclusions. What is Christian sacrifice? Once asked, the question proved very hard to *stop* asking.

Part III of this book follows this question—and its many answers—from the mid-sixteenth into the seventeenth centuries. The specific doctrinal controversies of the early Reformation now recede into the background. Even as they did so, the archive of Christian sacrifice grew ever more heterogeneous. The sacrificial imagination of the early Reformation was, as we have seen, mediated by the texts traditionally used in matters theological: Scripture, the writings of the ancient fathers, and other works canonized by long centuries of Christian reflection. Once the borders between Europe's major Christian communities stabilized and the "confessional" age had begun—an age characterized by the intransigence of religious difference—the sacrificial imagination grew in new directions, new materials made to answer newly urgent questions and concerns.

Humanist antiquarians had rediscovered the sacrifices of ancient Greece and Rome already in the fourteenth century, for example. By the early sixteenth century, these were compiled into vast miscellanies and compendia. It was only in the second half of the sixteenth century that these brought to bear explicitly on questions of *Christian* sacrifice, used to score the clear line between idolatry and faith so essential in an age where confessional differences seemed set in stone. By century's end, what chapter 5 will call "apophatic antiquarianism" came into its own, sustained efforts to *use* the sacrifices of Greece and Rome as dark shadows against which the uniqueness of Christ's death stood firm and bright. A version of comparative religion, and an effort to understand sacrifice in a more systematic fashion, were born out of this hot environment of confessional conflict.

Rich accounts of an empire of sacrifice in the New World likewise started early in the century, largely at the behest of the friars eager to understand (and to more effectively convert) the Mexica and the Inca. The ethnographic particulars of the earliest accounts—the apologetic histories of a Bartholomé de las Casas or the thick descriptions of Bernard de Sahagún's *Florentine Codex*—were mostly buried in Spanish archives, however, and their immediate impact on readers back in Europe blunted. But in the 1590s, chapter 6 argues, the amazing world of sacrifice in the Americas was drawn into the European imagination. What drew it in was the effort, common to both Catholic missionaries and Protestant theological geographers, to understand the durability of human sacrifice and idolatry even in the face of Gospel truth. Along the way, they collectively invented an anthropology of religion, designed to explain why humanity found itself ever-ready to sacrifice to gods of paste.

Since before the dawn of Christianity, the sacrificial imagination was also a political one. The laws of the Temple were also the laws of a Hebrew polity, or so the Bible was understood to say, Solomon the King the builder of altars. No less important was sacrifice to other ancient polities, to Greece and Rome, law and the sacred entwined in those ancient colleges of priests, but also embedded in city walls and boundary stones, the borders of political life marked with sacrifice. For their part, early Christians turned sacrifice against the state, martyrs seeking to transform judicial spectacle into an *imitatio Christi*. Such sacrifices meant something different in the early modern world, however, when the politics of sacrifice shattered the unity of the Church. By the later sixteenth century, when every political conflict staged a struggle between the laws of this world and the higher laws witnessed in the faith, a new politics of sacrifice was born, imagined by political theorists, lawyers, historians, and even playwrights from across the blood-lands of Europe. Convinced of the need for new distinctions between sacred and profane, they turned to an ancient archive—an archive of *kingship* and sacrifice—in the effort to move *beyond* the politics of martyrdom. Chapter 7 explores how Christianity's own king-priest, and the king-priests of ancient Greece and Rome, were together pressed into this frantic effort to coordinate sovereignty and sacrifice anew.

Chapter 8 returns us to a final crisis of sacrificial doctrine. Protestants and Catholics violently disagreed, but all clung tightly to the Crucifixion, the sacrificial foundation of Christian life. That Christ died for our sins supported a common vision of human salvation, and millennia of Christian prophecy, art, and exegesis. But again in the 1590s, the Crucifix began to tremble, shaken by a heresy that started first in Poland and then spread across Western Europe. What, by the eighteenth century, will be called Unitarianism provoked an astonishing counter-reaction, especially among Protestants who found themselves in the uncomfortable position of having to *defend* sacrifice against exactly the kinds of criticisms they had themselves perfected decades earlier. This sudden pivot, in which sacrifice became a norm, was again aided by texts and authors from beyond the Christian canon. In this case, it was the Hebrews—long subordinated to Christian typology, the sacrifices of the Hebrew temple made to serve the Christian Cross—who came to the rescue. With the materials of Hebrew antiquity, Protestants by the late century had begun to imagine sacrifice as fundamental to *all* religions, even their own.

What these chapters collectively describe, then, is the beginnings of a new epoch in the sacrificial imagination. By the late sixteenth century, a dynamic developed in which polemics between Christians were pulling ever-more disparate materials into its orbit. Christian efforts at *self*-definition thus came to depend on *other* stories, whether from pagan antiquity, the New World, or ancient Israel. The venerable practice of typology—long the keystone of the Christian sacrificial imagination—came undone. A new kind of theology was born alongside, one that depended on history, philology, and anthropology as foundational elements of evidence and argument. A new kind of sacrificial politics too began to emerge, populated less by ancient martyrs than by ancient kings, Christian and pagan. As a result, the Christian sacrificial imagination grew ever more heteronomous, ever less able to legislate its own contents, ever more populated by other histories, other anthropologies, other religions.

CHAPTER FIVE

The Way of the Negative

ANTIQUARIANISM AND THE SYSTEM OF SACRIFICE

Nothing that has once come into existence ever goes away.

—SIGMUND FREUD

IN 1598, THE Zürich theologian and scholar Johann Wilhelm Stucki published Europe's first dedicated treatise on sacrifice. Stucki walked in the mainstream of Swiss Protestantism, comrade of Calvinist luminaries and as doctrinally conventional as one had to be to hold the chair in Old Testament established by Reformation pioneer Huldrych Zwingli. Yet Stucki's work was also haunted by recondite passions. As a young man, he studied with Konrad Gessner, the polymathic natural historian and bibliographer of the classical world. Later in Strassburg, he enjoyed the company of the French legal historian Francois Hotmann, author of the *Francogallia* (1574) and pioneer of the comparative study of law. Then, in Paris, he hobnobbed with the great humanists of the age, from the classicist Adrian Turnebus to the logician Peter Ramus. He was a *homo trilinguis*, proficient in Latin, Greek, and Hebrew. And he was, above all else, a tireless, creative, and zealous antiquarian.[1]

The *Brief and Accurate Description of the Sacrifices and Sacred Rites of the Gentiles* dove deep into the world of gentile religion. So deep, in fact, that some, its author remarked, might wonder why a theologian should dedicate "so many words about those ancient idols, sacrifices, ceremonies, and superstitions of the gentiles, the memory of which it seems should not only be unrenewed, but also buried and abolished forever." Yet such work, he insisted, was "useful, fruitful, and fitting for Christian piety." Nary a page of scripture, especially in the Old Testament, can be found "without mention of the idols, foreign gods, angels, altars, temples, and sacrifices of the gentiles." For this reason, we find such intense interest in, and exploration of, even the most repellant gentile customs among Christian authors. From ancient church fathers like Tertullian, Cyprian, Arnobius, Lactantius, Augustine, and Clement of Alexandria, Stucki exclaimed, to Renaissance antiquarians like Alexander ab Alexandro, Polydore Vergil, Guillaume du Choul, and Lilio Giraldi, Christians have tirelessly shown how much "clearer and more manifest is the dignity and pre-eminence of the true religion when compared with superstition and idolatry."[2]

Both Stucki's book and his list of authorities index a new epoch in the sacrificial imagination. The notion that Christianity was always a comparative project should by now be familiar to readers. The Gospels; the letters of Paul; the writings of the early church fathers: the foundational texts of the Christian imagination were shot through with comparisons between Christians, Jews, and gentiles. Also familiar are Stucki's patristic authorities. As we saw, the patristic archive was key to the emergence of the new theological modalities of the sixteenth century, in which polemic about things sacrificial would be waged on the territory of the Christian past. Like Luther, Melanchthon, Calvin, Bullinger, and Bucer, our Zürich theologian defended Protestant verities about Christian sacrifice in traditional soteriological terms: only Christ's once-and-for-all death on the altar of the Cross had the power to break humanity's bondage to sin in harmony. No less than earlier reformers, Stucki supported his doctrinal commitments too on the foundations of the earliest, and most apostolic, churches.

But as the sixteenth century waned, this Christian archive expanded in new directions. The hegemony of the "patristic paradigm," as Dmitri Levitin calls it, yielded to increasingly more eclectic materials gleaned from across the ancient world.[3] Stucki's first guides to these materials were Renaissance collectors of curious pagan antiquaria: the Neapolitan lawyer Alexander ab Alexandro, author of a popular miscellany of antiquarian learning; the French numismatist and historian Guillaume du Choul, expert in ancient Roman religion; the Italian Polydore Vergil, obsessed with the "invention of things" in the classical world; Lilio Gregorio Giraldi, pioneer of gentile mythography. The world of *gentile* sacrifice was, for Stucki, crucial for adjudicating what Christian sacrifice had been, and should become.

On the face of it, this world of earlier humanist erudition was an unlikely ally for a Protestant like Stucki, eager to defend the truths of his tribe. From the fifteenth century onward—as we will discover below—scholars, writers, and artists had enthusiastically explored the religions of the classical world, pagan and Christian. So sympathetic did some scholars become to the gods of Greece and Rome, that there emerged various hybrids, Christian and pagan, in which the pious and profane blended in surprising and at times shocking ways.

For his part, the Calvinist Stucki abhorred syncretism. "Descriptions of those superstitions of the gentiles should rightly inflame and arouse our souls," he remarked, our pious zeal aroused when we learn how God "liberated us through his only begotten son, Jesus Christ, from these ancient ways, not only from the most burdensome and painstaking shadows of Jewish ceremonies, but also from the foulest and deadliest obscurities of gentile superstition."[4] The more we know just how miserable the Jews and gentiles were before the advent of Christ, the more our gratitude for His mercy grows. *Felix quem faciunt aliena pericula cautum*, as the adage went—"happy is he who learns prudence from the danger of others!" As our knowledge of superstition grows, so too grows our desire for the "true worship of the true and only God." How could it not? After all, if the gentiles can labor day and night at their devotion to vain and deadly gods, cannot Christians too spend "days and nights in the real, genuine, and salubrious worship of the true and only God"?[5] For Stuckius, antiquarian research was a form of apophatic piety, exposing all of the things that God is *not*, that we might better appreciate what He is.

The confessional reality of the mid-sixteenth century thus inspired new methods and objects of knowledge. What this chapter will call the *modus negandi*—the fundamental commitment to the *difference* between Christian truth and pagan superstition—came to dominate research into ancient sacrifice. From the gentler curiosities of Alexandro, Vergil, and du Choul, to the sharper distinctions of the Catholic Giraldi and the Protestant Stucki, the gentiles began to play an ever more negative role in the definition of Christian sacrifice.

It is tempting to view this darker turn in the history of religious erudition as a setback for the gradual growth of a properly secular appreciation of religious difference, the triumph of rigid purity over the gentle moderation so prized in our age. But in fact, this hot confessional environment proved immensely creative. For it was from this world that the first synthetic treatments of ancient sacrifice emerged. Earlier miscellanies, genealogies of paganism, histories of Rome, and works on ancient invention and discovery supplied the raw materials. But it was the confessional obsession with distinguishing between pagan and Christian that produced efforts to *organize* these materials, to describe the *system* that organized ancient sacrifice, and indeed, all of ancient religion.

This chapter follows in the footsteps of Stucki and his heroes, Vergil, Alexandro, du Choul, and Giraldi. As before, we start in the deeper past, with the pre-Reformation memories of paganism in Christian literary and interpretative traditions, and various creative symbioses of pious and profane that emerge in the Renaissance. This symbiosis was injured, if not destroyed, by the fragmentation of Latin Christianity in the sixteenth century. From this destruction emerged a new epoch in the sacrificial imagination. It was an epoch in which antiquarian research became an integral element of theological practice, doctrinal verities illuminated all the more brightly by the dark anti-types of paganism. It was an epoch too that made sacrifice into an organizing keystone of ancient religion, locking together the entire cultic system of the ancient world.

Afterlives of Pagan Sacrifice: Allegory, Art, Antiquarianism

The gods of Olympus were never forgotten in the long twilight of Greece and Rome. As "cosmic spirits, religious forces with a strong influence in practical affairs," in Aby Warburg's words, the ancient gods took shelter in the astrological tradition, for example, as "time gods, . . . mythically ruling every chronological unit in the annual round."[6] Jupiter, Venus, Mars, and Mercury migrated into the heavens, benevolent or demonic planetary deities that brought disease, governed weather, destroyed and sustained the institutions of human life. Saturn, ever hungry for human sacrifice, ruled the melancholic temperament. Those born under his sign, ancient and medieval astrology assured, were indolent, lonely, bitter, gloomy, and prone to dropsy and rheumatism.[7] Astrological manuals prescribed prayers to Kronos, "the Cold, the Sterile, the Mournful, the Pernicious." The ancient gods were also preserved in carved gemstones and cameos collected throughout the Middle Ages.[8] A seal belonging to Charlemagne bore the head of Jupiter Serapis, for example, and it was not uncommon to mount scenes of pagan antiquity on even the holiest of Christian artifacts, crosses, prayer books, and reliquaries.[9]

Traditions of allegory—the unearthing of moral significances hidden behind the surfaces of texts—were particularly effective in preserving the gods of Greece and Rome.[10] Already in late antiquity, creative allegorists transfigured even the most bloodthirsty of the old gods into moral models. When "Kronos swallowed his children," it suggested the god's intellectual nature, since "all intellect is directed against itself": so wrote the neo-Platonist Sallustius, friend of the Emperor Julian, in the fourth century.[11]

The Roman Macrobius saw in Saturn an allegory of time: "swallowing his sons and vomiting them back up . . . signifies that he is time, which by turns creates and destroys all things";[12] the North African mythographer Fulgentius instead thought that Saturn "devoured his own sons because every season devours what it produces."[13] This ancient allegorical tradition passed into the Latin Christian world through Martianus Capella's *Marriage of Philology and Mercury*, written by a North African contemporary of Augustine, revived by the Carolingians, and a popular textbook for later centuries.[14] Works like these remade the pagan gods into philosophically and morally pliable material for later Christian readers.

By the high Middle Ages, Christian poets and others were adept at weaving antique materials into pious tapestries. Homer, Vergil, and Ovid were resurrected in allegory, the gods turned into carnal figures for hidden spiritual truths. John of Salisbury—the student of Bernard of Chartres, one of the great Platonists of that age—took his lead from Capella in his philosophical poem *Entheticus* (1155?), for example, and insisted:

> that Philology be the companion of Mercury;
> not in order that reverence shall be paid to false divinities;
> but under the veil of words, truths lie hidden (*sub verborum tegmine vera latent*).[15]

That truths lie hidden behind a veil of words was how the Roman poet Vergil had already described the Sibylline prophecies, among the most opaque and thus most interesting of ancient texts. The same interpretive technique was then applied to Vergil in turn.[16] His so-called messianic eclogue proclaimed that "now hath the last age come, foretold by the Sibyl of Cumae;/ Mightily now upriseth a new millennial epoch./ Justice the Maid comes back, and the ancient glory of Saturn; /New is the seed of man sent down from heavenly places."[17] The "ancient glory of Saturn" returned as the "seed of man," Christ inaugurating a Saturnalia for a new dispensation. Indeed, the entire Vergilian corpus was made to serve Christian ethical and philosophical projects in the Middle Ages, "truth hidden behind a veil, *veritatem per integumenta occultat*," as the twelfth-century Platonist Bernardus Silvestris glossed Vergil's *Aeneid*.[18]

The allegorical urge was satisfied by Ovid as well, about whom the Carolingian bishop Theodolf had already written in the ninth century in nearly identical terms. "*Quanquam sint frivola multa/plurima sub falso tegmine vera latent*," he remarked, "although much may be frivolous, there are many truths hidden under the cover of lies."[19] The *Ovide moralisé*, over 70,000 lines of allegorical commentary written in the fourteenth century, was one of the most astonishing efforts to discover the truths that lay hidden behind the lies.[20] *Ovidus theologus, Vergilius theologus, Homer theologus:* "the old poets were prophets of God and . . . poetry is a second theology," as Ernst Curtius long ago remarked about the *poeta theologus* of the later Middle Ages.[21] The more secret, the more sacred: this allegorical key unlocked many ancient mysteries.

As the Middle Ages drew to a close, this allegorical tradition was supplemented by new ways of incorporating the ancient gods into the Christian imagination. Take, for example, Giovanni Boccaccio's 1375 *On the Genealogy of the Pagan Gods*, a Janus-faced work, *simul ante retroque prospiciens*, looking forward and backward, as his friend Petrarch put it.[22] One of the first books to be indexed, after the advent of print, it appeared in numerous Latin, French, and Italian editions and was an intellectual bridge from the mythographies of antiquity to the more systematic works of the sixteenth century.[23] The Tuscan too praised pagan poets as theologians, but not on account of their hidden *Christian* teachings.[24] Rather, it was the "physical and moral truth in their inventions" that interested Boccaccio.[25] "No creation of human genius was ever veiled in fiction more cleverly," the Italian wrote of the ancient myths, "nor adorned so beautifully in the splendor of words . . . Once the outer layer is peeled back . . . you will see aspects of nature, once shrouded in mystery, that will amaze you, as will the deeds of great men and customs now relatively obscure."[26]

On the Genealogy of the Pagan Gods revealed this hidden world of the ancients. "The remnants of the pagan gods strewn everywhere" like "fragments along the vast shores of a huge shipwreck" were in need of repair after long centuries of neglect.[27] Boccaccio vowed to knit the fragments back together and reconstruct the pagan gods as "first creations of the human mind," historical emanations of humanity as it developed over long centuries.[28] Saturn was the eleventh child of the Sky, it was said, but Boccaccio thought it more likely he was born to a powerful man named Uranus. He was perhaps a powerful king (here following Lactantius) and later venerated under the figure of an old man. Many stories were told about him. "He ate his children because age consumes spaces of time, as he is filled up insatiably by years passed," Boccaccio quoted Cicero. As for the children being vomited up:

> this refers to the fruits annually received from the earth, for fruits produced in season from the land, though they are all devoured in season, from that same season, through the agency of God, they return in the following year. On account of this fiction, not at all understood by the

ignorant, it was believed by some that the detestable rite of sacrifices arose among certain barbarian nations, where indeed for Saturn they used to sacrifice not just others but their own children, as if reenacting his deed.[29]

The cycle of the seasons—fruits received, devoured, and returning again—is the real heart of Saturnine sacrifice. But fictions produce fictions, stories about natural fecundity are absorbed by stories of nearly forgotten ancient kings. The barbarian nations sacrifice their children, reenacting a fiction about Saturn, himself a fiction dreamed up to describe how the earth renews and destroys its own creations.

At the heart of Boccaccio's story was the creative capacity of the human imagination. Because he was venerated in the form of an old man, Saturn attracted a set of associated attributes. Old men "have repulsive faces" and are "slow at walking, and slow to anger," so the god Saturn has a dark aspect, melancholic, sorrowful, repulsive, tending toward sloth and indolence.[30] History sediments these imaginative fictions and spreads them to new places, where they take on new forms. The man Saturn himself was driven out of Greece into Italy, where he "revealed many things not known previously," including metallic coin, for which reason the Romans always put the public treasury near the temple of Saturn.[31] Boccaccio combined poetry, anthropology, and history, in sum, to re-create "the religious beliefs of antiquity as a cultural production" and unveil "the hidden history of the human imagination."[32]

This history was concealed (and revealed) in more than literature. The memory of the gentiles and their sacrifices was preserved in Greek vases and Roman temples, from the Pantheon to the Forum, and throughout the material remains of the ancient Mediterranean.[33] It was laid on the mosaic floors of excavated villas, cast in stucco friezes, and carved in the marble prized by the discerning humanists of the fifteenth and sixteenth centuries. Nowhere were the sacrifices of the ancient world so well preserved and easily collected as in Rome. There, interested moderns could find on the Arch of the Argentarii a bull sacrificed at the behest of the Emperor Septimius Severus and his wife Julia.[34] The arch of Constantine was graced by sacrifices to Diana, Hercules, and Apollo, and a beautiful carving of a *lustratio* featuring Constantine and the *suovetaurilia*, the triple sacrifice of the swine, ram, and bull. Trajan's column also boasted an exquisite *suovetaurilia*. Another freestanding version of the triple-sacrifice, much emulated and copied, was later looted by Napoleon and brought to the Louvre (fig. 5.1). Fragments of friezes recovered from the

FIGURE 5.1. Roman *Suovetaurilia*, 1st century CE, marble. Louvre Museum. Erich Lessing / Art Resource, NY.

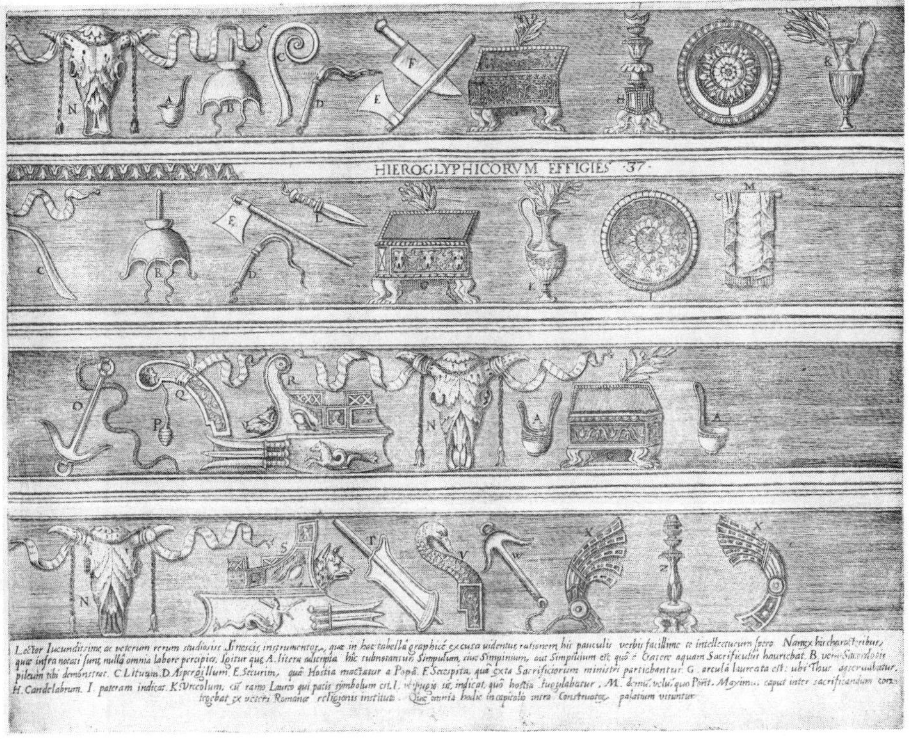

FIGURE 5.2. Sacrificial Instruments. Frieze from San Lorenzo fuori le mura, Rome. Reproduced in Hans Georg Hörwart von Hohenberg, *Thesaurus Hieroglyphicorum* (1610). Courtesy of Niedersächsische Staats- und Universitätsbibliothek Göttingen, Public Domain Mark 1.0 (PDM).

Roman church of San Lorenzo fuori le mura depicted a variety of tools—knives, axes, censers, cups—used in sacrificial rites (fig. 5.2).[35]

These remains came alive in the fifteenth century. Already in the 1930s, the marvelous art historian Fritz Saxl reconstructed the ways that painters and sculptors, especially in northern Italy, reanimated ancient sacrifices in creative and alarming ways.[36] They lavished ancient prototypes with exquisite attention in drawings and prints, as in this beautiful sketch of the Louvre *suovetaurilia* (fig. 5.3) or this anonymous homage to the Roman sacrifice to the manes—the shades of the underworld worshiped in the festivals of Feralia, Parentalia, and Lemuria—purporting to reproduce a stucco frieze from the Roman forum (fig. 5.4).

The Venetian engraver Girolamo Mocetto also copied the Louvre *suovetaurilia* frieze ca. 1500, but more significantly, created this scene of pagan sacrifice, part of a dyptich (fig. 5.5). Distinctive not only for its

FIGURE 5.3. Sketch of the Louvre *suovetaurilia* and triumphal procession. Amico Aspertini, late 15th century.

FIGURE 5.4. Roman Sacrifice to the Manes. Anonymous sketch, ca. 1500. bpk Bildagentur. Hamburger Kunsthalle. Christoph Irrgang. Art Resource, NY.

FIGURE 5.5. Sacrificial scene at the Piazza San Marco, Venice. Girolamo Mocetto, engraving ca. 1525–1530. © British Museum. All rights reserved.

FIGURE 5.6. Andrea Riccio, *Sacrifice to Asclepius*, 1516–1521, Della Torre tomb, Verona. Erich Lessing / Art Resource, NY.

setting—in the Piazza San Marco directly in front of the basilica—but also for its exquisite attention to the instruments of the sacrifice, Mocetto's engraving was modeled on a now lost, possibly antique Roman bas-relief. It imagined Roman sacrifice as alternatively solemn and festive, violent and restrained, pious and profane.[37]

Like the Roman exemplars he admired, Mocetto's image would also enjoy a reproductive afterlife in different media. When the Veronese bronze artist Andrea Riccio sculpted the Della Torre tomb monument (1516–1521) for a notable local family of doctors, for example, he turned to Mocetto, among others, for inspiration. The *Sacrifice to Asclepius* panel on the tomb—situated in the venerable San Fermo Maggiore church—was a resolutely classicist portrayal of another *suovetaurilia*, combining aspects of the triple sacrifice with visual elements from Mocetto's two engravings, especially the detailed instruments and the two men restraining a pig in the right foreground (fig. 5.6).[38]

Riccio's bronze was notable not just for its antiquarian detail, but also for its synthesis of Christian and Roman elements. Inside the image, for example, Riccio included a variety of quasi-Christian imaginative elements, not least the praying supplicant.[39] But one is left startled nonetheless by Riccio's free appropriation of pagan sacrifice for a Christian funerary monument, suggesting a certain permeability between Christian and pagan ways of honoring the special dead. He was not alone in such innovations—the painter Raphael had his tomb built inside of the Pantheon itself, a temple-turned-church whose Christian liturgical elements the painter expunged when visualizing the space ca. 1506.[40] But Riccio was bold to suggest that the sacrifices of Abraham and Abel so common in Christian art might be at least supplemented by altogether more foreign gods. Such boldness was on full display, finally, in Riccio's Paschal candelabra in the Basilica of St. Anthony in Padua, which placed a standing Christ on an altar, overseeing the sacrifice of a lamb.[41] The Last Supper and the sacrifices of the gentiles, joined at the hip.

This intimacy of Christian and Roman sacrificial visions thus created new imaginative hybrids. The association of the Eucharist with the sacrificial types of the Old Testament was common enough. But to put Christ in the same frame as Roman sacrifice was remarkable. Circa 1510, for example, the Veronese artist Galeazzo Mondella, called Moderno, cast a sumptuous silver plaquette that seated the Madonna and Christ child atop a pagan altar with a bull sacrifice engraved in relief.[42] Perhaps viewers were meant to see the victory of Christianity over the sacrifices of old, or a type of the Crucifixion. From a pictorial perspective, however, it seems no less plausible that the pagan altar served as Mary's throne, the sign of her majesty and power, just as she herself was depicted as the *sedes sapentiae* (the throne of wisdom) for the infant Christ in paintings by Duccio, Giotto, Cimabue, Hans Memling, and others. In which case, the pagan altar was the visual equivalent of the throne of Solomon, something to be embraced, not overcome.

For a final painterly experiment, let's continue in the footsteps of Fritz Saxl and observe Giovanni Bellini's *Blood of the Redeemer* (see fig. 5.7 and color plate 6). Like many in his northern Italian world, Bellini came from a background steeped in classical antiquity. His father Jacopo Bellini was an eager collector of the ancient Greco-Roman world, copying its inscriptions, coins, and images, what the traveler Ciriaco d'Ancona called the *sigilla historiarum*, the seals of history worthy of "more faith and notice than books themselves."[43] He also, like many in the powerful northern cities, looked to "Roman antique forms and motifs" in the effort to create a new Venetian Renaissance.[44] Jacopo Bellini injected Roman antique monuments, tombstones, and temples into his re-imagination of the

FIGURE 5.7. Giovanni Bellini, *Blood of the Redeemer*, ca. 1465. © National Gallery, London / Art Resource, NY.

Christian past, drawing the baptism of Christ, for example, in a landscape littered with classical ruins.[45] What Patricia Brown has called the father's "genius for accommodation and stylistic reconciliation" helped him to recreate the relationship with the pagan past, turning even pagan idols into "artifacts of history and objects of delight."[46]

Like paganism, Christianity too became an artifact of history in the son's paintings. The *Blood of the Redeemer* forced into the same frame the late medieval iconography of the Holy Blood, offered by the suffering Christ and received by the angels in the eucharistic chalice to be distributed for mankind's salvation, on the one hand. And on the other, background scenes of pagan sacrifice: an altar crowned by a sacred flame, libations celebrated by the traditional satyr with his double flute; and the self-sacrifice of Mucius Scaevola, hero of stoic fortitude and virtue, who let his hand be consumed, Livy reports, in a sacrificial fire to prove the valor of Rome.[47] The liveliness of the foreground, and the grisaille of the pagan sacrifices behind it, establish the familiar hierarchy between Christianity and its competitors. Yet their proximity also suggests a set of typological analogues between Christ and Roman sacrifice typically reserved for the Jews. The barely legible "*dis manibus*" inscribed on the altar established the link between the Paternalia and the Crucifixion, the sacrifice to the manes and the sacrament of the Mass, Christianity and paganism, as Saxl remarks, "represented as two stages of the same development, even in matters where to a less humanist believer they might seem most incompatible, namely in their view of sacrifice."[48]

Historians, finally, discovered the ruined remnants of ancient sacrifice in that pagan city whose devotion to piety and religion already Cicero had taken as emblematic of her glory.[49] The Romans were "our pagans," wrote the historian Flavio Biondo in 1459, in a work that celebrated a Rome seen by its author as a fortress guarding Christianity from the Turks who so recently conquered Constantinople.[50] Important for his arguments was the recently translated *Praeparatio evangelica* of the great patristic apologist Eusebius, whose work Biondo pillaged to paint a gloomy background against which Roman paganism might look less off-putting to a contemporary Christian reader. The Romans had abandoned the bloodthirsty cruelty of the Phoenicians, Rhodians, and Cretans—renowned since antiquity for their human sacrifice—and scrupulously devoted themselves "to religious observances (*sacra*), as of course they called them, and to religion," as Cicero observed.[51] And although Biondo did not praise the Roman pantheon, he was charitable to their *sacra*. Not only did he acknowledge a range of parallels between Christian and Roman liturgical life—similar clothes, similar kinds of offerings, similar confessions of guilt, similar prayers—but he also systematically unfolded an entire vocabulary of religious life shared among pagans and pious alike.[52] *Sanctus, sacra, religiosum, caerimoniae, adoratio, victima, sacrificare, litare, sacramentum, arcanum, immolatio*: this was just some of the lexical debt that Christianity owed to "our pagans." Immolation took its origin from the *mola*, for example, the salted meal made of ground emmer or spelt, toasted, and sprinkled on the consecrated victim.[53] More fancifully, *victima* are so called "because they fall under a strong blow (*ictae vi*) or because they are brought to the altar bound (*vinctae*)."[54] The semantic history of Christianity revealed its deep foundation in the pagan world of its birth.

Sacrificial Antiquarianism: The Curious Works of Alexandro, Vergil, and du Choul

"Nothing that has once come into existence ever goes away," wrote Sigmund Freud in 1929, captivated by the coexistence of Caesars and Popes in the Eternal City of Rome.[55] Already in the fifteenth century, humanist antiquarians had known a truth like this, known that our world bears traces of its past inscribed in literature, history, law, poetry, and the physical remains of antiquity. With specific regard to *sacrifice*, its past began to be recovered in earnest in the early decades of the sixteenth century. Its first pioneers were the antiquarians of ancient religion—Alexander ab Alexadro, Polydore Vergil, Guillaume du Choul, the heroes of Johann Stucki—who collected in miscellanies and treatises the sacrificial remains of antiquity. Their work, part philology, part history, prepared the ground for the new hybrids of theological and antiquarian learning of the later sixteenth century. For even as these erudites reconstructed the worlds of ancient religion, they also discovered the foundations of the present, binding the pagan and the Christian sacrificial imagination intimately together.

Alexander ab Alexandro. These learned explorers were, above all, *curious* about the peculiarities of ancient devotion and ways of worship. Take, for example, the Neapolitan lawyer Alexander ab Alexandro, who in 1522 published one of the era's most popular miscellanies of antiquarian learning. Hero to Stuckius, Alexandro mingled in the elite humanist circles that included Pomponio Leto, Francesco Filelfo, Flavio Biondo, Raffaele Maffei, and the other Italian erudites who collected the remains of classical antiquity. In print until well into the seventeenth century, Alexandro's *Festival Days* was loosely modeled on the *Attic Nights* of the late Roman writer Aulus Gellius, assembling anecdotes, quotations, and topical ruminations on a variety of subjects. For Alexandro, the subjects included antiquities, law, dreams, marriage, augury, ghosts, grammar, burial, cremation, bad omens, demons, and warfare. Included too were reflections on ancient sacrifice, especially among the Romans.[56]

Alexandro's reflections were occasional, not systematic. There was a chapter, for example, dedicated to "those sacrifices to the gods, in which ancient custom forbade the killing of victims or offerings (*hostiae*)." Here Alexandro seized on a single detail of Roman religious antiquity, and then assembled other details that struck him as related or simply interesting. So when Numa Pompilius—the mythical second king of Rome—instituted her temples and system of sacrifices, he excluded Terminus, the Roman god of the boundaries between fields, from the regime of blood: "it was once the custom that, in the rites of Terminus, nothing living was sacrificed, since they wanted this god, as the guardian of peace, to be exempt from slaughter."[57] Instead the ancient Romans offered cakes, flour, fruit, and salt to celebrate the rites of the fields. Similar rites, Alexandro noted, could be found across the ancient world. Pythagoras thought *only* flour, honey, fruits, and flowers should be offered in sacrifice, while the custom among the Egyptians was to offer prayer and incense, and they placated their god Serapis with herbs, wreaths, and cakes. The chapter mused on the origins of temples, and explored ancient practices of sacrificial substitution (animals, or garlic, or effigies in place of human beings), of humbling and humiliation during sacrificial rites (tears, downcast eyes, veiled heads) and a variety of other topics.

What resulted were learned rambles through ancient sacrifice, focused on curious and unusual institutions. In the days of the Roman kings, for example, the priests consulted monarchs on all things "concerning religion, sacrifices, and the ceremonies of the gods," so much so that the king assumed a quasi-sacerdotal status, "in the name of the king" offering a secular warrant for the efficacy of civic rites.[58] After the kings were vanquished, and the republic established, the sacrifices continued, now overseen by a new, purely nominal monarch, the *rex sacrorum* or *rex sacrificulus*. This special king, the only king in republican Rome, was forbidden any political role. "His power was held over matters of religion and temples alone"—he was made a lifetime member of the priestly college, subordinate only to the *pontifex maximus*, and performed a variety of ritual duties, including sacrificing a ram to Janus in January, designating days permissible (*fastus*) or prohibited (*nefastus*) for various legal and ritual activities, procuring materials for the sacrifices, including wool, wheat, fruits, herbs, and so forth.[59] Like the Roman rite of Lupercalia—where young men, anointed with the blood of the sacrifice, ran naked around the Palatine hill—or the bulls offered in the Alban hills in the ancient Latin festivals of confederation, the *rex sacrificulus* was interesting precisely because it was so bizarre.[60]

Only occasionally did Alexandro attempt anything systematic. His chapter on blood sacrifice, for example, occasioned the observation that, in many ancient cultures, "when [the priest] sacrifices to the gods, and performs sacred acts, he is first cleansed by washing his body, and abstains from Venus."[61] Examples included Romans (who abstain from meat), Egyptians (who cleanse themselves with water), the Samnites (who cut off their penises), and the gymnosophists (who eat only fruit, rice, and grain). Ascetic practices like this were, he noted, part of a wider regulation of purity around sacred sites and practices. Swineherds, servants, slaves, women, menstruating women, murderers, lepers: depending on the religious tradition, any of these might pollute, and must thus be excluded from, the sacrifices.

Such moments were unusual, however. Alexandro was more interested in, for example, the various plants used to decorate ancient altars (oak, laurel, olives, myrtle, ivy, heliochrysum, hyacinth, cinnamon, and papyrus flowers) than he was in systematic inquiry.[62] This cheerful curiosity about the gentile world disappeared only once in the *Festival Day*, when he reflected on the barbarity of the ancients.

> If we endeavor to lay out barbarian and foreign ceremonies and examine their SACRIFICES, what impious cults and unspeakable rituals will we discover in the different rites [found] among so many of the savage nations? The Scythotauri immolated foreigners as sacrifices to Diana; the Laodiceans, a virgin to Athena; the Arcadians, a young body to Zeus Lykaios. Near Borysthenes there were many people who, in their insanity, used to offer men and worship human bones in the sacrifices to their gods. The Blemmyae, the Cimbri, the Gauls, the Druids, & the Germans, on appointed days, sacrifice human victims, and smear their altars with blood of their captives.[63]

Phoenicians, Carthaginians, Rhodians, Cretans, Spartans, Celts, and Albanians were just a few of the ancient peoples who murdered in the name of piety. Burning and burying alive, beating, evisceration, strangling, decapitation: the crimes were legion. Their vanity, superstition, and cruelty served as the gloomy background, however, against which the light of Christ shone so bright. The barbarous rites of the gentiles made clear, the book concluded, "how much we owe to Christ, our lord, king, and physician."[64]

Polydore Vergil. Such criticisms of the gentiles were rare in the *Festival Days*, however. The same was true of Polydore Vergil (1470?–1555), another of Stucki's inspirations. An Italian who moved to England in 1502 as a representative of the papal court, Vergil spent the next fifty years there, serving the church, writing history, and mingling with the great humanists of the age, including Thomas More and John Colet.[65] His ticket to these lofty circles was a work called *On the Discovery of Things* (1499), which explored the origins of the gentile gods and institutions. The invention of gentile *sacrifice*, as Vergil discovered, was confusing. The Greek historian Herodotus discovered its paternity among the Egyptians, but according to Diodorus Siculus, it was the Ethiopians who "invented the rites, processions, gatherings and other activities that pay honor to the gods."[66] The Christian father Lactantius, however, taught "that Melissus, king of the Cretans, first made sacrifice to the gods." Others believed that Janus "showed how to worship the gods," but among the Romans, Numa Pompilius was said to found the rites and ceremonies. The church historian Eusebius argued *both* that Cadmus, "son of Agenor, first of all brought the mysteries and rituals of the gods . . . from Phoenicia to Greece" and that "Double-formed Cecrops, first of all called upon Jupiter, invented statues, set up an altar and immolated victims, none of which had ever before been seen in Greece."[67] Nor were pagans the only ones with claims on paternity. Cain and Abel "first made sacrifice to the omnipotent God whom we Christians worship," Vergil noted, while Eusebius and Jerome credit Enosh, who "first called on the name of the Lord" (Gen. 4.26). After Enosh, the Israelites "made sacrifice without initiation in any rites until God established the priesthood" with Aaron.[68]

In the 1499 edition of *On Discovery*, the origins of sacrifice were confusing, but untroubling. In 1521, however, Vergil published—with the help of Erasmus—a new and expanded edition of the work, now including the invention of *Christian* things.[69] This work raised more challenging questions about the ancient gods and their Christian replacement. Whatever the discontinuity between the reign of Saturn and Jesus, the *institutions*—priesthood, prayer, altar, and, crucially, sacrifice—endured. Vergil's hope was, he wrote in his introduction, to show "how the ancient Fathers of the Church, piously and for good reasons, accepted many of the religious rites inherited from the past."[70]

With Christianity in the picture, Vergil changed his focus. No longer satisfied with mere collection, now he sought to *explain* historical and religious transformations too. Like his friend Erasmus, Vergil turned to "accommodation," that tested strategy for blunting concerns about similarities between the pious and the profane. Rooted in the exegetical principle that Scriptures speak the language of man—*Scriptura humane loquitur*—accommodation insisted that the Bible talked in different ways to different people.[71] God did not *actually* repent that he made Saul king (1 Sam. 15.11), but Scripture uses the expression to accommodate a human way of understanding divine mysteries. The exegetical principle became a general strategy for mitigating ritual dissonance already among rabbinic authors, who, after the destruction of the second Temple and the end of Jewish sacrifice, began to describe the sacrifices as an unnecessary, "divine concession to polytheistic customs," rather than commandment.[72] Later, for Gregory the Great, accommodation became an important tool of the Christian missionary confronting gentile blood rites. Since the pagan Franks "are accustomed to killing many oxen while sacrificing to their demons, some solemn rites should be changed for them over this matter," he wrote in 601: "it is impossible to cut away everything at the same time from hardened minds, because anyone who strives to ascend to the highest place, relies on ladders or steps."[73] Like Gregory, then, Vergil buried the continuities between Jupiter and Jesus in the soft folds of charity, Christian hands outstretched to assist the barbarians up the ladder of salvation.

Accommodation enabled all sorts of intimacies between Christian and pagan things. Vergil's inquiry into Christian origins, for example, included a chapter on the ancient Roman priesthood. Like Alexandro, he was curious about the Roman *rex sacrificulus*, and how, "after the Kings were expelled from Rome, the Romans ordered that a king in charge of sacrifices be elected . . . so that they would in no way miss the sacrifices previously performed by the kings." Unlike Alexandro, however, he *connected* this *rex sacrificulus* to Christianity: Rome's priestly hierarchy, topped by a *pontifex maximus*, was a portent that "the city of Rome . . . would rule by pontifical authority." The chapter on Christian origins also explored other ancient Roman sacrificial customs, including the Terminalia festivals, which "celebrated the boundary markers set in the field" with bloodless sacrifices of cakes; the Lectisternium Festival, which included sacrificial rituals to the dark gods of the underworld; the banquets and sacrifices held during the *Taurilia* games; the Apollonian games, where oxen and goats were crowned in gold before their immolation; the way the Romans reclined on couches, holding sacrificial banquets in honor of Jupiter, Juno, and Minerva; and the familiar *suovetaurilia* festivals, with its triple sacrifice of "the bull, the ram and the boar." Such rites and ceremonies were at best superstitious, and at worst, "the works of evil demons." And yet, however dark their origins, Vergil concluded, "these were the beginnings of their sacred rites, *many of which we Christians have adopted*."[74]

Even human sacrifice, in this account, was an intimate of the Christian imagination. In between chapters on ancient Jewish sacrifice and the Christian Eucharist, Vergil inserted a survey of ancient barbarism:

> Oh, man's folly; oh, sad life! Who were these gods who defiled their worshipers by turning them into murderers and who generally brought harm to all? The father killed his only son, the mother the beloved daughter: sacrificing them like sheep to the demons. The Jews . . . used to offer their children and sacrifice to the demon Moloch by burning them. The Rhodians offered men in sacrifice to Saturn. On the island of Salamis it was customary to sacrifice a man in honor of Aglauros, daughter of Cecrops. In the Temple of Pallas, which was shared by Diomedes and Aglauros, they used to offer in sacrifice a man to Diomedes who, after being led three times around the altar by young people, was finally struck with an ax by the priest and placed in the pyre to burn.[75]

What followed was a vast geography of murder. In Rome, humans were sacrificed to Saturn, or thrown in the Tiber. The Carthaginians too killed in service of Saturn, and in one orgy of bloodletting, "offered in sacrifice to hundred of their noblest children . . . the cruelest act ever done since the beginning of mankind."[76] The Cypriots, the Gauls, the Egyptians, the Spartans, the Phoenicians, the Cretans, the Arabs, the Scythians: the ancient world was filled with such bloody altars.

Of course, Vergil found such rites a repulsive contrast to Christianity. Yet he made them fellow travelers in the sacrificial imagination. The entire Christian liturgical ceremony, with its "adoration and the honoring of God," was a "ritual of sacrifice." Although, he noted, "there are those who believe that the Eucharist instituted by Christ should not rightfully be called the sacrifice," nonetheless, "because from the beginning of its use, according to Tertullian, it was called sacrifice, we therefore want to observe this custom of religion." Christ "offered his body and blood so that each of [his apostles] would partake of it; and He commanded that such a sacrifice be made from then on in his memory."[77] After the crucifixion, Vergil reported, Christian sacrifice grew ever more complex. Worshipers were asked to stand and bow at the Mass at the behest of Pope Anastasius I (ca. 400); burning incense on the altar, the inheritance of Jews and Gentiles alike, became part of the sacrificial rite under Leo III (ca. 800);

washing the hands, a custom handed down either from the Jews or the Gentiles, Vergil remarked, entered Christian sacrifice later as well, as did new songs, new liturgical texts, the kiss of peace, and the priestly blessings. And finally, the chapter concluded:

> The practice of the priest at the altar to turn often toward the congregation and say "Dominus vobiscum" was clearly taken from the ceremonies of the Jews, whose priest, while performing his sacrifices, returned to the people, sprinkling the blood of the animal offered in sacrifice; which, according to the testimony of Apuleius, the priests of the Gentiles used to do in particular when they were giving divine replies, pretending to be moved by spirits. From this it is certainly clear that we have taken either from the Jews or the pagans the custom of turning around at the altar and facing the congregation.[78]

Vergil had no doubt about the superiority of the Gospels. Yet he thought Christianity flexible enough to incorporate heterogeneous ritual elements. He had no problem, therefore, explaining how the birthdays of the martyrs had roots in the funeral festivals of the Romans. After all, the latter had themselves adapted them from the Persians "where each person celebrated the day of his birth by offering many sacrifices and lavish meals." The concluding words to the Mass, *Ita missa es*, Vergil attributed to sacrificial ceremonies for the goddess Isis, brought to conclusion, according to Apuleius, by the Greek words *laois aphesis*, "which signified that it was now lawful for the ships to depart."[79] The origins of things were, for Christians and pagans alike, plural and heteronomous. No tradition—Vergil's message might be—can guarantee its own autonomy.

Guillaume du Choul. The intimacy of Rome and Christianity was no less fascinating for Guillaume du Choul, another luminary for our Swiss theologian Stucki. Du Choul was a fixture in the intellectual life of Renaissance Lyon, second city of France and center of humanist learning. He was also somewhat a man out of time. The 1550s in Lyon were a time of intense confessional strife, seething with the religious antagonisms that nearly destroyed France over decades of civil war. But du Choul turned his back on religious conflict, for the joys of antiquarian research. His greatest work, the *Discourse on the Religion of the Ancient Romans*, was issued by Guillaume Rouillé, the great "merchant-publisher" of the city, and intended as a contribution to an ambitious twelve-volume study of the antiquities of Rome.[80] It appeared in more than a dozen editions in French, Spanish, Latin, Italian, and Dutch, and it featured lavish illustrations of pagan religious life based on physical antiquities, above all coins, reliefs, and other objects. Through images like these, du Choul sought to recreate the totality of Roman "religion," that is, "the temples of the gods, the signs of their religion, & the priests, ceremonies, and the sacrifices."[81] Thus he wrote:

If it should be asked why the ancients began to sacrifice, I would reply that was for three reasons. First, to honor God; the second, for the utility of the sacrificer, who requests the health thought to belong to divine goods; & the third, to ask God's pardon for his faults, that he might become better in the future, & that he might receive medicine for a languishing soul. And in all of their sacrifices the priests began first with immolation, that is to say, sacrificing the victim, after having put on the front of the beast who is to be killed, a mixture of wheat, roasted barley [actually, spelt], and salt that was called *Mola*, which the ancients used in their sacrifices.[82]

Like Alexandro before him, du Choul had little interest in a *theory* of sacrifice. There were common elements to sacrificial practice—desires to honor the deity, to bring benefits to the sacrificer, to ask for pardon, and so on. But what really fascinated him was the mixture of wheat, spelt, and salt called *mola* that the Romans tossed on sacrificial beasts. His work patiently explored objects and practices like these, describing rather than analyzing the world of Roman sacrifice.

The sacrificial rite began long before knives flashed at the altar, for example. The purification of the sacrificial assistants with the *aspergillus*, the entry into the temples with their holy water vessels, the floral decorations on sacrificial altars, and the priestly vestments and hairstyles: du Choul set an elaborate ritual scene before the main act began. The immolation itself was a carefully wrought, formal ceremony. If the victim was a large one, it was marched with "gilded brow and horns, supplemented with small beads, and golden rosaries (*patenotres*)"; if a small one, it was "crowned with tree branches, which are dedicated to the God to whom the sacrifice was made."[83] Priests were attentive to the demeanor of the victim: if the victim struggled, it augured poorly, and the sacrifice would be halted. Docile victims indicated divine benevolence, by contrast, and good fortune to come.

Du Choul exhibited the drama of Roman sacrificial ritual with elegant reproductions of ancient art: the engravings on Trajan's column erected to celebrate the Emperor's victory in the Dacian wars (fig. 5.8) or a scene enlarged from a coin depicting the so-called secular games, a three-day festival of sacrifice re-established by the Emperor Augustus (fig. 5.9).[84] The sights, sounds, and smells of the sacrificial rite are captured in these elegant engravings, and some of their purposes too: the lustration of the

FIGURE 5.8. Scene from Trajan's column. Guillaume du Choul, *Discours de la religion des anciens Romaines* (Lyon, 1556). Courtesy of the Staats- und Universitätsbibliothek Dresden.

Roman army during war, the libations offered by priests and emperors, and the sacrifices held in celebration of the passing of the saeculum. Ancient sacrifice came alive in du Choul's hands, readers lead through its complex flows from beginning to the end when, "the sacred things are done, and the ceremonies complete, priest would say the last words . . . that is to say, *I licet*, to show that it is time to leave."[85]

Like Vergil, or the earlier artists and writers working in "sunlit years of fifteenth-century syncretism," du Choul also invited the ancient gentiles directly into the story of Christianity, embracing the resemblances between pagan ancients and Christian moderns.[86] The *I licet* with which Romans concluded their sacrifices, for example, found its analogue in Christianity, du Choul observed, when "our priests say at the end of the divine service, *Ita missa est*. And the phrase lets those attending the sacrifice know that it is time to leave."[87] "The flamine or the priest performing the sacrifice was dressed in a garment of pure linen, & white, which the Latins called *Alba vestis*, and common people an alb; because the color white is pleasing to God," he wrote, just as "today our priests in the ceremony of their sacrifices are dressed in white linens."[88] There were parallels throughout the ritual:

FIGURE 5.9. Sacrifice of the secular games of Augustus. Guillaume du Choul, *Discours de la religion des anciens Romains* (Lyon, 1556). Courtesy of the Staats- und Universitätsbibliothek Dresden. CC BY-SA 4.0.

in the holy water vessels, the orientation of the priest toward the east, the priestly covering of the mouth, the use of fire in the ceremonies, their occurrence in the morning, the distribution of food after the ceremonies, and more.

Du Choul not only offered what David Lupher has aptly termed a theory of "pagan survivals" in modern Christianity, he even embraced direct transference from the gentile to the Christian world.[89] The use of linens, for example, "was transferred (*translatée*) from Egyptian priests, who made their habits of a beautiful linen."[90] The Romans blessed the image of Jove's thunderbolt to ward off storms, and "that which the Gentiles did in their ridiculous superstition, we transferred to our Christian religion, when we consecrate and bless our little *Agnus dei* and our bells, which in this way assume the power to protect against storms and bad weather."[91] And in a final observation stolen nearly verbatim from the fifteenth-century Bolognese scholar Filippo Beroaldo, du Choul noted that, "if we observe carefully, we shall recognize that many institutions of our religion have been taken and transferred from the ceremonies of the Egyptians, and the gentiles: like the tunics and surplices, the tonsures that the priests wear, the bowing of the head around the altar, the sacrificial pomp, the temple music, the adorations, prayers, and supplications, the processions, and the litanies: and many other things which our priests take over (*usurpent*) for our mysteries."[92]

This last remark was extraordinary. From the ancient fathers to Calvin, Christians had made "pagan survival" a political and theological insult of high order. But like Moderno, Riccio, and Bellini before him, du Choul waved off the threat of paganism to piety. Like Flavio Biondo, du Choul saw the Romans as "ours," different from but intricately woven into the world of Christianity. The survival of paganism was, for him, hardly something to lament.

"Humanism is a stream into which flow all the waters of the past, mingling the most diverse forms and ideas," wrote Jean Seznec in 1953.[93] In literature, painting, and sculpture, and antiquarian study, humanist artists and scholars throughout much of the fifteenth and early sixteenth centuries freely experimented with the ancient gods and their sacrifices. As in the Middle Ages, ancient Greece and Rome provided the overwhelming majority of the materials relevant to these experiments, unsurprisingly, given the linguistic limits on the horizon of the "antique" in the period. But this horizon broadened over the period too, as new texts from the classical and Christian world came to supplement traditional authorities like Homer, Ovid, and Vergil. Collectors of antiquities like Alexandro, Vergil, and du

Choul tried to organize this ancient record, collecting fragments of ancient religions and their sacrifices, and compiling them for future generations. These writers were unafraid of the Greco-Roman sacrificial imagination, moreover, feeling little need to contrast paganism with the limpid piety of Christ and his martyrs. This experiment with antique sacrifice—this willingness to set pagan sacrifice into Christian devotional art, to observe casually Roman sacrificial benedictions behind the final words of the Mass, and so forth—was freer than it ever had been in the late antique world, or than it would become in the later sixteenth century.

Per Modum Negandi: Toward a System of Sacrifice

By 1548, when the Italian scholar Lilio Gregorio Giraldi (1479–1552) published his *History of the Gentile Gods*, this free atmosphere of experiment had, with relatively few exceptions, withered. Europe was a scene of large-scale and bloody warfare; the images and icons of an older Christianity destroyed or defended; a new cult of the martyrs growing among besieged religious minorities; the Bible translated anew; and the history of Christianity become an object of endless strife and struggle. In 1548 too, not far from where Giraldi lived in Ferrara, a great church council began to convene in Trent, a meeting that helped to consolidate the confessional divisions in European religious life.

For all that, the last of Stucki's guides to the ancient sacrificial past waged no explicit war on behalf of Rome, nor defended her ceremonies against Protestant vitriol. Rather, like the other popular Italian mythographies of its age, Giraldi's *History of the Gentile Gods* was a playground for those curious about the ancient Greco-Roman pantheon.[94] Giraldi was uniquely interested in sacrifice, however, appending to the end of his work a short treatise entitled simply *On Sacrifices*. Thre is some mystery about its composition. Giraldi had a colorful career, losing all of his books in the 1527 sack of Rome, losing his patron Gianfrancesco Pico della Mirandola in 1533 to assassination, bedridden from gout in Ferrara. Despite this, he remained a tireless collector of pagan antiquity, and among the first things he took up after fleeing Rome was ancient sacrifice. It was in this period, ca. 1538–39, that he likely composed his *libellus*, possibly publishing it (no known exemplars remain, however) in conjunction with his work on ancient burial, *De sepulchris & vario sepeliendi ritu* (1539).[95]

For a small book, it had a grander ambition, namely to collect and *organize* the words, the actions, and the intentions that together constituted the complex phenomenon that Giraldi (and, to a certain extent, also we) call sacrifice. His *libellus* was not just a hodgepodge of curious details, in other words. It was a *systematic* work that explored "where, by whom, what kind, how, and when, were the sacred rites (*sacra*) that the Gentiles rendered to their gods."[96] This effort to conceptualize sacrifice as a total phenomenon, "*in universum & per partes*," as Giraldi wrote,[97] represented a new phase in the sacrificial imagination, a new phase that emerged in the twilight of syncretism, when confessional tensions made the *very nature of Christianity* a subject of urgent concern. It was in this new age that curiosity gave way to system, syncretism abandoned for what we will call the method of negation.

Admittedly, from a modern perspective, the Italian scholar's treatise does not feel especially systematic. It has no generic explanation for why apparently all humans sacrifice, what a sacrifice is supposed to accomplish, or the impact that sacrifices might have on religion, culture, society, or politics. Like his humanist ancestors, Giraldi was interested in the *details*. Sacrifice was, he wrote:

> every duty toward the gods solemnly performed for the purpose of carrying out divine matters (*rei divinae faciendae*). Thus the word *sacrificare*, which (as Socrates said in the Euthyphro) meant to offer tribute (*munera*) to the gods: in order to make a vow, [or] to beseech the gods . . . Heraclitus in fact called sacrifice medicines, which can purge the soul of illness. A sacrifice, said Isidore, is a victim, & whatever things are burned or placed on an altar . . . It was called immolation by the ancients, from *mola* . . . or, as Isidore thought, because the victim was slain after being placed on the wall of the altar (*mole altaris*) . . . But in truth we call a sacrifice something sacred: to perform a sacred rite (*sacra facere*) . . . Some sacrifices were public, which were performed on behalf of people: these were also called popular sacrifices, as Labeo says, which all citizens performed . . . Others were private, which were done for individuals or families.[98]

As Giraldi saw it, a sacrifice could be a variety of things: a medicine, a victim, a sacred action, a gift or tribute. Different ancient authorities offered different views—from the philosophical perspective of Socrates to the naturalist views of Heraclitus to the more theological outlook of Isidore of Seville. Giraldi had little interest in settling the differences though. Like others of his tribe, he was fascinated by *particulars* of ancient sacrifice, and cast his net widely for the minutiae of Greek, Roman, Egyptian, Persian, and even Indians' religious devotions.

But now that these minutiae were *organized*, the miscellany became the treatise. Take, for example, Giraldi's discussion of the *where* of sacrifice. Above all, offerings happened in temples, the "*diversoria deorum*," the inns of the gods. Although some of the ancients—Persians, Germans, and various barbarians—thought the world fit enough to serve as temple to the gods, most peoples housed the divine in special places. "Having put off their barbarism," and begun to know the gods, primitive man thought it only fit to build beautiful buildings for them. Yet it was hard to say who first built a temple. Some said the gods themselves founded them—Janus or Dionysus. Others attributed their origins to particular peoples—the Cretans or the Phoenicians. Still others had a more functional explanation: "many think that temples have their beginnings in tombs," Giraldi wrote, with reference to his own earlier work on tombs and burials. Temples had specific locations depending on the gods they served, some inside the city walls, some on seashores, some on mountaintops. They had various shapes and particular spatial orientations, and could serve different functions: "the asylum was a certain kind of temple, from which no one could be removed . . . this was not the case for all temples, only those permitted by a law of consecration." Inside of the temple was, characteristically, an altar (*ara*), called such either from the "pure open spaces" (*purae areae*) or from the handles (*ansas*) gripped by the sacrificers, or even possibly because of the burning (*ardere*) of victims. And the altars themselves were ornamented in specific ways: "to Jove, with oak; to Apollo, with laurel; to Minerva, with olive; to Venus, with myrtle; to Hercules with poplar; to Bacchus, with ivy." Finally, the altars typically shared the temple space with statues, whose inventors Giraldi again addressed and whose multiform materials he laboriously documented.[99]

What had been distributed across earlier miscellaneous works was now, in short, ordered in a cohesive fashion. The "where" of sacrifice invited readers to understand the organization of sacred spaces in the ancient world, from altars to temples to tombs. Curious readers learned who was involved in sacrifices, and what they wore; to whom the sacrifices were made; what prayers were said during the offerings; what kinds of things were offered, to whom, and when; what the sacrifices were supposed to accomplish; what the festivals were in which the sacrifices were made; and much more.

Sacrifice thus supplied a deep structure to ancient pagan religions. The ancient (principally Roman) priesthood could be understood with reference to its different sacrificial roles; the all-important institution of augury too took shape around sacrifice; the festival calendar was, for Giraldi, a sacrificial calendar. Sacrifice organized the ancient treatment of the dead, both in terms of practical issues like burial and in terms of the divine beings awaiting the arrival of the dead in the underworld. Sacrifice even made sense of the ancient way of war. Giraldi paid special attention to the ritual of devotion, for example, in which Roman soldiers dedicated themselves, or an enemy, to the gods of the underworld:

> Father Dis, Veiovis, Manes, or by whatever other name it is right to call you . . . I dedicate and curse [our enemies] in place of the Roman people, our armies and legions, that you might vouchsafe the wellbeing of myself, my duty and command, our legions and our army on this campaign. If you do these things so that I know and understand them, then whoever has made this vow, wherever he has made it, may the appropriate action be performed with three black sheep.

Reprinting the oath of devotion found in Macrobius's *Saturnalia*, Giraldi commented that such devotions "were done not only in Italy, but also beyond it."[100] Around sacrifice, then, gathered all of the central features of the pagan religious—and even secular—imagination.

Unlike its predecessors, Giraldi *refused* to connect this sacrificial world with Christianity. A passionate confession opened the book: "I worship and venerate the one God (*unum Deum*), who, by his word commanded, by his reason arranged, and by his might was able to create from nothing this whole fabric [of the world] with all its equipment of elements, bodies, and spirits."[101] However sincere, this confession was also a defense against those, as Giraldi complained in the first words of the *Historia*, "who call themselves theologians" and believe the *studia humanitatis* inappropriate for the "true and sincere cultivator of Christian piety and religion."[102] To make this point even clearer, Giraldi recycled his confession directly from the Latin father Tertullian, one of the most energetic antagonists of *alienos deos* in the ancient world. Tertullian's confession was made in his *Apology* (late second century), a "demonstration of our religion" against the calumnies of the pagans.[103] But for Giraldi, the confession worked in an opposite fashion. It defended his interest in the *pagans* in a world of confessional strife.

Doubtless this confession sheltered him against accusations of impious curiosity. But it scored a bright line between the *unum Deum* and the *alienos deos* that would be the subject of Giraldi's *History*. "Dionysius, Eusebius, and the others rightly defined God in the negative (*per modum negandi*)," wrote Giraldi in his preface.[104] And so from the outset, he insisted that his work had nothing to say about Christian, or even Hebrew, antiquities:

> But when we discuss those who thought they were first to worship the gods, I deliberately remain silent about those things related in Hebrew, and our own, sacred history, lest I should let the most limpid spring flow into a sewer (*ne fontanam limpidissimam cloacae intermitterem*).[105]

The comparisons common in someone like Polydore Vergil were thus rare in the *History*. Giraldi did allow briefly as to the similarity between the Roman *I licet* and the Christian *Ita Missa Est*, and could not fail to mention that the word pontiff had a gentile origin. But he noted these in passing, moving on quickly "lest we mix the sacred and the profane."[106]

To illustrate this profanity, Giraldi reserved his one explicit reference to Christ, his Crucifixion, and the Eucharist for a final diatribe against the most "wicked and impious rites" of the gentiles and heathens.[107] There he offered a world-spanning geography of human sacrifice. The Scythians in the north sacrificed enemies, and those with the misfortune to shipwreck on their shores, to Diana; in far off Thule, victims were sacrificed to Mars. The Germans, the Druids, the Gauls, the Phoenicians, the Carthaginians, the Albanians, the Cretans, the British, the Romans, the Greeks: murderous sacrifice was everywhere. Even in the Americas—virtually Giraldi's only reference to the new world discovered "a few years ago . . . by Spanish sailors"—people "sacrificed infants and children to their gods, imprisoning and cruelly burning them inside the hollows of their statues and idols."[108] But "enough of this," his book concluded, "thus we give thanks to CHRIST, who, in order to free us from such foul and savage rites, instituted the life giving sacrifice of the Eucharist, which we offer daily to God his Father: who lives and reigns with the Father and Holy Spirit, through the world without end. Amen."[109]

Giraldi, therefore, was a more evident heir to patristic imagination than his earlier humanist predecessors. Not only was he deeply learned in the anti-pagan literature of the church fathers, but he was also committed to their sharp distinction between the *unum Deum* and the *alienos deos*. This may have been for strategic reasons. Interest in the wisdom secreted beneath pagan superstition, or in continuities between pagan and Christian ways of worship, was far riskier in the mid-sixteenth century than it had been fifty years earlier. Minimally Giraldi needed to guard against the suspicions of the "many theologians" who could have charged him with serving as a useful idiot for Protestants all too happy to discover the paganism lurking in Catholic Christianity. His *modus negandi* was thus characterized by a discrete silence about virtually anything Christian at all. "About our sacrifices, that is those of Christians and Hebrews," Giraldi firmly insisted, "I will report nothing beyond the minimal (*parergos*)."[110]

The *modus negandi* thus played a curious role in the history of the sacrificial imagination. In the first instance, it was clearly a product of new confessional constraints on research and scholarship. Giraldi was born in 1479, long before the Reformation shattered European Christianity, and he never shared the zeal for polemic so prevalent in the republic of letters of his later years. Nonetheless, by the 1540s, he had neither the ability nor perhaps the desire to experiment with syncretism. He simply set aside Christianity as an object of comparative interest, sharply distinguishing between the sacrificial rites of the gentiles and those of the Christians.

This "setting aside," however, enabled the construction of a synthetic picture of sacrifice as a total religious phenomenon. These were, in fact, two sides of the same coin. It was precisely *in order to* clarify the distinction between gentile and Christian that sacrifice was systematized, and made into the organizing principle of gentile religion. For its first six hundred pages, the *History of the Gentile Gods* explored a pantheon of exclusively pagan deities, with no fear lest it tread onto Christian toes. In its final chapter, Giraldi entered more perilous terrain, that zone of indistinction between Christian and gentile so long represented by sacrifice. It was as if, then, by organizing gentile sacrifice—and allowing it to become a coordinating system for gentile religion writ large—one could both understand gentile religion as an autonomous system *and* better see the difference between pagans and Christians. For this reason, we suspect, Giraldi reserved the most bloodthirsty of pagan rites for his concluding climax of the work, the difference he took to be evident between murder and the Eucharist confirming at last the radical distinction between superstition and piety.

Apophatic Antiquarianism

In the years after Giraldi's death, the counter-Reformation Church worked tirelessly to sharpen the distinctions between ancient paganism and the Christianity that emerged from it. An enormous project of Christianization began, especially in Rome where scholars were called on to document the ancient presence of Peter, to sort out Christian from pagan burial sites, to discover and later excavate ancient churches and papal houses, and to put an end to the loosely syncretic projects of people like Flavio Biondo. Giraldi was born a generation too early to participate in these

Church-sanctioned and -supported antiquarian enterprises, writing at precisely the moment when the Church had not yet determined either its theological or historical response to the furious attacks of the Protestant reformers. Among Protestants, however, theology and historical scholarship had been working hand-in-hand from the beginning. All of the giants of the early Reformation told new histories of Christianity, to show both how the Church strayed from righteousness and how a pious remnant preserved the memory of Christ. By the time that our Swiss theologian Johann Stucki took up his pen to write the *Sacrorum sacrificiorumque gentilium brevis et accurate descriptio*, then, it had long been clear that the ancient past had something to say to matters theological.

Yet few imagined quite how much. If early reformers started with doctrine and then turned to history, Stucki reversed the order, approaching theology from the world of erudition. His *Description* was published as an appendix to *the* late Renaissance text on ancient pagan feasting, for example, his *Antiquitatum convivialium libri III* (1582).[111] This latter work explored the ancient customs of banqueting, promising attention to all their "grammatical, physical, medical, ethical, economic, political, philosophical, and historical" details, not to mention customs still observed among Christians today.[112] It was in the *Antiquitatum convivialium* that Stucki first noted how powerfully meals and sacrifices—the Last Supper in both its culinary and its soteriological aspects—were associated in the ancient world. Was not the entire Mosaic law, he asked in his introduction, made up largely of culinary matters (*re cibaria*)? And were not its many sacrifices also "sacred feasts," its offerings also prophecies of the "only food fit for the good of our souls," the sacred food of body and blood that Christ offered on the Cross and that Christians enjoy in holy communion?[113] What would become a truism of late nineteenth century anthropology (see chapter 11) emerged, as Marc Kolakowski notes, for the first time at the end of the sixteenth century.[114]

More generally, Stucki converted a "practice of erudition [into] a practice of piety."[115] It was this transformation that made possible what we will here call *apophatic antiquarianism*. What is the use of writing so much, Stucki asked, "about those ancient idols, sacrifices, ceremonies, and superstitions of the Gentiles, the memory of which it seems should not only be unrenewed, but also buried and abolished forever?"[116] Christians need to know their ancient foes, he answered, because:

> we find almost no page in Scripture, above all in the Old Testament, in which the idols, foreign gods, high places, altars, temples, and the

> sacrifices of the gentiles are *not* mentioned. How, I ask, will a preacher or theologian be able to offer an intelligent and skillful explanation in these countless places? how will he apply them to the mores and customs of our times, unless he understands the idolatrous rites and ceremonies of those times?[117]

Whatever else they were, the sacrifices of the ancients unlocked the hermeneutical puzzles of Scripture, without which the text might not speak, as he remarked, to the "mores and customs of our times." Apophatic antiquarianism—the "antithetical model" of erudition that showed what *Christianity was not*—was, for Stucki, the sine qua non for theologians hoping to make sense of the world of Scripture and translate it for modern Christians.[118]

Even more emphatically than Giraldi, then, Stucki stressed the value of antiquarianism's *modus negandi*. Research on gentile religion offered the illumination of the "contrast of opposites": "the excellence and dignity of the true Religion becomes clearer and more manifest by comparison with superstition and idolatry," he remarked.[119] The contrast of opposites was, moreover, more than simply a list of differences. Stucki wanted to *explain* these differences too.

Unlike Giraldi, for example, Stucki was ever alert to the psychology of superstition, the economy of desires and fears that structured the errors of the ancients. "Even in the rudest and hellish fog of those errors and superstitions of the gentiles, certain clear and shining sparks (*scintillulae*) of truth shone forth." Stucki wrote:

> Thus, for example, even in their dreadful and damnable human sacrifices, the gentiles showed clearly that they knew that there was a God (*Numen*), and that it should be worshiped, and that it could not be finally placated except by a human victim, and that man could be expiated from sin by Him. . . . We Christians surely know and believe, that this victim is Christ, who offered not men, not goats, not first fruits, but himself on the altar of the Cross for the salvation of the human race.[120]

The errors of the gentiles teach that natural man, bereft of revelation and sunken in sin, knew there was a God, felt the psychological weight of sin, knew the sin must be expiated, knew that sacrifice was, in the end, the only thing that could alleviate his awful burden. The gentiles teach, as well, about piety: their error "kindles and inflames" our zeal for the true God, he wrote. Like the Jews, who show Christians their liberation from the burden of useless ceremony, the pagans demonstrate just how much

Christians gain by their affection for the "Sun of Justice," who relieved them from a world of violence and passion. And, finally, the pagans teach Christians about devotion. If the gentiles could dedicate themselves "night and day" to their vain superstitions, "how much more should we turn our days and nights, with enthusiasm, diligent zeal, and attention, to the real, genuine, and saving worship of the one true God?"[121]

This Protestant *modus negandi* was a pathway to new forms of comparison, toward what Kolakowski calls the "history of religion" more generally. Already in his 1582 *Antiquitatum convivialis*, Stucki began to develop a form of functionalism.[122] All ancient peoples observed important political and social endeavors with ceremonies. Treaties and contracts, in particular, were "initiated, established, and confirmed both with ceremonies, libations, and sacrifices, and with banquets." The tight bond between sacrificial banquets and treaty-making ran through the ancient world. Among the Hebrews, it was seen in the "blood of the covenant" that Moses spattered on Israel before his reception of the Law on Mount Sinai (Exod. 24.8). The Greek word *sponde* was a drink-offering, which in the plural, *spondai*, meant a treaty or a truce, and it was common to seal covenants with a sacrificial offering. This tradition of the drink offering Stucki traced to the Germans, the Persians, the Scythians, and other peoples. Bloodier rites were also common. The Romans, testified Festus, "were accustomed to seal their covenants by killing pigs." Others—like the Scythians, Armenians, and the "princes of the Saracens"—ratified their treaty by drawing and drinking blood. But the most common materials for sealing social and political bonds were salt and bread. Salt was a ubiquitous "symbol of peace, love, and friendship": Leviticus instructed Israel not to "let the salt of the covenant with your God to be lacking from your cereal offering" (2.13); the gospel of Mark (in some redactions) reported that "every sacrifice shall be salted with salt" (9.49); while Pliny told that "there is no sacrifice without the salted mola." And bread, "the sacrament of friendship (*mysterium . . . amicitiae*)," was held in high ritual regard among the Macedonians and Pythagoreans. And of course, among Christians, for whom the "mystical bread of the Lord's Supper" offered the federative feast par excellence, a feast "in which Christians, partly by the outward and physical eating of the bread and wine, and partly through communion by faith in the same spiritual body and blood of Christ, are joined together with God, and with each other, in a sacrosanct and imperishable bond." What could be "more sacred, more religious, more august" than the Lord's Supper, the perfect conjunction of sacrifice and feast?[123]

This was not a story of transference or syncretism. It was inconceivable for Stucki, as Kolakowski notes, that "Christian sacrifice derived from the gentiles."[124] Stucki instead took what we might characterize as a structural approach. What interested him were the *purposes* that different ritual behaviors, and ritual materials, served among various groups. Blood, bread, salt: all were agents of social bonding, symbols of friendship, markers of the desire for peace and comity. *Why* these apparently arbitrary things served such important functions was, of course, unveiled by the revealed word of God. As such, these were *scintillulae* of truth scattered among those deprived of the Word, that deep truth that organized the immense variety of ancient religious customs. There are patterns behind the wild diversity of beliefs and behaviors, in other words, patterns that theological antiquarians can make visible, and therefore useful, to the Christian reader today.

The project of apophatic antiquarianism was, in short, to map the subtle differences between superstition and religion. Even ancients like Cicero and Plutarch knew, Stucki wrote, that true religion was "positioned in the middle, between two extremes. One extreme is a lack, that is, *atheotes*, or *athreskeia*, irreligiosity . . . the other extreme is an excess . . . that is superstition, which is the opposite fault in religion." Atheism is easy enough, Stucki thought, to detect. The real challenge is to discern religion from its own excess. And while the gentiles, "above all their doctors and teachers, called Philosophers," had much to say about the difference between the two, "nevertheless they could never distinguish the true religion from the false, or from superstition," and thus always gave "their most indecent and monstrous superstition the august and sacred name of religion." The problem, as even Cicero knew, is that "superstition is so close [*propinqua*] to religion," that superstition is the "*imitatrix, aemulatrix, simulatrix, quasique simia*" of religion. And for just this reason, the God of Israel worked so hard to extract his people from this world of simulations and emulations, establishing the true religion "in one place, in one region, in one tabernacle and temple, at one altar, with one set of festivals and rites." And even then, Israel lapsed, lured by the Devil and its own base humanity back into the "impious and impure superstitions of the gentiles."[125] Sacrifice guides us through this uncanny valley between superstition and religion because it was the "leading element" (*praecipua pars*) of ancient religion "in general."[126] To understand sacrifice meant, in a deep sense, to understand religion.

The project was conceptually and practically ambitious. Stucki first assembled a tremendous archive of materials about sacrifice collected from both classical and modern authors, not least our authors above.[127] And then he *organized* this archive in a systematic fashion, mapping out the when (*quando*), the object (*ad quem*), the what (*quid*), the where (*ubi*), the who (*qui*), by what means (*quo modo*), and to what end (*cur*) of sacrifice.[128]

This "system" was hardly original. When, by what means, by whom, and to what end: these were the hallmarks of virtually all systematic thinking at an historical moment when, across many fields of knowledge, a premium was put on organizing the earlier miscellanies of the humanists. What Walter Ong once called the "method of method"—the organization of literature, science, the arts, and theology into broadly comparable systems by the Protestant logician Peter Ramus and his many emulators—was a broad European phenomenon of the waning sixteenth century.[129] Building on broadly Aristotelian categories, the method of method prized the ability to organize disparate materials under a fixed and finite set of topics. It was also a pedagogical project, concerned with packaging complex fields of knowledge for classrooms and universities. Stuckius's organizing framework was thus common in late sixteenth century education more generally.

But as applied to *sacrifice* it was original indeed. The *ad quem* of sacrifice was all of the objects to which sacrifice was addressed, for example, comprehending the entire world of "creatures, idols, and demons" that the gentiles called gods. To write the history of sacrifice was to write the history of idolatry, then, to comprehend all the

> natural things, both visible and corporeal, as well as invisible and incorporeal, things good, useful and beneficial, as well as things evil, pernicious, pestilential, execrable, and hateful . . . as well as artificial things, made by human hands and labor . . . images, simulacra, statues, columns, scepters, and other similar organs and instruments of superstition, made for the honor and worship of the gods.[130]

Idolatry too became a learned industry in the seventeenth century, as we will see later in this book. But already here, we can glimpse the new organization of religious knowledge that later made idols such an important topic. For Boccaccio, the study of the gentile gods was a literary project, essential to understand the divine characters that sprawled across ancient classical texts. For Stuckius, by contrast, the gentile gods were just one element in the total religious *system* of antiquity. This religious system included the origins and materials of pagan idols, the worship of demons, the natural objects worshiped as gods, the ancient priesthoods, the system of temples, the festival calendar, religious practices like prayer, and an infinite diversity of acts, materials, and beliefs.

This religious system revolved around sacrifice. Sacrifice led to prayer, for example, which in turn should be considered "diligently," by looking at "who prayed, for what, what kind, what manner, where, when, by what means, and to what end."[131] The cultic role of the ancient Roman priesthood invited consideration of its legal and political role, the Pontifex Maximus, according to the Roman historian Festus, being "judge and arbiter in matters divine and human."[132] To understand the sacrificing priesthood, in turn, we have to understand Roman law. Priestly regimes of continence inform about the nature of ancient purity, eating habits, and sexual practices. This expansiveness of vision made the *Descriptio* into not just an "encyclopedia of sacrifice," in Kolakowski's terms, but an encyclopedia of religion itself, coordinated around an act foundational to the religious imagination.[133]

The more expansive the vision, however, the more important it was that Christian readers not get lost in the valley between superstition and piety. Accordingly, Stucki leavened his erudition with editorial clarifications of the difference between pagan error and Christian truth. Some of these took the form of simple asides: the gentiles call their festivals "sacred, divine" but really they were "superstitious, impure, the greatest wickedness and scandals";[134] "the superstition of the Gentiles (which was the entirety of their religion) is more correctly called *deisidaimonia*, that is, fear of demons, as opposed to fear of God";[135] and so forth. Others were more reflective. Thus to Ovid's report that "the *victim* is so called because it is felled by a *victorious* right hand; the *hostia* takes its name from conquered foes,"[136] Stucki remarked:

> The sacrifice of Christ can be called host and victim following the specific significance of either of these words (if it is permitted to mix sacred and profane), since by it are overthrown, mastered, and defeated all the enemies of the human race, both visible and invisible, eg., the Devil, the World, Sin, Death, Hell, the curse of the Law.[137]

This mixture of "sacred and profane" might have been confusing had not his point been so clear: Ovid provides the *words*, but Christ supplies their *meaning*.

Contrastive exercises like this punctuated the *Descriptio*. Take the example of human sacrifice. As Kolakowski has observed, for Stuckius, "there isn't a single part of the world where we don't see the performance of human sacrifice."[138] This ubiquity compassed the gentile world: Carthaginians, Cretans, Gauls, Romans, and so forth. But it also included pious patriarchs, not least Abraham, who "was willing, to prove his singular faith (*pro singulari sua fide*), to kill and sacrifice his own son to God." It was in imitation of him, "or better in false imitation (*kakozelia*)," that the gentiles offered their "human, or actually inhuman, and purely diabolical victims." Abraham's devotion had a long afterlife not just among the gentiles, but even among his covenanted descendants. "This execrable custom of sacrificing human beings, and even their children, grew and strengthened not only among profane and barbaric Gentiles," Stucki pointed out, but "even among the people of God, the Jews and the Israelites," as evidenced in the Levitical prohibition against offering children to Moloch (20.2). These Jewish crimes were more than just a *kakozelia*, however. They were also *prophecies* (*vaticiniis*) of the real sacrifice, that of Christ, the "supreme human sacrifice, by which alone God is reconciled to us, and the sins of the world expiated."[139]

It was in this paradoxical spirit—both bringing gentile sacrifice into proximity with the peoples of God *and* holding them radically distinct—that Stucki ended the *Description* with a resounding survey of the antitheses between "gentilism or, as some call it, ethnicism, or paganism," on the one hand, and Christianity, on the other. Some of these antitheses were theological commonplaces. The gentiles worshiped many and false gods, but Christians worshiped the one true God, "Father, Son, and Holy Spirit, Creator, Conserver, Judge, and Master of the heavens." The gentiles have many mediators; the Christians have one. The gentiles have innumerable idols and images; the Christians have Christ, the very person of God. The gentiles make pilgrimages to their idols; the Christians find their God everywhere. The gentiles practice false worship; the Christians practice true worship. The gentiles live in an infinite universe of offerings and sacrifices; the Christians live under the blessings of the single, final, and true sacrifice, of Christ "himself of himself." The gentiles sacrifice a lamb to their false and fictive gods, hoping to placate their wrath. Their offering is "polluted and contaminated in the eyes of God," however, whereas we Christians have the one true Lamb, offered to abolish the sins of the world.[140]

Some of the contrasts, however, were much stranger, only visible in light of erudite antiquarian learning. The Greeks sacrifice thighs to their gods but we Christians "contemplate the thigh of Christ," as is written in Revelation, where the angry Christ appears, "and on his thigh he has a name inscribed, King of kings, and Lord of hosts" (19.16). The gentiles pluck the hair from their victims' heads, and consecrate it to their gods; we Christians know that every hair on our head is "counted by our God, the father who is in heaven," and meditate on the hairs of Christ, "white as white wool, white as snow" (Rev. 1.14). The gentiles consecrate the "viscera, intestines, vitals, and entrails to their gods," hoping to discover in them glimpses of the future; we Christians diligently contemplate the "viscera and entrails of God the father in heaven, and his only begotten son," as when Paul tells the Philippians "how greatly I long after you all in the bowels of Jesus Christ" (1.8).[141]

What apophatic antiquarianism taught, then, was *how to read Christian texts.* When the apostle Paul speaks of Christ as a "fragrant offering and sacrifice to God" (Eph. 5.2), we should be reminded of the fragrant plants common in gentile worship: frankincense, cinnamon, myrrh, and thyme. In the gentile world, these were used to cover the smell of blood and smoke that filled reeking pagan temples. But Stucki's "antithetical method" used them to fill the air with the fragrant smell of Christ.[142] The same method converted the methodical violence of pagan sacrifice into appreciation for the Passion of Christ. The gentiles, he reminded readers, select their victim from the herd, "lead it to the altar, crown it, bind it, sprinkle it with the *mola salsa,* kill it, chop it up, slit its throat, flay its skin, [and] dismember it." And Jesus underwent a similarly monstrous process, "captured, bound, . . . spit upon, whipped, wounded with a crown of thorns, tortured in horrible and miserable ways from his head to his feet." His body, "almost bloodless and lifeless . . . was led outside the city, like the remains of a sacrifice (κάθαρμα), to the place of suffering, called Golgotha, as if sent to the butcher's stall, stripped of his clothes with mockery and contumely, naked, affixed to the cross, and after many torments, slain."[143] The truth of Christian sacrifice is ultimately revealed in the Resurrection, when the victim is called back to life and summoned to the throne of heaven. And yet the stages of pagan ceremony let us see more clearly the terror of his Passion and the miracle of his rebirth.

The gentiles have much to teach us, in short, if only by contrast. And so to prove it, Stucki brought his immense work to conclusion with these words:

> Enough said of these antitheses between paganism and Christianity, which, if anyone wanted to pursue them individually, would grow into an immense oration. In it we see how great the differences were between them, and how much we should exert our care and attention, that we avoid and flee every gentile superstition (since, as Livy rightly said, *nothing is more deceptive in appearance than a false religion*) [and] constantly protect and conserve, intact and pure, the Christian religion.[144]

Nihil enim in speciem fallacius est quam prava religio: words pronounced by Postumius, a virtuous ancient Roman consul intent on taming a Etrurian religious swindler, whose invented Bacchic rites seduced women and men into nocturnal orgies, false prophecy, and ritual murder. "Every system of sacrifice except that performed in the Roman way" must be stamped out, the consul pronounced, since "nothing [is] so potent in destroying religion as where sacrifices [are] performed, not by native, but by foreign ritual."[145]

To give the last word to Livy's great Roman history *Ab urbe condita* might seem unusual. But the message was clear. Even the gentiles knew that false sacrifice was a poison. They did not have the antidote of Christ, so their cures were ultimately no less toxic than the poison itself. But from their struggle for healthy religion, and from their multitude of failures, Christians learn, *per modum negandi*, what true religion and real sacrifice should look like.

Conclusion: New Sacrifice, New Theology

Stucki had a powerfully normative view of what Christian sacrifice ought to look like, and it certainly did not look anything like a Catholic Mass. When he approvingly repeated Cyprian's view that the Lord's Supper is meant, not as an occasion for chewing on Christ's flesh, but as a meal sealing the bond between divine and human things, he surely had the Protestant theological verities about the Eucharist in mind.[146] And yet scoring confessional points against Catholic opponents was not his central concern. Nor was scoring points the concern of Lilio Giraldi. Both writers, Catholic and Protestant, sought first and foremost to explain the system of pagan sacrifice *in general*. This they accomplished not only by organizing the chaotic details of humanist learning, but also by setting it in relief with the true system of sacrifice to be found in Christianity.

From a contemporary perspective, such contrastive projects doubtless have a distastefully ideological feel, since they reject the openness to difference so agreeable to the modern imagination. And yet it must be confessed that the more appealing syncretism of the fifteenth century was possible only because the stakes were so low. When Bellini painted the sacrifices of Rome behind Christ the Redeemer, there was no thought that these intimacies might be a problem. The humanist delight in the heteronomy of the Christian archive posed no serious challenge to Christian hegemony. However conflictual the fifteenth-century Latin Church might have been, it was still *a* Church. Only with the coming of the Reformation did heteronomy became a real problem for Christianity, with serious political and religious consequences. Giraldi and Stucki wrote during this much hotter intellectual environment, when Christian fracture redrew the religious geography of Europe. The new demands of polemic made that older humanist syncretism—the blood of the redeemer in intimate dialogue with the altars of Rome—virtually unthinkable for them.

But, as so often, constraint is also a powerful imaginative stimulant. With confessional lines inscribed evermore deeply into European politics and culture, the clarifying impulses of polemic invited writers like Giraldi and Stucki to think sacrifice anew. The older humanists had voraciously collected data about the pagan gods, supplying thick descriptions of the rites, ceremonies, and institutions that played such vital roles in ancient religions. The apophatic antiquarians took this data and *organized* it. Sacrifice was an historically and functionally coherent system, the *modus negandi* insisted, one that structured the entirety of ancient religions. The religions of Greece and Rome are more than just curious assemblage of historical particulars. These particulars—the priests, the altars, the temples, the gods themselves—are all chained together by the rite of sacrifice.

Two final remarks. First, this turn to system was, as we have seen, the product of serious religious conflict. Organizing the eclectic world of ancient sacrifice enabled exactly the sharp distinctions—between Christian and pagan, Catholic and Protestant—so essential in the confessionalized world of the late sixteenth century. Once upon a time, the argument suggested, there was a *system* of ancient religion organized around sacrifice. And because it was a system, rather than a curious hodgepodge, it was (negatively) comparable to Christianity, now *also* redescribed as a coherent system, rather than an historical hodgepodge. The organization of ancient sacrifice thus went hand-in-hand with the organization of a normative Christianity, now freed—so the *modus negandi* affirmed—from any dependencies on the alien gods of the pagans.

Second, this turn to system had paradoxical consequences, however, not least for the practice of theology itself. When Boccaccio wrote that "not only is poetry theology, but theology is also poetry," he insisted on the importance of the *poetic* imagination to the pursuit of theological truths.[147] Writers like Stucki and Giraldi instead turned the *antiquarian* imagination into an essential feature of theological inquiry. The early Reformation made the archives of ancient Christianity newly salient, as we argued, to the adjudication of theological problems. By the late century, the practices and beliefs of ancient *pagans* entered the Christian archive, made useful and relevant to the urgent challenges of a confessional age. For the Catholic Giraldi, this was implicit, the proper Catholic teachings quietly illuminated by the contrast with the gentile gods. For the Protestant Stucki, this was explicit: antiquarian study was, he argued, a necessary element of theological training, a repository of knowledge relevant to the preacher and the teacher, an interpretive resource for readers of Scripture, indeed, a cornerstone of the Christian self-understanding.

By the late sixteenth century, then, the deep challenge of Christian sacrifice—and the specter of heteronomy that it invited in an age of Christian fracture—pushed theology to become an ever-more pluralistic language of inquiry. Older forms of doctrinal deliberation and scriptural exegesis never went away. But these methods were *shared* by Europe's confessional opponents, and so could never finally settle what exactly was Christian about Christian sacrifice. And so they were supplemented by new forms of evidence and argument. Philology, history, classical erudition, comparative religions: the expansion of the theological horizon, and the attendant growth of the Christian sacrificial archive, begun in the early years of the Reformation only accelerated as the century waned, as new worlds of learning were applied to older theological questions.

CHAPTER SIX

Gods of Paste

ANTHROPOLOGY AND THE SACRIFICES OF NEW SPAIN

For whilst they slew their children in sacrifices, or used secret ceremonies, or made revellings of strange rites . . . there reigned in all men without exception blood, manslaughter, theft, and dissimulation, corruption, unfaithfulness, . . . adultery, and shameless uncleanness. For the worshipping of idols not to be named is the beginning, the cause, and the end, of all evil.

—*WISDOM OF SOLOMON*, 14.23–27

Never were so great evils in the World, as those which Religion hath hatched and nourished.

—SAMUEL PURCHAS, *MICROCOSMUS, OR THE HISTORIE OF MAN* (1627)

Tantum religio potuit suadere malorum.

—LUCRETIUS, *DE RERUM NATURA*

IN THE EARLY 1520S, as European Christendom began to decompose, Hernan Cortés and his Spanish troops discovered an empire of sacrifice in the New World. In reports sent to his Emperor, the young Charles V, the adventurer spoke of a city and temple whose "magnificence no human tongue could describe." It was a temple dedicated to idols "made of dough from all the seeds and vegetables which they eat, ground and mixed together, and bound with the blood of human hearts which the priests tear out while beating."[1] In this city of priests, blood ran everywhere, all the time:

> Each day before beginning any sort of work they burn incense in these temples and sometimes sacrifice their own persons, some cutting their tongues, others their ears, while there are some who stab their bodies with knives. All the blood which flows from them they offer to those idols, sprinkling it in all parts of the temple, or sometimes throwing it into the air or performing many other ceremonies, so that nothing is begun without sacrifice having first been made. . . . whenever they wish to ask something of the idols, in order that their plea may find more acceptance, they take many girls and boys and even adults, and in the presence of the idols they open their chests while they are still alive and take out their hearts and entrails and burn them before the idols, offering the smoke as sacrifice. Some of us have seen this, and they say it is the most terrible and frightful thing they have ever witnessed.[2]

Everything, Cortés told his liege, "has an idol dedicated to it, in the same manner of the pagans who in antiquity honored their gods."[3]

This is the most iconic story of sacrifice in the early modern world, the astonishing story of the city of blood in Lake Texcoco in the Valley of Mexico. On the eve of its conquest, Tenochtitlan sat at the center of a mighty empire of tribute and war. It was a new empire. Only for two or three generations had the city and its masters commanded such power in the Valley. In less than a hundred years, however, it had created a world of sacrifice that stuns the imagination. From the bottom of society to the top, the Mexica—whom we have come to call the Aztecs—dedicated ferocious energy to the procuring and destruction of human beings. From the lowest ranks of society, fishermen and salt workers, to the highest priests and lords, the economy of blood circulated through the empire. In the service of the hummingbird god of war, Huitzilopochtli, and the rest of the Mexica pantheon, blood spilled from temple altars, foaming down the steps of the great pyramids alongside the eviscerated bodies rolled in its wake. Victims were flayed and their skins worn until they rotted. Children were raised for sacrifice, dressed and paraded, gifted to the gods as "bloodied flowers of maize." Special slaves were chosen, pampered and adorned in rich attire, bedecked with flowers, faces painted and sent to play their flutes and bells throughout the city, . . . and then their hearts cut out, heads skewered on skull racks.[4]

This dizzying world of ritual and violence has been an object of fascination ever since. Even today, anthropologists and historians struggle to recreate the religious and political cultures that made it possible. For the early moderns, however, the experience of the "New World" was curiously disjointed. The New World should have (and sometimes did) offer a real world laboratory for what erudites, antiquarians, and theologians had been thinking about sacrifice for a long time. Nowhere in Europe, after all, was there an active culture of sacrifice on a scale and complexity to rival that of Greece and Rome. Those who first encountered this culture of sacrifice—principally the Spanish conquerors, colonists, and especially missionaries, many steeped in humanist learning—witnessed an entire continent of people practicing religions wholly unknown, religions with such energetic commitment to sacrifice that it beggared thought. The Franciscan and Dominican missionaries were, for their part, among the most creative thinkers about sacrifice in the sixteenth century. They not only developed the archive of materials that still informs scholarship on pre-Colombian politics, society, and culture, but they also established a set of interpretive frameworks that were, context considered, extraordinarily innovative. From the detailed ethnographies of Bernardino Sahagún to the extraordinary apologetics of Bartholomé de Las Casas, it seems (to us) as if these should have reshaped how *all* early modern Europeans thought about sacrifice.

And yet they didn't. The humanist erudition lavished on sacrifice that we explored in the previous chapter, for example, showed virtually no interest in New World sacrifice. By and large, in fact, it took decades for the particulars of the sacrifices of New Spain to make themselves known, at least beyond the most garish stories. The ethnographically richest writings from the New World barely came to light, in fact, until the nineteenth century. This divergence—between, on the one hand, an immense archive built by the Spanish missionaries, and, on the other, the main currents of learned and theological reflection on sacrifice in Europe—is important, not least for what it tells us about the history of the sacrificial imagination writ large. The devil, as usual, is in the details.

The sacrificial imagination was and is, as we have seen, a complex terrain, haunted by the ghosts of ancient paganism and Christianity, and stained with the blood of theological and political conflict. We saw in the previous chapter how an era of innocent syncretism came to an end, and how a set of theological stakes energized antiquarian inquiry, creating by the end of the century a synthetic picture of sacrificial life. Among Protestants, for whom the problem of sacrifice was especially challenging, this amplified trends already ongoing in the confessional sphere, giving erudition and antiquarian learning a new theological relevance. With the New World, *anthropology* entered into the lists of theological conflict, first among missionaries who had practical reasons to concern themselves with the sacrifices of indigenous Amerindians. And then only later—indeed, much later—among the Protestants who, by the late sixteenth century, had their own reasons for thinking anthropologically about sacrifice.

This was not the anthropology of the nineteenth-century human sciences. It was a loose set of theories of religious behavior that compassed a terrain distributed across later disciplines that included anthropology, ethnography, ethnology, and comparative religion. These theories were meant to answer new questions urgently felt in that age. The first generation of reformers still envisioned a united Christianity purified of all traces of a pagan past. By 1590, the prospect of Christian unity had been abandoned, or at best postponed until some distant future. This age of stubborn confessional difference demanded answers to different problems: why, despite hearing the gospel rightly taught, do human beings so stubbornly cling to their errors? Why were superstition and idolatry so durable? Why do piety and impiety look so perplexingly alike?

The sacrifices of the New World were especially pertinent to questions like these. First, they supplied the means for late century Protestants to universalize their own dilemmas, to enfold the story of *Christian* error into that of *human* error. The idols that tyrannized the Americas, and the terrible sacrifices performed in their honor, witnessed the intractability of idolatry for the human imagination. Second, these same sacrifices also supplied the material through which Protestants might explain the maddening intimacy of the sacred and the profane, in their world and abroad. The sacrifice of a suffering God and the sacrifices of Tenochtitlan: nowhere were the holy and the horrifying in such proximity. As in antiquity, so in the modern, sacrifice scribed the delicate line between these, showing that human beings have always known God but failed to understand him, have always desired to worship Him but never known exactly how.

The Doughy Idols of Tenochtitlan

For centuries Tenochtitlan has lived on principally in the records that celebrated its destruction. From Cortés's laconic descriptions, the historians and propagandists for the Spanish conquest elaborated gruesome stories of what he had found there. In his position as official chronicler of the Royal Council of the Indies—the administrative heart of the Spanish Empire—the Italian historian Peter Martyr d'Anghiera, for example, wrote of idols "horrible beyond description," consecrated with a paste of maize and the blood of children. Their lips are "smeared with the blood that flows from the heart, and the latter burned, to appease, as they think, the anger of the divinity," he wrote in his *De orbo novo decades* (1511–1530).[5] A generation later, in 1552, another champion of the Spanish conquest, the historian Francisco Lopez de Gómara, offered other revolting stories of the great *teocalli* of Tenochtitlan and the temples that organized religious space among the Mexica, speaking of rooms "completely bathed in blood . . . [whose] walls were crusted with blood two fingers thick, and the floors a hands-breadth."[6]

These apologists for Spanish conquest occasionally tempered their gory descriptions with curiosity about this new world. Gómara, for example, wrote of a

> magnificent idol . . . [which] was the chief and greatest of their gods, and was made from the many types of the seeds found in that land . . . ground and kneaded with the blood of innocent children and of sacrificed virgins, opened at their chests to offer their hearts as first fruit (*primicia*) to the idol. The priests and ministers of the temple consecrated it with great pomp and ceremonies. The entire city and country are there for the consecration, rejoicing with incredible devotion, and after the consecration many of the devout come to touch the idol with their hands, and place in the dough precious stones, pieces of gold, other jewels and ornaments from their bodies . . . At times they renew the idol, and tear apart the old one; and blessed is he who gets pieces of it as relics and holy artifacts (*reliquias y devociones*), especially the soldiers.[7]

The greatest of Aztec gods was a doughy idol, Gómara told us, made of seeds and blood. Before this idol, hearts torn from living virgins were the firstfruits offered in an elaborate ritual of consecration. The doughy idol was then venerated and torn to pieces, its scraps distributed as relics to the faithful.

Although such doughy idols surely provoked a shudder among his readers, Gómara's description of this alien savagery was marked by something close to respect. The stately and pompous rite, the somber priesthood, the eager devotion to the doughy idol, and the careful collection of its pieces as holy artifacts: these were the trappings of religious life familiar to any Catholic (or just Christian) readers in the 1550s. His description suggested that the monstrous and the familiar shared a kinship of some sort.

Neither sympathy for, nor details about, Mexica rites were common in the writings of the official historians and chroniclers, however. It was only the Franciscan and Dominican friars who really preserved the archive of the customs of the Mexica, the Inca, and the other civilizations of the

New World, hoping, in the years after destruction, to understand what had disappeared.[8] Beginning in the 1550s, for example, the "first anthropologist" of New Spain, the Franciscan Bernardino de Sahagún, began to assemble the materials for what became the magnificent *Florentine Codex*.[9] For thirty years, he worked with indigenous informants to put together an immense bilingual Spanish-Nahuatl portrait of Mexica religious life, the second book of which "treateth of the feast and sacrifice by which these natives honored their gods." The portrait Sahagún and his local informants painted there was extravagant, a detailed calendar of feasts and festivals filled by dancing, parades, games, celebrations, mock warfare, and endless human sacrifice (fig. 6.1).[10]

FIGURE 6.1. Scenes of Aztec Ceremonial Life. Bernardino de Sahagún, *Florentine Codex*. World Digital Library.

The Franciscans and Dominicans were interested observers. They came to replace, not to document, the religious world of the Mexica. They also carried their own interpretive commitments, not least the robust curiosity about matters sacrificial that had flourished, as we have already seen, from the late medieval era onward. The apocalyptic scale of the Aztec sacrificial system may therefore be as much a product of the Christian imagination as indigenous reality.[11]

For Franciscans like Sahagún, at the very least, the brutality of Mexica sacrifice always served as a missionary foil to the salubrious effects of the Eucharist.

Missionary attention to sacrifice was not merely self-serving, however. It was also a response to political and legal issues on the ground. From the beginning of the conquest, land- and labor-hungry colonists on the ground in New Spain routinely invoked the savagery of native society both to justify warfare against it and to paint it as unworthy of Christian care. Already in 1512, the Spanish state had tacitly rebuked this latter view when it established its system of organized servitude known as the *encomiendas*, villages where native peoples were expected to live, work, and receive the Gospel. These were just the first of repeated efforts to bridle the looting and murder that characterized so much of Spanish colonial expansion in the Americas, and to fulfill the obligation of evangelization implicit in the *Patronato real*, the papal grant that gave the Spanish state control over its colonial churches. How much these efforts did to abate the wholesale destruction of indigenous peoples is unclear. But they were part of the struggle over the status of native peoples, as both potential converts and human beings, that occupied theologians and missionaries for decades after contact.[12] Even after the status of conversion was more or less settled at the doctrinal level—in 1537, Pope Paul III denounced those who "pretend[ed] that [the Amerindians] are incapable of receiving the catholic faith" as agents of Satan—it remained an open question for some time whether the Indians were truly human, and if so, what kind.[13]

To *these* questions, indigenous human sacrifice evoked a gloomy answer. The learned humanist Juan Ginés de Sepúlveda followed in the footsteps of many earlier theologians when he suggested, for example, that the Indians were "natural slaves," defending his argument not only with recourse to Aristotelian anthropology, but also to the barbarism of the Amerindians more generally.[14] The "customs and character of the Indians," he wrote in 1547, imply such corruption that it warrants the violent impunity that God approved when Israel confronted the worshipers of Moloch.[15] Instead of offering a pious heart to God, the savages took literally the command to offer hearts to God, thinking "that they should sacrifice human victims, and opening the chests of their victims, pull out their hearts, and offer them on their abominable altars." Crimes like these, he argued, "surpass all human depravity," a view that he shared not only with Aristotle, but also with the antiquarian literature on comparative religions, in which human sacrifice had already long served as a civilizational boundary stone.[16] The New World joined Scythians, Carthaginians, Druids, Greeks, and Romans as the newest entry in the annals of barbarism. What made the New World different, of course, was that human sacrifice was happening *now*. As such, it seemed to Sepúlveda, it was incumbent upon the Spanish Crown to put an end to it.

Early missionary attention to Mexica sacrifice developed, then, as a response to an implicit question: was it possible to be truly human, that is, capable of salvation and worthy of God's care, and still engage in practices that any decent person should find revolting? Sahagún's rich depictions of Mexica ritual life offered an oblique response to those who saw native peoples as beyond the pale, documenting the complexity of their civilization. The most forthright response came from the extraordinary mind of Bartolomé de Las Casas (1474–1566), a Dominican whose life traversed the first sixty years of the conquest. His father accompanied Columbus on his second voyage to what is now Haiti, and the son was already there by 1502. After early years as a colonist, he put on the friar's robes in 1510, and accompanied Velasquez in his conquest of Cuba in 1512. It was this experience that transformed Las Casas from profiteer to critic of the conquest. By 1516, he was given an official office as "Protector of the Indians," and, for the next fifty years, he fiercely defended the dignity of the New World civilizations that the Spanish destroyed, from the island peoples of the Caribbean to those of Florida, Mexico, and Peru.

This defense took many forms: collecting and digesting accounts of native customs, documenting Spanish atrocities, criticizing the Spanish crown, and even advocating the abandonment of the colonial project. At the core, however, was a tireless effort to render indigenous peoples worthy of the care that Sepúlveda so strenuously denied them. Las Casas's effort culminated in one of the great intellectual set pieces of the sixteenth century, a "debate" in Valladolid Spain in 1550–1551. This event has long attracted attention from scholars interested in the rise of international law, just war theory, human rights, and anti-colonialism. At the time, however, it was an erudite, even arid intellectual affair. At the behest of the emperor, Charles V, and organized by the royal Council of the Indies, the meeting convened a panel of learned judges: theologians, jurists, bishops, and bureaucrats. For five days, Las Casas stood before this panel and read aloud a text—what became his *Apology*, better known in English as *In Defense of the Indians*—that attacked the violence of the Spanish colonial project, and defended the value of the indigenous world it was destroying.[17]

For Sepúlveda, human sacrifice witnessed the depravity of the native peoples and the necessity of their subjection to the Spanish yoke. To answer him, Las Casas had to explain human sacrifice and, the harder task, *justify* it as a practice among human beings still worthy of God's affection. To defend the Indians demanded more than just the documentation of the richness of their religious lives, in other words, or the observation of parallels between the customs of natives and ancient pagans. It required an elaborate theory of human sacrifice, its origin, its logic, and its rationale.

The theory was developed—as one might expect from a pious Dominican—in terms theological. Already in the early eighth century, in his work *The Orthodox Faith*, the church doctor John Damascene had observed that "The knowledge that God exists has been naturally engrafted and implanted by him in all persons."[18] When nature writes God into our hearts, Las Casas concluded, she also prescribes that we *act* on this knowledge, that we "honor God by the best means available and . . . offer the best things in sacrifice."[19] For this reason, "offering sacrifices . . . is a very old practice, introduced by the natural law"; it is the "principal act of *latria* [worship]," so much so that "there has *never* been a nation so barbarous, brutal, and foolish as to offer sacrifice to anyone other than the one who is thought to be God."[20] Everywhere that humans worship God (or what they regard as God), there is also sacrifice.

And not just any sacrifice. The law engrafted in the human heart in fact inclines us to sacrifice *people*. Here Las Casas departed from John Damascene. Between man and God there is a "certain right of condescension . . . a certain kind of proportional equality" that obliges Him to man, Las Casas insisted, and man to Him. From this foundation of reciprocity, God gives man His gracious benefits, and expects the same in return. "By natural law, men are obliged to honor God by the best means available to offer the best things in sacrifice," wrote Las Casas. Yet nothing humans gave could ever "repay God for the benefits received, even if they were to give their property and endure labors, vigils, and finally life and death itself for God's glory."[21] As a result, there was no naturally determined form of sacrifice, since even "the best things in sacrifice" could not be enough to repay God for his favor.

All who lack the truth of revelation are thus in a difficult position. They want to give God their best but *they* have to determine what this is. It was "men themselves who, by means of human laws, teach what should be offered a sacrifice, that is, cattle or sheep or the like . . . some sacrificed swine to Ceres, horses to Phoebus, geese to Diana, asses to Priapus, and other such things."[22] Even the Bible showed that, before the covenant with Abraham, "each person could lawfully sacrifice what he willed," just as Cain chose to offer his firstfruits, and Abel the firstborn of his flock.[23]

For a people ignorant of revelation, but exquisitely sensitive to the debt they owe to God, choosing the *best* would take on a force of inexorability:

> nature teaches that it is just to offer God, whose debtors we admit we are for so many reasons, those things that are precious and excellent because of the surpassing excellence of his Majesty. But, according to human judgment and truth, nothing in nature is greater or more valuable than the life of man or man himself. Therefore *nature itself dictates and teaches* those who do not have the faith, grace, or doctrine, who live within the limitations of the light of nature, that, in spite of every contrary positive law, *they ought to sacrifice human victims to the true God or to the false god who is thought to be true*, so that by offering a supremely precious thing they might be more grateful for the many favors they have received.[24]

When human beings choose their own forms of sacrifice, then, nature will always suggest that there is something *even better* to be offered to God. The gods make clear that the first fruits of the harvest are not enough, the oracle told the ancient inhabitants of Greece, by continuing to afflict human beings with misery. Short of the arrival of worldly perfection, then, humans will always arrive at the same insight: the gods do not want vegetables. Rather they want "human offspring, a thing of all others most precious in the sight of the gods."[25] Like ancient pagans, then, New World peoples did not offer human sacrifice because either they or their gods were especially bloodthirsty. They sacrificed humans because they were as enthusiastic to venerate their deities as any lover of Jehovah.

Even child sacrifice fit this logic. The newborn babe owed God a life. "All men are obliged to give their blood and their life whenever God's honor demands it," Las Casas remarked.[26] There was no injustice with respect to God, then, in human sacrifice. Nor was there injustice in more provincially political terms. Because the native peoples lived in established political communities, and because the state could rightfully demand "that a man do or undergo all that he is capable of, that is, that he expose his life to the danger of death for [its] welfare," then citizens were all, in a sense, potential lawful victims. Any state that believed its welfare depended on human sacrifice would, in this case, be justified in levying this heavy obligation on its people. And in fact, the Indians believed exactly this, that "the universe of good and welfare of the whole state consists in sacrifices and immolations, that is, human victims" and so "when afflicted by needs, they sacrifice what in the judgment of all is most precious and pleasing to God, that is, men."[27]

Finally, Scripture itself intimated that human sacrifice might be acceptable to God. God commanded Abraham to "sacrifice to him his only son Isaac," Las Casas observed, suggesting that he "wished to indicate . . . that he would do no injustice to anyone in any way if he had commanded him to be offered in sacrifice."[28] That God had in the end saved Isaac did not mean that "everything, even human life, should *not* be offered up to him."[29] The harsh command to Abraham instead showed clearly the lawful status of human sacrifice even for God. Indeed, Las Casas concluded, "one might reasonably surmise that the practice of human sacrifice spread to all nations *because they heard* that the all-powerful God of the Jews ordered his dearest servant Abraham to sacrifice his own son to him."[30] God commanded human sacrifice; nature encouraged it; law sustained it; and politics permitted it. In this sense, human sacrifice was the paradigmatic form of pious veneration. No wonder that the native peoples built pyramids of blood to honor their gods.

Discoveries Deferred

To the history of the Western sacrificial imagination—indeed, for intellectual history more broadly—Las Casas poses a curious puzzle. Reading him now can feel as if the spirit of Marcel Mauss suddenly possessed a pious missionary, inspiring him to cast off his own cultural system and to embrace another, alien world of doughy idols and blood-crusted temples. Indeed, we should hope that a modern anthropologist could have such an appreciation for the customs of others, not to mention the courage to defend them against the powerful and unscrupulous. Las Casas's creativity, moreover, extended well beyond the anthropological. In his engagement with questions of natural law, human diversity, and political sovereignty, he also raised a host of questions that resonated broadly in the early modern period and indeed still resonate today. In recognition of this creativity, then, it is extremely tempting to take him—and thus the discovery of Amerindian life—as a catalyst for broad transformations in the European sacrificial imagination.

No less remarkable than Las Casas's views, however, was their *failure* to affect this imagination much beyond the world of the Spanish missionaries. Las Casas's major works were certainly creative. But they were largely unknown to the broader European public. Las Casas read aloud his early draft of the apology to the learned judges, and from this text he wrote a Spanish manuscript (now lost). A single Latin version of his apology was preserved in France—the earliest mention of it in the library catalog from the Abbey of St. Germain des Près is in 1740—but was not published until the nineteenth century. His other substantial project on New World religions, the *Apologética historia,* was written after 1551, but again disappeared into archives, only to reappear in the nineteenth century.[31] Pieces of this work were later published in Jerónimo Román y Zamora's *Republicas del mundo* (1575), but that text was suppressed by the Council of the Indies, put on the Index of Prohibited Books, and never translated into any other European language.[32] A summary of the Valladolid debate was published in Seville in 1552, but this included no more than a few paragraphs on the sacrifice issue.[33] The only one of Las Casas's major works to reach a wider European audience was his *Short Account of the Destruction of the Indies* (published 1552). This stirring polemic against colonial violence enjoyed a long afterlife in the so-called Black Legend of Spanish atrocities, but had none of the anthropological bravura that distinguishes his later writings.[34]

This pattern was not restricted to Las Casas. As a generation of historians have observed, the sixteenth-century European engagement with New World things was curiously deferred. The first years after contact saw a number of important works published: Columbus, Cortés, Peter Martyr, and pseudo-Vespucci, among them.[35] This early information about the sacrifices of New Spain was sketchy and sensational. The doughy idols, maize wafers drenched in human blood, the murder of children: these nightmares found their way into European broadsides and pamphlets from the 1520s onward.[36] One of the first German language pamphlets from 1522, for example, documented the great *teocalli* in Tenochtitlan featuring a graphic scene of child sacrifice, an image bursting with familiar motifs: sorceresses consulting the devil, evocations of Jewish blood-libel, and a restaging of the Massacre of the Innocents (fig. 6.2). The sacrifices of Tenochtitlan also proved visually useful in the polemics against the so-called idols of the churches of Catholic Europe, polemics that inaugurated the Reformation and would precipitate wide-scale violence throughout the sixteenth century (fig. 6.3). At an historical moment when the world turned on its head, and the devil lurked everywhere, this example of the depths to which human beings could fall under his thrall was doubtless instructive and thrilling.

But after an initial surge, the flow of printed information dried up. Publication of Cortés's first two letters was prohibited by the Royal Council of the Indies already in 1527, for example, and it was not until 1777 that a codex containing all five letters was found in Vienna by the Scottish historian William Robertson.[37] Later, the Spanish Crown clamped down even

Newe zeittung. von dem lande. das die Sponier funden haben ym 1521. iare genant Jucatan.

Newe zeittung vō Prussla/vō Kay: Ma: hofe 18 Martze. 1522.

Newe zceyt von des Turcken halben von Offen geschriben.

FIGURE 6.2. Frontispiece. [Anon.], *Newe Zeittung. Von dem Lande. Das die Sponier funden haben ym 1521. Iare genant Jucatan* (1522). Courtesy of the John Carter Brown Library.

harder on information from its colonies. Sepúlveda's *Democrates secundus* was judged too incendiary by religious and university censors when they saw it in the late 1540s. It was refused royal license (partly at the instigation of Las Casas) and would not appear in print until 1892. The other works that Sepúlveda *did* manage to print on these issues in the leadup to the Valladolid conference were likewise condemned and recalled.[38] After the

FIGURE 6.3. Frontispiece. Andreas Bodenstein, *Von Abtuhung der Bylder*, 1522, excerpt. Courtesy of the Staatsbibliothek zu Berlin Digitalisierte Sammlungen.

Valladolid conflict, Spanish efforts became even more restrictive. Gómara's *Historia general de las indias* was suppressed in 1553, immediately after publication: copies of the books were ordered seized, and a blanket prohibition issued on its printing, sale, possession, and reading.[39] In 1556, the new King Philip II and his Royal Council forbade any publication on the Indies without a license; in 1560, it began to confiscate relevant books still in circulation.[40] And the lavish works composed by the Spanish friars stayed in manuscript form until rediscovered centuries later in far-flung archives. The lavish ethnographies of Sahagún—product of such careful work and thought—simply disappeared for almost three hundred years, waking from archival hibernation only in the mid-nineteenth century.

No doubt readers back in Europe did know *something* about the new worlds across the Atlantic. But this knowledge was spotty, their attention fickle, and sacrifice seldom the main topic.[41] In the 1550s, for example, the cannibals of eastern Brazil suddenly monopolized public curiosity, information flowing back unconstrained by Spanish censors. Hans Staden, a German adventurer sailing with the Portuguese, for example, published a sensational account of his captivity among the Tupinambá people in 1557. The next year, the priest and explorer André Thevet, having accompanied French colonists to the Brazil coast, published his *Singularities of Antarctic France*, whose materials he reworked again for his 1575 *Universal Cosmography*. And in 1578 the French Huguenot Jean de Léry published his *History of a Voyage to the Land of Brazil*, an account of the disastrous attempt to set up the first Protestant mission in the New World. All of these works recounted hair-raising stories of the Tupinambá, part innocent forest peoples and part demonic devourers of human flesh.

Modern anthropologists usually describe their cannibalistic rites—captives in war fattened, slain, and consumed by their conquerors—as human sacrifices.[42] The first European reports on the Tupinambá barely mentioned sacrifice at all, however. They did not kill for religion or for hunger, Staden reported, but simply "from great hate and jealousy," feasting serving as an act of war by other means.[43] For someone who himself nearly ended up a meal, perhaps this is understandable: the distinction between sacrifice and murder can hardly be a sharp one for the victim. But Jean de Léry too put Tupinambá cannibalism into the domain of war, not religion, cycles of violence between warring tribes eating each other since time began.[44] Neither man saw much religion at all among the Tupinambá, in fact. "They believe in a thing, which grows like a pumpkin," Staden observed dryly, gourds they fashion into maracás that their soothsayers then make into gods.[45] They "neither confess nor worship any gods," have no rites, and do not pray; in fact, de Léry exclaimed, "there is no nation on earth that is further" from religion.[46] To the essayist Michel de Montaigne, these Brazilian peoples were thus a people out of time, a valiant race akin to the ancient Greeks, ferocious in war and courageous in suffering. They eat their enemies solely "as a measure of extreme vengeance," part of the natural exchange of violence between primitive men.[47]

Neither sacrifice nor religion played any role here. Indeed, it was the *contrast* between the solemn reciprocity of Tupinambá violence and the horrors of unrestrained human sacrifice found among the Aztecs (and, Montaigne observed, Europeans as well) that gave the cannibal tales their moral force.[48]

The so-called impact of the New World on the Old was, in short, contingent and sporadic. As regards the sacrificial cultures of New Spain, after an early rush of sensational literature, new information dried up.The rich ethnographies in the *Florentine Codex* and the comparative religious investigations of a Las Casas thus never made any substantive impact either on continental theological controversies for much of the sixteenth century. Even the long tradition of humanist curiosity—the curiosity that produced, as we have seen, such immense collections of ethnographic particulars from the ancient world—would include virtually none of the startling rites and ceremonies of the Mexica. For those sixteenth- century writers most directly engaged with matters sacrificial that we explored in the previous chapter, the New World was practically invisible. In 1548, the mythographer Lilio Giraldi afforded the briefest of mentions of an island called "Carolina," recently discovered by Spanish sailors, and the human sacrifices of its inhabitants.[49] Fifty years later, the Swiss theologian Johann Stucki cribbed the Giraldi story and added another minor reference to the Caribs and their customs that he took from the popular New World adventure story written by the Italian Girolamo Benzoni, and published in Latin as *Novae novi orbis historiae* (1578).[50] But that was it. Compared to those of Scythia and Carthage—not to mention Greece, Rome, and Jerusalem—the rich sacrificial world of Tenochtitlan was virtually absent from the erudite European geography of sacrifice.

The Doors Open: José de Acosta and the Sacrifices of New Spain

In 1590, however, this wider European world of letters finally discovered the sacrifices of New Spain. It did so through the work of José de Acosta, the former Provincial for the Society of Jesus and a prime mover in that order's mission in Peru. There Acosta helped oversee the creation of "reductions," which resettled indigenous people into towns overseen exclusively by the missionaries. The biggest of these, the town of Juli, would number some fourteen thousand souls, supervised by a dozen Jesuits who offered catechism and services in Quechua, Aymara, and Puquina.[51] In 1577, Acosta published a guide for the Peru mission entitled *De procuranda indorum salute*. Ten years later, after the Jesuit returned to Spain, this work grew into a much larger *Natural and Moral History of the Indies*. Cleared for publication by the Council of Castile, the work enjoyed broad success in Spain and beyond, translated almost immediately into Latin, Italian, Dutch, English, German, and French.[52] It was the first New World best-seller, and remained a touchstone in discussions of comparative religion—and sacrifice—for the next 150 years.

Why did the *Natural History* catch fire in Europe? Several answers seem plausible. By 1590, for example, the Spanish, the French, the Dutch, and the English had begun multipolar colonial struggles, giving the Americas a wide geopolitical relevance. The great Protestant collections of New World travel literature date from this period: Theodor De Bry's *Collectiones peregrinatiorum in Indiam orientalem et Indiam occidentalem* (1590–1634), Richard Hakluyt's *Divers Voyages Touching the Discovery of the Americas* (1582) and *Principall Navigations, Voiages, and Discoveries of the English Nation* (1589), books written to describe and defend the multiple fronts of colonial expansion in the Americas. The late sixteenth century too saw the emergence of partisan theoretical conflicts about the legal and political significance of the New World. The legality of empire itself became a broad concern as European powers jostled for legitimacy in places beyond their direct oversight and sovereignty. These disputes would have long-standing consequences for international law, just war theory, debates about slavery, and more.[53]

What truly drew the sacrifices of Acosta—and his "moral history" of the New World—into the imaginative horizon of learned Europeans, however, were the new Christian dilemmas of the late sixteenth century. For the first fifty years of the Reformation, the exigent question was: what is (and was) authentic Christianity? Catholics and Protestants struggled fiercely to come up with answers. Doctrinal orthodoxies about faith, the sacraments, Scripture, and ecclesiastical authority supplied some. Others, as we have seen, were supplied by history, in which authentic Christianity was discovered in the past, in the original teachings of Jesus, or the apostolic Church, or the community of saints, or the Church universal. By 1590, however, the doctrinal differences between the mainline Christian churches had hardened, given concrete form in texts like Confession of Augsburg, the Thirty-Nine Articles, or the Tridentine Confession that clarified exactly what it meant to be a Catholic, Lutheran, or a Reformed Christian.

The rise of what historians call the "confessional" churches put a particular premium on internal religious conformity. This was pursued politically and intellectually. Most churches merged symbiotically with territorial rulers, whether princes or city governments, who could be called upon to determine whatever local version of Christianity was deemed authentic. And the confessional churches—especially the Protestant ones—also engaged in intense processes of self-scrutiny, surveilling their members for lingering remnants of the old faith and for the new heresies that proliferated as the century waned.[54]

One general name for such lapses was *idolatry*, about which the New World mission had a great deal to say. Idolatry was a lingua franca of the whole enterprise, in fact, an interpretive tool that explained the New World pantheons that included familiar gods and goddesses, but also rocks, mountains, the moon, the sun, the dead, and more.[55] Already Las Casas had reframed the language of idolatry to suit his apologetic efforts to defend the peoples he sought to convert. For him, the earliest forms of Amerindian religion were idol-free, natural, simple, and oriented toward the true God. Only later—and here Las Casas cited Josephus—did the cult of false images dominate the Amerindian mind, the product of overweening political powers that drew "human beings away from the fear and hope of God and substitute[d] for this fear and hope [their] own power."[56] Idolatry was thus explained historically, the product of developing political institutions and the human desire for powers divine. It had a beginning, in other words, and might conceivably have an end.

For Acosta, idolatry was far more intractable. It was in fact the very axis of religion and culture around which Amerindian devotion and worship had *always* rotated, there from the very beginning. After his dominion was broken by the Gospels, the devil "retired to the most remote places" across the Atlantic Ocean and, in his new home, established an elaborate idolatrous pantheon designed to distract human beings from God. He convinced them to worship the dead and "made them believe that . . . noble creations—sun, moon, stars, elements—had power and authority of their own to do good or evil to men."[57] Ever the ape of God, however, the devil governed his realm with a host of rites and beliefs that looked startlingly familiar: temples, celibate priests, crosses, stories of a Flood, belief in judgment day, convents, penances, and sacraments. But "the chief way in which the enemy of God and men has always demonstrated his cunning," Acosta insisted, was "in the multitude and variety of offerings and sacrifices that he has taught the heathen for his worship."[58]

No book published in the sixteenth century thus rivaled the *Natural and Moral History* for its lavish account of the sacrificial ceremonies of Huitzilopochtli, Viracocha, and other members of the Amerindian pantheon. This account culminated in the mighty *teocalli* at Tenochtitlan, with its idol "made of dough of amaranth and maize, kneaded with honey, whose eyes were green beads and whose teeth were grains of maize." Around this idol, Acosta unfolded the resonant and gripping story of human sacrifice in the New World, which we recount at some length:

> a priest come out dressed in a short alb with many fringes [and . . .] went up to where those who were to be sacrificed were standing, and walked from side to side, showing that idol to each man individually and saying, "this is your God." . . . Six sacrificers appointed for this office came to the place of sacrifice: four to hold the feet and hands of the man who was to be sacrificed, another for his throat, and another to cut open the victim's chest and tear out his heart. . . . the sixth of these men was considered and revered as a supreme priest or pontiff . . . the name of their office was *papa* and *topilzin*; their apparel and clothing consisted of a red garment like a dalmatic with fringes on its edges, a crown of rich green and yellow feathers on their heads . . . [They] had their faces and hands thickly daubed with black; five of them had their hair tightly curled and in disarray, with strips of leather fastened around their heads . . . As they arrived the six sacrificers took each of them in order, one seizing one foot and another the other, one holding one hand and another the other, and threw him backward over that sharp pointed stone, where the fifth of these ministers placed the collar over his throat and the high priest used that [flint] knife to open his chest with extraordinary speed, tearing out the heart with his hands and holding it up still smoking to the sun, to whom he offered the heart's heat and steam. Then he turned to the idol and threw the heart on its face, and then they very easily sent the victim's corpse rolling down the temple steps.[59]

Acosta painted an extraordinary picture. A beautifully dressed priest steps to the top of the temple, doughy idol in hand, and descends slowly to his victims. These victims are lined up, awaiting their fate. The sacrificers, with their black daubed faces and unkempt hair, are organized and ready to start a long day of murder. In the hand of one, a razor-sharp flint knife; a "wooden collar carved in the likeness of a serpent" in the hand of another. The rhythm and violence of the rite is overwhelming: the sacrificers seize the victim, bind him to the altar stone, and cut out a still beating heart. Finally, the heart is thrown toward the doughy idol, and the body tumbled down the bloody steps.

Such descriptive richness nearly causes us to forget why Acosta found such details worth repeating. But we *should* remember. The Jesuit was a missionary, not an ethnographer, and he wrote at a key moment in the history of New World Christianity. The early missionaries encountered a world still alive with the cultures and customs of its first peoples, and sought, however ineffectively, to convert without destroying them. They also wrote at the time of apparent success, mass conversions that promised a new church of the Amerindians. Two generations later, the situation was different. Indigenous religion proved aggravatingly durable even in the face of energetic missionary work. The missionary project thus shifted its ambition away from accommodation, and toward extirpation. In the Yucatán in 1562, Franciscan friars tortured, flogged, and killed Indians who retained their pagan ways, finding in their confessions the signs of an idolatry that persisted beyond superficial Christianization.[60] The Tribunal of the Holy Office of the Inquisition was established in Mexico in 1571 to oversee the mission project, including the eradication of the "counter-religion," including sacrificial rites, of indigenous priests.[61] In Acosta's Peru, provincial church councils held after 1550 repeatedly sought to stamp out traces of Andean religiosity, mandating the destruction of mummies and other sacred objects and sites, erecting crosses on indigenous shrines, and so on.[62] Inca structures were quarried for churches, which were then often built on former sacred sites, most famously in Cuzco, where the convent of Santo Domingo squatted atop the Inca Golden Temple of the Sun. One ritual replaced another: the feast of Corpus Christi—celebrated as the "triumph over falsehood and heresy" in the 1551 words of the Council of Trent—usurped older Inca harvest festivals, young Peruvians trained to participate starting in the later sixteenth century.[63] Other institutions followed suit: the Peruvian Inquisition was established in 1570, soon followed by the division of Peru into dioceses and parishes, which in turn facilitated the practice of clerical visitation already pioneered in Europe to oversee orthodoxy.[64] Idolatry, as Pablo Joseph de Arriaga wrote in his 1621 compilation of indigenous backsliding, was "so ancient an evil, and one so deeply engrained and natural to the Indians," that it would take every ounce of clerical energy to drive it out.[65]

Acosta was the official theologian to the Third Provincial Council of Lima (1582–83), the so-called Trent of the Americas, which aimed at "adapting to the New World the discipline of that grand ecumenical council."[66] This Council—like its analogue in Europe—aimed to stabilize and standardize Catholic Christianity in the Americas, offering rules for visitations, prescribing clerical discipline, and producing catechisms, confessors' manuals, and exemplary sermons. Like its analogue in Europe too, this council sought to cleanse the church of those accommodations to local custom and religion that still carried the whiff of sulfur.

The *Natural and Moral History of the Indies*—deeply informed by the many manuscripts Acosta accessed in Peru and Mexico, but ultimately a missionary treatise—must be understood in this context. The details lavished on the sacrifices of Huitzilopochtli, Viracocha, and others supplied a post hoc explanation for both the failures and successes of Christianization. On the one hand, they dramatized the savagery of the devil's sovereignty. On the other, they showed the trap that God had set for his great adversary. For the very imitations that so pleased the ape of God left the native religious imagination open to the gospel message. No surprise, then, that even the "loftiest and most divine" of Christian sacraments, the Eucharist, had its parallels across the religious cultures of the New World.[67]

In Peru, for example, Acosta described how the solemn Andean summer festival called *capac raymi* culminated in a massive eucharistic celebration, in which participants were "offered communion" by "the priestesses of the sun, who . . . made small loaves of maize flour tinged and kneaded with the blood of white sheep that had been sacrificed that day. . . . all received and ate . . . and [swore that] such food would remain in their bodies as witness of the faith they kept to the sun and to the Inca their king."[68] And in Mexico, he highlighted the December festival of Panquetzaliztli, a celebration of the hummingbird god Huitzilopochtli:

> [out of amaranth and honey, they] made an idol of the same size as the wooden one, gave it green or blue or white beads for eyes, and for teeth grains of corn . . . they dressed it . . . they placed it upon a blue bench on a litter, to be carried on men's shoulders . . . [then] all the people set off on a procession as fast as they could [stopping at Chapultapec, Atlacuyauaya, and Coyoacán, before returning to the great *teocalli*] . . . they pulled the litter with the idol to the top of the temple with a great noise of flutes and blare of trumpets . . . This done, all the maidens came out . . . and took from their place of retreat pieces of dough made of toasted maize and amaranth . . . kneaded into the shape of large bones. These pieces of dough were called the bones and flesh of Huitzilopochtli . . . they were blessed and consecrated as that idol's very flesh and bones. When they had finished the blessing and rite of those

> pieces of dough representing the idol's bones and flesh, they worshiped them in the same manner as their God. Then the sacrificers came forth and perform the sacrifice of men . . . [sacrifices] more numerous than on any other day because the festival was so important.[69]

Again a doughy idol, the "bones and flesh of Huitzilopochtli," venerated with trumpets, celebrations, and sacrifices. Just as the blood of the Lamb was present in Christian eucharistic devotion, so too was the "blood of white sheep" mixed into the idol's bready flesh, which everyone received and ate, a bread that, like the Eucharist, signaled and sealed their devotion to their God. The communion established by the Inca Yupanqui, the Numa Pompilius of the Andes, as Acosta called him, would last until the Gospel of Christ "did away with all the superstitions, offering the true bread of life that joins souls together and unites them with God."[70] Among the Aztecs, the eucharistic resonance extended beyond just the amaranth and corn breads that anchor much of their devotion, but even to the Corpus Christi festival. As in that Christian ceremony, celebrants process with their doughy idol held high, carried on a float for all to see. The procession was a long one, starting at the central temple and winding through all of the surrounding towns, before returning back to the center, at which point pieces of the doughy idol—the "bones and flesh of Huitzilopochtli"—were collectively venerated. The entire ceremony culminated with a bloody sacrifice, human sacrifices "more numerous than on any other day."[71]

What Anthony Pagden has called Acosta's "program for comparative ethnology" thus unfolded inside a missionary horizon that tirelessly called attention to the similarities of ritual forms.[72] It was thus hardly radical, as one author has suggested about Michel de Montaigne, to link "eucharistic rites" and "cannibalistic ritual."[73] Missionaries did it all the time, and far more openly than the subtle French essayist. Ethnographic comparisons like this in fact supplied the missionary with a durable framework for New World religion and its sacrifices. They also oriented the missionary in practical ways: they suggested both shared imaginative horizons that the missionary might better translate the Gospel into local idioms, and practical forms of intervention, as when Spanish authorities forbade the cultivation of amaranth, the very stuff of Huitzilopochtli and his doughy idol.[74] Such comparisons were, moreover, tools developed in service of a particular late sixteenth century vision of the church—a vision shared among all of the churches of Europe—the vision of a confessional church determined above all to manage its own orthodoxy, and to ensure that those captured by this orthodoxy remain committed to it. And they were, finally, tools honed for a post-conversionary project of mission, its forensic efforts aimed at managing the *memory* of the sacrifices stubbornly clinging to life among New Spain's new Christians.

Protestants and the God of Paste

For Acosta and the Catholic missionaries, idolatry was fairly easy to discern. In the Latin tradition, the first commandment read as follows: "you shall have no other gods before me. You shall not make for yourself a graven image . . . you shall not bow down to them or serve them" (Exod. 20.3–5). The prohibition on images in verse 5 was thus a gloss on the general prohibition in verse 3; as long as an image did not represent an *alien* god, idolatry was of little concern. "Scripture," as the tireless Tridentine cardinal Robert Bellarmine wrote, "never gives the name of idols to true images, but only to the simulacra of the Gentiles, which refer to false Gods."[75] This view underlay the crucial distinction between image veneration (*dulia*) and image worship (*latria*). "Great profit is derived from all holy images," the Council of Trent unequivocally declared, because through them, people are moved to "adore Christ and venerate the saints whose likeness they bear."[76] In contentious cases, finally, the Church was there to clarify the distinction between idols and the holy images that were useful for pious worship.

Protestants were no less zealous than missionary Catholics to distinguish between pious and idolatrous worship. From the dawn of the Reformation, this zeal produced waves of iconoclasm that destroyed the statues, paintings, and stained glass that defiled properly Christian houses of worship.[77] And this violence was accompanied by tireless theological polemics against the sin of idolatry, a sin that, in Calvin's words, "does not merely deform the external form of the chapels (*sacrarii*), but pollutes and perverts the entire sanctity of the church . . . undermines the entire worship of God."[78] In treatises and sermons, Lutherans, but especially Calvinists, railed against Catholic images, rejecting as a subterfuge the "wily distinction" between *dulia* and *latria*.[79] Even the Eucharist was subjected to Protestant suspicion, what the Reformed preacher Pierre Viret called "the morsel of paste and flour" that Catholics "worship . . . instead of Jesus Christ, the true Son of God."[80] In satires, placards, libels, and theological treatises, Catholics were said to worship the "God of paste" held up in every Mass across Latin Christendom (fig. 6.4).[81] "Jean le blanc," as one French Protestant print described the Eucharist, "the god of paste is a god that poisons."

FIGURE 6.4. The Other God of Paste. Anonymous Pamphlet, 1560. Courtesy of the Leiden University Libraries Digital Collections.

The reformed had a much harder time, however, determining what idolatry *is not*. For the missionaries, idolatry was found beyond the Christian realm. For the reformed, it was found within it. Catholics worshiped the same God, after all, but they did it wrong. Two things followed. First, the second half of the traditional first commandment—"thou shall not bow down to them and serve them"—became so important that Protestants instituted it as its own separate commandment (now the second, following the Greek Orthodox church). The "*whole substance of the Christian religion* is brought into question" by the manner of worship, in Calvin's words. Right Christianity demands right worship.[82] Second, it grew exponentially more difficult to determine this very rightness. Since "serving the idols" entailed *all* impious transactions between human beings and God, campaigns against the idols were an exercise in frustration. Confessional churches worked hard to develop remedies, changing the physical layout of churches, replacing altars with communion tables, whitewashing the walls, removing statues and paintings, and reminding their flocks of the danger of the idols. But since the human mind itself was the "perpetual factory of idols," since the "the mind begets an idol [and] the hand gives it birth," as Calvin wrote, success receded to a distant theological horizon.[83]

To solve a problem, make it bigger, the saying goes. And the Protestants did just that, turning their doctrinal dilemmas into dilemmas for humanity writ large. Already in the sixteenth century, writers like Heinrich Bullinger explained how the early Christian cult of the dead gave rise to a culture of images, idols, and saint worship in the late antique churches.[84] By 1600, antiquarian work on idolatry had become a major intellectual project among learned Protestants, who explored the universe of (typically bad) religion found in the classical world. Much of the "history of religion" or "comparative religion" in the seventeenth century was, in fact, the history of idolatry, scholars describing the variety of ways that human beings have worshiped the wrong gods, and in the wrong ways. The English lawyer and polymath John Selden's *De diis Syris* (1617) and the Dutch philologian Gerhard Vossius's *De theologia gentilis et physiologia Christiana* (1641) are just two examples of an erudite late Renaissance literary culture that excavated Old World languages, cultures, and religions for the deep history of human error.[85]

Such learned works rarely left the horizon of the wider Mediterranean, however. The globalization of the doughy idols—and the universalization of the problem of error—only happened as Protestants themselves went abroad, discovering a world ripe for exploration and conquest. From the 1590s onward, ever-more expansive works collected, organized, and reprinted firsthand accounts of the geography, peoples, customs, and idolatrous religions of the New World, as well as those of Russia, Asia, the Middle East, and elsewhere. The first Latin translation of Acosta appeared in 1602 as the ninth volume of the Dutch engraver and publisher Theodor de Bry's sprawling *Collectiones peregrinationum in Indiam orientalem et Indiam occidentalem* (1590–1634). And those parts of Edward Grimeston's 1604 English translation of Acosta that dealt with Mexican and Peruvian religions found another home in the English cleric Samuel Purchas's *Purchas his Pilgrims* (1625). These global texts demonstrated the scope of idolatry's reign, showed how, in the words of the astronomer and antiquarian Edward Brerewood, "if we divide the known regions of the world into 30 equall parts, the Christians part is as five, the *Mahumetans*, as sixe, and the Idolaters as nineteene."[86] They also showed that the problem of idolatry—and the sacrifices that accompanied it—demanded more than ancient history. It demanded a theological *anthropology* to explain how humanity found itself ever-ready to sacrifice to gods of paste.

From Genesis to New Spain: Sacrifice and the Anthropology of Christianity

We find the most vivid and creative example of this new anthropology in the work of Samuel Purchas, a Church of England clergyman who never went anywhere, but who collected and reprinted rich archives of materials about the world, its peoples, and their religious customs.[87] His *Purchas his Pilgrims* expanded on Britain's first great travel collection, Richard Hakluyt's *Principall Navigations of the English Nation* (1589, 1598–1600), a work that followed the English overseas expansion across the Atlantic world. Purchas grew the geographical scope further, including a stunning range of New World materials. There English readers could discover, for the first time, some of the ethnographic richness of New Spain, in excerpts from Jerónimo Román y Zamora's *Repúblicas del Mundo* (1575), Garcilaso de la Vega el Inca's *Royal Commentaries of the Incas* (1608), Las Casas's *Short Account of the Destruction of the Indies*, and most dramatically, a full reprinting of the *Codex Mendoza*, an Aztec codex that Purchas acquired from Hakluyt, and a treasure trove of Mexica life.[88] The 1625 work was also an expansion of Purchas's own "theological and geographical history of Asia, Africa, and America," entitled *Purchas his Pilgrimage* (1613), a work so popular that it went through four editions between 1613 and 1625. Together these works became a literary and religious touchstone at least until Coleridge. And in them, the anthropology of sacrifice answered the question on every Protestant's mind: why, when the gospel has been renewed more powerfully than ever, do errors yet persist and multiply?

For Purchas, the question was present from the beginning. "One God, one truth" was the banner under which he exhaustively documented mankind's repeated loss of both God and truth alike. This anthropological *modus negandi* proceeded via contrast, using "the withered and fouler hue of passed [sic] out-worne rites, or present Irreligious Religions" to clarify the *unam veritam* of Christianity.[89] At the beginning of the world, religion was a "pure streame of Original Righteousnesse," the "whole Law . . . perfectly written on the fleshie Tables" of Adam's heart.[90] But after the Fall, human beings fell into diversity and error, and religion became onerous, demanding "paines and vexation of spirit to enquire and practice those things which *religare*, bind [us] surer and faster to God." Purchas's 1613 *Pilgrimage*—and the *Pilgrims* that came later—was a story about these rites and ceremonies, invented after the fleshy tables of the human heart lost their original righteousness.

A story needs a beginning, and for Purchas, the beginning was Genesis. There Purchas, like many learned Protestants, discovered the origins of ceremonies, why human beings invest in them, what unites them as common actions, and what ultimately distinguishes the pious from the sinful ones.[91] Nature and reason, Genesis told him, lead human beings ineluctably to the belief in God. No sooner did one "conceiveth that there is a God, but the will inferreth that he ought to be worshiped." And no sooner did man desire to worship, than he began to invent "outward ceremoniall effects," testament to the universal human intuitions that there is a God and He deserves our respect.[92]

These "ceremoniall effects" were not chance fancies. After God banished Adam, He left him with *specific* ways to worship. Christian anthropology dictated that nature came before law and grace, that human beings had to wait, first for the Decalogue, and then for the coming of Christ, before they would be ready for glory. But God did not leave mankind ignorant of what was to come. "We cannot see the Sunne without the sun, nor come to God but by God," as Purchas wrote.[93] So God "left a spark of that light covered under the ashes" that, already from the beginning of the world, alerted mankind to the suffering savior, through whose sacrifice they might be redeemed from sin. The "promise of this Seed slain from the beginning of the world"—the eternal presence of a crucified Christ—was "the seed of all true Religion."[94] God thus commanded Adam and Eve to sacrifice, and to "faithfully instruct their children," in honor of that future sacrifice that would end sacrifice altogether.[95]

Here anthropology echoed and replaced the older Christian hermeneutic of typology, that scrutiny of Hebrew texts for signs of Christ. Genesis revealed the anthropology of sacrifice in two ways. It showed the deep truth underlying the human urge to give to God. But it also explained how human beings *veered* from that truth. The piety of sacrifice, Purchas well knew, could not be reliably ensured even among Christians. No wonder, since even in the Garden, Adam and Eve sinned. In doing so, they "offered their *First fruits* to the Devill," Purchas wrote, an impious sacrifice that would accompany them as they fled Paradise, carrying ever after both the seed of Christ *and* the "seed of the Serpent."[96] This split first appeared among those ancient brothers, Cain and Abel, whose fraternal comity was sundered by sacrifice. Cain brought his fruits, and Abel his sheep, but God only "*respected Abel and his offering.*" The envy of the rejected Cain drove him to fratricide, thus "in this member bruising the heele of that blessed seed, as a type of that which the heade himself should after sustaine."[97]

From the beginning, then, there were *two* kinds of sacrifices, one holy, and one impious. The division begun in the Garden grew ever more complex. Of the holy sacrifices, for example, there were *also* two kinds, "the one called Gifts or oblations of things without life: the other Victims . . . Slain sacrifices of birds and beasts." Of these, further kinds: "propitiatorie, consecratorie, Eucharisticall, and so forth, whose kinds and rites *Moses* hath in his bookes, especially in *Leviticus*, so plainely declared."[98] After Adam, the story of mankind thus became an endless process of sundering and cleaving.[99] The Flood having destroyed mankind, Noah "*built an Altar to the Lord* . . . and offered burnt offerings upon the Altar. And the Lord . . . renewed the ancient blessings and promises to Noah and his posterity."[100] But again religion could not maintain its integrity, and split in two, Noah's cursed son Ham "the first Author, after the Floud, of irreligion," for "in these days they began to divine by the Starres, and to sacrifice their children by Fire."[101]

The result was a heteronomous history of mankind. It was a unified history, in the sense that all human beings are seen to proceed from the first family, all presumed to bear the memory of that holy time. But since all are also subject to this dynamic of sundering and cleaving, it was a history that constantly fissured (much like Protestantism itself!), holiness and impiety engaged in a constant war for preeminence. Purchas's works tracked this dynamic, following the "footsteps of Religion . . . [and] her wanderings from the truth" in a global theological geography.[102] After the Flood, religion wandered far from her innocent birth, as witnessed by the ancient Syrian gods and their cults. But she regained her way in ancient Palestine, where the Hebrews flourished, the "reall and verball teachers of the Truth, which they let fall, and we take up."[103] The many sacrifices of the Jews initially carried that first truth of Christ's sacrifice, but these "propheticall fountaines" were corrupted, the Jews falling prey to murmuring and idolatry already in the days of Moses and Aaron.[104] And again, the result was a sundering, the Jews falling into "divers sects, opinions, and Alterations of Religion," a dynamic of division that Purchas would find all over the world, in Arabia, Mongolia, Egypt, and India, religions forming and splintering over time.

Once Purchas departed the Old World, he was prepared for barbarism *and* piety, no people "so savage which have not their Priests, Gods, and Religion."[105] In New Spain, where Acosta was his most important source, he discovered how the great civilization of Tenochtitlan had grown out of a tribe of man-beasts, which lived on "Snakes and Lizards, which they offered likewise in sacrifice to the Sunne."[106] These gave birth to the fantastic cults of the Aztecs, Huitzilopochtli "appear[ing] in a dreame to an auncient priest" to lead the Mexica "to the place where their Citie should be built, to become famous through the world."[107] "Even as the pillar of Cloud and Fire conducted the Israelites in their passage through the Wildernesse," so did Huitzilopochtli appear to the Mexica.[108] The Mexica who grumbled at their God were punished, "their hearts were pulled out, and their Stomacks opened, which, after that, they observed in their Sacrifices." Even the most horrifying rites developed according to the logic of divine command, as when the Mexica tricked the treacherous King of Culhuacan into sending his daughter to become the "Queene of the Mexicans, and mother of their God," who, "by order of their God, she was murthered, and flayed, and a young man was covered with her skinne, with her apparrell thereupon, and being placed neer the Idoll, was consecrated a Goddesse, and mother of their God, ever after worshipping the same."[109]

The sacrifices of New Spain thus circulated dizzyingly between the alien and the familiar, the pious and the profane. Familiar offices, gestures, desires, and stories made the events on the great *teocalli* of Tenochtitlan all the more uncanny, stranger for being so near to the religion that Scripture prescribed. Like Israel, the Mexica had *its* priests in their sacred vestments, but *their* priests, "attyred in a Dalmatick robe of white," tied up their hair with laces of leather, and offering smoking hearts to the sun.[110] No less familiar in its strangeness was the story of Huitzilopochtli's doughy idol, which Purchas narrated at length, how the priests called the "morsels of paste, the flesh and bones of *Vitziliputzli*," how the idol was marched throughout the land, how the sacrifices of men followed in this "their most solemn Festivall," and finally how they took "the Image of paste . . . to the

Communion, beginning with the greater, and continuing unto the rest, both men, women, and children."[111]

Like Acosta (indeed, in his exact words), Purchas described how much the Mexica shared with everyone else, Jews, Christians, and pagans alike. Priests, temples, altars, consecrations, funerals, and festivals were the common idiom of religious practice for both Jesuit and Calvinist. These commonalities had different causes, however. For the Jesuit, they witnessed an *external* agent, Satan retired to the New World, tempting its peoples into savagery. In Acosta's New World, the line between piety and impiety was clear. Less so for the Calvinist. For Purchas, impiety flourished equally on the great *teocalli* as under the sign of the Cross. In the end, it was the devil *inside* that mattered most, the immanent logic of those first sacrifices playing out, just as they had for Cain and Abel, again and again.

Purchas's anthropology applied not just to other religions, moreover, but to Christianity too. The "bulkiest anti-Catholic tract of the age," as David Armitage calls Purchas's collection of travel writings, unfailingly compared Catholic rites with those of idolators ancient and modern.[112] Purchas dedicated the 1613 *Pilgrimage* on November 5, the anniversary of the Gunpowder Plot, and later wrote from the comforts of the King James I College of Divinity at Chelsea, the so-called college of controversy built to defend Protestantism against its Catholic foes.[113] And over the years of his publications, Purchas grew increasingly insistent that his readers should discover in the New World the same logic of error that they witnessed right at home.

"Mexican Lent" was how the first edition of the *Pilgrimage* described the doughy idols of Huitzilopochtli, which, Purchas wondered, "so much resembleth the Popish *Chimera* . . . of their *Corpus Christi* Feast with other their Rites."[114] Later editions were even more trenchant. By 1626, Purchas had rewritten the entire section on Mexican sacrifices, now under a subheading of "Their Feast of Transubstantiation, Lent, Bloudie Processions, and other Holy Times."[115] The morsels of paste torn from the body of Huitzilopochtli, the relics, the rites of consecration, the "kind of Communion": all of these were mirror images of Catholic rite, culminating in an orgy of human sacrifice. Even the otherwise direct translation of Acosta into Latin in 1602 wanted to make sure its readers saw this point, alerting them in advance that, when they read the final chapters of the *Natural History*, they should observe how there are *no* "festivals, celebrations, and rites in the Roman Church, whose likeness the terrible Satan will not have depicted and prescribed in those superstitions of the Indies: just as the author of this book, servant of the Society of Jesus, himself clearly shows."[116]

These polemics helped organize the Protestant response both to the ceremonies of foreign religions, and to the missionary enterprise that supplied the raw information for Purchas's global erudition. As Dominicans, Franciscans, and Jesuits globalized Christianity, they repeated at a new scale the old story of "Religion . . . and her wanderings from the truth." The "Christianity" preached in the New World, in Purchas's mind, hardly differed from the idolatry it discovered there. Indeed, the similarity between Catholic and gentile permitted the syncretism that late sixteenth century missionaries so lamented. Those same rites formerly used to "solemnize the Feasts of [the Inca] Kings" were now used to "solemnize the Feast of the most holy Sacrament, the true God our Redeemer and Lord."[117] The Jesuits, Purchas wrote memorably, merely offered "an exchanged Polytheisme in worshipping of Saints, Images, and *Hosts*."[118] Doughy idols, indeed.

Purchas's works were more than apologies for England's new colonial ambitions, therefore. They were also a modern-day *Panarion*, a breadbasket of heresies like that of Epiphanius of Salamis, raking the "rotten bones of the past, and stinking bodies of the Present superstitions" out of their graves to better demonstrate the breadth of human depravity.[119] Unlike ancient heresiologies, Purchas advanced his case genealogically, telling a story that began in the Garden and over time spread to encompass the entire world. The result was an eclectic mixture of materials, a biblical framework supplemented by scores of classical and modern authorities who afforded the historical, ethnographic, and anthropological scope to make good on this story of heteronomy.

Like ancient heresiologies too, Purchas was ultimately interested less in threats from outside, than threats from within. The "Historie of Religion . . . hath or should have God to be the *Alpha and Omega*," as Purchas wrote, and his exploration of the rites and ceremonies of the world's religions was a diagnosis of, and prophylactic against pluralism.[120] The aggravating stubbornness of Christian difference—the fact that, even after nearly a century of pointing out the many ways the Catholic Church had strayed from the Gospel, its power and scope seemed only greater—invited scrutiny of the deep roots of religious error.

Seen in this broader context, anthropology supplied what doctrine could not, a way of explaining the failure of the sacred to remain so. The proximity of the sacred and the profane that Purchas discovered in the story of Cain and Abel; the way that sacrifice, the manner of honoring God prescribed in the garden of Eden, immediately divided into sacred and profane types; the apparently arbitrary division of sacrifice into something beloved by God, and rejected by him: this logic could be generalized to compass entire globe. Every civilization discovered, every newly encountered religious culture, was invited into this anthropological framework, each showing the proximity between the holy and the impious. Precisely because sacrifice lived uneasily on that boundary between the true and the false, precisely because sacrifice was (and had always been) both inside and outside the horizon of the Christian, it disclosed the moments when truth tipped into error, past and present.

Conclusion: Polemics and Pluralism

Purchas was fervently anti-Catholic, but by his day, the problem of stubborn Christians was no longer restricted to Catholics alone. His Chelsea college was designed to controvert not only the Pope, but also dissension among the English Protestant ranks.[121] In his last work, *Microcosmus, or the Historie of Man*, he shared his fears of a "world of other Heresies, *Familists, Anabaptists, Tritheites*, and a nameless Number of Monsters" that joined the Roman Church in threatening the rule of piety.[122] He was not alone in this feeling. Across Europe, intra-Protestant political conflict was on the rise in the last decades of the sixteenth century. The Calvinist princes of central Europe, for example, began to demand a place for their churches among the officially recognized religions of the Holy Roman Empire, leading to violent anti-Calvinist sentiment in the Lutheran church. Even among Calvinists, by the first decades of the seventeenth century, the divisions were hard to miss. In the Empire, France, the Netherlands, and England, major theological conflicts about such key doctrines as predestination began to split communities into warring factions. The Dutch church nearly fractured, for example, divided between those hewing to more hard-line Calvinist views and those so-called Remonstrants who took their lead from the Amsterdam theologian Jacob Arminius.[123]

Purchas's England was no exception to this splintering. The Protestant wind that swept away the Spanish Armada in 1588 also swept away much of the existential Catholic threat to the Elizabethan state, leaving people freer to follow more schismatic tendencies. As Calvinist hegemony broke down, the English church split into Puritan and Arminian factions, a dynamic that drove much religious and political conflict through the whole century.[124] Theological conflict about doctrines seeped into broader intra-church conflicts about all manner of things, not least liturgy and worship. Already by 1613, in short, it was, sadly, clear that merely formalizing doctrine in catechisms and sermons went only so far in producing religious consensus, and that the sources of error were deeper than simply one's "beliefs."[125] Thirty years later, moreover, all illusions of English Protestant unity had collapsed, as political and religious communities fractured into outright war. The long list of new Christian sects—Quakers, Baptists, Ranters, Diggers, Seekers, Muggletonians and the like—brought Purchas's concerns about truth and error ineluctably back home.

What turned out to be very bad for Christian unity, however, was very good for learned curiosity about global religious pluralism. A final look forward to Purchas's epigone, Alexander Ross, is instructive in this light. Ross was a minister sympathetic to the Arminian faction of the English church, those who had fought more hard-line Calvinists (we call them Puritans) for ecclesiastical supremacy since the early seventeenth century. Ross's patrons included powerful churchmen like Lancelot Andrewes and William Laud, the Archbishop of Canterbury under Charles I executed for treason by the Long Parliament in 1645. Buffeted by the warfare of the 1640s, Ross played the role of a cranky polemicist against the English revolution until his death in 1654. When he died, he was still hard at work on a second edition of a text that became extraordinarily popular, with nine editions in English and multiple ones in French, German, and Dutch before 1700. His *Pansebia: Or, a View of all the Religions of the World*, continued Purchas's tradition of a global theological geography, reprising the story of Cain and Abel in the Garden, Huitzilopochtli's doughy idols, and many other particulars from the *Pilgrims*.

Compared with Purchas's earlier work, the *Pansebia* had little new to say about sacrifice. Its popularity rested on its simplicity and brevity, rather than any intellectual innovations, *pace* scholars who have looked to Ross as an avatar of the modern study of religion.[126] Ross was above all a heresiologist. The bulk of the work was a furious attack on Christian factionalism, dedicated to the proposition that the "Diversity of Religions beget envy, malice, seditions, factions, rebellions, contempt of Superiors, treacheries, innovations, disobedience, and many other mischiefs."[127] All seventeenth-century English editions of his work were bound, moreover, with a short book entitled *Apocalypsis: Or the Revelation of Certain Notorious Advancers of Heresie*, that denounced a long list of deviants including Thomas Müntzer, Melchior Hoffman, Michael Servetus, and Muhammad. Ross sent his readers abroad, in other words, in order to come back home better prepared to combat religious difference.

Sectarian conflict was, to put this another way, the midwife to the Protestant anthropology of religion. Polemicists solved a problem by making it bigger, resetting local dilemmas on a global stage. *We* struggle with the problem of religious error, the story went, because people have *always* struggled with the problem of religious error. Human beings walk the knife edge between piety and impiety, between a suffering savior and the sacrifices of Tenochtitlan, so the seventeenth-century anthropology of sacrifice taught. No wonder, since we have done so since the very beginning, when Adam offered his firstfruits to the Devil. We are simultaneous heirs of Cain and Abel, invited to sacrifice before God, but unsure *how* to do it. And from those first brothers grew the glorious and tragic story of humanity, inclined to the divine, but tempted by sin. Piety and human violence, the sacred rites of a revealed church and the bloodbath of human sacrifice: the human story will echo with both of these until the final end of things.

The encounter and conquest of the New World, in short, reshaped the early modern sacrificial imagination in unexpected ways. For all their shortcomings, the missionaries were the best at seeing what was actually there, creating a fund of materials that are still essential to research on pre-Columbian religion and society. But their rich ethnographies were by and large buried in libraries and archives, available only locally inside the Catholic orders. Very few documents that engaged Mexica culture directly, like the *Codex Mendoza*, saw the light of day in the seventeenth century; the majority lay unknown to Europe's wider reading public until centuries later. The sacrifices of New Spain thus came into European public view filtered, especially by the interpretive screens that the Jesuit José de Acosta laid over the manuscripts he had at his disposal. His was a generation fearful of stubborn indigenous customs, and far more pessimistic about the missionary project than the earlier Franciscans. This very pessimism, however, invited Acosta to make comparisons that might have seemed scandalous to earlier generations. Of course the Eucharist and the doughy idols resembled each other, the logic ran, how better for the Devil to lure men from a righteous path. Finally, these comparative materials were recycled yet again in the Protestant world, now made witnesses to a durable anthropology of sin. If idolatry was the problem, for Protestants, sacrifice supplied the materials for its resolution. For it stood exactly athwart the line between the holy and the horrifying, a structure of ritual life common to saint and sinner. In a world where the Gospel had finally been recovered from centuries of darkness, but where even *Christians* still resisted its evident truth, the sacrifices of New Spain afforded raw material for a universal story of human beings—ancient and modern—ever struggling to distinguish between the sacred and the profane.

CHAPTER SEVEN

Kings and Martyrs

SACRIFICE AND THE SEVENTEENTH-CENTURY POLITICAL IMAGINATION

No victim more choice or bounteous could be slaughtered to Jove than an unrighteous king.

—SENECA, *HERCULES*[1]

ONCE UPON A TIME, kings presided over the smoke of sacrifice. Before he built his mighty temple in Jerusalem, King Solomon offered "a thousand burnt offerings" in the high place of sacrifice at Gibeon. In the age of the heroes, taught Aristotle's *Politics*, when his power extended over "all things in city and country," the king oversaw the rites of sacrifice. Ancient Roman kings too were masters of the altar. The first king Romulus reserved for himself, Dionysius of Halicarnassus reported, "the supremacy in religious ceremonies and sacrifices and the conduct of everything relating to the worship of the gods."[2] Foundational figures in the Western political pantheon, the king-priest was an earthly echo of Jehovah, Zeus, and Jupiter, the power of the paternal divine quivering in the arms of man. No less essential, however, were the stories of their disappearance. Eventually, the king-priests vanished: the Temple was built, the age of the heroes came to an end, and the Roman kings fled. What was left behind, one story goes, was a world newly divided between prince and cleric, each now charged to oversee their *own* worlds, sacred and profane.

Christianity too had its king-priest. He did not burn offerings or slay animals, however, but sacrificed His own flesh to placate a Father angry with fallen mankind. This suffering sovereign also brought to an end the first age of sacrificing kings. The incarnate God was "living testimony . . .

of the irretrievable split" between the human and divine worlds, bridging heaven and earth in a way unfathomable to ordinary mortals. After His death, this bridge collapsed. Caesar and Christ went their separate ways, mortal kings ceding sacrifice to the King of Heaven.[3]

In theory. In fact, the sacrificing king—whether in its pagan, Jewish, or Christian forms—never really disappeared from the political imagination of the West. Nothing ever does, after all. Things like this, powerful and fundamental myths of political and religious life, simply wait until they are brought to life again, recalled by new circumstances from the archives where they sleep. The European wars of religion were the circumstance, reawakening these ancient sacrificing kings for efforts to rethink the nature of religion and politics.

It started with the martyrs. The Crucifixion never did sever the bridge between heaven and earth, after all, between sacred death and profane politics. The ancient age of martyrs, and the early modern age of martyrs (see chapter 4), both forced piety and politics into a tense intimacy. The suffering Christ, and the suffering saints who imitated him, witnessed against the legal and political order that condemned them, claiming the truth of conscience as a *new and better* tribunal for judging matters of ultimate value.

The scope of such judgments grew wildly between 1560 and 1650. Every major political conflict in that period—the wars of religion in France, the Dutch revolt, the political upheavals in England that culminated in its revolution, the slide into the continental bloodbath of the Thirty Years' War—could be imagined as a conflict between merely human, and another, higher law. Energetic literatures of resistance theory grew up around these conflicts, defending the right to protect the pious against persecution, the right to depose infidel kings and tyrants, the right to resist the state in the name of God. All of this was in dialogue with, and an elaboration of, the martyrological imagination, the sacrificing church now in arms against mundane human justice.

Against these holy warriors arose a generation of writers, frightened by disorder, and eager to fortify new distinctions between the political and the religious, between king and priest, against the violence of religious war. Lawyers, historians, political theorists, and playwrights from across Europe's blasted lands experimented restlessly with efforts to correct the relations of sovereignty and sacrality. Legal and political thinkers turned to the political and religious customs of Rome, and its culture of Stoicism, to reimagine kingship in an age of religious conflict. By 1600—these conflicts unabated—the sacrificing kings of Seneca, playwright for an age of disorder, took over the European stage. In them, the political imagination swelled with bloody sacrifices, reflections of an age when pious and profane seemed never closer. Experiment burst beyond literature and theory, moreover, when the English monarchy collapsed in the 1640s. The execution of Charles I in January 1649 unleashed a storm of creativity, frantic efforts to "re-halo" sovereignty under new crowns of thorns that competed with no less frantic efforts to disenchant sovereignty, and to put an end, once and for all, to the age of the martyrs.

By the middle of the seventeenth century, then, the ferocity of religious violence—and the urgency of stopping it —remade the sacred, the profane, and the sacrifices that coordinated them. An older political imagination rooted both in the metaphysics of Christian kingship and the exemplary lives of Christian martyrs yielded to something more unsettling and peculiar. A new Christian politics of sacrifice was built atop the *pagan* archives of Rome, figures from ancient Roman law and religion resurrected and then deployed against the very Christian ideal and institution of martyrdom. Ancient sacrificing kings—some sober, some murderous—were recalled from dusty obscurity to help rethink the proper order of kingship and priesthood, the political and the pious. And along the way, the archive of Christian sacrifice was once more expanded, and the sacrificial imagination transformed.

Christ the King, Subject of Rome

On virtually every Crucifix in western Christianity, the inscription *INRI—Iesus Nazarenus Rex Iudaeorum*—reminds viewers that the broken man in front of them is the King of Heaven. Indeed, two of Christ's three traditional offices, *rex* and *sacerdos*, unite on the Cross, for it was there that Christ, as "high priest forever after the order" of the ancient king-priest Melchizedek, offered himself up for the salvation of all (Heb. 6.20). On the Cross, the high priest brought himself low that he might ascend to his rightful throne on high.

This *rex-sacerdos* couplet had a long history in Christian political thought. In the Latin Middle Ages, for example, the two offices of Christ coordinated with the other double aspect of the Messiah expressed in the ancient creed of Chalcedon (451 CE). Christ is "truly God and truly Man" *and* Christ is truly king and truly priest. This doubling and redoubling unleashed a cascade of analogies between Christ and secular kingship throughout the long Middle Ages. If Christ is king, for example, then king too might be Christ. The two natures converged in king Melchizedek, *rex iusticiae*, king of righteousness, as one twelfth-century work described him, human priest-king but also type of the coming Messiah.[4] Written in the height of the investiture conflict, a struggle that pitted Pope against Emperor, the so-called Norman Anonymous "geminated" rulership, as the historian Ernst Kantorowicz observed. Even the pagan Emperor Tiberius, in that work, appeared

> as a "twinned" being just as much as the God-man himself . . . this imperial *gemina persona* is set against another *gemina persona*, that of Jesus Christ . . . Thus, the strangest chiasmus imaginable results . . . as though the *potestas* of Tiberius *qua* Caesar were "haloed," whereas Christ, in his human serfdom, remains without halo.[5]

Just as Christ shares a twinned nature as God and man, so does Tiberius participate in this twinning: *evil* as a man, but *divine* as an emperor. Thus the emperors were drawn into the imaginative orbit of Christian soteriology. The title *salvator mundi* thus could be (and was) applied to both Christ and the Carolingian emperors, who were described in turn as *christus per gratiam*, as the expression went, *Christ by grace*.[6] The political theology of that era, Kantorowicz shows, abounded in such curious admixtures, which "haloed" a pagan emperor, secularized Christ, and split the king into a body natural and a body eternal. The king is dead, long live the king: it was as easily said about Christ as any mortal monarch.

This *Christus-rex* analogy so important to the medieval political imagination did not long survive the destruction of Christian unity, however. In a world where monarchs were Christian to some, and infidels to others, older ways of configuring the relationship between sacred and secular power were subject to ruthless criticism. What resulted were *new* experiments with sacrifice, sacrality, and kingship, ones tailored for an age of Christian fracture.

As an opening example, let's begin in 1591, when the learned humanist Justus Lipsius returned to the Catholic Church. *Religio ac Fama*—religion and notoriety—drove him out of Leiden, the leading Dutch university and intellectual heart of Protestant Europe, he later wrote, after glorious years of learning there. His editions of Tacitus; his encomium to Stoic ethics, the *De constantia libri duo* (1584); and his political work, the *Politicorum sive civilis doctrinae libri sex* (1589): these products of his Dutch years established his reputation as Europe's leading Stoic thinker.

It was the last of these works that got him into trouble, however. Its advocacy of strict public conformity in matters religious created just the kind of local uproar that Lipsius, advocate of the Stoic virtue of *ataraxia*, equanimity, most disliked. The Catholic Church subjected it to correction through its Index of Prohibited Books. Meanwhile, Dutch Calvinists—already at war with Hapsburg Spain since the 1560s—angrily condemned its apparent call for the suppression of religious nonconformists. In this storm of controversy, Lipsius abandoned the Dutch world, turning back to his ancestral Church and to the open arms of the Catholic university of Leuven.[7]

Among the first things that Lipsius wrote after his readmission to the faith of his fathers was a learned treatise on the Crucifix. Since the dawn of the Reformation, the image of the crucified Christ had polarized Christian communities, between Catholics who venerated its depiction of the passion, and those reformed who saw only an invitation to idolatry. Lipsius's *De cruce,* dedicated to the State of Brabant and published in 1594, avoided this polemical minefield.[8] As he wrote in 1583, he viewed theology as elephants are said to view water: they delight in it, but "do not not enter it boldly, since they do not know how to swim."[9] In *De cruce,* his approach to this theologically vexed subject was therefore oblique. Take the standard doctrinal question: why was Christ crucified? Lipsius's answer was idiosyncratic. He did not say, for example, that He was crucified to atone for mankind's sins, or to prepare His victorious triumph over death. Rather, he turned the question into a purely *legal* one: what crime was Christ supposed to have committed for which he was crucified?

Asked in this way ("with piety, not curiosity," Lipsius quickly added), the Crucifixion looked quite different. All three synoptic Gospels report a trial of Christ before the Sanhedrin, the assembly of elders and judges in Jerusalem, who found him guilty of blasphemy. Per Leviticus, however, the Hebrew punishment for blasphemy was not crucifixion, but stoning. Philo Judaeus in his *Special Laws* did mention crucifixion, but for murder, not blasphemy.[10] This raised a puzzle, and suggested that the sentencing authority was *not* the Sanhedrin but the Roman state. Christ was punished, Lipsius ventured, according to "Roman laws and customs":

> Our innocent lamb was condemned as if in the name of sedition and pretended royal authority. Clearly by Roman law, *the authors of sedition or tumult, in accordance to their status, either are subject to the cross, or thrown to the beasts.* And indeed he was accused of this before Pilate, as Luke plainly writes: "We found this man subverting our nation, and forbidding that tribute be rendered to Caesar, and saying that he himself Christ is the King." Pilate believed it, and he didn't

believe it (*credidit nec credidit Pilatus*); and nevertheless, he had the title and the cause of His death inscribed, *Rex Iudaeorum*.[11]

The source was the jurist Paul, as recorded in the *Digest of Justinian*, one of the three pillars of the ancient Roman *Corpus iuris civilis*. It suggested that Christ had been found guilty of *lèse majesté*, an offense against the majesty of the state. The claim to the name "king of the Jews" would not have been a mere Jewish libel reported to the skeptical Pilate. Rather it was a serious legal offense, a usurpation of rightful Roman authority. And so it was that (believe it or not) Pilate inscribed Christ's name and sentence on the cross: *Iesus Nazarenus Rex Iudaeorum*.

Like the geminated figures of medieval political theology, Lipsius's *Christus-rex* was a strange composite. But its elements were altogether more mundane. He did not directly deny the soteriological significance of the Crucifixion. In fact, he supplemented doctrine with the quotidian and violent operations of law. *Iesus Nazarenus Rex Iudaeorum* was carved above Christ's head neither in mockery nor as a sign of Christ's divine kingship. Rather, it precisely named his crime and its punishment. Even the crown of thorns registered the nature of Christ's offense, a crown of punishment for a crown illegitimately assumed. Those who claim the crown for themselves commit sedition, even a messiah like Christ. By putting Christ's death into this ordinary legal setting, Lipsius gave the religious office of Christ, sovereign of heaven and self-sacrificing king, a worldly cast. The kingdom of Christ was not of this world, Lipsius suggested, but only of the next. In *this* world, Christ was a subject of Rome.

This learned treatise of the Crucifix thus accorded with Lipsius's politics of restraint and obedience. If government is the "sole pillar of human affairs," as Lipsius had written in his 1589 *Politica*, then religion is the sine qua non of civil peace, the "sole creator of unity." "In every commonwealth," Lipsius tendentiously repeated Aristotle, "*the care of sacred matters comes first*." For the prudent prince, then, the first goal is to preserve ancient customs: "*a wise man protects the traditions of his ancestors, by preserving their religion and rituals*," as Cicero observed. Above all, the *Politics* was committed to a political order unmoved by the passions of private conscience. To the martyrs who insisted that conviction warranted disobedience, even violence, Lipsius responded with the public cult of sacrifice found in ancient Rome. Cicero teaches us to "worship and preserve the ancient gods"; Tacitus that the sacrifices (*ritus sacrorum*) should be observed in both adversity and prosperity. This public *cultus*, as Lipsius called it, must be subject to public authority. As regards one's private religious convictions, however true they may be, Lipsius echoed the Roman Seneca, "*it is permitted to be silent*."[12] The preeminence of public order over private belief held even for the Messiah, who accepted his terrible punishment, after all, without a word of protest.

The Sacrificing King: Lessons from Roman Religion

In ancient times [the king's] power extended continuously to all things whatsoever . . . but at a later date they relinquished several of these privileges, and others the people took from them, until in some states nothing was left to them but the sacrifices.

ARISTOTLE, *POLITICS*, 1285B14–17

The fragmentation of the *respublica Christiana* shattered the medieval metaphysics of monarchy. It also put enormous strain on the traditional martyrological imagination, in which suffering and death witnessed the truth of faith against the injustice of state authority. For Lipsius, neither the metaphysics of kingship nor the ancient martyrs of the church supplied the tools for founding civil order. What was needed were *new* ways of imagining "the role of ruler as both *rex* and *sacerdos*," new ways of imagining the relationship between state power and the sacred.[13] Beyond the martyrological archives, then, and beyond the metaphysics of kingship, authors like Lipsius looked to pagan *Rome* to help them rethink the deep structures of kingship, sacrifice, and the sacred in an age of religious fracture. To Rome we go, then, on the trail of its sacrificing kings.

We already met Rome's "king of the sacrifices"—the *rex sacrorum* or *rex sacrificulus*—in chapter 5, when antiquarians like Alexander ab Alexandro and Polydore Vergil collected stories about this puzzling sovereign. The Greek historian Dionysius of Halicarnassus recounted how the founder of the Roman republic, Lucius Brutus, "appointed a king of sacred rites, exercising this single function, the superintendence of the sacrifices, and no other." Livy added that Lucius Junius Brutus, founder of the republic, had made this king "subordinate to the pontifex, lest the office, in conjunction with the title, might somehow prove an obstacle to liberty." And Plutarch remarked how the Romans "put up with royalty only to please their gods," linking the *rex sacrorum* to the Roman holiday of the *Regifugium*, celebrated on February 24 to commemorate the fleeing of the Tarquins from Rome. These classical sources suggested that there were kings in Rome before the Republic; these kings performed sacrifices and other sacred rites; when these kings were expelled, the new

Roman state established an officer, the *rex sacrorum*, whose duty was the performance of these rites; and this officer was the *sole* bearer of the name *rex* in the new republican and later, in the imperial Roman world, when the Emperor Augustus revived the institution once more. When Christ received His thorny crown, in ca. 33 CE in the Roman province of Judaea, there was only one king in Rome, this curious priest-king, a relic from the long-dead Roman monarchy.[14]

Already before the age of religious war, the *rex sacrificulus* had entered the European political imagination. In his *Discourses on Livy* (written ca. 1517), for example, the Florentine Niccolò Machiavelli (1469–1527) used it to think about about perils of political foundation. Rome, legend reported, had been founded by the warrior king Romulus. He built the first temple and began to organize the religious life of the ancient monarchy. Rome's second king, Numa Pompilius, had in turn softened the "fierce and warlike tempers" of the ancient Romans with "sacrifices, processions, and religious dances," consulted the gods before ascending the throne, and gave the Roman king the sanction of heaven.[15]

When the Roman republicans expelled the Tarquins, they thus realized that the long memory of kingship, blessed by the gods, posed a political challenge to the new state. Wisely, Machiavelli wrote, the republic recognized "the necessity of retaining at least a shadow of its ancient modes," lest the new political order seem "altogether alien to the past one."[16] The *rex sacrificulus* was one of these shadows:

> Since an annual sacrifice was offered in Rome that could not be done except by the king in person, and since the Romans wished the people not to have to desire anything ancient because of the absence of the kings, they created . . . the sacrificing king . . . by this way, the people came to be satisfied with the sacrifice and never to have cause, for lack of it, to desire the return of kings. This should be observed by all those who wish to suppress an ancient way of life in a city and to turn it to a new and free way of life.[17]

In a state founded on sacred origins, Machiavelli observed, preserve as many of these as possible in the name of civil peace. Since its sacrifices were essential to Rome's political constitution, the republicans wisely decided to keep them as intact as possible, appointing a titular king to preserve their force in the new political order.

The communal and social function of sacrifice reverberated throughout Machiavelli's politics of religion. Over the long history of Rome, the Florentine argued, religious sacrifice constantly created and recreated political life. The Roman consul Publius Decius (fourth century BCE), who devoted himself to death to destroy his Gallic enemies, was exemplary of the "simple virtue" that draws a republic "back to its beginnings."[18] Since all things grow old and ossified, Machiavelli pointed out, the life of the state demands periodic rejuvenation. New institutions built to check political corruption can provide this. But more often, rejuvenation demands more than wise policy. Rather, it depends on the actions of heroic men, who "without depending on any law" offer such powerful examples that "good men desire to imitate them." Publius Decius, and later his son and grandson—self-sacrificers all—were just such men, whose heroism "produced in Rome almost the same effect that laws and orders produced."[19]

Sacrifice thus stitched Rome's religious and political institutions together, founding new communities and renewing ones grown old and weak. All of this stood in sharp contrast with the religious politics of Machiavelli's world. Christianity, as he wrote, "disarmed heaven" and left men servile and weak, creating a world of endless disorder. Her trembling martyrs paled in comparison with the "blood and ferocity" of Roman sacrifice, whose terrible beauty "rendered men similar to itself."[20] The combination of a malignant Church and an ethic of servility, in his view, made Christianity a singularly bad foundation for new political and legal orders. "Unarmed prophets," as he memorably called them in *The Prince* (1513), can seldom found the new political and religious orders about which they dream.[21] To remake politics takes an "armed prophet" like Romulus or Moses, whose legal and religious innovations paired with ruthlessness toward their enemies.

The age of armed prophets began soon after Machiavelli died in 1527. The German peasants' war of 1525; the new Anabaptist Jerusalem violently established in Münster in 1533; the savage wars of religion that overwhelmed the Holy Roman Empire, France, and the Netherlands after the 1540s; new martyrs and judges who condemned them: this new age of religious fracture produced scores of people willing to kill and die for religious and political dreams.

These armed prophets not only destroyed the peace of Europe. They also made it abundantly clear to many that the older politics of sacrifice—whether rooted in Christly kingship or Christian martyrdom—needed serious re-imagination. As with Machiavelli, pagan Rome offered an historical archive for new projects in the political imagination, this time for those most eager to defang those armed prophets, and to secure political authority for new absolutist states.

The French lawyer, historian, and theorist of sovereignty Jean Bodin (1530–1596), for example, knew about the *rex sacrificulus*. His whole life unfolded under the shadow of France's religious conflicts. In his early days among the Carmelites in Paris, he witnessed his brothers arrested and executed for heresy. When he left the order to study law in Toulouse, he saw local authorities publicly strangle and burn stubborn adherents of the new Lutheran and later Reformed heterodoxies. When he arrived in Paris in the late 1550s to work in its ancient and powerful law court, the Parlement, he observed firsthand France's slow descent into civil war. And his 1576 *Six Books of the Republic*—the work that practically invented the modern concept of sovereignty—was overshadowed by the goriest episode of all, when, on St. Bartholomew's Day 1572, thousands of Huguenots were massacred at the behest of the Crown, their bodies dumped into the Seine, a bloody nadir of the conflicts that split France into violently antagonistic camps.[22]

Out of these civil wars emerged a new kind of Protestant martyr. The helpless victims celebrated by the martyrologies were now joined by armed prophets willing to kill for the faith. As the head of the Geneva church, Theodore Beza, concluded his radical 1574 pamphlet *Right of Magistrates*: "we must honor as martyrs not only those who have conquered without resistance, and by patience only, against tyrants who have persecuted the church, but also those who, authorized by law and competent authorities, devoted their strength to the true religion."[23] Beza's text was a cornerstone of Reformed resistance theory, a vibrant political literature that blossomed from the 1560s onward. When "the living temple of God should be delivered over to idols," then Christians are entitled to rise against their rulers, proclaimed so-called monarchomachs like the anonymous French author of the *Vindiciae contra tyrannos* (1579), another popular treatise that emerged from the crucible of St. Bartholomew's Day. Exemplary figures included the prophet Elijah, whose true sacrifices vanquished the idolatrous priests of Baal, after which he had them slaughtered, and Old Testament rebels like Mattathias, father of Judas Maccabee, who "waged war against [the Seleucid King] Antiochus for religion and country—for altars, I say, and hearths—[and] restored the true worship of God." Those that die in holy war are no less "martyrs than those who suffered the cross for the sake of religion."[24] "*Imitatio Christi* with a vengeance," one historian has aptly remarked, as the community of saints broadened to include the armed prophets of God.[25]

To such declarations of war on established government, Bodin offered a new foundation of political order, what he called *souveraineté* in French, or in Latin, *maiestas* or *summum imperium*, something that "neither jurisconsult nor political philosopher" had ever properly specified.[26] The arrangements that people invent to order their political lives, what Bodin called government, are various. But in all of these arrangements there exists *one* person (monarchy), *one* group of people (aristocracy), or *one* collectivity (democracy) that possesses the "true marks" of "the absolute and perpetual power of a republic."[27] These marks include the right to appoint magistrates, to grant powers, and "to have power of life and death": whoever possesses them is, by definition, the sovereign.[28]

On the face of it, Rome was a challenge to this unitary sovereignty, possessing what ancients and moderns called a "mixed constitution," whereby sovereignty was shared, or distributed, in ways that made opaque the true nature of a polity.[29] Rome was, as Machiavelli put it, a constitution in which "all three kinds of government . . . had their part."[30] The main ancient source for this view was the Greek historian Polybius, whose *Histories* extensively described the syncretic form of the Roman republic, blending the institutions of monarchy, aristocracy, and democracy equally.[31] Through Polybius, the longest lasting republic on earth might seem a terrible indictment of Bodin's project.

The *rex sacrorum*, however, helped to recruit Rome to the service of sovereignty. For Polybius was deceived, Bodin reported, having lived too close to Sparta, where the wise lawgiver Lycurgus had "translated souvereigntie unto the people [and] left unto the kings, the bare name and title alone." This transference retained the form "without any power at all to command," e.g., without the *substance* of the ancient monarchy.[32] The same thing, he pointed out, could be said about Rome: "in Rome, after the kings were driven out, they left the name of king to a certain priest, who they called the king of the sacrifices, in order to perform a certain sacrifice that only the king had been able to do earlier; this priest . . . could not, as Plutarch tells us, have any estate or bear any office."[33] When Rome became a republic, in other words, the transference of sovereignty was *complete*; all of the powers of the ancient kings were now to be held by the people of Rome. Rome was not a mixed constitution after all, so the sacrificing king showed, but a sovereign state.

As it turned out, the archives of both Roman kingship and Roman sacrifice had much to offer someone eager to combat the armed prophets of his day. The ancient powers of kings were codified, for example, in what was called the *lex regia*. For writers like Bodin, these laws helped specify the unitary nature of sovereign power. In the Roman Digest, for example, the jurist Ulpian confirmed that the people of Rome conferred their "entire authority" on the Emperor by virtue of the *lex regia* (Dig. 1.4.1). A bronze tablet inscribed with the *lex de imperio Vespasiani*—ceremonially installed in the Roman Church of St. John Lateran by the self-styled "tribune of Rome" and demagogue Cola di Rienzo in the fourteenth century—verified this.[34] This edict declared that the laws of the emperor Vespasian (69–79 CE) were "legal and valid, just as if they had been done by order of the people or plebs."[35] Sovereignty was singular, this showed, despite dramatic changes in government.

Roman regalian law applied directly, it seemed to Bodin and others, to Europe's civil wars of religion. Take for example the laws of Romulus, Numa Pompilius, and the other mythical Roman monarchs written down by the first *rex sacrorum,* Gaius Papirius.[36] Many in the later sixteenth century worked to reconstruct these. The pioneering French historian of Roman law François Baudouin, for example, in 1550 published an extensive commentary on the laws of Romulus.[37] The French jurist Louis Le Caron compiled the "laws of the ancient Romans" from "tablets" and other classical authorities, and published them in a short handbook in 1567.[38] Our Belgian antiquarian, Justus Lipsius, did the same, offering an even briefer synopsis of the laws of Romulus and Numa in 1589.[39] There readers learned that the first law of Romulus reserved for the king "supremacy in religious ceremonies and sacrifices and the conduct of everything related to the worship of the gods."[40] The laws of Numa Pompilius, for their part, were almost entirely about the regulation of sacrifice.[41] "*Sacrorum omnium potestas sub Regibus esto*. The power over all sacred matters [or, all *sacrifices*] shall fall to the kings," was the Romulan regalian law echoed in 1596 by the jurist Anne Robert, a successor to Bodin at the Paris Parlement.[42] The archives of ancient Roman law supplied solutions, it seemed, to the martyrological politics of the civil wars.[43]

Catholics were not the only ones to put Rome's sacrificing kings to work for new theories of kingship suitable to an age of armed prophets. From the beginning of its revolt against Spanish rule, the Netherlands rang with strident affirmations of the obligation to defend a suffering church against a tyrant king.[44] By 1615, however, the problems were *among* the Protestants themselves, now quarreling over the nature of right belief and worship. Conflict between factions—some more moderate Arminian and some more hard-line Calvinist—spilled into the political realm. The rioting that spread through Dutch cities, and the constitutional crises this caused, ultimately destroyed the most powerful politician in the Netherlands, Johan van Oldenbarneveldt, the Lands' Advocate for the States of Holland.[45] It also nearly dragged his young ally and protege, the humanist lawyer, historian, poet, and statesman Hugo Grotius, into an early grave (see chapter 8 for more on Grotius and the Arminian crisis). As the crisis unfolded, this pioneer of international law, and one of the great minds of the Dutch seventeenth century, responded with a treatise that would settle issues of church government, he hoped, and end Holland's troubles. Begun in 1614, Grotius's *On the Authority of the Sovereign with Regard to the Sacred* once again turned to Rome, and other ancient sacrificing kings, for help in re-imagining the Christian polity.

From the very beginning of things, and long before Christ became a king of Heaven, Grotius wrote, "nature and right reason" combined *rex* and *sacerdos* into a single office:

> In the earliest history of the world . . . the heads of the family held something like kingship and played the part of priests as well. On that basis Noah sacrifices to God when the earth is liberated from the Flood. God says of Abraham: *that he shall show his children and his household the way of pious living.* Thus we read of sacrifices by Job and other patriarchs . . . in the same period a kind of state had come into existence in the Canaanite region and there Melchizedek held the kingship and priesthood at the same time. . . . the most ancient peoples appear to have had the same rules of sacrifice . . . in Homer, too, heroes, that is rulers, do sacrifice . . . Dionysius of Halicarnassus and Livy inform us the Romans imitated this custom, and that is why, when kingship was abolished, the "rex sacrorum" remained.[46]

The primal right of sacrifice resided, at the beginning, in the natural power of fathers, sovereigns over families, as the Roman Law of the Twelve Tables proclaimed. Ancient patriarchs like Noah, Job, and Abraham exercised this right either through reason and natural instinct (as when Noah offered his sacrifices) or in response to divine command (as when Abraham brought Isaac to the Mount Moriah). Melchizedek—that type of Christ, king and priest alike—was just one of many such figures from this ancient world where sovereignty and sacrifice were joined in the king. Ethiopians, Spartans, Egyptians, Athenians: all ancient cultures evidenced the symbiosis that sustained the *rex sacrorum.*

What did this deep anthropology of kingship mean for a Christian polity? Theocrats might answer that "supreme authority and priestly office" must *always* be combined.[47] Grotius had had his fill of preachers fulminating against impious politicians, however. In the *rex sacrorum,* he thus discovered a middle way between theocracy and anarchy. There was indeed an ancient connection between king and priest, it showed, but these were easily separable. Royal authority was therefore *distinct* from the priesthood, Rome and Israel both demonstrated. "If nobody but the king himself had carried out the chief sacrifices, as the custom had been," Grotius pointed out, Israel would have been captivated (*haesissent*) by the grandeur of this king-priest. But when the ancient Israelite theocracy came to an end, the high priesthood was "stripped of its royal splendour" and subjected to the kings. Ultimately, Grotius piously concluded, this prepared the Hebrews "for a greater higher priest to come, who would also be king, as Melchizedek had been."[48]

In the Roman *rex sacrorum* and in ancient Israel, Grotius thus discovered a politics suitable to an age of armed prophets. On the one hand, the ancient connection between *imperium* and the priesthood suggested that kings had a "certain spiritual power."[49] "Kings are to be regarded as holy (*sanctos*)," Grotius later wrote in his *On the Law of War and Peace* (1625).[50] This holiness gave sovereigns authority over not only "secular [*profana*]" but also religious affairs. On the other hand, however holy the king, his *function* as priest was ultimately distinct from his sovereign office. The sovereign can be a priest in the same way he can be a physician, philosopher, astronomer, or poet. And although "no function is more excellent . . . than that of priest," Grotius wrote, still a king can delegate this function to others without diminishing his authority *circa sacra*.[51]

Neither earnest believers nor pious magistrates can therefore legitimately challenge the sword of authority. "It makes no difference whether the pretext for force and violence is religion or anything else," Grotius insisted, "for the supreme power remains liable for its own right." Even ancient Christian *martyrs* were witnesses, in his view, against rebellion in the name of holiness. When the Roman emperor Diocletian ordered the "burning of manuscripts of the Bible, the destruction of the churches, and the crucifixion of Christians themselves, there was only one Christian who tore up the edict," Grotius tendentiously cited the church father Eusebius: "when he received capital punishment for this, the other Christians declared that he had deserved death."[52]

The age of armed prophets, in short, reanimated the archives of pagan sacrifices. Machiavelli still imagined a servile Christianity unwilling to mobilize the power of sacrifice. Later writers were not so sanguine about Christianity's sacrificial politics. Abandoning an older metaphysics of Christian kingship, they turned instead to the histories and anthropologies of pagan kingship for new normative models for *rex* and *sacerdos*. The absolutist Bodin discovered in the historical *rex sacrorum* lessons about the unitary nature of sovereignty, learning that the power over sacrifice *and* sacred matters has always belonged to kings. Grotius—no less absolutist in leaning—hoped the sacrificing kings of Rome and Israel might afford new models for the peaceful relationship of politics and the sacred. In all cases, this ancient Roman king-priest displaced the sacrificing king native to Christian political thought, Christ himself.

The Monstrosity of the Sacrificing King

Avoid shedding human blood, all you who reign: your crimes are assessed with higher penalties.

—SENECA, *HERCULES*, 745–747

"Around 1600," the historian Gerhard Oestreich once wrote, "Stoicism became the ideology, almost the religion, of educated men." For Lipsius, Bodin, and Grotius, luminaries of this "Roman Century," the answer to the wars of religion—martyrs, armed prophets, civil war—was a "well defined order of commanding and obeying," as Lipsius defined *imperium*.[53] The fracture of Christianity demanded an ordered state, a prudent prince, and the ethics of clemency, restraint, and self-discipline, values no one expressed better than the Stoic author, Seneca, to whose political and ethical writings Lipsius gave much of his learned life.[54]

Stoic political theory could not contain the violence of this fracture, however. In the scholar's study, ancient sacrificing kings offered sober lessons of restraint and control. Outside the scholar's study, the disorder of Europe's religious life produced wilder visions of ancient sacrificial kingship, crazed sovereigns thirsty for blood and death. "Let the king desire what is honorable; everyone will want the same," Lipsius advised the readers of his *Politica* with the words of Seneca.[55] But the advice came not from the Roman's cool ethical doxa. They were instead those spoken to ancient King Atreus—father of Agamemnon and Menelaus—whose terrible crimes Seneca explored in his play *Thyestes*, an orgy of violence, human sacrifice, and cannibalism. It was Atreus whose monstrous mind devised the "unspeakable feast" known as the Thyestean banquet. "In my kingdom, death is something that people beg for," the King vowed, before tricking his usurping brother into eating his own sons in a magnificent banquet.[56] King Atreus prepared the feast with an unholy sacrifice of the boys:

> The incense is not missing, nor Bacchus' holy liquid nor the knife that touches the victims with salted meal . . . [and Atreus] himself is priest . . . Wine poured in libation on the fires changes as it flows to

> blood; the royal emblem slips repeatedly from his head; ivory statues weep in the temples. All are affected by these prodigies, but Atreus alone remains unaffected and constant [*immotus Atreus constat*].[57]

Atreus burned the incense, sprinkled the sacred *mola salsa*, and then fed the child-victims to their unwitting father. The sacrifice and the banquet—whose intimacy antiquarians like Stucki had already observed—here merged into monstrous piety. "What is normally a punishment becomes a prayer," sacred and profane exchanged places, the royal emblem slipped, and the earth groaned in protest.[58] Throughout Atreus was indeed *constant*, the poet said, that virtue so beloved by Stoics like Lipsius now bent toward insanity and slaughter.

"Stoic detachment is continuous," Gordon Braden remarks, "with the most paralytic kind of anger."[59] This was no less true in the age of Nero than it was in the late sixteenth century, when the furious sovereigns of Senecan drama stormed into Europe's literary and political imagination. Seneca's plays were reprinted in Latin, translated into English, Dutch, and German, and endlessly emulated in the tragic drama of the period. William Shakespeare, Christopher Marlowe, Joost van den Vondel, Hugo Grotius, Martin Opitz, Andreas Gryphius, Pierre Corneille, Jean Racine: nearly every major dramatist from the late sixteenth century onward staged the bloodthirsty tyrants, ritual sacrifice, cannibalism, incest, and other monstrous pathologies characteristic of the Senecan play.[60] "I consecrated and slaughtered this flock to you, wife of almighty Jove": so culminated the horror of Hercules, who, fury become frenzy, murdered his own wife and children in the name of the gods.[61] What Debora Shuger describes as the "undifferentiated, miasmatic cruelty" of late sixteenth century Passion plays found its analogue in the theater of political violence whose greatest classical exponent was Seneca.[62]

The monstrous sacrificing kings of Senecan drama upended the sober visions of a *rex sacrorum*, sternly coordinating sacred and secular realms. Solemn rites became instead instruments of vengeance for anger-crazed madmen.[63] When the Roman general Titus Andronicus—in Shakespeare's play—sacrificed the son of the Gothic queen Tamora to satisfy the "groaning shadows" of his own murdered children, he initiated a murderous cycle that drove the play into gory horror: "for their brethren slain/religiously they ask a sacrifice; To this your son is marked, and die he must."[64] Tamora's response was equally violent: the rape of Titus's daughter, hands and tongue severed to keep her silent. By the end, revenge came full circle: Titus Andronicus sacrificed the last of Tamora's murderous children, making of their flesh a new Thyestean banquet for their mother, now empress of Rome, to devour.

These sacrificing kings too haunted the seventeenth-century imagination, unsettling substitutes for the older metaphysics of Christian kingship. Already in the 1920s, the literary critic Walter Benjamin noted how the "tyrant and martyr in the Baroque age are the two Janus-faces of the crowned head," the frenzied violence of a Herod now translated into the idiom of a Passion play.[65] What he described as the "conflict" between the depravity of the tyrant and the "sacrosanct power of his role"—the unstable combinations of sacrality and profanity so striking in *Thyestes* and *Titus Andronicus*—was staged over and over, in plays like Andreas Gryphius's *Leo Armenius* (1650), Johann Christian Hallmann's *Mariamne* (1669), or Daniel Caspar von Lohenstein's *Sophonisbe* (1669), to remain only within the horizon of the German language plays that especially interested Benjamin.[66]

For Bodin and Grotius, the *rex sacrorum* suggested a clear organization of politics and the sacred. The martyr-kings of German tragic drama suggested that any such clarity was a fantasy. The hero of Gryphius's *Leo Armenius*—a usurping Byzantine emperor murdered on an altar during a Christmas Mass—was both a tyrant deserving death and a martyr in whose dying arms was clasped, the author fantasized, the very cross "on which our Savior sacrificed himself," supposedly preserved in Constantinople.[67] This admixture of sacred and profane lingered, sickly sweet, over the entire play. In its final act, for example, Armenius's murderers hacked off the same arms that cradled the Cross. Although dismembered saints are no strangers in the Christian archive, they are rarely dismembered *on a Christian altar*. Smearing the True Cross with the Emperor's own blood was the final, characteristic touch, a scene both disgusting and pious, "a miracle . . . and the most radical blasphemy."[68] This chimera of monster and saint was characteristic of the genre.

That sovereignty's halo was in trouble would have been lost on few people living in the Holy Roman Empire in the 1650s. The armed conflicts unleashed in 1618 in Bohemia devastated much of central Europe for the next three decades. Virtually every prince and principality in Europe was involved, from Spain to Sweden, and the principal battlegrounds were virtually all in central Europe, a scene of devastation by war's end in 1648. When the Silesian poet Christian Hoffmann von Hoffmannswaldau completed his scholarly peregrinations through Leiden, Amsterdam, Paris, and Rome in 1641, and returned to his home in the eastern city of Breslau (now Wroclaw, Poland), he found "the cities entirely ravaged." Indeed, that city lost nearly half of its population during the war, and greater Silesia over 20 percent by war's end.[69] "Men's lives should be compared to books/ where black marks are many, and white very few," he later wrote.[70] For anyone from Silesia—and Gryphius lived there most of his life—any sober theory of kingship ran aground on the impotence, hubris, and avarice that were the hallmarks of the Thirty Years' War.

For the dramas written in its shadow, there was nothing sacred about sacrifice or kingship. We will take as exemplary the work of another Breslau native, David Caspar von Lohenstein, who observed firsthand not only the devastation of the Thirty Years' War, but also the political aftermath that subjected this Protestant city to increasingly stringent control by its territorial overlords, the Catholic Hapsburgs. His 1669 play *Sophonisbe* again brought readers to Rome, restaging a story found in Livy's account of the Punic Wars. In the ancient text, Sophonisbe was a valiant defender of her homeland. Daughter of a Carthaginian general and wife of a Numidian king, at the defeat of her husband's army, she seduced the conquering general. Later, mistrusted by Roman authorities, and facing captivity in Rome, she fearlessly slaughtered herself rather than endure the shame.

In Lohenstein, however, all glory of sacrifice was gone. "Law lies with the conquerer," remarked his Sophonisbe about Rome, "to victorious violence is all injustice justice."[71] This bleak logic of power without right was mirrored in a series of awful sacrifices. "Come hither, children, whoever is worthy among you to climb upon the glowing grate, as sacrifice for the health of the fatherland": thus Sophonisbe—no longer Livy's pious pagan but now a bloodthirsty *regina sacrorum*—summoned her own blood as offerings to the goddess Baaltis. The young boys envision the sacrifice as a scene of transcendence: "out of your ashes will bloom the phoenix of joy," one son says to the other.[72] But their hopes are stymied by the officiating priest:

> In a moment of such need, the glowing idol of the gods
> must be moistened with the blood of others. Is there not another
> victim?
> Then sun and moon desire on their flaming altar
> as victims the firstborns of the prisoners.[73]

Instead of the boys, terrified Roman prisoners are led to the altar, cursing the "demonic house of idols," where the priest cuts out their hearts and offers them to the sun and moon. Sophonisbe, watching, echoes Christ's last words on the Cross and declares the sacrifice "finished (*vollbracht*)."[74] But the event that the sacrifice was supposed to forestall—the fall of the

Numidian kingdom—advanced ineluctably. Sacrifice and sovereignty were linked, but in a dark and terrible way. "Left to its own mercy, the human race is its own damnation," as Braden writes.[75]

Such disenchantments—where piety becomes abomination, sacrifice mere murder—organized the play's inevitable descent into brutality. We even find learned versions of this in the play's *footnotes*. Like most of his tragedian colleagues—Gryphius wrote a whole tragedy about the Roman law jurist Papinian!—Lohenstein was at home in this erudite world.[76] And his plays wore their learning ostentatiously, pairing drama with learned annotations. In *Sophonisbe*, these notes included classical and patristic authorities, as well as a cast of modern writers that included Lipsius, the geographer Samuel Bochart, the antiquarians Gerhard Vossius and John Selden, the Jesuit Athanasius Kircher, the historian Georg Hornius, and dozens of others from fields like mythography, rabbinics, music, and poetry.[77] Like the plot, this erudition made the sacrificing king more an object of horror than veneration.

In the first act, for example, Sophonisbe invokes her bloody goddess: "Baaltis, listen to me, who has always covered you with the noble blood of man, and the flesh of children."[78] In a lengthy note to this, Lohenstein rehearsed the bloody history of human sacrifice among the Carthaginians, the Gauls, the ancient Germans, cults of Saturn, even Peru and the Yucatan: "all the books are full of this sort of gruesome human sacrifice." Even *Abraham*, the note continued, supplies us with an example of sacrifice gone wrong:

> In this idolatry the blind and erring pagans sought to imitate not only Abraham, who wanted to sacrifice his son, and Jephta, who would sacrifice his daughter, but also the Jews who sacrificed their children to Moloch.[79]

Deep behind Sophonisbe's cry, then, we hear an echo of the *Akedah*, Abraham, that original sacrificing king, on the mountain with Isaac. Like Abraham, Sophonisbe too was ready to sacrifice her own; like him, she too was stopped at the very brink of a monstrous act; and like him, she too was offered the "proper" sacrificial object to complete the rite.

There is *no* original pious sacrifice, might be the moral of the story. Even Christian sacrifice was a question. The strangeness of the Gospel of John coming out of the mouth of a devotee of Baaltis would hardly have been lost on listeners. No less unsettling was the devotion that the Carthaginian priest showed to her cult, offering himself, like Leo Armenius, as a sacrifice on her own altar, and "kissing her noble cross." In another learned aside (and coming full circle), Lohenstein pointed his readers to Justus Lipsius's *De cruce*, and the distinctions he discovered there between traditions of Roman crucifixion, reserved for the rabble, and African crucifixion, the privilege of the nobility.[80]

For someone like Acosta, the surprising discovery of the cross in pagan Peru was reassuring. For Lohenstein, such surprises—the intimacy of the Cross of Christ and the cross of Baaltis, the proximity of sacred and profane—were less so. His world was one where piety and impiety were close neighbors, where the cosmos was disordered, where kingship was monstrous, and where sacrifices inevitably fail. "The whole order is changed, nothing lies in its proper place . . . nature is inverted, no lawfulness remains in the womb": these words, from Seneca's *Oedipus*, applied as much to the disordered world of ancient Thebes as to seventeenth-century Breslau.[81]

Conscience, Law, and the Sacrificed King

Sacrificing kings were not confined to the sober theory of imperial Roman Stoics, or the fevered plays of war-ravaged Breslau. The concerns that drove the Senecan revival—how to distinguish between sacrifice and murder, martyrdom and execution, justice and power, divine law and human law—had real-world analogues. When, after almost a decade of civil bloodshed, the English Parliament put their monarch on trial for levying war against Parliament and people, for example, it may not have been with the intention to kill him.[82] But kill him they did. Ten days of trial ended on the morning of January 30, 1649, when Charles Stuart was led to the scaffold before the Banqueting Hall at Whitehouse, laid his head on the block, and was beheaded before a watching crowd.

As soon as the news reached the continent, Andreas Gryphius began work on the play he titled *Murdered Majesty: or, Charles Stuart, King of Great Britain* (first ed., 1657). He based the play on the most effective royalist pamphlet in the revolutionary era, the *Eikon Basilike*: *the Pourtraicture of His Sacred Majestie in his Solitudes and Sufferings.*[83] Within a week of the execution, the first printing of the *Eikon* was already circulating. Before the year was out, there were thirty-five more printings in England alone. And by the end of 1649, readers of Latin, Dutch, Danish, French, and German had access to a work allegedly penned by the King for the occasion of his own martyrdom (fig. 7.1).[84]

That the "king's book" resonated for poets like Gryphius was testament not only to the prodigality of the event, the first judicial execution of a

FIGURE 7.1. The King-Martyr Charles I. [John Gauden], *Eikon Basilike* ([London?], 1649). Courtesy of the Folger Library Digital Collections.

king in European history. Almost as important was the rhetorical brilliance of the work, which offered the public, in the voice of Charles, a first-person *acta martyrum*. In it, the king protested his innocence, lamented his abuse, and offered lengthy prayers for his people and persecutors. The *Eikon* echoed the language of Psalms, so much so that its prayers were set to music in the 1657 *Psalterium Carolinum*.[85] It also echoed the complaints of Job, although for the protagonist of the *Eikon* a darker fate awaited. But this fate the author anticipated, concluding the work with Charles's meditation on the execution to come:

> If I must suffer a violent death, with my Saviour, it is but mortality crowned with martyrdome, where the debt of death, which I owe for sinne to nature, shall be raised, as a gift of faith and patience offered to

God. Which I beseech him to accept . . . [and so] to pardon their sins, who are most guilty of my destruction.[86]

Dying like Christ, Charles pronounced, he too would plead with heaven for the forgiveness of his tormentors, and the rebels of England.

This was not the first time that Charles had played the Christ-King. As the tide turned against the royalist cause in the 1640s, his political travails had swelled in religious portent and significance.[87] By 1647, they were versified after the manner of "The Sacrifice" by the poet George Herbert (1593–1633):

A king my title is, prefixt on high;
Yet by my subjects am condemn'd to die
A servile death in servile companie:
Was ever grief like mine?
—George Herbert, *The Sacrifice*

For my wrong'd Kingdom's sake: my very griefe
Doth break my heart, untill I finde reliefe,
Ile sue to heaven, Mercie from God my chiefe
Never was grief like ours.
—Charles (attrib.), *His Majesties Complaint*[88]

The reader of Herbert's poem was meant to feel the intimacy and inimitability of Christ's suffering. "Never was grief like mine," the poem ended, underscoring the "vast distance between God's behavior toward his creatures and those creatures' cruel treatment of their maker."[89] So too Charles's subjects, when asked to feel the king's inimitable suffering, sense their complicity in its making, and ultimately know their own subjugation.

The *Eikon* was the masterpiece of these efforts to recruit sacrifice to the royal cause, a virtuosic synthesis of the political treatise and the martyrology. In medieval political theology, the *Christus-rex* analogy turned on the regal office of Christ, in whose image the emperor might be *christus per gratiam*. The *Eikon* instead looked to the *suffering* Christ for its political theology, the Christ whose faith—like that of all martyrs—gave him the strength to resist the powers of the world.

The *Eikon* called this faith "conscience." From the outset of the troubles through his trial, Charles insisted, he had ever acted in service of the dictates of conscience. He defended the "Justice, which my Conscience suggested to me" and was steadfast against "Acts, wherein my Conscience is unsatisfied."[90] And it was conscience too that brought him to the scaffold:

Nor will I be brought to affirme that to Men, which in my Conscience I denied before God. I will rather Chuse to wear a Crown of Thornes with

> My Savior, than to exchange that of Gold (which is due to me) for one of lead, whose embased flexibleness shall be forced to bend, and comply to the various, and oft contrary dictates of any Factions.[91]

Here theological and political imaginations fused. In the background echoed the martyrological tradition in which the "testimony of conscience" played a starring role, in which "the transcendent importance of [the martyr's] beliefs" offered ground enough to resist the coercive force of law.[92] But in the foreground, it was the *King* who spoke, *lex loquens*, as James I was wont to say.[93] In this case, the "speaking law" insisted on an expressly political principle that the "absolute demands of sovereign conscience" should be the foundation of law itself.[94] "This last Parliament *I* called, not more by others advice, and necessity of *My* affaires, then [sic] by *My* owne choice and inclination": these were the opening words of the *Eikon basilike*, and they conveyed the political power of sovereign conscience.[95] The king, the royalist political theorist Robert Filmer argued, is bound only by the "equity of his conscience," swearing to "keep no law but such as in his judgment are upright."[96] As Kevin Sharpe observes, for Charles and the new royalism of the period, "the king's conscience was . . . never in theory at odds with his practice of government; it was the essence of his kingship."[97]

When the *Eikon* mapped the King's life onto the stations of the Cross, therefore, it coded a philosophy of political right. In a 1620 work dedicated to Charles, the late King James I had already meditated on the Passion recounted in the Gospel of Matthew, and the fearful symmetry between the "Croune of Thorns" and the "thorny cares, which a King . . . must bee subject unto."[98] As providence would have it, the reading from the Book of Common Prayer for the day of the execution was the Matthew Passion (chap. 27). Charles spent his last hours reading it.[99] The *Christus-rex* then climbed the scaffold and declared to his judges, executioner, and onlookers: "I am the Martyr of the People."[100] The fusion of Passion play and political treatise was complete.

This *Christus-rex* fusion was a precarious one, however, in an age accustomed to demystifying claims to sacrificial death, when tyrant-martyrs were as much part of the political imagination as pious kings and when the law of royal conscience could simply be rejected in favor of *other* laws. "Not the punishment, but the cause": it did not take long for this ancient Christian criterium for judging the truth of martyrdom to be applied to Charles. *Pseudo-Martyr Discovered* was the title of one of the many republican pamphlets that aimed to pry apart the royal crown and Crown of Thorns:

> by presenting his Book, with his picture praying in the Frontispiece, purposely to catch and amuse the people, magnifying all his misdeeds for pious actions, canonizing him for a Saint, and idolizing his memory for an innocent Martyr, and imposture without other parallell than that of *Mahomet*.[101]

The "icon" of the praying Charles was rather an *idol*, in the author's view, designed to charm the ignorant and halo a criminal. The *Pseudo-Martyr* aimed to demystify this piety. "What Conscience he made of bloodshed," it remarked, and exposed the litany of crimes that Charles (it argued) had unleashed in the name of "reason and conscience."[102]

By 1650, people were well practiced in demystifications like this. The title of the pamphlet recalled a 1610 anti-martyrology, for example, written by the churchman and poet John Donne. That earlier *Pseudo-Martyr* similarly aimed at pretenders to the martyr's palm, those who "like the . . . *Circumcellions* . . . running about . . . to urge and importune, and force men to kill them . . . and call all this Martyrdom."[103]

In Donne's world, the pretenders were the Catholics, especially Jesuits, who refused to swear James I's 1606 Oath of Allegiance. This was just the latest in a series of efforts to unmask religious claims as merely political and legal ones, to turn would-be martyrs into criminals. Already in 1583, the powerful advisor to Queen Elizabeth, William Cecil, had insisted that "questions of religion" had nothing to do with the "charges of treason" levied upon uncompromising Jesuits.[104] The 1606 Oath—a reaction to the Gunpowder Plot of the year before—required subjects to "abjure as impious and heretical, [the] damnable doctrine" that excommunicated princes might be "deposed or murdered by their subjects."[105] Those who refused were not heretics, but traitors, and, as Donne darkly remarked, "at Executions for Treasons, we may iustly say, No man dies for the Romane Religion, nor without it."[106]

In the special case of a *royal* martyr, however, things were trickier. If sovereign conscience was the same thing as law, after all, then there was no way to subordinate the king's "beliefs" to the law's power. Another poet, the revolutionary apologist John Milton, saw this clearly. Commissioned in response to the king's book, his 1649 *Eikonoklastes*—as the title suggested—violently attacked the "image" of the king, the "conceited portraiture before his Book . . . the Picture sett in Front [that] would Martyr him and Saint him to befool the people." This "civil kinde of Idolatry" deserved no less iconoclasm than any form of idol worship.[107] Just as the iconoclast reveals the idol as wood and stone when he destroys it, Milton too wanted to reveal Charles's martyrdom as no sacrifice at all.

To do this required a vigorous defense of the autonomy of law. The *law* had been on trial in January, in Milton's view, not the king: whether "the Testimony of one man in his own cause affirming . . . be of any moment to bring in doubt the autority [sic] of a Parliament denying." If the "reason and conscience" of a king were the rule of right, the result would be arbitrary government. "All Britain was to be ty'd and chain'd to the conscience, judgement, and reason of one Man," Milton wrote, "as if those gifts had been only his peculiar and Prerogative, intal'd upon him with his fortune to be a King." "Private reason," even of a king, "is to us no law." Why should justice be "more partial to him offending, then [sic] to all others of the human race," he asked? Justice "accepts no Person, and exempts none from the severity of her stroke. . . . Shee is the strength, the Kingdom, the power and majestie of all Ages."[108]

Eikonoklastes was written in tandem with Milton's great political treatise, the *Tenure of Kings and Magistrates*, published just two weeks after the *Eikon*. There too Milton argued, in line with many monarchomachs before him, that there must be laws higher than of the royal conscience: "the Law of nature justifies any man to defend himself, eev'n against the King in Person . . . justice don upon a Tyrant is no more but the necessary self-defence of a whole Commonwealth."[109] To those who saw in Charles "the Lord's anointed," Milton replied that there was not anointment enough for a tyrant to "charme" justice, the "onely true sovran and supreme Majesty upon Earth."[110] Indeed, in Britain, ancient kings *were* anointed but "*not of God, but such as were more bloody than the rest.*"[111] Blood was the true chrism of a kingship like Charles.

Tyrants were in fact always wont to play the priest, like "Pagan *Caesars* that deifi'd themselves." The "deepest policy of a Tyrant hath been ever to counterfeit religious," Milton observed in the *Eikonoklastes*, nodding to the simpering piety of Shakespeare's tyrant-king Richard III.[112] Small wonder that Charles too should seek to "erect *the Trophies of his charity over us*," to pray over an England that he himself destroyed, to enchant the credulous with a "new device of the King's picture at his praiers," to play the martyr to the "hapless herd."[113]

For a *rex-sacerdos* like this, punishment is an obligation, in defense of the majesty of justice and God. In Scripture we read how prophet Elisha anointed Jehu King of Israel and charged him to slay King Joram and "strike down the house of Ahab" (2 Kings 9). We read much the same in the pagan Seneca, Milton noted. "There can be slaine no sacrifice to God more acceptable than an unjust and wicked King," cried the triumphant hero of *Hercules Furens*, returned from vanquishing the tyrant king Lycus, a phrase repeated in Milton and across the literature of tyrannicide.[114]

If there was a sacrifice on January 30, 1649, then, it was a more ancient one than the Crucifix. "*The Land cannot be cleansed of the blood that is shedd therein*, but by the blood of him that shed it," wrote Milton in the language of Moses (Num. 35.33). No less than God himself "hath testifi'd by all propitious, & the most evident signes, that . . . such a solemn, and for many Ages unexampl'd act of due punishment, was no *mockery of Justice*, but a most gratefull and well-pleasing Sacrifice."[115] The scaffold at Whitehouse was not a Cross. It was rather the horned altar of propitiation, a righteous sacrifice for crimes committed.

The execution of Charles I thus unleashed a storm of creativity about kingship and sacrifice. In the place of older metaphysics of kingship arose creative but unstable fusions of the political and the religious. Neither the ancient martyrs nor the medieval emperors could have imagined the world that made "I am the Martyr to the People"—half republican political thought, half Christian ethics of suffering—into a banner of royalism. Nor would traditional republicans have found much recognizable about Milton's justification for tyrannicide, his "well-pleasing sacrifice" offered to God and to Justice alike. The instability of these fusions, and the vituperative politics of the era, invited, in turn, violent projects of demystification. King into tyrant, martyr into murderer, sacrifice into punishment: every effort to halo the king with sacrifice was demystified, countered, and redirected to new political ends. Enchantment called for disenchantment, vaunted holiness for profanation. In short, the regicide accelerated two opposing dynamics: the first, the frantic efforts to sacralize anew; the second, just as frantic efforts to show that what we call the sacred, is not sacred at all.

Kingship after Sacrifice, or, the Last Martyrology

> the slave is entitled by nature
> to rage against his own body
>
> —ULPIAN, *DIGEST*[116]

No one tried harder to control these new dynamics than the political writer Thomas Hobbes, who watched, horrified, from a self-imposed

Parisian exile as the English Parliament sentenced its king to death. His response was nearly instantaneous. He abandoned his work on geometry and optics, and turned his attention back to what he would call his "moral and civil science," the study of politics.[117] Around the nucleus of an earlier treatise grew a revolutionary work of the political imagination: the *Leviathan, or the Matter, Forme, & Power of a Commonwealth Ecclesiasticall and Civil* (1651).[118] The *Leviathan* was one of the great experiments in the seventeenth-century political imagination, a daring effort to immunize politics from Christian martyrs, to banish the crown of thorns to a distant past, and to reserve the power of sacrifice for the sovereign alone.

For a work written in their shadow, the *Leviathan* was reticent about the bloody events at Whitehall. Indeed, the word "regicide" appeared just once in its pages:

> [from] the books of Policy, and the Histories of the antient Greeks and Romans . . . , men have undertaken to kill their Kings, because the Greeke and Latin writers . . . make it lawfull, and laudable, for any man to do so; provided before he do it, he call him Tyrant. For they say not *Regicide*, that is, killing of a King, but *Tyrannicide*.[119]

Even in this brief aside, we discover Hobbes's distinctive method. However humanist his upbringing—and one of his first works was a translation of *Thucydides* (1628)—Hobbes rejected not just those ancient Greeks and Romans who made it "lawful and laudable" to kill a king, but the tradition of ancient political thought more generally. What was needed, he argued already in his 1642 *De cive*, was a *science* of politics, an account of "the very matter of civill government. . . . its generation, and form, and the first beginning of justice."[120] Instead of the ancient authorities that crowded the late-humanist political imagination, Hobbes offered the therapy of science.

Take the question of sovereignty. When Boden "discovered" it, he employed an army of historical examples. Hobbes's sovereign had no history at all. Rather it assembled *itself* from what we might crudely call anthropology (mankind in its natural state), psychology (the lust for domination and glory that makes this natural state so brutal), and sociology (the covenant that allowed exit from the state of war of all against all). The "great Leviathan called a Common-wealth or State" emerged—once, many times, always—from the crucible of nature, an "Artificial Man" created through covenant, the "Artificial *Soul*" of which is sovereignty.[121]

Compared to the syncretic works that we've explored in this chapter, then, Hobbes was startling in his reductive brilliance. The theological discussions that swelled the *Leviathan*—about the kingdom of God, the canon of Scripture, miracles, eternal life, the office of Christ, and so on—were almost comical in their theoretical frugality. That Christ was "both the sacrificed Goat, and the Scape Goat" needed no more demonstration, for Hobbes, than the scriptural witness of Leviticus 16 and Isaiah 53, proof-texts sufficient (apparently) to resolve the thorniest doctrinal issues of the day.[122] This evidentiary minimalism converged with his doctrinal minimalism: "the (*Unum Necessarium*) Onely Article of Faith . . . Necessary to Salvation, is this, that JESUS IS THE CHRIST."[123] And to the broader politics of Christian sacrifice, Hobbes applied this same spirit of reduction, imagining a state *structurally* immune to the armed prophets that he so feared.

Hobbes starts the *Leviathan*, recall, with a world before politics, a "state of nature," against whose violence human beings protected themselves by creating political order. This creation was not an accident. It grew inevitably from the nature of rights and obligations. As Hobbes wrote:

> The *Right of Nature* . . . is the Liberty each man hath, to use his own power, as he will himselfe, for the preservation of his own Nature; that is to say, of his own life . . . A *Law of Nature* is a Precept, or generall Rule, found out by Reason, by which a man is forbidden to do, that, which is destructive of his own life.[124]

The natural *right* to everything we deem essential to the preservation of our lives made the state of nature—in Hobbes's account—lawless and violent. But alongside this right emerged the *obligation* to do something about this, to restrain violence and create order. The "right of Nature" made covenant and commonwealth an option; the "Law of Nature"—a rule found out by reason—made them an obligation. "A real necessity of nature as powerful as that by which a stone falls downward" forces man to avoid death, Hobbes wrote in his 1642 *De cive*.[125] In *Leviathan*, this necessity became an imperative; man is *forbidden* to do anything destructive of his life. From this first obligation, then, follow others: to pursue peace, to "lay down [our] right to all things," and ultimately to alienate it to a sovereign willing to protect us.[126]

As so often in Hobbes, what seemed a familiar idiom (here of natural rights and obligations) was deceptively radical. One long-standing discussion considered the relation of life to liberty. Assuming that human beings are endowed with certain "rights" (*ius*) given by nature, how may these rights be disposed? Critics and proponents of colonial policy—principally the same Spanish theological milieu in which Las Casas wrote—fought over the legality of slavery, for example, by considering whether someone can legitimately alienate one's liberty to another.[127] Since nature "confers upon man the true *dominium* of his liberty," the Jesuit Francisco Suarez argued in 1612, we have the right to dispose of it as we see fit. Slavery is, on this view, entirely in accordance with natural right.[128]

Do we have the same dominion over our lives? Put another way, is suicide a live ethical option? Ancient Stoics clearly thought so, venerating the suicides of Cato and Seneca as heroic. Even the slave who owned nothing, the Roman jurist Ulpian argued, at least owned his life, and was free to destroy it if he wished.[129] Christians were more ambivalent. They roundly condemned suicide as injury to God, self, and even "natural inclination," as one theologian remarked. Yet the Christian archive also glamorized the desire for death, from Paul's "to live is Christ and to die is gain" (Phil. 1.21) to the suicide of Samson and various saintly virgins. For its part, the cult of the martyrs walked a very fine line between suicide and martyrdom. In Augustine's North Africa, recall, rules for defining the boundaries of Christianity's special dead emerged in order to police the line between impious self-homicide and righteous sacrifice for God.[130] In his *Acts and Monuments*, John Foxe made lists of Catholic and apostate self-murderers in order to better highlight the sanctity of his Protestant martyrs.[131]

This ambiguity about suicide could be recoded into the language of rights. Hugo Grotius—a great exponent of natural law—argued that life was inalienable, "belong[ing] so essentially to one man that [it] could not belong to another." This did not confer an unlimited right to dispose of it. The ubiquitous European laws against suicide were, in his view, thus well-justified. But it *did* allow a more passive right: "a man's life is so far his own that he may defend it even at the cost of injury to an aggressor; may forfeit it for crime; may sacrifice it in the service of his country."[132] For Grotius, this (limited) dominion meant that one was neither strictly obliged to protect one's own life, nor to sacrifice it. Indeed, self-sacrifice fell into the domain not of what Grotius called "expletive justice"—justice strictly speaking—but "attributive justice," that justice ruled by charity and sense of community. It was out of a sense of charity that God accepted Christ's sacrifice on the Cross. Out of the same sense of charity, an "innocent citizen" might allow himself to be "delivered into the hands of the enemy, in order to prevent the ruin otherwise threatening the state."[133]

Hobbes despised these efforts to defend a special space for self-sacrifice, whether by soldiers or martyrs. "Justice . . . , that is to say, Keeping of Covenant, is a Rule of Reason, by which we are forbidden to do anything destructive to our life; and consequently a Law of Nature," he insisted.[134] There is no special sphere of justice reserved for those who sacrifice their lives, in other words, whether for God or country. Lunatics who fail to hear the voice of reason might be so inclined. So too might rebels who ignore its clamor, who insist that if the kingdom of God might be gotten by violence, it could also "be gotten by unjust violence."[135] But nothing gives anyone the right to sacrifice one's life, nothing distinguishes the martyr from the suicide, or from the rebel. With respect to justice, natural law, and reason, these were all the same thing.

When Hobbes turned his iconoclastic attention to Christian martyrdom, he was thus ruthless. His criterium for martyrdom was a parodic version of Augustine's. "*Neque Mors est, quae Martyrem . . . facit, sed Testimonium*," as the Latin edition of *Leviathan* put it: It is not the death that makes a martyr, but the testimony.[136] And what testimony? The testimony reserved exclusively for the ancient disciples:

> that conversed with [Christ] on earth, and saw him after he was risen: For a Witnesse must have seen what he testifieth, or else his testimony is not good. . . . [the rest] are therefore but Witnesses of other mens testimony; and are but second Martyrs.[137]

The age of martyrdom *ended* with the death of the apostles, the last generation to witness Christ on earth and see him after the resurrection. To those who live after and seek the sanctity of the special dead, we must apply the judgment that we apply to everyone. "If a man by words, or signes, seem to despoyle himself" of his life, Hobbes wrote, "he is not to be understood as if he meant it, or that it was his will."[138] Such a man is either a madman or a fool.

Moreover, to seek martyrdom *now*—to refuse conformity in the name of a higher truth, whether in ancient Rome or Marian England—is to misunderstand the deep truth of Christianity. This truth we discover not in the martyrs, but in Naaman the Syrian, the pious Hebrew who obeyed the customs of his pagan king, and worshiped "before the Idol Rimmon" (2 Kings 5):

> whatsoever a Subject, as Naaman was, is compelled to in obedience to his Soveraign, and doth it not in order to his own mind, but in order to the laws of his country, that action is not his, but his Soveraigns . . . If he say, he ought rather to suffer death, then he authorizeth all private men, to disobey their Princes in maintenance of their Religion, true, or false.[139]

Doubtless Naaman felt the pull of conscience when he worshiped the Syrian god. But he did it *anyway*, subordinating his conscience to the demands of civil order and peace.

And this was, in the end, the lesson of *Leviathan*. Everyone has their particular views of the good, of the right way to honor God, whether in sacrifice or not. But once we are living a life in common, these particular views—like all those divisive desires that make nature so violent—must be given up. "Seeing a Common-wealth is but one Person," that is, the artificial person created by the covenant, "it ought also to exhibite to God but one Worship." This applied equally to infidel, Jewish, and Christian polities. Indeed, the Romans—and Hobbes named Numa Pompilius—were among the first to see that the prescription of "Ceremonies, Supplications, Sacrifices, and Festivals" was a part of "Policy," that is, key to the architecture of a commonwealth.[140] Laws of Christian worship were thus like the regalian laws of ancient Rome: *sacrorum omnium potestas sub regibus esto*. For the Roman martyr asked to sacrifice at the altar of the divine Augustus, then, Hobbes had an answer:

> the Worship which the Soveraign commandeth to bee done unto himself by the terrour of his Laws, is not a sign that he that obeyeth him, does inwardly honour him as a God, but that he is desirous to save himselfe from death . . . he doth it for fear . . . it is not his act, but the act of his Soveraign.[141]

When we are called publicly to sacrifice before foreign gods, as the pious Naaman showed, we recognize that our public acts are not our own. They are instead the acts of a sovereign who alone commands the worship that binds a political community together. The "greatest worship of all," "more acceptable to God than Sacrifice" (1 Sam. 15.23), is *obedience*.[142]

Hobbes's critics lamented this iconoclasm that, in the words of William Lucy, turned "all the blood of the holy Martyrs" into nothing but "fancies," foolishness and dreams.[143] No wonder that a man "so declared an Enemy to Martyrdom," the earl of Clarendon echoed, should charge thousands of primitive Christians with a "want of Wit and understanding."[144] And the critics had a point. Were a person to insist that conscience supplied an exemption to law, or that there was another kingdom, a spiritual kingdom, in whose name disobedience was warranted: such a person, in Hobbes's view, was nothing more than a rebel.[145]

Hobbes mentioned the regicide, we noted above, just once in the *Leviathan*. But the political imagination that grew around the regicide, royalist *and* republican, was a prime target of his work. Tyrannicide was no justification at all in a commonwealth where the sovereign alone distinguished between right and wrong, between idolatry and pious worship. But if this was royalism, it was a thoroughly disenchanted version. Charles had no more claim to martyrdom than anyone else. Nor was Christ's *worldly* kingship available to the royalist imagination. The kingdom Christ claimed "was to bee in another world," as Hobbes wrote.[146] No less disenchanted was Hobbes's view of the republican violence directed against the king. To Milton's "there can be slaine no sacrifice to God more acceptable than an unjust and wicked King," Hobbes might have pointed out what comes next in Seneca's play: Hercules goes mad, rebels against heaven, murders his wife and smashes out his own children's brains. Such amalgams—king-martyr, regicide-sacrifice—and the wider sacrificial archive on which they depended: the new science of politics rejected them all.

In a sense, then, Hobbes sought to free the political from its entanglements in theology and history. His urge was destroy, not creatively remake, the world of the martyr, to liberate sovereignty from the crown of thorns, and capture sacrifice for the state alone. The difficulty of accomplishing this—that is, some final liberation from time, from the archives of thought that we inherit—has made Hobbes a figure of perennial fascination to both critics and advocates of the contemporary secular. But his success or failure, whether he emancipated politics from theology or simply buried the theology even deeper, seems less important than the sensibility that informed his project, the sense, shared by so many, of just how saturated the political imagination was by the sacrifices of Christianity and paganism alike.

Conclusion: The End of Christus-rex

In his 1689 *Two Treatises on Government*, John Locke dryly remarked that mankind had never "dreamed of monarchy being *iure divino* . . . till it was revealed to us by the divinity of this last age."[147] A polemical observation to be sure, especially for someone living in the aftermath of a "Glorious Revolution" that had recently deposed another English king and sent him fleeing into exile. But also an astute one, for the cult of kings had, apparently, never been stronger than in the later seventeenth century. What Eric Nelson has called the "exclusivist republicanism" of the revolutionary decades had its counterpart in royalism, an ideological commitment to monarchy that would, in Britain, give rise to the Tory party, and, in significant corners of the intellectual world, a wild enthusiasm for all things crowned.[148] Nor was Britain alone in such royalism. In the Holy Roman Empire, the years after the Treaty of Westphalia began a "wave of regalisation" as its territorial princes sought the monarchical title that alone seemed to guarantee them equal sovereign status in that complicated political institution.

New crowns were forged for the Duke of Savoy and the Grand Duke of Tuscany; in a grand ceremony, the elector of Brandenburg added "King in Prussia" to his titles; the Elector of Saxony nearly bankrupted himself to become King of Poland; the Wittelsbach dynasty in the Palatine sought to gain regal status via the "royal throne of Armenia"; and so on.[149] And at the very summit of it all, the court of Louis XIV in Versailles, where the idols of absolute kingship were erected in gilded majesty. In place of the king's two bodies: *L'état, c'est moi.*

This new world of kingship produced new forms of the political imagination. The geminated fusion of *Christus-rex* did not entirely disappear: the restoration of the monarchy in England (1660), for example, saw the Office for King Charles Martyr added to the Book of Common Prayer. "Let his memory, O blessed Lord, be ever blessed among us," read the Collect, "our martyred sovereign" and the reading for the day was the Matthew Passion.[150] But by the 1660s, the apologists and ideologues of the new royalism typically looked elsewhere to sacralize their monarchy. Robert Filmer's *Patriarcha*, written during the revolution but only published during another crisis of kingship in 1680, turned to the biblical patriarchs for its political theology. Adam, Noah, Abraham, and the other ancient fathers supplied him and other late century royalists with a deep anthropology of kingship. In Adam could be found the first pillars of lordship, the subjection of women and children to a singular royal authority. In Noah and his sons could be discovered the dispersion of regal power across the globe. In Abraham was discerned the power to war against enemies and that "true mark" of sovereignty, the right over life and death.[151] Absent from this patriarchalism, however, were any traces of the older *Christus-rex* symbiosis.

This was not unique to Filmer.[152] As the century waned, what one historian has described as the "final phase of divine right theory" developed new foundations for sacred rule. "Providential divine right" looked to God's wise ordering of the world for its principles of monarchical legitimacy, for example. "God sets up a King, when by his Providence he advances him to the throne," in the words of the Anglican cleric William Sherlock.[153] In France, the divinity of the Sun-King Louis XIV's rule depended more on Apollo than Christ, his state-sponsored neo-paganism suffusing hundreds of paintings, sculptures, coins, ballets, and other pieces of visual iconography.[154] Nor did his chief ideologue, the bishop Jacques-Benigne Bossuet, much look to Christ when he defended the divine authority of his sovereign. The books of Kings, not the Gospel of Matthew, supplied him with proof enough of the sacrality of kings. Job, Moses, but above all David were the heroes of the genealogy of paternal kingship that he laid out in his 1709 *Politics Drawn from the Very Words of Holy Scripture*.[155] The last generation of kings who promised to heal the sick with their touch was also the last generation that felt the need to recruit the kingly office of Christ to their own banners.[156]

The age of sacrificing kings came to an end, in short. But sacrifice *itself* hardly vanished from the political imagination of the world that came after. "Thus [Christ] was faithful and affectionate," the bishop Bossuet wrote in his *Politics*, "to his ungrateful country, and to his cruel fellow citizens, who thought only of satiating themselves with his blood." Christ did have a role to play in this political vision, as it turned out. Not in connection with kingship, however, but with *citizenship*: "he shed his blood with a particular regard for his *nation*; and in offering up the great sacrifice, which was to effect the expiation of all the university, he willed that the love of country should find a place in it," as Bossuet wrote.[157] And so when that other king was hauled to the executioner's bench in 1793, the last great European regicide unfolded in a new imaginative terrain of citizenship, sociability, and sacrifice.

CHAPTER EIGHT

The Anthropology of the Atonement

SACRIFICE AND THE CEREMONIAL LAW IN THE SEVENTEENTH CENTURY

We have been commanded to slaughter the paschal lamb
and to sprinkle with its blood in Egypt the gates from outside,
so that we should bring forth the belief that the act, which
they deemed to be a cause of destruction, saves from destruction.

—MAIMONIDES, *GUIDE FOR THE PERPLEXED*

Tota licet Babylon destruxit tecta Lutherus,
muros Calvinus, sed fundamenta Socinus.

—FAUSTUS SOCINUS'S EPITAPH (APOCRYPHAL)

AT THE BEGINNING was the Crucifixion. Already in the Garden it was there, foretold in what Christians called the *protoevangelium*: "I will put enmity between you and the woman, and between your seed and her seed; he shall bruise your head, and you shall bruise his heel" (Genesis 3.15). The serpent bruised the heel of Eve's seed, but the seed of Mary will hold the serpent fast. In visual form, the story might look like this: the deadly apple and living Eucharist bound together in *one* divine economy (see fig. 8.1 and color plate 7). The blessing of Christ's sacrifice crosses time, knotting old and new covenants, past and future, into the tapestry of salvation.[1] "As in Adam all die, so also in Christ shall all be made alive," the Apostle Paul told the Corinthians, a glorious promise *to all*, not just those lucky enough to live after the miracle of the Resurrection: "Christ has been

FIGURE 8.1. Tree of Life and Death, *Salzburg Missal*, late 1450s–1494. Courtesy of the Bayerische Staatsbibliothek.

raised from the dead, the first fruits of those who have fallen asleep," mankind's generations past and future (1 Cor. 15.20–22). The painting also tells us that not all will *receive* salvation. Two futures are on display in Berthold Furtmeyr's late fifteenth century *Salzburg Missal*, the first for believers who accept His gifts, the second for the stubborn sinners who remain loyal to the fleshy Eve. A line of division bisects the circle of salvation and the choice is clear: law or grace, old or new covenant, Jew or Christian.

From a doctrinal perspective, the Tree of Life captured the drama of the atonement for late medieval Christians. Adam and Eve's betrayal of God, and descent into sin, left humanity in bondage to death, and naked to the justified wrath of their creator. In the long centuries after their expulsion, they and their progeny shared a divided fate, the sons of Abraham preserving the favor of God, the rest abandoned to damnation. Christ brought the human family back together, spirit becoming flesh in order to preach a Gospel of salvation, and to suffer cruelty and eventually death at the hands of a sinful mankind. He hung on the Cross as an offering, a sacrifice given to put an end to death's final power. In the words of the eleventh-century hermit Peter Damian:

> You are the priest and the sacrifice; you are the redeemer and the price with which the debt is paid. . . . Grant that I might receive the blood of highest price dripping in my mouth. O blessed sacrifice that breaks asunder the walls of hell![2]

By the later Middle Ages, the theological mechanics of this atonement were settled. Peter Damian's contemporary, Anselm of Canterbury, gave the Passion a theoretical shape it would possess well into the modern era. In his *Why God Became Man* (ca. 1098), sin was a debt owed to God, indeed such an infinite debt that humanity could not hope to repay it. The "least sin we can think of . . . [is] so monstrous" that "were there an infinite number of worlds as full of created existence as this," we should still be subject to the rigor of God's justice.[3] Satisfaction—Anselm's key concept—required a payment of a worth so incomparable as to outweigh even this terrible obligation, a debt "so great that, while none but man must solve the debt, none but God was able to do it."[4] God became man in order that He might die, each drop of His innocent blood sufficient to satisfy what we owe to God.

The Reformation abandoned some sacrifices, but *not* this one. In fact, reformers intensified the notion of satisfaction they inherited from Anselm. Where the medieval theologian understood sin as a debt, reformers instead saw it as a crime. God was not a creditor, but an angry judge, eager to levy punishment for the crimes of mankind. To satisfy His wrath, Christ abased himself completely, shouldering the worst of human crime in order that he might redeem them. As Luther memorably wrote:

> All the prophets did foresee in spirit, that Christ should become the greatest transgressor, murderer, adulterer, thief, rebel, blasphemer, &c. that ever was or could be in all the world. For he being made a sacrifice for the sins of the whole world . . . is not now the Son of God born of the Virgin Mary; but a sinner . . . [he] hath and beareth all the sins of all men in his body, that he might make satisfaction for them with his own blood.[5]

Murder, adultery, rebellion: Christ was a criminal for our sins. The sacrificial Crucifix was, Luther wrote, the site of "an expiatory offering, a shedding of blood that wrath may be turned aside."[6] Calvin echoed him: "to make satisfaction for our redemption," Christ was "arraigned . . . as a criminal."[7] And the Crucifix was, in turn, a sacrificial altar:

> that these things may take root firmly and deeply in our hearts, let us keep sacrifice and cleansing constantly in mind. For we could not believe with assurance that Christ is our redemption, ransom, and propitiation [ἀπολύτρωσις, ἀντίλυτρον, και ἱλαστηριον] unless he had been a sacrificial victim.[8]

This so-called doctrine of penal substitution reimagined the nature of the transgression and punishment, but preserved the deep logic of the Atonement.

Well into the sixteenth century, the Crucifixion underwrote the Christian doctrine of salvation. It also was the key that unlocked the mysteries of Scripture. Typology, we have remarked, was that creative strategy of violent commensuration by which Christians took over, and overcame, the sacrifices of the Jews. Already in the New Testament, the *Letter to the Hebrews* remade Israel with a familiar logic of integration and distinction. Speaking in the language of the Psalms, its author distinguished between the Hebrew priesthood and Christ who "did not exalt himself," but was appointed by God, who told him: "Thou art a priest for ever, after the order of Melchizedek" (Psalm 110; Heb. 5.5–6). In the letter, Christ himself spoke the language of Psalms: "Sacrifices and offerings thou hast not desired, but a body has thou prepared for me." Christ "abolishes the first in order to establish the second," the *Letter* explains, repeated Levitical sacrifices abolished by the "offering of the body of Jesus Christ once for all [*ephapax*]" (Psalm 40; Heb. 10.5, 9–10). Christ "enter[s] once for all [*ephapax*] into the Holy Place, taking not the blood of goats but his own blood, thus securing an eternal redemption," the *Hebrews* author wrote, asking readers to see Christ as abolition, repetition, extension, and perfection of the sacrifices of Israel (Heb. 9.12).

The desire to detect in past events latent portents of the future may be universal. Prophecy, allegory, and prefiguration all rely on some logic in which light from the future illuminates a shadowy past. Christians were particularly committed typologists, however, since their theological project always depended on maintaining the uneasy balance between the Hebrew Bible and the New Testament. Christology—the effort to understand exactly the meaning and nature of Christ—was an especially fertile field for the Christian typological imagination. Among the Calvinist churches of early modern Europe, for example, the "offices" of Christ were all construed typologically. Christ was appointed "Prophet, King, and Priest," Calvin wrote in the *Institutes*, and each of these roles was a prophetic fulfillment, or "antitype," of the "types" only obscurely understood by the Jews. "Christ to perform this office [of priest]," Calvin wrote, "had to come forward with a sacrifice. For under the [Hebrew] law too, the priest was forbidden to enter the sanctuary without blood."[9] The Puritan William Perkins agreed. Christ's priesthood depended on the satisfaction he rendered to God: "His sacrifice, which is an action of Christes offering himselfe to God the Father, as a ransome for the sinnes of the elect . . . In this sacrifice, the oblation was Christ, as he was man . . . The Altar also was Christ, as he was God." Typology thus took the unity of the Bible as writ—the ceremonial law of Leviticus *had* to make sense in a Christian interpretive framework, lest Christians lose their status as inheritors and perfectors of Israel.[10]

However violent the Reformation was to the sacrificial Mass and the cult of the saints, then, it left untouched the central drama of the Crucifixion. Whether its meaning was couched in the medieval language of debt, or the reformed language of crime, the Cross offered a set of concepts and metaphors that (then and now) intimately structure how Christians organized their relationship to God. The intractability of sin, the need for expiation, the gift of Christ's intercession, the humiliation of His passion, the blood of the Lamb satisfying a wrathful God, the priesthood of Christ, His prophetic fulfillment of ancient prophecy, the unity of Scripture, the Church's inheritance of the mission of Israel, the Christian supersession of the Jews: the list is practically endless. If anything, the Reformation concentrated the Christian sacrificial imagination even more fiercely on the final sacrifice of Jesus.[11]

But in the late sixteenth century, this final sacrifice of Christianity too was shaken to its foundation. The cause was a new heresy from within the ranks of the reformers, an enduring threat for Protestants for the next century and more. In the writings of the Italian heresiarch Faustus Socinus, mainstream reformers foresaw the end of the Atonement, Christ's de-divinization, the collapse of the Trinity, the destruction of the integrity of Scripture, indeed, the annihilation of Christianity itself. The response was immediate and long-lasting. Over the century, writers from across the Protestant world repeatedly sought to refound a theological commonplace—that Christ died for our sins—anew.

On the one hand, this refoundation accelerated the dynamics we have been tracing in this book. The archive of the Christian sacrificial imagination expanded again, to encompass not only the *types* of Hebrew sacrifices, but the *real things*, the actual sacrifices of the Hebrews from the patriarchs to the Levitical laws. Against the heresies of the age, Hebrew law was recruited as a Christian ally, summoned to aid the very event that supposedly *abolished* that Law in the name of Gospel liberty: the Crucifixion.

On the other hand, this effort at refoundation also collapsed the century-long project of learned apologetics. For the Atonement was more than just one sacrifice among many. It was the very thread that bound the Garden to the Crucifix, that rooted Christian ceremony in Scripture, and gave Christianity a deep history and anthropology. In the seventeenth century, for the first time, this earth-shattering event, the death of death, could no longer be taken for granted. To defend it, apologetes reached for history, law, and anthropology, supplementing and, eventually, supplanting the naive typologies that had long discovered portents of Golgotha in the sacrifices of the Hebrew patriarchs. In a word, the Crucifixion started to become ordinary, a sacrifice like others in the long history of human encounter with the divine. As it did so, these peculiar hybrids that we've been exploring so far—the admixtures of theology, history, antiquarianism, law, and anthropology—began to dissolve into the new religious and secular configurations that we will explore later in this book.

Learning Not to Sacrifice

In the late decades of the sixteenth century, an Italian writer emphatically rejected two thousand years of Christian sacrifice. He was a heretic, admittedly, who rejected any number of Christian truisms. The "commonly held view that, innate by nature in the human mind is a notion of a divinity, by whose power all things are ruled and directed" was, he thought, empirically false. Not only can one find examples of godless men in Scripture, but today in Brazil "whole populations have been recently discovered who have not the least notion or suspicion of any divinity."[12] But—judging from the reactions—it was the heretic's view of Christ that *really* caused a stir.

Born in Siena in 1539, Faustus Socinus was not trained as a theologian, or a philosopher, or really anything at all.[13] He came from a long line of of distinguished Italian jurists, and his uncle Laelius was a learned lawyer who turned to spiritual matters in the religious ferment of the 1540s. Like his nephew, Laelius was an unconventional thinker. He spent much of his adult life in the heartlands of the Swiss reformation, and included among his correspondents luminaries like John Calvin, Theodor Beza, and Heinrich Bullinger. A whiff of heterodoxy always accompanied Laelius, however, and he was suspected (rightly) of harboring sympathies with various undesirables, not least the Spanish humanist Michael Servetus, executed in 1553 for anti-trinitarian heresies at Calvin's behest.

Unlike Servetus, Laelius did not make the mistake of committing his heterodox views on the Trinity to print. When he died in 1562, he left a set of manuscripts to his nephew, then living as a merchant in Lyon. Faustus took the manuscripts to Florence in 1563, where he spent the next eleven years living a merry life in the entourage of Grand Duke Cosimo I of Tuscany, and a more secretive one of religious heterodoxy. When Cosimo died in 1574, Faustus left Italy, first following Laelius's footsteps to Basel, and by 1579, to Poland, then a welcoming place for religious radicals of various stripes. It was not until he was established there, well integrated in a community of anti-trinitarians in Rakov, that Faustus began to publish books, rumors of whose heterodoxy had already spread far and wide by clandestine manuscripts and word of mouth.[14]

From his first published work—*On the Savior Jesus Christ* (1594)—onward, Socinus waged a tireless war against the Tree of Life, the Crucifix, the atonement, satisfaction, penal substitution, in short, the very heart of the Christian sacrificial imagination. Historians have puzzled somewhat over where he obtained his arguments, since this "chief heresiarch of his age" was no trained theologian.[15] But on the fringes of the Reformation, where theology was as much a subject for peasants, bakers, miners, and cobblers, as learned schoolmen, views like his had circulated for decades. Already in the 1530s, the Spanish reformer Juan Valdés and his Italian admirer Bernardino Ochino elevated the ethical exemplarity of the Crucifixion over its atoning power.[16] Others—including the Dutch lawyer Cornelius Hoen and the Swiss schoolteacher Hans Denck—more daringly rejected the usual teachings on satisfaction to imagine a doctrine of universal salvation that might eventually even include the devil himself.[17] In Socinus, however, the heterodox found the "specific formulation" of what "many in the Radical Reformation as a whole were groping for half a century," a systematic demolition of the Atonement.[18]

However potent its impact, the argument was simple. Protestants all denied that God needed anything from man; Socinus simply applied this to the atonement as well. Sin is an injury to God, he agreed, but does God need *blood* to feel better? "Anyone can remit as much of his own right as he wants," Socinus insisted, and so God could have pardoned us "without having accepted satisfaction for [sin]." The two dominant ways to view the atonement, in Socinus's view, were absurd. If sin is a debt, as in Anselm, then God is a creditor. But surely God can forgive this debt, just as any creditor can forgive a debt, without needing bloody crucifixions. If sin is a crime, as in Calvin and Luther, then God is both judge and lawgiver. But in this case, Socinus insisted, "punishment is not owed [to the guilty], but to the state." The judge who fails to punish the guilty injures the framework of law; but the state, as the source of law, may pardon the guilty *ad libitum*. What is true of a state, must be true for God. Since He is the lawgiver, and "since no one can do injury to himself," his decision not to punish would injure no one.[19] There is no law other than the law of God, thus no other law that demands punishment.

For this reason, then, God was free to forgive humans of their debts—to absolve them of punishment—*without* the Crucifixion. "It was not the death of Christ itself, but his entry, through death, into heaven" that served as the "expiatory offering," Socinus insisted. The blood and the pain of the Crucifixion was instead nothing more than a "metonym" for the "universal offering" Christ made to God after the Resurrection.[20] The Crucifixion was no atonement, then. Rather, it was a sign of Christ's benevolent nature and thus means of reconciling man with man. Under the sign of the cross, man forms a community modeled on Christ's life. Virtue, not the blood of the lamb, reconciles man with God.[21]

Ridding Christianity of the Atonement required more than just a new theology, however. It would take philology, for example, to purge the sacrificial vocabulary from Christianity: to Calvin's stress on the *ransom* [ἀπολύτρωσις] Christ offered for our sin, Socinus replied that the Greek word *lutron* was simply a price paid for a captive, and had nothing to do with sacrifice.[22] And it would take a revolution in biblical exegesis and hermeneutics to disconnect the bloodless religion of the New Testament from the bloody sacrifices of the Hebrews. Neither the sacrifices of the patriarchs, nor Leviticus, nor any of the ceremonial laws of the Jews, in this new view, had anything to say about the death of Christ. Abel sacrificed "the firstlings of his flock . . . and the LORD had respect unto Abel and to his offering": so Genesis described the first biblical scene of sacrifice and, in the Christian typological imagination, the first explicit type of Christ's death. Socinus admitted Abel's sacrifice, but not its typological significance:

> Abel was beloved by God, so that if he committed a sin, God must have pardoned him for it. But why? Was it really on account of some actual satisfaction that either he or someone on his behalf, either already offered to God, or in the future, would offer to him? By no means.[23]

God favored Abel out of a free act of mercy, not because Abel's sacrifice either pleased him, or portented one that would. Similarly, when Aaron sent the scapegoat out into the desert bearing the transgressions of Israel, it did not prefigure the Atonement (as typology long suggested). Leviticus never speaks of "satisfaction," Socinus pointed out, and in any case, the transgressions relieved by the scapegoat were "what might be called [sins] of ignorance," not the "grave sins" that Christ can remedy.[24]

Virtually all of Christian sacrificial typology was, by this light, misplaced. What Socinus called the "empty figures" or the "empty shadows" found in the Hebrew Bible—above all, the Temple sacrifices—were just that: empty.[25] "The thing foreshadowing must correlate to the things foreshadowed," Socinus wrote, and systematically exploited the differences between Hebrew type and Christian antitype. The Hebrew Bible speaks of animal sacrifice, while the New Testament involves the death of a man; Levitical sacrifice relieves minor transgressions, while Christ relieves mortal sin; the ceremonial law speaks of purification, but never satisfaction; the sacrifices of the Hebrews never hint at the death of a messiah; and so forth.[26] In short, it is simply untrue that "in all of these ancient sacrifices for sin or transgression . . . the death of Christ was foreshadowed [*adumbratam*]."[27]

By prying apart Old and New Testament sacrifices, Socinus refashioned the Bible. He applied to the biblical books, for example, standards of historical credibility reserved for works of secular provenance.[28] He spoke of the "accommodation" of scriptural language to the time and place of its listeners, at times suggesting (like Spinoza later on) that the Bible had a provisional vocabulary, culturally and historically specific to antiquity.[29] And, most significantly, he emphatically distinguished between the two halves of the Christian Bible. Stressing the "complete abrogation and antiquation" of the Hebrew Bible, Socinus and his later followers established a way of reading Scripture that emphasized the utter originality of the Gospels and the person of Christ.[30] The authority of the Old Testament, Socinus wrote in an early work, rests entirely on its reception *as* authoritative by the New Testament.[31] The Old Testament has no independent authority, in other words, for Christian readers. Only as long as there is "a complete identity" between the two covenants can Christians profit by its reading.[32] The novelty of Jesus—His promise of eternal redemption, the universality of His intercession, the stunning fact of the resurrection—all of these sharply distinguished the revealed religion of Christ from that of Mosaic law.

The end of the Atonement, in other words, meant the end of traditional Christianity. Christ the mediator, His dying for mankind, His bearing our sins, the blood of the Lamb: fifteen hundred years of the Christian imagination would have to be revised. To put the Socinian project into effect would mean changing every liturgy, revising every sermon, changing every catechism, replacing virtually every piece of Christian art ever made. While likely fabulous, then, the epitaph allegedly carved into Socinus's gravestone—that he alone had destroyed the foundations of the "Babylon" of Christianity—sounds about right.[33]

In numbers, the Socinian movement was small. He and his writings found a receptive if precarious home among dissident anti-trinitarian churches in Poland, which thrived for some four decades before they were suppressed in the late 1630s. Although printing presses broadcast their anti-trinitarian writings across Europe, finding quietly receptive audiences in the Netherlands, Germany, and England, they remained an exile religion throughout the early modern era.[34] And yet, as so often in the history of Christianity, the heretical margins can set the terms for the orthodox center. Socinus had cut the sacrificial sinew that tied Christianity together, and to bind it back together involved far more than just political suppression and doctrinal stubbornness (although there was plenty of both of these). The Socinian crisis precipitated instead an extraordinary moment of paratheological creativity, in which a truth that Christians had long taken for granted would be defended with a heterogeneous arsenal of weapons drawn from history, philology, anthropology, and law.

Proving Typology

In 1614, a professor of theology of the University of Wittenberg began to preside over and author a series of theological dissertations on biblical typology. During the next two years, Wolfgang Franzius collected and published twenty of these in a book popular enough to warrant four separate editions over the century, very unusual for a collection of university dissertations.[35] Entitled *Schola Sacrificiorum Patriarchalium Sacra*, each of its disputations aimed to defend the "satisfying sacrifice of Christ . . . against the most recent Arians or Photinians," Faustus Socinus and his followers, who threaten to "wreck, shatter, destroy, and completely overturn" the very foundations of Christianity.[36] "One hundred years ago," Franzius wrote, "our divine theologian and our prophet of Germany, . . . [Martin] Luther" had restored the clear word of the Gospels, and purged the Church of its all-too-human things.[37] He commemorated the centenary with a 900+ page book on the sacrifices of the patriarchs, designed to show, against those modern Arians, that Christ's sacrificial role—the satisfaction that he offered an angry God and with which he redeemed humanity from sin—could be *proven* from the materials of the Old Testament.

The *Schola sacrificiorum* was not remarkable for its theological perspicuity or innovation. Franzius was an academic functionary writing in the homeland of traditional Lutheranism, and he defended a theological commonplace. All the more remarkable, then, that this functionary pursued his apologetic project in such comparatively novel manners.

Take the Christian truism that, after Christ's death on the Cross, the age of legitimate sacrifice came to an end. The *Letter to the Hebrews* said this, and it was witnessed prophetically in the book of Daniel. There the angel Gabriel spoke of the "seventy weeks of years . . . concerning your people and your holy city." Three periods mark the weeks: a "going forth of the word" for the seven weeks, sixty two weeks of building, and a final week, when:

> after the sixty-two weeks, an anointed one shall be cut off . . . for half of the week he shall cause sacrifice and offering to cease; and upon the wing of abominations shall come one who makes desolate, until the decreed end is poured out on the desolator. (Dan. 9.26–27)

For generations of Christian interpreters, this was pure Christology. The "going forth" that began the cycle was the *protoevangelium*—the start of sacrifice in Genesis 3.15—and it concluded with Christ's Passion (week 69.5) and Rome's destruction of the Temple in Jerusalem.[38]

This was more or less settled interpretation until Socinus.[39] After, it took *work* to defend. Was it the case that in fact Christ's death fell in the middle of week seventy, Franzius wondered? In his revolutionary work of chronology, *De emendatione temporum* (1583, 1598), the humanist Joseph Scaliger had declared that the division of Daniel's final week "had no more arcane a sense than the division of the *mina* into 25, 20, and 15 *shekels* in Ezekiel 45.12," and that the destruction of Jerusalem happened thirty-seven years after Christ died, a number indivisible by seven, and so could hardly be "half a week" after the Passion.[40] The precise dating of Christ's Passion was a topic of burning interest to learned humanists in the late sixteenth century.[41] But it would not have interested an orthodox theologian like Franzius had not Socinus so destabilized the very notion of typology. The moral meaning of shekels; the actual length of Daniel's "week"; whether Greeks should be considered authoritative witnesses to Persian history: in earlier times, Franzius could have played more peacefully in prophetic fields, rather than address such unusual subjects.[42]

And so the usual theological truisms were supplemented with new discussions: who performed the first sacrifices, whether Adam was immortal, how sacrificial rites spread around the world, why Hebrew sacrifice was limited to the Temple in Jerusalem, and what the various types, materials, and "external forms" of sacrificial ritual were. Some of these responded directly to Socinian heterodoxies. Others had more indirect links. Whether it was licit for *gentiles* to offer sacrifices after the Fall—the subject of *Dissertation IX*—was only an issue for Franzius, for example, because he gave sacrifice such an exclusively Christological lineage. If every sacrifice was, at the origin, a reference to Christ, were only *Hebrew* sacrifices the acceptable continuation of this tradition? Or could people "outside the lineage of the Israelites" also offer pious sacrifice?[43] His arguments ranged widely, exploring the Psalms that sing of *all people* celebrating God, the sacrifice of Alexander in Jerusalem as recounted in the Jewish historian Josephus, righteous gentiles like the priest king Melchizedek, even a short discussion on Amerindian human sacrifice, a perverted witness to the missionary zeal of David and his kin, who "declared his glory among the heathen" (Psalm 96).[44]

Even in the Lutheran fortress of Wittenberg, then, Socinus was a powerful intellectual reagent. In 1618, the faculty at Wittenberg collectively decided that these new Arians, as they were called, were the chief heresy of the age, even while Franzius's disputations apparently inspired Socinian sympathies among the students.[45] In 1615, while Franzius disputed, a nest of "crypto-Socinians" was discovered at the Lutheran Nuremberg Academy in the town of Altdorf, where clandestine connections with Poland had brought students and faculty into the Socinian fold. Various anti-trinitarian writings were publicly burned there in June 1616, and orthodoxy reimposed.[46] Meanwhile, the collection and publication of anti-Socinian writings became a mini-industry in the Lutheran seventeenth century. In 1945, the historian of Unitarianism Earl Wilbur counted some seven hundred dissertations written in German universities between 1595 and 1797, likely an undercount.[47] And these dissertations were astoundingly popular. The *Collegii anti-sociniani*, a massive collection of 154 dissertations gathered by the Leipzig Hebrew professor Johann Adam Schertzer, was printed first in 1672 and then again (expanded!) in 1684 and 1702.[48]

A Roman Law of Atonement

Lutherans felt an overwhelming need to answer Socinus. For the Reformed, it was even more urgent, since Socinian views fanned already-hot flames of theological conflict *inside* the church. This was especially true in the Netherlands, where the first decades of the seventeenth century saw conflict between rival Calvinist factions fierce enough to cause armed violence and near civil war. The precipitant was the work of Jacob Arminius, named professor of theology at Leiden in 1603. At that time, tensions across international Calvinism were high over the thorny question of predestination. Arminius was just one of many who were uncomfortable, morally and intellectually, with the most rigorous version of the doctrine. This so-called supralapsarian position proposed that God had predestined the elect, and cursed the damned, even *before* Adam's fall. Christ died only for *some* people, in other words, and He knew which before the fact. Moderating this doctrine involved rethinking the Crucifixion. "The death of Christ and its merit is antecedent, in nature and order, to predestination," Arminius insisted, since God gave Christ as a redeemer "*prior* to the decree, by which he determined to really apply to some, by faith, the grace obtained by the death of Christ."[49] This Christology was taken up by the moderate wing of Dutch Calvinists, the so-called Remonstrants. "Jesus Christ . . . died for *all and for every individual*, so that he has obtained for all, by his death on the cross, reconciliation and remission for sin," their 1610 *Five Articles of Remonstrance* declared. Hard-line opponents scoffed: "Christ through the blood of the cross . . . effectively redeem[ed] from every people, tribe, nation, and language *all those and only those* who were chosen from eternity for salvation," they replied.[50]

When Arminius died in 1609, these theological tensions boiled over. Who would replace him at the University of Leiden? The Remonstrants wanted an ally, recommending the German theologian Conrad Vorstius. Unfortunately, Vorstius was suspected by many (rightly, as it happens) of harboring Socinian sympathies. When this became public, thunderous denunciations of Vorstius and the Remonstrants rang from the lecterns and pulpits of the orthodox. One of these—Sybrandus Lubbertus, in Franeker—aggravated students sympathetic to Vorstius so much that they played a practical joke on him, publishing in 1610 a little book entitled *De officio hominis christiani*, by "an anonymous protector of the truth," e.g., Faustus Socinus. Lubbertus was so enraged at the joke that the next year he published an even *more* controversial work of Socinus, the *De Jesu Christo servatore*, accompanied by Lubbertus's own commentary, all the better to demonstrate the pernicious effects of Vorstius.[51] In a rich historical irony, then, Socinus's most heterodox work was first published in the Netherlands by a hard-line Calvinist. Ironies aside, the politics of this were fierce. Lubbertus and his faction were not just ideologues, but also canny opponents of Vorstius's political sponsor, the powerful Advocate of Holland, Johan Oldenbarnevelt and the same writer we met in chapter 7, Hugo Grotius.

It was these conflicts that drew Grotius into the orbit of Socinus and the Atonement. By the early 1610s, the Vorstius scandal, and the struggles between Remonstrant and Counter-Remonstrant factions, pitted Dutch cities and authorities against one another. They even spread internationally into the court of the English king James I, where, in fact, Grotius was on a mission of religious diplomacy when Lubbertus published yet another diatribe against Vorstius. Grotius's response was a blistering attack on Lubbertus and his orthodox allies.[52] And while it showcased Grotius's sharp tongue and formidable erudition, it did little for his cause, arousing a storm of controversy from both sides of the Channel.[53] To calm this down, Grotius went on the offensive, this time not against the Calvinist hard-liners, but against *Socinus* and his heretical teachings on the Crucifixion of Christ.

This treacherous political context explains why this learned humanist politician took up his pen in the winter of 1614, and wrote one of the most sustained defenses of Atonement in the early modern period: the *Defensio fidei catholicae de satisfactione Christi adversus Faustum Socinum*. For readers now, who may know Grotius only as the author of his 1625 *Laws of War and Peace*, a monument of legal scholarship for generations, the turn to "theology" likely sounds peculiar. But as his friend, the Leiden antiquarian Gerhard Vossius remarked, it was the legal training that rendered him particularly competent to defeat Socinus. "The subject cannot be treated substantially against that man but by one versed in jurisprudence," he wrote to Grotius in October 1614.[54] Socinus wielded the terms of law—remission, satisfaction, punishment—against the sacrificial atonement of Christ, and so it was with these same weapons that Grotius took up his defense. The result was a synthesis of law and theology, a new form of reasoning applied to old doctrinal questions.[55]

At the heart of the question, as both Socinus and Grotius saw it, was this: what kind of legal relationship exists between God, man, and Christ? To make his argument that God needs nothing from man and can remit his punishment freely and without satisfaction, Socinus had (according to Grotius) regarded God "as an offended party, as a creditor, as an owner," as if these were the same things. But this was a mistake. God does not punish sin as a creditor, for example. Debt occurs because "I lack something," and has no connection to any "moral wrongness." Unlike debt, sin is a *crime*, governed not by the civil law of contracts, but rather by penal law. This difference between equity and criminal statute is fundamental to law, Grotius pointed out. Even if the goods are restored or (in the case of God) the debt foresworn, the question of punishment still stands. And law does not leave punishment in the hands of the party whose rights are violated, but makes it "an act of the superior authority."[56] The real issue then was not whether God could remit a debt, but whether he could justly relax punishment for a crime.

Behind all of this discussion lurked Roman law, a subject in which Grotius was immensely learned.[57] "Emperors are judge of their own cause," Grotius summed up Socinus's jurisprudential argument, referring readers to the *Digest of Justinian*.[58] For Socinus, the implication was clear: if God can judge in his own cause, then why do we need Christ as a mediator? The answer, for Grotius, lay in the distinction between the rights of the *dominus*—the owner obliged only to himself—and those of the *rector*, the king or prince, with broader obligations to justice. The right of punishment, Grotius insisted, was not "the right of absolute ownership (*ius absoluti dominii*)." Rather it was an explicitly political right, as Debora Shuger has shown, one that "does not exist for the sake of him who punishes, but for the sake of the community."[59] God cannot avoid punishment for human sin, not because he lacks the *power* to do so, but because his jurisdiction demands an operating principle of justice. "It is not the case that the law could not be relaxed at all," Grotius declared, but "it should not be relaxed easily."[60] God's demand for Christ's death, in this context, might be seen as a concession to this demand for "difficulty," that relaxation cannot come without a price, and the price was the blood of the Lamb.

This did not quite undo the Italian heretic's knot, however. Socinus did not doubt that God had obligations to justice. He doubted whether God needed Christ *to die* in order to satisfy these. If legal punishment demanded "an equality suitable to order and the public good between a delict and an affliction," why was the affliction suffered by Christ the only thing that could satisfy God's obligations to justice?[61]

To answer this question, Grotius needed a new tool, which he found in the theological and legal term of art: "satisfaction." The "equality" demanded by Grotius's theory of punishment would be achieved only if God was satisfied that it was. But in what did this satisfaction consist? Again Roman law supplied an answer. Satisfaction, wrote the Roman jurisconsult Ulpian, "is tantamount to performance."[62] Satisfaction was in fact a special legal performance, arising in the case of a mortgage, when the debtor pledges collateral in exchange for a loan. Release from the mortgage can take place in two ways: either by paying off the loan or by handing over the collateral. But the two scenarios are not equivalent. In the first case, the creditor *must* discharge the debt. In the latter case, though, the debt is "satisfied" *only* if the "principal ratifies the transaction."[63] A "creditor who does not accept satisfaction but instead demands payment is in no way at fault," Ulpian noted, because the decision to accept the collateral (or some other good) in place of the debt was his alone.[64] Stated briefly, satisfaction demanded *two* elements: first the payment of the debt, and then "some act of the creditor or the ruler," by which the payment is accepted and the obligation remitted.[65]

On the one side stood God, then, mortgage-holder, injured party, and sovereign judge. On the other side, Christ, atoning for our sins by offering a payment far exceeding the debt of mankind's sin. And between them, the act of the satisfaction: God's free decision to accept Christ's death as an adequate substitute for our crimes. This was a decision God was in no way bound to make, just as Christ himself was in no way bound to offer himself in death to save mankind. Christ is the *lutron*, the *apolutrosis*, the *ransom* (per Calvin above), the "thing or act by which someone, who otherwise was going to inflict some inconvenience on someone, is induced to allow him to be liberated from it." And to Socinus's moral objection to penal substitution—the savagery of hostage taking and vicarious punishment—Grotius offered the historical reply that people have *always* done this. "Among all those we would call pagans there was no one who would regard it as unjust to punish someone for the delict of another," he wrote, noting how the Persians killed the family members of criminals, the Greeks killed the children of tyrants, and Romans murdered hostages by the hundreds.[66]

Yet the final—perhaps the most important—question still stood: did Christ have to die *like that* for God to be satisfied? Did God need the Crucifixion? This final question drew Grotius's *Defensio fidei* into the sacrificial world elaborated, as we have seen, across the intellectual terrain of the late Renaissance. The sacrificial act "primarily concerns God and not men," an observation that invited Grotius into the world of sacrifice proper, that is, the many things "done for man before God," from the Levitical sacrifices to the blood rites of the Canaanites, who "placate[d] Moloch by the slaughter of their own children," the Persians who "buried men alive," and the Albanians who "immolate[d] that man whom they believed to have the greatest power through his sanctity." Religions of the ancient world were, Grotius tells us, frenzies of bloodletting. Animals, virgins, children, beautiful men, holy men, all slain in varieties of ways in the hopes of placating vengeful deities. Even those Roman Decii, the noble consuls who died for Roman glory, "have the same origin," Grotius argued, as all other pagan violence. They were "expiatory offerings for all the 'wrath' of the gods."[67]

Here Grotius put the *modus negandi* of Christian antiquarianism—the perversion of ancient human sacrifice highlighting the true gift of the Cross we explored in chapter 5—to positive ends. Doubtless human sacrifice *was* perverse, originating in those years after the flood when the worship of many gods sprang up, and when the "the rites and ceremonies" of the true God were "transferred from a pious to an impious use." But it also developed—as Las Casas had argued decades earlier—as a natural response to a fundamental human problem. In the logic of satisfaction, payment never *guarantees* remission. The latter only comes at the pleasure of the ruler, in this case, God or the gods. The Jews made their offerings in the temple under rules laid down in Scripture, and might feel some (imperfect) security that their donations had their intended effects. But the nations of the gentiles had no security whatsoever. They owed a debt whose precise terms they could not fulfill and, sensing this, offered as much as they could. "Under the guidance of nature," Grotius wrote, "these nations realized that, the greater their gift to God, the more easily forgiveness could be obtained."[68] But how much was enough? An onion? A goat? A child? All the children? Precisely because they could *never* be sure that their gift was sufficient, they were driven to ever-wilder excesses of bloodshed.

Grotius's anthropology of sacrifice explained, then, the universality of sacrifice, the human response to a primordial sense of obligation with no guarantee of satisfaction. In the case of Christ, the difference was that his sacrifice *worked*. It worked because Christ became man, and then the God-man offered himself up to death. When Jesus offered his life to God on behalf of human sin, He fulfilled a natural and legal duty of performance. He performed this duty not as a debtor, however, since he owed nothing.

Instead, He offered himself in his office as *priest*, appointed to represent the community of man to God. He was the "lustral sacrifice," the death that "buys blood, i.e. redeems through blood." In this role as priest offering himself, finally, Christ abolished the ancient perversions of the pagans and the prescribed religious laws of the Jews. "As a true priest and a true victim . . . he surrendered himself to death," and made the offering "once and for all [*toties, quoties*]."[69]

As a theological intervention, the *Defensio fidei catholicae* failed. It did nothing to alleviate orthodox suspicions of the Remonstrants and their alleged Socinian leanings. Indeed, in later years, Grotius grew ever more sympathetic to the Italian heretic.[70] Nor did it diminish the political struggles between religious factions, struggles that, in the next years, swept Grotius's patron Oldenbarnevelt to the executioner's axe and Grotius into a Dutch prison. Nor, finally, was it even particularly successful as a *theory*. While it may have offered the only "fundamentally different alternative to the Anselmic theory of satisfaction" in the Reformed world, as the great church historian Jaroslav Pelikan wrote, it remained a "private theory" and was taken up by no public church.[71]

In the history of the sacrificial imagination, however, the *Defensio* was a milestone. The atonement had always entailed conceptual heterogeneity: economics, for Anselm, and later penal law, for Luther and Calvin, offering metaphors for this central mystery. But what was (and is) so startling about Grotius is how *literal* the metaphors became. Luther called Christ "the greatest transgressor, murderer, adulterer, thief, rebel, blasphemer, &c. that ever was," in order to dramatize just how far Jesus had to fall to shoulder the sins of humanity.[72] Grotius suggested that Christ was *actually* a ransom, by contrast, just like the "Tarentines [thrown] down from the Tarpeian rock, as Livy has it."[73] When he thought about the parallels between Christ's sacrifice and, say, those at the ancient Jewish Temple, he treated them literally. Christ's offering was

> twofold, like that of certain legal victims: the first part is the slaying, the second one the exhibition. In the case of legal victims, the former was performed in the temple, the latter in the innermost sanctuary itself; in the case of Christ, the former on earth, the latter in heaven; yet that former offering is not a preparation for the sacrifice, but the sacrifice; the latter not so much the sacrifice as the commemoration of the execution of the sacrifice.[74]

This was *not* typology. The sacrifice of Christ is a "species of the same genus," Grotius wrote, more perfect than the Temple sacrifices, but also the same kind of thing.[75] The death of Christ and the children of Moloch too were not just formally *similar*. They were in fact members of the same tribe.

Christ's Crucifixion was neither a normatively defensible act, in short, nor an element of the interpretive world of typology. It was rather one of the customs of the ancient world, which, as Shuger writes, "explicate theology because they supply documentary evidence for the moral logic of premodern societies and *not* because they state universally valid principles."[76] Methodologically, law, history, and anthropology had become more than a set of useful analogies. They were the very means by which theological problems might be solved.

Beyond Typology: Hebrew Sacrifices, Christian Sacrifice

Grotius and Franzius were symptomatic of a deep crisis that Protestants faced in the wake of Socinus. Without the Crucifixion, the Italian showed, the very structure of the Christian imagination began to unravel. To weave it back together, some redoubled their commitments to older forms of theological reasoning. But many others took off in new directions. Once the connection between sacrifices of the patriarchs and the Crucifixion of Christ could not be assumed as a literary and theological given, they looked instead for *other* imaginative resources, textual, historical, and anthropological.

Such resources were widely available by the late sixteenth century. In the third dissertation of the *Schola*—on prayer and song in the sacrifices—Franzius wondered why God accepted Abel's offering but rejected Cain's. To find out, he turned first to the Italian Dominican Santes Pagnino's 1528 Hebrew-Latin edition of the Old Testament, renowned for its literal fidelity. "And God regarded (*respexit*) Abel and his offering. And he did not look at (*aspexit*) Cain and his gift," Genesis read, suggesting that God did indeed respect the gifts of Abel, but not *why* He did.[77] Still puzzled, Franzius then reached for the so-called *Biblia regia* (1568–1572), an immense polyglot Bible published at the behest of King Philip II of Spain and supervised by his chaplain, Benito Arias Montano. This work included the Aramaic translation of the Torah called the *Targum Onkelos*, written in the first centuries CE. There, in the vernacular of ancient Palestine, Franzius found slightly different phrasing: "there was favor before the Lord toward Abel and his offering. But toward Cain and his offering there was no favor."[78] This seemed just right, to that Lutheran reader, since it

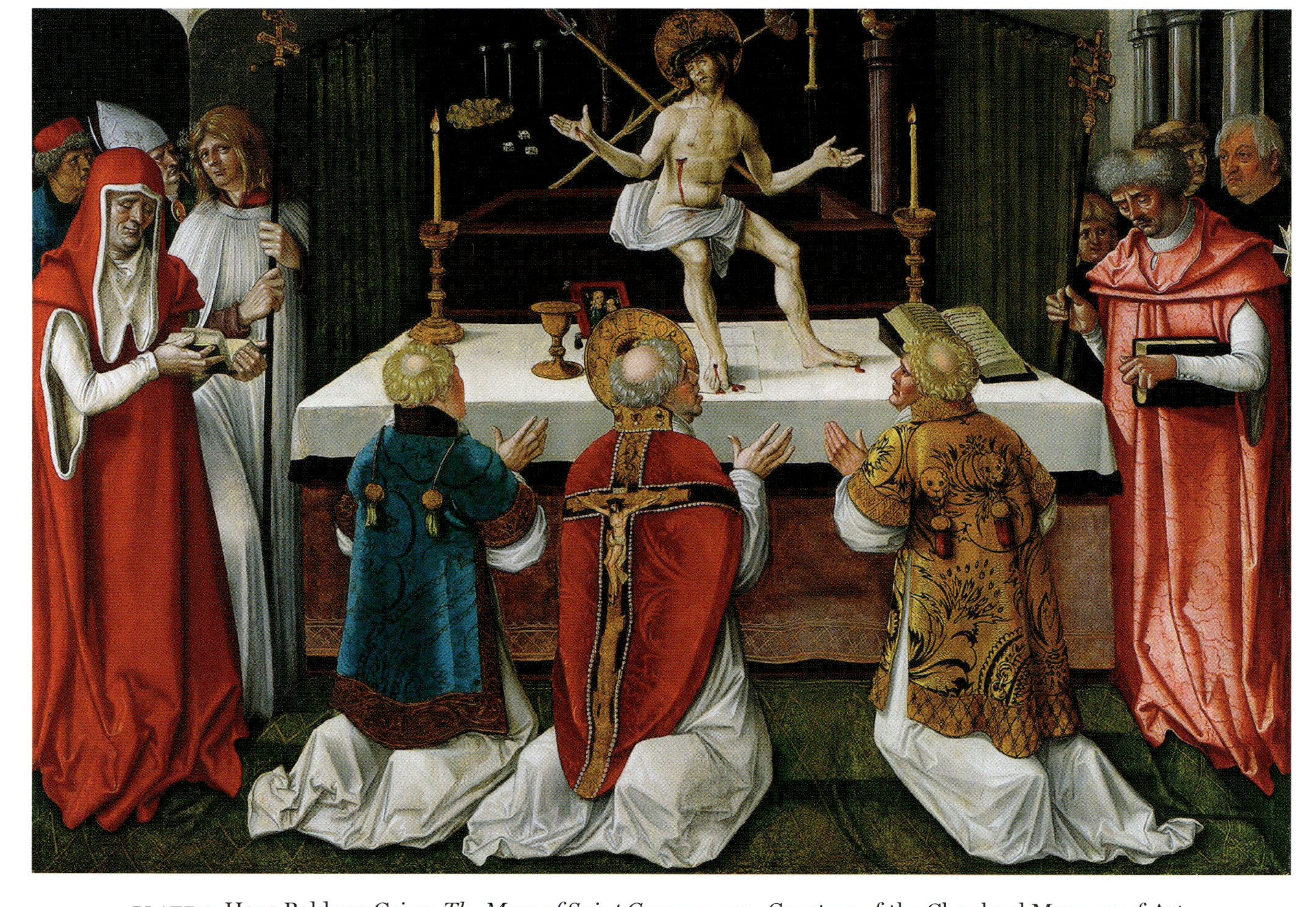

PLATE 1. Hans Baldung Grien, *The Mass of Saint Gregory*, 1511. Courtesy of the Cleveland Museum of Art.

PLATE 2. The Mass of St. Gregory. Hieronymus Bosch, *Epiphany Altarpiece*, outer wings. 1510. Museo del Prado, Madrid. The Yorck Project (2002) 10.000 Meisterwerke der Malerei (DVD-ROM), distributed by DIRECTMEDIA Publishing GmbH. Wikimedia Commons.

PLATE 3. The Adoration of the Magi. Hieronymus Bosch, *Epiphany Altarpiece*, retable. 1510. Copyright of the image Museo Nacional del Prado / Art Resource, NY.

PLATE 4. The Sacrifice of Abraham. Hieronymus Bosch, *Epiphany Altarpiece*, details. Copyright of the image Museo Nacional del Prado / Art Resource, NY.

PLATE 5. Weimar Altarpiece. Lucas Cranach and workshop. Church of Saint Peter and Paul, Weimar (1552–1555). bpk Bildagentur /St. Peter und Paul, Weimar / Photograph by Roland Dreßler/ Art Resource, NY.

PLATE 6. Giovanni Bellini, *Blood of the Redeemer*, ca. 1465. © National Gallery, London / Art Resource, NY.

PLATE 7. Tree of Life and Death, *Salzburg Missal*, late 1450s–1494. Courtesy of the Bayerische Staatsbibliothek.

PLATE 8. Rembrandt, *Sacrifice of Isaac*, 1635. Alte Pinakothek, Bayerische Staatsgemäldesammlungen. Munich, Germany. bpk Bildagentur / Alte Pinakothek / Art Resource, NY.

confirmed that the Lord favored Abel *before* favoring the gifts, and that this favor did not "come from any natural powers" that Abel might have to please God but was kindled in advance by the Holy Spirit.[79] Faith before works, already there in Genesis.

When a Lutheran theologian immerses himself in an ancient Middle Eastern vernacular to defend a doctrinal commonplace, change is afoot. The *Targum Onkelos* was just part of a large shift in the intellectual landscape of the early seventeenth century, as the trickle of Hebrew learning into European Christianity that began a century earlier flooded into universities, libraries, and the thought-world of theology.[80] By the 1530s, Hebrew had become a regular subject in early modern universities both Catholic and Protestant. Hebrew grammars and dictionaries rolled off of printing presses, and works like Pagnino's *Biblia* offered platforms for learned comparisons between Latin and Hebrew biblical texts. Ambitious polyglot Bibles—like the Complutensan Polygot (1514–17), the product of Spanish humanists and learned *conversos* at the university of Alcalá, the *Biblia Regia*, later the Paris and London polyglots—soon made possible direct comparison of Hebrew, Greek, Latin, Syriac, Samaritan, and even Ethiopic versions of scripture.[81] Nor was so-called Christian Hebraism restricted simply to the biblical texts. Over the course of the century, curiosity about Jewish Kabbalistic texts spread from Italy to the rest of Europe, creating peculiar hybrids of Christian-Jewish mysticism in writers like Heinrich Cornelius Agrippa (1486–1535), Guillaume Postel (1510–1581), Jakob Böhme (1575–1624), and others. Talmud, rabbinical commentary, Jewish chronicles, travel writings, philosophy, political works: nearly two thousand Hebrew titles were published throughout the sixteenth century.[82] Like the patristic texts of the early Reformation, this new archive afforded new resources for the Christian sacrificial imagination.

Take the temple and tabernacle, for example, rich sources of typological speculation since the dawn of Christianity. *Quam dilecta tabernacula tua, Domine virtutum*: "How lovely your tabernacles, O Lord of Hosts," read Psalm 84 (see chapter 2). Literally, the storage box for the Eucharist in the late medieval church, but figuratively, the Christian tabernacle was the Church militant, and typologically, the body of Christ, the one, final, and true sacrifice. When Erasmus wrote his commentary on this Psalm, *De sarcienda ecclesiae concordia* (1533), he moved easily across this landscape of analogies and figures. The Levitical feast of the tabernacle and the prophecies of Zechariah tied together the "holy convocation" of the church and sacrifices offered to the Lord (Lev. 23; Zech. 14). The temple was similarly charged with interpretive power. "The temple of Solomon signifies the blessed Maria," declared the popular late medieval handbook of typology, the *Speculum humanae salvationis*, and much attention was paid to the temple curtain, allegedly spun by Mary herself, to protect the holy of holies and rent asunder at the Resurrection.[83]

Here, by contrast, was the Church of England clergyman William Owtram, writing on the temple and tabernacle in 1677:

> As a moveable sanctuary [the tabernacle] was sufficiently adapted to the unsettled state of [Israel] in the wilderness, but it little comported with the fixed settlements and ample wealth that they acquired in Canaan. . . . expecting to illustrate his own name, David, the best of their kings, meditated the great work of erecting a fixed and splendid edifice as a temple for God. . . . [but the work was] not becoming a man engaged in war and stained with blood and slaughter. That honour was reserved for Solomon, a monarch born to peace and tranquility: who having ascended the throne, acquired great wealth, and . . . erected a magnificent temple to Jehovah.[84]

The two books of Owtram's *De sacrificiis* began with straightforward historical descriptions like this, using the lived experience of ancient Israel and her sacrifices as defenses of the "universal church . . . against Faustus Socinus and his followers." History and theology were intimately linked. To show that "what was shadowed forth by the types was really accomplished in the antitype," Owtram argued, first it was "necessary to examine the sacrifices of the Jews, and carefully to inquire, what the particular logic [*ratio*] of the sacrifices is . . . for which reasons, and with what ceremonies, and in what place the sacrifice was to be immolated; what was the design [*ratio*] of the sacred tabernacle, of the temple at Jerusalem, of the consecrated altar, and of the sacred table."[85] He sought, in other words, to resecure the shaky foundations of typology in the historical world of the Hebrews.

Owtram was not the first to try this. The 1572 *Biblia regia*, for example, concluded with a set of critical appendices written by the Spanish scholar Arias Montano. Later reprinted separately as the *Antiquitatum iudaicarum* (1593), they included a treatise on "the construction and structure of temples." The heavenly temple is the "church of God," Montano affirmed, but on earth, temples are made by human hands: funded by powerful kings, staffed by clergy, built according to specific designs, and populated with functional objects.[86] His exemplary case was the temple of Solomon, whose textual and visual reconstruction he accomplished using the materials of Hebrew antiquity, especially the Mishnah—an ancient

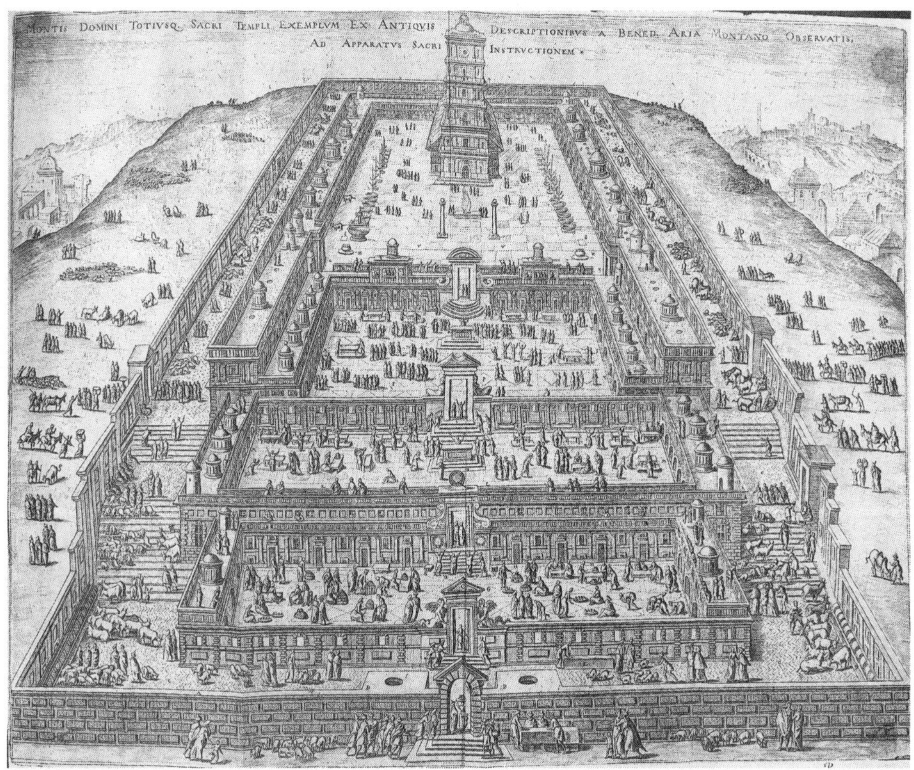

FIGURE 8.2. Solomon's Temple. Benito Arias Montano, *Antiquitatum Iudaicarum Libri ix* (Leiden, 1593). Courtesy of the Herzog August Bibliothek, Wolfenbüttel, 58.4 Hist.

work of rabbinic learning—and its tractate on temple measurements (the *Middoth*).[87] Montano illustrated this temple as a spare building, with a lofty but undecorated porch, and a sanctuary pierced by small windows. Scenes of the temple in use augmented this quotidian sensibility (fig. 8.2).

On the outside, the "*Mons domus*," an area for animals and commerce; then the "atrium of the profane," where trading and exchange were permitted; the "atrium of the women," with its "throne of the pontifex"; the "atrium of the Israelites," with the "throne of the king"; the interior section open only to the Levites; and finally the enclosed sanctuaries themselves. At the very center of it all was the Levitical high priest whom Montano also lovingly illustrated with all of the "apparatus for performing the sacrifices" (see fig. 8.3). The smoking altar, the wood for the fire, the bellows to keep it going, the knives for the killing, the trumpets and harps for the celebration, and at the center, the priest himself piously awaiting the arrival of the victim.

FIGURE 8.3. Hebrew High Priest. Benito Arias Montano, *Antiquitatum Iudaicarum Libri ix* (Leiden, 1593). Courtesy of the Herzog August Bibliothek, Wolfenbüttel, 58.4 Hist.

Montano's temple was, in short, the kind of building made by, and filled with, *people*. His depiction of the tabernacle was no less prosaic, embedding this site of worship in the everyday life of an ancient nomadic people, driving their sheep and goats, fetching water, and caring for their children. In all of this, sacrifice was a quotidian affair. It required skill with a knife, the feeding the holocaustal flames, and the disposal of the carcasses. The Christian reader of the *Biblia* was thus asked to keep *two* temples and *two* tabernacles always in mind, one mystical, one mundane, one whose truth was supplied dogmatically, the other with the materials of Hebrew antiquity.

Over the course of the seventeenth century, this became a norm. When the clergyman Thomas Fuller published his theological geography of the Holy Land—the *Pisgah Sight of Palestine* (1650)—he laboriously recounted every construction detail of the ancient Temple. Relying on Montano and others, he described the finances of Solomonic temple building, the weight of the nails used to build the Holy of Holies, the ceremonial utensils found in the temple, the priestly refectories, and the musical instruments used during the rites.[88] Ten years later, Samuel Lee published an even more explicit effort to map typology onto historical and geographical particulars. His 1659 *Orbis Miraculum, or, the Temple of Solomon pourtrayed by Scripture-Light* saw the Temple as an immense representational knot. While the ultimate tool for loosening this knot was Christ, whose coming revealed the "Sacred Mysteries lodged within these Palaces," the modern Christian also needed a very precise set of learned tools to assist in the project. On the one hand, the Temple had to be located in a global space. "[T]he exact distance . . . of this famous City *Jerusalem*" was crucial, argued Lee, "that we may know whereabouts in the World our Discourse lies." After some calculations, Lee determined that his Temple lay exactly "2717 miles, 7 furlongs, 30 poles, and 1/2" from the city of London.[89] From this global space, Lee then moved inward. Beginning at the "Porch" of the Temple, he unwrapped the mysterious center of the place, describing first the inner sanctuary, and then the Holy of Holies, that part of the Temple reserved only for the high priest on the day of atonement. From the interior, Lee then pulled back, diagramming the courts that surrounded the Temple building and assigning to each their proper ritual objects and holy men.

Only *after* this tour of the Temple's sacred geography did Lee weave "this Sacred pile" into a synthetic Christological prophecy. The final chapter, for example, explained what Lee called the "Jewish Gospel, or the streaming forth of the glorious beames of Christ incarnate, whilst he walked under the Vail of *Moses*." The Sanctuary typified the "Church Militant on Earth," while the Holy of Holies signified "the place and state of Saints in Glory," and its veil the "vaile of *Christ's Flesh*," and the Temple festivals and sacrifices indicating the final perfection of the Cross.[90]

As above, however, these typological commonplaces were less assumed than *proven*. That the "birth of our Saviour answer[s] to the Feast of the Tabernacles" Lee demonstrated with complex astrological calculations and learned references to ancient calendars. That "no sacrifice could expiate for the sin of man, but man himself" he demonstrated with historical comparisons to the ancient Gauls and Achilles's slaughter of the Trojan youths after the death of Patroclus. To understand the curious (likely corrupt) phrase in the the Gospel of Mark—that "every sacrifice shall be salted with salt" (9.49)—Lee unleashed a torrent of analysis: an antiquarian observation that ancient sacrifices were all accompanied by salt; a typological, that "every true Christian is an evangelical *Sacrifice*, and is to be salted . . . that he might become savoury . . . to God"; and a philological, hinging on manuscripts suggesting the reading "salted with fire" might be more accurate. To make a "compendious Map of . . . the unknown Land of the Gospell," typology needed the resources of geography, history, chronology, ancient customs, rites, and ceremonies. It needed, in short, an entire edifice of learning drawn from Hebrew antiquity.[91]

By the 1670s, then, the prophetic imagination of temple and tabernacle had been supplemented, not least by the rabbinic materials circulating widely in seventeenth-century Europe. Already in 1649, the Talmudist John Lightfoot explored the "temple service" in the age of Christ, with the rabbis as his guide. Lightfoot declared of the temple sacrifices that their first purpose was to "represent and be a memoriall of the great sacrifice of Christ."[92] Then it supplemented this truism with a cornucopia of particulars. It described the methods and instruments used to flay the slain sacrifices; the ways that blood was sprinkled on the altar; and a host of sacrificial practices that Lightfoot collected from every rabbinical source he could find.[93] Owtram too reveled in these rabbinic details. The temple was a finite space, he wrote, so "stationary men" (*viri stationarii*) were appointed to attend "the public sacrifices as representatives of the whole nation." These men included gatekeepers, custodians of the musical instruments, ticket keepers, aqueduct inspectors, incense makers, curtain weavers, clothiers, and doctors to care for the priests "who, from walking without shoes on the pavement of the sanctuary, were frequently troubled with dysentery."[94]

What had once been reflex, in short, was now reflexive. Christology still bound together Old and New Testaments; the sacrifice on the Cross was still the fulfillment of Levitical law; the world of Israel was still valuable to the extent that it was superseded by the new covenant: but the truth of these teachings now depended on the very Hebrew ceremonial law that Christianity had long prided itself on abolishing.

Maimonides, Sacrifice, and the Founding of Christian Ceremony

Ceremonial law was, as it happened, an especially vexing matter for Protestants—and especially English Protestants—in the seventeenth century. In part this was an extension of older conflicts. The sacrificial Mass was an early victim of Protestant orthopraxis, as were many of the ceremonial trappings that accompanied it. The sacrality of the altar, the veneration of relics, priestly vestments, the use of incense, the consecration of churches: all things with taproots into the sacrificial cultures of gentile and Hebrew antiquity were endless points of contention. Contention was violent not only between Catholics and Protestants, moreover, but also *among* Protestants, who often disagreed vehemently whether one or another ceremony was actually Christian at all. Repeated efforts to settle the issue—by insisting, for example, on a range of ceremonies as "adiaphora," unrequired but also unoffensive, and thus not worth division and conflict—tended to fail when tensions ran high.

In England, the monopoly on doctrine that Calvinists enjoyed by the late sixteenth century did little to resolve these tensions. The so-called Elizabethan settlement involved repeated liturgical compromises: whether to allow crucifixes, rood screens, images, vestments, altars, rogation ceremonies, and many other flash-point issues. These compromises inevitably pleased one faction at the expense of another. When, as in the Netherlands, this church split into Puritan and Arminian groups at century's end, conflicts over ceremony and public worship were pushed to the forefront of English religious and political controversy. From Richard Hooker's *Laws of the Ecclesiastical Polity* (1593) to Thomas Hobbes's *Leviathan* (1651), advocates of ecclesiastical unity rebranded ceremonial issues as adiaphoric, demoted them as irrelevant to a pious Christian life, and recommended their control by clerical and political authorities. These efforts typically failed, with charges of crypto-Catholicism, crypto-paganism, and crypto-Judaism leveled at those who failed to distinguish properly between pious and impious Christian rite.

At the same time, the first decades of the seventeenth century were also a period of wild ceremonial experimentation. On the one hand, there emerged explicitly "judaizing" sects of Calvinists, who revived the Saturday sabbath, Levitical proscriptions in diet, even the practice of circumcision (!). Other splinter groups of English antinomians banished "the [Mosaic] Law entirely from the field of Christian worship," equally rejecting *all* civil or ecclesiastical control over their liturgical practices.[95] Confusion only grew over the decades. The re-replacement of communion tables by altars—the "greatest place of God's residence upon earth," as the Arminian Archbishop William Laud commented in 1637—marked just one of the fault lines that, in the next few years, yawned between sides in England's civil wars.[96] Neither the parliamentary rule of the 1640s or 1650s, nor the restoration of the monarchy in 1660, did much to diminish the issue. Indeed, the later seventeenth century would see repeated top-down efforts to enforce conformity—the Clarendon Code of the 1660s, the Test Acts of 1673 and 1678—in matters of both doctrine and liturgy, and repeated conflicts between dissenting sects and the established church.

When William Owtram wrote his *De sacrificiis libri duo . . . contra Faustum Socinum*, therefore, he gave pride of place to the question of ceremony. The majesty of God, he opened his inquiry, lends a "character of holiness [*sanctitas*], not only to *persons*, but also to *things* and *times* and *places*, and even to *rites* and *ceremonies*," and most importantly sacrifice.[97] This affirmation of holiness was no neutral statement of fact. It was instead a polemical broadside against Socinus, and against the Quakers, Ranters, Seekers, Diggers, Muggletonians, Fifth-Monarchy Men, and other radical sects that had peopled the revolutionary landscape, threatening not only the ecclesiastical authority, but even the very concept of worship itself. By 1670, in other words, the early shock of Socinus was now refracted through broader circumstances that demanded that "holy ceremony" be more than an oxymoron.

Once again, it was the rabbis who came to the rescue, most importantly, the late medieval (1135–1204) Andalucian rabbi Moses Maimonides. Indeed, no postclassical Jewish writer exercised the early modern Christian imagination as much as this philosopher, doctor, and codifier of Jewish law, known as Rambam.[98] Like all rabbinic works, his writings on Jewish law, the *Mishneh Torah* and the *Commentary on the Mishnah*, were at best ignored and dismissed in the Christian Middle Ages, and at worst condemned by churchmen as blasphemy. By the late sixteenth century, however, they found a home in the Christian canon. Read first in Hebrew by theologians and scholars, parts of them became visible to a wider Latin readership over the course of the seventeenth century. The Mishnaic treatise *Middoth*—on the measurements of the ancient Temple—was translated by the Leiden Hebraist Constantijn l'Empereur in 1630, for example, and included rich references to Maimonides's legal writings. The *Middoth*, he argued, both "illustrat[ed] the religious ceremonies of the Old Testament" and shone "a bright light on the Gospel narratives."[99] It supplied Calvinist magistrates with resources to combat "the heresies of the Arians and Socinians" and afforded a clear analogy between the tabernacle of ancient Israel, and *tabernaculum Dei* of the living Reformed church awander through Europe.[100]

Over the next decades, parts of Maimonides's *Mishneh Torah* were translated directly into Latin, both in the Netherlands and in England, serving a host of different agendas.[101] Indeed, it was one of the leaders of the English separatist community in Amsterdam, the community that eventually populated the Puritan New World adventures, who first integrated Maimonides into a vernacular biblical commentary. Nearly every page of Henry Ainsworth's 1618 *Annotations upon Leviticus* relied on "Maimony, treat. of the Dayly Oblations"—the *Ha Korbanot*, later translated as *De sacrificiis* in 1683—for every last detail of the ancient sacrificial cult of Israel. From the religious dissenter Ainsworth at the beginning of the century, to high church Anglicans like Simon Patrick and Richard Kidder at its end, when it even reached learned readers in Boston, Maimonides's vision of the Talmud provided a foundation of Christian sacrificial typology and its sacrificial imagination more generally.[102]

For writers like Owtram, the *Guide for the Perplexed*—Maimonides's philosophical masterpiece—was essential reading. Translated from Arabic into Latin already in the Middle Ages, the *Guide* was introduced into the early modern print-public sphere first by the Corsican bishop Agostino Giustiniani in 1520, and then again in 1629, at the hands of the Swiss Calvinist Hebraist Johann Buxtorf the Younger.[103] By the middle of the seventeenth century, it was a touchstone for learned Calvinists from Hugo Grotius to John Selden.[104] And while Christian readers could find many points of interest in the *Guide*, from Hebrew philology to biblical hermeneutics, Maimonides's historico-anthropological account of the *origins* of Mosaic Law proved critical for Christians eager to keep their ceremonies sacred.

The early modern imagination was obsessed with origins. As man's fate is ruled by Adam, the nature of things is ruled by their beginnings. The Amerindians were innocents, the Franciscan friar Bartholomé de las Casas argued, because their bloody sacrifices had origins in nature and human reason. His near contemporary Francisco de Vitoria argued the opposite: since "no argument from reason can be given for any kind of sacrifice . . . *no sacrifices existed in the state of innocence*."[105] The missionary José de Acosta discovered the origins of Amerindian sacrifice in diabolical imitation, but his near contemporary, the Cardinal Robert Bellarmine, defended the sacrificial Mass by insisting that sacrifice was rooted in nature: since "every religion, true or false, in all times and places, have used sacrifice in the worship of God," it must come from "the light and instinct of nature."[106]

Most Protestants believed that sacrifice had its origin in revelation, not reason. There was often disagreement about *when* this revelation might have happened, however, since Scripture was silent on the matter. As we saw in chapter 6, the theological geographer Samuel Purchas thought that there was a tacit revelation to Adam in the Garden. Franzius disagreed, and like Vitoria, insisted that "in the state of innocence" Adam neither needed nor performed any sacrificial rite, and it was only afterward that (somehow) God made it known that he desired sacrifice.[107] For his part, Grotius took the more "Catholic"—or, as he would have argued, patristic—view that "it was not by any divine command, but by the dictate of reason" that Cain was inspired to make offerings to God.[108]

Maimonides clarified this confusion. Rationality governed the confusion of biblical particulars, the *Guide for the Perplexed* taught. There is "a cause for all the commandments," said Maimonides, because nothing that God does can be devoid of purpose. If God willed there to be 613 commandments, as the ancient rabbis taught, these were "consequent upon wisdom and . . . given in view of some utility." This was easy to see with the major commandments: *thou shalt not kill* ensured a peaceful and pious community, for example. For every commandment whose "utility was clear to the multitude," however, there were dozens of commandments with no apparent rhyme or reason. The reasons for *these* commandments Maimonides discovered in the "study of the doctrines, opinions, practices, and cult" of an ancient group of sun-worshiping idolaters he called the Sabians.[109]

It is unclear who these Sabians actually were.[110] Like the Romans for Christian antiquarians, however, they served Maimonides as a proxy for "paganism," for the religious and cultural matrix from which the people of Israel struggled to emerge. Documented in a tenth-century work called the *Nabatean Agriculture*, "their festivals, their sacrifices, their prayers, and other matters belonging to their religion" clarified the nature of the commandments "considered to be without cause." Indeed, the "foundation of the whole of our Law and the pivot around which it turns," Maimonides daringly argued, could *only* be discerned through the historical and anthropological materials found in this supposedly ancient Babylonian text. For the *Nabatean Agriculture* documented a way of life and worship "customary in the whole world" of antiquity. Since the people of Israel endured a long childhood in this ancient world of idolatry and error, and since man "is not capable of abandoning suddenly all to which he was accustomed," God imposed the Law to efface "these opinions from the minds" of ancient Israel.[111] In short, he *accommodated* his Law to the history and anthropology of Israel.

That "the Scriptures speak the languages of man" was, we have observed, an ancient exegetical commonplace.[112] "It befitted God to request sacrifices in earlier times," Augustine wrote, "now, however, things are different." Every epoch has its appointed institutions, each accommodated to their time, and to one another, that history might unfold "like a beautiful melody."[113] Medieval writers like William of Auvergne and Thomas Aquinas supplemented typological interpretations of the ceremonial law with the principle of accommodation, especially when they sought to understand the value of the law for the Jews themselves.[114] Later Calvin augmented Christology with an accommodationist reading of the Law. He spoke of God's "lisp," for example, the way He spoke to humans "as nurses commonly do with infants," and how God "has accommodated himself to men's capacity, which is varied and changeable," the Law an instrument for the childhood of mankind, and the Gospel for its maturity.[115] For a skeptic of typology like Socinus, finally, accommodation was an attractive way to hold the sacrifices of the Hebrew Bible at an historical distance, and weaken their traditional link to the Atonement.[116]

Maimonides turned accommodation into a total theory of revelation. The central puzzle of the Law, as he saw it, was its appearance of utter contingency. "No cause"—no moral cause, that is—"will ever be found for the fact that one particular sacrifice consists in a *lamb* and another in a *ram*," and anyone who looks for one will be "stricken with a prolonged madness."[117] Since presumably the governor of all things needs neither rams nor lambs, his choice of either seems utterly arbitrary. All ceremonial sacrifice suffers the same confusion. Why does God command the slaughter of oxen and goats, and not wild animals? Why does He forbid the offering of leavened bread? Why does He require all sacrifices to be salted with salt? Why aren't the uncircumcised allowed to partake in the sacrifice? Why is blood used for purification? There must be *some* reason why He insisted on one over the other, lest the contingency of ceremonial prescription overwhelm the orderliness of God's wisdom.

Maimonides discovered this reason in history and anthropology. The Mosaic law began in Exodus, when God liberated Israel from Egypt. Pharoah let the people go, but Israel was no longer, and not yet, the people of God. The Hebrews in Egypt were no less "Sabian" than the Egyptians themselves: prone to idolatry, tempted toward astral worship, eager to propitiate demonic djinns, liable to superstition. The project of freeing Israel from the religious and psychic effects of bondage would take generations to accomplish.

The Mosaic law was not a general set of prescriptions for holy living, therefore. It was *specifically* targeted to historical Israel, a set of ritual countermeasures introduced to wean the ancient Jews from their idols and bring them back to God. The Egyptians "forbade the slaughter of sheep": Sabians worshiped the djinn under the form of goats; oxen were held "in great esteem" by ancient idolators. The great Temple sacrifices of sheep, and goat, and oxen were designed to overcome these ancient taboos, inverting the order of pagan holiness to create a new people of God. An "extreme act of disobedience was [now] the one through which one came near to God": Israel's worship of the golden calf was cured by a systematic cult of calf-killing, the holy things of Egypt turned into their opposite. Idolators sacrificed wild animals, so Levitical law forbade it; The Sabians "seasoned their sacrifices with honey," so the Hebrews used salt; the Sabians thought blood was the most unclean thing of all, so Israel used it to purify its altars.[118] In this way, the ancient Temple was a ritual laboratory designed to remake the religious and psychic constitution of Israel.

To understand the ceremonial law, then, we must become historians. "For in the day that I brought them out of the land of Egypt, I did not speak to your fathers or command them concerning burnt offerings and sacrifices. But this command I gave them, 'Obey my voice, and I will be your God'": these words of Jeremiah had long puzzled the rabbis, since the entire law of Moses treated just such matters (Jer. 7.22–23). To this Maimonides explained that Jeremiah was speaking *historically*. "In the first legislation given to us there was nothing at all concerning burnt-offerings and sacrifices"—that is, in the days of Abel and Abraham, there was no need for ordinances like these. Only later were such ordinances given, that an idolatrous Israel might once again hearken to the words "Obey my voice, and I will be your God."[119] Scripture alone does not reveal the nature of the ceremonial law. This requires historical research:

> Just as ... the doctrines of the Sabians are remote from us today, the chronicles of those times are likewise hidden from us today. Hence if we knew them and were cognizant of the events that happened in those days, we would know in detail the reasons of many things mentioned in the *Torah*.[120]

The *Nabatean Agriculture* opened a window on the ancient world of Israel, Maimonides thought, but other documents might reveal other things. He who would understand the Torah must assume *reasons* for its rules, and seek them in the "chronicle of those times."[121]

A medieval rabbi might seem an unusual recruit to the cause of the Anglican establishment. But Maimonides provided valuable new ways to defend the Atonement and Christian ceremony at the same time. Three things were suggested by the *Guide*: first, that God never commanded sacrifice until the Israelites departed Egypt; second, that sacrifices must have been there *before* the law was given at Sinai; and third, that *even if* the origin of sacrifice was all-too-human, nonetheless it was pious.

For a reader like William Owtram, the first points helped to resolve that long-standing puzzle about the origins of sacrifice. Although Scripture did not afford a clear answer, he admitted, Maimonides showed that the injunction to sacrifice came *late*, the product of God's "great selection, both of things and of rites, for his sacrifices" to counteract the Hebrew addiction to Egypt. There was an idiom of worship common to gentiles, Jews, and even Christians. Eucharistic sacrifices, votive sacrifices, sin- and trespass-offerings: these "were directed to the same end, as prayers and thanksgivings uttered by their lips; only with this difference, that the same intention was expressed with different signs, in the latter by articulate sounds, in the former by significant rites."[122] Neither the result of divine command nor diabolical imitation, together these were part of the "natural worship of God," a common way of recognizing that God was the "maker, preserver, and sovereign of the universe."[123] Ceremony was, in a sense, the natural order of things.

Even more significant, however, was Maimonides's final point. Despite their natural origin and their historical contingency, the Levitical sacrifices were nonetheless *true*. For the medieval rabbi, they were true in the sense that they were essential to the formation of Israel and thus worthy of veneration on their own account. For Owtram, they were true in a very different way. They were not just a divine ruse to end idolatry. They were also, at the same time, the divine revelation of the great truth to come, God's way to "shadow forth the great sacrifice of Christ." The profane and the pious could walk hand in hand. But to grasp the latter—to prove, in essence, what Christians had always "known" about the Law—now the theologian must first explore and explain the former. From the Hebrew sacrifices, Owtram wrote, reversing the usual order of operations, "we may learn the true power and rationale [*propria vis et ratio*]" of Christ's sacrifice.[124] The two books of Owtram's *De sacrificiis libri duo* followed just this order: *first*, the history and anthropology of Jewish sacrifice, *then* the synthetic treatise on Christian typology. The road to theology ran through history and anthropology.

John Spencer and the Anthropology of Atonement

In 1685, the Anglican Hebraist John Spencer published a work he titled *De legibus Hebraeorum ritualibus*. This was the culmination of the learned Latinate effort to recruit Maimonides, and Jewish antiquity, for the sacrificial and ceremonial imagination of Christianity.[125] Spencer is a figure of some posthumous notoriety. His "Latin work on the ritual law of the Hebrew . . . laid the foundations of the science of comparative religion," wrote the Semitist William Robertson Smith in 1894 (see chapter 11).[126] Since then, he has been seen as an intellectual pioneer of the secular study of religion, someone who "begins to speak the language of Enlightenment" from the folds of a dense antiquarianism, as Jan Assmann writes.[127] Seen contextually, however, Spencer was less a radical than "an active partisan of the Church of England," who defended the exclusive legitimacy of the Restoration church against the antinomianism of the revolutionary period.[128] He was inspired to write the work, Spencer remarked, in order to "curb the obstinacy of the fanatics," the "multifarious sects" who insist that "no communion should be cultivated with the Anglican church."[129] That such an effort demanded nearly a thousand pages of bristling historical and anthropological erudition shows in stark form just how heterogeneous the apologetic project had become by the late seventeenth century.

God did not deliver Israel "by straight lines to their original state and religion," but rather brought back a people afflicted "by the crimes and errors of Egypt" through a delicate process of toleration, accommodation, and redirection.[130] Thus began Spencer's treatment of the "reason and origin of the sacrifices" in the Jewish ritual law. He nested this view in a thicket of Christian patristic authorities. But at the heart of his book were the historico-anthropological arguments of Maimonides. The Mosaic law was a form of ritual therapy for the Hebrews, recreating them as a people of God; it was the product of a gracious ruse, and a concession to human frailty; it used the rites of the gentiles against the gentile gods; and so forth. Only these could explain why Scripture at times so clearly rejected exactly the sacrifices that the Law required. "Will I eat the flesh of bulls or drink the blood of goats?" asked the Psalmist (50.13), showing just how little God valued the sacrifices per se.[131] The ceremonial law was an historical event, so Maimonides taught, handed down at a particular time for particular purposes.

But Spencer wrote under new intellectual and religious circumstances. His work was part of the well-known reevaluation of "natural religion" among later seventeenth-century Anglican writers, for example. The emergence of pious natural philosophy after 1660—witness the English Royal Society, with its collection of virtuosi like Robert Boyle eager to reconcile natural knowledge with the ways of God—was only one dramatic site of transvaluation of things natural. Members of the Society included so-called latitudinarian theologians like John Tillotson, made archbishop of Canterbury in 1691, who focused on the reasonability of Christianity and its compatibility with natural law. Christianity is "the same in Substance with the Law of Nature," Tillotson wrote in a late-century sermon, arguing, on the one side, that atheism was a crime against nature and, on the other, that the exercise of natural reason should inexorably deepen Christian faith. A more natural religion, as he wrote, might bring the "Nation . . . back to a more sober sense of Religion . . . from a factious contention about things indifferent." And among the most natural expressions of human devotion was sacrifice, he remarked in the same work, the practice *all* men are "most apt to chuse" to pacify the deity.[132]

Spencer defended views like this on historical and anthropological grounds. If the sacrifices of ceremonial law were a late intervention, per Maimonides, where did sacrifice come from in the first place? Again, the answer lay in Hebrew antiquity. Sacrifice was there, Spencer argued, already a few years after mankind exited from the Garden, "commanded by no revelation of god, but by the pious inclination of their souls." Abel, Noah, and all the ancient Hebrews "who worshiped God with sacrifice before the Law" invented *sua sponte* the most fitting manner to venerate the one true God. Cain worked in the fields, so he chose his firstfruits; Abel was a shepherd, so he chose his finest sheep. Both were moved by the "spontaneous witness of their grateful souls" to give their best to God. The Church fathers, the rabbis, and modern authors all showed that, at the origin of sacrifice lay "human custom and will," governed by pious inclinations and free of divine command.[133] Later, gentiles applied this insight in ways often horrifying. But considered in its own right, sacrifice was the innocent product of a natural man, yearning for God. As Tillotson wrote in a 1691 sermon, the religion of Israel was a tool to "keep alive in the World the primitive Tradition and Belief of the *One true God*."[134]

Gospel zealots, antinomians, would-be prophets, scriptural literalists: all believed that only those sacraments, rites, and ceremonies *commanded* by God can serve in the liturgy of His church. The natural history of sacrifice proved otherwise, proved that the merely human can supply the foundations of properly pious devotions. What had been one of the standard Protestant charges against Catholics—that they had transferred gentile rites to the worship of God—now looked like a general principle of "religious evolution, where the incorporation of previous non-sacred traditions into the sacred was presented as standard practice," in the word of one perceptive commentator.[135] That "many sacred things are tempered with human rites and ceremonies" is not a surprise, as Spencer put it, since many sacred things *start* with human rites and ceremonies. Ancient and natural man had developed a set of sacred traditions all on its own, after all, through its own devices. It was not God who invented the things that would become sacred, but mankind. God was now the follower, rather than the governor, of men.

Put so baldly, the idea might have felt blasphemous to these clergyman-scholars. But it was the inevitable conclusion of their claims. The road to the Atonement ran through the historical and anthropological circumstance of a human antiquity, gentile and Hebrew alike. For Spencer, God's accommodation of the idolatrous Jews was the "primary" purpose for the Mosaic Law; the "secondary" purpose was so that "by the rites and institutions of that Law, certain mysteries might be shadowed forth." This view required the pious researcher to carefully discern *which* elements of the Law had a prophetic purpose, and which did not. This could not be determined, however, on a priori dogmatic grounds. "Socinians and modern Jews . . . reject and scorn all the mysteries and hidden senses of the Law," Spencer argued, while fanatics and spiritualists run to the other extreme, believing the "entire Law is pregnant with everlasting mysteries and allegories."[136] Discerning the space of the properly typological required some *other* method, beyond mere doctrinal assertion.

How do we know whether the wildly specific descriptions of the Tabernacle, with its veils, doors, screens, pillars, and gates, should be minutely mapped onto Christological fulfillments, for example? Does the "least particle of the Law" have a typological meaning? To decide this, we need to know what was simply contingent—what was "accommodated to the childishness" of the idolatrous Jews—and what was more broadly significant.[137] By 1685, history and anthropology had become essential propaedeutics to the defense of pious Christianity.

Conclusion: The Coming Collapse

This hybrid of history, anthropology, antiquarianism, and theology did not remain behind the walls of Latinate learning. By the 1690s, the Archbishop of Canterbury was publicly preaching its conclusions, that there was an "ancient and common Notion" among Jews and gentiles that God should be honored with sacrifice; that God "was pleased to comply" with this notion when He promulgated the Law; and, most remarkably, that:

> when *God sent his son, in the Fulness of time*, he was pleased likewise, in the dispensation of the Gospel . . . to have so much regard for these common Notions, and Apprehensions of Mankind, as to provide for the supply of those two great Wants, which they seem'd always to have laboured under, and concerning which they were at so great a loss, *viz.* an effectual expiatory Sacrifice for Sins upon Earth, and a powerful Mediator and Intercessor with God in Heaven.[138]

Coming from the highest prelate in England, the argument that *Christ himself*, and the manner of his death, was an accommodation to the "common Notions and Apprehensions of Mankind," was shocking. So shocking, in fact, that Tillotson and others who embraced this syncretic form of apologetics were charged with the heresy they were most eager to eradicate: Socinianism.

For Charles Leslie, an Irish Jacobite and gadfly of the established church, for example, it was precisely the argument—that Christ's death was of a piece with ancient human sacrifice—that demonstrated the Socinian leanings of Tillotson. To imagine the Atonement as God's effort "to indulge those Wild and Diabolical Notions of Mankind" was the view of a "rank Socinian," a view that "makes *God* to be the *Devil's Ape*," as Leslie colorfully wrote in a 1695 tract entitled *The Charge of Socinianism against Dr. Tillotson Considered*.[139] Nor was Tillotson alone in his endeavor to topple the Cross, thought Leslie. When the latitudinarian Bishop of Salisbury Gilbert Burnet defended the Atonement in a 1694 discourse "on the divinity and death of Christ," for example, he also described a "Sacrificatory Style" common to the ancient Jewish and pagan world out of which the New Testament emerged, even suggesting a certain "Poetical Liberty" that might surround the expiation of Christ.[140] Grounds enough, thought Leslie, for a charge of Socinianism and apostacy for the Bishop.

Over the 1690s, in fact, these Socinian controversies spread so widely that there were calls for a general convocation to determine what, exactly, the Church of England's doctrine of the trinity ought to be.[141]

Leslie's tract had one more enemy, however, and a new one. Named Charles Blount, he was not a churchman eager to defend the Atonement and Christian sacrifice. He was rather a freethinker and author of a much-reprinted and scandalous pamphlet entitled *Great is Diana of the Ephesians: Or, the Original of Idolatry Together with the Politick Institution of the Gentile Sacrifices* (1680). *Cum sis ipse nocens, moritur cur victima pro te? stultitia est morte alterius sperare salutem*—"Why dies a victim for you in your sin? Grace through another's blood fools hope to win"—read the epigraph, which well summarized Blount's view of sacrifice more generally. "Before Religion, that is to say, Sacrifices, Rites, Ceremonies, pretended Revelations and the like, were invented among the Heathens, there was no worship of God except in a rational way," he wrote, putting the syncretic truisms of Owtram, Spencer, Tillotson, and others to far less pious uses.[142] Blount adopted their Maimonidean line as well, describing how the "sweetness of Sacrifices" that the Hebrews discovered in Egypt was, "through divine permission," used to wean them from gentile idols.[143] Sacrifice was not the product of divine revelation or a typological prophecy of the Savior, however. Rather, "all sacrifices seem to be the invention of Priests," a way for men to cast tyranny in the guise of the holy.[144] The suggestion was clear: such sacrificial impostures were as much part of the Christian past as the pagan. As Leslie put it, Blount was a member of the "Atheistical Club," and his work designed "to Blaspheme, and like a Mad Dog, to Curse and Reproach the whole Institution of God."[145]

Leslie had a point. By the 1690s, new and even more unsettling applications of gentile, Jewish, and Christian antiquity were legion. In the *Guide for the Perplexed*, for example, one can find the puzzling suggestion that, not only did gentile sacrifice preexist the Law, but that gentiles *themselves* might have preexisted the biblical first man and father of the human race.[146] This suggestion was given the force of an outrageous theory in 1655, when an avant-garde heretic from Bordeaux named Isaac La Peyrère finally published a work he had circulated in manuscript since the early 1640s. The English title said it all: *A Theological System Upon that Presupposition that Men Were Before Adam*. The *Prae-Adamitae*, as it was known in Latin, was the public face of a largely clandestine world of impious literature circulating from the 1650s, a dark underbelly of the learned world of Spencer and his ilk. Five editions were published in its first year, and it was as quickly translated as it was condemned, its author arrested in Brussels. Forced publicly to abjure the work, La Peyrère converted to Catholicism to avoid grim consequences.[147]

The *Prae-Adamitae* offered a quirky exegesis of Paul's *Letter to the Romans*, when the apostle wrote, "sin indeed was in the world before the law was given, but sin is not counted where there is no law" (5.13). This traditional proof text for the Christian doctrine of original sin, La Peyrère argued, actually showed the opposite: that the "law" must have meant the law given to *Adam*, not Moses. Because there *was* sin before Adam, he concluded, there must have been *men* before Adam. The Gentiles were the "promiscuous buds of the first Creation . . . and the off-spring of that earth which likewise brought forth other creatures," he wrote lyrically, and the Jews uncreated "in the beginning of things, but form'd out of the clay in *Adam*."[148]

Fleshing out this argument took La Peyrère into biblical exegesis, the history of ancient religions, the anthropology of native Americans, and contemporary learned works from Scaliger to Grotius. Biblical set pieces formerly deployed for pious purposes were turned to more profane ends. If there was no one in the world besides these two sons of Adam, La Peyrère reasoned, where did Cain get the sword to kill Abel? Whom did he fear when he fled from his crime? who were the companions that he gathered east of Eden, as the Jewish historian Josephus reported? whom did he marry to father Enoch and the generations to come? Melchizedek too played his role, the ancient type of Christ's priesthood made, by La Peyrère, into a natural man, else he be a "Man-monster . . . without Father or Mother, or without Original."[149] Ancient chronologies showed the world far more ancient, modern voyages of discovery showed that human origins were far more plural, than anyone had imagined. Nor did La Peyrère fail to use these materials, in the final section of the work, in service of an extraordinarily convoluted defense of the sacrificial death of Christ. We need not rehearse this here, or try to assess whether La Peyrère was sincere in his professions of orthodoxy. More significant is the imaginative space shared by La Peyrère and his clerical contemporaries, who together set conventional Christian claims into entirely new frameworks of justification and exploration.

By the late 1600s, in short, the Protestant effort to re-found the central mystery of Christianity—how a dying God might redeem the sins of the world—had produced a creative yet combustible mix of history, anthropology, philology, antiquarian research, and theology. Socinus was the initial instigator, and a century later, remained a specter haunting Protestant Christology. But the issue was far broader than one doctrinal heterodoxy.

The wound that Socinus opened did not heal because mainline Protestants *themselves* could never agree on what, exactly, it would take to resecure the foundations of the Christian sacrificial imagination.

The violent disputes about ceremony; the pluralization of Protestant sects; disagreements among different schools of authoritative theologians; the politics of worship: all of these added more urgency to the issues that Socinus raised, but did little to resolve them. Like many moments of crisis, however, this one produced spectacular creativity, as both doctrinal and exegetical truisms were embedded in new intellectual constructs. Like many moments of crisis, this spectacular creativity would come with unpredictable consequences, as late century freethinkers and other members of the so-called Atheistical School began to turn these constructs to altogether different ends and, as we will see, as new movements inside the Protestant churches developed a new, affective theology of Christ's sacrifice shorn of the anthropology and history so characteristic of the seventeenth century. These movements would, in tandem, begin to disaggregate the hybrids we've explored here, loosening the sacrificial imagination from the gravity of Christian doctrine.

PART IV

Sacrifice *ad saeculum* *ca. 1685–1915*

SACRIFICE . . . but not like that. From the deep Christian past, the challenge had always been to work out the terms of this difficult thought. From this thought grew the archives of Christian sacrifice from the Reformation onward, as generations of writers grappled with that essential but impossible question: what belongs to Christianity, and what does not? What I have called the heteronomy of Christianity—the ways that it incorporated and sedimented inside itself the world of its opponents—was put on full display as Christians, and especially Protestants, in Europe discovered that what they had thought was Christianity was, surprisingly, nothing of the sort. Sacrifice thus split the churches apart, each seeking to delimit which sacrifice belongs and which does not, which should be preserved and which eliminated. Like the history of Christianity itself, sacrifice was simply too important to lose. How to save it was the problem.

Over time these archives grew, swollen with material first about the early church and its ultimately failed efforts to patrol the boundaries of the new faith. Early conflicts about the Eucharist, liturgical reforms, and eventually the blood of the martyred pulled Christianity into relationship with its own deep time. Theology joined forces first with history, antiquarianism, and then anthropology, a dynamic that only accelerated in the seventeenth century. New problems, confessional and otherwise, made new questions urgent: why is sacrifice apparently universal? Is sacrifice a human invention or a divine one? Are the sacrifices of the ancient Mediterranean, the New World, and the sacrifices of Christ all part of *one* story? If so, what story is this? Comparative histories of idolatry, anthropologies of worship from the ancient Mediterranean to the New World, problems of sovereignty and sacrality: the archives of sacrifice were endlessly pressed into new political, religious, and intellectual service.

However various the questions, problems, and materials, what knit them all together were the sinews of Christianity's sacrificed deity. By the later seventeenth century, these began to fray. The gradual waning of confessional polemic, for example, diminished the theological stakes of the sacrifice problem. Meanwhile, the norms of theological practice themselves began to change. From within the Christian churches, new and dynamic religious movements emerged for which the elegantly assembled archives of historical, antiquarian, and anthropological *comparanda* were simply irrelevant to the understanding and pursuit of true piety. From outside the churches, moreover, scandalous advocates of free thought wondered whether theology has anything to do with truth at all, and began to exploit these archives themselves for entirely impious ends. The history and anthropology of sacrifice did not witness the truth of Christianity, in their hands, but the error of *all* religions. Finally, and perhaps most decisively, a deep structure of the Christian imagination began to collapse. Still defended on historical ground in the seventeenth century, as we saw, what Christians knew as typology or *figura* collapsed as an interpretive scheme by the eighteenth century. *Figura*, in the words of the great literary critic Erich Auerbach, "remove . . . the concrete event, concretely preserved as it is, from time, and transpose . . . it into a perspective of eternity."[1] Genesis and Calvary, Abraham and Christ, Levitical sacrifice and the Lord's Supper—the figural imagination held past and present intimately together, and suggested that, beneath all the variety we might find in human history, *one* story unites it all.

This collapse (or, if you prefer, escape) into pluralism is what I call Enlightenment. A proliferation of new spiritualisms beyond the older confessional churches transformed the religious landscape, even as a new world of skeptical free thought challenged the very nature and authority of all religion. Alongside and enabling these pluralizations came new forms of print and media, from the learned journal to the encyclopedia, which emerged in the last decades of the seventeenth century. Together these helped create a new vernacular public sphere that made the apologetic Latinate treatises of the sixteenth and seventeenth centuries seem dusty and dated. The result was a world of experiment, in which a set of older problematics were at times discarded, but more often repurposed for unpredictable imaginative ends.[2]

Where stories of sacrifice were once variants of the *singular*—a story that began in Genesis and climaxed in Jerusalem, in whose aftermath the world still labors—now they chronicled the *many*. These new stories were overwhelmingly about human beings, the anthropologies that unite them, the institutions they create, the histories they inhabit, the politics they produce. This was, in short, a reorientation of sacrifice "toward the world, *ad saeculum*," in the words of Amos Funkenstein.[3]

Our final part of this book explores, then, the *secular* imagination of sacrifice from the Enlightenment to the nineteenth-century world of the human sciences. For the new religious movements of the early eighteenth century, the release of sacrifice from an older Christian imaginative order freed it to do new religious work, unencumbered by the problem of Christian heteronomy. For others, this release opened up new ways of thinking sacrifice *beyond* the world of normative Christianity. Chapter 9 explores both, showing how the older archives of sacrifice, and the older questions they were designed to resolve, were repurposed for new ends. Why, for example, is sacrifice (apparently) universal? Christianity had had an answer for this, one that unified the human experience from beginning to end. But in the eighteenth century, *new* answers emerged, no less concerned to preserve the unity of the human experience, but now in different terms. Some answers were, broadly speaking, critical. The freethinkers of the eighteenth century made the blood rite central to an assault on religion itself. All religions sacrifice, they agreed, and so all religions are equally products of human superstition. Others were more constructive, making sacrifice central to new anthropologies and psychologies of religion oriented *ad saeculum*. The result was a set of "secular experiments" in the sacrificial imagination, new logics that made sacrifice central to the very constitution of human life.

Sacrifice slipped the symbolic chains of Christianity, then, and began to roam free. This was true in intellectual terms but also *political* ones. For much of this book, the politics of sacrifice have been governed by a logic of scarcity. Martyrs are martyrs because they are special, athletes of the faith who exemplify Christian fortitude for the rest of us. Or, alternately, sacrifice is for sovereigns, those assigned to manage the rites of religion in an age of holy war. In the eighteenth century, chapter 10 argues, the politics of sacrifice were democratized, made available to all. New Enlightenment ideals of sociability, sentiment, and virtue wove sacrifice, and especially *self*-sacrifice, into a broader and inclusive political imagination. The emergence of what the chapter calls ethical republicanism—a republicanism disconnected from concrete political institutions—made the willingness to sacrifice for others, and for the state, into a norm of political community. Older Roman and Christian models were wrenched in new directions, creating a new language of citizenship, and new ideals of what began to be called "civil religion." The chapter explores this political imagination as it expanded across the eighteenth century, from the political treatises, plays, and novels of the early period, to the age of revolution, when the killing of a king put excruciating pressure on the secular hope for a political sacrifice that builds, rather than destroys, human community.

"Secular," finally, does not mean autonomous, as I understand it, freed of dependency on the Christian past. The secular is no more free of its own history than Christianity was. It is no less original for all that. Our final chapter explores this thought—the complex braiding of repetition and innovation—in the context of the human sciences of the nineteenth century. There we find entirely new horizons of the sacrificial imagination: new philosophies of sacrifice, new ways of thinking about sacrifice in evolutionary and historical terms, new sociologies and anthropologies of sacrifice that carry us far beyond the horizons of Christianity. But we also discover a question by now familiar to us: is sacrifice something alien and better left in the past, or something essential to our shared world? The question of *heteronomy*—exactly what had made sacrifice so generative yet unsettling for the Christian story we explored—persists, in other words. And so too persists that creative tension between those who dreamed of a human world finally liberated from sacrifice, rational and self possessed. And those for whom this dream is only that, a repression of those deep truths that sacrifice reveals about human dependence, irrationality, and violence.

CHAPTER NINE

The Enlightenment

SECULAR EXPERIMENTS IN THE SACRIFICIAL IMAGINATION

In the night of thick darkness enveloping the earliest antiquity, . . . there shines the eternal and never-failing light of a truth beyond all question: the world of civil society has certainly been made by men, and that its principles are therefore to be found within the modifications of our own human mind.

—GIAMBATTISTA VICO, *THE NEW SCIENCE* (1744)[1]

"REASON'S DOMAIN IS truth and wisdom; Theology's is piety and obedience."[2] It was a startling proposal. In 1670, when the Dutch philosopher Benedict Spinoza wrote his *Tractatus theologico-politicus*, theology was still an expansive intellectual project, whose methods of inquiry drew from traditional scriptural and doctrinal sources, but also philology, antiquarianism, history, anthropology, and politics. "Mathematical demonstration" was just the latest addition, the rationalist efforts to harmonize the truths of Scripture with the new philosophies of, among others, René Descartes. To this variety of truth-seeking methods, Spinoza proposed a dramatic simplification. For truth was *irrelevant* to theology, he argued. "Faith requires not so much true doctrines, as pious doctrines" and so how "doctrines are to be understood, with respect to their truth, it leaves to be determined by reason." This was not just a doctrinal minimalism, an effort to reduce Christianity (or all religion) to a set of incontestable universal maxims like "Jesus is the Christ," "God exists," or "God pardons the sins of those who repent." It was a *methodological* minimalism that rendered theology politically inert. If truth was no longer at stake, men would no longer "think up new doctrines," no longer quarrel over religion at all. All theology need do, in Spinoza's view, was teach "the practice of loving-kindness and justice."[3]

A retiring lens-grinder living in a small Dutch town—worse, an "impudent atheist . . . [and] apostate Jew," as one of his contemporaries called him—was in no position to dictate terms to Christian theology.[4] But like many outsiders, Spinoza was alert to the fractures of the culture he inhabited. His *Tractatus* probed these relentlessly, exploiting the materials sedimented over 150 years of theological controversy.[5] He spoke the language of accommodation, for example, already well established from Erasmus to Socinus to later Christian readers of Maimonides. Yet he concluded heretical notions from it: that the prophetic revelation was accommodated to the temperament of the prophet, happy prophets predicting happy things; gloomy ones, gloomy things. He was interested in the ancient priest-king Melchizedek, not as prooftext of Christ's eternity, but as evidence that Abraham had learned his "worship, precepts, institutions, and laws" from other ancient peoples. And he too paid attention to the similarities between Jews and ancient pagans. Prophecy was "not particular to the Jews, but common to all the nations"; Jews separate themselves from others by circumcision, the Chinese by their long queues.[6] All the anthropological and historical materials so meticulously collected for theological ends witnessed, in Spinoza, not a common revelation, but the common stock of humanity.

Spinoza held sacrifice in low regard. At best, it was an unnecessary ceremony; at worst, a superstitious practice antithetical to true religion.[7] In this, he was hardly alone. For his English translator Charles Blount, too, sacrifice was nothing more than a hoax perpetrated by priests on their gullible flocks. Both writers joined a flowering of free thought in the late seventeenth century that challenged Christianity, and even religion, itself. In this radical tradition, the historical and anthropological materials of the Christian sacrificial archive—the mythography of a Giraldi, the antiquarian compendium of a Stucki, the explorations of ancient paganism found in Grotius, the Hebrew antiquities of a Spencer—were made to serve new masters. Rather than elevating Christianity from the world of lesser religions, they became a means for humbling it . . . all religions were equal, and all equally bad. Far from a mark of original piety, sacrifice marked nothing more than human folly.

Free thought flourished even as confessional conflict within Christianity declined. Beginning in the 1650s, but accelerating quickly as the century waned, the thick interconnection of politics, religion, and intellectual life central to this book came unravelled. New territorial, commercial, and imperial rivalries—violent warfare between the Dutch and the English both at home and abroad, for example, or the expansionism of France in the age of Louis XIV—destroyed older religious alliances. At the same time, new Christian reform movements gathered strength in the wake of the Thirty Years' War: Jansenism among the Catholics, and varieties of Pietism and spiritualism among the Protestants. These criticized, often fiercely, the older established churches. The old habits of confessional polemics began to seem like a barrier, not a path to true Christianity. In its place, new, experimental forms of theological inquiry set aside history, anthropology, and doctrinal niceties in favor of affective practices of piety. Christian sacrifice was less something to be explained than simply *experienced.*

In this chapter, we explore this afterlife, when sacrifice slipped its older symbolic chains, and those lush archives assembled over 150 years of theological controversy lost their animating purpose. These archives were irrelevant to the true understanding of Christian life, said the new spiritualists, who then created their own sacrifices free from the burden of the past. These archives were nothing at all, said the skeptics, beyond monuments to human irrationality. The first half of the chapter focuses on this unravelling, ending with the great literary engine for the destruction of older certainties, the encyclopedia.

The second half of the chapter surveys efforts of reconstruction, when, already in the early century, a new symbolic order of sacrifice began to be imagined. Sacrifice might obey neither the logic of the Crucifix, nor the deep metaphysical truths of nature, but it had a rationality *different* from the "reason" so beloved to a thinker like Spinoza. This *human* logic explains why it is an enduring, apparently universal, and endlessly creative feature of human life. Its principles were "to be found within the modifications of our own human mind," to echo the Neapolitan philosopher Giambattista Vico, to be found above all in the *history* and *anthropology* of humanity.

This was a sacrificial imagination turned *ad saeculum*, discovering in the older archives new uses for ancient Christian and pagan histories; new anthropologies of human religions; new explanations for the origins of human religious, social, and political institutions. The chapter follows this sacrificial imagination through a diverse cast of philosophers, historians, missionaries, poets, publishers, encyclopedists, and collectors of religious customs. Their projects, and the secular imagination they helped create, were eclectic and conjectural, like much of Enlightenment history and anthropology. Nor were these projects ever "autonomous," that is, liberated once-and-for-all from the Christian past. They were indeed as heteronomous as Christianity itself had always been, incorporating yet remaking what they inherited from a world now on the wane. Sacrifice discarded, sacrifice reborn: as in Christianity, so too in the age of the encyclopedia.

Part I: Beyond the Christian Archive

A Christianity Beyond History

In 1699, a Wittenberg educated historian-turned-theosophist, religious mystic, and separatist named Gottfried Arnold published the last great church history of the early modern period. The *Impartial History of Church and Heresy* recalled such great ecclesiastical works of the Reformation as Matthias Flacius Illyricus's *Magdeburg Centuries* (1559–1574), John Foxe's *Acts and Monuments* (1563, first ed.), or Cesare Baronio's *Annales ecclesiastici* (1588–1607). But where those older books told the story of right-belief persevering in the face of persecution and heresy, Arnold described the opposite, how "so-called right belief" (as he called orthodoxy) had repeatedly conspired with political power to crush the true piety of the heretics.

Arnold's vision of Christian history was, in a word, heterodox. Even more startling, heterodoxy itself was the hero in his story. Pluralism and variety were the *strength*, not the weakness, of Christianity. In the first centuries after Christ, ante-Nicene fathers like Clement of Rome, Ignatius of Antioch, Clement of Alexandria, and Irenaeus "were bound to no particular community, but rather traveled around, teaching and doing what was necessary in all places." Christians were disorganized and idiosyncratic. Reading Paul's letters, Arnold remarks, it is clear that "there was hardly a single Christian, especially at the outset of his conversion, who did not diverge from the others." The "teachers themselves . . . were not free from major errors," in an era when Christian truths and Christian peoples were tangled among "Jews, Greeks, and their sects and philosophers." Indeed, even the most learned of these "spoke so scandalously and differently about theological matters, that many often proposed things that later one would call heresy."[8]

These diverse and mobile communities held onto their ceremonies loosely. Even to the Eucharist—the rite most strongly associated with the unity of Christian communion—"they did not bind themselves strictly . . .

but rather left it free" to celebrate as each wanted. Some Christians used water rather than wine in their ceremonies. Some apostles celebrated Easter "according to the Jewish custom," like a Passover feast; others did not. This liturgical heterogeneity endured right into the era of Christian martyrdom, when local Christian communities were forced to meet "in cemeteries, in prisons, in caves and cellars" and celebrate their rituals in ways that commemorated, as best they could, the deaths of the faithful. Some made offerings for the dead, *oblationes pro defunctis*. Others baptized each other in the blood of their martyrs, the so-called "blood baptism, which was in this time and long after so cherished that it was treasured as much as, and even more than, baptism by water."[9]

The creative heterodoxy of the earliest Christian era came to a painful end. Under the pressure of repeated Roman persecutions, Christians defensively developed a strong concept of the Church. The emergence of creeds and formularies began to define the so-called right believers against those who dared to differ. Christians then became heresiologists, more interested to exclude than correct, to excoriate than comfort. The final collapse came at the moment of Christianity's apparent triumph. The emperor Constantine took this renegade religion into the bosom of Babylon, and made it an instrument of imperial domination. Thereafter, "Christians began to bite and feed on each other . . . to judge and to damn, to wreak robbery and murder."[10] Orthodoxy triumphed.

The *Impartial History* was Arnold's last work of scholarship. He resigned his professorship of universal history in the town of Gießen. And he turned his back on learning in favor of a *praxis pietatis*, the experimental combination of asceticism, mysticism, and spiritualism that swept the wider Atlantic world at the turn of the eighteenth century.

This renewal movement was broad and eclectic. In the Catholic Church, it included followers of the Belgian bishop Cornelius Jansen, whose severe Augustinian theology inspired lay and clerical followers in France, Italy, and beyond into lives of pious withdrawal.[11] Among Protestants, as one might expect, it was even more heterogeneous, including religious utopians like the English prophetess Jane Lead or the German Johann Gichtel, devotee of the cobbler-mystic Jakob Böhme and founder of Amsterdam's Angel Brethren. It included ascetic radicals who took vows of celibacy and withdrew from the established churches, inspired alike by the ancient Desert Fathers and modern Catholic mystics. Some of these innovators found shelter in the more tolerant Netherlands; others led semi-clandestine lives, or lived under the protection of local princes in places like Sayn-Wittgenstein-Berleburg in the Holy Roman Empire.

Some formed new intentional religious communities, in Herrnhut, Saxony among the Moravians, and the Ephrata Cloister in the wilds of colonial Pennsylvania. Yet other important figures, like John and Charles Wesley in England or Philip Jakob Spener in Prussia, remained within the older churches, but forged new pathways for the devout life, stressing lay reading in conventicles, camp meetings, communal singing, and other innovative practices of piety.[12]

In this improvisational religious environment, Christian sacrifice was unchained from earlier doctrinal and confessional controversies. Among these new Protestant groups—hardly formal enough to call churches—an eclectic theological and ceremonial imagination thickened around, for example, the idea of spiritual martyrdom. "Often I have wished to die for my brethren," wrote Johann Gichtel in 1694, "often I have sacrificed my soul for them as an anathema and curse."[13] Deep in the theological background lurked the fifteenth-century Catholic writer Thomas à Kempis, whose *Imitatio Christi* had more than 400 editions in the seventeenth century, mostly from Protestant presses.[14] Practices of celibacy, sleep deprivation, and prayer vigils entered into a repertoire of Protestant ascetic practices designed to mortify the self, but also, like Christ, to intercede on behalf of the spiritual unregenerate. As the quietist Charles de Marsay wrote, "Suffer! Die! . . . by this you will serve them and the secret virtue of your blood shed will give them a tincture of life."[15] The devout would become, in Gichtel's words, *anathema*, simultaneously cursed and consecrated, set apart for sacrifice. From this grew the "Office of the Melchizedek Priesthood," an ideal of a regenerated priesthood able, through mortification, to "stand in the [wine] press for his brethren," both spiritual sacrifice and spiritual Levites, appointed to the offices of the temple of Christ.[16]

This newly affective *imitatio Christi* took a variety of forms among these experimental Christianities that emerged in the first decades of the eighteenth century. Disagreements between the heterodox theologian and alchemist Konrad Dippel—a denier of Christ's atonement in the manner of Socinus—and the founder of the Moravian Brethren, Nikolaus Zinzendorf, for example, enflamed the latter's zeal for the Holy Blood. Devotion to the wounds of Christ regenerated the sinner, "cauter[izing] sinful members as the believer is covered in the blood and sweat of Jesus."[17] "Powerful wounds of Jesus, so moist, so gory, bleed on my heart so that I may remain brave," read the 1744 *Litany of the Wounds*. This liturgical text beloved by Zinzendorf and integrated deeply into Moravian spirituality opened with the exhortation to "Look at his five holy, red wounds . . . the payment and ransom for the whole world." The glistening, cavernous, warm, soft, and juicy wounds of Christ—so the *Litany* went—were portals to rebirth, openings from which poured the blood and spirit of baptism on the new believer.[18] For Zinzendorf and his followers, the Socinian challenge to the Atonement did not elicit a learned defense of the Christly *lutron*, in other words. Rather, it engendered a set of devotional practices, and a richly sacrificial imaginative world, that hearkened more to late medieval piety than Protestant erudite doctrinalism.

Affective attachment to the Atonement was no less powerful for the early Methodists, who similarly invited the faithful to participate imaginatively in the sacrifice of Christ. Charles Wesley's "Passion Hymn" asked readers and singers to *feel* the suffering of Christ, to "sympathize," in the eighteenth-century semantics of sensibility, with his wounds:

Give me to feel Thy agonies,
One drop of Thy sad cup afford:
I fain with Thee would sympathise,
And share the sufferings of my Lord.[19]

The tradition of Passion poetry was a long one, but among Wesley and other Methodists, it was an essential means of thinking about the sacrifice of Christ. "There is a fountain filled with blood," wrote the poet William Cowper in 1772, reborn into evangelical Christianity after one of his many suicide attempts, "Drawn from Emmanuel's veins / And sinners plunged beneath that flood / Lose all their guilty stains."[20] In the tradition of "heart religion," the Atonement was not something to be defended in doctrinal terms (indeed, Wesley seems to have had no settled doctrine in this regard). Rather, it was something to be *experienced*.[21]

The latitude for theological and liturgical experiment in these new Christianities mirrored the heterodoxy of Arnold's early church. Indeed, the *Impartial History* itself supplied some materials for this experimentation, not least the para-sacramental "love feast" that developed among many groups. The *agape* meal survived in the archive of ancient Christianity, when banquets and feasts were held either before or directly in conjunction with Eucharistic communion.[22] Arnold excavated this, describing a ritual of communal banqueting, hymn-singing, holy kissing, rebaptism, and foot-washing "in connection with Communion." By the first decades of the eighteenth century, the rite began to spread among the various new "awakened" sects, first the quasi-Anabaptist Schwarzenau Brethren, a splinter group of which founded in 1732 the quasi-monastic Ephrata Cloister in Pennsylvania. Later the Community of True Inspiration, the

Moravians, and the Methodists, all embraced the rite as part of Eucharistic celebration.[23]

This variety of religious experimentation defies easy summary. Disagreements, both inside and among these groups, were as fierce and rancorous as one might expect for communities often led by charismatic visionaries. Whatever their differences, we can discern a common contempt for the doctrinalism of the earlier Reformation, an embrace of a cross-confessional theological library, and a stress on affective connection between believer and Christ. Above all, these experiments decisively rejected the modes of theological argument that we have explored until now. The erudite historical, comparative, and anthropological materials that so suffused earlier doctrinal deliberation were distractions from the more direct experience of Christ that these reformers craved. Instead, outpourings of spirit, mortifications, wound-theology, ecstatic trances, re-enactments of biblical scenes—in short, the immediate connection between the human and the divine—was at the center of this new piety.

Even for the less enthusiastic wings of these new reform movements, the premium was on immediacy. Sober German Pietists like August Hermann Francke, who helped to found the University of Halle in 1694, had little patience for Gichtel and his kind. But he too looked to shrink the distance between believer and Word. *Sola scriptura* returned as a watchword for this new generation of reformers, who began the largest vernacular Bible publication project of the eighteenth century. At Halle's *Collegium orientale theologicum*, founded in 1702, history and anthropology were pushed aside in favor of "the words of scripture" in biblical languages and later in modern ones as well.[24] In England, John Wesley's brand of biblicism also rejected "all curious and critical inquiries, and all uses of the learned languages." "Let *me* think and speak as a little child! Let *my* religion be plain, artless, and simple," he exclaimed, and his own corpus of theological writings swelled with letters, journals, and sermons, not the learned disputations so common in the seventeenth century.[25]

When Gottfried Arnold abandoned history for theosophy and spiritualism, then, it marked a moment in this wider transformation in religious life circa 1700. A new, post-confessional, and experimental theology promiscuously combined Catholic mysticism and asceticism, Calvinist doctrines of regeneration, and Lutheran theologies of the cross. In the community of the reborn, the older doctrinal niceties that had loomed so large for generations of thinkers were largely irrelevant. Forms of writing, as well as liturgical and devotional practices, grew more various and unpredictable. Arnold's personal library shows evidence of this eclecticism: it included the usual works of the church fathers, eminent reformers, church histories, as well as many of the antiquarian works we have encountered so far, including Grotius, Vossius, and others. But it also included Jesuit hagiographies, the alchemical writings of Paracelsus, Catholic mystics like Henry Suso and John of the Cross, Jewish Kabbalistic texts, a huge collection of writing from the sixteenth-century Anabaptist David Joris, neo-Platonist writers like Iamblichus, not to mention the numerous theosophical, spiritualist, apocalyptic, prophetic, and millennialist works authored by his radical contemporaries.[26]

This studied eclecticism let Arnold imagine a world, in his *Impartial History*, where Christian sacrifice had *never* been a settled affair. Among the first Christians, neither Eucharist nor martyrdom were governed by doctrinal standard, rule of faith, or liturgical canon. So too among Arnold's peers did Christian sacrifice take on a new imaginative form, largely unconstrained either by the doctrinal quarrels of a previous generation or the theoretical means of their adjudication. The anthropology, the history, the religions of the gentiles and the Jews: none of these were, in the minds of an Arnold, a Gichtel, or a Zinzendorf, of any consequence to the truth of Christianity.

Most of these new religious movements were marginal to the state-churches, which remained powerful institutions in the eighteenth century. And the tradition of erudite theology remained a strong one in Protestant university faculties in places like Cambridge, Oxford, Leiden, later Göttingen, and elsewhere. Yet these alternative Christianities had profound effects on the fate of modern Protestantism. The Methodists became one of the most dynamic denominations of the eighteenth and nineteenth centuries, for example, laying foundations for what we now call evangelicalism. On doctrinal issues, no doubt, Protestants continued to disagree fiercely: Wesley's (Arminian) doctrine of universal atonement was (and is) anathema to the stricter Calvinist wings of this broad eighteenth-century reform movement.[27] But virtually all of these "new lights," as they were sometimes called, utterly rejected the forms of theological reasoning so essential to the earlier ages of polemic. Here was born an ideal of a Christianity *without history*, a Christianity enlivened not by its own past, but by the spiritual energies of the present. These energies were channeled above all into experiential forms of the religious imagination, where the wounds of Christ throbbed, alive in the minds of the devout.

Sacrifice and the Archives of Nonsense

In one respect, however, these new Christianities clung to tradition. My religion, wrote John Wesley, is "the one old religion; as old as the Reformation, as old as Christianity, as old as Moses, as old as Adam."[28] Arnold's heterodoxy was acceptable because it was *original*, original to the early Church, and in that sense, the original revelation of God. Indeed, Christian primitivism was all the rage in the last decades of the seventeenth century, including new editions and translations of early Church apocrypha, collections of "apostolic antiquities," and proposals for "societies for promoting primitive Christianity."[29] Some of this enthusiasm for the primitive grew directly out of old confessional conflicts. Anti-Catholic controversialists like the Calvinist Jean Daillé had already compiled, by the 1630s, enormous lists of early Christian heterodoxies. After the English Revolution, lists like these were the terrain of furious disputes, not just between Protestants and Catholics, but especially among those various Protestant groups struggling over the primacy and authority of what began to be called Anglicanism.[30] The struggles produced new compendia of ancient Christian life: William Cave's *Antiquities Apostolicae* (1676), for example, or Joseph Bingham's ten-volume *Origines ecclesiasticae* (1708–1720).

Freethinkers too were interested in the origins of Christianity, albeit for very different reasons. When the political radical and erstwhile Spinozist John Toland published his *Nazarenus* in 1718, for example, he purported to discover the "original plan" of Christianity not in the early Church, or even in the writing of Paul, but among a group of ancient Jews called the "Nazarenes or Ebionites," whose teachings he discovered in the apocryphal Gospel of Barnabas.[31] The earliest Christians were, from this perspective, not Christians at all! Indeed, to freethinkers like Toland and others, the pious industry of patristics provided just more proof of the tyranny of priestcraft. We should be unhappy indeed, deist Matthew Tindal remarked in his 1730 *Christianity as Old as Creation*, if we were "oblig'd to take our religious sentiments from Men, who . . . have, even from the earliest times . . . left nothing entire on which they cou'd lay their foul hands."[32] Far from supplying convincing evidence of an original orthodoxy, for freethinkers, the early Church was just one more scene of fraud and deceit.

Early Christianity was not the only victim of this skepticism. Throughout the early modern period, tradition held that, at some remote beginning, there was a first, true revelation. Whether caused by sin, the devil, or plain forgetfulness, human error always came *after* this "original plan." Since

"Truth is certainly more ancient than Errour," wrote the jurist Matthew Hale in his 1677 *Primitive Origination of Mankind*, "even before the ancientest Form of Idolatrous Worship in the World, even that of the Heavenly and Elemental Bodies, there was a True Worship of the True GOD."[33] Error cannot be a "seed of *Truth*," declared the cleric William Lucy, for "the greater growth it hath, the greater is the *Errour*, but it never grows into Truth."[34] *First* truth, *then* error, however introduced. The Garden comes before the Fall; the piety of Noah's religion collapsed into idolatry after his sons colonized the world. Time corrupts, the world "being once amisse grows daily worse and worse," in the words of the poet Edmund Spenser.[35]

In the late seventeenth century, however, a new idea appeared among the intellectual *enfants terribles*: perhaps there *was* no first truth of religion. This was the "foundation laid for Atheism" that William Lucy discovered in the works of Thomas Hobbes.[36] The "seed of Religion," Hobbes had written in 1651, is "onely in Man," in the "Opinion of Ghosts, Ignorance of second causes, Devotion towards what men fear, and Taking of things Casuall for Prognostique."[37] The gods, temples, and sacrifices of the pagans were not deformed versions of a true religion, since such a religion had *never existed* in the first place. By the late century, others joined Hobbes in this idea. There were parallels in the polygenetic visions of Isaac La Peyrère (see chapter 8), whose 1655 speculations about the "pre-Adamites" shattered the unity of human history and anthropology, the gentiles now an entirely different stock of humanity, "men of the first Creation, Atheists . . . without a God."[38] Spinoza too detected nothing divine behind the multitude of "sacrifice and prayers" dreamed up by humans enslaved by superstition, who "invent countless things and interpret nature in amazing ways, as if the whole of nature were as crazy as they are."[39] Even someone like John Spencer seemed, to suspicious readers, to be suggesting much the same. Who could believe that God "patch'd up" the religion of Israel, thundered the Calvinist John Edwards in 1699, from the "Obscene, Irreligious, Impious, Prophane, Idolatrous, Execrable, Magical, Devillish Customs . . . first invented . . . by the most Barbarous *Gentiles*, the Scum of the World, the Dregs of Mankind"?[40]

Once upon a time, Cain and Abel explained the deeper truths of sacrifice, its universal pull on the human imagination. But if sacrifice was *not* the child of revelation, then perhaps the universality of sacrifice had nothing to do with truth at all. Certainly this was the view of the freethinker Charles Blount, who saw the biblical patriarchs, and the generations of priests and politicians that followed their lead, as no more than clever swindlers. "Sacrifices were the most ancient and universal, so the greatest and most mysterious fourbs [impostures] that were ever invented or imposed upon mankind," he wrote.[41] John Toland set this idea to verse:

Natural religion was first easy and plain,
Tales made it mystery, Offrings made it gain,
Sacrifices and Shows were at length prepar'd
The Priests at Roast-meat, and the People star'd.[42]

Other writers were more direct in their jibes at the scriptural story of sacrificial foundation. According to the Huguenot Pierre Bayle's 1697 *Historical and Critical Dictionary*, for example, both of Adam's sons slept with their mother Eve. When Cain later wanted to marry his own daughter, Adam decided to let God unravel the incestuous knots. He sent the brothers off to a mountaintop, "that the success of their sacrifices might decide their differences." But losing the contest, Cain slew Abel and took his daughter off to the wilderness. The saucy moral Bayle took from Horace: "before Helen's day, a wench (*cunnus*) was the most dreadful cause of war."[43] And the cause of sacrifice too, was the implication.

What has come be known as the radical Enlightenment thus happily dismissed the long history of sacrificial thought and practice as a monument to human credulity. Sacrifices were no more than the invention of cunning priests who dreamed up gods unsatisfied by simple piety, and forced their foolish flocks to offer the fruits of labor and loins. In the eyes of a Spinoza, a Blount, a Toland, or a Bayle, there was simply no *reason* for sacrifice. Rather, as Girolamo Imbruglia remarks, sacrifice "belonged to the sphere of *déraison*."[44] *Primus in orbe deos fecit timor*—"fear first made gods in the world" was the ancient saying revived by the skeptical critique of sacrifice.

The Reorganization of the Sacrificial Imagination

By the early eighteenth century, then, we observe a curious conjunction. On the one hand, new forms of Christianity emerged that no longer needed (indeed actively rejected) the histories and anthropologies of sacrifice that had seemed so essential to earlier defenders of orthodoxy. On the other hand, radical skeptics too discarded the archives of sacrifice as the fever dreams of primitive man. Put another way, one of the major intellectual productions of the Reformation and confessional ages—a sacrificial archive sedimented with theological, historical, and anthropological findings—was set adrift, neither central to the newest Christianities of the age, nor, for radical critics of religion, signifying anything more than the folly of man.

And yet the question—why do people sacrifice?—persisted. Fear-addled humans might be prone to all sorts of superstitious behavior: yet why should this fear (apparently everywhere and always) incline them to *sacrifice*? Nor was it clear how foolishness could be so religiously and culturally creative. The priesthoods, temples, altars, rituals and rites, feasts and banquets, the endless variety of things sacrificed, its many ends and purposes: did all of this amount to *nothing*? Was human history simply bunk? The eighteenth century was full of answers to the contrary, experiments in a sacrificial imagination turned *ad saeculum*.

One experiment had to do with archive itself. In the age of confessions, this archive was held together by the sinews of Christ, the Crucifix ordering the relations between Abraham and Calvary, the Levites and the Eucharist, the pagan shadows and the truth of Christianity. Absent this order, the archive was confusing. Readers might reasonably conclude from it: (1) that sacrifices were founded on fear or they were founded on gratitude; (2) that they were about giving something away or they were about destroying something; (3) that the burning is the most important act of destruction, or the slaying is; (4) that sacrifices originally served to placate angry gods or that they served to create friendships with benevolent ones; (5) that the archetypal sacrifice was the bloodless offering of food, or that it was the bloody killing of animals; (6) that sacrifice was a merely mechanical action to satisfy the gods, or it was a moral one that demanded a virtuous offerer; (7) that sacrifices should be understood principally as meals, or acts of covenanting, or confessions of guilt, or communal purifications.[45] Each argument had different consequences for our understanding of religion and mankind. Christ had once organized them; now they needed a new organization.

One approach was simply bibliographical. The late seventeenth and early eighteenth centuries teemed with works—especially in the German language world—that organized knowledge by organizing books. What was called *historia literaria* sought a "universal history of all learning across all ages," taking stock of the history of works on philosophy, theology, law, philology, medicine, and other disciplines.[46] The result was large-scale bio-bibliographies: Theodore Hase and Friedrich Lampe's eight-volume *Bibliotheca Historico- Philologico- Theologica* (1717–1727), Christoph August Heumann's *Conspectus reipublicae literariae* (1718), or Johann Friedrich Reimann's *Historia universalis atheismi* (1725), to name a few.[47] Thus the Hamburg professor and bibliophile Johann Albrecht Fabricius collected, in his *Bibliographia antiquaria* (1713), those earlier works on sacrifice written in the heat of fierce confessional conflict, now simply presented as literary history.[48]

Even more useful in organizing the older sacrificial imagination, however, was that avant-garde Enlightenment literary technology, the *encyclopedia*. Beginning in the late 1720s, these became ubiquitous across Europe, large-scale efforts to repurpose the older Latinate world of learning for new vernacular audiences. These encyclopedias of the Enlightenment afford a first, and vivid, example of how the world of religious controversy began to be reoriented *ad saeculum*, its remainders reassembled for new intellectual projects.

To begin, let's briefly return to Wolfgang Franzius, the anti-Socinian theologian who wrote hefty works in the late sixteenth century proving the atoning sacrifice of Christ (see chapter 8). Before he died, Franzius drew up the notes for a commentary on Leviticus. These were unpublished until 1696, when they were rediscovered by a cranky Leipzig professor of theology named Valentin Alberti. By that late date, virtually all of Franzius's preoccupations were long out of fashion, and the work would have vanished into dusty obscurity, if Alberti (in all likelihood) had not reorganized Franzius's notes into new explanatory tables. These tables echoed and elaborated the organizational schemes we found in the apologetics of the antiquarian Stucki (see chapter 5), but now applied them to *all* sacrifices, gentile and Christian alike.

Thus the materials of sacrifice, the ends a sacrifice might serve, the people involved and the proper times of sacrifice: these made up one table (fig. 9.1). And the other laid out, for example: "sacred things, perpetual and temporary" and "purification, communal and individual" and so forth (fig. 9.2).[49] The result was a grid of sacrificial operations organized by time, place, manner, person, and materials. Eucharistic sacrifice is a voluntary, temporary, sacred thing, for example, whereas holocausts are perpetual sacred things.

Four decades later, these tables reappeared in a new guise, in the eighteenth century's largest encyclopedia. Begun in 1732 and finished in 1754, the German language *Grosses Vollständiges Universal Lexicon aller Wissenschaften und Kunsten* was symptomatic of the Enlightenment ordering of knowledge. The brainchild of a Hamburg publisher and author, Johann Heinrich Zedler, the work offered a thorough compilation of the world's knowledge, from the "letter A" in volume 1 to "Zzeune" (apparently a city in Egypt) in volume 64. The anonymous entry "sacrifice," and the

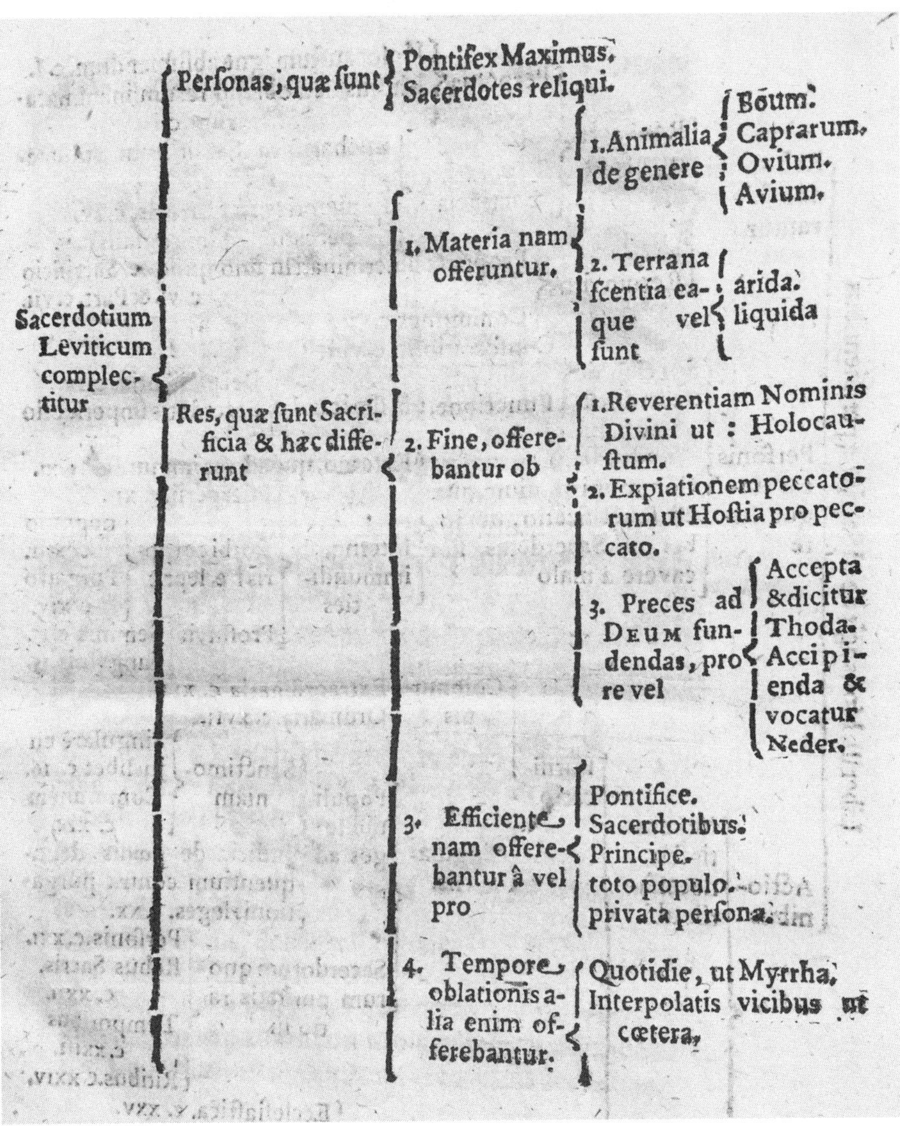

Sacerdotium Leviticum complectitur

- Perſonas, quæ ſunt
  - Pontifex Maximus.
  - Sacerdotes reliqui.
- Res, quæ ſunt Sacrificia & hæc differunt
  - 1. Materia nam offeruntur.
    - 1. Animalia de genere
      - Boum.
      - Caprarum.
      - Ovium.
      - Avium.
    - 2. Terrana ſcentia eaque vel ſunt
      - arida.
      - liquida
  - 2. Fine, offerebantur ob
    - 1. Reverentiam Nominis Divini ut: Holocauſtum.
    - 2. Expiationem peccatorum ut Hoſtia pro peccato.
    - 3. Preces ad DEUM fundendas, pro re vel
      - Accepta & dicitur Thoda.
      - Accipienda & vocatur Neder.
  - 3. Efficiente, nam offerebantur à vel pro
    - Pontifice.
    - Sacerdotibus.
    - Principe.
    - toto populo.
    - privata perſona.
  - 4. Tempore oblationis alia enim offerebantur.
    - Quotidie, ut Myrrha.
    - Interpolatis vicibus ut cœtera.

FIGURE 9.1. Table of Sacrifices I. Wolfgang Franzius, *Commentarius in Leviticum* (Leipzig, 1696). Staatsbibliothek zu Berlin. Author's photograph.

dozens of sub-entries arranged beneath it, spanned ninety pages. After an opening generality—"sacrifices are sacred actions (*Handlungen*) that consecrate to God specific earthly things with specific ceremonies prescribed by Him"—the entry organized sacrificial practice using Franzius's (or Alberti's) tables as a guide.[50] The entry was a narrative, but if we render it schematically, it consists of two interlocking tables (figs. 9.3 and 9.4).

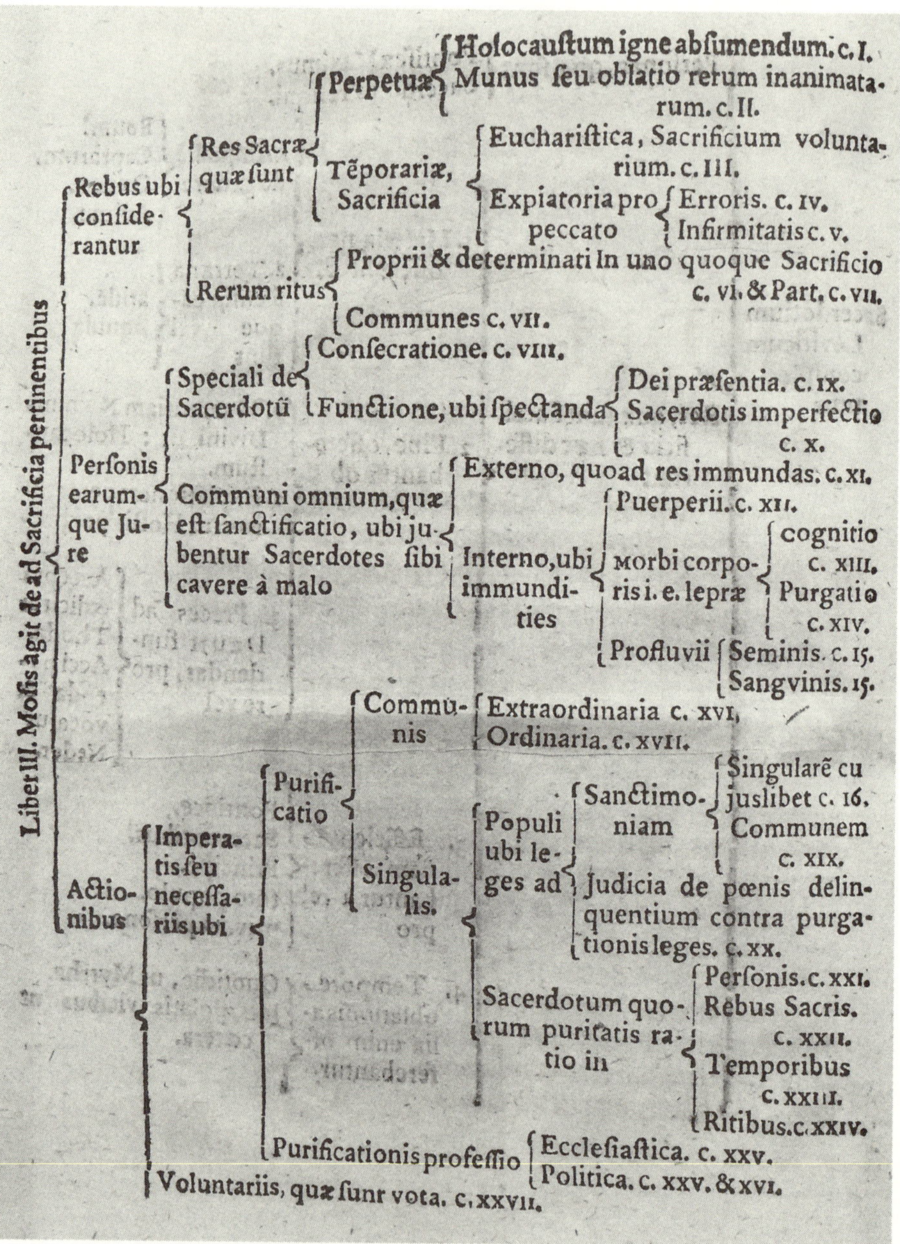

Liber III. Mosis agit de ad Sacrificia pertinentibus

- Rebus ubi considerantur
  - Res Sacræ quæ sunt
    - Perpetuæ
      - Holocaustum igne absumendum. c. I.
      - Munus seu oblatio rerum inanimatarum. c. II.
    - Tēporariæ, Sacrificia
      - Eucharistica, Sacrificium voluntarium. c. III.
      - Expiatoria pro peccato
        - Erroris. c. IV.
        - Infirmitatis c. V.
  - Rerum ritus
    - Proprii & determinati In uno quoque Sacrificio c. VI. & Part. c. VII.
    - Communes c. VII.
- Personis earumque Jure
  - Speciali de Sacerdotū
    - Consecratione. c. VIII.
    - Functione, ubi spectanda
      - Dei præsentia. c. IX.
      - Sacerdotis imperfectio c. X.
  - Communi omnium, quæ est sanctificatio, ubi jubentur Sacerdotes sibi cavere à malo
    - Externo, quoad res immundas. c. XI.
    - Interno, ubi immundities
      - Puerperii. c. XII.
      - morbi corporis i. e. lepræ
        - cognitio c. XIII.
        - Purgatio c. XIV.
      - Profluvii
        - Seminis. c. 15.
        - Sangvinis. 15.
- Actionibus
  - Imperatis seu necessariis ubi
    - Purificatio
      - Communis
        - Extraordinaria c. XVI.
        - Ordinaria. c. XVII.
      - Singularis. pro
        - Populi ubi leges ad
          - Sanctimoniam
            - Singularē cujuslibet c. 16.
            - Communem c. XIX.
          - Judicia de pœnis delinquentium contra purgationis leges. c. XX.
        - Sacerdotum quorum puritatis ratio in
          - Personis. c. XXI.
          - Rebus Sacris. c. XXII.
          - Temporibus c. XXIII.
          - Ritibus. c. XXIV.
    - Purificationis professio
      - Ecclesiastica. c. XXV.
      - Politica. c. XXV. & XVI.
  - Voluntariis, quæ sunt vota. c. XXVII.

FIGURE 9.2. Table of Sacrifices II. Wolfgang Franzius, *Commentarius in Leviticum* (Leipzig, 1696). Staatsbibliothek zu Berlin. Author's photograph.

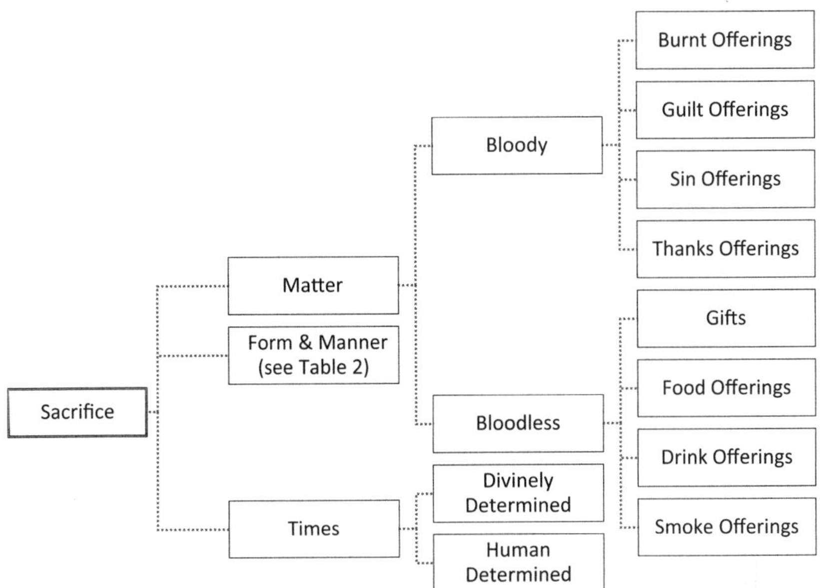

FIGURE 9.3. The General Organization of Sacrifice. Zedler, *Universal Lexikon* (1732–1754), s.v. "Opffer."

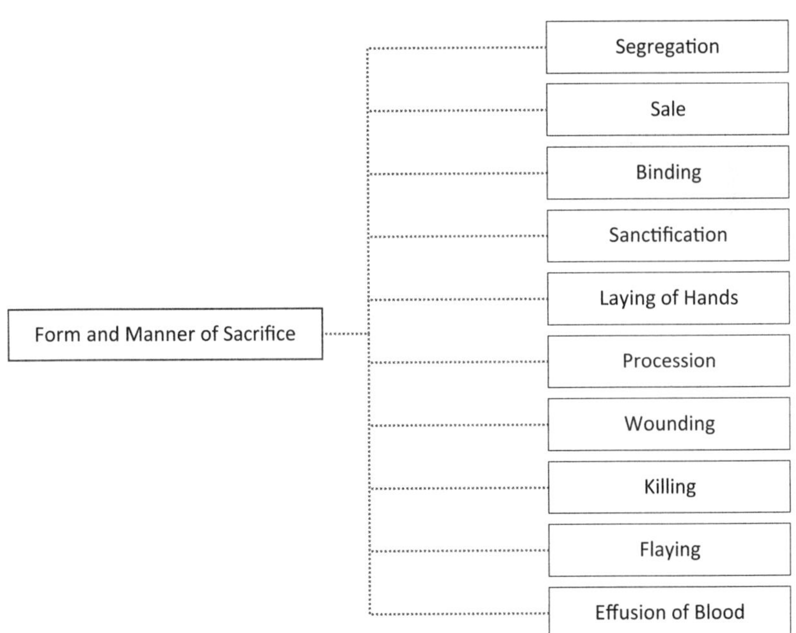

FIGURE 9.4. The Structure of Sacrificial Action. Zedler, *Universal Lexikon* (1732–1754), s.v. "Opffer."

Judging from his citations, the anonymous author was a pious Lutheran with Franzius's commentary sitting on his bookshelf. But the shift to the encyclopedia transformed the anti-Socinian polemics of the older theologian into something new. The organization of sacrifice mapped by figure 9.4 invited consideration, for example, of what we would now call "ritual." It laid out in systematic detail the prescribed order of "sacred actions," which included: the segregation of the victim, its purchase, binding, and sanctification, the laying of hands on it, the leading-out and wounding of the victim, and so forth. The author was committed to Christology, but the organization of the materials suggested an abstract order of ritual sacrifice applicable in *all* circumstances.

Similar abstractions shaped the accompanying sub-entries. In the entry on the "sacrifice of the lepers," for example, the author repackaged Leviticus 14 as a narrative of twenty-three "actions and ceremonies" performed in these rituals of purification. This account was purged of Christology. It simply recounted the enduring structures of sacred action.[51] The sub-article, "sacrificial equipment," was even less biblical in its focus. A translation from a contemporary French numismatic work, it laid out common Roman equipment for sacrifice, including vases used for libations, and the tools used for killing, sprinkling holy water, and the collection of flesh and entrails.[52] The entry on "pagan sacrifice" emphasized its diabolical origins, but the one on "sacrificial meals" merely remarked that these were celebrated "with particular joy after the completed sacrifice among both Jews and pagans," and neutrally referred readers to heterodox works that would have incensed Franzius, the neo-Platonist Ralph Cudworth's extraordinary comparative tract on the Lord's Supper (1642) and even Spencer's *De legibus hebraeorum*.[53] The article on "sacrificial knives" included findings from grave excavations in northern Europe while the cross-referenced article on "altar" was general and abstract: "a place elevated above the ground, on which one sacrifices and before which one prays."[54] When transposed into the world of the encyclopedia, in short, frameworks developed to defend the Crucifix could be reoriented toward more worldly purposes, sacrifice treated in fundamentally *human* terms.

The encyclopedia offered a flexible means of reorganizing older bodies of literature. In doing so, however, it also transformed this older literature. A treatise could swell to as many pages as patience permitted, but an encyclopedia entry had to be economical, synthetic rather than comprehensive. This in turn encouraged efforts at precise definition. In the first encyclopedia, Ephraim Chambers's English-language *Cyclopaedia* (1728), for example, sacrifice was

> an Offering made to God on an Altar, by means of a regular Minister, as an Acknowledgment of his Power, and a Payment of Homage. *Sacrifices* differ from mere *Oblations*, in that in a *Sacrifice* there is a real Destruction or Change of the Thing offered, whereas an Oblation is only a simple Offering of Gift. . . . See OBLATION.[55]

This sharp distinction between sacrifice and oblation owed at least as much to formal constraints as to any deep theoretical commitment. It allowed Chambers to reorganize, however, the sedimented literature on sacrifices by selecting only those materials in which a "real Destruction or Change" featured centrally. When Chambers wrote that "*sacrifices* were ordinarily nothing else but Holy Banquets," therefore, he did not have the Eucharist in mind, but simply the dietary history of mankind.[56] This elevation of the functional had other advantages too. It set aside origins as objects of interest, indifferent as to whether Noah or the Egyptians were the inventors of the rite. It avoided all of the doctrinal conundrums introduced when sacrifice was understood along the axis of human-divine relations, as variously eucharistic, expiatory, propitiatory, and so forth. And it meant that the "New Law" of bloodless sacrifice could be mentioned without further comment. The tiresome polemics around Christian sacrifice were, in this way, formally dissolved.

The encyclopedia also encouraged new connections between the older sacrificial archive and other, formerly unrelated things. Chambers's cross-reference "See OBLATION" suggested that readers would find clarity on the nature of religious gifts there. (In vain, as it turned out, since the oblation entry remarked only that they "properly denote *Sacrifices*, or things offer'd to God," and referred them back to the "sacrifice" entry.)[57] But the cross-reference introduced the possibility of new and and unexpected associations between historically religious concerns and other ones. The "Law of Sacrifices . . . made Man a carnivorous animal. See CARNIVOROUS"— from a discussion of Porphyry and ancient vegetarianism, a reader was invited to consider the natural history of the teeth and the intestines, the world of ancient religious taboos set into dialogue with the most modern natural philosophy.[58] Alienated from Christology, sacrifice was in this way given new and more human histories.

No encyclopedia pursued this strategy of alienation more deliberately than the French *Encyclopédie* (1751–1772). Edited by Denis Diderot and Jean Rond d'Alembert, the most famous encyclopedia of the eighteenth century drew widely on the French republic of letters and transformed the intellectual culture of the mid-century. It also made explicit its own effort to unsettle common frames of reference using the formal means of the cross-reference. Cross-references, Diderot wrote:

> will confront one idea with another; they will contrast principles; they will attack, undermine, and secretly overthrow those ridiculous opinions that no one would dare insult openly . . . [From these] the entire work will receive an inner force and secret utility, whose silent effects will necessarily become sensible with the passage of time.[59]

The *Encyclopédie* thus offered a brief main entry on sacrifice: "worship (*culte*) offered to the divinity by the offering of some victim, or by some other gift," augmented by various sub-entries on the sacrifices of the pagans, of the Hebrews, and on the Christians. The topic of sacrifice was also distributed across a network of cross-references. "Sacrifice of the pagans" pointed to an article on the *hostes*, for example. Indeed, there were *two* articles on "hosts": the Christian Host, the "word incarnate," and the "hosts" of paganism, "enemies . . . [that] in the first barbarous centuries, were sacrificed before a battle to propitiate the gods."[60] What Diderot called the "secret utility" of the cross-reference lay here, in the proximity that it established between barbarian battle-sacrifices and the Crucifixion. A cross-reference to "human victims" was not less suggestive. "There is no act so atrocious that man will not commit it when cruel fanaticism arms his hand," that article argued, a lesson that held true for ancient Carthage, the New World, and the Spanish Inquisition.[61] Other articles in the *Encyclopédie* pointed back to the sacrifice entry, including "altar," "Eucharist," "expiation," and "offerings." But so did the article on "anthropophages," a more scandalous entry that connected "people who live on human flesh" with the Eucharist, communion, and sacrifice.[62]

It is possible to reconstruct a general view of sacrifice from these various articles.[63] But the novelty of the *Encyclopédie* lay less in such general theories than in the way it alienated and remade older orders of knowledge. Written in the vernacular, it aimed at a popular readership uninterested in erudite subtleties. Rather, it put a premium on economy, inviting reductions of sacrifice to synthetic definitions. Sacrifice is a sacred action that consecrates things to God; sacrifice is an act of destruction; sacrifice is an offering of a victim or a gift: such generalizations flattened older hierarchies—Christian-Jew-gentile—and set all sacrifices on broadly the same footing. Across multiple entries, moreover, writers divided formerly connected materials into discrete topics. Readers might learn about different epochs and traditions of sacrifice depending on their interests. This disaggregation of older hierarchies also distinguished between different *kinds* of knowledge. Christian sacrifice was denoted as "theological" in the *Encyclopédie*, while the sacrifices of the gentiles fell under, variously, "sacred criticism," "mythology," "antiquity," or the "history of religious superstitions."

Finally, the open format of the encyclopedia invited entirely new imaginative connections. For *Encyclopédie*'s "sacrifice of Abel" entry, Jaucourt discarded the traditional effort to discover in Adam's offerings an ancient foundation of religious worship. For Jaucourt, the primal scene of sacrifice illuminated not biblical history, but human psychology. His main source for the entry was thus a work of literature: Salomon Gessner's 1758 German prose-poem *The Death of Abel*, wildly popular in the later eighteenth century. The poem focused on the inner life of Cain, whose austere melancholy made him ever more resentful of his brother, whose charmed life bore witness to the divine favor he enjoyed. God's rejection of his sacrifice crushed Cain's fragile spirit, overwhelming him with sadness, guilt, and eventually murderous anger. For Gessner and Jaucourt, the sacrifices of Abel and Cain taught a universal lesson about the nature of vulnerability and the pain of abandonment.[64]

Viewed negatively, then, the encyclopedia was thus a powerful intellectual solvent. It broke down the older Christian archive, reordered its materials, and coordinated them with the intellectual concerns of post-confessional age. More positively, it was also an experiment in literary form, a new way to coordinate the "multitude of books" written in the heat of early modern religious controversy, and thus to create new possibilities for a sacrificial imagination no longer tied to the Crucifixion.[65]

Part II: Secular Experiments in the Sacrificial Imagination

History: Sacrifice and the Afterlives of Antiquity

The Enlightenment was full of such experiments, redirection of the sacrificial imagination *ad saeculum*. These experiments were often tentative, and even contradictory in their impulses. They were nonetheless creative, turning the heterogeneous materials deposited in that Christian archive toward new, more human ends. Take, for example, the efforts to imagine anew the *history* of sacrifice, and more specifically, the sacrificial worlds of antiquity. For Christians, as we have seen, sacrifice bore an uneasy relationship to the past. On the one hand, it was something left behind, an *old* way of communicating with God now abandoned: first law, then

Gospel. On the other hand, it was something carried forward, re-enacted in dialogue with ancient ways. Antiquity, Jewish and pagan, had something to *teach* Christianity, either by negative or positive example. For better or worse, sacrifice had bound Christianity and antiquity tightly together.

What did the history of ancient sacrifice teach when it was no longer a servant to Christian concerns? Three Enlightenment answers stand out, three secular afterlives of the sacrifices of antiquity.

1. One was (at least from a modern perspective) obvious. The ancient world simply teaches us about *itself.* There is an antiquity "as such," that is a mostly Greco-Roman past whose oblations and deities we can enjoy from the happy remove of the present. Such a view organized the voluminous works of an unusually creative French Benedictine monk named Bernard de Montfaucon. Often credited with founding both the sciences of paleography (the study of ancient handwriting) and archaeology, Montfaucon was a "Gargantua of research," as one historian has observed.[66] His most ambitious work, *Antiquity Explained and Represented in Figures,* was published between 1719 and 1724, appeared first in French, then in a French-Latin bilingual edition, and then was almost immediately translated into English. Its five volumes were filled with images, ancient visual remains—sculpture, ceramics, mosaics, and coins—that Montfaucon gathered from collections across Europe. These volumes had a long afterlife, appreciated not least for their strong sense that antiquity should be treated *separately* from Christianity.

Classical antiquity was (and is!) a curious and powerful notion. On the one hand, it was supposedly inclusive, embracing the long history of the ancient Mediterranean world. On the other hand, it typically divorced the ancients from any connection to the Christian story. The Hebrews did not belong to Montfaucon's antiquity, for example, since their history was so uncertain that one is reduced to "guessing about almost everything." Nor did the older interest in connecting the ancient gentile gods and Scripture. "I have no taste for such erudition," the monk remarked, separating Christian and pagan in ways foreign to the more heteroclite antiquarianism we explored earlier. What he called "the *belle antiquité*" began deep in the Bronze Age and extended until the reign of Emperor Theodosian II (450 CE).[67] But this was a world, in his view, entirely pagan in character.

For centuries, then, writers had explored the porous boundaries between Christianity and its gentile surroundings, showing how the church of Christ preserved liturgical instruments, vestments, architecture, and rites from its pagan surround. *Antiquity Explained* ignored this shared terrain of ancient religious life, and the doctrinal troubles that it invited. Despite the scandalous beliefs and behaviors of the ancients, its voice was thus neutral and largely free of opprobrium. It described the sacrificial instruments and rites of Greece and Rome with detached curiosity and even appreciation. It registered no more offense at the lustier sacrificial rituals of Bacchus—whose details Montfaucon discovered in a Roman marble statue that had belonged to Queen Christina of Sweden—than at the more austere ones of Ceres.[68] Ancient religion was a cultural form in its own right, in this view, with its own values, practices, and organization.

Gentle amazement was the dominant tone of *Antiquity Explained.* So the sacrificing king, the *archeontes*, was devised in ancient Athens to administer "all the sacred and divine things" with "purity and piety," as witnessed in an ancient inscription from the collection of Jean Baptiste Colbert. No mention of Christ, no worries about kings and priests, simply a curious fact about Athenian history. The sheer variety of ancient altars struck Montfaucon as wonderous: some round, some triangular, some square, some high, some low, and so forth. Some were made of wood, some stone, some "no more than a heap of ashes." Sacrificial instruments were magical in their multiplicity. Take the beautiful libation bowls, the *paterae*, that Montfaucon gathered from various European collections—delicately engraved, they poured wine over the victims, or collected the blood from the sacrifices (fig. 9.5).[69]

No less remarkable were the sacrificial mallets, axes, and knives deposited in the collections of European aristocrats, which Montfaucon lovingly described to a curious audience: the *malleus*, the *securis*, the *acieres*, the *secespita*, the *lingula*, all the tools of the ancient sacrificial trade. And so too, finally, the variety of sacrificial rituals. A feeble gesture toward organization—there are "two kinds" of sacrifice, one involving the immolation of "living things," the other, "inanimate and insensible" things—devolved into loving description of particulars. Female victims were more highly prized than male; the Romans sacrificed black sheep to the infernal gods, white ones to the celestial gods; if a white oxen had spots, they were covered with chalk, and so on. There is "such a great variety of sacrifices, and in so many different places, that it is almost impossible to describe them all."[70] The pleasure of the book lay in its trying.

Except for one significant exception, then, Montfaucon refused to compare, or even connect, pagan and Christian worlds. This was the Roman *taurobolia* of the Great Mother Cybele. In this rite, the high priest deposited himself in an underground chamber below an altar. At the sacrifice, the blood of a bull dripped down on the waiting prelate, sanctifying him

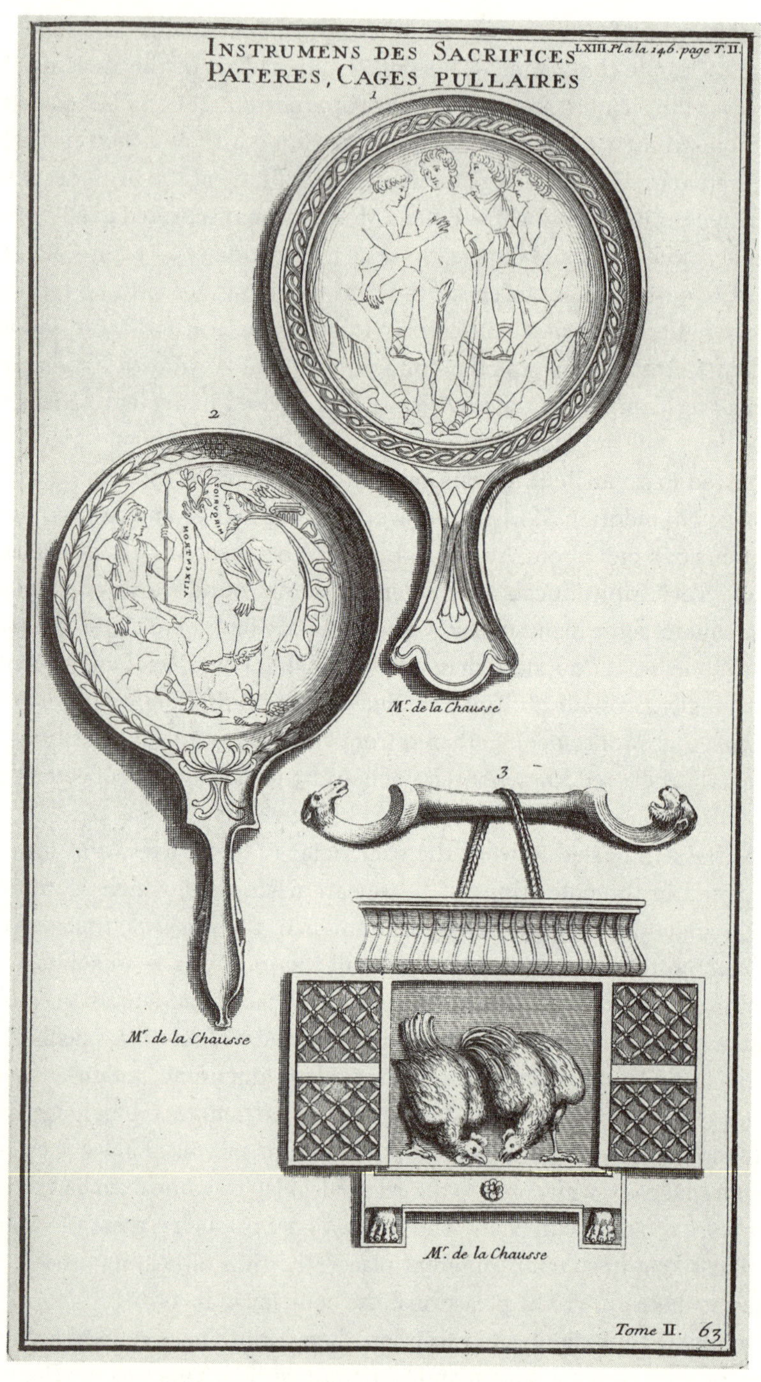

FIGURE 9.5. Sacrificial Libation Bowls. Bernard de Montfaucon, *L'antiquité expliquée, et représentée en figures* (1719–1724). Courtesy of the Wellcome Collection.

in gore. Earlier writers described it as an ancient consecration ritual dating back to the early Roman republic, but in 1702, the Dutch scholar Antony van Dale showed that it was a late addition to the ritual forms of antiquity. Many Christian rites derived from the gentile world, including baptism, pilgrimage, vigils, mysteries, sacred feasts, and colleges, van Dale observed.[71] But the *taurobolia* went the other way, the rare ritual that *began* in Christianity and spread to the pagan world. *This* was the sort of connection our Benedictine author found compelling. The *taurobolia* "began late in paganism," Montfaucon echoed van Dale, as a "baptism of blood, which [the gentiles] apparently invented in opposition to the baptism of Jesus Christ."[72] The implication, then, being that paganism learned from but had nothing to teach the Christian world.

For three centuries, as we have seen, the intimacy of Christian and pagan sacrifices had troubled and intrigued writers. *Antiquity Explained* left this uneasy world of comparisons behind. It presented instead an early version of what came to be called "classics," that is, a Greco-Roman world blissfully free of the controversies of Christian history. The *belle antiquité* was a happy world of refinement, Greece and Rome preserved in the amber of appreciation. The other side of this coin was hidden but no less important. "Classical antiquity" protected Christianity, now freed from the scandal of its proximity to the sacrifices of the pagan gods.

2. This Enlightenment science of antiquity thus offered a new way to manage the dangers that ancient religion had always posed to Christian self-possession. These dangers only grew in the eighteenth century, moreover, as freethinkers began writing increasingly *critical* histories of the ancient world. Their antiquity was a world of ignorance and terror, a world where sacrifice seemed the only way to manage forces beyond human control. Writing its history was a form of therapy, a cure for the collective neuroses we inherited from the ancients, the neuroses we call religion.

The Enlightenment rang with voices who discovered in the sacrifices of the ancient world the seeds of humanity's discontents. In his epic *Henriade* (1723), for example, the young Voltaire described the fiend "*Fanaticism* . . . Unusual Offspring of Religion," who inspired the sacrifices of Moloch and Jephthah's rash vow, "demanded Iphigenia's death," begat the "Holy Homicides" of the Druids, inspired the violent enthusiasm of the Protestant Ranters and the Catholic Inquisition alike.[73] Fanaticism, Alexandre Deleyre later wrote in the French *Encyclopédie*, was

> born in the forests, in the shadows of the night; & and panicked terrors built the first temples of Paganism . . . But without investigating . . . if

> it was politics or superstition that demanded victims; . . . if the bloody sacrifices of paganism come from Hell, that is to say, the ferocity of dark and turbulent passions, or the derangement of the imagination . . . that is, wherever the idea of satisfying the divinity with blood came from, it is certain that, as soon as it began to run over the altars, it was impossible to stop it.[74]

From ancient paganism, to Muslim conquest, the persecution of the Jews, the destruction of the New World, and the violence of European religious wars—the genealogy of the "holy vertigo" that overwhelmed "innumerable nations atop the tomb of a God of peace" began in the sacrifices of antiquity.[75]

For Deleyre and others, then, the ancient world revealed the dark truth of Christianity, indeed all religion. When the Scottish philosopher David Hume wrote his *Natural History of Religion* (1757), for example, he made "polytheism or idolatry" into the "first and most antient religion of mankind." Because the human mind expects regularity, anything strange "alarms him from its novelty; and immediately sets him a trembling, and sacrificing, and praying." But life is such a stream of inexplicable strangeness that *everyone* (save the philosopher) imagines a world plagued by a "constant combat of opposite powers." The gods first protect and then abandon us: "prayers and sacrifices, rites and ceremonies" are our efforts to manage this uncertainty:[76]

> A sacrifice is conceived as a present; and any present is delivered to the deity by destroying it and rendering it useless to men; by burning what is solid, pouring out the liquid, and killing the animate. For want of a better way of doing him service, we do ourselves an injury; and fancy that we thereby express, at least, the heartiness of our good will and adoration.[77]

Sacrifice should be seen as a special form of gift-giving, in which the invisible gods can be satisfied only by rendering the gift useless to mankind. At root, however, it amounts to no more than a fancy, the all-too-human hope that, by doing ourselves injury, we might propitiate the powerful.

The most radical critique of antiquity and its sacrifices, however, came from the posthumous pen of the French engineer and freethinker, Nicolas-Antoine Boulanger (1722–1759). His 1766 *Antiquity Revealed*—the title an echo of Montfaucon—was republished a remarkable six times between 1768 and 1778, a near bestseller of the Enlightenment.[78] "Wrapped in an apparatus of etymological erudition," as one contemporary reviewer put it, *Antiquity Revealed* was a frontal attack on Christianity.[79] Indeed it was long attributed to one of the great atheists of the eighteenth century, Paul Henri Thiry, the Baron d'Holbach, whose own *Christianity Revealed* (1766)—an explicit assault on the "strange sacrifice" of Christ—was published in London . . . under the name of Nicolas-Antoine Boulanger.[80]

Religious institutions were children not of truth, Boulanger argued, but of trauma. Specifically, the trauma of the ancient Flood, which so frightened early mankind that it created a "new species of man," "sad, melancholy, and excessively religious."[81] This new man feverishly invented "religious ceremonies and rituals" to pacify the terrible gods of nature.[82] Human customs were designed to protect mankind by keeping the memory of this ancient disaster alive. Sacrifices, ritual calendars, and festivals reflect the "liturgical" or "commemorative spirit" that haunts mankind still living in the shadow of the Flood. Noah's sacrifice after the Flood was the first of repeated efforts to ward off, by sacrifice, divine vengeance against the world and mankind. Even the cruelest human sacrifices align with this deep structure. From the ancient Roman Saturnalia to the modern Mexican *teocalli*, the "times of great expiation and great sacrifice" are the times when the "world was menaced by the greatest danger . . . the time when the God of vengeance was unleashed."[83]

The most important Christian ceremonies were no different. All festival calendars, for example, "recall to men that the world was once destroyed and devastated, that it must be destroyed once more . . . & that it must be prepared for by appeasing the gods." The Saturnalia ritually appointed a new king to acknowledge that the new post-diluvial age would have new gods. The Christian celebration of Epiphany was a "remainder" of this ancient conviction. The pagans celebrated the birth of Mithras as a festival of the return and rebirth of the sun after the winter solstice, recalling man's reprieve from universal destruction. The same festival migrated into Christianity, which presented "the image of the end of days at the end of each year; Advent is a time of sadness that prepares us for a time of joy." Hebrew, Christian, and pagan use of water in libation, purification, and expiation (from sacrifice to baptism) similarly recalled the Flood; "expiation was an artificial deluge" used to prevent divine punishment, sacrifice the recollection of violence that, through ritual, was transformed into new life. We are still living under the shadow of this disaster, Boulanger concluded, our modern religions perpetuating the same "crime against the human race" perpetrated by the gloomy ancients, "needlessly troubling the happiness that [mankind] should enjoy on this earth."[84]

For Boulanger, then, happy antiquity had never existed. The ancient world was rather a time of primal terror. The flood was the "tomb of reason and of philosophy, the tomb of the arts, sciences, and legislation," antiquity and its religions was the "first taint of evil"—*prima mali labes*, in Vergil's words—from which humanity is only gradually recovering.[85]

3. Released from its Christian service, then, those ancient sacrifices were invested with new historical purpose. For Montfaucon, they witnessed a beautiful past, far from our own. For Boulanger, they tyrannized an unhappy humanity. For a third group, however, antiquity and its sacrifices offered an *alternative* to Christianity itself, an ideal of divinity and humanity liberated from the Cross.

When he arrived in Rome in November 1755, the young German Johann Joachim Winckelmann—a "pagan spirit," as the poet Johann Wolfgang von Goethe later described him—had already fallen in love with ancient Greece, its art, and its gods.[86] He adorned his *Thoughts on the Imitation of Greek Works in Painting and Sculpture*, published in the same year, with a sacrifice of Iphigenia. In the frontispiece sat the ancient artist Timanthes of Kythnos at work in his studio, painting a veil over Agamemnon's face to protect him against the sight of his daughter destroyed (fig. 9.6).[87]

The veil so common in ancient ritual sacrifice was interesting not as a liturgical instrument for Winckelmann, but as a representation of Greek aesthetic perfection. The Greeks refused, he famously insisted, to depict a beautiful body tormented and agonized. The "anguish appropriate to Agamemnon," wrote a critical admirer of Winckelmann in 1766, "would have to be expressed through distortions, which are always ugly."[88] The veil thus preserved the beauty of sacrifice intact, the bare-breasted virgin reclining in the arms of Calchas, peacefully prepared for the holocaust that will assuage the anger of Artemis and send the Greeks to victory.

Indeed, the magic of Greek religion was its superhuman beauty. The "first founders of religion, who were poets," Winckelmann wrote in *History of the Art of Antiquity* (1764), "bestowed exalted concepts on . . . images, and these gave wings to the imagination to elevate their achievement . . . above the sensuous."[89] The ancient divinities were not hungry for the entrails of the dead, in this view. They were beings that transcended matter, beings from which "all signs of flesh and blood existence had been purged."[90] The fleshy idols that outraged Christians for millennia were now objects of adoration, their beauty sublimating the stench of blood that had long clung to their feet. Small wonder that Winckelmann helped create the first "Museum of Pagan Antiquities"—packed with the idols that

FIGURE 9.6. The Painting of Iphigenia and Agamemnon. Frontispiece, Johann Joachim Winckelmann, *Gedanken über die Nachahmung der Griechischen Werke* (Dresden and Leipzig, 1756). Courtesy of the Getty Research Institute.

had so long unsettled Christian viewers—in the heart of the Vatican in 1767.[91]

Winckelmann was not alone in this aptly termed "aesthetic paganism."[92] The Greeks offered an especially attractive alternative to Christianity among various intellectual elites, who flocked to Italy starting in the 1750s to experience the spirit of pagan antiquity for themselves. In the "foreign, free world of the Greeks," artists, architects, poets, and many others discovered a space apart for their own imaginative and spiritual projects.[93] Winckelmann's fellow Germans were particularly enthusiastic for the "beautiful world" of the ancient gods, in the 1788 words of Germany's great poet, Friedrich Schiller. So his "Gods of Greece":

> *Your* temples smiled like palaces,
> The hero's games exalted you,
> In the laureled festivals of the Isthmus,
> And the chariots thundered to their end.
> Beautiful twining soulful dances,
> Circled round the blazing altars . . .

Each offered the best they had,
The shepherd his beloved lamb . . . [94]

These were gods of nature and light, whose "blazing altars" were bedecked with flowers, dancing, and the "beloved lamb" freely given by each joyful celebrant. What a difference between this beautiful world and the "mournful stillness" of the Christian God: "gloomy, like himself, is his form / my renunciation alone are his revels."[95]

In the beautiful world of antiquity, the gods did not look for expiation or propitiation. Theirs was a world of gifts and banquets, sacrificial feasts extinguished by the arrival of Christianity, and its "joyless culture of sacrifice."[96] Later, in his 1797 hair-raising ballad the "Bride of Corinth"—the story of a young pagan who falls in love with a hungry Christian vampire—the poet Johann Wolfgang von Goethe sharpened the contrast:

And the joyous throng of ancient gods
has abandoned the now silent house.
There is one alone, invisible, in the heavens,
And one savior worshiped on a cross.
There are sacrifices here,
neither lamb nor steer,
but human sacrifices, never-ending.[97]

Christianity did not, as it had so long proclaimed, end the blood sacrifices of primitive man. Rather, the new religion sanctified them, putting first its God and then all of humanity up on the Cross. The ancient gods were gods of joy; the dead Christ grim, bloodthirsty, and silent. "Joy is not for me," says the Christian bride of pagan Corinth.[98]

In the early eighteenth century, to summarize, the archive of antiquity, its gods and their sacrifices, was released from the services it had long offered Christian apologetics. It was liberated to perform novel imaginative work for new cultural and intellectual projects. Some of these projects still supported Christian ends, if in new ways. But others roamed further afield. For Enlightenment skeptics and freethinkers, ancient sacrifice showed the deep irrationality of *all* religion. The altars of Carthage, the fires of the Inquisition, the zealots and holy warriors of the recent past: these were the shared patrimony of religious enthusiasm. By the end of the century, however, the sacrifices of antiquity re-emerged as *alternatives* to Christianity, a transvaluation that played out in the aesthetic realm, but also (as we will see in the following chapter) in the world of politics.

Anthropology I: Custom, Comparison, and the Universality of Sacrifice

History was just one new secular space of the sacrificial imagination. What will later be called anthropology (see chapter 11) was another. As we have seen, after all, the older Christian archive was stuffed with anthropology, the customs, rites, and rituals found across human societies, ancient and modern. Holding together this infinity of examples was the powerful conviction that sacrifice was a universal constant, a durable feature of all human cultures. How to explain this universality absent the older interpretive resources of sacred history? Already in the 1720s, a new "science" of comparative religion tried to do just this, tentatively if creatively seeking to describe the deep logic of religious behavior in broadly human terms.[99]

Christian anthropology took for granted the fundamental unity of the human story. The origin of the religions and peoples of the Americas was, for the Jesuit José de Acosta, a religious and historical puzzle whose parameters were firmly established by the stories of Genesis. Which ancient stock gave birth to the indigenous Americans was uncertain. The Canaanites, the lost tribes of Israel, the Phoenicians, the Tatars, the Spanish, the Ethiopians, the Chinese, the Welsh, and the Norwegians were all mooted with various degrees of seriousness.[100] But what no one doubted—with the exception of the arch-heretic Isaac La Pèyrere—was the "peopling of the world from Adam," as the cleric Edward Stillingfleet wrote in his 1662 *Origines Sacrae*.[101] No less than anyone, the peoples of the New World shared the stock of Adam, and benefited from the "original plan" of salvation and sin that God deposited in the first father.

When Joseph-François Lafitau wrote his 1724 *Customs of the American Indians Compared to the Customs of the Previous Times*, he too was committed to the unity of mankind. Small wonder for a pious Jesuit, who entered the order at the age of 15 and spent another fifteen years studying languages and theology before embarking on his mission to the Iroquois in Sault St. Louis. During his six years in New France, he collected unique ethnographic materials and used them to paint a comparative portrait of the religious, political, and social customs of the native Americans. His work also leaned hard on the ancient, patristic, and early modern authors by now familiar to us.

Customs of the American Indians bore no trace, however, of the confessional conflict that so energized the Christian sacrificial imagination. The Catholic priest was not worried about Protestants. His concern was the freethinkers who consigned *all* of religion to the ash heap of superstition.

To combat them, he developed what he called a "system," an effort to show that even the most apparently irrational forms of religious life had a logic of their own.

This system took as writ the common descent of mankind from Adam and Eve, a "common history," as Jacques Revel notes, grounded in scriptural commitments.[102] Lafitau could no more imagine there were men before Adam than he could imagine that the world was abandoned by God. God "imprinted the idea of his existence indelibly on the most ferocious hearts," he rebuked freethinkers.[103] And yet Lafitau also took to heart the challenge of freethought, which defied the pious to explain the consonance of religious customs in new ways.

The biblical story was true, Lafitau thus argued, but it did not *have* to be true to explain the regular patterns in religious practice. Yes, God revealed himself to all human beings, but "the spirit of man, limited and bounded, could not collect, under a single point of view, the infinity of his attributes, except in a vague manner." Confronted by the infinity of God, Lafitau contended, the human sensorium created "palpable images [*images sensibles*] . . . symbols lifting us up to him." The very truth of that first religion—God's oneness, his superiority, his infinite wisdom, his omnipotence—forced humans to produce a "hieroglyphic theology," a theology consisting of these palpable images (e.g., the sun) and a set of connected names (Saturn, Vesta, Isis, Ceres, and the Iroquois Horakouannentakton were just a few that Lafitau mentioned) that wove the symbols into more complex mythologies.[104]

The hieroglyphic theology entailed practices too. It created what Lafitau called "cult," that "assemblage of duties by which man, recognizing the superiority of a God, makes Him a humble vow of dependence, by the homage rendered to the dignity of His being."[105] At the heart of cult lay sacrifice:

> an act of religion, an offering made to the divinity through the same motives as are included in the obligation that men have, in general, to render him the cult He is owed; and especially through the motive of recognition of the benefits which they receive. *It is as old as religion itself and as widespread as the nations subject to religion*, since there is not one in which sacrifice is not customary, and in which, at the same time, it is not a proof of that religion.[106]

Lafitau does not seem to have known the ethnographic work of that Dominican friar Bartholomé de las Casas we discussed in chapter 6. But he began with a similar observation: *all* men recognize a felt obligation to the divinity. They naturally respond by offering Him something of their own. From this first principle, Lafitau developed an elaborate anthropology of sacrifice. At first, peoples offer small things (flowers, plants, animals) to God. As they grow wealthy and powerful, their offerings grow in magnificence. The most developed societies offer the most: hecatombs of animals or, later, their most prized possessions, their children. From these sacrifices come other cultic practices, for example, the bacchanals of the Greeks and Romans, the dances performed by the Egyptians and Israelites, and the war-feasts of the Iroquois. All of these coordinate ritually with the practice of sacrifice. The drums used to celebrate sacrificial festivals can be found, Lafitau argued, in such different contexts as Apollonius of Rhodes, the priests of Phrygia, the Brazilians, the Egyptians, and the Iroquois.

"At first it will seem surprising that things which appear profane to us such as the dance and so far from the spirit of religion as warfare, have been united almost inseparably with the solemnity of the sacrifices," Lafitau observed. Yet these are common elements of the hieroglyphic theology. Similar customs emerge in different societies because each society produces a similar response to a similar problem. Savage customs have their analogies in David's dance before the ark, for example, and in the name of the Hebrew God himself, the Lord of Hosts; the mysteries of Ceres and Bacchus are analogues of the Eucharist; the lustrations of the Lacedaemonians are analogues of both the self-flagellations during the Eleusinian mysteries and the initiation rites of the Iroquois, Carib, and Tupi tribes. This theory of the "palpable image" supplemented the Bible with a speculative and conjectural system, in other words, that rooted human similarities in man's shared cognitive capacities.[107]

To the modern eye, Lafitau's "system" is pretty unsystematic. And yet it indexed a new era in the sacrificial imagination. Lafitau ignored the elaborate regimes of distinction that had so energized earlier scholars. Rather, he sought to understand the organization of *all* religious institutions, to understand how, even absent revelation, diverse human societies might establish the *same* customs of behavior and thought.

To be sure, the Jesuit was no modern anthropologist. He discerned a Christian kernel deep in human life, a vague intuition of truth found in all peoples, however remote or barbaric. Eleusinian, Lupercalian, Iroquois, and Inca initiation rites shared such remarkable affinities because they reflect a universal longing for "atonement for past sins." Only Christianity accurately diagnosed and resolved the human desire for atonement. But if this intuitive longing explained the shared *motivations*, it did not explain the shared *institutions* that arose—everywhere and independently—to resolve them. Not revelation, but shared human capacities, encouraged "general" customs to emerge without diffusion or contact, simply as products of ordinary men and women confronting a puzzling world.[108]

What the Enlightenment called "customs" thus became central to efforts to explain the universality of sacrifice. In this, Lafitau was typical. As Europeans expanded their territorial power and their commercial networks, a literature of travel described customs from all over the world: in the Americas, in China, the Ottoman Empire, India, Russia, and the like. Some of this literature was explicitly comparative, like Noël Alexandre's *Conformity of Chinese Ceremonies with Greek and Roman Idolatry* (1700) and [Nicolas?] de la Crèquiniére's, *Conformity of the Customs of the East Indians with the Jews and Other Peoples of Antiquity* (1704), which pursued what Margaret Hodgen has called the "argument from similarity," the documentation of behavioral correspondences among peoples far-flung in time and space.[109] The correspondences that interested most were religious ones, so much so that, by the early eighteenth century, interested readers could consult a dictionary of such things, one that offered for the "readers' entertainment," the "particular Officers, Offices, and Functions in Religion; divers peculiar Rules, Customs, and Ceremonies; as also several sacred Rites, Utensils, and Festivals" collected and organized for "all Nations in all Ages."[110]

The most ambitious collection of customs, however, was the nine-volume *Religious Customs and Ceremonies of All the People of the World* (1723–1737). This work was a product of the French Protestant exile community that took refuge in Amsterdam after their expulsion from France in 1685. Bernard Picart, who lavished the work with hundreds of engravings, was a convert from Catholicism, albeit a heterodox one. Jean Frederic Bernard, who supplied the text, was a no less heterodox Huguenot.[111] He was also an entrepreneurial publisher alert to a literary marketplace hungry for compilations. Indeed, the first decades of the new century were a golden age of compilations, exemplified in the rash of new literary journals comprised largely of excerpts from other works. Pierre Bayle's *Nouvelles de la république des lettres* began its print run in 1684, but by the 1720s, there were dozens of others in many European vernaculars. Bernard himself edited at least three different such journals before tackling his herculean effort to compile *all* of the customs and ceremonies of the world's religions.

The *Customs and Ceremonies* was as close to a global history of religion as was possible in the early Enlightenment. Starting with the customs of the Jews, it explored Christianity in its various forms, the religions of the New World, and the religions of "idolatrous peoples" (by which was meant the religions of Asia and Africa). Each volume worked systematically through these traditions, summarizing beliefs, customs of worship, funeral customs, marriage customs, manners of dress, and other observations gathered from the accounts then available. Lavish images supplemented the text and supplied Europeans with a visual repertoire of world religion until well into the nineteenth century (fig. 9.7).[112]

Religious customs had their distant origin in a first man "implor[ing] divine mercy" out of guilt for his sins.[113] "All the peoples of the world sense the necessity of adoring a sovereign Being," Bernard remarked, "this necessity presupposes a dependence of mankind . . . [that] gives even the most savage some knowledge of sin."[114] This sense of sin was *not*, however, the lingering afterlife of the Fall. "We shall not distinguish divine institution from that which is purely human," because similar beliefs and customs appeared to arise independently among peoples far flung in time and space.[115] So even if Adam *had* preserved his innocence, Bernard proposed the shocking counterfactual, he *still* would have "implored the aid of his Creator, and addressed his supplications to him."[116] A natural sense of guilt and dependency was—for Bernard as for Lafitau—a seed from which all religious life grew.[117]

The first fruit of this seed was prayer, and the second was sacrifice. The ancient voice of supplication was the "origin of the Sacrifices of Cain and Abel," the primal act of devotion in nearly every human society, no matter how disparate in time and space. From prayer and sacrifice arose a host of practices, all oblique references to the sense of dependency that stands at the origin of religious life. Early patriarchs celebrated their sacrifices in woods and fields to encourage that "silence and contemplation" so necessary for devotion. Later they moved to mountaintops, which better conveyed "the elevation of God above us." "Extraordinary emergencies of state" inspired peoples "to appease the rage of the gods by the voluntary death of one person for the whole." From this sense of expiatory obligation grew the custom of human sacrifice, practiced by so many peoples ancient and modern. The desire to solemnize certain aspects of quotidian life—to set it apart as belonging to the gods—was no less an outgrowth of the primal sense of obligation. Every religion has specific hours and days set apart for worship, moments marked as different than the others. "If the sacrificer noticed any work going on during the sacrifice, the ceremony

FIGURE 9.7. The Great Sacrifice [Bernard Picard and Jean Bernard], *Cérémonies et coutumes religieuses de tous les peoples du monde* (Amsterdam, 1723). Courtesy of the Library of Congress, Jay I. Kislak Collection.

was profaned," Bernard wrote about the Romans, but the point was more general. Rules about bathing, ritual ablutions, covering the head and veiling the face, the wearing of white, processing barefoot, entering temples with the right foot forward, orienting churches to face the sun, casting the eyes downward, prostrations, dances, hymns, and laurel crowns are the common signs of supplication to the gods before whom mankind stands, guilty and dependent.[118]

Bernard's universalism drew on the older Christian archive. That ancient lustral sacrifice grew out of a universal desire for atonement was a dogmatic point in Johann Lomeier's *De veterum gentilium lustrationibus syntagma* (1681), for example, another defense of the Atonement against the Socinian heresy.[119] The Calvinist Lomeier supplied Bernard with rich materials for his discussion of lustration, highlighting the importance of water, for example, in rites of purification.[120] Bernard shared neither Lomeier's fear of Socinus, however, nor his confidence in traditional typologies. The first man's desire to atone was *not* a sign pointing to a future Messiah. It was instead a natural or psychological fact, one that helped to construct the great patterns of religious behavior found across the world. A sense of the majesty of God explains why people naturally make gestures of respect in the presence of the sacred, why "we uncover [our heads] when we pray to God and when we approach sacred things." A sense of shame explains why people naturally make gestures of supplication, since "nature endowed mankind with certain movements with which he expresses, almost without will or reflection, the affliction of his heart and the disquiet of his spirit."[121]

The Huguenot Bernard was far from even-handed in his treatment of religious cults. He often found ancient religions foolish, and regularly dismissed Catholic cult as superstitious nonsense.[122] Nor did he apply the secular universalism of the preface consistently across the vast terrain of the *Customs and Ceremonies*. There, descriptions of sacrifice were as various as the materials collected from travel writers, missionaries, antiquarians, and historians. In one account of our familiar doughy idols, for example, Bernard offered a dispassionate description of how the "blood of certain young children" was kneaded into dough, fractured by the priests, and distributed to the devotees. A few pages later, he redescribed it, however, now with an outrage familiar from earlier texts. The doughy idols were distributed, he exclaimed, "in the manner of a sacrament . . . so like that practiced among Christians, that one can hardly avoid explaining this idolatry as a usurpation of the Devil over the mysteries of the Christian religion."[123] As for human sacrifices more generally, Bernard wrote with some puzzlement:

> This manner of serving God, established among all nations of the world before the birth of Jesus Christ, might have been preserved by tradition in America after the arrival of the first colonies. About the human victims, that have bloodied the altars of the peoples of both hemispheres, it is difficult to say anything reasonable. Might we detect any kind of humanity [*idée d'humanité*] in the barbarism of these Sacrifices? And yet it is likely that first victims of this sort were offered to invite divine mercy on those occasions where nothing but human blood seemed capable of appeasing the angry gods.[124]

Two explanations compete in this short passage. Perhaps human sacrifice was a legacy of the ancient world, carried to the New by the peoples who moved there in the deep past. Or, possibly, it was a custom invented time and again, the extreme consequence of that human sense of dependency on the divine. The lack of certainty was significant, however. Works like the *Customs and Ceremonies* were conjectural rather than conclusive.

These early Enlightenment anthropologies invite some broader remarks. First, we observe how they both depended on and departed from that older Christian sacrificial archive. Released from confessional service, this archive was plundered for new cultural and intellectual projects, some more obviously pious, others far less so. These universalist projects were oriented *ad saeculum*, however, experimental efforts to understand the durability of sacrifice in the long history of the human experience.

Second, we note how, in the early decades of the eighteenth century, sacrifice helped coordinate a new comparative literature on religion. Sacrifice supplied the archetype of ceremony, both because of its status as the first ceremony, and because it was the ceremony around which so many other aspects of religious life—priests, altars, temples, and so forth—were understood to collect. To understand the origin of sacrifice was, in a sense, to understand the origin of religion itself, whether in the Garden, in the Mosaic Law, or in natural human impulses. The practice of sacrifice thus supplied the code that constructed *all* religious life.

And third, we see how this Enlightenment anthropology of sacrifice reproduced that double temporality with which Christians had long struggled. Sacrifice once and for all, sacrifice everyday: was Christianity the religion that overcame sacrifice? Or the religion that made it more powerful than ever? In the works of Lafitau and Bernard, echoes of these questions sounded loudly. Was sacrifice merely a primitive ceremony, an ancient way of relating to the divine that the moderns have thankfully overcome? Or was it a perennial phenomenon, an ineluctable product of the human struggle to understand the divine? The uncertainty about the right answer—and the experiments with *different* answers—echoed the uncertainties that Christians had long felt about the sacrificial archive they too had inherited and remade.

Anthropology II: The Sacrificial Foundations of Human Culture

The first secular *theory* of sacrifice likewise emerged out of the corpse of confessional scholarship. What does sacrifice *do* in the making of a human world? In an older framework, the answer was evident—sacrifice orients us toward an ultimate salvation. But in the post-confessional era, the question was far more puzzling. The most creative answer came from the original mind of Giambattista Vico (1668–1744). Dismissive of freethinkers like Hobbes and Bayle; an avid reader of seventeenth-century erudition; a nominal Catholic with little apparent fondness for the historical or modern Church: the Neapolitan Vico was an exemplary post-confessional thinker, someone who completely transformed the materials sedimented over two centuries of Christian polemics. [125] In Vico too we can see a hazy portent of the theories of sacrifice that later populate the speculations of modern anthropology and sociology.

"There has never been a nation of atheists," Vico wrote in the first version of his *New Science* (1725), "because all nations begin in some single religion."[126] This sounded like a pious commonplace: Cicero had spoken of humanity's natural religious instinct; Christian apologists of a first revelation lurking in the deep time of human history. But Vico was thinking along radically different lines. There has never been a nation of atheists because *nations themselves*—the social, legal, and political institutions that organize human collective life—are rooted in the primitive responses of human beings to their environment, responses that we call religion.

As in Boulanger, Vico's story began with the violence of the Flood, which split mankind into two races, one of proper men—pious adherents of Noah that preserved the memory of revelation for their progeny, those who became the Hebrews—and the other of *giants*. Vico set the Hebrews aside in favor of these giants: monstrous in shape, memories of God obliterated, customs reduced to nullity, they were also the distant ancestors to the civilized nations of Greece and Rome. How did this happen? How could a savage race, ignorant of Adam and oblivious of Christ, utterly cut off from the people of God and their revelations, nonetheless develop "uniform" institutions from its *own* resources?[127] How did the giants become gentiles, inventing patterns of life that, ages later, converged with those of their long-lost Hebrew brethren?

The answer lay in the *imagination*, the basic storytelling capacity common to all human beings. To be human is to possess a "mental language" [*lingua mentale*] that delimits the "things feasible in human life and expresses it with as many diverse modifications as these same things may have diverse aspects." These shared imaginative resources served as a springboard out of raw nature and into social life. To the thundering heavens that followed the universal flood, men responded with the story of Jove, a "king and father of men and gods" hurling his thunderbolts from the sky. The "corporeal imagination" was powerful enough in those days to quicken this first story into life. "So popular, disturbing, and instructive that its creators themselves believed in it," this story was mankind's first idol, a human creation so perfect it bewitched its own makers. Rooted in the imagination, a "poetic theology" and a "crude metaphysics" in time yielded the full complexity of human institutions.[128] In this story, sacrifice was foundational, the root of all human politics, law, religion, and culture.

The original giants roamed the world, so Vico's story went, until the terror of the gods ended their nomadic ways. First sheltering from the thunderbolts in caves, and then imagining the gods confined to mountains, coarse humanity settled in arable lands. There, their fertile imaginations invented new gods. The Greeks had their Cybele, mother of the gods and patron of cultivated lands. And the Romans—the most significant of ancient gentile peoples—had their Vesta:

> goddess of divine ceremonies, for the lands ploughed at that time were the first altars of the world. Here the goddess Vesta, armed with a fierce religion, watched over fire and spelt, which was the grain of the ancient Romans. . . . On these first lands Vesta sacrificed to Jove the impious practicers of the infamous promiscuity [of women and things], who violated the first altars (the first fields of grain). These were the first *hostiae*, the first victims of the gentile religions. Plautus called them *Saturni hostiae*, Saturn's victims . . . and they were called *hostes* because such impious men were rightly held to be enemies of the whole human race. And among the Romans it remained the custom to cover with spelt the brow and horns of sacrificial victims. . . . On this account,

> Vesta is the goddess of divine ceremonies among the Romans, for the first *colere* or cultivating, in the world of the gentiles was the cultivation of the land, and the first cult (*culto*) was raising these altars, setting this first fire to them, and sacrificing upon them the impious men.[129]

In the deep time of gentile humanity, cult and cultivation arose together. They began with the goddess Vesta, "goddess of divine ceremonies," in whose name the fields, the "first altars of the world," were planted. The violators of those fields were also the "first victims of the gentile religions," sacrificed to Jove or Saturn as *hosti humani generis*, enemies of the human race. Romans sanctified their deaths—and later the animals sacrificed too—with the *mola salsa*, the spelt raised on Vesta's fields. Thus were agriculture and sacrifice founded together, culture and religion partners in the making of man.

Vico's theory of the sacrificial origins of culture expanded from here. Because the fields served as sacrificial altars, early man fixed their boundaries, forcing themselves into stable communal arrangements. "Bloody ceremonies . . . consecrated [the] first walls," in turn, as boundaries marked with stones or hedges. From this came "the so-called sanctity of the walls" (a reference to Roman law) and from that, "the sanctity of the laws of war and peace." Over time, these altar-walls gathered together more people, "even as beasts driven by intense cold will sometimes seek salvation in inhabited places," so "men in their feral state . . . came to pass from their bestial liberty into human society."[130] From these fixing of the fields then emerged agrarian laws, and later the principles of authority that govern political life, those sacrificers on the first altars holding sovereign dominion over the lands that they had hedged off from the chaos of nature.

These sacrificial foundations of Rome explained *all* gentile religious and social developments. In the allegorical frontispiece to the 1744 *New Science*, Vico pictured how the altar supported every institution of gentile civil life (fig. 9.8). It supported the practices of divination and the practices of sacrifice, "from which came later all their human things," including marriage, human burial, the division of the fields, the "distinction of cities and peoples and finally of nations." As Vico unfolded his allegory, the altar grew in significance: the "plough rests its handle against the altar" to show that plowed lands were the first altars, the rudder bows at the foot of the altar, "the first cities were almost all called altars." Indeed, the altar organized the entirety of what he called the age of the gods, the foundational age of gentile societies. It is from the sacrificial altar, then, that Vico

FIGURE 9.8. Frontispiece, Giambattista Vico, *Principi di scienza nuova* (Naples, 1744). Courtesy of the Beinecke Rare Book and Manuscript Library, Yale University.

developed his universal logic of human cultural and social development, his "rational civil theology of divine providence."[131]

What kind of theology was this? To the extent that it was a theology at all, it hearkened back to the poetic theology of a Petrarch (see chapter 5). Doctrinal matters were absent, and the historical and anthropological materials that had sustained them were reoriented for new imaginative ends. God did not exit the story: "divine providence initiated the process by which the fierce and violent were brought from their outlaw state to humanity . . . by awaking in them a confused idea of divinity."[132] But this providence was radically emptied of biblical materials. No shadowy types of Christ's Cross, no long-forgotten ritual laws, no faint memories of the Flood or the Garden: none of that explained the universal patterns of human institutions.

That sacrifice was so essential to this philosophical anthropology was no accident—centuries of reflection on Christian sacrifice informed and shaped this. But now the animating issues were different. "In the night of thick darkness enveloping the earliest antiquity," wrote Vico, "there shines the eternal . . . light of a truth beyond question: that the world of civil society has certainly been made by men." We are *homo faber*, creating the social and political institutions through the operations of our own imaginations. From this primal creative force, humans have created their pantheon of customs, laws, and institutions, all of which collectively founded the "world of nations."[133] Sacrifice was thus a durable witness of both the inventive power of the imagination and the creative role of religious institutions in the making of human civilization.

Conclusion: Sacrifice ad saeculum

For centuries, the European sacrificial imagination circled eccentrically around the Crucifix. The sacrificial imagination of the Enlightenment instead turned *ad saeculum*, the doctrinal concerns that had so swelled the sacrificial archive moving to the periphery, history and anthropology to the center of the story. This imagination was, however, no more autonomous than Christianity had ever been. Just as Christianity inherited hierarchies, connections, ideals, and images from the Hebraic and gentile world of *its* birth, so too was the secular imagination of Enlightenment heir to centuries of Christian reflection on that most puzzling part of its patrimony. The turn toward the *saeculum* did not mean a final emancipation from the Christian past, but rather the reworking of that inheritance, its re-purposing for new intellectual projects.

Freethinkers and skeptics, for example, dismissed the entire world of sacrifice—Christian, Hebrew, and gentile—as no better than superstition and priestcraft. In one sense, they simply exploited the hierarchy of gospel over law that had always been present in Christianity. The critique of Catholic ceremony sharpened by decades of Protestant scorn was generalized into a critique of ceremony, full stop. Writers like Blount, Toland, Bayle, or Boulanger had to reach no further than a Bullinger to find the materials they needed to write sacrifice off as the deluded mania of primitive mankind. There was a distinct path from "Christian apologetics to deism," as Joan-Pau Rubiés has remarked.[134]

Rather than abandon the sacrificial archive, however, others *refashioned* it. New literary technologies reorganized the huge body of sacrificial materials that Christians had collected in the long effort to understand their own history. They condensed this body of materials into secular formulae, universal explanations of the sacrificial phenomenon on human terms alone. They broke down these materials in novel ways, unstructured by the older hierarchies of gentile, Jew, and Christian. And they forged new imaginative connections between sacrifice and other aspects of human anthropology and history: the natural history of teeth, ancient vegetarianism, the psychology of early mankind, and so on.

The liberation of antiquity from Christian doctrinal preoccupations also opened new interpretive pathways. On the one side, the most dynamic forms of eighteenth-century Christian piety abandoned the antiquity so important to older confessional theology, and thus invented new ways of thinking about Christian sacrifice. Later, the evangelicalism of the late eighteenth and early nineteenth centuries, with its new doctrine of Atonement put into the service of economic rationality, cared little for the ancient world so essential to the confessional age.[135] On the other side, secular writers reimagined anew the world of antiquity and its sacrificial religions. For some, this antiquity now evidenced the dark savagery of ancient mankind, all the better to highlight the progress of human reason in the age of Enlightenment. For others, antiquity could be reimagined in purely aesthetic terms, a classicism fundamental to the triumph of philhellenism by century's end. Indeed, the sacrifices of antiquity came to serve, for some, as models for a new religious sensibility freed of the grim shadow of the Crucifix.

The universality of sacrifice—once abstracted from the framework of Christian doctrinal concerns—also proved an immensely generative issue for the secular imagination. Lafitau's "system" sought to explain this universality in terms of human psychology and cognitive capacities, for example. Convergence between Iroquois, Greek, Jewish, and Christian customs could be imagined in quotidian, rather than salvific terms. Bernard's *Ceremonies and Customs* likewise looked to ground the sacrificial instinct in primal human responses to the world, that obscure sense of guilt and dependency that this massive collection detected across all the world's religions and cultures. Writers like these thus asked and answered a question that became urgent for the modern human sciences as they emerged in the nineteenth century: why do apparently *all* human beings sacrifice?

Finally, the Enlightenment saw the first efforts to *theorize* sacrifice in secular terms. By this I mean, the effort to explain in universal terms the centrality of sacrifice to human culture. Some explanations were deflationary. They saw sacrifice as a problem—a superstition, a neurosis, or a primitive sensibility—that humanity had to overcome to achieve autonomy and liberation. In the Christian vocabulary, sacrifice was an *ephapax*, a relic of an ancient era when man was not ready for the truth of things. Other explanations were more charitable to the sacrificial history of mankind, seeing sacrifice instead as an integral part of the human experience of the divine. Thus sacrifice might arise from a shared sense of obligation, or perhaps a shared desire to pay homage, to powers greater than ourselves. Sacrifice was, in this anthropological view, simply part of the human inheritance, as essential as sex or death in the grand scope of human life. Most ambitious was the effort to imagine sacrifice *itself* as a creative force in human history. For a writer like Vico, sacrifice founded human institutions, from agriculture to human settlement and political life. Few writers in the eighteenth century took this view, but by the early nineteenth century, this became more common, as we will see in chapter 11, when philosophers, philologians, later anthropologists and sociologists imagine sacrifice as an activity constitutive of humanity itself.

In short, then, the Enlightenment exploited the heteronomy of the Christian archive, opening new horizons for the sacrificial imagination. When the assemblage of doctrinal, scriptural, anthropological, and historical materials that had swelled the theologies of the confessional age collapsed, thinkers distributed its parts toward different ends. Some of these were explicitly Christian. But most of them were efforts to turn sacrifice *ad saeculum*, to understand its meaning in distinctly human terms. The story of sacrifice became a story of the modifications of the human mind, in Vico's language. It was this insight that put sacrifice at the very center of the human sciences as they took their modern form in the century to come.

CHAPTER TEN

The Deaths of Cato

CITIZENS, KINGS, AND THE REPUBLIC OF ENLIGHTENMENT SACRIFICE

The virtue of Socrates is that of the wisest of men;
But . . . Cato resembles a god among mortals.

JEAN-JACQUES ROUSSEAU, 1755[1]

IN AUGUST 1759, A Prussian officer named Ewald Christian von Kleist died in the village of Kunersdorf, east of Berlin. It was a thoroughly unromantic affair. Shot from his horse, he lay helpless overnight in the mud, while Cossacks robbed him of his clothing. In the morning, he was finally discovered and brought to a surgeon, who splinted his shattered bones. But ten days later, the splint failed, an artery burst, and Kleist died, just one of the twenty-three men in his aristocratic Pomeranian family killed in the wars of their Prussian King, Frederick the Great.[2]

Kleist was not a typical Prussian officer, however. He was a popular poet, an author of the idylls, rhapsodies, and elegies that packed German bookshelves of the mid-eighteenth century. The stars included Friedrich Klopstock, Gotthold Lessing, Salomon Gessner, and Karl Ramler, and hundreds of lesser lights. In this sentimental firmament, Kleist was the rare soldier, as ready to celebrate the violence of warfare as the beauties of spring. His songs of *Cissedes and Paches* (1759), set in the wars of ancient Greece, celebrated the unique love between warriors, the joy at defending the homeland, and the special world of sacrifice found only on the battlefield. This was a poetry awash in tears, young men declaring their friendship to the grave and beyond. It was equally awash in blood, blood that, in Kleist's poem, slaked the thirst of the dying Cissedes. "Death is our wish and joy," Kleist's heroes proclaimed. After they reached this happy end, their ashes were mixed in a devotional urn, a "glorious monument" for generations to come "Warriors!," the songs concluded, "You who, in later times, see the grave of my heroes, scatter roses on it, and sow around a forest of laurels! Death for the fatherland deserves eternal honor."[3]

Death was on the minds of many in the late 1750s. For three years already, the violence that killed Kleist had raged across the Holy Roman Empire, the European theater of a global conflict. In the Atlantic colonies, what became known as the Seven Years' War decisively rebalanced power between the British and the French, and laid the political, economic, and ideological foundations for the two great revolutions of the late century. The stakes were no less high on the continent, where Kleist's King envisioned a Prussia, weak in resources but fiercely militarized, equal to France, Britain, and Austria in the European concert of nations. Frederick's defeat at Kunersdorf almost destroyed his armies, and his ambitions for great-power Prussia. Everything depended on one final decisive effort, the King wrote in despair four days after the battle, as Russian forces marched toward Berlin. "If I had more lives, I would sacrifice them for my fatherland," but "if this blow fails, I have firmly decided to put an end to myself."[4]

Sacrifice had a long afterlife in the early modern political imagination. The age of the Christian martyrs sealed confessional communities in the blood of the special dead, new martyrologies recording stories of suffering in the name of faith. The age of armed prophets unleashed a new politics of sacrifice in the seventeenth century, whether in those king-priests monopolizing sacrifice and the sacred for the state, or in the king-martyr Charles, shedding his innocent blood for the sins of England. None of these sacrifices were easily accomplished, as we saw. Sacrifice is not a definite action, after all, so much as an *interpretation* of an action. What distinguishes the butcher from the priest is not the killing, but the meaning of the killing, blood transformed to something higher and better. All the more so when the sacrifices are of a subjective sort, the self-sacrifices so essential to the Christian imagination. Since anyone can (and everyone does) die, only interpretation distinguishes the sacrifice from the murder, the execution, or the suicide. And because sacrifice operates in this realm of the symbolic, it is vulnerable to skepticism, the sacrality of the death always open to contest and struggle.

In the age of confessional politics, such struggles were everywhere. No martyrology without an anti-martyrology; no claim for the sacrality of kingship, without a counterclaim to profane it. The more closely entwined Christian truth was with the legitimacy of rule, the more difficult it became to enact the strange interpretive alchemy by which human beings, living and dead, became something more than that, an incarnation of the divine. The deep structure of both early modern politics and religion, then, constrained the sacrificial imagination, always subjecting its grander ambitions to withering criticism and suspicion.

By 1700, however, the confessional age was drawing to a close. This was a difficult business, in both practice and theory. The new wars over empire, colonies, and commerce were no less violent than the religious and civil wars they replaced. Nor was being a religious minority easy virtually anywhere in Europe for at least another century and more. Difficult too was the imaginative work this change entailed. A literature on toleration, for example, sought to protect religious commitment from the supervision of public authorities. "Conscience," in John Locke's language as well as that of other contemporaries, belonged to a private domain, irrelevant to the proper operations of state power. To the extent that the state became absolute, as the historian Reinhard Koselleck observed, it became (or was supposed to become) "a field of moral neutrality," disinterested in private matters like belief.[5] This put a burden on states to disregard matters of private conscience and a burden on individuals to sequester moral life from political action.

And yet "the striving of morality to *become* political," Koselleck continued, was also "the great theme of [the] eighteenth century."[6] Generally shut out of direct participation in absolutist government, the ascendent commercial and middling classes of the early Enlightenment rooted their political imagination in moral and ethical principles. Political institutions were secondary, in this view, to what we would now call political *culture*, the shared "civic morality" binding on a political community.[7] In a world of "citizens without sovereignty," as it has been aptly called, citizenship was imagined less in terms of political-institutional rights and protections.[8] Rather, it was imagined as a thick form of *social* association, rooted common sensibilities, affections, and virtue.

In this new political landscape, sacrifice escaped from its older conceptual constraints. What this chapter will call the Enlightenment's "ethical republicanism" drew on a long tradition, running back through the civic humanists of the Renaissance to the classical republicanism of antiquity, which had long elevated self-sacrifice, *amor patriae*, into the highest of political virtues. The austere severity of a Cato, dying to preserve a fading republic; the suicidal charges of the Roman Decii; the unflinching courage of a Mucius Scaevola, who proved his dedication to Rome by thrusting his hand into Etruscan sacrificial fires: such were the heroes of Roman citizenship. The Enlightenment tempered such rigors by stressing the affections and feelings that bind a people—from ordinary merchant to crowned head of state—into a moral and political whole. Sacrifice was *democratized*, the chapter shows, no longer reserved for heroes like Cato. It became not just an aspiration, but an expectation for the citizens who share a common moral and political community.

It was this new sacrificial imagination that shaped the stories of Kunersdorf. If Frederick had indeed died in that battle—as some accounts report he nearly did—no one would have enrolled him as either a king-priest or Christian martyr. Instead he would have joined the ranks of the Kleists, those other citizens whose mutual affections, and love of a shared nation, carried them boldly from life into a glorious death. With Christian truth no longer at stake, put another way, the sacrificial imagination slipped its older symbolic chains. What had once constrained the honor of "sacrifice" to a special few expanded instead into an *inclusive* political vision, in which all citizens were now invited to sacrifice themselves for that most human of things, a common political community.

This chapter explores this expansion of political sacrifice *ad saeculum*, from the rarified world of priest-kings and martyrs, to the mundane world of citizens, patriots, and poets. It begins in the early century in England, with the emergence of a new moral landscape in which sensibility, sentimentality, and the horizontal bonds of fraternity were imagined essential to the proper political life. It follows the expansion of this "soft republicanism" into more unlikely places, into the absolutist worlds of France and Prussia, where new languages of virtue, new forms of sentimental writing, and new anthropologies of politics, wove sacrifice into the fabric of the political imagination. It takes us finally into the age of revolutions, when the ideal of citizenship—and the sacrifices it necessarily demanded—expanded again, becoming the common way of imagining national solidarity across the older boundaries of *ancien régime* Europe.

What is the relationship between virtue and politics? Is virtuous citizenship reserved for republics alone? What is virtue in the age of commerce and self-interest? What sacrifices are we willing to make for community and country? In these eighteenth-century questions and their answers, we discover the seeds of some distinctively modern ways of imagining political sacrifice. It was a world far removed from the *Christus-rex*, but no less peculiar for that, populated with martyrs for liberty, citizen-saints, and vengeful *manes* of the dear departed. The archives of sacrifice lived on, transformed for the new projects of the Enlightenment and beyond.

Part I: Sacrifice and the Ethical Imagination

Sacrifice in an Age of Sentiment

The Enlightenment was the "age of reason," it is said. It was an age of science, which replaced the warmer affections with the cool rationality of the machine. It was an age of self-interest, in which collective solidarities and commitments were dissolved by utilitarian calculations of pain and pleasure. It was an age of individualism, finally, that elevated personal liberty and self-expression over the good of the whole.

And yet for a cool age of reason, historians have long observed, it was fascinated by the heat of human feeling, affection, sympathy, and sociability. From the very beginning of the eighteenth century, the literary marketplace swelled with works that elevated these into the highest forms of human expression. Plays, poetry, novels, philosophical and moral treatises: all were vehicles for what G. J. Barker-Benfield has called the "culture of sensibility." It took root first in England and Scotland, and then spread so widely that, by century's end, virtually nowhere in western Europe was immune to this "sentimental fashion."[9] The ethics and politics of modern sacrifice took root here, in this other Enlightenment, more passionate, more virtuous, more social, and more concerned with understanding how human beings collectively shape their lives.

While a movement this broad can be birthed by no single author, Anthony Ashley Cooper, the third Earl of Shaftesbury, played at least the role of sturdy midwife. This student and critic of John Locke, cosmopolitan classicist, and idiosyncratic moralist pioneered—first in his *Inquiry Concerning Virtue* (1699) and later in *Characteristics of Men, Manners, Opinions, Times* (1711)—the study of the social virtues.[10] "To have one's affections right and entire not only in respect of oneself but of *society and the public*: this is rectitude, integrity or virtue," he wrote, a view that proved powerfully attractive to the Enlightenment moral imagination.[11]

No less repelled by fallen Adam than by Hobbes's brutish mankind, Shaftesbury discovered in sociability a politics as well. Our "political and social capacity . . . [is] natural and essential in our species," Shaftebury wrote, a "natural affection" that propels human beings from loneliness into society and government alike.[12] A political community is not a mere "multitude held together by force" but a "social league," a people united by shared moral sentiments and affections:[13]

> The relation of countryman, if it be allowed anything at all, must imply something moral and social. The notion itself presupposes a naturally civil and political state of mankind, and has reference to that particular part of society to which we owe our chief advantages as men and rational creatures, such as are *naturally* and *necessarily* united for each other's happiness and support.[14]

Basic anthropology—the "naturally civil and political state of mankind"—disposes us naturally to serve *each other* rather than just ourselves. To be a countryman is thus to share a common foundation of social and moral life that sustains the political life of a people.

The stress on the virtuous foundations of political life was not unique to Shaftesbury. What James Hankins calls "virtue politics" had deep roots in the ancient world and more proximate ones in the world of the Renaissance. Italian humanists of the fifteenth century, in particular, made "moral virtue . . . a necessary condition for the legitimate exercise of political power." The history of this civic tradition was not continuous, however. The humanist praise of republicanism, for example, was open to the variety of constitutional forms that a legitimate government might take.[15] By the seventeenth century, a more "exclusive" and more bellicose vision of republicanism—as the *sole* form of legitimate government—took hold, above all in the context of the English Civil War and its aftermath.[16] As it happened, Shaftesbury's grandfather was a founder of the Whig parliamentary faction, born in the 1680s out of the failed effort to exclude the Catholic brother of King Charles II from regal lineage. In their early, oppositional days, Whigs like Algernon Sidney wielded this exclusivist republicanism to indict the Stuart dynasty for tyranny.[17]

By the younger Shaftesbury's day, however, the Whigs had moved into government. As they did so, they shed the Spartan republicanism of their early days for a "soft republicanism" that emphasized the essential role of civility, culture, and above all, mutual affection in the flourishing of political life.[18] In this soft republicanism, we find the foundations of a new kind of political sacrifice, now imagined in terms of the horizontal affections that bind humans together in community.

Dulce et decorum est, pro patria mori—from antiquity resonated the Horatian epithet, which recognized acts of exceptional sacrifice for the sake of Rome. The virtue of such men was heroic, reserved for the few and fortunate. Theirs was "a path denied to others," a virtue that "spurns the vulgar crowd."[19] When his terrified cavalry fled their foes, the ancient Roman consul Publius Decius Mus put an end to their panic by devoting himself to death, offering up "the legions of the enemy, to be slain with myself as victims to Earth and the Manes."[20] It was this exemplary sacrifice, valuable because rare, that "produced in Rome almost the same effect that laws and orders produced," as Machiavelli later wrote, rejuvenating civic life through almost impossible heroism.[21]

By contrast, Shaftesbury's *pro patria mori* was scaled down to a more ordinary, human frame. "Of all human affections," he wrote, "the noblest and most becoming human nature is that of love to one's country."[22] True virtue disdains calculation, thus his 1709 *Sensus communis*, and acts regardless of self-interest or salvation:

> No premium or penalty being enforced . . . the virtue was a free choice, and the magnanimity of the act was left entire . . . He who would frankly serve his friend or country, at the expense even of his life, might do it on fair terms. *Sweet and proper it is* was his sole reason. It was inviting and becoming. It was good and honest.[23]

Sacrifice does not require heroes, in short. It is rather a free act of honest generosity, an extension of the "sweet and proper" affections that constitute the naturally political state of mankind: love and common concern for mutual happiness. Even the savagery of battle does not distinguish the hero from the knave. Rather, it amplifies these shared virtuous affections, war having the "force of [a] confederating charm," a "combining principle" that tightens the "knot of fellowship."[24] At the heart of political sacrifice is not valor, in other words, but something like friendship.

We find in this early sentimentalist, then, an ethics and politics of sacrifice turned *ad saeculum*, founded in this-worldly social virtues. Even the Christian martyrs, in Shaftesbury's view, followed the inclinations of these virtues. "He who yields his life a sacrifice to his prince or country, the lover who for his paramour performs as much, the heroic, the amorous, the religious martyrs who draw their views, whether visionary or real, from this pattern and exemplar of divinity": all of these are motivated by the same virtue, that of "pure friendship."[25] Martyrs, lovers, and patriots all enjoy the horizontal bonds of affection that make sacrifice meaningful in human terms. Sacrifice depends on the *feelings* that motivate it, the shared human affections that lie at the foundation of political life.

This turn toward the secular, affective foundations of sacrifice opened new avenues in the eighteenth-century political imagination. Theological polemic and austere political science yielded to more experimental genres of writing that crossed between the philosophical and the literary. Shaftesbury himself balanced on the boundary, presenting alternately as aesthete, moralist, literary critic, and philosopher. More significant for our study was the investment of intimate affections with political significance. This made imaginative *literature* into a newly powerful site for reflecting on the nature of citizenship and sacrifice.

Two months after Shaftebury died, for example, in April 1713, theatergoers applauded a version of his "tender masculinity" on the London stage. Written by that extraordinary social being, polite flaneur, and chronicler of urban London, Joseph Addison, *Cato: A Tragedy* discovered in its austere Roman hero the materials of domestic melodrama. The innovation evidently worked. In London, the play was performed over two hundred times in the coming decades. It was the first English play translated into French and Italian; Jesuits turned its neoclassical declamations into Latin; and performances in Ireland, Scotland, Germany, the Netherlands, and across the new American colonies together made *Cato* into *the* theatrical event of the eighteenth century.[26]

In contrast with the carnage of Senecan tragic drama, *Cato* was restrained, "a succession of just sentiments in elegant language," as Samuel Johnson later wrote.[27] The play was made moving less by the blood of the ancient patrician, who, as every schoolboy knew, fell on his sword rather than kneel to the tyrant Caesar. Rather, the *tears* welling out of masculine eyes stirred the sympathies of its viewers.[28] As poet Alexander Pope wrote in its prologue:

> Here Tears shall flow from a more gen'rous cause,
> Such Tears as Patriots shed for dying Laws.
> He bids your breasts with ancient ardor rise,
> And calls forth *Roman* drops from *British* eyes.[29]

These tears ran for thwarted lovers, whose story Addison invented to make a melodrama of the austere confrontation between Cato and Caesar. Above all, however, they flowed for friendship, along the channels of fraternal sociability that knit together the community of rebels that Cato commanded on the North African shores.

Cato the Younger (95–46 BCE), in Plutarch's classical biography, was a stiff-necked, hectoring hero whose superhuman rectitude aggravated his enemies and infatuated his admirers. The Enlightenment Cato was more approachable. To be sure, in Cato, we discover "to what a Godlike height / The *Roman* Virtues lift up mortal Man."[30] But the relationship between Cato and those men who joined his doomed resistance was not that of king to subject, or father to son. *Cato: A Tragedy* was the story of *fraternity*, not patriarchy. On the occasion of the death of his son, for example, Cato offered this advice:

> How beautiful is Death, when earn'd by Virtue!
> Who wou'd not be that Youth? What pity is it
> That we can die but once to serve our Country!
> . . .
> Alas my Friends!
> Why mourn you thus? Let not a private loss
> Afflict your Hearts. 'Tis *Rome* that requires our tears.[31]

Cato feels no "private loss" for his son, whose beautiful and virtuous death serves the cause. Friends should shed no tears for such death, he says, but only for Rome, in whose defense they are bound together in affection. To die for the fatherland is to affirm the horizontal solidarity that holds together a community of citizen-friends.

Even Cato's suicide—in Addison's retelling—was not an expression of honor, *amor patriae*, or any other abstract virtue. Rather, he died to protect his friends from the wrath of Caesar:

> *How shall I save my Friends*! Tis now, O Caesar, I begin to fear thee
> . . . I my self, with tears, request it of [Caesar],
> The Virtue of my Friends may pass unpunish'd.[32]

Enlightenment melodramas like *Cato*, in short, invested their sacrifices with the thick ties of solidarity and sentiment. The greatness of Cato did not rest on otherworldly heroism. His ideals were the intimate ones that bound *all* human communities together, from a small band of brothers, to nations, even to mankind itself. And his sacrifice grew from the becoming and honest sentiments that, for Shaftesbury, made dying for the fatherland *dulce et decorum*. "There fell the greatest Soul that ever warm'd / A *Roman* breast," his ally Lucius cries on finding the lifeless corpse, "*O Cato!* O my Friend!"[33]

Already in these early-century English writers, we find a new spirit of political sacrifice turned *ad saeculum*. There were faint echoes from the Christian archives, the distant majesty of Cato softened by tender suffering, a kind of Roman Man of Sorrows. And so Addison spoke of "Godlike" Cato; described him as "an off'ring fit for Heav'n"; and invested his final contemplations on death with the language of piety: "The Stars shall fade away, the Sun himself / Grow dim with age, and Nature sink in years; / But thou shalt flourish in immortal youth."[34] But all of this trafficked merely in the realm of metaphor, Christian sacrifice now slipping free into the domain of the symbolic. The audience had no idea which God awaited the dying hero, Jupiter or Christ. Nor did it matter, since the *stakes* that had made such distinctions so essential in previous eras had now largely vanished. At stake was not Christian truth, or the political power of Christian kingship, but the human bonds that Addison's Cato cemented in the mundane world of civil affections. Political sacrifice thus became an evermore mobile notion, freed of the older constraints that reserved its power for the martyrs and the heroes. It became too ever more human, given meaning by horizontal ties that bind us into ethical communities.

Republicanism as a Form of Life

When Americans hear *Cato* now, we hear the voices of our revolutionary patriots. Thus Patrick Henry in 1775 spoke in the language of Addison: "Is life so dear, or peace so sweet, to be purchased at the price of chains and slavery?" as did Nathan Hale at the gallows in 1776: "I only regret that I have but one life to lose for my country." From their lips, the sacrifices of Addison's *Cato* became a common idiom in the later age of revolutions.[35]

That it was less the fearsome Roman of classical sources than the Cato of a sentimental play, who captured the imagination of Enlightenment patriots, suggests something distinctive about the republicanism of that era. Few remember now just how *weak* republicanism was as a live political option in Europe ca. 1750. Its very few "republican" polities—places like the Low Countries, Genoa, or Venice—were in relative economic and political decline, and in any case, were hardly ideal models of civic equality and representative government. The most dynamic political actors in the eighteenth century were centralized monarchies and expansionist empires: France, the United Kingdom, Austria, and Prussia. As a result, eighteenth-century republicanism was only feebly associated with concrete projects of political reform. In the words of Franco Venturi, "in the middle of the century the word 'republic' found an echo in the minds of many people, but as a *form of life*, not as a political force."[36]

Republicanism was a creature of the imagination, in other words, and above all, the *ethical* imagination of the eighteenth century. For, as Venturi continues, it was the "ethical aspect of the republican tradition" that so appealed to the writers of the Enlightenment, especially those disoriented or disgusted by the new commercialism of the early century.[37] Classical republicanism had always depended on austerity, a willingness to foreswear desire in the name of individual and political autonomy. Republican strength came not despite but because of poverty, privation the forge of collective solidarity and military valor. The great enemy of republicanism was thus wealth and credit, which created relations of dependency—rich and poor, borrowers and lenders—in which the very "foundations of personality themselves appeared imaginary."[38] Classical republican ethics depended on self-control and sacrifice in the face of austerity and deprivation.

This ethic supplied a powerful platform from which to criticize the age of affluence that dawned in the early decades of the eighteenth century. In November 1720, for example, John Trenchard and Thomas Gordon began to publish their aptly named *Cato's Letters*. The frenzy of market speculation that seized London in the first months of that year had collapsed by the fall. The South Sea Bubble, as it was known, launched a fury of recrimination toward the crooked brokers, rapacious company directors, and irresponsible politicians that had sold the nation for a handful of silver. "A thousand stock jobbers, well trussed up, besides a diverting sight, would be a cheap sacrifice to the Manes of trade," Trenchard and Gordon exclaimed.[39]

This fiasco exposed the challenge of coordinating public virtue and private interests in the age of the market. Some, like the Dutch writer Bernard Mandeville, began publicly to argue that only private *vice* leads to public virtue. A community becomes stronger, he wrote in his 1714 *Fable of the Bees*, when people follow their desires, however base these might be. Indeed, only villains "preach up Publick-Spiritedness," to better "reap the Fruits of the Labour and Self-Denial of others."[40] *Cato's Letters* denounced cynical views like these. The wealth of rogues and villians is the "manifest plunder of the people . . . let it be restored to the people and let the publick be their heirs."[41] A vicious people will make a vicious *civitas*, they insisted, for the "people's interest is the publick interest."[42]

However fervent their outrage, *Cato's Letters* were not republican in any *institutional* sense. Indeed, Trenchard and Gordon seemed perfectly content with the limited monarchy consensus that had long dominated Whig politics.[43] The republicanism of the *Letters* instead made up "in moral fervor for what it lack[ed] by way of a specific program."[44] The Roman Cato would have—one suspects—been surprised at this political complacency.

This displacement of republicanism out of concrete politics and into the realm of the ethical imagination was an eighteenth-century commonplace. In an important sense, "republicanism" became a free-floating imaginative language, a way of talking about virtue portable *across* political systems. This helps explain why it thrived not just in places like the United Kingdom, which had some semblance of representative government, but even in the France of Louis XIV, which had none at all. But even there, in the early decades of the century, a loosely republican semantics of *patrie*, *nation*, and *société civile* entered into the intellectual mainstream (for details, see below).[45] With it developed a broad "politics of virtue," a normative discourse that invited a "public" excluded from participation in the affairs of government to imagine itself as politically engaged.[46]

Republicanism thrived in the imaginative realm of virtue. This virtue was partly individual, demanding self-restraint for the greater good. It was also collective, seen as essential to the development of sociability and civil society. Shaftesbury had already made this point in 1709, but it clearly resonated with his later admirers, including the young French philosopher Denis Diderot, who translated the *Inquiry on Virtue* in 1745. What Shaftesbury called "natural affections," Diderot translated as "*social* affections," insisting that "participation in the joys of others and the desire for their esteem" created a social unity that was the true foundation of political right.[47] Virtue coordinated private and public, self and other, into a system of reciprocal dependency and community.

Essential to this virtue was the willingness to sacrifice, even to sacrifice one's own life. Ancient republicanism had always said this, but again, it meant something new in the context of the eighteenth century. Across an intellectual avant-garde, after all, we can find many writers insisting, with Hobbes, that the preservation of one's life is the first law of nature and the most essential of human interests. In Diderot's circle, it was the *enfant terrible* of the *philosophes*, Claude Helvétius, who most vigorously defended this disenchanted view of humanity. It is "impossible to love virtue for the sake of virtue," he wrote in a rebuke of all sentimentalism.[48] Just as "the physical universe is subject to the laws of motion, the moral universe is no less to that of *interest*," a "powerful enchanter" that vitiates our distastes, and haloes our preferences.[49] In this world of pure interest, sacrifice—that is, giving up with no expectation of return—meant little.

Against the calculations of interest, writers like Shaftesbury and his French translator insisted that there *was* no virtue without sacrifice, that virtue stood apart from interest and desire. It might seem that "love of one's life" is the "one private affection" that we must set above all things, Shaftesbury wrote and Diderot echoed. But "there is no other [affection] whose excess produces such great disorders and is most fatal to felicity."[50] To be sure, the love of life was good in moderation. But in abundance, it makes a man the "cruelest enemy of himself."[51] It deprives him of self-mastery, incites superstition, and elevates impulsive desire over considered choice. Liberty thus itself depends on sacrifice, on the ability *not* to follow the dictates of self-interest.

"What is virtue?" Diderot later asked in a eulogy to England's great sentimental novelist, Samuel Richardson. "It is, however one considers it, a sacrifice of the self," he answered, "the sacrifice of the self made in the mind is a fixed disposition to immolate the self in reality." Imaginative literature, again, proved crucial for expounding the virtues essential to republicanism as a form of life. Richardson "sows in our hearts the seeds of virtue," Diderot exclaimed about his novel *Clarissa*; it awakens in us a moral sensibility that we did not even know we had, love of the good, and rage at injustice.[52] By trying the moral worth of its characters, testing their ability to navigate the tension between duty and desire, eighteenth-century novels regularly made domestic scenes of sacrifice, above all sacrifice for friendship and love, into key sites of moral reflection.[53]

In France, the most popular of these was authored by Diderot's collaborator and sometime friend, Jean-Jacques Rousseau. In the 1761 *Julie: Or the New Heloise*, passionate but thwarted love prompted flights of the sacrificial imagination, as its heroes, Julie and her tutor St.-Preux, pursue a romance doomed by circumstance. "Virtue must be but an empty name, or it must require sacrifices": so Julie schooled her lover on the claims of the heart.[54] "Happiness must be immolated to duty," to put it another way, self-interest sacrificed to the stern claims of right.[55] This immolation, the romance of impossible desire, drew endless tears from this epistolary novel's admirers, whose fondness for Julie and St. Preux made it *the* literary sensation of the French eighteenth century.[56]

Rousseau also made the connection between the travails of love and the rigors of republican political sacrifice unusually explicit. When the distraught St. Preux meditated on suicide, for example, he reached for the example of the "great and divine Cato . . . whose august and sacred image used to inspire the Romans with holy virtue and make tyrants quake." "I do not pretend that all of humankind should immolate itself by common consent," but "once the weariness of life overcomes the horror of dying, then life is obviously a great evil." St. Preux's interlocutor was astonished at the comparison. "Did Cato rip out his entrails for his mistress?," he exclaimed. He "owed his blood . . . to the fatherland," not to a lover.[57] But the comparison—sacrifice for love, sacrifice for country—was also natural in an age when the politics of republicanism were routinely translated into the languages of sentiment and virtue. Sacrifice *ad saeculum*, again, slipping into the realm of the symbolic, making available to all an act once reserved for heroes, kings, and martyrs.

PART II Sacrifice and Republican Political Culture

Montesquieu and the Anthropology of Republicanism

Imaginative literature was one important site of this transformation. No less important was the world of Enlightenment political thought, above all in France, where a dynamic set of mid-century writers wrestled with questions of republicanism, virtue, and citizenship. Here again we discover the migration of sacrifice down from its lofty heights to the more intimate spaces of shared affection.

To begin, then, with the French Enlightenment's most influential political thinker, Charles-Louis de Secondat, the Baron de Montesquieu. In traditional political theory, political societies were categorized by what Aristotle had called their "constitutions," a basic structure of rule that distinguished republics from monarchies and oligarchies. It was Montesquieu's insight that such constitutions were important, but ultimately *secondary* to the real factors that distinguish one political society from annother. More important was the rich sediment of law, informal institutions, character traits, and shared social conventions that sustain and support constitutional arrangements. Culture came before constitution.

Already in 1716, Montesquieu had begun to explore this view. In his *Dissertation on Roman Politics in Religion*, he plumbed the archives of Roman religion to discover the political "genius of the republic." Like Machiavelli, he focused on Numa Pompilius and other early kings, who instituted ceremonies and sacrifices "so wise that when the kings were expelled the yoke of religion was the only one from which this people, in clamoring for freedom, dared not emancipate itself."[58] This intuition that polities found, develop, and depend on a culture—what he called the "general spirit, the mores, and the manners of a nation"—lay at the heart of his 1748 *Spirit of the Laws*.[59]

To a modern reader, reading the *Spirit of the Laws* can be a strange experience. It offers little of the analytical clarity, for instance, that has made Hobbes's *Leviathan* or Locke's *Two Treatises on Government* into cornerstones of the Western political canon. Montesquieu's work instead sprawled through ancient and medieval history, mapping political institutions onto the character of the communities that sustain them. "Climate, religion, laws, the maxims of the government, examples of past things, mores, and manners": the nature of the people to be governed always preceded the government they find acceptable.[60] It was not a treatise on political right, but a political *anthropology*, one that sought the "spirit" of laws in the contingent experiences of human communities.

Its thesis can be put simply: "laws regulate the actions of the citizen, mores regulate the action of the man." Mores create and constrain political order, and political order in turn reinforces the mores that sustain it. The three types of political systems—"republican, monarchical, and despotic," according to Montesquieu—were not an abstract menu of constitutions, therefore, available to all. They were possibilities determined by the history and anthropology of the people who inhabit them. The "customs of a slave people are part of their servitude," he memorably declared, "those of a free people are part of their liberty." And just as every people has its character, each political system has its culture, a "spring" that coordinates and animates the polity.[61]

For republics, this spring was what Montesquieu called "political virtue." This was neither a moral virtue nor a Christian virtue. Indeed it was not an individual virtue at all. "Love of homeland, that is, love of equality"—the spring of republicanism—was instead a *social* virtue, anchored in the collective. It is a "feeling" that animates everyone in the body politic to love the republic above all else: "Love of equality in a democracy limits ambition to the single desire, the single happiness, of rendering greater services to one's homeland than other citizens . . . At birth one contracts an immense debt to it that can never be repaid."[62]

This unpayable debt orders the life of a republican citizen around sacrifice. Love of equality subordinates individual interest to collective goods; love of frugality limits "the *desire to possess* to the mindfulness required by that which is necessary to one's family." The less we can satisfy our own interest, the more we give ourselves over to "passions for the general order." In monarchies, "politics accomplishes great things with as little virtue as it can," but in republics, the "sacrifice of one's dearest interests" was at the heart of the political project. In short, "virtue asks for the continuous sacrifice to the state of oneself and ones' aversions." Lose virtue, and the "republic is a cast-off husk."[63]

Republicanism depended on a robust *culture* of sacrifice, then, an integrated system of ethics, politics, and religion. Indeed, Montesquieu's political anthropology made little distinction between these spheres. They were all means of cementing social cohesion, itself both precondition and product of political order. "Religion and the civil laws should aim principally to make good citizens of men," he wrote, both should be "bound with the principles of society." *Which* religion did not matter particularly to his point. "I am not a theologian, but one who writes about politics," he wrote, and treated the "various religions of the world only in relation to the good to be drawn from them in the civil state."[64] Republicanism was foundationally sacrificial, then, in just this way. An ethic of selfless obligation, a politics of austerity, and a religion that demanded both personal devotion and public sacrifice: out of these was woven the social and political fabric of the republican civil state.

Montesquieu's own political views are opaque.[65] He was no better than ambivalent about the austere sacrifices of classical Greece and Rome, wondering at ancient laws that "sacrificed both the citizen and the man and thought only about the republic."[66] He was ambivalent too about the self-destructive heroism of a Cato. True, the Roman culture of devotion produced great acts of heroism, he wrote in his 1734 *Considerations on the Greatness of the Romans*, but it also proceeded out of a confused overveneration of the self, "an obscure natural instinct that makes us love ourselves more than we love life itself."[67] There was something deeply unstable about ancient republicanism, a fragility in this culture of sacrifice that runs so athwart "natural bodies and their wants."[68]

Whatever his own politics, however, Montesquieu's anthropology of politics excavated the thick set of ethical commitments that underlay the republican form of life. Republican political institutions could no more survive without these than a plant could survive the destruction of its roots. Without a political culture founded in virtue and committed to sacrifice, republicanism would wither away.

Rousseau: Sacrifice and Civil Religion

A synonym for this political culture—coined in the mid-eighteenth century by our sentimental novelist and "critical disciple" of Montesquieu, Jean-Jacques Rousseau—was *civil religion.*[69]

Civil religion became a sociological term-of-art in late twentieth century America, in the wake of the turbulent 1960s, when the social fabric seemed in dire need of repair.[70] After the sociologists came historians of political thought, who discerned a long tradition of civil religion—"the appropriation of religion by politics for its own purposes"—dating variously to Numa Pompilius, Machiavelli, Hobbes, and others.[71] If it is understood in this manner, in fact, there are *no* thinkers of significance in Western political philosophy who fail to pay attention to civil religion.

But the historian must point out that the concept of "civil religion" was dreamed up in a *particular* moment. It was a moment, for example, when the very idea of the "civil" had grown in power and complexity. We see this in the new eighteenth-century meanings of "civil government." For Hobbes, civil government was simply a synonym for the state, however constituted.[72] By the 1680s, the "civil" started to shoulder new political and conceptual burdens. "Absolute monarchy . . . can be no form of civil government at all," John Locke wrote in his *Second Treatise on Government*, since it subjected "civil society" to the rule of arbitrary power.[73]

The simple statement concealed a sophisticated and novel point of view. The concept of "society"—the abstraction was an eighteenth-century neologism—named that special form of human association that exists before and beyond the reach of government. As we saw in Montesquieu already, it had powerfully ethical components that rested on the moral pillars of politeness, sociability, and sympathy so important in the dawning age of sentiment.[74] It also had political overtones, denoting the immanent order of connection and, at times, subordination that made political life imaginable.

The modifier "civil" gave society an explicit political value. It both hearkened to the *civitas* so important to earlier, especially republican political thought, and suggested that *beyond* the institutions of government lay another politically relevant body, "civil society." Thus the first entry for "civil" in Samuel Johnson's 1755 dictionary of the English language read, "relating to the *community*, political."[75] The French *Encyclopédie* stated it thus: "by civil society is understood the political body that men of the same nation, the same state, the same city or other place, form together, and the political bonds that tie them together."[76] Civil society is then something different than civil government, a "body" that ties together a political community. Like "society," moreover, the "civil" also had an associated ethics. To be civil was, Johnson also wrote, to be "complaisant, civilized, gentle, well-bred." Civility is the "way of acting and conversing with other men in society," in the terms of the *Encyclopédie*, a way of "marking the regard one has for another," an "interior sentiment conforming to reason . . . a practice of the natural law."[77] The notion of civil society, in short, twisted politics and ethics into a tight knot.

Religion was part of the knot as well. In the seventeenth century, the "civil" stood *opposed* to religion, as when Milton's God ordained laws to Israel, "part, such as appertain / To civil justice; part, religious rites / Of sacrifice."[78] In the eighteenth century, civil became more porous to the sacred. "The authority of religion is absolutely necessary, not only for supplying society with a thousand sweetnesses and amenities," declared the entry "society" in the *Encyclopédie*, "but also to ensure the observance of duties and maintain civil government."[79] "Man was *made* for living in society": his Creator designed him to be a social and political being.[80] This was not the Machiavellian functionalism—"where there is religion, arms can easily be introduced," as the Florentine famously wrote—now associated with the term "civil religion."[81] It was rather a form of theological anthropology that described the thick set of associations that make a "society" into a species of religion.

From early on, Rousseau was fascinated by this knot of politics, ethics, and religion. We see it already, for example, in his early 1755 article "economy, political" for the fifth volume of the *Encyclopédie*. The first rule of "legitimate or popular government" is to "follow the general will in all things," he echoed the *Spirit of the Laws*.[82] For the general will to be accomplished, for the general will to have real political effect, one thing above all: "make virtue reign."[83] But it is not enough simply to *tell* people to be good, Rousseau confessed. Rather, they have to be taught, and the most effective school for this was love of country:

> [T]he greatest prodigies of virtue have been produced by love of country. Let us dare to compare Socrates himself to Cato: the one more a philosopher, the other more a citizen. Athens was lost, and Socrates was left with no country but the whole world; Cato always carried his in his bosom; he lived only for her and could not survive without her.[84]

Rousseau signed the article "citizen of Geneva"—the homeland that had cast him out—and indeed, "citizenship" was at the heart of the matter. Socrates was a man without a country, the cosmopolitan philosopher. Cato was a *citizen*, by contrast, Cato whose love of country ran so deep that he could not imagine life without it.

Citizen Cato was also the model for ordinary political life, one we must emulate if we want virtue to reign. This virtue was grounded in what Rousseau's friend Alexandre Deleyre, librarian to the Duke of Parma and later revolutionary regicide, called the "cult of the home," with its "customs, laws, religion."[85] At its limit, this cult of the home invited, even demanded, sacrifice, each virtuous citizen a Cato who "consecrates himself *voluntarily* and *out of duty* to death" for the sake of all.[86] That there was a "cult of the home" appropriate to the citizen, and that this cult was like *other* religions: these insights were fundamental to Rousseau's 1762 *Social Contract*, in whose pages he first invented this long-influential idea of "civil religion."

In the *Social Contract*, Rousseau devised a state in which citizens regained the freedom and autonomy that they lost when they first exited nature and entered society. Living together, his 1755 *Discourse on Inequality* had complained, comes at a very high cost. It curtails our natural liberties, it shackles us with laws, and it creates social hierarchies. The solution was a new constitution, one in which each put "his person and all his power in common under the supreme direction of the general will," creating the "public person" called a *republic*. In this free state, each citizen was both the object and subject of law. He was "master of himself" because he obeyed the law that *he* authored.[87] Even the ultimate power of the state, the right over life and death, was subject to this dynamic of self-legislation:

> [Citizens] have only exchanged to their advantage . . . natural independence for freedom, the power to harm others for their personal safety; and their force, which others could overcome, for a right which the social union makes invincible. Their life itself, which they have dedicated to the State, is constantly protected by it; and when they risk it for the State's defense, what are they then doing but except to give back to the State what they have received from it?[88]

To be a citizen is to devote oneself to the service of the state. The social union gives us each our freedom and an "invincible" right of protection. But in exchange for this, we are obliged to the state, compelled to return to the state what it gives to us, namely our lives. "Life is no longer only a favor of nature, but a conditional gift of the State," as Rousseau wrote.[89] Natural life is offered to the moral community, and political life received in exchange.

In theoretical terms, this was a quid pro quo, personal liberty given for collective security received. From Montesquieu, however, Rousseau had learned that citizenship was above all a social and moral condition, a set of shared affections and sensibilities that made a *people* from a mere collection of self-interested humans. Could we reasonably imagine citizens, facing mortal danger, to recall the fair bargain they had made for their security? How, as Rousseau wrote in an early fragment, to kindle such zeal for the fatherland that "the honor of shedding their blood" in its defense would be counted not a *cost*, but itself a blessing?[90]

His answer came in a chapter excluded from the intitial manuscript of the *Social Contract* sent to the publisher Marc-Michel Rey in autumn 1761. The exclusion must have been deliberate, since Rousseau had already drafted this chapter several years before, in an early (ca. 1756) version of the book. In that draft, he had written:

> A people has never subsisted nor ever will subsist without Religion . . . In every state that can require its members to sacrifice their lives, anyone who does not believe in the afterlife is necessarily a coward or a madman. But we know only too well the extent to which the hope of an afterlife can bring a fanatic to scorn this life. Take away this fanatic's visions and give him the same faith as the reward for virtue, and you will turn him into a true citizen.[91]

A people collectively depends on religion; the state requires the full measure of their devotion; a citizen is a virtuous fanatic: the words were scribbled in hasty handwriting, either an afterthought or an inspiration, on the back of the chapter "On the Legislator." On the front side of the pages, Rousseau spoke of the "great soul" of the legislator, that uncommon gift of creating in people a "moral body" ready to "obey with freedom and bear with docility the yoke of public felicity."[92] *How* this moral body was constituted Rousseau left for the other side of the manuscript, materials that became, in his last-minute addition to the *Social Contract*, the chapter entitled "On Civil Religion."

Civil religion was, in short, an answer to the question: how do naturally self-interested humans form a moral community? As one scholar writes, civil religion had a magical power, "capable of ontologically transforming man into citizen."[93] From persons it created a people, committed to the shared virtues that precede the institutions of political life. In the ancient Roman world, Rousseau wrote, this civil religion had gods, tutelary patrons, a cult prescribed by law, and extended "the duties and rights of man as far as its altars." This was, however, a barbarous world, one in which "to die for one's country is to be martyred, to violate the laws is to be impious," and the result was a people "bloodthirsty and intolerant."[94] In the improved world of Rousseau's social contract, civil religion involved instead:

> a civil profession of faith, the articles of which are for the Sovereign to establish, not exactly as Religious dogmas, but as *sentiments of sociability* without which it is impossible to be a good Citizen . . . Without it being able to obligate anyone to believe them, the sovereign can banish from the State anyone who does not believe them. The sovereign can banish him not for being impious, but for being *unsociable*: for being incapable of sincerely loving the laws, justice, and of giving his life, if need be, for his duty. If someone who has publicly acknowledged these same dogmas behaves as though he does not believe them, he should be punished with death.[95]

Civil religion consisted, then, of the "sentiments of sociability" required for citizenship in a polity. These sentiments included shared commitments to an order of law and justice, but also a common affection for the state and its ways. A state requires our *love*, in other words, not just our obedience. Only love can bind us to a state so firmly that we are ready, if need be, to sacrifice everything on its behalf.

For Rousseau, this readiness to give one's life became the sine qua non of citizenship, the deepest expression of the sincere affections that bind citizens horizontally to each other, and vertically to the state. Small wonder that Rousseau was quick to compare the trials of love with the rigors of republican life. "Virtue must be but an empty name, or it must require sacrifices": the words came from Rousseau's romantic novel, but they applied just as much to his *Social Contract.*[96]

Civil religion thus fused a set of concepts and concerns highly specific to the Enlightenment. The neologism paralleled other, similar ones, like "civil society." And like these, it suggested that there must be a deep structure to politics, before, beyond, and perhaps more important than the institution of government. This deep structure included the pre-political affections necessary for a people *to be a people*, and thus capable of the demands of republican politics. And it installed sacrifice at the heart of citizenship, which, as we will see, crucially shaped the *actual* politics of the age of revolutions.

Boulanger: Republicanism as Theocratic Remnant, or the First Secularization Theory

What kind of "religion" was this, however? Rousseau was sure that it was *not* Christianity. Christianity had broken the ancient synthesis of theology and politics, he argued, first destroying the "unity of the [ancient] State," and then, having conquered it in the name of a "supposedly otherworldly kingdom," erected in its place the "most violent despotism in this world."[97] Civil religion was thus a political *therapy* for Christianity, a point that pious readers of Rousseau were quick to observe. "How could [Christianity] destroy the unity of the state," wondered the abbé Nicolas Bergier, when Christ never commanded anything more clearly than obedience to Caesar? The Genevan condemnation of the *Social Contract* was more straightforward: it was "scandalous, impious, tending to the destruction of the Christian religion."[98]

But if it was not Christianity, then what was civil religion? This was an important question with a long interpretive afterlife. Perhaps it was a *form* of Christianity, but transposed into a new secular idiom, older ideals of martyrdom recruited for a republican state. Or perhaps it was a new kind of religion altogether, the state itself made into a transcendental value. Historians and theorists of nationalism still struggle to answer this.[99] But interestingly enough, it was a question *already* asked in the middle of the eighteenth century, in the first recognizably modern theory of secularization.

We first glimpsed Rousseau's idea of civil religion in his 1755 *Encyclopédie* article on "economy, political," where he praised Cato, and the rule of virtue. The article was published when Rousseau and Diderot still shared both friendship and intellectual purpose. Ten years later—the friendship now broken and obviously disappointed in Rousseau—Diderot commissioned a *second* article on the same topic. "Political economy" appeared in volume eleven of the *Encyclopédie*, and its author was the antiquarian freethinker whom we met in chapter 9, Nicolas-Antoine Boulanger.

Rousseau had opened his chapter on civil religion with this bold claim: "Men at first had no other Kings than the Gods, nor any Government than Theocracy."[100] Boulanger agreed. But he wondered whether humans had even been *cured* of this need for a god to run their lives. No matter the form, whether republican, monarchical, oligarchic, or despotic, government *itself* had begun in that golden "age of holiness" when men proclaimed God their king, when man "wanted there to be no other master and no other sovereign on earth, as in heaven."[101]

At first, what Boulanger called the "god-monarch" was a good thing, "one of the first ideas of sociable and reasonable man." Over time, however, humans forgot that they had elected God their king. Instead, the "principles of the reign above were applied to the reign below." Mighty temples were built for their kings, their thrones were raised on high, he was given officers and ministers: "religion absorbed government, and the reign of heaven gave religion the reign on earth."[102] And so, humans became the slaves and victims of their own creation, the god-monarch now ruling like a God himself over all.

Once crowned, the god-monarch corrupted everything. Ordinary human acts were infused with divine portent, and thus debased. Gifts, for example, began simply. But once people came to believe they "owed everything to their divine king," they assumed a sinister form:

> After the fruits, one offered animals, and when this latter custom made men familiar with the cruel idea that the divinity loves blood, it was but a short step to slitting the throats of men, in order to offer him what was doubtless in his eyes the dearest and most precious blood.

> Unable to rise to a higher apex, ancient fanaticism thus slit the throats of human victims. It presented the palpitating organs to the divinity as an offering that was agreeable to him. What's more, man ate of it himself, and after extinguishing his reason, he ended up overcoming nature to participate in the banquets of the gods.[103]

First fruits, then animals, then men, then the hearts of men, then cannibalistic brutality: since the god-monarch cannot be satisfied with ordinary things, he must have *everything* given in his honor. The simple gratitude of a gift was transformed into a banquet of blood.

Modern man has not left these perversions behind. The germ of the god-monarch still blooms in modern political forms. It does so in despotism, for example, which grants the tyrant the crown of heaven, afforded sole power to dominate his enslaved subjects. This persistence Boulanger called *secularization*. The despotic state emerges from the "secularization [*la sécularisation*] of the ancient theocracies' great priests," the "throne nothing but the altar itself secularized [*sécularisé*]."[104]

But even *republics*, in Boulanger's view, secularized the ancient god-monarch. Indirectly, to be sure, but no less insidious for that. "Obliged to preserve the shadow of kingship when they were annihilating its reality," the liberated Athenians raised a statue to Jupiter and "gave him the title of king."[105] Here our *rex sacrificulus* returns, albeit with new meaning. The Roman king of the sacrifices fused king and priest, offered a "theocratic image" to satisfy those ancient desires for the god-monarch. And so:

> When these first republicans destroyed the kings while still preserving royalty, they were again led to this by a vestige of that ancient prejudice that had pushed primitive societies to live in expectation of the reign of the god-monarch, whose arrival the ruin of the world made them believe to be urgent and imminent.[106]

From its beginning, then, republicanism was infected by the germ of the god-monarch. The ancient Delphic oracles and Roman sibyls spoke of a once and future king, for example. Under the banner of theocratic expectations, the Roman republic marched its legions, first to imperial domination and eventually to its own destruction.

Even republican ideals, such as liberty, equality, and the reign of virtue, bore traces of this original sin. They invited men to imagine themselves kings, legislators, even gods: "for a time, the republican had to raise himself above himself . . . his legislation aimed to regenerate the golden age that had been the reign of virtue." As such, republican government too was a theocracy under another name, a violent wrenching of heaven to earth to serve human needs.[107]

Boulanger's article offered the earliest version (that I know) of "secularization" in a key modern sense, that is, a name for the illegitimate preservation or transposition of the sacred in properly civil contexts. The cult of republicanism—with what Rousseau called its "holy rage of virtue"—and the sacrificial demands of republican citizenship are nothing more, in Boulanger's view, than theocratic remnants, the secret yearning for divine power that tempts every form of modern politics. Civil religion, in this view, was not an *alternative* to Christianity. It was a *repetition* of the same Christian urge that "haloed" the secular emperors, that crowned them with the title of *salvator mundi*.[108] It was another name for the rule of the god-monarch, now hidden in the fabric of a republican state. Had Boulanger lived to read Rousseau's *Social Contract*, one can imagine his reaction.

Small wonder, finally, that Boulanger found republicanism so distasteful. Republicanism caused "the shedding of . . . more blood than the cruelest despotism," not because it sets too *low* a value on mankind, but rather the opposite. Because republics aim to "regenerate the golden age that had been the reign of virtue" and raise mankind to the divine heights, they always come to a dismal end. The true heir of Cato was Caligula, a monster come to earth. Only a secular *monarchy* "is made for earth," disenchanted enough to allow "man . . . to become man again."[109]

Part III: Sacrificial Citizenship in the Age of Revolutions

Citizen-Kings and the First War of Sacrifice

Every citizen is King, under a citizen-King.

—CHARLES SIMON FAVART, *SOLIMAN SECOND* (1761)[110]

Boulanger was not the only monarchist in the late 1750s. But he was one of the few intellectual critics of the politics of virtue and sacrificial citizenship in those years, in the middle of Europe's first global war. This war—what people later called the Seven Years' War—transformed the virtuous sacrifices of republican dreamers into the common currency of the European political imagination, in monarchies and republics alike. Montesquieu was adamant that perfectly decent governments might well live without much virtue at all. The patriotic paroxysms of the later 1750s made such sentiments a distinctly minority view.

The war was years in the making, rooted in European imperial expansion abroad and great power politics back home. The 1748 peace of Aix-la-Chapelle—the most recent effort to resolve the military and political conflicts that attended the inexorable decline in the power of the Hapsburg emperors—unraveled at first slowly, and then decisively in 1756. Open warfare erupted in North America and the Mediterranean between France and Britain, and in central Europe between Austria and Russia, on the one side, and the energetic military of the Prussian King Frederick II.

In France, the disastrous losses to the British in North America, and virtual collapse of her overseas empire, provoked an unprecedented political change. Not in French institutions, however, which remained as hidebound as ever. Rather, it transformed the French political imagination. The sense of national disaster, and national grievance against the victorious English, as David Bell and others have shown, elevated *all* the people of France from subjects to citizens. Subjects of this absolute monarchy were, enthusiasts for the cause declared, as liable to "patriotic zeal" as any republican had ever been.[111] Patriotism is "more alive and more generous in the French citizen than it was in the most Patriotic Roman," insisted one Rossel, author of an eight-volume work on French patriotism published in 1769. Indeed, for Rossel, the history of French patriotism *was* the history of France.[112]

Similar views populated the cultural landscape, actively promoted by the French absolutist goverment. Take, for example, the death of the French officer Joseph Coulon de Jumonville in 1754 in the woods of Pennsylvania. American readers might remember this as the first act in the career of the young George Washington, then British officer and later hero to the American cause. But in France, it began a transformation in the public culture of the nation, as Jumonville was elevated from soldier to saint, citizen martyr to the cause of the French. His death was celebrated in epic poems, and became part of a broader atrocity literature, often supported by the French foreign ministry, aimed at mobilizing sentiment for the war.[113]

Works of the imagination like this were central to a new politics. The most popular French play of the eighteenth century, the *Siege of Calais* (1765), was written during the last months of the war, and was performed broadly in its aftermath.[114] An extended homage to citzenship, sacrifice, and sociability, this first "national tragedy" transformed the fourteenth-century burghers of Calais into modern heroes.[115] "Martyrs to the fatherland, follow me, the palms are prepared," pronounced their leader, ready to sacrifice himself to the tyrant English king that Calais might be saved.[116] The language was republican; the politics was anything but. The *Siege of Calais* was underwritten by the royal ministry and performed at military garrisons throughout France. As one observer later remarked, the play had "taught the French that patriotism does not belong to Republics alone."[117]

This absorption of republicanism by Europe's Old Regime was a remarkable moment in the political imagination. In France, the concept "citizen" grew in power over the eighteenth century as it was newly coordinated with other keywords like fatherland, patriotism, virtue, and happiness.[118] In the abstract, this language of citizenship threatened the bloodlines that had traditionally structured European society, setting aristocratic elites apart from the common man. But it also afforded new political opportunities. Many of the French nobility had, for example, long defended their status against the leveling solvents of absolutism. For early eighteenth-century aristocratic writers like Henri de Boulainvilliers, for example, classical republicanism supplied a new terrain on which to defend the importance of the noble classes to the life of the nation. These classes were, in his view, the repository of the virtue and patriotism so important to the republican project, representing a "virtuous citizenry in the ongoing battle against civic decrepitude and . . . despotism," as Jay Smith remarks.[119] Cato was a *senator*, after all, before he was a martyr for Rome.

Like the nobility, the crown too found ideals of virtue, sacrifice, and citizenship appealing. And so a peculiar chimera grew inside the European political imagination, that of "monarchical patriotism," which "invited men to act as Roman citizens while being subjects in a Christian absolute monarchy."[120] On this view, Montesquieu was mistaken in his political anthropology. In a proper monarchy, no less than a republic, sacrifice, virtue, and citizenship reigned supreme.

Thus we return to 1759, to the bloody battlefield of Kunersdorf, when Prussia—arguably the *least* republican, the most militarized, aggressive, and hierarchical of the European monarchies—suddenly discovered that it too was a home of citizenship and patriotic sacrifice. "What a pity is it / that we can die but once to serve our country": the young Prussian Thomas Abbt began his 1761 *On Death for the Fatherland* in the words of Addison's *Cato*. He wrote the work in Frankfurt on the Oder, four miles from the battlefield that had claimed the life of the poet-soldier-martyr, Ewald Christian von Kleist, only two years before.

The book launched the young Abbt onto the public stage. The philosopher Moses Mendelssohn gave it high praise in *Briefe, die neuste*

Literatur betreffend, the most important literary journal of the Berlin Enlightenment. It was with Mendelssohn that Abbt prepared a translation of the Earl of Shaftesbury's essays. And it was Shaftesbury who in turn inspired Abbt's "aesthetic patriotism," organized around a "beautiful idea of [the] harmonious political community of citizens."[121]

The problem of modern monarchy was that it was *too* rational, Abbt thought, too much the calculating community of interests that so attracted Montesquieu. Beauty supplied an alternative moral order to that of interests, a ground for "genuine virtue without . . . the presence of a legislator."[122] As Mendelssohn wrote, "Beauty is the self-empowered mistress of all our sentiments . . . the animating spirit which transforms speculative knowledge of the truth into sentiments and incites us to active decision."[123] For Abbt, more specifically, it was the beautiful image of the *king* that transformed speculation into sentiment, incited action, and cemented a national moral community:

> All the glory that flows to him, all the radiance that surrounds him, also wafts a clear breath of heaven around the entire nation . . . The more sensuous the objects that arouse our passions are, the longer they remain before our eyes in a blazing passion, the stronger, the more lively our sentiment becomes. . . . What patriotic breast would not beat hard, when we see the man after which our century calls itself . . . offer himself as a sacrifice to the fatherland, which he himself represents in all his earnest majesty![124]

The Roman Decii were important less for their *own* sacrifices than for the sacrifices they inspired in others. Like these ancients, the radiant Frederick II—the warrior king of Prussia—was the sensuous example to which no heart could fail to warm. From him blows the breath of heaven, arousing the sentiments of a patriotic heart. In the light of this king, "the difference between farmer, townsman [*Bürger*], soldier, and noble [disappears]. All unite . . . under the glorious name of a *citizen* [*Bürger*]."[125] As Mendelssohn put it, "in a warring monarchy, all are citizens."[126]

Aesthetic response similarly moved Abbt to admire the "holy" battlefields of Zorndorf and Kunersdorf.[127] With respect to war-fighting, admittedly, these were not scenes of glory. The first was at best a draw for Frederick; the other was his worst defeat. But glory lay less in *winning* battles than in losing them, in becoming (nearly) the martyr that Prussia yearned for. The king himself seems to have felt almost the same way: "if I had more lives, I would sacrifice them for my fatherland," we recall him writing after the disaster of Kunersdorf, but "if this blow fails, I have firmly decided to put an end to myself."[128] Rumors of the king's death were the call to arms for Ewald Kleist (so Abbt believed), rumors that "flooded men's souls with melancholy pleasure."[129] That it was a *poet* who died in battle for the beautiful king was, therefore, almost too good to be true. The beauty of Kleist's sentiments, the beauty of his writings, and the beauty of his death all converged on the battlefield of Kunersdorf:

> If I should walk the lonely paths, among the noisy and heedless crowd, to your grave, and past your grave, immortal Kleist: then I would count those wounds you received for the fatherland . . . and pay you the gratitude, which we owe those patriots who sacrificed themselves for our safety.[130]

That war was a poetic experience would have surprised most of those who fought and died in the armies of Prussia. These armies were enormous—fully 35 percent of Prussia's national income, estimates suggest, was spent on the military in 1760. Ninety percent of the officers were from the nobility, part of the great integration of the second estate into the project of Prussian nation-building that began in the early decades of the century. Many officers died, like Kleist and his cousins. But the real victims were the commoners, as always, captured by Prussia's brutal system of conscription, which subjected all men between ages 16 and 30 to twenty years of service either in the military or in forced labor on vast noble estates. Their lot was a dismal one. Frederick himself observed that the common soldier should "have more fear of his officer than the enemy" and there is little to suggest that they were impressed by the beauties of war. Desertion rates were high, casualties no less so, and the bodies of the dead were dumped in common pits or simply burned.[131] Far cry from the tender and melancholy grave of the poet-warrior Kleist.

Yet the poetry of war laid laurels over the armies and battles of Frederick. The *Prussian Warsongs of a Grenadier* began to appear in the late 1750s, for example, first as pamphlets, then as a book. The author was a "common soldier," possessed in equal parts of "heroic courage and poetic genius," wrote Gotthold Ephraim Lessing, prince of the German Enlightenment. (In fact, the author Johann Wilhelm Gleim was no soldier at all, but a poet.) "War is my song / since the world wants war, let it be war!" the collection opened. The poems that followed sang the heroism of sacrificial death, and the heroism of Frederick. "A hero I fall / and even dying, my hand its saber wields / death makes immortal the hero / death for the fatherland!"—the poetry was repetitive, but its sentiments clearly struck a chord in the age of Frederick's wars, reprinted several times in the next decades, and even set to music.[132] Kleist's "Ode to the Prussian Army" was written in March 1757, and likely the most influential poet of the age, Friedrich Klopstock, had already written his own "War Song" in 1749:

> The battle begins, the enemy near
> Onward to victory in the field!
> Leading us the foremost man
> In the entire fatherland!
> . . .
> Let thunder fall! Frederick drives
> The swarms before him.
> Welcome, death for the fatherland!
> When our sinking head,
> Already drenched in blood, then we die
> With glory for the fatherland.[133]

Most startling about these were the new forms of sentimental attachment that they promoted. When kings sacrifice, or were sacrificed, in the century past, they did so as *sovereigns*, Christian and pagan, *Christus-rex* and *rex sacrificulus* in equal measure, always remote. When they did so in the eighteenth century—once monarchical republicanism had made its inroads across the concert of nations—they did so as fellow *citizens*. The demand that we leave interest behind in the name of something greater falls no less on the shoulder of the patriot king than on those of the ordinary soldiers. The monstrous sovereigns of Seneca have become our familiar intimates. "[We] miss the presence of the king," Abbt concluded his work, like a mother who misses her "tender child, too early torn away from her into the cohorts of the god of war . . . so too longs the fatherland, filled with devoted yearning, long for you, O King, our joy!"[134]

There was something new about this, neither quite classical nor Christian. Again, in the older sacrificial imagination, sacrifice was reserved for the few and privileged, those martyrs and heroes "either strengthened by firm conviction in the promise of Christianity, or encouraged by sounds of posthumous glory already ringing in their ears."[135] But Abbt envisioned a *universal* project of citizenship, a Ciceronian "model of active public life" reimagined for the age of monarchs at war.[136] Everyone, from peasant to king, was thus invited to embrace the bonds of sacrificial citizenship. To build this community, other "passions," as Abbt called them, were needed to conquer the natural fear of death. "Fear [of death] sets all the nerves into trembling motion," but in patriotism, we discover a new conviction, that our death will "add more to the sum of our pleasures than we would ever achieve through a longer life" and so the "dark fears of the imagination disappear."[137] This emotional alchemy accomplished, and man is transformed: "we learn to die for others, rather than teaching others to live for us."[138]

In the era of the Seven Years' War, then, there occurred an astonishing political transformation, in which it became possible—in some respects necessary—to imagine the most rigid ancien régime politics in sacrificial terms. From the royal sponsorship of the *Siege of Calais* to Frederick II's sense of himself as sacrifice for the fatherland, the crowns of Europe recruited the power of sentiment and sacrifice for their own political projects. In many cases, this worked. Even though Frederick was a remote figure in the later years of his reign, his death in 1786 saw a stupendous outpouring of heartbreak, recorded in vast commemorations of his life. Volumes of Fredrician anecdotes were collected and published, his life celebrated in printed images, drinking mugs, watches, tobacco tins, jewelry, and calendars. By the end of the century, huge memorial temples were planned to honor the dead Frederick. Let this image from the *Göttinger Taschenkalendar* for 1792 stand for this wider apotheosis of Frederick, the dead King here laying down his torch and carried aloft by the genius of death, crowned by the genius of glory (fig. 10.1).[139]

As monarchy became republican, however, it too was transformed. That monarchs might sacrifice *neither* as sovereign priests nor as types of Christ, but as familiar friends: this dissolved the distinction between conquering Caesar and suffering Cato, and that between citizen and king. Kings did not lose their privileges, of course. They clung to the lands and thrones that elevated them far above commoners and nobility. But the lateral chain of affections that tied citizen to citizen tightened around the monarchies of the late century, the kings no longer distant and terrible, now citizens too in a community of virtue. Sacrifice *ad saeculum* invited all to belong inside its common political horizon.

Violence, Sacrifice, and the Age of Revolutions

By the late eighteenth century, then, a new secular sacrificial imagination had expanded through the political sphere. It was assembled from a heterogeneous set of cultural materials, including novels, plays, poetry, letters, encyclopedia articles, political pamphlets, and ethical treatises. No less eclectic were the intellectual sources that it welded together. Fragments of that older Christian archive were stitched to classical republicanism, and both were reprocessed by the era's fascination with virtue,

FIGURE 10.1. The death of Frederick the Great, *Göttinger Taschenkalender* ([Göttingen], 1792). Gift of Dr. Dieter Erich Meyer. Public Domain. Courtesy National Gallery of Art, Washington, DC.

sentiment, and sociability. No longer reserved for heroes or martyrs, anyone with the claim on citizenship could enjoy its comforts. Whether we call this patriotism or nationalism, it wove citizenship and sacrifice permanently into the fabric of modern political life. What made this permanent were the late century revolutions, the republican experiments that upended the ancien régime and birthed the liberal political order in the West, both its political institutions and its political imagination.

These experiments were both terrifically creative and terrifically violent. The Seven Years' War in North America had scarcely ended before popular unrest over the Stamp Act—imposed to fund, it was said, the military costs of protecting the colonies—and various military quartering requirements began to swell in the colonies.[140] Mob violence in places like Boston took aim at customs officials and later colonial elites, destroying property and hanging officials in effigy. The gradual escalation through the later 1760s—armed militias confronting British troops, and most iconic, the bloodshed of the 1770 Boston massacre—culminated in bloody war. Campaigns of terror and torture against loyalists waged by patriot "committees of safety," naval bombardment and burning of cities, the murder of prisoners, the extirpation of Indian tribes, battlefield atrocities of every sort: this was a ferocious conflict. Indeed, as a percentage of population, it killed far more Americans than either of the world wars of the twentieth century.[141]

If modern nostalgia obscures the violent birth of the American republic, the same cannot be said of France. There revolutionary violence became a thing of legend. The collapse of France's monarchy too had its distant origins in the Seven Years' War: the destruction of France's North American colonies, compounded by its support of the Americans in their war for independence, and other financial misadventures that paved the way for calling the Estates to Paris in May 1789. With a few notable exceptions—the July 1789 storming of the Bastille and the massacre at the Champs de Mars in 1791—the first three years were relatively peaceful. But after war erupted in early 1792, events accelerated. The overthrow of the monarchy in August 1792, the prison massacres in September, the trial and execution of Louis XVI in January 1793, the mass conscriptions of February, the revolt in the Vendée and its bloody suppression, the formation of the Committee of Public Safety, the beginning of the Terror, all against the background of endless warfare with other European nations: violent convulsions endured, for many in France, until the fall of Napoleon in 1815.

Out of the violence of these republican experiments came an enduring political culture of sacrifice. In the American context, for example, the words of Cato echoed loudly among the elite patriots who staffed the revolutionary army and supplied it with its political martyrs. "Empty all your veins for LIBERTY," wrote Joseph Sewall Mitchell in his *New Epilogue to Cato*, a rousing call to join the military cause in 1781.[142] In eulogies, poems, pamphlets, and broadsides, a public culture of sacrifice grew up around the revolutionary conflict that would give an enduring shape to the nationalism of early America. There were, as we might expect, both Roman and Christian aspects to this culture, the Elysian fields no less a martyr's destiny than the arms of Christ. When the Connecticut pastor Thomas Brockway preached his *America Saved, or Divine Glory Displayed* thanksgiving sermon in 1784, he was moved to offer these words of praise:

> They have shared the fate of war, paid the debt to nature and their country, the silent mansion of the grave is their habitation . . . Shall these, my friends, ever be forgotten by us, who reap the purchase of their blood? Forbid it humanity . . . Let their memory be held dear to posterity, and the liberties of our country, the price of their blood, be ever treated as sacred.[143]

The funeral oration of Pericles, the panegyric to the city of Athens in the first Peloponnesian war, rang out in a Christian idiom, blood spilled in "the lofty theater in which God acts," which already Brockway imagined as extending "three thousand miles" to the Pacific ocean.[144] This broader culture of sacrifice grew stronger in the early national period, a world of revolutionary memorials that included triumphal arches, cenotaphs, parades, fireworks, and an array of other ways of celebrating and commemorating the revolution's special dead.[145]

A *national* vision of citizenship was, however, slow to come to the American colonies. There were those who passionately advocated that there ought to be one standard of belonging that applied to all people equally. On the ground, though, the individual states long remained the main arbiters of rights and duties. The 1789 Constitution never specified the parameters of citizenship, neither who counts as a citizen, nor the privileges that might belong to him. The Bill of Rights could have been a platform for such ideals, but it was immediately restricted by the Eleventh Amendment to the US Constitution (passed 1795, implemented 1798), which enshrined the states as the final arbiters of law and citizenship. It was only after the Civil War—with the brutal fights about citizenship occasioned by sectionalism, slavery, and reconstruction—that the Fourteenth Amendment, ratified in 1868, finally defined the contours of American citizenship.[146]

And it was a certain version of national citizenship, as the French example powerfully shows, that so supercharged the sacrificial imagination. The patriotism of the mid-century was politically *inclusive*, its notion of citizenship trafficking in the realm of the symbolic rather than that of practical politics. Thus peasant, burgher, and king were all entitled to what Thomas Abbt called the "glorious name of a citizen." The violence of the French Revolution destroyed these imaginative equivalences. In an *actual* republic, those lateral bonds of affection, friendship, virtue, and sacrifice could compass neither a king nor his advocates. What the Viscount Bolingbroke had called a "patriot King" became an oxymoron.[147] "No man can reign innocently," as the young revolutionary firebrand Saint Just declared in late 1793.[148]

In this great experiment of European republican founding, citizenship and the virtues that had come to define it thus became *exclusive*, necessarily limited to those politically committed to the revolution. These limits were formally defined from the outset, in the French *Declaration of the Rights of Man and Citizen* (1789), which enshrined national citizenship at the heart of the revolutionary project. Its preamble spoke of the collectivity—the "members of the Social body"—whose rights and duties the *Declaration* defended. Its articles defended the rights of "citizens" to equal justice, political participation, and free speech. They spoke of the need for a citizen army, and the liability of all citizens to taxation. And they announced a collective aspiration to found a *nation*. "Sovereignty resides essentially in the nation," article 3 insisted.[149]

The *Declaration* completed a transformation in French citizenship from a legal to a political category, historians have observed. Privilege was at the heart of the ancien régime society of orders, in which citizens were principally bearers of specific juridical rights. To destroy this, revolutionaries redefined citizenship in political terms. They imagined a "fundamentally novel . . . construction of the citizen as a public and political being." For the French revolutionaries, but also for most modern liberal societies, to be a citizen is *both* to have legal rights and to affirm an active role in determining the nature of the national polity. When the first French constitution was enacted (1791)—which established France as constitutional monarchy governed largely by a powerful and elected Legislative Assembly—the "status of citizens" was therefore among its principal concerns.[150]

Revolutionary citizenship, however, entailed more than just a set of political rights. It was above all a normative project, as Carla Hesse points out, one that sought to *create* the citizens who might then enjoy the fruits of republican liberty. The Revolution's most notorious legal institution—the revolutionary tribunal that tried and executed some 17,000 people for counter-revolutionary crimes—was a crucial site of this civic education, a way of shaping the "people" into revolutionary citizens.[151] Revolutionary citizenship was thus less defined by the rights enshrined in founding constitutional documents, than by shared norms, the virtues and social affections fundamental to republican politics. One such norm was, again, *sacrifice*: to be a citizen was (and is) to be willing to sacrifice personal interests to the "Social body" to which a citizen belongs. The more contested citizenship grew over the course of the revolution, the more important sacrifice became in the republican political imagination.

To see this, we close the chapter with an exemplary crisis in revolutionary citizenship, unleashed on August 10, 1792, when, after a thousand years, the French monarchy collapsed. That day, the Parisian National Guard and street fighters, driven wild by the coming of war and suspicions of their king, destroyed the king's Swiss Guards at the Tuileries Palace in Paris. Louis and his family escaped the bloodshed only by taking refuge in the Legislative Assembly. After the king was put in prison, the question facing the Assembly was the same one that had faced the English Parliament in 1649, namely, what to do with a deposed monarch?

If the questions were the same, the contexts were entirely different. The English parliament could, for example, draw on a long history of its own legal and political authority to justify the king's trial. In France, by contrast, the legal and political landscape was tremendouly uncertain. There was no Parliament, and the hated ancien régime law courts had been dismantled.[152] Since their replacements were as yet undetermined, it was unclear from the beginning who had legal authority over the person of the king, or under what law he might be tried. Indeed, the constitution that did exist, reluctantly signed by a chastened Louis XVI in September 1791, seemed to immunize the king against any such trial, since it stipulated that the "person of the King is inviolable and sacred." Only if the king abdicated the throne—whether by explicit renunciation or implicit attack on the republic—was he to be relegated to "the class of citizens [that] can be indicted and judged like other citizens for crimes committed *after his abdication*."[153] Whether he had abdicated; whether his crimes had taken place before or after the abdication; whether he was now a citizen liable to trial: all of these disputed issues were taken up by the National Convention, which replaced the Legislative Assembly in September 1792 in order to rewrite the constitution in the aftermath of the king's fall. Long before it accomplished this task, however, it found itself in the role of political tribunal in the case of the indicted *Citizen Louis Capet.*

Citizenship was, in other words, at the heart of the king's trial. Even Louis recognized this. Unlike Charles I, who refused the terms of the indictment, and confronted his opponents as a *Christus-rex* figure (see chapter 7), Louis never reached for the martyr's crown. Instead, he confronted the Convention on the legal terrain of the Constitution. In that text, his kingship was declared "sacred and inviolable." Once removed he was now a citizen, protected by the law. But this law did not apply—his advocates argued—to the alleged crimes committed *before* his abdication. "In order to judge him according to our institutions, there must be a statute which can be applied to him," argued Charles-François Morisson, "yet there is no law."[154]

For their part, the key promoters and organizers of the king's trial—the Girondin faction of deputies in the National Convention—scorned the royal inviolability, but on similarly constitutional terms. The nation had granted this right through the National Constituent Assembly that had written the 1791 Constitution, and could, therefore, rescind it through the legislature.[155] Having now abdicated, the Girondins continued, the citizen Louis Capet was as vulnerable to indictment and conviction as any other citizen. Their long debates in the National Convention about the fate of citizen Louis Capet thus revolved around technical legal issues: whether the former king could be tried for crimes committed before he abdicated, the nature of royal inviolability, whether the Convention was the proper forum for the trial, how the trial should be conducted, and so forth.

By the late eighteenth century, in short, the ghost of *Christus-rex* that still haunted the seventeenth century had become faded and ragged. Only the Jacobins—the radicals in the Convention—breathed some faint life into it. From the beginning, they opposed the trial, because it made the king *too* ordinary, too much a regular citizen. Legal process assumed that the king enjoyed protections. But the king should not be "judged as an ordinary citizen," the Jacobin firebrand Louis Antoine de Saint Just declared on November 13, but as "*an enemy*." He was "not a citizen before his crime . . . since his crime, he is still less a citizen." There is "no natural bond" between the people and the king, he exclaimed, no justice "common to humanity and Kings." Assassination, "no formality but thirty dagger blows," was the right response to such a tyrant. A people "does not hand down sentences, it hurls down thunderbolts," Robespierre proclaimed in early December.[156] The king's sacrality (if it can be called that) was of a monstrous sort.

Their objections were not, however, rooted in some repressed Christian sensibility. They stemmed rather from their sensitivity to the peculiarities of sentimental citizenship. For once you granted citizenship to the king, did you not also include him in the affective and moral community that made up the nation? The Girondins too were aware of the issue. The moderate Jean-Bapiste Maihle wrote passionately about the "echoing voices of the citizens" who died in the morning of August 10, the "cries of many a new Decius, patriots who, in giving their lives for their country," thirst for vengeance against the king.[157] The king was a citizen, in their view, only in the narrowest legal sense. But the Jacobins suspected that you could not have it both ways. If the deposed king was now a citizen, his voice too might join the lineage of patriots who had died in defense of the *patrie.* "The effect of tyranny," Robespierre insisted, "is to break completely all bonds with the tyrant."[158] And once broken, the king stood outside the polity, no citizen at all.

These uncertainties climaxed when, on January 21, 1793, Louis Capet was brought to the guillotine at the Place de la Revolution in Paris and executed. What ensued was an outpouring of ambivalence. Louis-Marie Prudhomme—the editor of the radical newspaper *Révolutions de Paris*—captured this nicely. On the one hand, he could already imagine the regicide in thoroughly sacrificial terms. The priests "are already looking for place in their calendars" to put Louis XVI among the martyrs, he drolly observed. The people tore his garments, like the Jews in Jerusalem tore those of Christ, *scinderunt vestimenta sua* (John 19), but in a "pure spirit of republicanism." "Look at this little morsel of cloth," grandfathers will say to their petits enfans, and remember how the last tyrant died as a traitor on the scaffold.[159] More gruesome comedy followed, he reported, as citizens clambered atop the guillotine and, with hands like aspergilla, sprinkled their comrades with the blood of Louis Capet. People will say that the blood of Louis Capet is on our heads, one rascal shouted, well, so be it! He "washed his hands many times in our blood! Republicans, the blood of a king brings good luck."[160]

But he also described the events in far more quotidian terms. "Work stopped for a moment" in Paris, Prudhomme remarked, but then "started almost immediately, as if *nothing had even happened.*" Vegetables and milk were sold in the market, he reported, and although citizens sang and celebrated, the civic mood was relaxed. Later, his account grew even more restrained. The execution of Charles I failed to kill the lure of royalty, he cautioned, because he died *as king*. But for Louis Capet, it was a "death as common as the most vile of criminals; it was not his royalty that was punished, but his *guilt.*" He was "alone with his crimes," no one "raised his voice in his favor," no one offered to take his place.[161] Louis died not as a blood sacrifice, not even as a king, but merely as a scoundrel.

Was the king a traitor? an expiatory offering? a criminal? a martyr? The crisis that beset revolutionary citizenship made it hard for Prudhomme to figure out. The Convention was in the middle of an extraordinary political emergency, after all. The 1791 Constitution had been signed *after* the king had attempted to flee France, and had never developed any real political standing. The final collapse of the constitution and the monarchy came just as revolutionaries were fielding armies to fight Austria and Prussia. In the National Convention, Girondin and Jacobin factions disagreed furiously about the war, the trial, and the broader nature of the revolution. Just a few short weeks after the trial, civil war exploded in the western province of Vendée, and the problem of counter-revolution became ever more exigent. In March of 1793, the revolutionary tribunals were established in the name of "revolutionary justice," which aimed both to manage popular violence and to teach people how to become the citizens that the revolution required.[162] When, two months later, Girondin deputies were forcibly ejected by Parisian crowds, and later sentenced to death by the Paris tribunal as false republicans, it became crystal clear that revolutionary citizenship entailed far more than mere political or legal rights. Above all, it was a *moral* project, dependent on the ideal of virtuous community and the willingness to sacrifice all on its behalf that was so central to the republican imagination of the eighteenth century.

No one sensed this as clearly as the Jacobins, who emerged triumphant from the trial of the king. For the Jacobins, the regeneration of political life and virtue were synonymous.[163] It was as an enemy of virtue that Saint-Just condemned Louis Capet, "shadowed in darkness, kings persecuted virtue; but we judge kings before the eyes of all."[164] This shadowy evil tormented Jacobins; there is "no system of tyranny" like the one "built on kindness and the appearance of goodness."[165] "Men of feeling," Saint Just continued, will be tempted to sympathize with kings like this, but, as Rousseau had written long before, "pity for the wicked is a great cruelty to men."[166] The "final proof of devotion" owed the nation, Robespierre declaimed, is "to sacrifice the first natural movements of sensibility to the safety of a great people."[167] What was needed was "public conscience" or "public spirit," that is, the spontaneous upwelling of virtue into public view, inner moral truths made visible to all.[168]

Public demonstrations of virtue (spontaneous or staged) became a signature of Jacobin political life. The first great festival of the Revolution was held already in July 1790, to celebrate the fall of the Bastille. There was no official system of festivals, however, until the Jacobins took power in early 1793. Eager to showcase the nature of republican virtue, they organized a series of monumental events. The Festival of Republican Reunion was held on August 10, 1793, celebrating the new republican Constitution in an eclectic rite that included a gigantic Egyptian-themed statue of nature, from whose breasts water gushed and celebrants drank, as well as revolutionary altars, and funeral pyres.[169] In November, there followed the Festival of Reason, with its statues of Liberty and parades of young women throwing flowers in her honor, and the following June, the Festival of the Supreme Being, to be held in every town in France. Designed by the artist David, the last included a ceremonial burning of the "Hideous Atheism," a monumental statue of Wisdom, Hercules on a pillar, processions, hymns, women holding their babies up to the sun, an enormous mountain built on the Champs de la Réunion, speeches, and civic banquets.[170] What coordinated these eclectic events—and there were hundreds more in the provinces—was the effort to create a new republican citizen, motivated by virtue, sensibility, solidarity, and sacrifice. "Liberty and virtue together sprang from the breast of divinity," Robespierre declared at the Festival, let us "give to the world the example of republican virtues . . . our blood runs for the cause of humanity: this is our prayer; these are our sacrifices; this is the cult that we offer."[171]

The result was a great overflowing of the sacrificial imagination. Jacobin speeches endlessly eulogized the blood they were prepared to offer (or had offered) for the cause of nation and humanity. The cult of the Jacobin Michel Le Pellietier, assassinated on the eve of the *ci-devant* king's execution, prompted an extraordinary public funeral where the murder weapon, "sanctified by the blood of a patriot," was displayed alongside the Declaration of the Rights of Man. The corpse itself was laid on the pedestal of a deposed statue of Louis XIV, and Jacques-Louis David's portrait of Le Peletier was hung alongside that of Jean-Paul Marat, two martyrs of liberty displayed "in perpetuity" in the hall of the Convention (fig. 10.2).[172] "Heaven . . . calls me perhaps to trace with my blood the route which must lead my country to happiness and to Liberty," Robespierre announced in 1792, "I accept with transports that sweet and glorious destiny."[173] Two years later, he got his wish. "Who am I? . . . a slave to liberty, a living martyr of the republic," Robespierre declared the night before his arrest and execution at the Place de la Révolution in July 1794.[174]

This imagination had its dark side. The *manes* of republican martyrs—the ghosts or shades of the special dead regularly invoked by Jacobin orators—had at times a terrible thirst for vengeance. The "bleeding shades," the "plaintive shades," the "sacred shades" of August 10 and other scenes of revolutionary violence were among the spectral accusers of Louis Capet at his trial. The "day of vengeance has arrived" for these sacred dead, declared the deputy Antoine Girard at his regicide vote. Revolutionary firebrand Camille Demoulins cried for the immediate execution of the

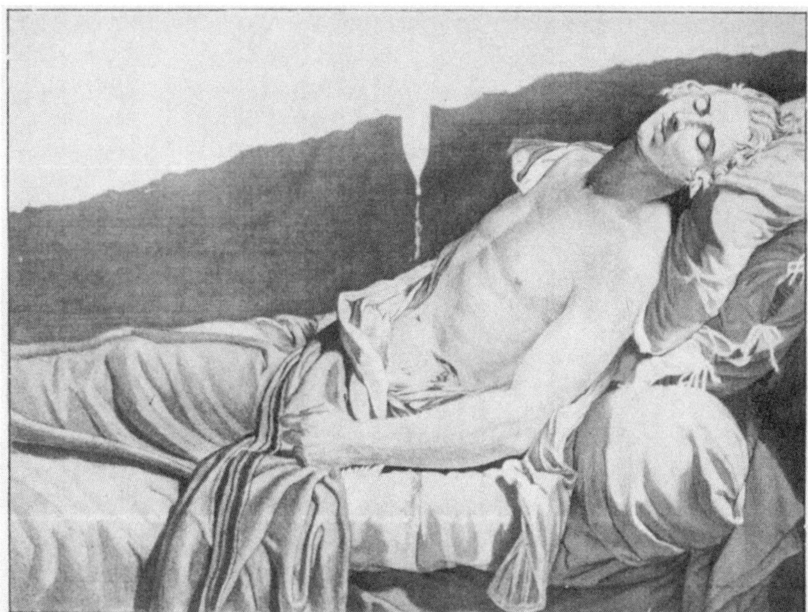

FIGURE 10.2. Engraving after Jacques-Louis David, *The Death of Louis Michel Le Peletier de Saint-Fargeau*, 1793. Original lost. *Source*: Aristide Déy, *Histoire de la ville et du comté de Saint-Fargeau, Perriquet et Rouillé* (Paris, 1856). Courtesy of the Getty Research Institute.

king "to appease the shades of one hundred thousand citizens he caused to perish." After the execution, new shades, among them Marat, were hungry for more blood. May the blood of his assassin "be poured to satisfy the shades of the martyr of liberty," wrote the Republican Society of Tonnerre. When the Comte de Custine, general in the revolutionary army, was executed in August 1793, it was commemorated with this print: "to the *manes* of our brothers sacrificed by the traitor . . . his impure blood waters our fields."[175] The echo of the French battle anthem *La Marseillaise* was doubtless deliberate (fig. 10.3).

It is a mistake to view this as the "atavistic return" of "Old Regime habits" among the revolutionaries, and little better to describe it as an outcome of their "profound spirituality." It was the all-too-human ideal of citizenship, grown in the ethical and political matrix of eighteenth-century republicanism, that put a sacrificial frame around dying for the revolution. The revolutionary *manes* did not so much reproduce "an ancient tradition of believing in the immortality of the soul."[176] Rather, citizen-revolutionaries saw themselves in sacrificial terms *while they were still*

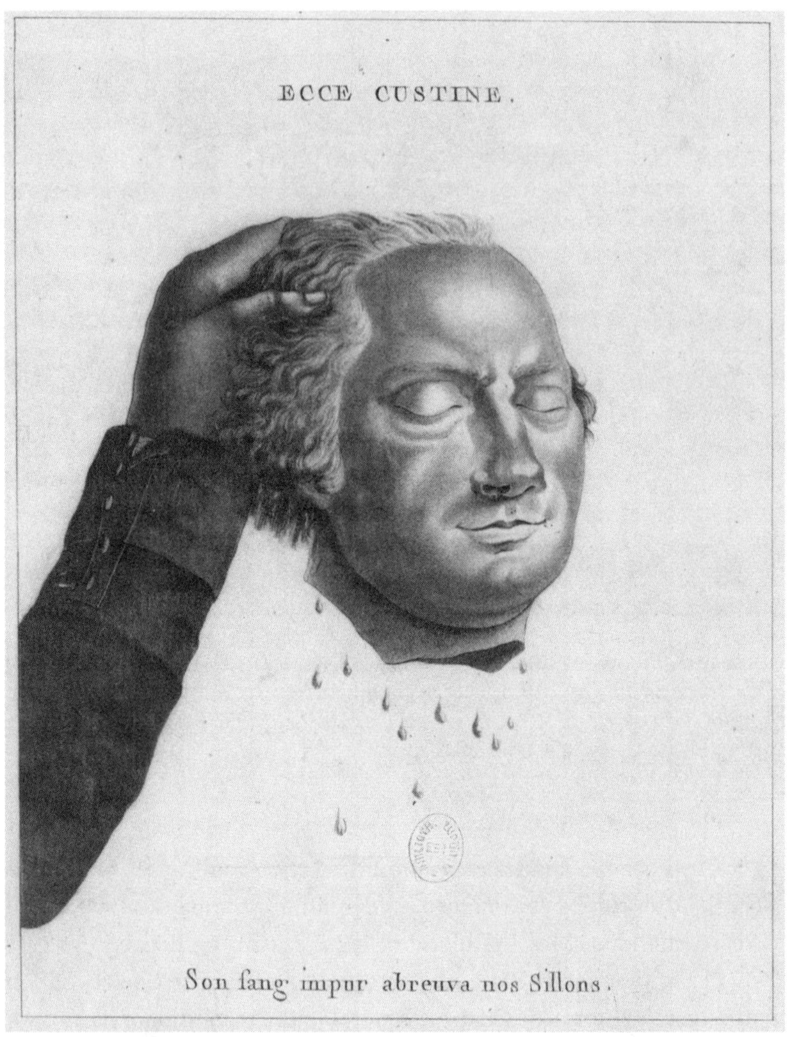

FIGURE 10.3. *The Execution of the Comte de Custine*, 1793. Courtesy of the Bibliothèque nationale de France, Département Estampes et Photographie.

alive. Revolutionary sacrifice was a wild experiment, combining things sacred and profane, Roman and Christian, ancient and modern. Pouring out blood to feed the special dead would have been familiar to any reader of the *Odyssey*; the Roman *manes* were no less bloodthirsty than the French republican ones.[177] But if we discern in revolutionary martyrs and *manes* echoes of Christian and pagan pasts, we also detect something different, their turn *ad saeculum* toward a human world bound horizontally together by shared ideals of citizenship, virtue, and sacrifice.

Conclusion: History and the Deep Logic of Sacrifice

The execution of Louis XVI casts a long interpretive shadow over the revolution and its afterlives. Almost immediately the Savoyard aristocrat and Catholic reactionary Joseph de Maistre saw it as the secret of modern liberal politics, founded in sacrifices and violence that it can neither stop nor justify. He lamented the innocent king in his 1797 *Considerations on France*, both a victim criminally murdered, and a vengeful Christ-figure whose death would "cost torrents of French blood."[178] Later, in his 1821 *St. Petersburg Dialogues*, he grew even more extreme. "Following [Louis XVI], millions of innocents were harvested and gathered *into the granary* by this dreadful revolution," the first sacrifice unleashing a torrent of blood unconstrained by the Gospel of Christ. As he colorfully wrote, "whenever the true God is not known and served by virtue of an express revelation, men will always sacrifice men and often eat them."[179]

Speculations like this have enjoyed a strangely enduring afterlife. Thus, for example, one political scientist describes the regicide as the "violent founding act" of the republic, in which revolutionaries "transferred the unified, transcendent, and sacred power of the king to the people." Revolutionaries "subject[ed] the king to a sacrificial process" to "capture" the king's "sacred power," making him a ritual scapegoat and co-opting "Catholic purification and initiation rites" for their own purposes.[180] Most influentially, the historian Lynn Hunt describes the execution as a "ritual sacrifice," pointing again to the words of revolutionary journalist Louis Prudhomme: "The blood of Louis Capet, shed by the blade of the law on 21 January 1793, cleanses us of a stigma of 1300 years . . . Liberty resembles that divinity of the Ancients which one cannot make auspicious and favorable except by offering it in sacrifice the life of a great culprit."[181] Here we discover the "psychosexual foundation of the political order," she suggests with Sigmund Freud in mind, in which killing the Father and cleansing the community of guilt produces a new republic founded in the blood of Louis XVI.[182] Whether rooted in theology, anthropology, or psychology, a deep "logic" of sacrifice is essential, in these accounts, to the dynamics of political foundation.[183]

Arguments like these are more metaphysics than history, however. It takes serious gymnastics to turn the eclectic views of a Prudhomme into a coherent "theory" of the revolution, for example, let alone the modern republic.[184] More seriously, such views also depend on an unbelievable story about the Christian imagination. They suggest, for example, that once upon a time, there was a coherent Christian theology of sacrifice, rather than, as we have seen, an endless field of struggle over what sacrifice was and should be. Even worse, they suggest that the Christian imagination existed somehow outside of time, that it forms a spiritual "foundation" that survives even the most dramatic historical transformations. Whether we speak about the "transfer of sacrality," or declare that "the social edifice rests entirely on the cross," or insist that there is "no significant difference" between pre-revolutionary "royal religion . . . and the sacralized politics of nationalism," we are trafficking in what the philosopher Hans Blumenberg would call a "substantialist" view of spiritual things.[185]

But if we recognize that there is *no substance of spiritual things*, no repository of the sacred to be exhausted or preserved or transferred, a new story is possible. Religion and the sacred—no less than the political and the ethical—are constant creations. Older forms of life are recycled and repurposed, their material pressed into service for the new. These new forms supply people with new ways of imagining their lives. They offer new horizons of expectations, new forms of solidarity, new ethical priorities, new distinctions between sacred and profane. They are nevertheless *heteronomous*, that is, they are haunted by the histories they have inherited. *Ex nihilo nihil fit*—nothing comes from nothing, whether religious or secular.

Republicanism was just such a new form of life in the eighteenth century. On the one hand, it affirmed an ethical and political vision that challenged the hierarchies of the ancien régime, its three estates, its society of orders, its crowns and mitres. Sensibility, sympathy, society, the civil, the public: these creatures of the Enlightenment created an ideal world of affections and obligations beyond hierarchy. This was a secular world, in the sense that it *rejected* Christian political and social organizations as part of a world best left behind. But it was also a secular world in the sense that it *incorporated* aspects of its religious surround, putting them to new ethical and political uses.

Political sacrifice in the Enlightenment thus slipped the chains of an older Christian imagination, one that reserved its privileges for the very few, the heroes and martyrs of the faith. It became thereby something new, the older archive of ideas and practices now democratized for new uses. Cato and Christ were among its components; so too the Roman Decii, the ancient martyrs, the burghers of Calais, and others. Sacrifice helped assign a value to virtue in an age of self-interest. It affirmed the shared set of affections and obligations that sustain an ethical and political community. It defined the limits of that community, those to whom we owe enough that we might sacrifice ourselves on their behalf. It sustained a new ideal of citizenship, no longer simply a set of legal entitlements, but a rich and demanding moral project. And it shaped the modern meanings of war and political violence, both for the age of revolutions and for the age of nineteenth-century nationalism, whose own imaginative projects transformed and repurposed once again those older archives of sacrifice.

"Deep logic" stories of sacrifice thus do serious disservice, in my view, to the history of the sacrificial imagination in the eighteenth century. And yet they are interesting for all that. For they are *themselves* symptomatic of what sacrifice will become in the nineteenth century, when new disciplines like anthropology, psychology, and sociology will take it up as one of the central puzzles of human life. Freud was no de Maistre, after all, and it was with new tools that he and others imagined new roles for sacrifice in the making of human instititutions. It is here that we bring this book to a close, then, with the vexed efforts to theorize sacrifice in secular terms—to develop *new* logics and histories of sacrifice—that together engendered some of the most ingenious and creative work in the modern human sciences.

CHAPTER ELEVEN

The Heteronomy of the Secular

SACRIFICE AND THE EUROPEAN SCIENCES OF MAN

> *. . . History may be servitude,*
> *History may be freedom. See, now they vanish,*
> *The faces and places, with the self which, as it could, loved them,*
> *To become renewed, transfigured, in another pattern.*
>
> —T. S. ELIOT, "LITTLE GIDDINGS"[1]

ON THE EVE of World War I, the Russian composer Igor Stravinsky dreamt of ancient gods, pagan ancestors, and a sacrificial virgin who "danced herself to death" to propitiate the sky.[2] The "Great Sacrifice"—as the ballet *Rites of Spring* was initially titled—was performed in Paris in May 1913, to the astonishment of its audience.[3] Vaslav Nijinsky's choreography was upsetting, the stomping, whirling, and slapping that bore little resemblance to the balletic *plié*. The music too was overwhelming, "eccentric and demonic," as one reviewer wrote, with bassoons playing "like perforated skulls in the nimble fingers of cannibal improvisers."[4] It projected, wrote another, the "savage energy of a youthful humanity not yet sundered from the umbilical cord that unites them with Mother Earth, and the force of the dark, ill-defined sensations that possess them."[5]

Over the following years, other savage energies sundered much of Europe's young humanity from its mortal life, the machines of twentieth-century war inspiring different and bleaker poetries of sacrifice. But for Stravinsky and other modernists in 1913, the blood rites of ancient Scythia offered a fountain of youth for a dilapidated Russian and European culture. The dancing maiden, under Nijinsky's direction, leaped high and pounded the earth, swirling in jerky ecstasy until her collapse. The waiting ancestors gathered her up, and lifted her high to the waiting gods. From an ancient and darker past, so this tableau imagined, might awaken a new springtime for humanity.

In June 1913, meanwhile, at the Vienna Psycho-Analytical Society, Sigmund Freud presented the final paper of what became *Totem and Taboo*. He too was fascinated by sacrifice, and by the obscure ways that past and present are entangled. The religious psyche was formed already in the deep time of humanity, he declared, when men first worshiped and then sacrificed the totem animal in whose name the earliest clans took shape. This sacrifice transformed early man from a "patriarchal horde" into a fraternal clan founded on a "common complicity" in the killing of the totem animal.[6]

Naturally, for Freud, the animal was not really an animal at all. It was both the tribal *god* and the tribal *father*, whose violent rule the sons determined to overthrow. The murder of God-the-Father became, in the twisted ways of the human psyche, the regular sacrifices of religion, repeated both to commemorate primitive violence and to cover it beneath the cloak of piety. "The importance which is everywhere, without exception, ascribed to sacrifice," Freud remarked, "lies in the fact that it offers satisfaction to the father for the outrage inflicted on him in the same act in which the deed is commemorated." And the memory of this "first great act of sacrifice" never fades away, recurring under new guises in every religious culture.[7] Christianity is only unusual for how explicitly these substitutions took place: the death of the Son placated the wrathful father and, in so doing, took His place on the throne of Heaven.

Composer and psychoanalyst: for each, sacrifice shaped a common imaginative terrain. This was an imagination turned *ad saeculum*, that is, deliberately confining its concerns to what was taken to be a common human world. Over the course of the nineteenth century, this common human world came to be described with different tools. The post-Enlightenment human sciences paid attention to shared practices and beliefs (ethnography, anthropology, comparative religion), human institutions (sociology), and mental structures and habits (psychology). Across these, sacrifice stood as both *explanans* and *explanandum*, something to be explained by, and also an explanation of, the deep structures of human religion, culture, society, and history.

This secular sacrificial imagination stood in uneasy relationship to a past understood as Christian. On the one hand, it was imagined *against* this past, by new human sciences antagonistic to theological concerns and questions. Religion is an "infantile prototype," and its "store of ideas" born from "man's need to make his helplessness tolerable," Freud wrote in his 1927 *Future of an Illusion*, a dreamworld from which the psychoanalyst hopes to awaken humanity.[8] On the other hand, the sacrifices of the nineteenth-century human sciences also were intimately connected with the imaginative archive we've explored in this book. In this sense, the sciences of sacrifice repeated figures, topics, and instincts developed deep in the Christian past.

What shall we make of these repetitions? From one perspective, they are a problem. Like the reforming Christians who looked back at the early church and were dismayed to discover how much it shared with the religions it abandoned, what we call "modernity" tends to be uncomfortable with its debts to the past. This is true in general. Ever since the famous eighteenth-century "quarrel of the ancients and the moderns," originality and autonomy have been hallmarks of a certain kind of modern sensibility.[9] Repeating the past shows dependence, not autonomy. And this is specifically true with respect to religion. After all, for the modern human sciences, another name for the past we must overcome is religion itself. The value of philosophy, as Immanuel Kant wrote in his 1798 *Conflict of the Faculties*, lay in its freedom from the subordination that afflicts theology, beholden as it is to church and government. That the human sciences might echo the imaginative world of theology might demonstrate not only their bad faith, in this view, but their illegitimacy as ways of knowing.

Yet echoes are never just more of the same. When a pious poet weaves a biblical verse into her work, she both repeats *and* distinguishes between Scripture and poetry. Parody and blasphemy are, for that matter, no less forms of repetition than appreciation or praise. When the apostle Paul quoted the Hebrew Psalms and Prophets, it was an act of both homage and violence, the *spolia* of the Jews turned Christian trophy.[10] The power of Giovanni Bellini's *Blood of the Redeemer* (see fig. 5.7) lies in its resetting of ancient sacrifice in a new imaginative frame. Culture itself might be understood as thick structures of repetition, in which older forms are repurposed for new imaginative work.[11]

This final chapter explores these dynamics as they expand toward our own era. It brings to a close our story of the secular imagination: its emergence from a world of Christian polemic, its reinvention of the Christian sacrificial archive, and its organization of the unruly Enlightenment experiments with imagining sacrifice *ad saeculum*. And it does with particular references to those European sciences of man, organized in the nineteenth century as new ways of describing and knowing human experience. It takes three case studies as exemplary: new philosophies of sacrifice, from Kant to Kierkegaard; the emergence of the "higher criticism" of the Hebrew Bible and the afterlives of Hebrew sacrifice; and the early disciplines of ethnography, anthropology, and sociology, which collectively put sacrifice at the heart of human religion and culture. As again, it will be that unsettling ambivalence—that sense of a savage world abandoned yet hauntingly present—that will invest sacrifice with so much imaginative power.

The Scandal of Sacrifice: Philosophy and the Ethics of the Negative

Then Abraham put forth his hand,
and took the knife to slay his son.

GEN. 22.10

The Dutch painter Rembrandt was a master of the dramatic moment (see fig. 11.1 and color plate 8). His 1635 painting *Sacrifice of Isaac* captured an Abraham interrupted, his enormous hand covering, almost crushing the face of his son as he held him down in preparation for slaughter. So committed was the father to fulfill the command to offer his son as burnt offering in the land of Moriah, and so shocking the angel's appearance, that Abraham let fall his knife in surprise. This is not a typological painting, where Isaac's near-death figures the real sacrifice of the Son on the Cross. Even the ram, "caught in a thicket by his horns" (Gen. 22.13) to relieve Abraham of his grim task, is barely visible in the scene. Instead Rembrandt forces his viewers to confront directly the terror of the *Akedah*, Abraham trapped between his obligations to his son and to the Lord.

In a sense, Rembrandt painted the Abraham that Enlightenment skeptics later detested, an Abraham willing to "slaughter his own son . . . contrary to every expectation," as Voltaire put it in his 1764 *Philosophical Dictionary*.[12] "Is it agreeable to the Character of the infinitely good and wise God, to give a Command which at once dissolves two of the strongest Ties in Nature, the reciprocal Affections of Parents and Children," asked one anonymous eighteenth-century pamphleteer, and the clear answer was *no*.[13] Such sentiments got their most powerful formulation late in the century, in the moral philosophy of Immanuel Kant. In two works from the 1790s—*Religion Within the Bounds of Mere Reason* (1793) and the *Conflict of the Faculties* (1798)—Kant explained how terribly Abraham's sacrifice violated moral and religious obligations. Key to Kant's rational

FIGURE 11.1. Rembrandt, *Sacrifice of Isaac*, 1635. Alte Pinakothek, Bayerische Staatsgemäldesammlungen. Munich, Germany. bpk Bildagentur / Alte Pinakothek / Art Resource, NY.

ethics, after all, were the principles of *autonomy*, that moral obligations must be self-imposed, and *universality*, capable of being extended to everyone in all circumstances. Abraham violated both, subordinating himself to another and (almost) performing a deed that, if universalized, would be monstrous.[14]

Suppose that one morning a man—call him Abraham—woke up and heard God telling him to slaughter his only son. How was he supposed to respond? First of all, Kant suggested, he should have asked whether this was *really* the voice of God. In the best of circumstances, after all, it is "quite impossible" to apprehend God with mere human senses. But surely a person can know when "the voice he hears is *not* God's," that is, when the voice commands a moral atrocity:

> [Take], as an example, the myth of the sacrifice that Abraham was going to make by butchering and burning his only son at God's command (the poor child, without knowing it, even brought the wood for the fire). Abraham should have replied to this supposedly divine voice: "That I ought not to kill my good son is quite certain. But that you, this apparition, are God—of that I am not certain, and never can be, not even if this voice rings down to me from . . . heaven."[15]

What had been traditionally Abraham's virtue—his immediate and relentless response to God's command—marked instead a "consummate expression of heteronomy," the self-subordination to the monstrous demands of another.[16] In this sense, the sacrifice of Isaac supplied a *negative* moral maxim. It showed what must at all costs be avoided in the interests of human dignity.

That sacrifice stood as reason's dark opponent is not a new view, of course. It was there already in the ancient world, and was a staple in Christian polemics against paganism and Judaism. If sacrifice cleanses sin, the *Hebrews* author mocked, then why do the Hebrews keep sinning (and sacrificing)? Sacrifice epitomized what writers, from Cicero to Hume, called superstition, that is, the *lack* of reasonability in religious duties.

Throughout, however, *self*-sacrifice retained much of its normative value. This was true of even as skeptical a writer as Diderot, as we saw. Virtue is a "sacrifice of the self," he wrote in 1766, the suppression of desire and interest in the name of something higher and better. For Kant, this was more troublesome. As he saw it, moral duty required the sacrifice of desire. And yet it was easy to imagine how self-sacrifice might *itself* become desirable. People routinely deny themselves, after all, out of no higher feelings than pride, or spite, or shame. Nor did self-sacrifice necessarily avoid the problem of heteronomy. Imagine that God had asked Abraham to kill himself, for example, rather than Isaac. The problem of heteronomy would remain, Abraham still unsure whether to regard the voice as a divine, diabolical, or simply a delusion.[17]

We leave Kant's complexities to the philosophers. For our purposes, we simply note how sacrifice became, in the early nineteenth century, a subject of distinctive philosophical attention. In part, this had to do with the broader shifts in the organization of knowledge, especially for Kant and the philosophical traditions that grew up in his wake. Although the "conflict of the faculties," as Kant described it, had been at play at least since Spinoza, the late eighteenth century saw a new phase in philosophy's struggle to establish itself as the queen of the sciences. This entailed not only a struggle for institutional emancipation from the church (Kant's two essays were both written under the threat of ecclesiastical censorship). It also involved the explicit philosophical appropriation of an intellectual terrain seen as once belonging to the theologians. Abraham's sacrifice was a sharp example, a traditional figure of faith extracted from Scripture and translated into a negative ethical precept. It became, in short, a figure of the *secular* imagination.

This figure was not invented *ex nihilo*, however, but rather exploited interpretive possibilities latent in the archives of Christian sacrifice. There too sacrifice was a figure of ambivalence, alternately pious and profane; alien and familiar; ancient and modern. Christ crucified was the *skandalon*, so wrote the apostle Paul to the Corinthians, the "stumbling block to Jews and foolishness to gentiles" (1 Cor. 1.23). Abraham's sacrifice was hardly less scandalous—murder and eternal life join hands on the altar at Moriah. Indeed, these scandals often merged: "In the city of Jerusalem, at the tomb of Christ, there is the site of Calvary," wrote a German pilgrim in the sixth century, "where Abraham offered his son as a holocaust."[18] For Luther, Abraham both embraced and resolved the scandal: "though I am killing my son, I have him alive." This interpretive reversal made Abraham an exemplary Christian figure, in Luther's view, witnessing the "unique teaching of the church."[19] By binding Calvary and Moriah into *one* figure—the near-death of Isaac resolved by the death and resurrection of Christ—the scandal of Abraham became a reassuring figure of faith.

Like Rembrandt, however, Kant left the scandal of Abraham exposed. The same behaviors that once made the patriarch a paragon of trust now made him monstrous. From the Christian archives, then, something new and stranger was born, a horror that philosophical ethics felt compelled to unravel. For the story of Abraham, in Kant's reading, did not point to any higher truth. Rather, it stood as a bleak warning about human pride and weakness, the ease with which we ignore the quiet voice of conscience, and are seduced by heteronomy.

Christianity was not the only means of resolving the scandal of sacrifice, however. It was no less liable to *secular* resolutions, its negativity transformed into something of value. From almost the beginning of his writerly life, for example, Georg Friedrich Hegel appreciated the possibilities that sacrifice might offer to philosophical projects. Already in his "Tübingen Essay" from 1793, the young seminarian discovered especially in pagan sacrifice a "solemn awe of the holy being," a sense of dependency on the gods critical for the intensification of piety and social cohesion.[20] Schiller's "Gods of Greece" poem rang in the background, perhaps, or the poetry of Hegel's young friend Friedrich Hölderlin, who sang hymns to the gods of Olympus.

Later, in Hegel's 1807 *Phenomenology of Spirit*, sacrifice lost this whiff of nostalgia. Instead, its very negativity was refashioned into a powerful force advancing the human spirit.[21] Negation was integral to the story the *Phenomenology* told, of the "path of natural consciousness" journeying toward "true knowledge," its purification "for the life of the Spirit." Just as the ascetic denies himself in the name of spiritual progress, so does the soul realize itself through instances of negation. Awareness of self first emerges through the violent negation of another, a "trial by death," as Hegel wrote, such that by "staking one's life . . . freedom [might be] won."[22]

What Hegel called "determinate negation" was thus fundamental to his method of dialectics, where things antithetical to consciousness—sacrifice, struggle, conflict, violence, and so forth—energize its development and spiritual progress. By surrendering oneself to the power of another, for example, through an "actual sacrifice" of self, consciousness also realizes that it has *power* over itself, and "obtain[s] relief from its *misery*." Indeed, it is through this dynamic that reason itself is discovered, a universal principle that exists both beyond and inside the self.[23]

What was true for individual consciousness was also true for the human species, a view that Hegel developed in the *Phenomenology* and the later *Lectures on the Philosophy of Religion* (1821–31). Seen as an anthropological practice, sacrifice emerges at the stage of "religion in the form of art," when "the self gives itself the consciousness of the divine Being descending to it from remoteness."[24] In the beginning, Hegel argued, the divine and the human were entwined. For early humanity, everything was a form of worship, since worship itself did not "constitute something distinctive, set apart from the rest of life."[25] But at some point there developed what he called "Cult," that is, a way of simultaneously recognizing the otherness of the divine, and keeping it close at hand.

Sacrifice was the first cult, "the pure *surrender* of possession which the owner, apparently without profit whatever to himself, pours away or lets rise up in smoke." A determinate negation of ordinary life, the first sacrifice announced that we are neither nature nor god. Rather, we *take* from nature and *give* to the gods, and thereby establish our place beyond both. In this surrender, we carve the gods out of the world. Before sacrifice, divinity saturated everything. After sacrifice, "divine Being in its immediacy . . . Perishes," transformed into an abstract and distant being, Zeus or Bacchus. With the creation of the gods, human beings too achieve their independence. The destruction of the animal is only the first phase of the sacrifice after all. Next comes "the preparation of the offering for a meal, the feast that cheats the act out of its negative significance."[26] After killing comes the eating: human beings thereby gather and form *themselves* into distinctive communities.[27]

In surrendering what is precious, in short, we come to possess ourselves. A history that is distinguishably human starts here. Sacrifice leaves human and divine beings each free to pursue their own distinct destinies. This history culminated again in sacrifice, when what Hegel called "Spirit" learned "how to sacrifice [it]self" at the end of its journey into self-knowledge. This sacrifice, the *Phenomenology* concluded, "is the externalization in which Spirit displays the process of its becoming Spirit in the form of *free contingent happening*," a final renunciation that coordinated the Spirit with both nature and history.[28] The history of sacrifice, in an important sense, was the history of history.

In Hegel, then, dialectics resolved the scandal of sacrifice. Here the simultaneous intimacy of, and conflict between, the Christian and secular imaginations are hard to overlook. On the one hand, the Crucifixion looks like a model for dialectics, destruction converted into higher creation. On the other hand, it is also just an *example* of dialectics, that is, a historical or figurative rendering of a process much bigger than the events on Calvary. The dialectic of sacrifice did not end with Christ, after all, but with *human* transcendence. The violence and irrationality of sacrifice—the giving without the receiving—is only apparent, for by giving we are assured the greatest gifts of all, human freedom and autonomy.

Sacrifice entered the German philosophical lexicon as something that must be overcome, its negativity either excluded or turned toward human benefit. This was no less true in England, where new moral sciences of utilitarianism struggled endlessly either to domesticate or eliminate sacrifice in its ethical calculations. "Private ethics has happiness for its end," observed Jeremy Bentham in 1823, and the "only interests which a man at all times and upon all occasions" should consult "are his own."[29] The sacrifice of happiness for something else seems an irrational, if not an unethical, position from this point of view. Later, John Stuart Mill confronted the issue squarely in his 1863 *Utilitarianism*, noting that while utilitarian morality recognizes "in human beings the *power* of sacrificing their own greatest good for the good of others," it "refuses to admit that the sacrifice is *itself* good." It applauds only the sacrifice that increases "the sum total of happiness."[30]

By the later nineteenth century, this urge to rationalize sacrifice was common. In his 1871 *Descent of Man*, for example, Charles Darwin took up what became the "altruism" problem in evolutionary theory. How the "most noble of all attributes," sacrificial behavior, could advance the evolutionary success of an individual was simply puzzling.[31] Inside the biological sciences, the theories of group selection made popular in the early twentieth century started as efforts to solve this problem. Outside the biological sciences, meanwhile, evolutionary human scientists turned this altruism issue into a general defense of religious institutions. In his 1894 *Social Evolution*, the British sociologist Benjamin Kidd discovered that the "social system [was] founded on a form of religious belief," that is, the conviction that sacrifice was essential to group life. Meanwhile the Finnish moral philosopher Edward Westermarck (1862–1939) suggested that human sacrifice was a "method of life-insurance," a developmental advantage for all human moral communities.[32] What is today called "effective altruism" continues this effort to rationalize sacrifice, to translate its apparent excesses and costs to the ultimate benefit of humanity.[33]

Such rationalizations, such efforts to abolish heteronomy from human affairs, also elevated sacrifice into modernity's dark double, however. Already for the conservative Savoyard Joseph de Maistre, writing in the wake of the French Revolution, the persistence of blood sacrifice shattered all modern pretensions of rationality. More richly, however, it was the Dane Søren Kierkegaard who discovered in the *Akedah* an alternative to the "mercantile soul" of the modern world.[34]

"Abraham I cannot understand," Kierkegaard wrote in his 1843 *Fear and Trembling*, "I can learn nothing from him except to be amazed."[35] He had no interest in resolving the apparent monstrosity of Abraham, so obedient to God that he would murder his beloved son. The monstrosity was precisely the point. Modern ethics—Kantian, Hegelian, or utilitarian—subordinates individual acts to general rules. But Abraham destroys the rules. "In the moment Abraham is about to sacrifice Isaac," Kierkegaard tells us:

> the ethical expression for what he is doing is: he hates Isaac. But if he actually hates Isaac, he can rest assured that God does not demand this of him . . . He must love Isaac with his whole soul . . . only then can he *sacrifice* him; for it is indeed his love for Isaac that makes his act a sacrifice by its paradoxical contrast to his love for God.[36]

Love universally demands we sacrifice ourselves for another. But Abraham did the opposite. *Because* he loved Isaac, he was asked (and agreed) to kill him. The more he loved Isaac, however, the more terribly he violated his ethical obligations. Yet only by loving Isaac could what Abraham planned to do even *be* a sacrifice, rather than simply an act of murder.

Worse still, Abraham did not even know *why* he should slaughter his beloved son. Tragic heroes like the Greek Agamemnon and the Hebrew Jephthah killed their children for a higher purpose, whether the conquest of Troy or the destruction of the Ammonites. Abraham simply heard a command, and obeyed it. This command vitiated the promise that God himself had made, however, that Abraham and his posterity would be as numberless "as the dust of the earth" (Gen. 13.16). Abraham faced his dreadful decision alone, in other words, comforted neither by God, ethics, or hope of the future. "One cannot weep over Abraham," Kierkegaard wrote, "one approaches him with a *horror religiosus*."[37]

The horror of Abraham reveals, however, the truth of faith. A faith where Abraham was *guaranteed* the substitution of the ram would, after all, be a weak faith indeed. Abraham had to "act by virtue of the absurd," in a space beyond calculation of interest, and beyond certainty that what he was about to do was not a terrible crime. This "knight of faith," as Kierkegaard called him, had to place his own feeble judgment "higher than the universal."[38] In Abraham's sacrifice, then, Kierkegaard discovered the weakness of the modern soul, confident in its own autonomy and rationality.

Sacrifice thus came to play a double role, as it long had in Christianity, something both abandoned and conserved. Heroic efforts to exclude it inspired no less heroic efforts to recall it to mind. So a philosophical counter-tradition extended from de Maistre to Kierkegaard to the late nineteenth century revolutionary socialist Georges Sorel, who saw in sacrificial violence a means to "regenerate morality" in an age of bourgeois decadence.[39] The same urge returned in writers like the idiosyncratic French "excremental philosopher" Georges Bataille, whose 1930s secret society *Acéphale* proposed (it was rumored) to carry out a human sacrifice in order to liberate the primitive from its modern shackles.[40] "The filthy aspects of the torn-apart body guarantee the totality of disgust where life subsides," Bataille wrote ca. 1933, the blood of sacrifice supplying the energy for a resurrected self and society.[41] For him and others, the negativity of sacrifice consisted in its ostensible irrationalism, the eruption of violence into the smooth operations of bourgeois liberalism and capitalism.

Hebrew Sacrifice and the German Sciences of the Higher Criticism

That it was an ancient Jewish patriarch who provoked such controversies in the moral sciences was no accident. For centuries, sacrifice had held Jew and Christian together in tense intimacy. Christianity had (it claimed) superseded the bloody sacrifices and fetishistic legalism of the Jews, but then wove the Levitical temple service into the fabric of its theology, liturgy, art, and poetry. This complex structure slowly came apart over the seventeenth and eighteenth centuries, and the Hebrew Bible—and with it, Jews, ancient and modern—became ever stranger for European readers.[42] As it did, a new secular science of sacrifice arose within the walls of biblical criticism.

Already in the eighteenth century, the normative value of the Hebrew Bible was fading. Enlightenment critiques of clericalism and intolerance often took aim at its supposedly primitive and theocratic peoples. Voltaire, for example, looked for the deep roots of clerical prejudice in the (supposed) savagery of the ancient Hebrews. "The sacrifice of human victims was customary among the Jews," he remarked in his article on Abraham, a piece of exemplary barbarism for a people (he wrote) "descended from parricidal and idolatrous forefathers."[43] He was not alone in this. Rationalist theologians began to dismiss more emphatically the moral value of the Hebrew Bible for Christian readers, seeing in it a superstitious book for a backward people.[44] The "vital conceptual space of that which is mostly deeply antithetical to reason," as Adam Sutcliffe has remarked, "was occupied above all by the Jew."[45]

By the early nineteenth century, a new "liberal" Protestantism—pioneered in German lands by, among others, the Berlin theologian Friedrich Schleiermacher—turned this critical project to more positive theological ends. This took the form of a latter day Gnosticism, a new, self-sufficient Christian theology liberated from the shackles of the Hebrew

Bible. Schleiermacher proposed the "complete abandonment" of the "traditional proof of Christian doctrines through Old Testament passages," for example, effectively the abandonment of figural, prophetic, and typological readings of the Hebrew Bible.[46] As he put it in 1811, "to include the Jewish codex in the [Christian] canon is to see Christianity as an extension of Judaism, and contradicts the idea of the canon."[47]

What was to become of the Hebrew Bible in this new imaginative terrain? One answer came from the biblical scholars, who began to make the Hebrew Bible into a monument of philological and historical inquiry. Already in 1753, the French scholar Jean Astruc discovered in the book of Genesis two textual layers distinguishable by the different names of God used by the historical communities that produced them. By century's end, this project had broadened to compass the entire Hebrew Bible. In the preface to his *Introduction to the Old Testament* (1787, 2nd ed.), the Jena professor of Oriental languages, Johann Gottfried Eichhorn, gave these efforts the name that remains today: "the higher criticism."[48]

In theory, the higher criticism aimed to reconstruct the "history of the culture and enlightenment of an ancient people" from its literature. The problem with Israel, however, was that its literature was unreliable. The disastrous fall of the ancient Hebrew state and temple dispersed a once vibrant literary tradition. What we know as the Hebrew Bible is simply the "detritus" of this tradition, Eichhorn observed, the "fragments" of the materials gathered in the wake of Israel's first destruction.[49] Given that we can trust neither the text of the Hebrew Bible, nor the history that it purports to represent, what should we do?

One searching answer came from Schleiermacher's colleague at the newly founded University of Berlin, the theologian Wilhelm de Wette. De Wette *embraced* the fragmentation, pioneering the view that still dominates liberal biblical criticism, namely, that what we call the Hebrew Bible is a collage. It is a set of texts collected from many different eras, edited many times, and assembled long centuries after the events they describe.[50]

This approach rested on a bedrock thesis about ancient Israel. Other ancient peoples were interested in many things: nature, poetry, politics, and philosophy. But *religion alone* mattered to the Hebrews; it was "the flower and the fruit" of their history, the means by which an "insignificant nation of Jews elevated itself to a universal-historical rank." For ancient Israel, "*nothing* was more important and noteworthy" than its "temple and cult."[51] The text of the Hebrew Bible was thus a monument to Israel's maniacal documentation of the worship proper to God.

For the historian of the Bible, this mania was invaluable for it conserved the wildly different pictures of "temple and cult" found in various epochs. These differences were most evident in the ways that the Hebrew Bible described sacrifice. Scripture recounted the building of Solomon's temple twice, for example. In Kings, the author reports that "three times a year Solomon used to offer up burnt offerings and peace offerings upon the altar which he built to the Lord, burning incense to the Lord. So he finished the house" (1 Kings 9.25). Nearly the same story appears in 2 Chronicles:

> Then Solomon offered up burnt offerings to the Lord upon the altar of the Lord which he had built before the vestibule, as the duty of each day required, offering according to the commandment of Moses for the sabbaths, the new moons, and the three annual feasts—the feast of the unleavened bread, the feast of weeks, and the feast of tabernacles. (8.12–13)

The devil was in the details, however. Examined closely, the details of these two passages offered antithetical norms of ceremonial life. In the first, the king offers sacrifices of *his* choice in a place that *he* builds; in the second, the king has the altar built by others, and makes his offerings according to Mosaic Law.

What do these conflicts tell us about the Hebrew Bible? Given the Hebrew obsession with religious propriety, de Wette observed, the author of the earlier passage from Kings could not have omitted *anything* of religious significance.[52] Evidently then, the Mosaic rules for sacrifice found in Chronicles came *later*, after the feasts, commandments, priesthood, and law were established facts of Hebrew religious life. The two books were, in other words, written at different times, by different authors, and for different audiences. The spiritual condition described in the book of Chronicles was "entirely Mosaic-Levitical," de Wette argued, while the books of Samuel and Kings offer "little or nothing at all of Levitical ceremonialism."[53]

Throughout his *Contributions*, de Wette discovered the different layers of biblical texts using Israel's sacrificial prescriptions. "History shows indisputably that in the earlier period a complete freedom of worship dominated," he wrote: "as with the patriarchs and the Homeric Greeks, God's open heavens was his temple, every mealtime a sacrifice . . . That one should make sacrifices only in one sacred place, at the tabernacle or temple: no one had any notion of this."[54] With sacrifice as his scalpel, De Wette peeled apart the layers of scripture, their relative time of composition now indicated by the different ritual practices they admired.

Put more generally, the higher criticism repurposed an older Christian imagination. Certain elements are familiar: the Christian conviction that there was a *better* sacrifice than those ceremonies performed in the ancient Temple was patent, the celebration of the original "free" state of worship, the evident distaste for Levitical ceremony. But the framework is new. No longer is Scripture bound together by the sinews of Christ, but instead is an historical palimpsest, a record of discordant epochs in human worship papered over by the contingent act of editors and scribes.

This decisively reshaped the modern understanding of the Hebrew Bible. For the first time, European readers began to appreciate "the distinctive characteristics of Old Testament religion," rather than see it as an imperfect and early species of Christianity.[55] This was, as Suzanne Marchand has observed, doubtless a "lopsided" project.[56] The Hebrew Bible, as it lost theological cachet, was far more vulnerable to historical critique than was the New Testament. But the result was an explosion of creativity by writers like Heinrich Ewald, Heinrich Vatke, Karl Heinrich Graf, Abraham Kuenen, Abraham Geiger, John William Colenso, most in Germany but elsewhere as well.[57] Together they invented entirely new approaches to Scripture, relying on materials drawn from archaeology, the history of ancient Israel, and Semitic philology.

This epochal shift in secular biblical studies—and the central role that sacrifice played in it—is decisively witnessed in the late-century work of Julius Wellhausen. Trained as a theologian, later a controversial teacher at universities in Griefswald and Göttingen, Wellhausen's 1878 *Prolegomena to the History of Israel* became the gold standard of Hebrew Bible criticism.

Like de Wette, Wellhausen was fascinated by the ages of biblical sacrifice, the contrast between epochs of "naive" and "legal" sacrifice. In the beginning, he observed, was an offering in the form of a "meal prepared in honor of the Deity" in which the "altar is also called a table." Later came the "bloody offering" in which atonement was achieved through "the vicarious power of the life destroyed." Worship arose first "from ordinary life," celebrated "earthly relationships," and created lateral social bonds among the Israelites. Later, it developed "a manifoldness of rites" dedicated to atonement for felt sins, a culture of guilt overseen by a priestly caste. In short, "before the cult was spontaneous; later it became statute." The "beginning" Wellhausen found in parts of Exodus, the books of Samuel and Judges, and prophets like Hosea and Amos. The "later" he found above all in Deuteronomy and Leviticus.[58]

These epochs echoed familiar Christian hierarchies. Wellhausen himself confessed to a deep unease with ancient Judaism. Already as a young man, the Jewish Law had felt like a "ghost" that "spoiled the pleasure" of the Hebrew Bible.[59] Over time, however, he transformed this ancient Christian prejudice into something more interesting. Jewish legalism was not, he discovered, merely a symptom of obstinacy, hard-heartedness, or chauvinism. Rather, it was the product of *history-making* itself.

In pre-exilic Israel, as Wellhausen told it, sacrifice was performed naively. The Hebrews worshiped the same way as all ancient peoples, distinctive solely for *whom* they worshiped. When a prophet like Jeremiah railed against Israel's attachment to sacrifice, therefore, it was not an attack on priestly legalism (as Christians had traditionally understood it). He merely sought to redirect Israel back toward the God who, in Jeremiah's words, "did not command [your fathers] concerning burnt offerings or sacrifices" (7.21). Jeremiah admonished Israel to remember *its own* God, who did not (unlike many other gods) command about sacrifice.[60]

After the Babylonian exile, Israel was burdened with the duty to remember not just God, however, but also its *own past*. "As long as sacrifice continued as a praxis," Wellhausen wrote, "no one dealt with it in theoretical fashion, nor was there any cause for codification." But the exile ended this continuity. Those who came after rebuilt the Temple in the Jerusalem. An ascendent priestly caste had to reinvent the older sacrificial codes in a project of memorialization that Wellhausen called "denaturalization." These priests and the project of memorialization froze into prescriptions the rites that had once been performed in a spontaneous fashion by early Hebrews. And now the *authority* of these rites depended exclusively on the power of an imagined past. The sacrifices, festivals, ceremonies found in Levitical law were thus the institutions of a people living in what *they themselves* now saw as an afterlife. They were "shadows," mere pendants on a past world of vitality, truth, and revelation.[61] Ritual became "legal," in other words, by becoming historical.

The past as fetish—this was something that the priestly Levites shared with Wellhausen's theological ancestors, not to mention the many university historians and philologians who populated his intellectual world. Indeed, the higher criticism depended on it, for without the fetishized past, there would be no Hebrew Bible to study. Ancient redactors and editors so venerated the received texts, that is, that they revised them only lightly, and kept even the passages that did not conform to their new religious reality. Prophets, wrote Wellhausen, live in the "storm of world history, that sweeps away the institutions of man"; they have no need for an historical pedigree. Later, priests turn the prophets into institutions, turn the voice of prophecy into written canon. Deuteronomy was written "to acquire public authority *as a book*," Wellhausen remarked.[62] The irony here—that the higher criticism, and indeed historical thought, was itself a species of Levitical fetishism—was not lost on Wellhausen.[63]

In the higher criticism, in short, the Christian sacrificial imagination returned to haunt itself, its own prejudices directed *against* the normative authority of Scripture. No wonder this technical biblical philology resonated powerfully with nineteenth-century critics of religion. The "philosopher of sacrifice," Friedrich Nietzsche, was one careful reader of the *Prolegomena*, for example, his marginalia and repeated underlinings revealing the debt that his 1888 *Anti-Christ* owed to Wellhausen.[64] "All things of life are so ordered that the priest is *everywhere indispensable*," Nietzsche railed against Second Temple Judaism, "at all the natural events of life, at birth, marriage, sickness, death, not to speak of 'sacrifice' (meal-times), there appears the holy parasite to *denaturalize* them—in his language, to 'sanctify' them." In the face of "the radical *falsification* of all nature, all naturalness, all reality," the older system of "festival worship" collapsed. And "the same phenomenon again and in unutterably vaster proportion" took place in the Christian Church, which destroyed everything that was life-affirming about Jesus Christ.[65] Whatever nobility His death on the Cross might have had, "the deranged reason" of the early Church betrayed with a "downright terrifying" idea:

> God gave his Son for the forgiveness of sins, as a *sacrifice*. All at once it was all over with the Gospel! The *guilt sacrifice*, and that in its most repulsive, barbaric form, the sacrifice of the *innocent man* for the sins of the guilty! What atrocious paganism! . . . All at once the Evangel became the most contemptible of all unfulfillable promises.[66]

The vigor of Nietzsche's attack—on Judaism, on Christianity, on theology, on Germany, on philosophy—could hardly have been anticipated by the sober Wellhausen. And yet the biblical scholar had sharpened the knives that Nietzsche cheerfully applied to the idols of the nineteenth century. The language of denaturalization, the critique of biblical sacrifice, even the ironic mode in which sober philological learning was conducted: these were as much Wellhausen as Nietzsche.[67]

We should beware modernist triumphalism. The disaggregation of the Christian sacrificial imagination lent itself to the work of a theoretical avant-garde. But it also sustained new and durable forms of anti-Semitism.

Debates about whether it was even possible for Jews to convert to Christianity, for example, erupted at the end of the eighteenth century—a Jew will "remain always a Jew" even if baptized, declared Schleiermacher in 1799.[68] If the Hebrew Bible was no longer normative for Christians, as he thought, the shared imaginative horizons of Jewish and Christian life withered away. Wilhelm de Wette was more pointed: "Christianity was born out in antagonism to Judaism," because "neither tolerates the other in their presence; their fundamental ideas, their innermost essence, are different."[69] Disagreement about what, if anything, Christianity owed to Judaism raged throughout the nineteenth century, as indeed it does today.[70]

It was in this context that Hebrew sacrifice was turned to violently anti-Semitic ends. In 1764, Voltaire had already suggested that human sacrifice "was customary among the [ancient] Jews."[71] By the late 1830s, a certain strain of atheist radicalism argued that this savagery persisted even among *modern* Jews. The writers were often eccentric, but no less significant for that. The Nuremberg Bible scholar and poet Georg Friedrich Daumer violently rejected his Pietist upbringing, for example, "discovering" that the ancient Jews worshiped the fire god Moloch, that the sabbath was originally a day of human sacrifice, that early Christianity continued the cannibalistic and sacrificial cult of the Hebrews, and, most unpleasantly, that this deep history *continued* through the Middle Ages and into the modern period.[72] His Nuremberg colleague Friedrich Ghillany agreed, supporting his 1842 speculations on the savage practices of ancient and modern Jews with the authority of de Wette and other leading biblical critics.[73]

Together, moreover, these writers combined critical histories of Hebrew sacrifice with the Christian tradition of blood libel, in which Jews were accused of, among other things, sacrificing Christian children for their own religious rites.[74] Indeed, the 1840 Damascus affair—the supposed ritual murder of a Catholic priest—and similar examples of Jewish violence against ancient and modern Christians, amply proved that it was still "a general custom among the Jews to martyr and sacrifice purchased or stolen children for their Passover, and to use their blood for superstitious purposes."[75]

In April 1842, for example, Georg Daumer wrote to his friend, Ludwig Feuerbach, to report on the bloodthirsty Jews. Not only had the ancient Hebrews sacrificed children; not only did the festival of Purim celebrate the crushing of human beings in wine presses and drinking their blood; not only did the Talmud recommend cannibalism; but even modern Jews were guilty. "I recently examined the old cellars and subterranean ovens of the Jews in Nuremberg," Daumer concluded, "and found remarkable results." The human sacrifice of the Jews was likely still happening, and right around the corner.[76]

It was no accident Daumer thought he had an ally in Germany's most prominent philosophical atheist. At the root of *all* religions, Daumer insisted, lay the blood cult.[77] Ludwig Feuerbach's 1841 *Essence of Christianity* concluded much the same thing: "bloody human sacrifices are in fact the rude and material expression of the secrets of religion." In sacrifice, man offers to the gods what he holds most dear, a human life. Conclusive proof of Feuerbach's great thesis: *homo homini deus est*, man is a god to man, religion nothing more than the projection of human desires and values onto the divine. Or, more succinctly, "the secret of theology *is* anthropology."[78]

In the nineteenth century, in short, the biblical world of Hebrew sacrifice—long cherished for its Christological portents—was released from its older theological home. What was to become of it afterward was less certain: textual histories of the Bible, creative reflections on history and memory, cutting critiques of Christianity, violent anti-Semitic atheism. These were doubtless innovations, unthinkable in the thought-world of early modern Christianity. But they also participated in a pattern now familiar to us, sacrifice living a double life, both marking a past that has been (or must be) overcome, and persisting nonetheless. What we called the heteronomy of sacrifice—that unwilled presence, that foreign legislation of a world long gone—was at work no less in the secular than it had been in the Christian imagination. It animated the higher criticism, and indeed all those new sciences of man that the nineteenth century bequeathed to our contemporary world.

The Disciplines of Sacrifice

The Enlightenment experimented with new ways to imagine sacrifice *ad saeculum*; the nineteenth century gave these experiments disciplinary shape. What we now call anthropology grew in the rich soil of European imperial and colonial projects, for example, and aided the administration of political power across the globe. A new geography of political power emerged, in which large parts of South Asia, Africa, and Oceania came under direct European governance, and with them, new fields for anthropological research. Alongside came new efforts to create sciences of the so-called savage slot, that is, the study of peoples relegated beyond European norms.[79] Ethnography and ethnology were the early names for this science, and then later anthropology. New institutions, funded by governments and churches, were designed to study what the Enlightenment called the "ceremonies and customs" of the world's peoples: new societies for ethnographic research (Paris in 1838, London in 1843), scientific journals, museums of ethnography and later anthropology, university chairs, colonial offices, and new missionary organizations.[80]

These sciences of sacrifice developed under new political conditions. When Bernard and Picart wrote about religion in India in 1728, for example, they briefly discussed the custom of *sati*, a "kind of voluntary sacrifice" where the Hindu widows "burn themselves on the body of their husbands." This evidenced the "shame and inhumanity" of the heathens, they noted, but also a Stoic valor unseen since the days of the Roman Mucius Scaevola, who thrust his own hand into fires of sacrifice.[81] A century later, curious, even appreciative asides about *sati* were rarely thinkable. *Sati* instead instigated one of *the* great debates in British missionary, colonial, and anthropological circles, as imperial authorities struggled over whether to ban the practice outright.[82] The debate turned on whether such sacrifices were prescribed by classical Hindu legal and religious texts, and, as importantly, whether these were sacrifices at all. As one Baptist missionary remarked, *sati* was not a sacrifice, but a *crime* perpetrated by the husband's relatives, who trick or force the grieving widow into this monstrous act.[83] Elsewhere, the ascetic practice of "hookswinging" preoccupied colonial authorities in southern India, while the festival of Jagannath—in which worshipers threw themselves under the wheels of "Juggernaut"—did the same for authorities in Bengal.[84] The direct regulation of Indian religious life, in short, made distant and, to Europeans, bizarre sacrificial practices into pressing political issues.

It would be instructive, if daunting, to explore how sacrifice shaped European imperial projects in the nineteenth century. Daunting especially, I believe, because such a project would require serious expertise not just in modern European colonialism but, as importantly, also in the religious imaginations of the cultures colonized.[85] Possessing neither, I will instead limit our focus to our key question: what is the relationship between the sacrificial imagination of these new human sciences and the deep Christian past?

Anthropology, comparative religion, comparative philology, comparative law, sociology, and history: all nineteenth-century human sciences took sacrifice seriously as a question to be answered and a puzzle to be unraveled. They did so, no doubt, in deep dialogue with that centuries-long Christian project to understand its *own* sacrificial imagination. This imagination was, as we have seen, a heterogeneous one, an archive of conflicting histories and problems, many of which were originally no more "Christian" than they were pagan or Jewish. Exactly because this archive was so heterogeneous, even contradictory in its constitution, however, it intensified the creativity of the secular sciences of sacrifice.

In the first instance, the very *concept* of sacrifice that the human sciences set out to explain arguably owes its existence to this archive. As we mentioned in our introduction, the classical semantics of sacrifice describe an embarrassment of customs and notions including (minimally) the Greek *thusia* (things burned for the Olympian gods), *sphagia* (things offered to the infernal gods), *aparchai* (offerings of firstfruits), *spondai* (pouring out of libations), and *askesis* (giving something up); not to mention the Hebrew *korban* (draw near), *olah* (burnt offering), and *minha* (gift), and the Latin vocabulary that came later. These semantics unfolded across a thousand years, used by peoples living across the wider Mediterranean, and collected in a library of different texts and writers. But in the early modern period, spurred by intense religious controversy, this chaotic terrain was organized. A miscellany of practices and beliefs was thus gathered under one conceptual umbrella named "sacrifice." And then this miscellany was *explained*, given a logic that coordinated this diversity. This logic was "historical," that is, grounded in the story of Adam and his children, the first sacrificers. It was also "theological," that is, founded in the atoning sacrifice of Christ, whose death would unite and make meaningful all of these various activities.

The secular human sciences adopted neither logic. But they did adopt the conviction that there was *some* logic that organized this universe of practices. What that logic was, however, was very hard to specify. Take, for example, the work of Edward Tylor, first professor of anthropology at Oxford. His 1871 *Primitive Culture* marked a milestone in the creation of the modern discipline. Writing in the wake of Darwin, Tylor described how religion evolved "upwards from the simplest theory"—what he called animism—to arrive at last at the notion of a "Supreme being ordering and controlling" the cosmos.[86]

Animism proceeds from the conviction that "all nature is possessed, pervaded, crowded with spiritual beings."[87] Sacrifice has its origin in the animistic age, in the "early period of culture," and it did so in the form of gifts. "Gift-theory . . . take the first place," as the "most rudimentary form of sacrifice," a "childlike kind of offering" appropriate for an early mankind who believed that the spirits pervading things were like enough to humans to need such things.[88] Over time, this simple sacrifice grew complex, as humans decided first that the gods wanted homage, and later that they wanted to see humans deprive themselves of something valuable.

A simple and powerful story. But it also ignored many of the things long captured by the concept of sacrifice. Tylor was too honest, for example, not to realize that some things were given more often than others. If animists considered spirits to have "the ethereal nature of smoke or mist," then why, for example, did so much sacrifice consist in *food*? Perhaps because their spirits live on "steam and vapours," which would explain why food was often burned, why incense and tobacco smoke are so often part of sacrificial rites, and why the blood (the material form of spirit, in his view) was a privileged substance for the gods.[89] Yet much sacrificial food is not burned, but instead eaten by the priests or the community, or simply flung (or poured) on the ground. And many things sacrificed are not edible at all: cloth, precious stones, incense, he mentions.

Nor was it clear how animistic gifts related to the propitiatory sacrifices common in many religions. To explain *this*, Tylor pivoted toward a new explanation of the gods, by "the analogy of man's dealings with man." Here the gods were not the spirits of nature, but rather human beings apotheosized. Sacrifices were, in this theory, either acts of propitiation, like "the common man's present to the great man, to gain good or avert evil."[90] Or they were acts of self-abnegation, as when we find pleasure simply in giving things away, regardless of whether the gift benefits another.[91] This theoretical pivot helped to explain other forms of sacrifice, to be sure, but at considerable cost to the coherence of Tylor's project. It was devilishly difficult, in short, to explain the logic of sacrifice without the theological investments that created the sacrificial archive in the first place.

Efforts to do so produced some of the most creative work in the early human sciences, however. From the theological perspective, sacrifice beyond the Christian frame was always a form of error, at best a shadow of Christian truth. The human sciences insisted instead that a practice as (apparently) universal to human society as sacrifice *must* have a positive function in the making of a human world. Disagreement about the nature of this function was, in turn, the engine of theoretical curiosity for generations of researchers.

To remain in Britain, work on sacrifice flourished during the Victorian "crisis of faith," the decades after the 1859 publication of Darwin's *Origin of the Species* and the 1860 publication of the *Essays and Reviews*, which unleashed the higher criticism into the British public sphere.[92] The Scottish biblical scholar and Semitist William Robertson Smith fell victim to this crisis in the late 1870s, tried for heresy and forced out of his university chair. This good friend of Wellhausen became an editor at the *Encyclopedia Britannica*, writing the 1886 entry on "sacrifice," and expanding his views in his 1889 *Lectures on the Religion of the Semites*.

The most common way that early anthropologists explained sacrifice was in reference to belief. Early mankind, said Tylor and others, shared a cosmology that invited sacrifice. Robertson Smith was less interested in beliefs than social practices, however. Sacrifice was "primarily a meal offered to the deity," he wrote, a meal shared *among* human beings, and *between* people and their gods. "Gods and worshippers together make up a society of commensals," a form of kinship in which "the circle of common worship is also the circle of social duty and reciprocal moral obligation."[93] The sacred feast was "the sacrifice of a clan, and so the sacrificial meal had pre-eminently the character of a public feast." In this sense, worship was "essentially social," a way of confirming who belongs inside a given social and political order. All those who share in the meal are "brethren," friends and kinsmen committed to living together in common worship and solidarity.[94]

Taken individually, these were not new ideas. That sacrifice had something to do with eating was a commonplace in a Christian world obsessed with the edible elements of the Eucharist.[95] Early moderns also knew quite a bit about the federative power of sacrifice. Republicans had always known this, and it was key to the Enlightenment politics of sacrifice. But in the nineteenth century, these various notions were recombined in the name of a new functionalism. Sacrifice was everywhere in human society, the argument went, because it helped create and sustain the most basic features of human life: the formation of kinship groups and the development of social organization.

That sacrifice grounded social order became a truism across the nineteenth-century human sciences. Legal historian Henry Sumner Maine suggested in his 1861 *Ancient Law* that social and political groups "consecrat[ed] their association by common sacrifices," which also served as the means of exogenous recruitment when "strangers [were] amalgamated with the brotherhood" by participation in them.[96] The French classicist Numa Denis Fustel de Coulanges agreed. In his 1864 *The Ancient City*, he described how families first formed around common sacrifices, how these sacrifices grew the household through marriage and adoption, and finally how they founded the ancient city "as a sanctuary for this common worship."[97] Most important to Robertson Smith, however, were the works of Scottish anthropologist John McClennan, who discovered in the late 1860s—with evidence drawn from American and Australian indigenous peoples—that early human social groups coalesced around totems, common objects of veneration and worship.[98] All "ancient nations came through the totem stage," and there were as many totem gods "as there were stocks" of human beings.[99]

Robertson Smith inserted sacrifice into the heart of the totem.[100] Sacrificial feasting was hedged, he observed, by specific prohibitions and requirements. Certain foods may be eaten, other must not be. This was characteristic of the "totem system of belief," in which "a man may not eat the totem animal of his clan."[101] Sacrificial feasting not only preserved the totemic status of deity, then, but it also tightened communal bonds among those who gathered in its name. In this sense, sacrifice created kinship—an "older thing than family life"—solidifying kin ties internally and defending the kin group against those that threaten from the outside.[102] "For one totem group to feast on the carcase [sic] of a hostile totem is to express their social and religious particularism," he wrote, "to honour their own totem and cast scorn on that of the enemy."[103] Sacrifice was thus essential to the constitution and strength of *all* early human societies.

Other late century human scientists were no less creative in their refashionings of their sacrificial inheritance. Robertson Smith's friend and fellow Scotsman, the classicist James Frazer, was the most exuberant of these. In 1887, Robertson Smith recruited Frazer to write the articles on "taboo" and "totemism" for the *Encyclopedia Britannica*. Over the next years, the first of these ballooned into a work that Frazer called *The Golden Bough: A Study in Magic and Religion* (1st ed., 1890). "Modest origins followed by riotous growth" became the pattern of Frazer's writerly life, the four pages on taboo in the *Encyclopedia* expanded to twelve fat volumes by 1911.[104]

The Golden Bough was a book about sacrifice, and specifically, the sacrifice of *kings*. In the ancient grove of Nemi, a strange and terrible drama unfolded, the book began, a priest-king armed with a sword kept lonely watch for the one who would kill and replace him. Just as his path to the sacred crown had passed through murder, so the priest-king too would eventually fall to his successor: "surely no crowned head has ever lay uneasier . . . than his." For the next 1500 pages, Frazer sought to explain "the strange rule of this priesthood," drawing on every source, classical and modern, he could imagine. The first place he looked to solve this puzzle was familiar: "at Rome and in other Italian cities there was a priest called the Sacrificial King . . . appointed after the expulsion of the kings in order to offer the sacrifices which had been previously offered by the kings."[105]

The *rex sacrorum*, the curious hybrid of the pagan and the Christological we explored earlier, thus returned in the nineteenth century. For some, it exemplified the logic of secularization, that new story told across the human sciences about the gradual emancipation of human life from the bonds of religion. Henry Sumner Maine, for example, insisted that ancient law always moved from status to contract, from divine and personal power to secular codification. The "king of sacrifices" was a tool in this transformation. As a "mere formal hierophant," it helped the ancient Romans shrug off

> that persuasion which clung so long and so tenaciously to the human mind, of a divine influence underlying and supporting every relation of life, every social institution. In early law, and amid the rudiments of political thought, symptoms of this belief meet us on all sides.[106]

As the monarch lost his monopoly over sacrifice, he also lost his divine aura and thereby his monopoly over law. The result was the incipient "severance of law from morality, and of religion from law," that ultimately culminated in that triumph of legal autonomy, the Roman Code.[107] What the great nineteenth-century German historian of Rome, Theodor Mommsen, called the "secularization of sovereignty," then, was embodied in the *rex sacrorum*.[108]

For Frazer, however, the sacrificial king was more akin to Boulanger's "god monarch," that is, a witness to the deeply *political* organization of the divine. The "combination of priestly functions with royal authority" is ubiquitous across human history, Frazer pointed out. Kings were charged to "offer public sacrifices" in Asia Minor, China, Greece, Rome, Madagascar, east Africa, and Central America, confirming the early union of spiritual and temporal power. Indeed, kings were not just representatives of the divine, but were often "themselves gods," charged with a primitive sacrality and able to bestow the blessings reserved for "superhuman and invisible powers."[109]

Sacrifice, sovereignty, and sacrality were thus universal intimates in primitive societies (ancient and modern). Why, Frazer asked, are kings themselves so often offered as sacrificial victims? "It was as a god that the king had to die," his "divine afflatus" qualifying him as a sufficient offering to the heavens. This aura of sacrality reached beyond the royal person. In Cambodia, Vietnam, ancient Greece, and Israel, it was thus common to offer the king's children, or "temporary kings," in human sacrifice. The sacrifice of first-born, and especially noble, children, those especially "sacred to God," was a further extension of the "afflatus" principle. Even the Passover rite, Frazer remarked, preserved a trace of these ancient roots. Once upon a time the Hebrews sacrificed their own sacred first-born; Passover now both hides and manages that "vivid memory of the horrors of those fearful nights."[110]

That the king died *as a god* pointed, moreover, toward a deeper truth of sacrifice. For even the gods must be killed and reborn in Frazer's story of ancient nature cults, the rebirth of the world through the death of divinity. Lurking behind the Sacrificing King was the Roman rite of Saturnalia, the god of sowing whose altars were "stained with the blood of human victims." His merry festivals featured a mock king—"originally representing Saturn himself"—forced at the end of the celebration to cut his own throat.[111] That Christianity put its god up on a Cross, and then celebrated His slaying with weekly sacramental celebrations, was just one example of a universal constant, that the sacrifice of the gods repeats the eternal cycles of nature, the hidden secret of human religion and culture.

Was sacrifice *still* fundamental to human religious, social, and political organization? The secular sciences of sacrifice were ambivalent. For evolutionary anthropologists like Tylor, Robertson Smith, and Frazer, humanity had once needed sacrifice, but now no longer did. To the extent that it persisted, it was a "survival," in anthropological terms, a remnant of an older world preserved by unconscious habit or tradition. The Roman funeral feast "was succeeded by the feast at the martyr's tomb," wrote Tylor in 1871, a survival that both preserved and remade an older ritual form.[112] The gifts to the poor at modern funerals, the pagan *Diis Manibus* carved on Christian tombs, various modern European rites of haircutting and bloodletting, the Catholic use of holy water: these survivals were the "threads of continuity which connect the faiths of the lower with the faiths of the higher world."[113] But they also show a world disappearing. Sacrifice—like religion itself—was bound to disappear along with the "army of spirits" that once dwelled among us, Frazer declared, now "gone even from their last stronghold in the sky." "Only in poet's dreams is it given to catch a glimpse of the last flutters of the standards of the retreating host."[114]

But many things survive for a reason: why had sacrifice survived? For the French sociologists Émile Durkheim and Marcel Mauss, uncle and nephew, sacrifice survived (and would always survive) because it was a "social fact."[115] It was fruitless—so Mauss and his collaborator, the archaeologist Henri Huber, argued—to organize sacrifice into the developmental stages found in Tylor, Robertson Smith, and Frazer. Not only were the documents faulty, and the variety of recorded sacrifices nearly infinite, but the developmental model missed the structural "unity of the sacrificial system."[116] At its most basic level, Huber and Mauss argued, sacrifice was "a means of communication between the sacred and profane worlds through the mediation of a victim." Sacrifice was the hinge between two worlds; thanks to it, the sacred and the profane could "interpenetrate yet remain distinct."[117] This was not a "religious" operation, however. It was fundamentally a *social* one:

> These expiations and general purifications, communions and sacralizations of groups, . . . give—or renew periodically for the community, represented by its gods—that character, good, strong, grave and terrible, which is one of the essential traits of any social entity . . . [through sacrifice, individuals] confer upon each other, upon themselves, and upon those things they hold dear, the whole strength of society.[118]

Rites of expiation and purification confer on the social body a transcendent character, a status beyond the merely temporal. For this reason, society needs the magic of sacrifice—or something like it—to transform a disorganized horde into a unified moral community. In this sense, sacrifice survives because *society* survives.

That society was the source of the sacred was also the major premise of Durkheim's 1912 *Elementary Forms of the Religious Life*. Durkheim was a reader of Robertson Smith but turned the biblical scholar's developmental framework inside out.[119] The story of sacrifice showed not the waning of religious institutions, in his view, but their durability. For social life itself "arouse[s] the sensation of the divine." We experience this social divine as both a restriction and an enlargement of ourselves. On the one hand, society "exacts . . . concessions and sacrifices" beyond our desires and interests. It alerts us that there is something bigger than ourselves at work in the world. On the other hand, society "uplifts [our being] and brings it to maturity." We sense this uplift when we participate in collective life, enjoying the intensity and "effervescence" that lifts us out of ourselves.[120]

Sacrifice intensifies, effervesces us. As in a totemic society, when the "Australian uses [sacrifices] to regenerate himself spiritually," so do all peoples experience spiritual regeneration through collective sacrifice. Sacrifice thus allows man to participate in the sacred, and to invigorate himself and the social order in which he lives. For this reason, cults have "endure[d] as long as human societies have," recreating "a moral being on which we depend, as it depends on us," that is, the moral being called society.[121]

Sacrifice belongs firmly to the past; sacrifice is an unavoidable feature of our present. In this ambivalence, we again hear the echoes of Christianity, caught as it was between the *semel* and *quotidie*, the sacrifice that ends sacrifice, but never quite does so. Sacrifice survived in Christianity as both stumbling block and inspiration. And it survived again the secular imagination of the human sciences, both as a necessary aspect of our common humanity, and as something alien and ancient still at work, that "old catastrophe," in the poet Wallace Stevens's words, haunting the dreamer of *Sunday Morning*.

This Verily Is That: A Methodological Coda

> *Hiesos Kristos, magician of the beautiful, the Logos*
> *Who suffers in us at every moment. This verily is that.*
> *I am the fire upon the altar. I am the sacrificial butter.*
>
> —JAMES JOYCE, *ULYSSES*

> *Jesus died for somebody's sins . . . but not mine*
>
> —PATTI SMITH, *GLORIA*

It is this catastrophe that has so enlarged the sacrificial imagination, from the Christian era to the age of anthropology. Even the ancients, Robertson Smith suggested, never felt quite at home in their sacrificial world. Yes, their rites joyfully celebrated the union of the clan, with one another and with their totem god. But this was no less a terrible celebration, the priest and the hangman in uneasy proximity as they violated the most primal taboo, the killing of kinsman and deity. No surprise that this most ancient sacrificial rite should, with the passage of time, become altogether less joyful, filled rather with "painful and scrupulous anxiety."[122]

That we might never feel at home in the world we create: here Freud discovered his historical analogue with the human psyche. The mind too is often uncomfortable with the world it creates, our past persisting even (especially!) when we seek to put it aside. Repression works until it doesn't, at which point the past comes back, in often disconcerting ways. The murder of Moses, so Freud wrote in his late *Moses and Monotheism*, was the original crime of the ancient Hebrews, made even more powerful by its disavowal in public memory. So powerful, in fact, was this crime that it created not one, but *two* religions:

> this crime deserving death had been the murder of the primal father who was later deified. But the murder was not remembered: instead of it there was a phantasy of its atonement . . . a son of God had allowed himself to be killed without guilt and had thus taken on himself the guilt of all men. It had to be a son, since it had been the murder of a father.[123]

Jesus died for somebody's sin, but not mine: so sang poet-rocker Patti Smith in 1975. This disavowal is an ancient one, Christ dying for a sin buried deep in the past, the ancient murder-sacrifice of Moses, the totem god of ancient Israel. Out of that first repressed murder was born the Hebrew people, and later Christianity too, the great religions of the Mediterranean born of human neuroses.

Whether such a sacrifice is a neurosis to be overcome, or the very heart of human culture: here again a Christian afterlife, an echo of questions never resolved despite millennia of efforts. But such echoes now sound in new and unexpected places. In the Jewish psychoanalyst from Vienna; in Stravinsky's *Rites of Spring*, whose "Scythianism" leveled the savagery of the ancient world against the decadence of the modern; in the lyrics of a lascivious punk anthem, the chorus "GLORIA" a raised middle finger to 1950s American prudery. "I am the fire upon the altar. I am the sacrificial butter": James Joyce's vision of the "life esoteric" saw new horizons for the imagination in the sacrificial secrets of Christ and the Vedas, Buddha and Plato.[124] The new primitivism of early twentieth century art movements; the cascade of visual and poetic works that followed on the violence of the First World War; the poetry and prose of the Holocaust: the history of the secular imagination is rich with the power of sacrifice, that old catastrophe, to unsettle and provoke.

This history—and all the histories we have explored in this book—is a specific one. It pertains to the Mediterranean world that made Christianity, to the world that Christianity itself made in the Latin West, and to the new worlds that were made in Europe in its wake. Yet it also, I hope, affords general lessons about the stories we scholars tell about religion and its place in the world we hold in common.

In many of these stories, what matters are the sharp distinctions: Christianity, not Judaism; Christianity, not paganism; true religion, not idolatry; the secular, not religion. Such distinctions matter a great deal. They often constitute religious and secular identities, for example, by their rejection of other ways of life. As such, they are also essential to religious and secular hierarchies, organizing injustice and inequality, repressing one people in favor of another. What we now call "criticism" understandably spends much time showing how such distinctions function, and the power they exert over those subjected to them.

Take, for example, the German Egyptologist Jan Assmann, whose wonderful work has been an interlocutor for me over many years. The "Mosaic distinction"—that distinction between truth and false in religion—emerged first in the ancient world, he argued in his 1997 *Moses the Egyptian*, a creature of a new thing called monotheism. The distinction was Mosaic in two ways. First, for its immediate association with the familiar Hebrew lawgiver; and second, for its mediated association with the Egyptian Pharaoh Akhenaten, the memory of whose monotheistic iconoclasm was absorbed (it is argued) by Moses, that son of Egypt, and carried into the deserts of Israel. The details are less important than the model. Monotheism was the "first distinction," out of which grow the many others that infect the world with conflict and strife: distinctions between the one and the many, revelation and reason, natural and supernatural, this world and the world beyond, the sacred and the profane, religion and the secular.[125]

But distinctions come in various kinds. In G. Spencer Brown's 1969 *Laws of Form*—the somewhat peculiar work that affords Assmann's framework—a distinction severs, and so creates a universe, built around the border between one side and another. This border can be a hard one, creating differences of absolute and exclusive kind, true and false, reason and revelation, the immanent and the transcendent, or similar. But it can also be something softer, more permeable. "A universe comes into being when a space is severed or taken apart," Brown announces, just as "the skin of a living organism cuts off an outside from an inside."[126] But the skin of an organism is soft. It is a space of interaction between outside and in, the precondition for touch, inclusion, and intimacy.

What kind of distinction is the "Mosaic distinction"? On the one hand, in conceptual terms, it seems absolute and exclusive: *my* religion, *your* idolatry, a boundary that founds violence and hierarchy. On the other hand, in *historical* terms, the distinction was anything but. It was under the robes of Moses—to take Assmann's example—that the (pagan) religion of a Pharaoh was smuggled into the promised land, beginning a series of transformations and conversions that will hold Egypt and Israel in an uneasy interpretive intimacy that will last for millennia. The Mosaic distinction therefore at once creates and confounds difference; it is not a wall, but a skin.

The Mosaic distinction thus entails what the philosopher Nancy Levene calls a "dualism of inclusion," that is, "a distinction both from positions that distinguish invidiously and from those that do not distinguish at all." This kind of dualism is not independent of the exclusive one. Rather it stands *between* the invidious (*my* religion, *your* idolatry) and *no distinction at all* (ancient polytheism, in Assmann's terms, in which everything can be translated into everything else). It invites consideration on what might be *shared*, what Levene calls the "histories in common" that are produced through transformation, critique, and interpretation.[127]

"Religion" and the "secular" are also conditioned by these two distinctions. The sharp one, predicated on autonomy and hierarchy, insists both that there is a "special or ontologically distinct sphere of human activity," call it secular or religious, and that this sphere (whichever one it is) is prior, more authentic than the other. The soft one depends on but also undoes the first, referring "to what can be shared—the problems of otherness, knowledge, limit, difference—among the regnant spheres of humanistic investigation," in Levene's words.[128] One distinction invites the other, exclusion creating possibilities of intimacy, however vexed.

For its part, the modern literature on religion and the secular pays most attention to the sharp distinctions. Early social scientists and scholars of religion insisted on the necessary autonomy of the secular, for example, taken both as a methodological and a moral position. The secular stands *opposed* to religion, and it is *better* to be secular than not. Since the 1990s, this particular distinction has been eroded, if not entirely undone, by new critiques of secularism. Genealogy, as this critique often calls itself, insists that the secular always fails to live up to its promise of autonomy, that the secular is a form of European or Christian governance, that the secular relies on (indeed advances) normatively Christian commitments. This critique has been most forceful in the space of colonial encounter, Christianity offering the "language in which . . . possibilities are formulated" and exerting thereby "specific forms of power or subjection" over those captured by European empire, as the anthropologist Talal Asad memorably wrote.[129] Politically salutary, perhaps, but methodologically not much of an advance over its opposite. After all, the force of the critique also depends on the sharp distinction, the imagined autonomy of the secular reinforced in its very undoing. No less the religious, for that matter.

As regards sacrifice, much ink has been spilled in efforts to show how, for example, liberal politics always requires more than rational consensus and law. It depends, it is said, on a foundation of sacrifice that can neither be admitted or denied. For Western liberal societies, wrote the political and legal philosopher Paul Kahn in 2007, "absent sacrifice there is no sacred presence of the sovereign." The very essence of popular sovereignty is the willingness to die for one's country; this foundational sacrifice supplies, he concludes, a repressed alibi for liberalism's *own* violence toward others.[130]

Perhaps. A thick *history* of the modern sacrificial imagination would, I suspect, upset some of the neatness of these formulations. In political terms alone, such a history would have to engage the various nineteenth-century nationalist imaginaries, the slow death of European royalism, the cultures of military commemoration, the poetry of revolution and war, American slavery and abolitionism, the violence of the American Civil War, the rhetoric of populism and anti-Semitism, the sacrificial imagination of socialism and pacifism, and, not least, the culture and politics of sacrifice that attended what came to be known as the Holocaust. Not to speak of the Cold War, the politics of nuclear weapons, the war on terror, the so-called clash of civilizations, and the new politics of suicide-bombing.[131] Too much for the end of an already very long book.

Whether true or not, however, Kahn's views—like those of Asad and the genealogists—are still instructive. For they repeat, in form, the indictment of heteronomy that has so long structured the sacrificial imagination, applying it now not to Christianity, but to the secular liberal world. "Nowhere in liberal accounts of the state does anyone die," writes Kahn, "there is only protection from the state; there is no dying for the state."[132] Liberal politics thus always demands what it cannot justify, the accusation charges, that every citizen be ready to sacrifice life and limb for the fatherland. In a deep sense, then, modern political culture is—like Luther's Catholics or Freud's Hebrews—still haunted by that ancient religious scandal of sacrifice. The power of the critique depends again on the sharp distinction, the failure of liberalism chalked up to its inability to preserve the distinctions it cherishes, to preserve the distinction that gives the critique its edge.[133]

This book has tried to imagine the *other* distinction, to take heteronomy as precondition rather than problem. It has sought to write less as a judge than as an historian sympathetic to the worlds that people find themselves living inside and making. For it has been above all the intimacies—uncomfortable, strained, even violent—created by, and persisting across, hard borders that have proven especially powerful. Sacrifice was like Moses the Egyptian priest, the smuggler of the secrets of Egypt into Jewish and Christian Scriptures. It was and is a space where distinctions were made and undone, the *semel* and *quotidie*, the sacrifice that ended sacrifice and created it anew. It kept Christianity in perpetual intimacy with the worlds that it abandoned, the patriarch and the Levites living on the altars in Christianity's holiest places. And by doing so, it sustained endless imaginative creation among artists, poets, theologians, philosophers, historians, scholars and others. This is no less true for the secular imagination as well, the old catastrophes returning as dreams of a bygone world that inspire and haunt our inner lives.

In any case, to imagine that we—Christians or moderns—ever *could* leave sacrifice (or religion) altogether behind is to imagine ourselves autonomous, free to invent and dispose of the meanings that shape our lives. "We know no time when we were not as now; know none before us, self-begot, self-rais'd"—thus John Milton's Satan, crying out a fantasy of independence as deceiving as it was delusional.[134] If it does anything, after all, history shows that we are not masters of ourselves, that we are subject to questions and problems, cares and concerns, that we have inherited (knowingly or not) from others.

This verily is that, as Joyce wrote. Indeed, we might not even *want* to be autonomous in that Satanic fashion. Surely it is under conditions of heteronomy, after all, that the human imagination truly thrives. The long struggle with sacrifice created *worlds*. For centuries now, poets, prophets, painters, theologians, historians, anthropologists, missionaries, novelists, and philosophers labored to understand something so alien yet so intimate. This labor catalyzed one of the greatest eras of theological creativity in Christian history. It helped revolutionize Christian theology and liturgy, upending habits of Christian life and thought that had endured for centuries. It shaped new forms of the political imagination, from the age of martyrs to the age of revolutions. It spurred missionaries into tortured efforts to understand their converts and themselves. It catalyzed searching inquiry into the history and anthropology, not just of Christianity, but of all religions. It inspired astonishing works of visual art, from Bellini's *Blood of the Redeemer* to Rembrandt's *Sacrifice of Isaac*, to the works of modern artists like Käthe Kollwitz, Paul Klee, Jacques Lipchitz, Jose Orozco, Marc Chagall, Romare Beardon, and many others. It aroused endless poetic creativity, from the baroque poetry of seventeenth-century drama, the war poetry of the Enlightenment, the decadent verse of Charles Baudelaire, and the lean Christian modernism of T. S. Eliot.

> . . . History may be servitude,
> History may be freedom. See, now they vanish,
> The faces and places, with the self which, as it could, loved them,
> To become renewed, transfigured, in another pattern.[135]

Thus Eliot wrote in 1942, under a hail of German bombs, in a poem on sacrifice and resurrection, history and memory, death and renewal. The history of the imagination *is* this history of renewal, transfiguration, in other patterns. Neither quite freedom nor servitude, it stages the commerce of the old and the new, debts inherited yet paid off in other currencies. As regards Christianity—another past that we inherit and remake, another heteronomous present haunted by its own history—we cannot, as Eliot writes, "ring the bell backwards."[136] The original state of blessed self-sufficiency, whether sacred or profane, never did exist, anyway. Thankfully so, for the human imagination depends on it.

ACKNOWLEDGMENTS

THE ACKNOWLEDGMENTS FOR a book that has taken as long as this one to write feels like an inventory of my intellectual life. At the beginning lies a set of seminars and conversations with the historian Amos Funkenstein (1937–1995), who gifted me with his curiosity, generosity, and life of the mind. It was Funkenstein who made me into an early modernist, and turned religion, for me, from a scandal into a question. I have been in dialogue with him, wittingly or unwittingly, for over three decades. This book is dedicated to his memory.

These early conversations happened at Berkeley in the mid-1990s, and they began a relationship with a place that has indelibly shaped my life and work. Since my return to Berkeley in 2007, I have been the beneficiary of its astonishing community, whose imprint on this book is evident, at least to me, across all its pages. At its center are Carla Hesse and Thomas Laqueur, who have together been precious partners in writing and thinking for decades. Large parts of this book were talked through and written in a mountain cabin in their apple orchard near Santa Cruz, a study hall just far enough away from the world to allow some perspective. Ethan Shagan has been my cherished partner-in-thought since we both arrived in Berkeley. He is an incisive reader, a brilliant critic, and a great friend. Speaking of great friendships, Mark Peterson left Berkeley before the book was finished, but our conversations continued over the years, and the book shows it, not least in what it does *not* say. Susanna Elm was one of my first readers, and has worked valiantly ever since to keep me from embarrassing myself too much when talking about late antique Christianity. Abhishek Kaicker and Stacey Van Vleet both know far more now about Christian sacrifice than I wager they ever planned, and I'm grateful for all their energies. David Bates, Kinch Hoekstra, and Victoria Kahn spent many years with this project, giving generously of their insights and pushing me to think both more clearly and capaciously. Randy Starn, David Hollinger, and Marty Jay have all been models of the learned life, ever generous with a younger colleague. And from just outside the guild, Cynthia De Nardi has read each chapter, encouraged me to write better, and enriched my imagination at every turn.

Berkeley has many mansions. Its group of early modernists, including especially Timothy Hampton, Niklaus Largier, David Marno, and Diego

Pirillo, have created a world of conversation and critique second to none. After founding the Berkeley Center for the Study of Religion (BCSR) in 2012, I had the good fortune to spend seven years co-directing it with Mark Csikszentmihalyi, whose generous intelligence remains, for me, an ideal to emulate. BCSR also gathered a stellar community of scholars. Karen Barkey, William Hanks, Ron Hendel, Charles Hirschkind, Saba Mahmood, Christopher Ocker, and Devin Zuber are just a few of those from whom I've learned much. So too the many BCSR visitors, with generous support from the Henry Luce Foundation, who came to Berkeley and helped us to imagine theology in new and exciting ways. In the History Department, Diliana Angelova, Janaki Bakhle, Cathryn Carson, John Connelly, Brian Delay, John Efron, Victoria Frede-Montemayor, Stefan-Ludwig Hoffman, Ethan Katz, Carlos Noreña, and Wen-hsin Yeh have all been wonderful collaborators in many projects. Teaching at Berkeley has also been transformative. Over the years, a remarkable group of Berkeley graduate and undergraduate students have helped me think harder and better about the stories that I tell. They have also assisted practically, as research assistants, bibliographers, translation checkers, note and fact checkers, and curator of images. I owe particular thanks to Simon Brown, Lily Callender, Talia DiManno, Shterna Friedman, Rhiannon Graybill, Robert Harkins, Grace Harpster, Hannah Hartt, Caleb Longacre, Sara Ludin, Kyle Martin, Min-shu Lin, Graham Nelson, Jenny Smith, Samuel Stubblefield, Norman Underwood, Timothy Wright, and Madeleine Wyse. The University, finally, has been very generous with this project, including with support from the Townsend Center for the Humanities; the Humanities Research Fellowship from the College of Letters and Sciences; and the History Department's Shepherd and Chip Robertson Funds.

The earliest seed of the book that I can recall came in a conversation with Mary Elizabeth Berry on the porch of the Townsend Center for the Humanities in 1999. The first strata of research were laid down shortly afterward, at UCLA, where I spent a fantastic year reading in the William Andrews Clark and Henry Huntington Libraries trying to figure out the peculiar world of seventeenth-century antiquarianism. There I also learned much from conversations with Peter Reill, sadly now deceased, with Vincent Pecora, and with Debora Shuger, whose work has been a constant inspiration ever since. My first academic home, Indiana University, was an essential incubator for the book, not least because of Dror Wahrman, with whom I later co-wrote a book and who has been my closest confidant and interlocutor ever since. There too I had the privilege of knowing Constance Furey and Nancy Levene, both of whom have pushed me to think harder and deeper about religion. Constance read the manuscript in multiple drafts, even when she had better things to do, and has been a model critic from the beginning. And it was Nancy who once asked me an offhanded question that stopped me in my tracks: what is theology anyway? I've been trying to answer it for almost twenty years. Later, at the University of Michigan, Katherine Ibbett and Tomoko Masuzawa became the great comrades that they have been ever since, in affairs of both life and the mind.

I have been lucky, moreover, to enjoy the generous support of three other marvelous learned institutions. In 2011–12, the ACLS Frederick Burkhardt fellowship funded me to spend the year at the Folger Shakespeare Library, where the earliest draft chapter of the book was written. Its director, Michael Witmore, the other fellows, especially David Loewenstein and William Sherman, and the incredible collections there supplied a congenial and stimulating place for quiet thought. The *Wissenschaftskolleg zu Berlin*, in conjunction with the European Union Institute for Advanced Study, generously invited me to spend 2015–16 in this remarkable home of learning. There I finally figured out what the book might actually be about, and how to write it. Tatiana Borisova, Karol Berger, Jane Burbank, Anna Busse-Berger, Luca Giuliani, Michael Gordin, Leor Halevi, Ina Hartwig, Daniel Jütte, Naoko Matsumoto, Erika Milam, Richard Prum, Barbara Stollberg-Rilinger, Ralf Ubl, and Constanta Vintila together made the year both delightful and productive. And finally, in 2020–21, I took shelter from the COVID pandemic in Princeton, at the School of Historical Studies at the Institute for Advanced Study. This very strange year was made bearable, even enjoyable, by the company and conversation of Francesca Trivellato, Lawrie Balfour, Simona Cerutti, Pamela Long, Valeria López-Fadul, and Arnaud Orain. In Princeton, Anthony Grafton too once again extended the generosity of spirit that has, since my days in graduate school, been so foundational to my own intellectual development. On a smaller scale, I am also grateful for the Hermann und Marianne Straniak Stiftung, the Fritz Thyssen Stiftung, the Herzog August Bibliothek, and the Social Science Research Council, all of which supported at important moments the making of this book.

One of the joys of academic life is the privilege of joining conversations that circle around the world. My own republic of letters has included, in addition to those above: Joseph Blankholm, Giovanna Ceserani, Annelien De Dijn, Dallas Denery, Beate Fricke, Martin Gierl, Alice Goff, Jan-Lodewijk Grootaers, Dmitri Levitin, Avi Lifschitz, Kathryn Lofton, Suzanne Marchand, Martin Mulsow, Hannah Murphy, Jane Newman,

Ilana Pardes, Matthias Pohlig, Joan-Pao Rubiés, Sarah Shortall, Daniel Stolzenberg, Nomi Stolzenberg, Winnifred Sullivan, Yunus Telliel, Lorenz Trein, Henning Trüper, Mark Valeri, Jonathan van Antwerpen, Dorothea von Mücke, Daniel Weidner, Mario Wimmer, and Robert Yelle. Jacob Sheehan, Avi Sheehan, Benjamin Ipsen, Michael Ipsen, Zoë Sheehan Saldaña, Michael Sheehan, and Denise Saldaña have been a different sort of republic of letters, sharing philosophy, poetry, and literature, high and low. Susanne Lachenicht invited me as a senior fellow to the University of Bayreuth from 2017–2020, where I profited greatly from conversations with her, her colleagues, and her students. I have also learned tremendously from the many discussants and audiences at the institutions where I was kindly invited to present earlier versions of these arguments. These include: the Folger Institute; Washington University, St. Louis; Northwestern University; Villanova Law School; University of California, San Diego; the Graduate Theological Union; Indiana University; the University of Chicago; the University of Virginia; the University of Notre Dame; Columbia University; Yale University; the SUNY Buffalo Law School; the American Historical Association; the Berkeley Institute; the Online Enlightenment Club; the Institute for Historical Research at the University of London; the Mandel School for Advanced Study at the Hebrew University; the Zentrum für Literaturforschung in Berlin; the Ludwig-Maximilian-Universität in Munich; the Wissenschaftskolleg zu Berlin; the Humboldt University in Berlin; the Max Planck Institute for Human Development in Berlin; the Helsinki Institute for Advanced Study; CRASSH at the University of Cambridge; the University of Edinburgh; and the Gotha Research Center at the University of Erfurt.

Finally, my sincere thanks to Fred Appel, Karen Carter, James Collier, Kathleen Strattan, Karen Verde, and the anonymous readers for Princeton University Press. Fred stewarded this book for far longer than he planned, and I'm grateful for his patience and critical encouragement. It has been a pleasure to work with him for now almost twenty years.

NOTES

Introduction: Christianity and the Secular Imagination

1. Wallace Stevens, "Sunday Morning," in *Collected Poems* (New York: Knopf, 1954), 66–67.

2. Valerio Valeri, *Kingship and Sacrifice: Ritual and Society in Ancient Hawaii* (Chicago: University of Chicago Press, 1985), esp. chap. 7.

3. William Robertson Smith, *Encyclopedia Britannica*, 9th ed. (Edinburgh: Adam and Charles Black, 1875–1889), s.v. "Sacrifice," 132.

4. Thus the Revised Standard Version of Leviticus chaps. 1–7. For the complexities of Hebrew sacrifice, see Jacob Milgrom, *Leviticus, 1–16: A New Translation with Introduction and Commentary*, Anchor Bible vol. 3 (New York: Doubleday, 1991), part I, "The Sacrificial System."

5. David Frankfurter, "Egyptian Religion and the Problem of the Category 'Sacrifice'," in Jennifer Wright Knust and Zsuzsanna Várhelyi, eds., *Ancient Mediterranean Sacrifice* (Oxford: Oxford University Press, 2011), 75.

6. On the history of kinship in anthropology, see Hans Hummer, *Visions of Kinship in Medieval Europe* (Oxford: Oxford University Press, 2018).

7. Guy Stroumsa, *The End of Sacrifice* (Chicago: University of Chicago Press, 2009).

8. Sigmund Freud, *Der Mann Moses und der monotheistische Religion* (Amsterdam: Allert de Lange, 1939), 239.

9. Sigmund Freud, *Das Unbehagen in der Kultur* (Vienna: Internationaler Psychoanalytischer Verlag, 1929), 14.

10. Immanuel Kant, "Groundwork of the Metaphysics of Morals," in Mary J. Gregor, ed. and trans., *Practical Philosophy* (Cambridge: Cambridge University Press, 1996), 4:441.

11. Charles Taylor, *Modern Social Imaginaries* (Durham, NC: Duke University Press, 2004), 26.

12. Giambattista Vico, *The New Science of Giambattista Vico*, trans. Thomas Goddard Bergin and Max Harold Fisch (Ithaca, NY: Cornell University Press, 1948), 104. On Vico and "maker's knowledge," see Amos Funkenstein, *Theology and the Scientific Imagination* (Princeton, NJ: Princeton University Press, 1986), 328. More generally on poetics and making, see Victoria Kahn, *The Trouble with Literature* (Oxford: Oxford University Press, 2020).

13. Vico, *New Science*, 116, 117.

14. Nelson Goodman, *Ways of Worldmaking* (Indianapolis, IN: Hackett, 1978), 6.

15. Vico, *New Science*, 100.

16. Euripides, *Iphigenia at Aulis*, ed. and trans. David Kovacs (Cambridge, MA: Harvard University Press, 2002), lines 1397–99, p. 319.

17. See José Casanova, "The Secular and Secularisms," *Social Research* (76.4): 1049–1066.

18. The literature here is vast and complex. Important studies include: Talal Asad, *Genealogies of Religion* (Baltimore, MD: Johns Hopkins University Press, 1993) and *Formations of the Secular: Christianity, Islam, and Modernity* (Stanford, CA: Stanford University Press, 2003); William Connolly, *Why I Am Not a Secularist* (Minneapolis: University of Minnesota Press, 2000); Hent de Vries and Lawrence E. Sullivan, eds., *Political Theologies: Public Religions in a Post-Secular World* (New York: Fordham University Press, 2006); Charles Taylor, *A Secular Age* (Cambridge, MA: Belknap Press, 2007); Janet Jakobsen and Ann Pelligrini, eds., *Secularisms* (Durham, NC: Duke University Press, 2008); Elizabeth Shakman Hurd, *The Politics of Secularism in International Relations* (Princeton, NJ: Princeton University Press, 2008) and *Beyond Religious Freedom: The New Global Politics of Religion* (Princeton, NJ: Princeton University Press, 2015); Saba Mahmood, *Politics of Piety: The Islamic Revival and the Feminist Subject* (Princeton, NJ: Princeton University Press, 2004) and *Religious Difference in a Secular Age* (Princeton, NJ: Princeton University Press, 2015); Joan Wallach Scott, *Sex and Secularism* (Princeton, NJ: Princeton University Press, 2018).

19. Spirited discussions of this issue include Grace Davie, *Religion in Britain since 1945: Believing Without Belonging* (Oxford: Blackwell, 1994) and *The Sociology of Religion* (London: Sage, 2007); Peter Berger, *The Desecularization of the World: Resurgent Religion and World Politics* (New York: Wm. Eerdmans, 1999); Callum Brown, *The Death of Christian Britain: Understanding Secularisation, 1800–2000* (London: Routledge, 2001); Steve Bruce, *God Is Dead: Secularization in the West* (Oxford: Wiley-Blackwell, 2002); Philip Jenkins, *The Next Christendom: The Coming of Global Christianity*, 3rd ed. (Oxford: Oxford University Press, 2011),

20. See most importantly Karl Löwith, *Meaning in History: The Theological Implications of the Philosophy of History* (Chicago: University of Chicago Press, 1949) and Hans Blumenberg, *The Legitimacy of the Modern Age*, trans. Robert M. Wallace (1st German ed., 1966; Cambridge, MA: MIT Press, 1985).

21. See, e.g., the essays in Winnifred Fallers Sullivan et al., eds., *The Politics of Religious Freedom* (Chicago: University of Chicago Press, 2015).

22. Again, the literature here is large. Good introductions would include Asad, *Genealogies of Religion*; Russell McCutcheon, *Manufacturing Religion: The Discourse on Sui Generis Religion and the Politics of Nostalgia* (Oxford: Oxford University Press, 1997); Tomoko Masuzawa, *The Invention of World Religions, or, How European Universalism Was Preserved in the Language of Pluralism* (Chicago: University of Chicago Press, 2005); Carlin A. Barton and Daniel Boyarin, *Imagine No Religion: How Modern Abstractions Hide Ancient Realities* (New York: Fordham University Press, 2016); Brett Nongbri, *Before Religion: A History of a Modern Concept* (New Haven, CT: Yale University Press, 2013).

23. On sovereignty, see Yvonne Sherwood, "The God of Abraham and Exceptional States, or the Early Modern Rise of the Whig / Liberal Bible," *Journal of the American Academy of Religion* 76 (2008): 312–343; on rule of law, see Asad, *Formations of the Secular*; on tolerance, see Wendy Brown, *Regulating Aversion: Tolerance in an Age of Identity and Empire* (Princeton, NJ: Princeton University Press, 2006); on religious freedom, see Hurd, *Beyond Religious Freedom* and Anna Su, *Exporting Freedom: Religious Liberty and American Power* (Cambridge, MA: Harvard University

Press, 2016); on feminism, see Mahmood, *The Politics of Piety* and Scott, *Sex and Secularism.*

24. Gil Anidjar, "Secularism," *Critical Inquiry* 33 (2006): 52–77.

25. Marcel Gauchet, *The Disenchantment of the World: A Political History of Religion*, trans. Oscar Burge (Princeton, NJ: Princeton University Press, 1997), 18, 77, 101. See also my "When Was Disenchantment? History and the Secular Age," in Craig Calhoun, Michael Warner, and Jonathan Van Antwerpen, eds., *Varieties of Secularism in a Secular Age* (Cambridge, MA: Harvard University Press, 2010), 217–242.

26. Jonathan Sheehan, "In the Christian Archives: Sacrifice, the Higher Criticism, and the History of Religion," *Modern Intellectual History* 19 (Winter 2022): 1226. See also Jonathan Sheehan, Henning Trüper, and Mario Wimmer, "Beyond Secularized Eschatology: Introductory Remarks," *Modern Intellectual History* 19 (Winter 2022): 1182–1190.

27. Blumenberg, *Legitimacy of the Modern Age*, 74.

28. Already in the 1930s, the biblical scholar Walter Bauer, for example, argued that heresy preceded orthodoxy across much of the ancient Christian world; see *Rechtgläubigkeit und Ketzerei im ältesten Christentum* (Tübingen: J. C. B. Mohr, 1934).

29. Here a word on languages and translations: in general, if there exists what I judge to be a standard English translation of a work, I have happily used it. If I have modified these standard translations in some way, this will be noted. All other translations are my own.

30. Johann Wolfgang von Goethe, *Faust: Eine Tragödie* (Tübingen, 1808), 50.

Chapter 1: In the Archives of Ancient Sacrifice

1. Eusebius, *The Proof of the Gospel*, ed. and trans. W. J. Ferrar (Grand Rapids, MI: Baker Book, 1981), 1:7.

2. Throughout this chapter, and the book, I will use the words "pagan" and "paganism" advisedly, to describe the various local and state religions of the Mediterranean, even though, of course, this was a specifically *Christian* way of describing these things. In other words, "pagans" would hardly have described themselves in this way. For a discussion of the word and its evolution, see Alan Cameron, *The Last Pagans of Rome* (Oxford: Oxford University Press, 2011), 15ff.

3. On the "novelty" of Christianity, see Daniel Boyarin, *Border Lines: The Partition of Judea-Christianity* (Philadelphia: University of Pennsylvania Press, 2004), 17.

4. A few important terminological and bibliographical notes: First, throughout this book, I will generally refer to the twenty-four books called in Hebrew the *Tanakh* as the "Hebrew Bible," but occasionally, when context suggests, I will use the Christian terminology of "Old Testament." Second, unless otherwise noted, all biblical references are to the Revised Standard Version.

5. There is a huge literature on when "religion" became a term of art, primarily among Christians. Here I am using the term loosely, simply to designate the overlapping, if not identical, semantic and imaginative terrain of that space where humans

traffic with the divine. For the former, see, especially, Brett Nongbri, *Before Religion: A History of a Modern Concept* (New Haven, CT: Yale University Press, 2013).

6. I use these terms of orthodoxy and heterodoxy advisedly—not only did it take a long time for something like "orthodoxy" to emerge, as we will see, but "heterodoxy" is at best an etic term, used by the orthodox to reject what might have, in another history, itself become the norm.

7. In the English-speaking world, this revolution was pioneered above all in the work of Peter Brown. From his early biography of Augustine (Berkeley, 1967), to his 1971 *The World of Late Antiquity* (London), to the more recent *Through the Eye of a Needle: Wealth, the Fall of Rome, and the Making of Christianity in the West, 350–550 AD* (Princeton, NJ: Princeton University Press, 2012), Brown virtually created the field of late antique studies, expanding well beyond the traditional world of patristics. Now the study of the late antique world is one of the most dynamic fields around. For some representative English language works, I would point to Boyarin, *Border Lines;* Claudia Rapp, *Holy Bishops in Late Antiquity: The Nature of Christian Leadership in an Age of Transition* (Berkeley: University of California Press, 2005); Brent Shaw, *Sacred Violence: African Christians and Sectarian Hatred in the Age of Augustine* (Cambridge: Cambridge University Press, 2011); Susanna Elm, *Sons of Hellenism, Fathers of the Church: Emperor Julian, Gregory of Nazianzus, and the Vision of Rome* (Berkeley: University of California Press, 2012).

8. Plutarch, *On Superstition*, in *Moralia*, trans. Frank Cole Babbitt (London: William Heinemann, 1954), vol. 2, p. 455 (164e). On this essay, see J. B. Rives, "Human Sacrifice Among Pagans and Christians," *Journal of Roman Studies* 85 (1995): 77–78; and more recently, Dale Martin, *Inventing Superstition: From the Hippocratics to the Christians* (Cambridge, MA: Harvard University Press, 2004), 93–108.

9. Plutarch, *On Superstition*, 469 (167d).

10. Plutarch, *On Superstition*, 489 (170e).

11. Plutarch, *On Superstition*, 493 (171b-c).

12. Robert M. Berchman, *Porphyry Against the Christians* (Leiden: Brill, 2005), 135. On the Porphyry text, see most recently Irmgard Männlein-Robert, *Die Christen als Bedrohung? Text, Kontext, und Wirkung von Prophyrios'* Contra Christianos (Stuttgart: Franz Steiner Verlag, 2017).

13. Timothy D. Barnes, *Constantine and Eusebius* (Cambridge, MA: Harvard University Press, 1981), 210.

14. Berchman, *Porphyry Against the Christians*, 168.

15. The fourth-century *Apocriticus* of Macarius Magnes, a text discovered in the fifteenth century, preserves a set of anti-Christian screeds that some scholars, most notably Adolf von Harnack, have directly attributed to Porphyry; see Adoph von Harnack, "Porphyrius: 'Gegen die Christen,'" *Abhandlungen der königlichen preussischen Akademie der Wissenschaften: Philosophisch-Historische Klasse* no. 1 (1916): 6.

16. Berchman, *Porphyry Against the Christians*, 181.

17. The dating here is controversial. While the *bishop* lived in the second century, the best recent scholarship shows that the martyrology only dates from the mid-third century. See Candida Moss, "On the Dating of Polycarp: Rethinking the Place of the *Martyrdom of Polycarp* in the History of Christianity," *Early Christianity* 1 (2010):

539–574; and *The Myth of Persecution: How Early Christians Invented a Story of Martyrdom* (New York: Harper Collins, 2013).

18. "The Martyrdom of Polycarp," in *The Apostolic Fathers*, ed. and trans. Bart D. Ehrman (Cambridge, MA: Harvard University Press, 2003), §9, 1:379.

19. Justin Martyr, *The First and Second Apologies*, trans. Leslie William Barnard (New York: Paulist Press, 1997), 26, 27.

20. Clement of Alexandria, "Exhortation to the Greeks," in G. W. Butterworth, trans., *Clement of Alexandria* (London: William Heinemann, 1919), 47.

21. "The Martyrs of Lyon," in Herbert Musurillo, trans., *The Acts of the Christian Martyrs* (Oxford: Clarendon, 1972), 67.

22. Marcus Minucius Felix, *The Octavius*, trans. G. W. Clarke (New York: Newman Press, 1974), 65. For more on Thyestian banquets, see Athenagoras, *Legatio*, ed. William R. Schoedel (Oxford: Clarendon Press, 1972), 9 (3.1); Tertullian, "Apology," in Gerald H. Rendall, trans., *Tertullian*, (London: William Heinemann, 1953), 45 (8.6–8). More generally, see Andrew McGowan, "Eating People: Accusations of Cannibalism Against Christians in the Second Century," *Journal of Early Christian Studies* 2.4 (Winter 1994): 413–442.

23. Minucius Felix, *Octavius*, 107. Italics mine. On this charge, see this bibliography from Rives, "Human Sacrifice," fn. 6.

24. Tertullian, "Apology," 47 (9.2).

25. Eusebius, *Oration in Praise of the Emperor Constantine*, in *Nicene Fathers*, 2nd series, 1:601–2 (chap. 13). For a similar late apologetic attack, see, e.g., Prudentius, "Contra Symmachos," in *Prudentius*, trans. H. J. Thomson (London: William Heinemann, 1953), 1:379ff (1.379–99).

26. Clement of Alexandria, *Exhortation*, 91.

27. Clement, *Exhortation*, 97.

28. Origen, *Contra Celsum*, trans. Henry Chadwick (Cambridge: Cambridge University Press, 1980), 153 (3.37).

29. E.g., "no craft, therefore, no profession, no form of trade contributing anything to the equipment or formation of idols will be free from the charge of idolatry . . ."; Tertullian, *De Idololatria*, trans. J. H. Waszink and J.C.M. van Winden (Leiden: E. J. Brill, 1987), 45 (11.8).

30. T. D. Barnes, "Legislation Against the Christians," *Journal of Roman Studies* 58.1–2 (1968): 48. The obscurities of this letter and, generally, the Roman legal management of Christianity before the reign of Decius (250 CE) have given rise to a substantial scholarship on the legal basis of Roman persecution. See Barnes, but also A. N. Sherwin White, "The Early Persecutions and Roman Law Again," *Journal of Theological Studies* 3.2 (October 1952): 199–213 and G.E. M. de Ste. Croix, "Why Were the Early Christians Persecuted?" *Past and Present* 26 (November 1963): 6–38.

31. Ste. Croix, "Why Were the Early Christians Persecuted?," 20.

32. On the philanthropy of sacrifice, see K. W. Harl, "Sacrifice and Pagan Belief in Fifth- and Sixth-Century Byzantium," *Past and Present* 128 (August 1990): 9. On how the decline in financial support affected the institution of sacrifice in late antique Rome, see Alan Cameron, *The Last Pagans of Rome* (Oxford: Oxford University Press, 2011), 51, 65.

33. Pliny, *Letters*, trans. William Melmoth (Cambridge, MA: Harvard University Press, 1935), 2:403 (10.96).

34. On the absence of such a law, see Ste. Croix, "Why Were the Early Christians Persecuted?," 14.

35. Just how much the authorities worked to get stubborn Christians to sacrifice can be seen in the *passio* of Pionius; see "The Martyrdom of Pionius," in Musurillo, trans., *Acts of the Christian Martyrs*, esp. p. 161–3.

36. See G.E.M. de Ste. Croix, "Aspects of the 'Great' Persecution," *Harvard Theological Review* 47.2 (April 1954): 80–82.

37. Marie-Zoe Petropoulou, *Animal Sacrifice in Ancient Greek Religion, Judaism, and Christianity, 100 BC–AD 200* (Oxford: Oxford University Press, 2008), 247.

38. J. B. Rives, "The Decree of Decius and the Religion of Empire," *Journal of Roman Studies* 89 (1999): 153. More generally, on the changing culture of sacrifice in the Roman world, see Jan N. Bremmer, "Transformations and Decline of Sacrifice in Imperial Rome and Late Antiquity," in M. Blömer and B. Eckhardt, eds., *Transformationen paganer Religion in der Kaiserzeit* (Berlin and Boston: de Gruyter, 2018), 215–256, and Guy Stroumsa, *The End of Sacrifice: Religious Transformations in Late Antiquity* (Chicago: University of Chicago Press, 2009).

39. Libellus no. 1, in John R. Knipfing, "The Libelli of the Decian Persecution," *Harvard Theological Review* 16.4 (October 1923): 363.

40. Cyprian, *De Lapsis* and *De Ecclesiae Catholicae Unitate*, trans. Maurice Bévenot, S.J. (Oxford: Clarendon Press, 1971), 13 (chap. 8).

41. On the variety of evasions, see Ste. Croix, "Aspects of the 'Great' Persecution," 100.

42. On this conflict, see Ronald E. Heine, "Cyprian and Novatian," in *The Cambridge History of Early Christian Literature* (Cambridge: Cambridge University Press, 2004), 154–155. On Novatian, see Johannes Quasten, *Patrology*, vol. 2, *The Ante-Nicene Literature after Irenaeus* (Westminster, MD: Newman Press, 1953): 212–232; also *Theologische Realenzyklopädie* (Berlin: Walter de Gruyter, 1994), s.v. "Novatian."

43. Cyprian, *De Lapsis* (Oxford: Clarendon Press, 1971), 39.

44. John Milbank, "Stories of Sacrifice," *Modern Theology* 12 (January 1996): 41.

45. Herodotus, *Herodotus*, trans. A. D. Godley (London: William Heinemann, 1921), 261 (4.62).

46. Euripides, *Euripides*, trans. David Kovacs (Cambridge, MA: Harvard University Press, 1999), 187.

47. See J. Rives, "Human Sacrifice Among Pagans and Christians," *Journal of Roman Studies* 85 (1995): 69. More generally, on the real practice (or the real absence) of human sacrifice in the ancient Greek world, see Dennis D. Hughes, *Human Sacrifice in Ancient Greece* (London: Routledge, 1991). In ancient Carthage, archaeological evidence indicates that child sacrifice was indeed a reality: see Susanna Shelby Brown, *Late Carthaginian Child Sacrifice and Sacrificial Monuments in Their Mediterranean Context* (Sheffield: Sheffield University Press, 1991), esp. chap. 3.

48. Plutarch, *On Superstition*, 493 (171c-d). For another version of this story, see Diodorus Siculus, *Bibliotheca historica*, trans. Francis R. Walton (London: William Heinemann, 1956–67), 117 (20.14.1–15).

49. Plato, *The Republic*, trans. Paul Shorey (London: William Heinemann, 1946), 1:127 (362c).

50. Plato, *The Republic*, 1:219 (390d).

51. Lucretius, *De rerum natura*, trans. W.H.D. Rouse with revisions by Martin Ferguson Smith (Cambridge, MA: Harvard University Press, 1992), 5.1197, 471–472.

52. Virgil, *Aeneid*, trans. Robert Fitzgerald (New York: Random House, 1981), 35–40.

53. Lucian, "On Sacrifices," *Lucian*, trans. A. M. Harmon (London: William Heinemann, 1936), 5:171.

54. Porphyry, *On Abstinence from Killing Animals*, trans. Gillian Clark (Ithaca, NY: Cornell University Press, 2000), 56 (2.5), 57 (2.7).

55. Iamblichus, *De mysteriis*, trans. Emma C. Clarke, John M. Dillon, and Jaskson P. Hershbell (Leiden: Brill, 2004), 239 (5.9).

56. Cicero, *De natura deorum*, trans. H. Rackham (London: William Heinemann, 1933), 193, 2.28.

57. Augustine, *City of God Against the Pagans*, ed. R. W. Dyson (Cambridge: Cambridge University Press, 1998), 180 (4.40).

58. Athenagoras, *Legatio*, trans. William Schoedel (Oxford: Oxford University Press, 1972), 9 (4.1).

59. Clement, *Exhortation*, 49. More generally on ancient atheism, see *Reallexicon für Antike und Christentum* (Stuttgart: Hiersemann Verlag, 1950), s.v. "Atheismus."

60. Justin Martyr, *The First and Second Apologies*, trans. Leslie William Barnard (New York: Paulist Press, 1997), 26.

61. Plato, *Apology of Socrates*, in *Plato*, 1:99 (26c-d), 133 (37e).

62. Tertullian, *Tertullian*, trans. Gerald H. Rendall (London: William Heinemann, 1953), 77 (14.7).

63. More generally on Christian Platonism, see Alexander J. B. Hampton and John Peter Kenney, *Christian Platonism: A History* (Cambridge: Cambridge University Press, 2021). On Justin Martyr specifically, see Denis Minns, "Justin Martyr," in Lloyd P. Gerson, ed., *Cambridge History of Philosophy in Late Antiquity* (Cambridge: Cambridge University Press, 2000), 258–269.

64. Justin Martyr, "Hortatory Address to the Greeks," in *The Ante-Nicene Fathers*, Alexander Roberts and James Donaldson, eds. (Grand Rapids, MI: Wm. B. Eerdmans, 1956), 1:281.

65. Justin, "First Apology," 55.

66. Minucius Felix, *Octavius*, 83, 85.

67. Tacitus, *The Annals*, trans. John Jackson (London: William Heinemann, 1951), 4:283 (15.44).

68. Minucius Felix, *Octavius*, 66.

69. Robert M. Berchman, *Porphyry Against the Christians*, 135.

70. Julian, "Against the Galileans," in *The Works of the Emperor Julian*, trans. Wilmer Cave Wright (London: William Heinemann, 1923), 3:343–345 (106c-d). On Julian more generally, and this text specifically, see Elm, *Sons of Hellenism*, esp. chaps. 3 and 7.

71. Ignatius of Antioch, "Letter to the Philadelphians," in *The Apostolic Fathers*, Bart D. Ehrman, ed. and trans. (Cambridge, MA: Harvard University Press, 2003), 1:291 (8.2).

72. See, e.g., the *Odyssey*, 3.51. Also see *Theologische Wörterbuch zum Neuen Testament*, ed. Gerhard Kittel (Stuttgart: W. Kohlhammer, 1933–79), s.v. κοινωνός. Against this view, see Wendell Lee Willis, *Idol Meat in Corinth: The Pauline Argument in 1 Corinthians 8 and 10* (Chico, CA: Scholars Press, 1985), esp. 201ff. Willis's strenuous efforts to prove that Paul was not advocating a fully sacrificial Eucharist seems, to me, beside the point given how quickly the early church subscribed exactly to this view. Just as beside the point, it seems to me, is the strenuous *defense* of the "sacramental" (a loaded term if ever there was one) character of *koinonia* in George Heyman, *The Power of Sacrifice: Roman and Christian Discourses in Conflict* (Washington, DC: Catholic University of America Press, 2007), 115f.

73. Dennis E. Smith, *From Symposium to Eucharist: The Banquet in the Early Christian World* (Minneapolis, MN: Fortress Press, 2002), 85.

74. See C. S. Mann, trans. and commentary, *Mark: A New Translation* (New York: Doubleday, 1986), 415, 418–419, and Morna D. Hooker, *The Gospel According to Saint Mark* (Peabody, MA: Hendrickson, 1991), 248–249. Also see *Theologische Wörterbuch zum Neuen Testament*, s.v. λύω, λύτρον.

75. See, e.g., Flavius Josephus, *Antiquities of the Jews*, trans. Ralph Marcus (Cambridge, MA: Harvard University Press, 1963), 16.7.1, p. 75. More generally on the *hilasterion*, see the measured and learned discussion in Douglas L. Moo, *The Epistle to the Romans* (Grand Rapids, MI: William B. Eerdmans, 1996), 231–238.

76. One of the most sacrificial of the fathers, Origen, seized on just this connection in his *Commentary on the Epistle to the Romans, Books 1–5*, trans. Thomas P. Scheck (Washington, DC: Catholic University Press, 2001), 216–217 (3.8.1).

77. "Didache: The Teaching of the Twelve Apostles," in *The Apostolic Fathers*, ed. and trans. Bart D. Ehrman (Cambridge, MA: Harvard University Press, 2003), 1: 439 (14.1–3). More generally, see here Paul Bradshaw, *Eucharistic Origins* (New York: Oxford University Press, 2004), esp. chap. 2, and Anders Ekenberg, "The Eucharist in Early Church Orders," in David Helholm and Dieter Sänger, eds., *The Eucharist—Its Orders and Contexts: Sacred Meal, Communal Meal, Table Fellowship in Late Antiquity, Early Judaism, and Early Christianity* (Tübingen: Mohr Siebeck, 2017), 2:958–992.

78. Clement of Rome, "First Letter of Clement to the Corinthians," in Bart D. Ehrman, ed. and trans., *The Apostolic Fathers* (Cambridge, MA: Harvard University Press, 2003), 1:107 (40.1–2).

79. Bradshaw, *Eucharistic Origins*, 83.

80. "Didache," in *Apostolic Fathers*, 1:439 (14.3).

81. Tertullian, "Apology," 97 (19.2).

82. Justin, "First Apology," 60.

83. Augustine, *City of God*, 396 (10.4).

84. Augustine, *City of God*, 398 (10.6).

85. Augustine, *City of God*, 834 (18.12).

86. Augustine, *City of God*, 729 (16.22).

87. Isabel Speyart von Woerden, "The Iconography of the Sacrifice of Abraham," *Vigiliae Christianae* 15.4 (December 1961): 229.

88. Tertullian, "Apology," 97 (19.1).

89. von Woerden, "The Iconography of the Sacrifice of Abraham," 220, 219.

90. "Epistle of Barnabas," in *Apostolic Fathers*, 2:27 (5.2), 39 (7.9). See also Justin Martyr, "Apology," 57.

91. Augustine, *City of God*, 858–59 (18.29). See also Eusebius, *Oration in Praise of the Emperor Constantine*, in *Nicene Fathers*, 2nd series, 1:605 (15.11). More generally on the passage and its application to things Christian, see William H. Bellinger, Jr. and William R. Farmer, *Jesus and the Suffering Servant: Isaiah 53 and Christian Origins* (Harrisburg, PA: Trinity Press, 1998). For a skeptical take on the suffering servant, see Morna Hooker, *Jesus and the Servant: The Influence of the Servant Concept of Deutero-Isaiah in the New Testament* (London: SPCK, 1959).

92. Augustine, Letter 35, in *Letters*, trans. Roland Teske, S.J. (Hyde Park, NY: New City Press, 1994), 2.1:137.

93. Cyprian, *De Lapsis*, 41.

94. Augustine, *City of God*, 397 (10.5).

95. Augustine, *City of God*, 400 (10.6).

96. Origen, *Contra Celsum*, 464 (8.17).

97. Julian, "Against the Galileans," 405 (305d–306a).

98. Augustine, "Answer to an Enemy of the Law and the Prophets," in *The Works of Saint Augustine*, trans. Roland J. Teske, S.J. (Hyde Park, NY: New City Press, 1994) 1.18:382, 383.

99. "Moysi litterae verba sunt Christi"; Irenaeus, *Adversus haereses*, ed. Norbert Brox (Freiburg: Herder Verlag, 1997), 4:22 (4.2.2).

100. On Abraham, see Irenaeus, *Adversus haereses*, 4: 62 (4.8.1).

101. On Malachi, see Irenaeus, *Adversus haereses*, 4:134–5 (4.17.5).

102. Irenaeus, *Adversus haereses*, 4:138 (4.18.1–2).

103. Augustine, "*Answer to Faustus, a Manichean*," in *Works*, trans. Roland Teske, 1.20:97.

104. Augustine, "Answer to Faustus," 1.20:264.

105. Epiphanius, *Panarion*, trans. Frank Williams (Leiden: E. J. Brill, 1987), 86.

106. Epiphanius, *Panarion*, 86.

107. Augustine, "Heresies," in *Works*, trans. Roland J. Teske, S.J., 1.18:38.

108. Quoted in Andrew McGowan, *Ascetic Eucharists: Food and Drink in Early Christian Ritual Meals* (Oxford: Clarendon Press, 1999), 187.

109. McGowan, *Ascetic Eucharists*, 89.

110. McGowan, *Ascetic Eucharists*, 98.

111. McGowan, *Ascetic Eucharists*, 203. More generally on sacrifice and eating, see Marcel Detienne and Jean-Pierre Vernant, eds., *The Cuisine of Sacrifice among the Greeks*, trans. Paula Wissing (Chicago: University of Chicago Press, 1989).

112. McGowan, *Ascetic Eucharists*, 240.

113. Cyprian of Carthage, *Ep. 63.15.2*, quoted in McGowan, *Ascetic Eucharists*, 206.

114. Ignatius of Antioch, "Letter to the Ephesians," in *Apostolic Fathers*, 1:227 (8.1).

115. Ignatius of Antioch, "Letter to the Romans," in *Apostolic Fathers*, 1:273 (2.2), 275 (4.2).

116. "The Martyrs of Lyon," in Musurillo, trans., *Acts of the Christian Martyrs*, 75, 79.

117. Augustine, Sermon 312, "On the Birthday of the Martyr Cyprian," in *Works*, 3.9:83.

118. "The Martyrdom of Pionius the Presbyter and His Companions," in *Acts of the Christian Martyrs*, 165 (compare with 159). This comparison comes first in 1 Cor. 9:25.

119. Tertullian, "The Crown," in Robert D. Sider, ed., *Christian and Pagan in the Roman Empire* (Washington, DC: Catholic University Press, 2001), 129 (9.1). More generally on the incorporations of the pagan crown, see Karl Baus, *Der Kranz in Antike und Christentum: Eine religionsgeschichtliche Untersuchung mit besonderer Berücksichtigung Tertullians* (Bonn: Peter Hanstein, 1940).

120. "The Martyrdom of Bishop Fructuosos and His Deacons, Augurius and Eulogius," in *Acts of the Christian Martyrs*, 183–185.

121. "The Martyrdom of Bishop Fructuosos," 185 fn.15.

122. Prudentius, "Peristephanon liber," in *Prudentius*, trans. H. J. Thomson (London: William Heinemann, 1953), 2:169 (4.189–198).

123. Prudentius, "Peristephanon liber," 2: 317 (11.169ff).

124. "Martyrdom of Polycarp," in *Acts of the Christian Martyrs*, 393 (18.2–3).

125. Peter Brown, *The Cult of the Saints: Its Rise and Function in Latin Christianity* (Chicago: University of Chicago Press, 1981), 9. See also Ann Marie Yasin, *Saints and Church Spaces in the Late Antique Mediterranean: Architecture, Cult, and Community* (Cambridge: Cambridge University Press, 2009).

126. See Vincenzo Fiocchi Nicolai, "The Origin and Developent of Roman Catacombs," in *The Christian Catacombs of Rome: History, Decoration, Inscriptions*, ed. Vincenzo Fiocchi Nicolai, Fabrizio Bisconti, and Danilo Mazzoleni (Regensburg: Schnell and Steiner, 1999), 14.

127. Eusebius, *Ecclesiastical History*, trans. J.E.L. Oulton (London: William Heinemann, 1953), 2:150 (6.11.10).

128. See Richard Krautheimer, "Mensa-Coemeterium-Martyrium," *Studies in Early Christian, Medieval, and Renaissance Art* (New York: NYU Press, 1969); Graydon F. Snyder, *Ante Pacem: Archaeological Evidence of Church Life before Constantine* (Macon, GA: Mercer University Press, 2003). Not all churches housed martyr's bodies or other tombs, especially if they were within city walls where burial was generally forbidden; see Yasin, *Saints and Church Spaces*, 69–70.

129. Quoted in William Tabbernee, *Montanist Inscriptions and Testimonia: Epigraphic Sources Illustrating the History of Montanism* (Macon, GA: Mercer University Press, 1997), 237.

130. See Thomas W. Laqueur, *The Work of the Dead: A Cultural History of Mortal Remains* (Princeton, NJ: Princeton University Press, 2015), 95–96. Also Nicolai, "The Origin and Development of Roman Catacombs," 53.

131. On the Carthage discovery, see William Tabbernee, "Epigraphy," in *The Oxford Handbook of Early Christian Studies*, ed. Susan Ashbrook Harvey and David G. Hunter (Oxford: Oxford University Press, 2008), 120–139. More generally, see, André Berthier, *Les vestiges du christianisme antique dans la Numidie centrale* (Algiers: Imprimerie Polyglotte Africaine, 1943).

132. On these relations, see Candida Moss, "Christian Funerary Banquets and Martyr Cults," in *The Eucharist—Its Origins and Contexts*, 2: 819–828. Also Ramsay

MacMullen, "Christian Ancestor Worship in Rome," *Journal of Biblical Literature* 129 (Fall 2010): 597–613.

133. On Salona, see Snyder, *Ante Pacem*, 167–168.

134. Nicolai, "The Origin and Development of Roman Catacombs," 45; Fabrizio Bisconti, "The Decoration of Roman Catacombs," in *Christian Catacombs of Rome: History, Decoration, Inscriptions*, 80, 109–13. For various interpretations of these Roman catacombs, see the work of Nicola Denzey Lewis, both *The Bone Gatherers: The Lost Worlds of Early Christian Women* (Boston: Beacon, 2007) and *The Early Modern Invention of Late Antique Rome* (Cambridge: Cambridge University Press, 2020).

135. See Krautheimer, "Mensa-Coemeterium-Martyrium," 46–47; Nicolai, "The Origin and Development of Roman Catacombs," 50.

136. Augustine, sermon 310, "On the Birthday of the Martyr Cyprian," (date unknown) in *Sermons*, trans. Edmund Hill (Hyde Park, NY: New City Press, 1994), 3.9:69.

137. In general, see Kenneth John Conant, "The Original Buildings at the Holy Sepulchre in Jerusalem," *Speculum* 31.1 (January 1956): 1–48.

138. Eusebius, *Life of Constantine*, trans. Averil Cameron and Stuart G. Hall (Oxford: Clarendon Press, 1999), 132–133 (26.1–28.1).

139. Eusebius, *Life of Constantine*, 135 (33.3).

140. Justin E. A. Kroesen, *The Sepulchrum Domini Through the Ages: Its Form and Function* (Peeters: Leuven, 1975); Colin Morris, *The Sepulchre of Christ and the Medieval West: From the Beginning to 1600* (Oxford: Oxford University Press, 2005); and Robert Wilken, *The Land Called Holy: Palestine in Christian History and Thought* (New Haven, CT: Yale University Press, 1992).

141. For Constantine's edict, see Eusebius, *Life of Constantine*, 109 (40.1).

142. See here Krautheimer, "Mensa-Coemeterium-Martyrium."

143. Nicolai, "The Origin and Development of Roman Catacombs," 63–64.

144. Quoted in Yasin, *Saints and Church Spaces*, 153.

145. "The Martyrdom of Saints Perpetua and Felicitas," in Musurillo, *Acts of the Christian Martyrs*, 117.

146. Origen, *Exhortation to Martyrdom*, trans. John J. O'Meara (Westminster, MD: Newman Press, 1954), 171.

147. Cyprian, *De lapsis*, 29.

148. Prudentius, hymn 1, to Emeterius and Chelidonius of Calagurris, in *Prudentius*, 2:101 (1.18); on propitiation, see the hymn to St. Vincent, 2:191 (5.357–364).

149. Augustine, *City of God*, 1134 (22.9); on the miracles, see 1128 (22.8).

150. Origen, *Exhortation to Martyrdom*, 183.

151. Cyprian, *The Unity of the Catholic Church*, trans. Maurice Bévenot, S.J. (Oxford: Clarendon Press, 1971), 79, italics mine. Later, Prudentius put this sentiment directly in the mouth of the martyr Hippolytus; see "Peristephanon liber," in *Prudentius* 2:307 (11.29–31).

152. Cyprian, *The Unity of the Catholic Church*, 85–86.

153. Cyprian, *The Unity of the Catholic Church*, 85.

154. On Origen, see Elizabeth Clark, "New Perspectives on the Origenist Controversy: Human Embodiment and Ascetic Strategies," *Church History* 59.2 (June 1990): 147.

155. On the situation of the North African Church, and the conflicts between dissident and Catholic groups, see especially Brent D. Shaw, *Sacred Violence: African Christians and Sectarian Hatred in the Age of Augustine* (Cambridge: Cambridge University Press, 2011). Donatism is an epithet that has grown into a historical descriptor, as Shaw shows. Nevertheless, since it will have a long afterlife, I will use it here, with caution.

156. Shaw, *Sacred Violence*, 82.

157. Optatus quoted in Shaw, *Sacred Violence*, 166.

158. Augustine, Sermon 313e, "Discourse on the Birthday of Saint Cyprian" [410] in *Sermons*, 3.8:113.

159. Augustine, Sermon 313e, "Discourse on the Birthday of Saint Cyprian," 3.8:111.

160. Augustine, letter 173 to Donatus [ca. 411], in *Letters*, vol. 2.3:127.

161. See, e.g., Augustine, letter 204 to Dulcitius, in *Letters*, vol. 2.3:204.

162. For the parable, see Augustine, letter 173 to Donatus, in *Letters*, vol. 2.3:129.

163. E.g., Clyde Pharr, trans., *The Theodosian Code, Novels, and the Sirmondian Constitutions* (Union, NJ: Lawbook Exchange, 2001), 16.2.5.

164. Shaw, *Sacred Violence*, 224–226. For one formalization of these bans, see Pharr, trans., *The Theodosian Code*, 16.10.4. The efficacy of these bans is hard to assess, since emperors felt compelled to repeat them well into the sixth century. On the long decline of pagan sacrifice, see K. W. Harl, "Sacrifice and Pagan Belief in Fifth- and Sixth-Century Byzantium," *Past and Present* 128 (August 1990): 7–27. For revisions to this, see also Cameron, *Last Pagans of Rome*.

165. Pharr, trans., *The Theodosian Code*, 16.5.6 [dated 379 CE].

166. Eunapius, "Lives of the Philosophers," in *Philostratus and Eunapius: The Lives of the Sophists*, trans. Wilmer Cave Wright (London: William Heinemann, 1952), 425.

167. Julian, "Against the Galilaeans," 415 (335c).

168. Origen, *Contra Celsum*, 157 (3.43).

169. Clement of Alexandria, "Exhortation to the Greeks," 99–101.

170. Prudentius, "Contra Symmachos," in *Prudentius*, 1:365 (1.190–92).

171. Eusebius, *Life of Constantine*, 146 (57.2).

172. Athenagoras, *Legatio*, 75 (30.3); this was made all the more juicy because it came from a pagan source (see Callimachus, *Hymn to Zeus*, in *Callimachus: Hecale, Hymns, Epigrams* (Cambridge, MA: Harvard University Press, 2022), 181 (8–9).

173. Augustine, *City of God*, 354 (8.26).

174. Augustine, *City of God*, 1135 (22.10).

175. Augustine, "Answer to Faustus," 1.20:263 (20).

176. Augustine, "Answer to Faustus," 1.20:29 (20).

177. Augustine, sermon 277, "On the Feast of the Martyr Vincent," in *Sermons*, 3.8:33.

178. Krautheimer, "Mensa-Coemeterium-Martyrium," 47.

179. Augustine, sermon 310, "On the Birthday of the Martyr Cyprian," 3.9:69.

180. Augustine, sermon 311 "On the Birthday of the Martyr Cyprian," (405), in *Sermons*, 3.9:73 (see also 79, fn. 8).

181. Augustine, letter 29, in *Letters*, 2.1:97, 99.
182. Augustine, "Answer to Faustus," 1.20:280.

Part II: Sacrifice and the Deep Time of Christianity

1. For this transformation, see Rachel Fulton, *From Judgment to Passion: Devotion to Christ and the Virgin Mary, 800–1200* (Ithaca, NY: Cornell University Press, 2002). On the passion during the Carolingian period, see Celia Chazelle, *The Crucified God in the Carolingian Era: Theology and the Art of Christ's Passion* (Cambridge: Cambridge University Press, 2001).

2. See, e.g., Gerhard Lutz, "Late Medieval Spaces and the Eucharist," in *A Companion to the Eucharist in the Middle Ages*, ed. Ian Christopher Levy et al. (Leiden: Brill, 2012), 471–497; Justin E. A. Kroesen, *The Sepulchrum Domini Through the Ages: Its Form and Function* (Peeters: Leuven, 1975); also, Eamon Duffy, *Stripping of the Altars: Traditional Religion in England, c. 1400–c. 1580* (New Haven, CT: Yale University Press, 1992), 29ff.

3. Fulton, *Judgment to Passion*, 18, 107. See also Miri Rubin, *Corpus Christi: The Eucharist in Late Medieval Culture* (Cambridge: Cambridge University Press, 1991), 51–52.

4. On the origins, development, and elaboration of Corpus Christ, see Rubin, *Corpus Christi*. See also Gary Macy, "Theology of the Eucharist in the High Middle Ages," in *A Companion to the Eucharist in the Middle Ages*, ed. Ian Christopher Levy et al. (Leiden: Brill, 2012), 365–398.

5. Carolyn Walker Bynum, *Wonderful Blood: Theology and Practice in Late Medieval Northern Germany and Beyond* (Philadelphia: University of Pennsylvania Press, 2007).

6. Rubin, *Corpus Christi*, 302, 304, 308.

Chapter 2: From the Thesaurus to the Archive

1. Desiderius Erasmus, *The Correspondence of Erasmus*, trans. R.A.B. Mynors, in *Collected Works of Erasmus* (Toronto: University of Toronto Press, 1988), 8:73. Hereafter *CWE*.

2. Peter of Lombard, *Libri IV sententiarum*, 2nd ed. (Florence: Ex Typographia Collegii S. Bonaventurae, 1916), 2:812 (4.12.5). Translation after Francis Clark, *Eucharistic Sacrifice and the Reformation* (Westminster, MD: Newman Press, 1960), 75–76, with my changes.

3. Peter of Lombard, *Libri IV sententiarum*, 2:812 (4.12.5). Translation after Francis Clark, *Eucharistic Sacrifice*, 75–76, with my changes.

4. James W. Thompson, "EPHAPAX: The One and the Many in Hebrews," *New Testament Studies* 53, no. 4 (October 2007): 566–581.

5. See, e.g., Marius Lépin, *L'Idée du sacrifice de la messe* (Paris: Gabriel Beauchesne, 1926), chap. 4; Bruce D. Marshall, "The Whole Mystery of Our Salvation: Saint Thomas Aquinas on the Eucharist as Sacrifice," in *Rediscovering Aquinas and the Sacraments: Studies in Sacramental Theology*, ed. Matthew Levering and Michael

Dauphinais (Chicago: Hillenbrand Books, 2009), 41–42. More generally, Miri Rubin, *Corpus Christi: the Eucharist in Late Medieval Culture* (Cambridge: Cambridge University Press, 2002), and Ian Christopher Levy, Gary Macy, and Kristen Van Ausdall, eds., *A Companion to the Eucharist in the Middle* Ages (Leiden: Brill, 2012).

6. Peter of Lombard, *Libri IV sententiarum*, 2:813.

7. Marcia Colish, "Systematic Theology and Theological Renewal in the Twelfth Century," *Journal of Medieval and Renaissance Studies* 18, no. 2 (Fall 1988): 136 (arguing against this view—see p. 137 for examples).

8. Jacques-Guy Bourgerol, "The Fathers and the *Sentences* of Peter Lombard," in *The Reception of the Church Fathers in the West: From the Carolingians to the Maurists*, ed. Irena Backus (Leiden: Brill, 1996), 1:115. Even the Sorbonne, one of the great manuscript libraries of Europe, only had a very partial copy of book I of the *City of God*; see E. L. Saak, *Creating Augustine: Interpreting Augustine and Augustinianism in the Later Middle Ages* (Oxford: Oxford University Press, 2012), 31.

9. E. Ann Matter, "The Church Fathers and the *Glossa Ordinaria*," in *The Reception of the Church Fathers*, ed. Irena Backus, 1:102–103.

10. Ivo of Chartes, *Decretum*, in *Patrologiae Cursus Completus*, ed. J. P. Migne (Paris, France: J. P. Migne, 1855), 161: 142–143 (2.6.D). The quotation is repeated in the *Panormia*, the more condensed version of the *Decretum*; see Ivo of Chartes, *Panormia*, in *Patrologiae*, ed. J. P. Migne, 161:1077 (chap. 141).

11. Gratian, *Decretum Magistri Gratiani*, 2nd ed., ed. Aemilius Ludwig Richter and Emil Albert Friedberg (Leipzig: Bernhard Tauchnitz, 1879), 1:1333 (3.2.53).

12. The 1603 print edition, in fact, has a quotation from Ambrose and from Chrysostom; see *Bibliorum Sacrorum cum Glossa Ordinaria iam ante quidem a Strabo Fulgensi collecta nunc autem novis, cum graecorum, tum latinorum partum expositionibus, Locupletata*, ed. Franciscus Feuardentium OFM, Joannes Dadraeus, and Iacobus Cuilly (Venice, 1603), 6:903, commenting on Hebrews 10.

13. On Aquinas as a firsthand reader of the fathers, see Leo J. Elders, "Thomas Aquinas and the Fathers of the Church," in *The Reception of the Church Fathers*, ed. Irena Backus, 1:343.

14. Monika Asztalos, "The Faculty of Theology," in *Universities in the Middle Ages*, ed. Hilde de Ridder-Symoens (Cambridge: Cambridge University Press, 1992), 414.

15. Colish, "Systematic Theology," 151–155.

16. On the odd position of the theology faculty, see Olaf Pedersen, "Tradition and Innovation," in *The History of the University in Europe*, ed. Hilde de Ridder-Symoens (Cambridge: Cambridge University Press, 1996), 2:474; also Antonio García y García, "The Faculties of Law," in *Universities in the Middle Ages*, 1:400–401; Monika Asztalos, "The Faculty of Theology," in *Universities in the Middle Ages*, 1:414. More generally, see James Brundage, *Medieval Origins of the Legal Profession: Canonists, Civilians, and Courts* (Chicago: University of Chicago Press, 2008).

17. On Fourth Lateran Council, see Clare Monagle, *Orthodoxy and Controversy in Twelfth-Century Religious Discourse: Peter of Lombard's* Sentences *and the Development of Theology* (Turnhout: Brepols, 2013), chap. 5; on the later reception, see Spencer E. Young, *Scholarly Community at the Early University of Paris: Theologians, Education, and Society, 1215–1248* (Cambridge: Cambridge University Press, 2014), 28, 52–55.

18. On the *Sentences* and Lombard, see Marcia L Colish, *Peter Lombard* (Brill: Leiden, 1994), 1:33f, and on systematics more generally. Stephan Kuttner, *Harmony from Dissonance: An Interpretation of Medieval Canon Law* (Latrobe, PA: Archabbey Press, 1960).

19. Peter Abelard, "*Prologus*" in *Sic et Non: A Critical Edition*, trans. and ed. Blanche B. Boyer and Richard McKeon (Chicago: University of Chicago Press, 1976), 97. "*cum ipsos etiam prophetas et apostolos ab errore non penitus fuisse constet alienos.*"

20. Peter Lombard, "*Prologus*" in *Libri IV sententiarum*, 1:2–3. This is a near quotation from Hilary of Poitiers, *De Trinitate libri duodecim* in *Patrologiae Cursus Complectus*, 10:1–2.

21. See especially Young, *Scholarly Community*, 30–31; G. R. Evans, *Old Arts and New Theology: The Beginnings of Theology as an Academic Discipline* (Oxford: Clarendon Press, 1980), chap. 4; Jaroslav Pelikan, *Growth of Medieval Theology (600–1300)* (Chicago: University of Chicago Press, 1978), 255.

22. Lombard, *Libri IV sententiarum*, 2:818 (4.13.1: lines 130–131).

23. See Andrea Riedl, *Kirchenbild und Kircheneinheit: Der dominikanische "Tractatus contra Graecos" (1252) in seinem theologischen und historischen Kontext* (Berlin: Walter de Gruyter, 2020), esp. chap. 3.

24. Walter Berschin, *Greek Letters and the Latin Middle Ages: From Jerome to Nicholas of Cusa*, trans. Jerold C. Frakes (Washington, DC: Catholic University Press, 1988), 257.

25. Charles Stinger, "Italian Renaissance Learning and the Church Fathers," in *The Reception of the Church Fathers*, ed. Irena Backus, 2: 483. On Coluccio's library, see B. L. Ullmann, *The Humanism of Coluccio Salutati* (Padua: Edictrice Antenore, 1963), chap. 9.

26. On Traversari, see Charles L. Stinger, *Humanism and the Church Fathers: Ambrogio Traversari (1386–1439) and Christian Antiquity in the Italian Renaissance* (Albany, NY: State University of New York Press, 1977).

27. See Henry Chadwick, *East and West: The Making of a Rift in the Church: From Apostolic Times to the Council of Florence* (Oxford: Oxford University Press, 2003), 268.

28. John Monfasani, *George of Trebizond: A Biography and a Study of His Rhetoric and Logic* (Leiden: E. J. Brill, 1976), 47–48. See also Christina Abenstein, *Die Basilius-Übersetzung des Georg von Trapezunt in ihrem historischen Kontext* (Berlin: Walter de Gruyter, 2014).

29. On Trebizond as translator of Eusebius, see Monfasani, *George of Trebizond*, 78.

30. George of Trebizond, prefatory letter to Pope Nicholas V to his translation of Eusebius's *Praeparatio Evangelica*, in John Monfasani, ed., *Collectanea Trapezuntiana: Texts, Documents, and Bibliographies of George of Trebizond* (Binghamton, NY: Medieval & Renaissance Texts & Studies, 1984), 291–922, italics mine.

31. On the preprint environment, see Nikolaus Staubach, "*Memores pristinae perfectionis*: The Importance of the Church Fathers for *Devotio Moderna*," in *Reception of the Church Fathers in the West*, ed. Irena Backus, 1:405–469; Charles Stinger, *Humanism and the Church Fathers.*

32. Charles Stinger, "Italian Renaissance Learning and the Church Fathers"; Eugene Rice, "The Humanist Idea of Christian Antiquity: Lefèvre d'Étaples and His Circle," *Studies in the Renaissance* 9 (1962): 126–160.

33. On Valla's life and the conflict with Neapolitan church authorities, see Girolamo Mancini, *Vita di Lorenzo Valla* (Florence: G. C. Sansoni, 1891), chap. 7.

34. Salvatore Camporeale, "Lorenzo Valla between the Middle Ages and the Renaissance: The *Encomium of St. Thomas*," in *Christianity, Latinity, and Culture: Two Studies on Lorenzo Valla*, trans. Patrick Baker (Leiden: Brill, 2014), 169, 173.

35. Camporeale, "Lorenzo Valla," 183.

36. Lorenzo Valla, *Encomium of St. Thomas*, trans. Patrick Baker, in *Christianity, Latinity, and Culture: Two Studies on Lorenzo Valla*, 308.

37. Valla, *Encomium of St. Thomas*, 311.

38. On Chrysostom in the fifteenth century, see Sam Kennerley, *The Reception of John Chrysostom in Early Modern Europe: Translating and Reading a Greek Church Father from 1417 to 1624* (Berlin: Walter de Gruyter, 2023).

39. Desiderius Erasmus, *Convivium religiosum*, in *CWE*, 39:182.

40. Martin Luther, "Eyn sermon von dem newen Testament, das ist von der heyligen Messe," in *D. Martin Luthers Werke: Kritische Gesammtausgabe* [WA] (Weimar: Hermann Böhlau, 1888), 6:353, italics mine.

41. Erasmus read Luther's 1520 tirade against the sacraments, the *Babylonian Captivity of the Church*, in August 1521; See Erasmus, "Letter to Marcus Laurinus, 1 February 1523," in *Correspondence* 9:395 (letter 1342).

42. Erasmus, *Convivium religiosum*, in *CWE*, 39:188.

43. Erasmus, *Convivium religiosum*, 39:190.

44. Erasmus, *Convivium religiosum*, 39:191.

45. Erasmus's letters from the summer of 1522 are quite mixed about Luther, not least because many were demanding that he declare emphatically for one side or the other (see Wolfang Capito, "The Letter from Wolfgang Capito," in *The Correspondence of Erasmus*, 9:166–67 [letter 1308]). For a good example of the ambivalence, and the care with which Erasmus manages his audience, see Erasmus, "The Letter to Duke George of Saxony," in *The Correspondence of Erasmus* 9:178–83 (letter 1313).

46. For Erasmus on Theophylact, see M. A. Screech, *Ecstasy and the Praise of Folly* (London: Duckworth, 1980), 145–148.

47. Erasmus, *Correspondence*, 7:147, 148.

48. Erasmus, *Correspondence*, 7:153.

49. Eugene Rice, *Saint Jerome in the Renaissance* (Baltimore, MD: Johns Hopkins University Press, 1985), 116, 118.

50. Lisa Jardine, *Erasmus: Man of Letters: The Construction of Charisma in Print* (Princeton, NJ: Princeton University Press, 1993), 64.

51. The literature on Erasmus's interest in the Fathers is tremendous. See, inter alia, John Olin, "Erasmus and the Church Fathers," in *Six Essays on Erasmus* (New York: Fordham University Press, 1979); Jan den Boeft, "Erasmus and the Church Fathers," in *The Reception of the Church Fathers*, 2:537–572; Irena Backus, "Erasmus and the Spirituality of the Early Church," in *Erasmus' Vision of the Church*, ed. Hilmar M. Pabel (Kirksville, MO: Sixteenth Century Journal Publishers, 1995), 95–114; Robert Peters, "Erasmus and the Church Fathers: Their Practical Value," *Church*

History 36, no. 3 (Sept. 1967): 254–261; André Godin, *Érasme lecteur d'Origène* (Geneva: Librairie Droz, 1982).

52. For the thickening of this archive in the five editions of Erasmus's *Annotations on the New Testament*, see Erika Rummel, *Erasmus'* Annotations *on the New Testament* (Toronto: University of Toronto Press, 1986), chap. 2.

53. Erasmus, *Convivium religiosum*, in *CWE*, 39:184.

54. Erasmus, *Paraclesis*, in *Christian Humanism and the Reformation: Selected Writings of Erasmus*, ed. John Olin (New York: Fordham University Press, 1987), 103.

55. On this text, see most recently Thomas P. Scheck, "Erasmus' Program for Theological Renewal," in *Erasmus' Life of Origen*, trans. and ed. Thomas P. Scheck (Washington, DC: Catholic University Press, 2016), 1–42.

56. Erasmus, *Ratio seu Methodus compendio perveniendi ad veram Theologiam* in *Ausgewählte Schriften*, ed. Werner Welzig (Darmstadt: Wissenschaftliche Buchgesellschaft, 1967), 3:158, 164.

57. Erasmus, *Ratio*, 3:170.

58. Erasmus, *Ratio*, 3:184.

59. Erasmus, *Ratio*, 3:222.

60. Erasmus, *Ratio*, 3:230–232. Also 3:294–296.

61. Erasmus, *Ratio*, 3:296.

62. Erasmus, ed., *Opera divi Caecilii Cypriani episcopi Carthaginensis* (Basel: Froben, 1540), 508.

63. Erasmus, ed., *Opera divi Caecilii Cypriani*, 509–510.

64. Erasmus, ed., *Opera divi Caecilii Cypriani*, 515.

65. Erasmus, ed., *Opera divi Caecilii Cypriani*, 522.

66. Erasmus, ed., *Opera divi Caecilii Cypriani*, 523.

67. Silvana Seidel Menchi, "Un'opera misconoscuta di Erasmo? Il trattato pseudo-ciprianico '*De duplici martyrio*,'" *Rivista storica italiana* 90, no. 4 (October–December 1978): 709–743.

68. See here Brad S. Gregory, *Salvation at Stake: Christian Martyrdom in Early Modern Europe* (Cambridge, MA: Harvard University Press, 1999), 212–213.

69. Cyprian, "Exhortation to Martyrdom," in *Treatises*, ed. and trans. Roy J. Deferrari (Washington, DC: Catholic University Press, 2007), 316.

70. Cyprian, *De lapsis*, trans. Maurice Bévenot, S.J. (Oxford: Clarendon Press, 1971), 23.

71. See index to Erasmus, *Opera divi Caecilii Cypriani*, b3 verso.

72. Tertullian, "The Chapelet," in *Disciplinary, Moral, and Ascetical Works*, trans. Rudolph Arbesmann, O.S.A., Sister Emily Joseph Daly, C.S.J., and Edwin A. Quain, S.J. (Washington, DC: Catholic University Press, 1959), 248.

73. Tertullian, "The Chapelet," 254.

74. Tertullian, "The Chapelet," 237.

75. See Ernst von Dobschütz, ed., *Das Decretum Gelasianum: De libris recipiendis et non recipiendis* (Leipzig: J. C. Hinrichs, 1912), 12.

76. On Tertullian in the Middle Ages, see Paul Lehmann, "Tertullian im Mittelalter," *Hermes* 87, no. 2 (Aug. 1959): 231–246.

77. On Rhenanus's editions, and the manuscripts, see Irena Backus, *Historical Method and Confessional Identity in the Era of the Reformation (1378–1615)* (Leiden:

Brill, 2003), 152ff; John D'Amico, "Beatus Rhenanus, Tertullian, and the Reformation: A Humanist's Critique of Scholasticism," *Archiv für Reformationsgeschichte* 71 (1980): 37–63. On Rhenanus's biography of Erasmus, written as a preface to the 1538–40 *Opera omnia*, see Karl Enenkel, "A Blueprint for the Reception of Erasmus: Beatus Rhenanus's Second *Vita Erasmi* (1540)," in *The Reception of Erasmus in the Early Modern Period*, ed. Karl Enenkel (Leiden: Brill, 2013), 25–40.

78. John D'Amico, "Beatus Rhenanus," *Archiv für Reformationsgeschichte*, 42, 41.

79. Beatus Rhenanus, *Opera Q. Septimii Florentis Tertulliani inter Latinos ecclesiae scriptores primi* (Basil, 1521), a3recto.

80. Beatus Rhenanus, *Opera Q. Septimii Florentis Tertulliani*, a4verso.

81. Beatus Rhenanus, *Opera Q. Septimii Florentis Tertulliani*, a4verso.

82. Beatus Rhenanus, *Opera Q. Septimii Florentis Tertulliani*, a4verso.

83. Beatus Rhenanus, *Opera Q. Septimii Florentis Tertulliani*, 410.

84. Beatus Rhenanus, *Opera Q. Septimii Florentis Tertulliani*, 411.

85. Beatus Rhenanus, *Opera Q. Septimii Florentis Tertulliani*, 411.

86. Beatus Rhenanus, *Opera Q. Septimii Florentis Tertulliani inter Latinos ecclesiae scriptores primi* (Basil, 1539), 506.

87. The number of such documents is startling; see George Huntston Williams, *The Radical Reformation* (Kirksville, MO: Truman State University Press, 2000), 1401–1403.

88. For more on the *Confession*, see chapter 3.

89. See Jaroslav Pelikan and Valerie Hotchkiss, *Creeds and Confessions of Faith in the Christian Tradition* (New Haven, CT: Yale University Press, 2003), vol. 2.

90. Erasmus, *Ratio*, 3:222.

91. Erasmus, *Explanatio symboli apostolorum sive catechismus*, in *CWE*, trans. Louis A. Perraud, 70:242.

92. Erasmus, *Explanatio*, 70:252, 253, 254–255.

93. Erasmus, *Explanatio*, 70:273ff, 293–295, 331.

94. Erasmus, *Explanatio*, 70:302–303.

95. Erasmus, *Explanatio*, 70:302–303.

96. On the publishing, see Emily Kearns's introduction to *De sarcienda ecclesiae concordia*, in *CWE*, 65:131.

97. Psalm 83 in the Catholic/Greek numbering.

98. The Revised Standard Version translates the Hebrew word *mishkan* in various ways ("booths," "dwelling place," e.g.), but in the Latin tradition, this was always rendered "tabernaculum." As a result, I will silently amend the translations below better to bring this into conversation with Erasmus's world.

99. On the tabernacle, see Nathan Mitchell, O.S.B., *Cult and Controversy: The Worship of the Eucharist Outside Mass* (New York: Pueblo Publishing, 1982), 168; Kristen Van Ausdall, "Art and Eucharist in the Late Middle Ages," in *Companion to the Eucharist in the Middle Ages*, 610. On the parallel between the tabernacle and the womb of Mary, see Barbara Lane, *The Altar and the Altarpiece: Sacramental Themes in Early Netherlandish Painting* (New York: Harper & Row, 1984), 27–35; Achim Timmermann, *Real Presence: Sacrament Houses and the Body of Christ, c. 1270–1600* (Turnhout, Belgium: Brepols, 2009).

100. For the Fourth Lateran decree, see Norman P. Tanner, S.J., ed., *Decrees of the Ecumenical Councils* (Washington, DC: Georgetown University Press, 1990), 1:244. More generally, see Timmermann, *Real Presence*, esp. chap. 2; Klaus Gamber, *Sancta sanctorum: Studien zur liturgischen Ausstattung der Kirche, vor allem des Altarraums* (Regensburg: Kommissionsverlag Friedrich Pustet, 1981), 84–85.

101. Quoted in van Ausdall, "Art and Eucharist," 610.

102. Erasmus, *De sarcienda ecclesiae concordia*, in *CWE*, 65: 139. That the Psalm had such prophetic intent was, for Erasmus, confirmed by its curious dedication, "for the wine presses," *pro torcularibus*, taken widely as prediction of Christ's triumphant death on the Cross and a visual motif extensively elaborated in the later Middle Ages.

103. Desiderius Erasmus, *Paraphrase on the Epistles to the Corinthians*, in *CWE*, trans. Edward A. Phillips, Jr., 43: 113.

104. Erasmus, *De sarcienda ecclesiae concordia*, in *CWE*, 65:301, 140.

105. Erasmus, *De sarcienda ecclesiae concordia*, 65:172, 173–174, 197.

106. Erasmus, *De sarcienda ecclesiae concordia*, 65:208, 209, 216.

107. Erasmus, *Ennaratio psalmi 14 qui est de puritate taburnaculi sive ecclesiae christianae*, in *CWE*, 65:264, 267.

108. Erasmus, *Ennaratio*, 65:264, 246. Italics mine.

109. Erasmus, *Ennaratio*, 65:146–47, 150–51.

110. Marcus Minucius Felix, *The Octavius*, trans. G. W. Clarke (New York: Newman Press, 1974), 65.

111. For more on Thyestian banquets, see Athenagoras, *Legatio*, ed. William R. Schoedel (Oxford: Clarendon Press, 1972), 9 (3.1); Tertullian, "Apology," in *Tertullian*, trans. Gerald H. Rendall (London: William Heinemann, 1953), 45 (8.6–8). More generally, see Andrew McGowan, "Eating People: Accusations of Cannibalism Against Christians in the Second Century," *Journal of Early Christian Studies* 2, no. 4 (Winter 1994): 413–442.

112. See especially Magda Teter, *Blood Libel: On the Trail of an Antisemitic Myth* (Cambridge, MA: Harvard University Press, 2020).

113. Erasmus, *De sarcienda ecclesiae concordia*, 65:151.

114. Erasmus, *Correspondence*, 8:73.

Chapter 3: Sacrifice Abandoned, Sacrifice Redeemed

1. John Bossy, *Christianity in the West, 1400–1700* (Oxford: Oxford University Press, 1985), 141.

2. Cyrille Vogel, *Medieval Liturgy: An Introduction to the Sources*, trans. William G. Store and Niels Krogh Rasmussen, O.P. (Washington, DC: Pastoral Press, 1986), 80. On the reception of the Roman rite, see also Joseph Andreas Jungmann, S.J., *Missarum Sollemnia: Eine genetische Erklärung der Römischen Messe*, 3rd ed. (Freiburg: Verlag Herder, 1952), vol. 1.

3. John the Deacon, *Sancti Gregorii magni vita*, in J. P. Migne, ed., *Patrilogiae cursus completus: series Latina* (Paris: Migne, 1844–1902), 75:94 (hereafter *PL*).

4. Jungmann, *Missarum Sollemnia*, 2: 128.

5. H. A. Wilson, ed., *The Gregorian Sacramentary under Charles the Great* (London: Harrison & Sons., 1915), 2.

6. Wilson, ed., *The Gregorian Sacramentary*, 3.

7. Wilson, ed., *The Gregorian Sacramentary*, 3.

8. Theodosius, *De situ terrae sanctae* (ca 530), quoted in Isabel Speyart Van Woerden, "The Iconography of the Sacrifice of Abraham," *Vigiliae Christianae* 15, no. 4 (Dec. 1961), 229, 239.

9. On these developments, see Jungmann, *Missarum Sollemnia*, 2:127–31.

10. Jungmann, *Missarum Sollemnia*, 2:174 (silence); 177 (elevation), 179 (signs of the cross, prescribed since early tenth century).

11. Paul the Deacon, *Sancti Gregorii Magni vita*, in *PL*, 75:52–53.

12. On the reception of this story into medieval exempla, see Caroline Walker Bynum, "Seeing and Seeing Beyond: The Mass of St. Gregory in the Fifteenth Century," in *The Mind's Eye: Art and Theological Argument in the Middle Ages*, ed. Jeffrey F. Hamburger and Anne-Marie Bouché (Princeton, NJ: Princeton University Press, 2006), 235 n.14. For doubts about the connection between the early medieval vitae and the later Mass, see Esther Meier, "Ikonographische Probleme: Von der 'Erscheinung Gregorii' zur Gregorsmesse," in *Das Bild der Erscheinung: Die Gregorsmesse im Mittelalter*, ed. Andreas Gorman and Thomas Lentes (Berlin: Dietrich Reimer, 2007), 39–57.

13. On this image, see Michael Heinlen, "An Early Image of a Mass of St. Gregory and Devotion to the Holy Blood at Weingarten Abbey," *Gesta* 37, no. 1 (1998): 55–62.

14. Susanne Wegmann, "Passionsandacht und Messeerklärung: Die Verwendung der 'Visio Gregorii' im Buch," in *Das Bild der Erscheinung*, 416ff; for the *Te igitur*, see Ernst Günther Grimme, *Der Aachener Domschatz* (Düsseldorf: L. Schwann, 1972), 114.

15. Flora Lewis, "Rewarding Devotion: Indulgences and the Promotion of Images," in *The Church and the Arts*, ed. Diana Wood (Oxford: Blackwell, 1992), 184.

16. Thanks to Leor Halevi for pointing this out.

17. On the idea of this sacramental viewing, see Aden Kumler, *Translating Truth: Ambitious Images and Religious Knowledge in Late Medieval France and England* (New Haven, CT: Yale University Press, 2011), 156ff.

18. Bynum, "Seeing and Seeing Beyond," 210. See also Joseph Leo Koerner, *The Reformation of the Image* (Chicago: University of Chicago Press, 2004), 355.

19. These images of the *arma Christi* were similarly indulgenced in the later Middle Ages; see Lewis, "Rewarding Devotion," 181.

20. On blood and painting, see Beate Fricke, "A Liquid History: Blood and Animation in Late Medieval Art," *RES: Journal of Anthropology and Aesthetics* 63/63 (Spring/Autumn 2013): 64.

21. On this piece, see Reindert Falkenburg, "Hieronymus Bosch's Mass of St. Gregory," in *Das Bild der Erscheinung*, esp. 191ff.

22. On the expansion of the Gregory Mass motif, from a fixed object in a church, to a mobile image in private houses, books, and so on, see Esther Meier, *Die Gregormesse: Funktionen eines spätmittelalterlichen Bildtypus* (Wien: Böhlau, 2006), chap. 3.

23. See Bodleian Library MS. Acut. D. inf. 2. 11. Image URL here: https://digital.bodleian.ox.ac.uk/objects/322fec41-5285-4057-a37d-cc2543d577eb/surfaces/58707fbc-d37c-4c06-857e-f99c6d12b487/

24. Susanne Wegmann, "Passionsandacht und Messeerklärung," in *Das Bild der Erscheinung*, 407.

25. Peter of Lombard, *Libri IV Sententiarum*, 2:813.

26. For the media history of the pamphlet, see Claudine Moulin, "*Ein Sermon von Ablass und Gnade* (1518): Materialität, Dynamik und Transformation," in Irene Dingel and Henning P. Jürgens, *Meilensteine der Reformation: Schlüsseldokumente der frühen Wirksamkeit Martin Luthers* (Gütersloh: Güterloher Verlagshaus, 2014), 113–119.

27. On the image in the context of the indulgence debate, see Wegmann, "Passionsandacht," 430–431.

28. Martin Luther, *D. Martin Luthers Werke: Kritische Gesamtausgabe: Tischreden* [WATr], 1:272 (nr. 584); Luther, WATr, 3:666 (nr. 3862).

29. Luther, WATr, 1:18 (nr. 51); Luther, WATr, 2 :230 (nr. 1824).

30. Martin Luther, *The Babylonian Captivity of the Church, 1520*, trans. A.T.W. Steinhäuser, in *Luther's Works*, ed. Abdel Ross Wentz and Helmut T. Lehmann (Philadelphia: Fortress Press, 1959) 36:35; and also 36:51. (For the major treatises, I will use this edition; the minor ones, the standard German Weimar Ausgabe [WA]).

31. Luther, WATr, 4:175–176 (nr. 4760).

32. Luther, *Misuse of the Mass*, in *Luther's Works*, 36:147, 177, 178.

33. Luther, *Babylonian Captivity*, in *Luther's Works*, 36:52.

34. Luther, WA 3: 646, quoted in Wolfgang Simon, *Die Messopfertheologie Martin Luthers: Voraussetzungen, Genese, Gestalt, und Rezeption* (Tübingen: Mohr Siebeck, 2003), 186.

35. Luther, "Formula missae et communionis pro ecclesia Vuittembergensi," *Formula missae et communis*, in WA, 12:211.

36. Luther, *Ein Sermon von dem neuen Testament, das ist von der heiligen Messe*, in WA, 6:355.

37. Luther, *Babylonian Captivity*, in *Luther's Works*, 36:52–53; Luther, *De Captivitate*, in WA, 6:524.

38. Luther, WA, 3:646, quoted in Simon, *Messopfertheologie*, 187.

39. Luther, *Admonition Concerning the Sacrament of the Body and Blood of Our Lord, 1530*, in *Luther's Works*, 38:105, 108.

40. Luther, *Admonition*, 38:111–112.

41. For a systematic theological exploration of this, see Reinhard Meßner, *Die Meßreform Martin Luthers und die Eucharistie der Alten Kirche: Ein Beitrag zu einer systematischen Liturgiewissenschaft* (Innsbruck: Tyrolia-Verlag, 1989), 172–185.

42. Augustine, *City of God Against the Pagans*, ed. R. W. Dyson (Cambridge: Cambridge University Press, 1998), 269 (10.5).

43. Augustine, *City of God*, 273, 277 (10.6).

44. Just for Augsburg printings, see Lee Palmer Wandel, *The Eucharist in the Reformation: Incarnation and Liturgy* (Cambridge: Cambridge University Press, 2006), 69–79.

45. George Hunston Williams, *The Radical Reformation* (Kirksville, MO: Truman State University Press, 2000), 116.

46. Williams, *Radical Reformation*, 128.

47. Williams, *Radical Reformation*, 180. On Zwingli's 1523 "Canon of the Mass," see also Bruce Gordon, *Zwingli: God's Armed Prophet* (New Haven, CT: Yale University Press, 2021), 100–101.

48. On Strassburg, see Nicholas Thompson, *Eucharistic Sacrifice and Patristic Tradition in the Theology of Martin Bucer, 1534–1546* (Leiden: Brill, 2005), 96.

49. Williams, *Radical Reformation*, 191.

50. Williams, *Radical Reformation*, 208.

51. John D. Rempel, *The Lord's Supper in Anabaptism: A Study in the Christology of Balthasar Hubmaier, Pilgram Marpeck, and Dirk Philips* (Waterloo, ON: Herald Press, 1993), 77–78.

52. Huldrich Zwingli, "Auslegen und Gründe der Schlußreden" [1523], in *Sämtliche Werke*, ed. Emil Egli and Georg Finsler (Leipzig: Heinsius, 1908), 2: 118. On Zwingli and Eucharistic sacrifice, see Keith D. Lewis, "*Unica Oblatio Christi*: Eucharistic Sacrifice and the first Zürich Disputation," *Renaissance and Reformation* 17, no. 3 (1993): 19–42.

53. On Fabri's work in the libraries in 1522, see Giovanni Mercati, "Scritti ecclesiastici greci copiati da Giovanni Fabri nella Vaticana," *Bessarione* 37 (1921): 88–119. In general, on the Irenaeus reception in the Reformation, see Jean-Louis Quantin, Agnès Molinier, Pierre Petitmengin, and Olivier Szerwiniack, "Irénée de Lyon entre humanisme et Réforme: Les citationes de l'*Adversus haereses* dans les controverses religieuses, de Johann Fabri à Martin Luther (1522–1527)," *Recherches Augustiniennes* 27 (1994): 131–185.

54. Irenaeus, *Adversus haereses*, ed. Norbert Brox (Freiburg: Herder Verlag, 1997), 4:138 (4.18.1). For Faber on Irenaeus, see Johann Faber, *Ain warhaft underrichtung* (Freiburg/Breisgau: Wörlin: 1523), f recto. Gregory the Great reports Irenaeus as lost in his letters, see Pope Gregory I, *Letters of Gregory the Great*, trans. and ed. John R. C. Martyn (Toronto: Pontifical Institute of Medieval Studies) 3:787 (11.40).

55. Faber, *Warhaft underrichtung*, e4verso.

56. This becomes, for example, a leitmotif in Johann Eck's 1526 *De sacrificio missae*; see Thompson, *Eucharistic Sacrifice*, 18.

57. Luther, *Misuse of the Mass*, in *Luther's Works*, 36:136; Luther, *Vom Missbrauch der Messe*, in WA 8:484.

58. Peter Fraenkel, *Testimonia Patrum: The Function of the Patristic Argument in the Theology of Philip Melanchthon* (Geneva: Librairie E. Droz, 1961), 18. See also the essays on Melanchthon collected in Günter Frank, Thomas Leinkauf, and Markus Wriedt, eds., *Die Patristik in der frühen Neuzeit: Die Relektüre der Kirchenväter in den Wissenschaften des 15. Bis 18. Jahrhunderts* (Stuttgart: Bad-Canstatt, 2006).

59. Fraenkel, *Testimonia Patrum*, 23.

60. Fraenkel, *Testimonia Patrum*, 72, 73.

61. Fraenkel, *Testimonia Patrum*, 170.

62. For a survey of this, see Michael J. Hollerich, *Making Christian History: Eusebius of Caesarea and His Readers* (Berkeley: University of California Press, 2021), chap. 6.

63. For an excellent survey of Protestant church histories, see Matthias Pohlig, *Zwischen Gelehrsamkeit und konfessioneller Identitätsstiftung: Lutherische Kirchen- und Universallgeschichtsschreibung 1546–1617* (Tübingen: Mohr Siebeck, 2007); on

Eusebius, see Arnaldo Momigliano, "The Origins of Ecclesiastical Historiography," in *The Classical Foundations of Modern Historiography* (Berkeley: University of California Press, 1990), esp. 149ff. See also Alexandra Kress, *Johann Sleidan and the Protestant Vision of History* (Aldershot: Ashgate, 2008). On Reformed Church histories, see Gustav Adolf Benrath, *Reformierte Kirchengeschichtsschreibung an der Universität Heidelberg im 16. und 17. Jahrhundert* (Speyer: Zechnersche Buchdruckerei, 1963).

64. *The Augsburg Confession* in *Creeds and Confessions of Faith in the Christian Tradition*, ed. Jaroslav Pelikan and Valerie Hotchkiss (New Haven, CT: Yale University Press, 2003), 2: 85.

65. On the history of this document, see Christian Peters, *Apologia Confessionis Augustanae: Untersuchungen zur Textgeschichte einer lutherischen Bekenntnisschrift* (1530–1584) (Stuttgart: Calwer, 1997).

66. Melanchthon, *Apologia confessionis augustanae.* 1st ed. [Aug. 1530], in *Corpus reformatorum* (Leipzig: M. Heinsius, 1834–), 27:297–298 (hereafter CR).

67. Melanchthon, *Apologia confessionis augustanae*, 2nd ed. [Sept. 1530], in CR 27:611.

68. Melanchthon, *Apologia*, CR 27:620.

69. Melanchthon, *De ecclesia et autoritate verbi dei*, CR 23:600–601.

70. Melanchthon, *De ecclesia*, CR 23:600, 626.

71. Melanchthon, *De ecclesia*, CR 23:615.

72. Melanchthon, *De ecclesia*, CR 23:615.

73. In general, see Hughes Oliphant Old, *The Patristic Roots of Reformed Worship* (Zürich: Juris, 1975).

74. Throughout, I will use "reformed" to signify Protestants more generally, and "Reformed" to mean, broadly, the Calvinist faction.

75. On Bullinger's histories of idolatry, see Marco Cavarzere, "A Comparative Method for Sixteenth-Century Polemicists: Cults, Devotions, and the Formation of Early Modern Religious Identities," *Journal of Early Modern History* 19 (2015): 385–407.

76. Heinrich Bullinger, preface to *De origine erroris, in negocio eucharistiae, et missae* (Basil: Wolffius, 1528), a2recto.

77. Lactantius, *Divinarum Institutionem*, in PL 6:729 (Book 6, chap. 25, A).

78. On Pliny, see Bullinger, *De origine erroris*, a7verso, and a8recto.

79. Bullinger, *De origine erroris*, b5recto.

80. Bullinger, *De origine erroris*, b5verso.

81. Bullinger, *De origine erroris*, c1verso.

82. Theodore Mommsen, ed., *Liber Pontificalis: Pars Prior in Gestorum Pontificum Romanorum* (Berolini [Berlin]: Apud Weidmannos, 1898), 1:38.

83. Bullinger, *De origine erroris*, c4verso.

84. Bullinger, *De origine erroris*, c2verso.

85. See Thompson, *Eucharistic Sacrifice*, 120.

86. Bullinger, *De origine erroris*, c3verso.

87. Bullinger, *De origine erroris*, c5recto.

88. Lactantius, *Divinarum Institutionem*, in *PL* 6: 635 (6.1). Passage quoted in Heinrich Bullinger, *De origine erroris libri duo* (Zürich: Froschauer, 1539), 26recto.

89. Bullinger, *De origine erroris libri duo*, 26verso, 27recto.

90. Bullinger, *De origine erroris libri duo*, 26verso.

91. "Martyrdom of Polycarp," in *Acts of the Christian Martyrs*, 393 (18.2–3).

92. See Bullinger, *De origine erroris libri duo*, 29recto.

93. Bullinger, *De origine erroris libri duo*, 29 recto.

94. Bullinger, *De origine erroris libri duo*, 58 recto.

95. See Jerome, *Contra Vigilantium admonitio*, in *PL*, 4: 337–355. For Bullinger on the Jerome-Vigilantius debate, see *De origine erroris libri duo*, pp. 58r, 60r, 67r, 71r, 72r, etc. Viz. the broader debates about early relics, see, recently, Robert Wisniewski, *The Beginnings of the Cult of Relics* (Oxford: Oxford University Press, 2019), and the classic Peter Brown, *Cult of the Saints: Its Rise and Function in Latin Christianity* (Chicago: University of Chicago Press, 1981).

96. Bullinger, *De origine erroris libri duo*, 59recto.

97. Augustine, *City of God*, 398 (10.6).

98. Thompson, *Eucharistic Sacrifice*, 95.

99. Thompson, *Eucharistic Sacrifice*, 99.

100. Eck quoted in Irena Backus, "Martin Bucer and the Patristic Tradition," in *Martin Bucer and Sixteenth Century Europe: Actes du colloque de Strasbourg (28–31 août 1991)*, ed. Christian Krieger and Marc Lienhard (Leiden: E. J. Brill, 1993), 56.

101. Thompson, *Eucharistic Sacrifice*, 66.

102. Bucer quoted in Thompson, *Eucharistic Sacrifice*, 115.

103. See Thompson, *Eucharistic Sacrifice*, 122.

104. Thompson, *Eucharistic Sacrifice*, 285; see p. 232 for the five sacrifices, and the rest of chapter 10 for an exploration of each of these in light of Bucer's theology and ecclesiology. On Bucer's engagement with Gropper and Witzen, see chapters 7–9. See also Irena Backus, "Martin Bucer and the Patristic Tradition."

105. John Calvin, *Institutes of the Christian Religion*, trans. Ford Lewis Battles (Louisville, KY: Westminster John Knox Press, 1960), 1042 (4.2.2).

106. Calvin, *Institutes*, 1431 (4.18.3), 1435 (4.18.7).

107. Calvin quoted in Christian Grosse, *Les rituels de la cène: Le culte eucharistique réformé à Genéve (XVIe–XVIIe siècles)* (Librairie Droz: Geneva, 2008), 143.

108. Raymond A. Mentzer, "Reformed Liturgical Practices," in *A Companion to the Eucharist in the Reformation*, ed. Lee Palmer Wandel (Leiden: Brill, 2013), 238.

109. Grosse, *Les rituels*, 169–170.

110. "La forme des prières ecclésiastiques," in Grosse, *Les rituels*, 648.

111. Grosse, *Les rituels*, 199.

112. Calvin, *Institutes*, 851, 852 (3.20.2).

113. Calvin, *Institutes*, 873 (3.20.16).

114. Calvin, *Institutes*, 875 (3.20.18).

115. Calvin, *Institutes*, 888 (3.20.28).

116. For Calvin's complicated relationship to the church fathers, and generally to "tradition" in the church, see R. Ward Holder, *Calvin and the Christian Tradition: Scripture, Memory, and the Western Mind* (Cambridge: Cambridge University Press, 2022).

117. John Calvin, *Commentaries on the First Book of Moses Called Genesis*, trans. John King (Grand Rapids, MI: Eerdmans, 1948), 192; John Calvin, *In primum Mosis*

Librum, qui Genesis vulgo dicitur, Commentarius Iohannis Calvini in *Ioannis Calvini Opera quae supersunt omnia*, ed. Eduardus Cunitz, Eduardus Reuss, and Paulus Lobstein (Braunschweig: Schwetschke et Filium, 1882), 23:84.

118. Calvin, *Commentaries*, 193; *Opera*, 23:84.

119. Calvin, *Commentaries*, 196; *Opera*, 23: 86.

120. Calvin, *Institutes*, 1281 (4.14.6).

121. Calvin, *Institutes*, 1361 (4.17.1).

122. Calvin, *Institutes*, 1363 (4.17.3); 1364 (4.17.5).

123. Calvin, *Institutes*, 1368 (4.17.8); 1370 (4.17.10).

124. Calvin, *Institutes*, 1367 (4.17.7).

125. Calvin, *Institutes*, 1441 (4.18.13).

126. Calvin, *Institutes*, 1443–1444 (4.18.16).

127. Wandel, *The Eucharist in the Reformation*, 159, 165.

128. Koerner, *The Reformation of the Image*, 232.

129. Susan Karant-Nunn, *The Reformation of Ritual: An Interpretation of Early Modern Germany* (London: Routledge, 1997), 97–98.

130. Ruth Slenczka, *Die gestaltende Wirkung von Abendmahlslehre und Abendmahlspraxis im 16. Jahrhundert*, in *Europäische Geschichte Online* (EGO), published by the Institut für Europäische Geschichte (IEG), Mainz 12/9/2010. Available online at http://www.ieg-ego.eu/slenczkar-2010-de. More generally, see Barbara Stollberg-Rilinger, *Rituale* (Frankfurt: Campus Verlag, 2013), 84–85.

131. Irena Backus, "Calvin and the Greek Fathers," in *Continuity and Change: The Harvest of Late Medieval and Reformation History*, ed. Robert J. Bast and Andrew C. Gow (Leiden: Brill, 2000), 254 fn.8.

132. See Anthony N. S. Lane, "Justification in Sixteenth-Century Patristic Anthologies," in *Auctoritas Patrum: Zur Rezeption der Kirchenväter im 15. und 16. Jahrhundert*, ed. Leif Grane Alfred Schindler, Markus Wriedt (Mainz: Verlag Philipp von Zabern, 1993), 69.

133. Calvin, *Institutes*, 1435–36 (4.18.7).

Chapter 4: Polycarp's Bones

1. Frank Lestringant, *Lumière des martyrs: Essai sur les martyre au siècle des réformes* (Paris: Honoré Champion, 2004), 12.

2. Quoted in Brad Gregory, *Salvation at Stake: Christian Martyrdom in Early Modern Europe* (Cambridge, MA: Harvard University Press, 1999), 162.

3. "The Martyrdom of Polycarp," in *The Apostolic Fathers*, Bart D. Ehrman, ed. and trans. (Cambridge, MA: Harvard University Press, 2003), 1:393. On Polycarp's martyrdom, and issues with its textual transmission, see Candida Moss, *Ancient Christian Martyrdom: Diverse Practices, Theologies, and Traditions* (New Haven, CT: Yale University Press, 2012), 57–75.

4. Peter Brown, *The Cult of the Saints: Its Rise and Function in Latin Christianity* (Chicago: University of Chicago Press, 1981), 6–7, 70.

5. Thomas W. Laqueur, *The Work of the Dead: A Cultural History of Mortal Remains* (Princeton, NJ: Princeton University Press, 2015), esp. 95–96.

6. Prudentius, "Peristephanon liber," in *Prudentius*, trans. H. J. Thomson (London: William Heinemann, 1953), 2: 317 (11.169ff).

7. Bernhard Kötting, *Die frühchristliche Reliquienkult und die Bestattung im Kirchengebäude* (Cologne: Westerdeutscher Verlag, 1965), 17ff.

8. Eugene A. Dooley, *Church Law on Sacred Relics* (Washington, DC: Catholic University of America Press, 1931), 23; Robert Bartlett, *Why Can the Dead Do Such Great Things? Saints and Worshippers from the Martyrs to the Reformation* (Princeton, NJ: Princeton University Press, 2013), 240–241.

9. On Gregory and relics, see John M. McCulloch, "The Cult of Relics in the Letters and 'Dialogues' of Pope Gregory the Great: A Lexicographical Account," *Traditio* 32 (1976): 148. More generally, see Arnold Angenendt, *Heilige und Reliquien: Die Geschichte ihres Kultes vom frühen Christentum bis zur Gegenwart* (Munich: C. H. Beck, 1997).

10. McCulloch, "Cult of Relics," 150, 161–162 (on *sanctuaria*).

11. Julia M. H. Smith, "Old Saints, New Cults: Roman Relics in Carolingian Francia," in *Early Medieval Rome and the Christian West: Essays in Honour of Donald A. Bullough*, ed. Julia M. H. Smith (Leiden: Brill, 2000), 318. See also Felice Lifshitz, *The Name of the Saint: The Martyrology of Jerome and Access to the Sacred in Francia, 627–827* (Notre Dame, IN: University of Notre Dame Press, 2006), 75–76.

12. Patrick J. Geary, *Furta sacra: Thefts of Relics in the Central Middle Ages* (Princeton, NJ: Princeton University Press, 1978), 42–44, 153.

13. Einhard, "Translation of the Relics of Sts. Marcellinus and Peter," trans. Barrett Wendell and ed. David Appleby, in *Medieval Hagiography: An Anthology*, ed. Thomas Head (New York: Garland, 2000), 209.

14. Geary, *Furta sacra*, esp. chap. 3.

15. Geary, *Furta sacra*, 28; G.J.C. Snoek, *Medieval Piety from Relics to the Eucharist: A Process of Mutual Interaction* (Leiden: Brill, 1995), 46.

16. On the ancient genre of historical acts, see Hippolyte Delehaye, *Les Passions des martyrs et les genres littéraires* (Brussels: Bureaux de la Société Bollandistes, 1921).

17. Bartlett, *Such Great Things*, 19–21.

18. On legendaries, see Bartlett, *Such Great Things*, 547ff.

19. Jacobus de Voragine, *The Golden Legende* [*Legenda aurea*], trans. William Caxton (Westminster, 1483), ccccxvii verso.

20. Bartlett, *Such Great Things*, 506–507.

21. Lifshitz, *The Name of the Saint*, 97 (on litanies).

22. For an exception, see an early poetic version of the martyrology of Bede which has it on February 1: Henri Quentin, *Les martyrologes historiques du moyen age* (Paris: Victor Lecoffre, 1908), 123.

23. Felice Lifshitz, "Introduction to Bede's *Martyrology*," in *Medieval Hagiography: An Anthology*, 171.

24. [Anon.], *Viola sanctorum* (Basel, 1475), unpaginated, s.v. Januarius 26.

25. [Anon.], *Martilogium [sic] der heiligen nach dem kalendar* (Straßburg: Johann Prüss, 1484), unpaginated, s.v. Genner 26.

26. In general, see André Vauchez, *La sainteté en Occident aux derniers siècles du moyen age: d'après les procès de canonisation et les documents hagiographiques* (Rome: École Français, 1981).

27. On 1096 and Jewish martyrdom, see especially Jeremy Cohen, *Sanctifying the Name of God: Jewish Martyrs and Jewish Memories of the First Crusade* (Philadelphia: University of Pennsylvania Press, 2004); also see Israel Yuval, *Two Nations in Your Womb: Perceptions of Jews and Christians in Late Antiquity and the Middle Ages* (Berkeley: University of California Press, 2008).

28. For the numbers, see Gregory, *Salvation at Stake*, esp. chap. 3. On the Catholic numbers under Elizabeth, see Geoffrey F. Nuttall, "The English Martyrs: 1535–1680: A Statistical Review," *Journal of Ecclesiastical History* 22, no. 3 (July 1971): 191–197. On martyr trials and judicial executions, see Paul Friedland, *Seeing Justice Done: The Age of Spectacular Capital Punishment in France* (Oxford: Oxford University Press, 2012), chap. 5.

29. For the violence, see Barbara B. Diefendorf, *Beneath the Cross: Catholics and Huguenots in Sixteenth-Century Paris* (Oxford: Oxford University Press, 1991), chap. 6.

30. For a rich description of all these various martyrological sources, see Gregory, *Salvation at Stake*. On Rabus, see Peter Burschel, *Sterben und Unsterblichkeit: Zur Kultur des Martyriums in der frühen Neuzeit* (Munich: R. Oldenbourg Verlag, 2004), chap. 2; on Crespin, see David El Kenz, *Les bûchers du roi: La culture protestante des martyrs (1523–1572)* (Seyssel: Champ Vallon, 1997) and Jean François Gilmont, *Jean Crespin: Un éditeur réformé du XVIe siècle* (Geneva: Droz, 1981); on van Haemstede, see J. F. Gilmont, "La genèse du martyrologe d'Adrien van Haemstede (1559)," *Revue d'Histoire Ecclésiastique* 63, no. 2 (Jan. 1968): 379–414.

31. Gregory, *Salvation at Stake*, 73.

32. Elizabeth Evenden and Thomas S. Freeman, *Religion and the Book in Early Modern England: The Making of Foxe's 'Book of Martyrs'* (Cambridge: Cambridge University Press, 2011), 56–59, 77–78, 83, 95–98. On Grindal, see Patrick Collinson, *Archbishop Grindal, 1519–1583: The Struggle for a Reformed Church* (Berkeley: University of California Press, 1979).

33. John Foxe, *The Unabridged Acts and Monuments Online or TAMO* (1563 edition) (The Digital Humanities Institute: Sheffield, 2011), book 5, p. 1120. Available at: https://www.dhi.ac.uk/foxe/index.php. Subsequent references to this resource will simply read: Foxe, *TAMO*, with parenthetical reference to relevant edition and online pagination. I am also silently correcting the English orthography for clarity.

34. Foxe, *TAMO* (1563), 1131.

35. Foxe, *TAMO* (1563), 1132.

36. Gilmont, *Jean Crespin: Un éditeur réformé du XVIe siècle*, 165.

37. For Haemstede as an historian, see Andrew Pettegree, "Adriaan van Haemstede: The Heretic as Historian," in *Protestant History and Identity in Sixteenth-Century Europe*, ed. Bruce Gordon (Aldershot, UK: Scolar Press, 1996), 2: 59–76. For Crespin, see David Watson, "Jean Crespin and the Writing of History in the French Reformation," in *Protestant History and Identity in Sixteenth-Century Europe*, 2:39–58; also, Charles H. Parker, "French Calvinists as the Children of Israel: An Old Testament Self-Consciousness in Jean Crespin's *Histoire des Martyrs* before the Wars of Religion," *Sixteenth Century Journal* 24.2 (Summer 1993): 227–248. For Rabus's historical project, see especially Matthias Pohlig, *Zwischen Gelehrsamkeit und konfessioneller Identitätsstiftung: Lutherische Kirchen- und Universalgeschichte 1546–1617* (Tübingen: Mohr Siebeck, 2007), chap. 5.

38. Thomas Fuchs, "Protestantische Heiligen-Memoria im 16. Jahrhundert," *Historische Zeitschrift* 267, no. 3 (Dec. 1998): 587–614, esp. 591–593.

39. See Harald Bollbuck, "Einleitung," *Historische Methode und Arbeitstechnik der Magdeburger Zenturien* (Wolfenbüttel: Herzog August Bibliothek, 2012), available online at http://diglib.hab.de/edoc/ed000086/start.htm; and Harald Bollbuck, *Wahrheitszeugnis Gottes Auftrag und Zeitkritik: Die Kirchengeschichte der Magdeburger Zenturien und ihre Arbeitstechniken* (Wiesbaden: Harrassowitz, 2014).

40. On Reformation history writing, see, inter alia, Gregory Lyon, "Baudouin, Flacius, and the Plan for the Magdeburg Centuries," *Journal of the History of Ideas* 64 (Spring 2003): 253–272; Pohlig, *Zwischen Gelehrsamkeit und konfessioneller Identitätsstiftung*; Anthony Grafton, *What Was History? The Art of History in Early Modern Europe* (Cambridge: Cambridge University Press, 2007); Anthony Grafton, "Past Belief: The Fall and Rise of Ecclesiastical History in Early Modern Europe," in *Formations of Belief: Historical Approaches to Religion and the Secular*, ed. Philip Nord, et al. (Princeton, NJ: Princeton University Press, 2019), 13–40.

41. Miles Huggarde, *The displaying of the Protestants & sondry their practices* (London: Robert Caly, 1556), 69v.

42. Nicholas Harpsfield, *Dialogi sex contra summi pontificatus, monasticae vitae, sanctorum, sacrarum imaginum oppugnatores, et Pseudomartyres* (Antwerp: Christopher Plantin, 1566), 744.

43. Luther quoted in Robert Kolb, *For All the Saints: Changing Perceptions of Martyrdom and Sainthood in the Lutheran Reformation* (Eugene, OR: Wipf & Stock, 2020), 13. Luther, *Vorlesungen über 1. Mose von 1535–1545*, in WA, 44:521.

44. John Calvin, *An Admonition Concerning Relics* [1543], in *Tracts and Treatises on the Reformation of the Church*, trans. Henry Beveridge (Grand Rapids, MI: Eerdmans, 1958), 291.

45. Foxe, "Ad doctum lectorem," in *TAMO* (1563), 10.

46. Calvin, *An Admonition Concerning Relics* [1543], 290, 292.

47. Gregory, *Salvation at Stake*, 316.

48. Foxe, *TAMO* [1563], 889.

49. Foxe, *TAMO* [1563], 900.

50. Jean Crespin, *Histoire des vrays Tesmoins de la verite de l'evangile, qui de leur sang l'on signée, depuis Jean Hus iusques au temps present* (Geneva: L'ancre de Iean Crespin, 1570), book VI, 425ff.

51. See Thomas S. Freeman, "'Great searching out of bookes and autors': John Foxe as an Ecclesiastical Historian" (PhD diss., Rutgers University, 1995). See also Thomas Fuchs, "Protestantische Heiligen-memoria im 16. Jahrhundert," 587–614.

52. John Bale, "The Second Examination of Anne Askewe," in *Select Works of John Bale*, ed. Henry Christmas (Cambridge: Cambridge University Press, 1849), 187.

53. Foxe, "Dedication to Queen Elizabeth," in TAMO (1563), unpaginated.

54. Foxe, TAMO (1563), 1119, 1131.

55. Foxe, TAMO (1563), 1132.

56. Foxe, TAMO (1563), 1132.

57. Bullinger, *De origine erroris libri duo* (1539), 29recto (on Polycarp); 58recto (on bones).

58. Harpsfield, *Dialogi*, 383.

59. Harpsfield, *Dialogi*, 751.

60. Harpsfield, *Dialogi*, 780.

61. Harpsfield, *Dialogi*, 780.

62. Eusebius wrote in Greek, but until 1544, his *Ecclesiastical History* would only have been available in the early fifth century Latin paraphrase of Rufinus. On Foxe and Eusebius, see esp. Freeman, "'Great Searching Out of Bookes and Autors': John Foxe as Ecclesiastical Historian"; also Gretchen E. Minton, "'The Same Cause and like Quarell': Eusebius, John Foxe, and the Evolution of Ecclesiastical History," *Church History* 71, no. 4 (December 2002): 715–742.

63. In 1647, the Archbishop of Armagh James Ussher published the *editio princeps* of the letter: on the textual history here, see Ehrman, ed., *The Apostolic Fathers*, 1:357ff.

64. Compare, e.g., Foxe, *TAMO* (1570), 75, and Matthias Flacius Ilyricus, *Ecclesiastica Historia* (Basil: Oporinus, 1559), 2.175.

65. Foxe, *TAMO* (1570), 61–62.

66. Foxe, *TAMO* (1570), 113.

67. Foxe, *TAMO* (1570), 94.

68. Foxe, *TAMO* (1570), 113, 114.

69. Foxe, *TAMO* (1570), 113.

70. Foxe, *TAMO* (1570), 100. For the story of Origen and the Jews, see Epiphanius, *Panarion*, trans. Frank Williams (Leiden: Brill, 1994), 132–133 (book 2, sect. 64).

71. James Calfhill, *An answer to J. Martiall's Treatise of the Cross (1565)*, ed. Richard Gibbings (Cambridge: Cambridge University Press, 1846), 270.

72. Thomas Cartwright, *The second replie of Thomas Cartwright: agaynst Maister Doctor Whitgiftes second answer, touching the Churche discipline* (Heidelberg, 1575), 6.

73. Cyprian, *The Unity of the Catholic Church*, trans. Maurice Bévenot, S.J. (Oxford: Clarendon Press, 1971), 79; Prudentius puts this sentiment directly in the mouth of the martyr Hippolytus; see Prudentius, *Peristephanon liber*, in *Prudentius*, 2:307 (11.29–31).

74. Augustine, letter 173 to Donatus [ca. 411], in *Letters* in *The Works of Saint Augustine*, Part 2, 3:127 (2.3:127).

75. Eunapius, *Lives of the Philosophers*, in *Philostratus and Eunapius: The Lives of the Sophists*, trans. Wilmer Cave Wright (London: William Heinemann, 1952), 425.

76. Augustine, *Answer to Faustus, a Manichean*, in *The Works of Saint Augustine*, 1.20:263.

77. Augustine, Sermon 311, "On the Birthday of the Martyr Cyprian" (405), in *Sermons* in *Works*, 3.9:73 (see also 79, fn.8). Augustine, Letter 29, in *Letters* in *Works*, 2.1:97, 99.

78. Brad Gregory, "Saints and Martyrs in Tyndale and More," in *Martyrs and Martyrdom in England c. 1400–1700*, ed. Thomas S. Freeman and Thomas F. Mayer (Woodbridge: Boydell Press, 2007), 116.

79. Alison Knowles Frazier, *Possible Lives: Authors and Saints in Renaissance Italy* (New York: Columbia University Press, 2005), 64ff.

80. On the Catholic effort to authenticate their saints, see Simon Ditchfield, *Liturgy, Sanctity, and History in Tridentine Italy: Pietro Maria Campi and the Preservation of the Particular* (Cambridge: Cambridge University Press, 1995), 31, 35–36.

81. On the martyrology, see Giuseppe Antonio Guazzelli, "L'immagine del *Christianus Orbis* nelle prime edizioni del *Martyrologium Romanum*," *Sanctorum* 5 (2008): 261–284; Giuseppe Antonio Guazzelli, "Baronio attraverso il *Martyrologium Romanum*," in *Cesare Baronio tra santità e scrittura storica*, ed. Giuseppe Antonio Guazzelli, Raimondo Michetti, and Francesco Scorza Barcellona (Rome: Viella, 2012), 67–110; and Giuseppe Antonio Guazzelli, "Cesare Baronio and the Roman Catholic Vision of the Early Church," in *Sacred History: Uses of the Christian Past in the Renaissance World*, ed. Katherine van Liere et al. (Oxford: Oxford University Press, 2012), 72–97.

82. Stefano Zen, *Baronio storico: Controriforma e crisi del metodo umanistico* (Naples: Vivarium, 1994), 129. See also Simon Ditchfield, "Reading Rome as a Sacred Landscape, c. 1586–1635," in *Sacred Space in Early Modern Europe*, ed. Will Coster and Andrew Spicer (Cambridge: Cambridge University Press, 2005); Stefania Tutino, "'For the Sake of Truth of History and of the Catholic Doctrines': History, Documents, and Dogma in Cesare Baronio's *Annales Ecclesiastici*," *Journal of Early Modern History* 17 (2013): 125–159; Jan Michielsen, "An Aspiring Saint and His Work: Cesare Baronio and the Success and Failure of the *Annales Ecclesiastici* (1588–1607)," *Erudition and the Republic of Letters* 2.3 (2017): 233–287.

83. Simon Ditchfield, "Baronio storico nel suo tempo," *Cesare Baronio*, 13.

84. See, e.g., the notes to the martyrdom of Ignatius of Antioch, Feb. 1, Cesare Baronio, *Martyrologium romanum, ad novam kalendarii rationem & Ecclesiasticae Historiae veritatem restitutum* (Venice: Marcus Zalterius, 1597), 63ff.

85. Guazzelli, "L'immagine del *Christianus Orbis* nelle prime edizioni del *Martyrologium Romanum*," 261–284.

86. On the *Tractatio*, see Silvia Ronchey, "Baronio e gli antichi Atti dei Martiri: dottrina ufficiale e realtà storica," in *Baronio e le sue fonti*, ed. Luigi Gulia (Sora: Centro di studi sorani Vincenzo patriarca, 2009), 301–325; on the notarial history, see esp. 312–318.

87. Cesare Baronio, *De Martyrologio Romano, Praecapitulatio dicendorum*, in *Martyrologium romanum*, IX. This story is repeated in Robert Parsons, *A Treatise of Three Conversions of England from Paganisme to Christian Religion* (Saint Omer: François Bellet, 1603–4), part III, 32–33.

88. Negro quoted in Giovanni Mercati, *Ultimi contributi alla storia degli umanisti* (Vatican: Bibliotheca Apostolica Vaticana, 1939), 2: 70, n.3 (translation from Frazer, *Possible Lives*, 64. See also Platina, *Platinae Hystoria De Vitis Pontificum Perjucundae Diligenter Recognita Et Nunc Tantum Integre Impressa* (Lyon: 1512), s.v. Antherus (xxxii recto-verso), Fabianus, (xxxiii recto–xxxiiii recto).

89. See Cesare Baronio, *Annales ecclesiastici* (Romae: Typographia Vaticana, 1588), 1:698. See also Ditchfield, "Reading Rome," 176.

90. Baronio, *Martyrologium romanum*, III.

91. Baronio, *Martyrologium romanum*, II.

92. Baronio, *Martyrologium romanum*, II. See Tertullian, *De Baptismo*, in *Quinti Septimi Florentis Tertulliani Opera*, ed. August Reifferscheid and Georg Wissowa (Vienna: F. Tempsky, 1890), 1:215.

93. Ernst von Döbschutz, *Das Decretum Gelasianum: De libris recipiendis et non recipiendis* (Leipzig: J. C. Hinrichs, 1912), 11.

94. In his *Annales*, Baronio traced their provenance back through Pope Innocent (378–417) and into the earlier church [5.236]. Modern scholarship traces the MS tradition back to the eighth or ninth century; see von Dobschütz, *Das Decretum Gelasianum*, 184ff.

95. Baronio, *Martyrologium romanum*, II.

96. Baronio, *Martyrologium romanum*, II. See here Döbschutz, *Das Decretum Gelasianum*, 9.

97. Quoting canon 13, "Liceat etiam legi passiones martyrum, cum anniversarii dies eorum celerantur," Baronio, *Martyrologium romanum*, II.

98. Cesare Baronio, *Martyrologium Romanum: ad novam Kalendarij rationem, & Ecclesiasticae historiae veritatem restitutem* (Cologne: Ioannem Gymnicum, 1603), IV.

99. Baronio, *Martyrologium romanum* (1597), V.

100. Baronio, *Martyrologium romanum* (1597), V.

101. Baronio, *Martyrologium romanum* (1597), V.

102. John R. C. Martyn, trans., *The Letters of Gregory the Great* (Toronto: Pontifical Institute of Mediaeval Studies, 2004), 2: 522–523 (8.28).

103. Baronio, *Martyrologium romanum* (1597), X.

104. Baronio, *Martyrologium romanum* (1597), 51.

105. Baronio, *Martyrologium romanum* (1597), 13 (vigils), 22 (Pope), 42–43 (*equuleum*), 45–46 (Trajan).

106. See Charles L. Stinger, *The Renaissance in Rome* (Bloomington: Indiana University Press, 1985), chap. 4; also Philip Jacks, *The Antiquarian and the Myth of Antiquity: The Origins of Rome in Renaissance Thought* (Cambridge: Cambridge University Press, 1993), 238 (*urbs sacra*), 244 (Ugonio).

107. See, inter alia: Ingo Herklotz, *La Roma degli antiquari: cultura e erudizione tra cinquecento e settecento* (Rome: De Luca Editori d'Arti, 2012); Jetze Touber, *Law, Medicine, and Engineering in the Cult of the Saints in Counter-Reformation Rome: The Hagiographical Works of Antonio Gallonio, 1556–1605* (Leiden: Brill, 2014); Kelley Magill, "Reviving Martyrdom: Catacombs in Cesare Baronio's Patronage," in *Death, Torture, and the Broken Body in European Art, 1300–1650*, ed. John R. Decker and Mitzi Kirland-Ives (Farnham, UK: Ashgate, 2015), 87–115; Giuseppe Antonio Guazzelli, "Roman Antiquities and Christian Archaelogy," in *A Companion to Early Modern Rome, 1492–1692*, ed. Pamela M. Jones, et al. (Leiden: Brill, 2019), 530–545; Talia Di Manno, "Christian Archaeology and the Invention of the Early Church in Rome, 1561–1636" (PhD diss., University of California, Berkeley, 2020).

108. Platina, *Liber pontificalis* (1512) s.v. Damasus (xlvii verso–xlix verso). See also L.V. Rutgers, *Subterranean Rome: In Search of the Roots of Christianity in the Catacombs of the Eternal City* (Leuven: Peeters, 2000).

109. J. Osborne, "The Roman Catacombs in the Middle Ages," *Papers of the British School at Rome* 53 (1985): 278–328. But see especially Irina Oryshkevich, *The History of the Roman Catacombs from the Age of Constantine to the Renaissance* (PhD diss., Columbia University, 1993). I'm grateful to Dr. Oryshkevich for the help she generously offered in thinking through these materials.

110. See Oryshkevitch, *History of the Roman Catacombs*, 205. More generally, see Stinger, *The Renaissance in Rome*, 33–43.

111. Simon Ditchfield, "Text before Trowel: Antonio Bosio's *Roma sotterranea* Revisited," in *The Church Retrospective*, ed. R. N. Swanson (Woodbridge, UK: Boydell Press, 1997), 348; see also Simon Ditchfield, "Reading Rome as a Sacred Landscape, c. 1586–1635," in *Sacred Space in Early Modern Europe*, ed. Will Coster and Andrew Spicer (Cambridge: Cambridge University Press, 2005), 167, 171.

112. Onofrio Panvinio, *De ritu sepeliendi mortuos apud veteres Christianos* (Cologne: Maternum Cholinum, 1568), 16, 24. On Panvinio, see William Stenhouse, "Panvinio and *Descriptio*: Renditions of History and Antiquity in the Late Renaissance," *Papers of the British School of Rome* 80 (Oct. 2012): 233–256; Stefan Bauer, *The Invention of Papal History: Onofrio Panvinio between Renaissance and Catholic Reform* (Oxford: Oxford University Press, 2020).

113. For the cemetery churches, see Louis Reekmans, "L'implantation monumentale chrétienne dans la zone suburbaine de Rome du IVe au IXe siècle," *Rivista di archeologia cristiana* 44 (1968): 182; more generally, see Umberto M. Fasola and Vincenzo Fiocchi Nicolai, "Le necropoli durante la formazione della città cristiana," in *Actes du XIe congrès international d'archéologie chrétienne*, vol. 2 (Rome: Pontificio instituto di archeologia cristiana, 1989).

114. See Panvinio, *De ritu sepeliendi*, 20.

115. The classic source on the catacombs is Giovanni Battista de Rossi, *Roma sotterranea: or, An Account of the Roman Catacombs*, 2 vols., trans. J. Spencer Northcote and W. R. Brownlow (London: Longmans, Green, and Co., 1879). See, inter alia, Ingo Herklotz, "Christliche und klassische Archäologie im sechzehnten Jahrhundert: Skizzen zur Genese einer Wissenschaft," in *Die Gegenwart des Altertums: Formen und Funktionen des Altertumsbezugs in den Hochkulturen der Alten Welt*, ed. Dieter Kuhn and Helga Stahl (Heidelberg: Edition Forum, 2001), 292ff.

116. Gregory Martin, *Roma sancta* (1581), ed. George Bruner Parks (Rome: Edizione di storia e letteratura, 1969), 44.

117. Baronio quoted in Magill, "Reviving Martyrdom," 94.

118. Simon Ditchfield, "Thinking with Saints: Sanctity and Society in the Early Modern World," *Critical Inquiry* 35, no. 3 (Spring 2009): 555

119. Ditchfield, "Reading Rome as a Sacred Landscape," 167.

120. For simplicity's sake, I'll refer to Bosio as the author of the *Roma sotterranea*. For more on the Oratorian editorship of the book, see Ingo Herklotz, "Antonio Bosio e Giovanni Severano. Precisazioni su una collaborazione," *Studi romani. Rivista trimestrale dell'Istituto di Studi Romani* 56 (2008): 233–248; Giuseppe Finocchiaro, "La *Roma sotterranea* e la Congregazione dell'Oratorio," in *Messer Filippo Neri, santo, l'apostolo di Roma*, ed. Tellini Santoni (Rome: Biblioteca vallicelliana, 1995): 189–193; Lorenzo Spigno, "Considerazione sul manoscritto Vallicelliano G. 31 e la

Roma sotterranea di Antonio Bosio," *Rivista di archeologia cristiana* 51 (1975): 281–311.

121. Antonio Bosio, *Roma sotterranea, opera postuma* (Rome: Appresso G. Facciotti, 1632), 531 (book 3, ch. 61).

122. Bosio, *Roma sotterranea*, 607 (book 4, ch. 9) (see 608 for the patristic references).

123. Severano notes that the vessels could not be found among Bosio's effects, so included reproductions of those supposedly found by Jacobo Crescentio in the catacomb of St. Callixtus, also on the Via Appia; see Severano's editorial note, *Roma sotterranea*, 197 (book 3, ch. 23).

124. [Giovanni Severano], preface to *Roma sotterranea*,10.

125. Antonio Gallonio, *Trattato de gli Instrumenti di Martirio* (Rome: Ascanio e Girolamo Donangeli, 1591); on Gallonio, see Touber, *Law, Medicine, and Engineering.*

126. [Severano], preface to *Roma sotterranea*, 6.

127. Bosio, *Roma sotterranea*, 593.

128. Bosio, *Roma sotterranea*, 594.

129. The Orpheus-Christ connection was, in fact, well established already in the late antique period, with Orpheus seen as an early monotheist, or a type of Christ for his travels to the underworld, his ability to resurrect the dead, and so on. See Bernhard Huss, "Orpheus," in *Mythenrezeption. Die antike Mythologie in Literatur, Musik und Kunst von den Anfängen bis zur Gegenwart* in *Der Neue Pauly, Supplement*, ed. Maria Moog-Grünewald (Stuttgart: J. B. Metzler, 2008), 5: 522–553; Christoph Markschies, "Odysseus und Orpheus christlich gelesen," in *Mythenkorrekturen. Zu einer paradoxalen Form der Mythenrezeption*, ed. Bernd Seidensticker and Martin Vöhler (Berlin: Walter de Gruyter, 2005), 69–92; John Block Friedman, *Orpheus in the Middle Ages* (Cambridge, MA: Harvard University Press, 1970). Many thanks to Professor Ralf Behrwald from the University of Bayreuth for references and guidance.

130. Bosio, *Roma sotterranea*, 627–628.

131. See, generally, J.M.C. Toynbee, *Death and Burial in the Roman World* (Ithaca, NY: Cornell University Press, 1971), chap. 3; also Ramsay MacMullen, "Christian Ancestor Worship in Ancient Rome," *Journal of Biblical Literature* 129, no. 3 (Fall 2010): 602f.

132. Bosio, *Roma sotterranea*, 391.

133. Bosio, *Roma sotterranea*, 632.

134. Bosio, *Roma sotterranea*, 634.

135. Bosio, *Roma sotterranea*, 635.

136. Martin, *Roma sancta*, 44.

137. Robert Parsons, *A Treatise of Three Conversions of England from Paganisme to Christian Religion* (1603), 2:73.

138. Antonius Paulus, *De adventu sancti spiritus deque Christianae reipublicae stabilitate oratio* (1606) quoted in Frederick J. McGinness, *Right Thinking and Sacred Oratory in Counter-Reformation Rome* (Princeton, NJ: Princeton University Press, 1995), 131.

Chapter 5: The Way of the Negative

1. For Stucki's biography, see Marc Adam Kolakowski, "Johann Wilhelm Stucki (1542–1608): De l'histoire antiquaire à l'histoire des religions," (PhD diss., University of Lausanne, 2020). This is the authoritative work on Stucki and his treatise on sacrifice, and the author is grateful to Kolakowski for sharing the dissertation in advance of its publication. My first draft of this chapter was written before I had the chance to read Kolakowski, but my debts to this important work should be clear below.

2. Johann Wilhelm Stucki, *Sacrorum sacrificiorumque gentilium brevis et accurate descriptio, universae superstitionis ethnicae ritus cerimoniasque complectens* (Zürich: Johann Wolfius, 1598), unpaginated preface.

3. Dmitri Levitin, "What Was the Comparative History of Religions in 17th-Century Europe (and Beyond)? Pagan Monotheism/Pagan Animism from *T'ien* to Tylor," in *Regimes of Comparatism: Frameworks of Comparison in History, Religion, and Anthropology*, ed. Renaud Gagné, Simon Goldhill, and Geoffrey E. R. Lloyd (Leiden: Brill, 2019), 57.

4. Stucki, *Sacrorum sacrificiorumque gentilium . . . descriptio*, unpaginated preface.

5. Stucki, *Sacrorum sacrificiorumque gentilium . . . descriptio*, unpaginated preface. Adage found, among other places, in Erasmus's *Adages*, as an explanation of Pliny's "*Optimum aliena insania frui*." See Erasmus, *Adages*, in *CWE*, 33:150.

6. Aby Warburg, "Pagan-Antique Prophecy in Words and Images in the Age of Luther," in *The Renewal of Pagan Antiquity: Contributions to the Cultural History of the European Renaissance*, ed. Steven Lindberg and trans. David Britt (Los Angeles: Getty Research Institute, 1999), 598–599.

7. Raymond Klibansky, Erwin Panofsky, and Fritz Saxl, *Saturn and Melancholy: Studies in the History of Natural History, Philosophy, and Art* (London: Nelson, 1964), 144–145.

8. Jean Seznec, *The Survival of the Pagan Gods: The Mythological Tradition and Its Place in Renaissance Humanism and Art*, trans. Barbara Sessions (Princeton, NJ: Princeton University Press, 1981), 53 (prayer), 55 (gems).

9. [Anon.], *Karl der Grosse: Werk und Wirkung* (Aachen: Schwann, 1965), 186 (340b); Seznec, *The Survival of the Pagan Gods*, 55; I. H. Garipzanov, *The Symbolic Language of Authority in the Carolingian World (c. 751–877)* (Boston: Brill, 2008), 217; W. S. Heckscher, "Relics of Pagan Antiquity in Mediaeval Settings," *Journal of the Warburg Institute* 1, no. 3 (January 1938): 204–220.

10. See generally Robert Lamberton, *Homer the Theologian: Neoplatonist Allegorical Reading and the Growth of the Epic Tradition* (Berkeley: University of California Press, 1986).

11. Sallustius, *Concerning the Gods and the Universe*, trans. Arthur Darby Nock (Cambridge: Cambridge University Press, 1926), §4, p. 5.

12. Macrobius, *Saturnalia*, ed. and trans. Robert A. Kaster (Cambridge, MA: Harvard University Press, 2011), 1:91 (1.8.10).

13. Leslie George Whitbread, trans., *Fulgentius the Mythographer* (Columbus: Ohio State University Press, 1971), (I.2), 49.

14. Martianus Capella, "The Marriage of Philology and Mercury," in *Martianus Capella and the Seven Liberal Arts*, ed. and trans. William Harris Stahl, Richard Johnson, and E. L. Burge (New York: Columbia University Press), 2:22; also see Andrew Hicks, "Martianus Capella and the Liberal Arts," in *The Oxford Handbook of Medieval Latin Literature*, ed. Ralph Hexter and David Townsend (Oxford: Oxford University Press, 2012).

15. John of Salisbury, quoted in Ernst Robert Curtius, *European Literature and the Latin Middle Age*, trans. Willard Trask (Princeton, NJ: Princeton University Press, 1953), 206.

16. Generally, see Domenico Comparetti, *Vergil in the Middle Ages*, trans. E.F.M. Benecke (Princeton, NJ: Princeton University Press, 1997).

17. Quoted from Craig Kallendorf, "From Virgil to Vida: The *Poeta Theologus* in Italian Renaissance Commentary," *Journal of the History of Ideas* 56, no. 1 (Jan. 1995): 46.

18. Seth Lerer, "John of Salisbury's Virgil," *Vivarium* 20, no. 1 (1982): 29–31.

19. Theodolph quoted in Seznec, *Survival of the Pagan Gods*, 91.

20. Seznec, *Survival of the Pagan Gods*, 93.

21. Curtius, *European Literature*, 216, 219.

22. Seznec, *Survival of the Pagan Gods*, 220. On Boccaccio, see David Lummus, "Boccaccio's Poetic Anthropology: Allegories of History in the *Genealogie deorum gentilium libri*," *Speculum* 87, no. 3 (July 2012): 724–765.

23. Jon Solomon, "Introduction" in Giovanni Boccaccio, *Genealogy of the Pagan Gods*, ed. and trans. Jon Solomon (Cambridge, MA: Harvard University Press, 2011), 1:X–XII.

24. On the poeta theologus in the Renaissance, see Ronald Witt, "The *Poeta-Theologus* from Mussato to Landino," *European Legacy* 20, no. 5 (2015): 450–461.

25. Charles Osgood, *Boccaccio on Poetry* (New York: Liberal Arts Press, 1956), 122.

26. Boccaccio, *Genealogy of the Pagan Gods*, 1:21.

27. Boccaccio, *Genealogy of the Pagan Gods*, 1:19.

28. David Lummus, "Boccaccio's Poetic Anthropology: Allegories of History in the 'Genealogia deorum gentilium libri,'" *Speculum* 87, no. 3 (July 2012): 728.

29. Boccaccio, *Genealogy of the Pagan Gods*, 2:275.

30. Boccaccio, *Genealogy of the Pagan Gods*, 2:279.

31. Boccaccio, *Genealogy of the Pagan Gods*, 2:281.

32. Lummus, "Boccaccio's Poetic Anthropology," 738, 743.

33. See Inez Scott Ryberg, *Rites of the State Religion in Roman Art* (Rome: American Academy in Rome, 1955).

34. See Guillaume du Choul, *Discours de la religion des anciens Romains* (Lyon: Guillaume Rouille, 1556), 290.

35. See Phyllis Pray Bober and Ruth Rubinstein, *Renaissance Artists & Antique Sculpture: A Handbook of Sources* (London: Harvey Miller, 1986), 180, 189ff.

36. Fritz Saxl, "Pagan Sacrifice in the Italian Renaissance," *Journal of the Warburg Institute* 2, no. 4 (April 1939): 346–367.

37. The sacrifice might also be a reference to Venetian carnival—during *Giovedi grasso*, pigs were slaughtered on the Piazza San Marco. See Edward Muir, *Civic Ritual*

in Renaissance Venice (Princeton, NJ: Princeton University Press, 1981), 160–161. My thanks to Randolph Starn and Loren Partridge for this suggestion.

38. Gert Jan van der Sman, "Girolamo Mocetto and the Antique," *Print Quarterly* 30, no. 2 (June 2013): 165–170.

39. See Rebekah Anne Carson, "Andrea Riccio's Della Torre Tomb Monument: Humanism and Antiquarianism in Padua and Verona" (PhD thesis, University of Toronto, 2010), 146.

40. See Arnold Nesselrath, "Impressions of the Pantheon in the Renaissance," in *The Pantheon from Antiquity to the Present*, ed. Tod A. Marder and Mark Wilson Jones (Cambridge: Cambridge University Press, 2015), 257.

41. See Davide Banzato, "Il candelabro pasquale di Andrea Riccio. Note sulla storia, la committenza, la lettura, le derivazioni dall'antico e da altri fonti figurative," in *Rinascimento e passione per l'antico: Andrea Riccio e il suo tempo*, ed. Andrea Bacchi and Luciana Giacomelli (Trent: Museo diocesano tridentino, 2008), 109–110.

42. See Saxl, "Pagan Sacrifice," 349f. To see the image, follow this link: https://www.khm.at/objektdb/detail/87306/.

43. Patricia Fortini Brown, "The Antiquarianism of Jacopo Bellini," *Artibus et Historiae* 13, no. 26 (1992): 69. See also Fritz Saxl, "Jacopo Bellini and Mantegna as Antiquarians," *Lectures* (London: Warburg Institute, 1957), 1:151–160.

44. Patricia Fortini Brown, *Venice and Antiquity: The Venetian Sense of the Past* (New Haven, CT: Yale University Press, 1996), 108.

45. See, e.g., Brown, "The Antiquarianism of Jacopo Bellini," 80.

46. Brown, *Venice and Antiquity*, 134–135.

47. Livy, *Ab urbe condita*, II.12.

48. Saxl, "Pagan Sacrifice," 352.

49. Marcus Tullius Cicero, *De Haruspicum Responsis*, in *Orations: Pro Archia. Post Reditum in Senatu. Post Reditum ad Quirites. De Domo Sua. De Haruspicum Responsis. Pro Plancio*, trans. N. H. Watts (Cambridge, MA: Harvard University Press, 1923), 341 (IX.19).

50. Frances Muecke, "'Gentiles nostri': Roman Religion and Roman Identity in Biondo Flavio's 'Roma Triumphans,'" *Journal of the Warburg and Courtauld Institutes* 75 (2012): 93–110. Angelo Mazzocco, "A Reconsideration of Renaissance Antiquarianism and Light of Biondo Flavio's '*ars antiquaria*' with an Unpublished Letter from Paul Oskar Kristeller," *Memoirs of the American Academy in Rome* 59/60 (2014/2015): 121–159.

51. Biondo Flavio, *Rome in Triumph*, ed. Maria Agata Pincelli and trans. Frances Muecke (Cambridge, MA: Harvard University Press, 2016), 53.

52. Muecke, "'Gentiles nostri,' " 102.

53. Biondo, *Rome in Triumph*, 77.

54. Biondo, *Rome in Triumph*, 97.

55. Freud, *Das Unbehagen in der Kultur* (Vienna: Internationaler Psychoanalytischer Verlag, 1929), 14.

56. On Alexandro, see Domenico Maffei, *Alessandro d'Alessandro: Giureconsulto umanista (1461–1523)* (Milan: Giuffrè, 1956).

57. Alexander ab Alexandro, *Geniales dierum libri sex varia ac recondita eruditione referti* (Paris: Ioannem Petrum, 1532), 47 recto.

58. ab Alexandro, *Geniales dierum libri sex*, 87 recto.

59. ab Alexandro, *Geniales dierum libri sex*, 87 recto. The description is extracted largely from Ovid's *Fasti*.

60. ab Alexandro, *Geniales dierum libri sex*, 107 recto (Lupercalia); 130 recto (Monte Albano). On the institution itself, see, e.g., Christopher Smith, "The Religion of Archaic Rome," in *A Companion to Roman Religion*, ed. Jörg Rüpke (Oxford: Blackwell, 2007), 39–40. On Roman religion more generally, though equally puzzled about the *rex sacrorum*, see Jörg Rüpke, *Pantheon: A New History of Roman Religion* (Princeton, NJ: Princeton University Press, 2018).

61. ab Alexandro, *Geniales dierum libri sex*, 112 recto.

62. ab Alexandro, *Geniales dierum libri sex*, 112 verso.

63. ab Alexandro, *Geniales dierum libri sex*, 193 verso–194 recto (all capitals in original).

64. ab Alexandro, *Geniales dierum libri sex*, 194 verso.

65. Catherine Atkinson, *Inventing Inventors in Renaissance Europe: Polydore Vergil's* De inventoribus rerum (Tübingen: Mohr Siebeck, 2007), 76–79.

66. Polydore Vergil, *On Discovery*, ed. and trans. Brian Copenhaver (Cambridge, MA: I Tatti Renaissance Library, 2002), I.5, p. 73.

67. Vergil, *On Discovery*, I.5, p. 73, 75.

68. Vergil, *On Discovery*, I.5, p. 75.

69. Atkinson, *Inventing Inventors*, 79.

70. Polydore Vergil, *Beginnings and Discoveries*: *Polydore Vergil's De inventoribus rerurm*, ed. and trans. Beno Weiss and Louis C. Pérez (Nieuwkoop: De Graaf, 1997), 247. (I will use this edition for the last 5 books only.)

71. Amos Funkenstein, *Theology and the Scientific Imagination from the Middle Ages to the Seventeenth Century* (Princeton, NJ: Princeton University Press, 1986), 213ff.

72. Vergil, *Beginnings and Discoveries*, 222.

73. Gregory I, *The Letters of Gregory the Great*, trans. John R. C. Martyn (Toronto: Pontifical Institute of Mediaeval Studies, 2004), 3:802 (letter 11.56, to Mellitus 18 July 601).

74. Vergil, *Beginnings and Discoveries*, 316, 314–315, 318, 319, 322.

75. Vergil, *Beginnings and Discoveries*, 356.

76. Vergil, *Beginnings and Discoveries*, 359.

77. Vergil, *Beginnings and Discoveries*, 362, 372–373.

78. Vergil, *Beginnings and Discoveries*, 377.

79. Vergil, *Beginnings and Discoveries*, 378.

80. Natalie Zemon Davis, "Guillaume Rouillé, Businessman and Humanist," in *Editing Sixteenth-Century Texts*, ed. R. J. Schoeck (Toronto: University of Toronto Press, 1966), 72–112. See also Margaret M. McGowan, *The Vision of Rome in Late Renaissance France* (New Haven, CT: Yale University Press, 2000), 71–81.

81. Du Choul, *Discours*. On du Choul, see Felix Bourriot, "Un ouvrage lyonnais de la Renaissance: Discours de la religion des anciens Romains par G. du Choul, Lyon, 1556," *Revue du Nord* 66 (April–Sept. 1984): 653–675.

82. Du Choul, *Discours*, 264.

83. Du Choul, *Discours*, 275, 277.

84. On this last image, and more generally on the afterlife of sacrificial images on coins, see Martin Mulsow, "Tempel, Münzen und der Transfer von Bildern: Zur Rolle der numismatischen Illustration im religionsgeschichtlichen Antiquarianismus," in *Architektur- und Ornamentgraphik der Frühen Neuzeit: Migrationsprozesse in Europa*, ed. Sabine Frommel and Eckhard Leuschner (Rome: Campisano Editore, 2016), 295–312. In general, on du Choul's sources for the illustrations, see Richard Cooper, *Roman Antiquities in Renaissance France, 1515–1565* (London: Routledge, 2016), 181ff.

85. Du Choul, *Discours*, 304.

86. Anthony Grafton, *Inky Fingers: The Making of Books in Early Modern Europe* (Cambridge, MA: Harvard University Press, 2020), 115.

87. Du Choul, *Discours*, 305.

88. Du Choul, *Discours*, 273.

89. David A. Lupher, *Romans in a New World: Classical Models in Sixteenth-Century Spanish America* (Ann Arbor: University of Michigan Press, 2003), 285.

90. Du Choul, *Discours*, 273.

91. Du Choul, *Discours*, 262.

92. Du Choul, *Discours*, 312. On Beroaldo, see Grafton, *Inky Fingers*, 114.

93. Seznec, *Survival of the Pagan Gods*, 121.

94. See especially Natale Conti's *Mythologiae sive explicationis fabularum libri decem* (Venice, 1551) and Vincenzo Cartari's *Le imagine con la sposizione de i dei degli antichi* (Venice, 1556).

95. Karl A. E. Enenkel, "The Making of 16th-Century Mythography: Giraldi's 'Syntagma de musis' (1507, 1511, and 1539), 'De deis gentium historia' (ca. 1500–1548) and Julien de Havrech's 'De cognominibus deorum gentilium' (1541)," *Humanistica Lovaniensia* 51 (2002): 28.

96. Lilio Gregorio Giraldi, *De deis gentium varia & multiplex Historia* (Basel: Oporinus, 1548), 649.

97. Giraldi, *De deis gentium*, 649.

98. Giraldi, *De deis gentium*, 666.

99. Giraldi, *De deis gentium*, 649, 649–650, 653, 655, 656, 657–658.

100. Macrobius, *Saturnalia*, II:69–70 (III.10–11); Giraldi, *De deis gentium*, 696.

101. Giraldi, *De deis gentium*, 2.

102. Giraldi, *De deis gentium*, 1.

103. Tertullian, *Apology*, in *Tertullian: Apology, De Speculis*, 87 (16.13).

104. Giraldi, *De deis gentium*, 2.

105. Giraldi, *De deis gentium*, 11.

106. Giraldi, *De deis gentium*, 732, 658.

107. Giraldi, *De deis gentium*, 760–761.

108. Giraldi, *De deis gentium*, 761.

109. Giraldi, *De deis gentium*, 764.

110. Giraldi, *De deis gentium*, 739.

111. On the composition history, and its entanglement with various episodes of confessional violence, see Kolakowski, "Johann Wilhelm Stucki," 269–293.

112. Johann Wilhelm Stucki, *Antiquitatum convivialium libri III. In quibus hebraeorum, graecorum, romanorum aliarumque nationeum antiqua conviviorum*

genera, nec non mores, consuetudines, ritus ceremoniaeque conviviales, atque etiam aliae explicantur, & cum iis, quae hodie cum apud Christianos, tum apud alias gentes a Christiano nomine alienas in usu sunt, confereantur . . . (Zürich: Christoph Froschauer, 1582).

113. "Praefatio ad lectorem pium & candidum," in Stucki, *Antiquitatum*, unpaginated.

114. Kolakowski, "Johann Wilhelm Stucki," 341.

115. Kolakowski, "Johann Wilhelm Stucki," 333.

116. Stucki, "Prefatio" in *Sacrorum sacrificiorumque gentilium . . . descriptio*, unpaginated.

117. Stucki, "Prefatio" in *Sacrorum sacrificiorumque gentilium . . . descriptio*, upaginated.

118. Kolakowski, "Johann Wilhelm Stucki," 332.

119. Stucki, "Prefatio" in *Sacrorum sacrificiorumque gentilium . . . descriptio*, unpaginated.

120. Stucki, "Prefatio" in *Sacrorum sacrificiorumque gentilium . . . descriptio*, unpaginated.

121. Stucki, "Prefatio" in *Sacrorum sacrificiorumque gentilium . . . descriptio*, Unpaginated.

122. On history of religion, see Kolakowski, "Johann Wilhelm Stucki," 416; on functionalism, see Kolakowski, "Johann Wilhelm Stucki," 343.

123. Johann Wilhelm Stucki, *Antiquitatem Convivialium Libri III, editio secunda* (Zürich: Apud Iohannem Wolphium, 1597), 108recto, 109recto, 110recto, 111recto, 111verso–112recto, 111verso, 112verso–113recto.

124. Kolakowski, "Johann Wilhelm Stucki," 334.

125. Stucki, *Antiquitatem Convivialium Libri III* (1597), 6recto, 7 recto.

126. Stucki, *Sacrorum sacrificiorumque gentilium . . . descriptio*, 1recto.

127. For Stucki's authors, see Kolakowski, "Johann Wilhelm Stucki," 307–320.

128. Marc Kolakowski, "*Humana, seu potius inhumana sacrificia.* Le sacrifice humain à la croissée des discours dan l'oeuvre du polyhistor Johann Wilhelm Stucki (1542–1607)," in *Sacrifices humains. Dossiers, discours, comparaisons: Actes du colloque tenu à l'Université de Genève, 19–20 mai 2011, eds. Agnes A. Nagy and Francesca Prescendi* (Turnhout: Brepols, 2013), 92.

129. Walter J. Ong, S.J., *Ramus: Method and the Decay of Dialogue* (Cambridge, MA: Harvard University Press, 1983), 225.

130. Stucki, *Sacrorum sacrificiorumque gentilium . . . descriptio*, 15verso. For Stucki on idolatry, see Kolakowski, "Johann Wilhelm Stucki," 380–389.

131. Stucki, *Sacrorum sacrificiorumque gentilium . . . descriptio*, 83recto.

132. Stucki, *Sacrorum sacrificiorumque gentilium . . . descriptio*, 96verso.

133. Kolakowski, "Johann Wilhelm Stucki," 92.

134. Stucki, *Sacrorum sacrificiorumque gentilium . . . descriptio*, 14recto.

135. Stucki, *Sacrorum sacrificiorumque gentilium . . . descriptio*, 15recto.

136. Stucki, *Sacrorum sacrificiorumque gentilium . . . descriptio*, 8recto. Quoting Ovid, *Fasti*, trans. James George Frazer (Cambridge, MA: Harvard University Press, 1996), 27 (I.335).

137. Stucki, *Sacrorum sacrificiorumque gentilium . . . descriptio*, 8recto.

138. Kolakowski, "Johann Wilhelm Stucki," 94.

139. Stucki, *Sacrorum sacrificiorumque gentilium . . . descriptio*, 42verso–43recto, 43 recto, 43verso.

140. Stucki, *Sacrorum sacrificiorumque gentilium . . . descriptio*, 154 verso, 155verso, 156recto.

141. Stucki, *Sacrorum sacrificiorumque gentilium . . . descriptio*, 157verso, 158recto. The RSV translates the metaphor as "how I yearn for you with all the affection of Christ Jesus." Early modern translations, like the King James here, keep the literal expression.

142. Stucki, *Sacrorum sacrificiorumque gentilium . . . descriptio*, 158verso; Kolakowski, "Johann Wilhelm Stucki," 332.

143. Stucki, *Sacrorum sacrificiorumque gentilium . . . descriptio*, 156verso.

144. Stucki, *Sacrorum sacrificiorumque gentilium . . . descriptio*, 166recto.

145. Livy, *ab urbe condita*, ed. and trans. J. C. Yardley (Cambridge, MA: Harvard University Press, 2018), 11:265 (XXXIX.16).

146. Stucki, *Antiquitatem Convivialium Libri III* (1597), 123recto.

147. Curtius, *European Literature*, 218, 226.

Chapter 6: Gods of Paste

1. Hernan Cortes, *Letters from Mexico*, trans. and ed. A. R. Pagden (New York: Grossman Publishers, 1971), 106.

2. Cortes, *Letters from Mexico*, 35.

3. Cortes, *Letters from Mexico*, 106.

4. Inga Clendinnen, *Aztecs: An Interpretation* (Cambridge: Cambridge University Press, 1991), 138, 147; See also Davíd Carrasco, *City of Sacrifice: The Aztec Empire and the Role of Violence in Civilization* (Boston: Beacon Press, 1999).

5. Peter Martyr d'Anghiera, *De Orbe Novo: The Eight Decades of Peter Martyr D'Anghera*, trans. Francis Augustus MacNutt (New York: G.P. Putnam's Sons, 1912), 2:117 (Fifth Decade).

6. Francisco López de Gómara, *Conquista de Méjico* (Barcelona: Biblioteca clásica española, 1887), 1:191.

7. de Gómara, *Conquista de Méjico*, 1:92–193.

8. Most recently, historians have begun to explore the annals written by indigenous authors themselves, typically Nahuatl elites who were themselves products of a Franciscan education; see here Camilla Townsend, *Fifth Sun: A New History of the Aztecs* (New York: Oxford University Press, 2019).

9. Miguel León-Portilla, *Bernardino de Sahagún: First Anthropologist*, trans. Mauricio J. Mixco (Norman: University of Oklahoma Press, 2002).

10. Bernardino de Sahagún, *General History of the Things of New Spain*, trans. Arthur J. O. Anderson and Charles E. Dibble (Santa Fe, NM: School of American Research and the University of Utah, 1981), book 2. For a brief account of the work's composition, see Townsend, *Fifth Sun*, 221ff; also Tom Cummins, "Sacrifice and Idolatry in Pre-Columbian and Colonial America: 'Because the worshipping of abominable idols is the cause and the beginning of all evil'," in *Sacrifice and Conversion in the Early Modern Atlantic World*, ed. Maria Berbara (Florence: I Tatti, 2022), 38–52.

11. Townsend, *Fifth Sun*, 221–222.

12. More generally, see Anthony Pagden, *The Fall of Natural Man: The American Indian and the Origins of Comparative Ethnology* (Cambridge: Cambridge University Press, 1982); Sabine MacCormack, *Religion in the Andes: Vision and Imagination in Early Colonial Peru* (Princeton, NJ: Princeton University Press, 1991).

13. Paul III, "Sublimis Deus," in *New Iberian World: A Documentary History of the Discovery and Settlement of the Latin America to the Early 17th-Century*, ed. John H. Parry and Robert G. Keith (New York: Times Books, 1984), 1:387.

14. Carina Johnson, *Cultural Hierarchy in Sixteenth-Century Europe: The Ottomans and the Mexicans* (Cambridge: Cambridge University Press, 2011), 13. See also Carina Johnson, "Idolatrous Cultures and the Practice of Religion," *Journal of the History of Ideas* 67, no. 4 (October 2006): 597–622.

15. Juan Ginés de Sepúlveda, *Democrates secundus sive de iustis belli causis apud Indos,* in *Obras completas,* ed. and trans. A. Coroleu Lletget (Pozoblanco: Excmo. Ayunamiento de Pozoblanco, 1997), 3:67.

16. de Sepúlveda, *Democrates secundus,* 3: 68.

17. Francisco Castilla Urbano, "The Debate of Valladolid (1550–1551): Background, Discussions, and Results of the Debate between Juan Genés de Sepúlveda and Bartolomé de las Casas," in *A Companion to Early Modern Spanish Imperial Political and Social Thought*, ed. Jörg Tellkamp (Leiden: Brill 2020), 229.

18. Bartolomé de las Casas, *In Defense of the Indians: the Defense of the Most Reverend Lord Don Fray Bartolomé de las Casas, of the Order of Preachers, late Bishop of Chiapa, against the Persecutors and Slanderers of the Peoples of the New World discovered across the Seas,* trans. Stafford Poole (DeKalb: Northern Illinois University Press, 1974), 226.

19. Las Casas, *In Defense of the Indians*, 228.

20. Las Casas, *In Defense of the Indians*, 231, 229. Italics mine.

21. Las Casas, *In Defense of the Indians*, 228.

22. Las Casas, *In Defense of the Indians*, 231.

23. Las Casas, *In Defense of the Indians*, 232.

24. Las Casas, *In Defense of the Indians*, 234. Italics mine.

25. Dionysius of Halicarnassus, *Roman Antiquities* (Cambridge, MA: Harvard University Press, 1960), I:77 (I.24.1); quoted in las Casas, *In Defense of the Indians*, 235.

26. Las Casas, *In Defense of the Indians*, 235.

27. Las Casas, *In Defense of the Indians*, 238.

28. Las Casas, *In Defense of the Indians*, 239.

29. Las Casas, *In Defense of the Indians*, 240.

30. Las Casas, *In Defense of the Indians*, 241.

31. For the curious publication history of both the Apology and the *Apologética historia*, see Henry Raup Wagner and Helen Rand Parish, *The Life and Writings of Bartolomé de las Casas* (Albuquerque: University of New Mexico Press, 1967), 278–279, 286.

32. See MacCormack, *Religion in the Andes*, 245. On the suppression, see Fidel Villarroel, "Jerónimo Román, historiador del siglo de oro," *Estudio Agustiniano* 9 (Sept.–Dec. 1974): 429.

33. Bartholomé de las Casas, *Aquí se contíene una disputa, o controversia entre el Obispo don fray Bartholome de Las Casas . . . y el Doctor Gines de Sepulveda* (Seville, 1552). The "eleventh reply" in the text summarizes chapters 34–37 of the *Argumentum/In Defense of the Indians.*

34. More generally, see V. Afanasiev, "The Literary Heritage of Bartolomé de Las Casas," in *Bartolomé de las Casas in History: Toward an Understanding of the Man and His Work*, ed. Juan Friede and Benjamin Keen (DeKalb: Northern Illinois University Press, 1971), 539–578.

35. For the print history of these from 1492–1532, see Rudolf Hirsch, "Printed Reports on the Early Discoveries and Their Reception," in *First Images of America: The Impact of the New World on the Old*, ed. Fredi Chiappelli (Berkeley: University of California Press, 1976), 2:553–560.

36. See Carina Johnson, *Cultural Hierarchy*, chap. 1.

37. A. R. Pagden, "Introduction," in Cortes, *Letters from Mexico*, lxxvi, lxxii.

38. Urbano, "The Debate of Valladolid (1550–1551)," 241, 223ff.

39. Cristián Andrés Roa de la Carrera, *Histories of Infamy: Francisco López de Gómara and the Ethics of Spanish Imperialism* (Boulder: University Press of Colorado, 2005), 55.

40. Pagden, *Fall of Natural Man*, 238 fn. 2.

41. J. H. Elliott, *The Old World and the New, 1492–1650* (Cambridge: Cambridge University Press, 1970), 12.

42. See, e.g., Neil L. Whitehead and Michael Harbsmeier, "Introduction," in Hans Staden, *Hans Staden's True History: An Account of Cannibal Captivity in Brazil* (Durham, NC: Duke University Press, 2008), xv–civ; and Florestan Fernandes, "La guerre et le sacrifice humain chez les Tupinamba," *Journal de la Société des américanistes* 41, no. 1 (1952): 139–220.

43. Staden, *True History*, 127.

44. Jean de Léry, *History of a Voyage to the Land of Brazil, Otherwise Called America*, trans. Janet Whatley (Berkeley: University of California Press, 1992), chap. 15 (which mentions sacrifice only once, and this with respect to New Spain).

45. Staden, *True History*, 125.

46. de Léry, *History of a Voyage*, 134, 136.

47. Michel de Montaigne, *Essays*, ed. and trans. J. M. Cohen (Baltimore, MD: Penguin, 1958), 113.

48. See here Frank Lestringant, *Cannibals: The Discovery and Representation of the Cannibal from Columbus to Jules Verne*, trans. Rosemary Morris (Berkeley: University of California Press, 1997), 118. There is also a literature that discovers in Montaigne's essay a commentary on the Eucharist; see George Hoffmann, "Anatomy of the Mass: Montaigne's 'Cannibals,'" *Publication of the Modern Language Associations of America [PMLA]* 117, no. 2 (March 2002): 207–221. For my part, I find the *absence* of sacrifice more startling than its presence.

49. Lilio Gregorio Giraldi, *De deis gentium varia & multiplex Historia* (Basel: Oporinus, 1548), 761.

50. Johann Wilhelm Stucki, *Sacrorum sacrificiorumque gentilium brevis et accurate descriptio, universae superstitionis ethnicae ritus cerimoniasque complectens* (Zürich: Johann Wolfius, 1598), 42r, 128r.

51. Simon Ditchfield, "What Did Natural History Have to Do with Salvation? José de Acosta SJ (1540–1600) in the Americas," *Studies in Church History* 46 (2010): 154–155.

52. See Andrés I. Prieto, *Missionary Scientists: Jesuit Science in Spanish South America, 1570–1810* (Nashville, TN: Vanderbilt University Press, 2011), 147.

53. See, e.g., Lauren Benton, *Law and Colonial Cultures: Legal Regimes in World History, 1400–1900* (Cambridge: Cambridge University Press, 2002) and *A Search for Sovereignty: Law and Geography in European Empires, 1400–1900* (Cambridge: Cambridge University Press, 2010).

54. The literature here is substantial. For a start, see Joel F. Harrington and Helmut Walser Smith, "Confessionalization, Community, and State Building in Germany, 1555–1870," *Journal of Modern History* 69 (March 1997): 77–101. Also Thomas Brady, "Confessionalization: The Career of a Concept," in *Confessionalization in Europe, 1555–1700*, ed. John M. Headley and Hans J. Hillerbrand (London: Rutledge, 2004) and Heinz Schilling, "Confessional Europe," in *Handbook of European History, 1400–1600. Late Middle Ages, Renaissance and Reformation. II. Visions, Programs and Outcomes*, ed. Thomas A. Brady et al. (Leiden: Brill, 1995), 641–675.

55. See, e.g., Carmen Bernand and Serge Gruzinski, *De l'idolatrie: Une archéologie des sciences religieuses* (Paris: Éditions du Seuil, 1988).

56. MacCormack, *Religion in the Andes*, 219.

57. José de Acosta, *The Natural and Moral History of the Indies*, ed. Jane E. Mangan and trans. Frances M. López-Morillas (Durham, NC: Duke University Press, 2002), 260.

58. De Acosta, *Natural and Moral History*, 288.

59. De Acosta, *Natural and Moral History*, 295. De Acosta seems to have gotten most of his information on Mexico from fellow Jesuit Juan de Továr, whose manuscript on the Indies copied liberally from an earlier manuscript of Diego Durán—again, a great example of both what was hidden, and what de Acosta brought to light. See Elizabeth Boone, "Incarnations of the Aztec Supernatural: The Image of Huitzilopochtli in Mexico and Europe," *Proceedings of the American Philosophical Society* 79, no. 2 (1989): 1–107.

60. John Lynch, *New Worlds: A Religious History of Latin America* (New Haven, CT: Yale University Press, 2012), 39ff.

61. Richard E. Greenleaf, "The Mexican Inquisition and the Indians: Sources for the Ethnohistorian," *The Americas* 34, no. 3 (Jan 1978): 319.

62. MacCormack, *Religion in the Andes*, 254; Carolyn Dean, *Inka Bodies and the Body of Christ: Corpus Christi in Colonial Cuzco, Peru* (Durham, NC: Duke University Press, 1999), 16.

63. On Trent, see H. J. Schroeder, O.P., trans., *Canons and Decrees of the Council of Trent* (St. Louis, MO: Herder Books, 1941), 76 (Session 13, chap. 5, "The Worship and Veneration to Be Shown to This Most Holy Sacrament"). On Corpus Christi in the New World, see Carolyn Dean, *Inka Bodies*, chap. 3.

64. See L. Clark Keating, "Introduction" to Pablo Joseph de Arriaga, *Extirpaton of Idolatry in Peru*, trans. and ed. L. Clark Keating (Lexington: University of Kentucky Press), xiii.

65. Arriaga, *Extirpation of Idolatry in Peru*, 8.

66. Ditchfield, "What Did Natural History Have to Do with Salvation?," 156; Enrique T. Bartra, S.J., "Introduction" to *Tercer Concilio Limense, 1582–83* (Lima: Facultad Pontifica y Civil de Teológia de Lima, 1982), 21 (Decrees of the Second Session, 15 August 1583, chap. 30, 73).

67. De Acosta, *Natural and Moral History*, 300.

68. De Acosta, *Natural and Moral History*, 300–301.

69. De Acosta, *Natural and Moral History*, 302–303; on the festival, see Boone, "Incarnations of the Aztec Supernatural," 37.

70. De Acosta, *Natural and Moral History*, 301.

71. De Acosta, *Natural and Moral History*, 303; Acosta mistakenly gives May as the date of the Aztec festival, perhaps to bring it in better alignment with Corpus Christi, traditionally held in early June.

72. Pagden, *Fall of Natural Man*, 146.

73. Hoffmann, "Anatomy of the Mass," 212.

74. Boone, "Incarnations of the Aztec Supernatural," 36.

75. Robert Bellarmine, *Septima controversia generalis de ecclesia triumphante tribus libris explicata* in *Ven. Cardinalis Roberti Bellarmini Politiani S.J. Opera Omnia Ex Editione Veneta, Pluribus tum Additis tum Correctis*, 12 vols., ed. Justinus Fèvre (Paris: L. Vivès, 1870), 3:213.

76. Schroeder, trans., *Canons and Decrees of the Council of Trent*, 216.

77. See Margaret Aston, *England's Iconoclasts Laws Against Images*, vol. 1 (Oxford: Oxford University Press, 1988); Carlos Eire, *War Against the Idols: The Reformation of Worship from Erasmus to Calvin* (Cambridge: Cambridge University Press, 1986); Lee Palmer Wandel, *Voracious Idols and Violent Hands: Iconoclasm in Reformation Zürich, Strasbourg, and Basel* (Cambridge: Cambridge University Press, 1995); for idolatry as a problem of representation, see Stuart Clark, *Vanities of the Eye: Vision in Early Modern European Culture* (Oxford: Oxford University Press, 2007).

78. Calvin quoted in Eire, *War Against the Idols*, 200 fn. 22.

79. John Calvin, *Institutes of the Christian Religion*, trans. Ford Lewis Battles (Louisville, KY: Westminster John Knox Press, 1960), 111 (I.11.11).

80. Viret quoted in Christopher Elwood, *The Body Broken: The Calvinist Doctrine of the Eucharist and the Symbolization of Power in Sixteenth-Century France* (Oxford: Oxford University Press, 1999), 94.

81. The *dieu de paste* was an integral part of French Protestant attacks on the Mass, and examples could be multiplied ad infinitum from all the leading reformers, among them Calvin, Beza, Estienne, etc., e.g., John Calvin, *Sermon XLI: sur le Chap XI de Daniel v. 36–38*, in *Ioannis Calvini Opera quae supersunt omnia*, ed. William Baum et al., *Corpus reformatorum* (Braunschweig: C.A. Schwetschke, 1890), 42: 92 (*Corpus Reformatorum* vol. 70).

82. Calvin quoted in Eire, *War against the Idols*, 199.

83. Calvin, *Institutes*, 108, (I.11.8).

84. Heinrich Bullinger, *De origine erroris libri duo* (Zürich: Froschauer, 1539), chap. 13.

85. On idolatry, the bibliography is substantial, and includes: Peter Miller, "Taking Paganism Seriously: Anthropology and Antiquarianism in Early Seventeenth-Century

Histories of Religion," *Archiv für Religionsgeschichte* 3 (2001): 183–209; Martin Mulsow, "John Seldens *De Diis Syris*: Idolatriekritik und vergleichende Religionsgeschichte im 17. Jahrhundert," *Archiv für Religionsgeschichte* 3 (2001): 1–24; Guy Stroumsa, "John Spencer and the Roots of Idolatry," *History of Religions* 41, no. 1 (August 2001): 1–23; Francis Schmidt, "Polytheisms: Degeneration or Progress?," *History and Anthropology* 3 (1987): 9–60; Jonathan Sheehan, "Sacred and Profane: Idolatry, Antiquarianism, and the Polemics of Distinction in the Seventeenth Century," *Past and Present* 192 (August 2006): 37–66; Jonathan Sheehan, "The Altars of the Idols: Religion, Sacrifice, and the Early Modern Polity," *Journal of the History of Ideas* 67 (October 2006): 648–674; Joan-Pau Rubiés, "Theology, Ethnography, and the Historicization of Idolatry," *Journal of the History of Ideas* 67 (October 2006): 571–596.

86. Edward Brerewood, *Enquiry Touching the Diversity of Languages and Religions* (London, 1614), 118.

87. Purchas is also oddly understudied. In Peter Harrison's otherwise excellent *'Religion' and the 'Religions' in the English Enlightenment* (Cambridge: Cambridge University Press, 1990), for example, an entire chapter on travel and religious diversity in seventeenth-century England omits even a single mention. An important exception is David Armitage, *Ideological Origins of the British Empire* (Cambridge: Cambridge University Press, 2004), esp. chap. 3.

88. On the codex, see Frances F. Berdan and Patricia Rieff Anawalt, *The Essential Codex Mendoza* (Berkeley: University of California Press, 1992), xii; the work passed from the cosmographer Thevet, to Richard Hakluyt, to Purchas, and later to John Selden. More generally, see Colin Steele, *English Interpreters of the Iberian New World from Purchas to Stevens* (Oxford: Dolphin Press, 1975).

89. Samuel Purchas, "Dedication to George Abbott, Archbishop of Canterbury," in *Purchas his Pilgrimage, or Relations of the World and the Religions Observed in All Ages and Places Discovered from the Creation unto this Present* (London: William Stansby, 1613), unpaginated.

90. Purchas, *Purchas his Pilgrimage* (1613), 16.

91. For the broader use of the Genesis framework for explaining religious diversity, see Harrison, *'Religion' and the 'Religions' in the English Enlightenment*, chap. 4; also Colin Kidd, *The Forging of Races: Race and Scripture in the Protestant Atlantic World, 1600–2000* (Cambridge: Cambridge University Press, 2012), esp. chap. 3.

92. Purchas, *Purchas his Pilgrimage* (1613), 26.

93. Purchas, *Purchas his Pilgrimage* (1613), 28.

94. Purchas, *Purchas his Pilgrimage* (1613), 27.

95. Purchas, *Purchas his Pilgrimage* (1613), 28.

96. Purchas, *Purchas his Pilgrimage* (1613), 21, 27.

97. Purchas, *Purchas his Pilgrimage* (1613), 28.

98. Purchas, *Purchas his Pilgrimage* (1613), 28.

99. Purchas, *Purchas his Pilgrimage* (1613), 28.

100. Purchas, *Purchas his Pilgrimage* (1613), 36. Italics in original.

101. Purchas, *Purchas his Pilgrimage* (1613), 45–46.

102. Purchas, *Purchas his Pilgrimage* (1613), 87. On the early modern tradition of theological geography more generally, see Zur Shalev, *Sacred Words and Worlds: Geography, Religion, and Scholarship 1550–1700* (Leiden: Brill, 2012).

103. Purchas, *Purchas his Pilgrimage,* (1613), 89.

104. Purchas, *Purchas his Pilgrimage* (1613), 111, 116 (Golden Calf).

105. Purchas, *Purchas his Pilgrimage* (1613), 639.

106. Purchas, *Purchas his Pilgrimage* (1613), 659.

107. Purchas, *Purchas his Pilgrimage* (1613), 661.

108. Purchas, *Purchas his Pilgrimage* (1613), 660.

109. Purchas, *Purchas his Pilgrimage* (1613), 661.

110. Purchas, *Purchas his Pilgrimage* (1613), 668.

111. Purchas, *Purchas his Pilgrimage* (1613), 680.

112. David Armitage, "Samuel Purchas," *Oxford Dictionary of National Biography,* https://doi.org/10.1093/ref:odnb/22898, accessed October 18, 2020.

113. Armitage, *Ideological Origins of the British Empire,* 83. On Chelsea College, see Simon Brown, "Useful Subjects: Theology, Education, and Practical Knowledge in Seventeenth-Century Britain" (PhD diss., University of California, Berkeley, 2022).

114. Purchas, *Purchas his Pilgrimage* (1613), 680.

115. Purchas, *Purchas his Pilgrimes in Five Bookes* (London: William Stanby, 1625), 880.

116. Jean-Theodor de Bry et al., "Praefatio ad lectorem," *Americae nona et postrema pars* (Frankfurt: Matthew Becker, 1602), unpaginated.

117. Purchas, *Purchas his Pilgrimage,* 4th. ed., (London: William Stansby, 1626), 946. The reference is to the mestizo informant Garcilaso de la Vega.

118. Purchas, *Purchas his Pilgrimage* (1613), 43.

119. Purchas, "Letter to the Reader," in *Purchas his Pilgrimage* (1613), unpaginated.

120. Purchas, *Purchas his Pilgrimage* (1613), 1.

121. Brown, "Useful Subjects," 30.

122. Samuel Purchas, *Microcosmus, or the Historie of Man* (London: Tho. Alchorn, 1627), 696–697.

123. More generally, see Philip Benedict, *Christ's Churches Purely Reformed: A Social History of Calvinism* (New Haven, CT: Yale University Press, 2002), esp. chap. 10.

124. Nicholas Tyacke, *Anti-Calvinists: The Rise of English Arminianism c. 1590–1640* (Oxford: Oxford University Press, 1989).

125. If, as Ethan Shagan has argued, belief became harder, not easier, in the long aftermath of the Reformation, then Protestants needed other tools for understanding the failure of truth to vanquish error. See *The Birth of Modern Belief: Faith and Judgement from the Middle Ages to the Enlightenment* (Princeton, NJ: Princeton University Press, 2018).

126. For a brief list of those who have read Ross in this way, see R.J.W. Mills, "Alexander Ross' *Pansebeia* (1653), religious compendia, and the seventeenth-century study of religious diversity," *The Seventeenth Century* 31, no. 3 (Aug. 2016): 289.

127. Alexander Ross, *Pansebeia: Or, A View of all Religions in the World*, 2nd ed. (London: John Saywell, 1655), 506.

Chapter 7: Kings and Martyrs

1. Seneca, *Hercules*, in *Tragedies* (Cambridge, MA: Harvard University Press, 2018), trans. John G. Fitch, 1:89 (lines 922–924).

2. 1 Kings 3.4; Aristotle, *Politics*, in *The Complete Works of Aristotle*, ed. Jonathan Barnes (Princeton, NJ: Princeton University Press, 1984), 1285b10; Dionysius of Halicarnassus, *Roman Antiquities*, trans. Earnest Cary (Cambridge, MA: Harvard University Press, 1961), 2.14.

3. See Marcel Gauchet, *The Disenchantment of the World: A Political History of Religion* (Princeton, NJ: Princeton University Press, 1997) for a sophisticated version of this. Here quoted from p. 77.

4. George Huntston Williams, *The Norman Anonymous of 1100 AD: Toward the Identification and Evaluation of the So-Called Anonymous of York* (Cambridge, MA: Harvard University Press, 1961), 128–129.

5. Ernst Kantorowicz, *The King's Two Bodies* (Princeton, NJ: Princeton University Press, 1957), 55.

6. Kantorowicz, *King's Two Bodies*, 87.

7. On Lipsius's departure from Leiden, see Mark P. O. Morford, *Stoics and Neostoics: Rubens and the Circle of Lipsius* (Princeton, NJ: Princeton University Press, 2017), chap. 4.

8. On the history of *De cruce*, see especially Jeanine de Landtsheer, "Justus Lipsius's *De Cruce* and the Reception of the Fathers," *Neulateinisches Jahrbuch* 2 (2000): 99–124.

9. Letter to Cornelius Prunius, quoted in Harro Höpfl, "History and Exemplarity in the Work of Lipsius," in *(Un)masking the Realities of Power: Justus Lipsius and the Dynamics of Political Writing in Early Modern Europe*, ed. Erik de Bom et al. (Leiden: Brill, 2011), 54.

10. Philo, *The Special Laws*, trans. F. H. Colson et al. (Cambridge, MA: Harvard University Press, 1937), 3.28.152, p. 57.

11. Justus Lipsus, *De cruce libri tres ad sacram profanamque historiam utiles*, 2nd ed. (Antwerp: Plantin, 1595), 45–46. The Roman law source is *Digest* 48.19.38.

12. Justus Lipsius, *Politica: Six Books of Politics, or Political Instructions*, ed. and trans. Jan Waszink (Assen: Royal van Gorcum, 2004), 295, 389, 387 (referring to Aristotle, *Politics*, 1328b22), 389, 267, 399.

13. Ronald G. Asch, *Sacral Kingship between Disenchantment and Reenchantment: The French and English Monarchies 1587–1688* (New York: Berghahn, 2014), 9.

14. Dionysius of Halicarnassus, *Roman Antiquities*, 2.4.74, p. 499; Livy, *Ab urbe condita* (Cambridge, MA: Harvard University Press, 1988), 1.2.2, p. 221; Frank Cole, trans., *The Roman Questions of Plutarch* (Oxford: Clarendon Press, 1924), question 63, p. 147.

15. Plutarch, *Lives*, trans. Bernadotte Perrin (Cambridge, MA: Harvard University Press, 1967), 1:331. Livy, *ab urbe condita*, 1.I.10 (Romulus), 1.1.18 (Numa Pompilius). On this story, see also Mark Silk, "Numa Pompilius and the Idea of Civil Religion in the West," *Journal of the American Academy of Religion* 72 (December 2004): 863–896. See also my "The Sacrificing King: Ancients, Moderns, and the Politics of Religion," in *For the Sake of Learning: Essays in Honor of Anthony Grafton*, ed. Ann Blair and Anja-Silvia Goering (Leiden: Brill, 2016), 344–363.

16. Machiavelli, *Discourses on Livy*, trans. Harvey C. Mansfield and Nathan Tarcov (Chicago: University of Chicago Press, 1996), 60.

17. Machiavelli, *Discourses*, 60–61.

18. Machiavelli, *Discourses*, 211. On Decius, see Livy, *Ab urbe condita*, 10.28.13,

19. Machiavelli, *Discourses*, 211.

20. Machiavelli, *Discourses*, 131.

21. Machiavelli, *The Prince* (1513), in *Essential Writings of Machiavelli*, ed. and trans. Peter Constantine (New York: Random House, 2007), 24 (chap. 6). On Machiavelli, Savonarola, and unarmed prophets, see John T. Scott, "The Fortune of Machiavelli's Unarmed Prophet," *Journal of Politics* 80.2 (March 2018): 615–629. More generally, see James Hankins, *Virtue Politics: Soulcraft and Statecraft in Renaissance Italy* (Cambridge, MA: Harvard University Press, 2019), esp. 466ff.

22. See Howell Lloyd, *Jean Bodin: 'This Pre-eminent Man of France: An Intellectual Biography* (Oxford: Oxford University Press, 2017), 15, 21, 53, 108.

23. Theodore Beza, *Right of Magistrates* (1574), in *Constitutionalism and Resistance in the Sixteenth Century*, ed. and trans. Julius Franklin (New York: Pegasus, 1969), 135.

24. [Stephanus Junius Brutus], *Vindiciae contra tyrannos*, ed. and trans. George Garnett (Cambridge: Cambridge University Press, 1994), 50, 65. The references are to 1 Kings 18 and 1 Maccabees 2. More generally on resistance theory, see Martin van Gelderen, *The Political Thought of the Dutch Revolt, 1555–1590* (Cambridge: Cambridge University Press, 1992), chap. 3.

25. Donald Kelley, "Martyrs, Myths, and the Massacre: The Background of St. Bartholomew's," *American Historical Review* 77.5 (Dec. 1972):1328.

26. Jean Bodin, *Les six livres de la republique* (Paris, 1576), 152. Later references will also cite Jean Bodin, *Six Bookes of a Commonweale*, trans. Richard Knolles (London, 1606), which combined the Latin and French versions. I have also consulted the modern partial translation: Jean Bodin, *On Sovereignty: Four Chapters from* The Six Books on the Commonwealth (Cambridge: Cambridge Univers ity Press, 1992).

27. Bodin, *Les six livres*, 125.

28. Bodin, *Six Bookes*, 163.

29. Richard Tuck, *The Sleeping Sovereign: The Invention of Modern Democracy* (Cambridge: Cambridge University Press, 2015), 22; see also Julius Franklin, "Sovereignty and the Mixed Constitution: Bodin and His Critics," in J. H. Burns and Mark Goldie, eds., *The Cambridge History of Political Thought, 1450–1700* (Cambridge: Cambridge University Press), 298–328.

30. Machiavelli, *Discourses*, 14.

31. Polybius, *The Histories*, trans. W. R. Paton (Cambridge, MA: Harvard University Press, 2010), book VI, chap. 11–14.

32. Bodin, *Six Bookes*, 186. For the importance of Polybius to Bodin, see Lloyd, *Jean Bodin*, 137.

33. Bodin, *Les six livres*, 221–222.

34. On Cola di Rienzo and the tablet, see Ronald G. Musto, *Apocalypse in Rome: Cola di Rienzo and the Politics of the New Age* (Berkeley: University of California Press, 2003), 112ff.

35. Allan Chester Johnson et al., *Ancient Roman Statutes* (Austin: University of Texas Press, 1961), 149. For the Vespasian law, and the *lex regia* more generally, as a source for political thought, see Daniel Lee, *Popular Sovereignty in Early Modern Constitutional Thought* (Oxford: Oxford University Press, 2016), chap. 1.

36. Dionysius Halicarnassus, *Roman Antiquities*, (Loeb) 3.36.4; 4.1.4; for the identification here, see Alan Watson, "Roman Private Law and the Leges Regiae," *Journal of Roman Studies* 62 (1972): 104. The identification was already made in the early modern period: see François Baudouin, *Libri duo ad leges Romuli Reges Rom. Leg. XII. Tabularum* (Lyon: Simon Gryphius, 1550), 14.

37. Baudouin, *Libri duo*.

38. Louis Le Caron, *Veteres Romanorum leges* (Paris, 1567).

39. Justus Lipsius, *Leges regiae et leges X. virales*, 2nd ed. (Antwerp, 1601). This short text only offered "headings" of the *lex regia*, rather than filling them out, but readers of classical sources could be expected to fill them in.

40. Dionysius of Halicarnassus, *Roman Antiquities*, II.14; Lipsius, *Leges regiae*, 3.

41. For the sources of this ancient law, see Salvator Riccobono, ed., *Fontes Iuris Romani Antejustiniani* (Florence: Barbèra, 1941), 1:4–14; for the translation, see Johnson et al., *Ancient Roman Statutes*, 3–4.

42. Anne Robert, *Rerum iudicatarum libri IIII* (Paris: Robert Fouet, 1611), book 3, p. 1 recto. This book went through at least seven editions: 1596, 1597, 1599, 1602, 1604, 1611, 1620. On Anne Robert, see Marie Houllemare, "Un avocat parisien entre art oratoire et promotion de soi (fin xvie siècle)," *Revue Historique* 306.2 (April 2004): 283–302. For a similar version of this argument in the English context, see John Hayward, *A Reporte of a Discourse Concerning Supreme Power in Affaires of Religion* (London: F.K., 1606), 18ff.

43. This Romanization of Christian politics, it has to be confessed, pleased no one. The work was condemned by the Catholic Holy Office in 1592, and in 1596, completely (*omnino*) forbidden by the Index of Prohibited Books, and it was no less reproached in Geneva, especially for its clear critique of the politics and ethics of martyrdom. On Bodin's condemnations by the Church—as an atheist, crypto-Jew, anti-papalist, Machiavellian, and heretic—see Michaela Valente, "The Works of Bodin under the Lens of Roman Theologians and Inquisitors," in *Reception of Bodin*, ed. Howell Lloyd (Leiden: Brill, 2013), 219–235. On the censorship of Bodin in Geneva, see Ingeborg Jostock, *La censure négociée: le contrôle du livre a Genève, 1560–1625* (Geneva: Droz, 2007), 208ff. The Geneva preface to the 1577 edition of Bodin was especially critical on the issue of resistance; see J.H.M. Salmon, "Bodin and the Monarchomachs," in *Jean Bodin*, ed. Horst Denzer (München: C.H. Beck, 1973), 362.

44. See van Gelderen, *Political Thought of the Dutch Revolt*, esp. chap. 3.

45. More generally, see Jonathan Israel, *The Dutch Republic: Its Rise, Greatness, and Fall 1477–1806* (Oxford: Clarendon Press, 1995), esp. chap. 19.

46. Hugo Grotius, *De imperio summarum potestatum circa sacra*, ed. and trans. Harm Jan van Dam (Leiden: Brill, 2001), 1:189–191.

47. Grotius, *De Imperio*, 1:197.

48. Grotius, *De Imperio*, 1:193. On Grotius and Israel's theocracy, see Eric Nelson, *The Hebrew Republic: Jewish Sources and the Transformation of European Political Thought* (Cambridge, MA: Harvard University Press, 2011), 101ff.

49. Grotius, *De Imperio*, 1:203.

50. Hugo Grotius, *De jure belli ac pacis* (Paris, 1625), 108. For the English translation, see Hugo Grotius, *De jure belli ac pacis libri tres*, trans. Francis Kelsey (Oxford: Clarendon Press, 1925), vols 2–3.

51. Grotius, *De Imperio*, 1:157, 1:199, 1:189.

52. Grotius, *De Imperio*, 1:231.

53. Lipsius, *Politica*, 295.

54. Gerhard Oestreich, *Neostoicism and the Early Modern State* (Cambridge: Cambridge University Press, 1982), 37, 9.

55. Lipsius, *Politica*, 317, quoting Seneca, *Thyestes*, in Seneca, *Tragedies*, vol. 2, trans. John G. Fitch (Cambridge, MA: Harvard University Press, 2004), line 213.

56. Seneca, *Thyestes*, line 272–273; 247–248.

57. Seneca, *Thyestes*, lines 687–80; 700–705.

58. Seneca, *Thyestes*, line 752.

59. Gordon Braden, *Renaissance Tragedy and the Senecan Tradition: Anger's Privilege* (New Haven, CT: Yale University Press, 1985), 30.

60. See Braden, *Renaissance Tragedy*; Curtis Perry, *Shakespeare and Senecan Tragedy* (Cambridge: Cambridge University Press, 2021); Joachim Harst, "Germany and the Netherlands: Tragic Seneca in Scholarship and on Stage," in *Brill's Companion to the Reception of Senecan Tragedy: Scholarly, Theatrical and Literary Receptions*, ed. Eric Dodson-Robinson (Leiden: Brill, 2016), 149–173.

61. Seneca, *Hercules*, in *Tragedies*, vol. 1, lines 1036–1037.

62. Debora Kuller Shuger, *The Renaissance Bible: Scholarship, Sacrifice, and Subjectivity* (Berkeley: University of California Press, 1995), 95.

63. On the link between ritual sacrifice and vengeance, see especially Jennifer Waldron, *Reformations of the Body: Idolatry, Sacrifice, and Early Modern Theater* (New York: Palgrave Macmillan, 2013), chap. 4.

64. William Shakespeare, *Titus Andronicus*, ed. Alan Hughes (Cambridge: Cambridge University Press, 2006), 1.1.124–125.

65. Walter Benjamin, *Origin of the German Trauerspiel*, trans. Howard Eiland (Cambridge, MA: Harvard University Press, 2019), 55.

66. Benjamin, *Origin of the German Trauerspiel*, 57. The bibliography on the *Trauerspiel* is substantial, but of specific interest viz. the martyr-king, see Ferdinand van Ingen, "Andreas Gryphius' *Catharina von Georgien*: Märtyrertheologie und Luthertum," in *Studien zur Literatur des 17. Jahrhunderts: Gedenkschrift für Gerhard Spellerberg (1937–1996)*, ed. Hans Feger (Amsterdam: Rodopi, 1997), 45–70; Daniel Weidner, "Aufführung des Wortes: Theater und Sakrament," in Stefanie Erz, Heike Schlie, and Daniel Weidner, *Sakramentale Repräsentation: Substanz, Zeichen, und Präsenz in der Frühen Neuzeit* (Munich: Wilhelm Fink, 2012), 179–208; Peter-André Alt, *Der Tod der Königin: Frauenopfer und Politische Souveränität im Trauerspiel des 17. Jahrhunderts* (Berlin: De Gruyter, 2004). On Seneca in Germany, see Wolf-Lüder Liebermann, "Die deutsche Literatur," in *Eckhard Lefèvre, Der Einfluss Senecas auf das europäische Drama* (Darmstadt: Wissenschaftliche Buchgesellschaft, 1978), 371–449.

67. Andreas Gryphius, *Leo Armenius*, in *Gesamtausgabe der deutschsprachigen Werke*, ed. Marian Szyrocki and Hugh Powell (Tübingen: Max Niemeyer, 1965), 5:4; on this scene, see Daniel Weidner, "'Schau in dem Tempel an den ganz zerstückten Leib, der auf dem Kreuze lieget': Sakramentale Repräsentation in Gryphius' *Leo Armenius*," *Daphnis* 39.1–2 (2010): 302–304.

68. Gryphius, *Leo Armenius*, 5: 82 (lines 164–170); Weidner, "Sakramentale Repräsentation," 311.

69. Population for Silesia from Peter H. Wilson, *The Thirty Years War: Europe's Tragedy* (Cambridge, MA: Harvard University Press, 2009), 788.

70. Lothar Noack, *Christian Hoffmann von Hoffmannswaldau (1616–1679): Leben und Werk* (Tübingen: Max Niemeyer, 1999), 123.

71. Lohenstein, *Sophonisbe*, in *Afrikanische Trauerspiele*, ed. Klaus Günther Just (Stuttgart: Anton Hiersemann, 1957), 343. See also my "When Is a Sacrifice Not a Sacrifice?," in *Opfer im Leben und Tod. Sacrifice Between Life and Death*, ed. Walter Schweidler (Weingarten: Academia, 2008), 83–101.

72. Lohenstein, *Sophonisbe*, 271, 272.

73. Lohenstein, *Sophonisbe*, 273.

74. Lohenstein, *Sophonisbe*, 274.

75. Braden, *Renaissance Tragedy*, 58.

76. Alberto Martino, *Daniel Casper von Lohenstein: Geschichte seiner Rezeption* (Tübingen: Max Niemeyer, 1978), 70.

77. On Lohenstein as philologian, see Jane O. Newman, *The Intervention of Philology: Gender, Learning, and Power in Lohenstein's Roman Plays* (Chapel Hill: University of North Carolina Press, 2000).

78. Lohenstein, *Sophonisbe*, 271.

79. Lohenstein, *Sophonisbe*, 359.

80. Lohenstein, *Sophonisbe*, 304, 383.

81. Seneca, *Oedipus*, in *Tragedies*, vol. 2, lines 366–371.

82. There is a vigorous debate on this issue, however; most recently, see Sean Kelsey, "Instrumenting the Trial of Charles I," *Historical Research* 92 (Feb. 2019): 118–138; and his opponent, Clive Holmes, "The Trial and Execution of Charles I," *Historical Journal* 53 (June 2010): 289–316.

83. On Gryphius's sources for *Carolus*, see Stackhouse, *The Constructive Art of Gryphius's Historical Tragedies* (Bern: Lang, 1986), chap. 3.

84. Francis F. Madan, *A New Bibliography of the Eikon Basilike of King Charles the First* (Oxford: Oxford University Press, 1950).

85. Elizabeth Skerpan Wheeler, "*Eikon Basilike* and the Rhetoric of Self-Representation," in *The Royal Image: Representations of Charles I*, ed. Thomas N. Corns (Cambridge: Cambridge University Press, 1999), 134–135. More generally on the cult of Charles, see Andrew Lacey, "The Office for King Charles the Martyr in the Book of Common Prayer, 1662–1685," *Journal of Ecclesiastical History* 53:3 (July 2002): 510–526; and Andrew Lacey, *The Cult of King Charles the Martyr* (Suffolk, UK: Woodbridge, 2003).

86. [Anon.], *Eikon basilike: The Pourtraicture of his Sacred Majesty in his Solitudes and Sufferings* ([London], 1648/49), 264.The authorship issues of the pamphlet have been long debated. For purposes of clarity, I am going to refer to its author as Charles, although there is clear evidence that the cleric John Gauden was at least the co-author, if not the author outright. See Laura Lunger Knoppers, "'Paradise Regained' and the Politics of Martyrdom," *Modern Philology* 90 (Nov. 1992): 204.

87. See Andrew Lacey, *Cult of King Charles*, chap. 2 and Andrew Lacey, "'Charles the First, and Christ the Second': The Creation of a Political Martyr," in *Martyrs and Martyrdom in England, c. 1400–1700*, ed. Thomas S. Freeman and Thomas F. Mayer (Woodbridge, UK: Boydell Press, 2007), 203–220.

88. Charles I (attrib.), *His Majesties Complaint Occasioned by his Late Sufferings* (n.p., 1647), 4.

89. Michael Schoenfeldt, "'That spectacle of too much weight': The Poetics of Sacrifice in Donne, Herbert, and Milton," *Journal of Medieval and Early Modern Studies* 3 (Fall 2001): 573.

90. [Anon.], *Eikon*, 8, 9.

91. [Anon.], *Eikon*, 39.

92. Brad Gregory, *Salvation at Stake: Christian Martyrdom in Early Modern Europe* (Cambridge, MA: Harvard University Press, 1999), 124.

93. See, e.g., King James IV and I, *Political Writings*, ed. Johann P. Sommerville (Cambridge: Cambridge University Press, 1994), 161, 171, 183.

94. Lacey, "'Charles the First, and Christ the Second,'" 209.

95. [Anon.], *Eikon*, 1.

96. Robert Filmer, *Patriarcha* in *Patriarcha and Other Writings*, ed. Johann P. Sommerville (Cambridge: Cambridge University Press, 1991), 43. For the difficulties in dating the *Patriarcha*, see pp. xxxii–iv.

97. Kevin Sharpe, "Private Conscience and Public Duty in the Writings of Charles I," *Historical Journal* 40 (Sept. 1997): 653.

98. James I, "Epistle Dedicatorie," *Two Meditations of the Kings Maiestie* (London, 1620).

99. For the Matthew reading, see William Cobbett and Thomas Bayly Howell, eds., *Cobbett's Complete Collection of State Trials* (London: Hansard, 1809), IV: 1132. See also Helen W. Randall, "The Rise and Fall of a Martyrology: Sermons on Charles I," *Huntington Library Quarterly* 10 (Feb. 1947): 137.

100. *King Charles His Speech Made upon the Scaffold at Whitehall Gate* (London, 1649), 6. On gallows speeches in seventeenth-century England, see J. A. Sharpe, "'Last Dying Speeches': Religion, Ideology, and Public Execution in Seventeenth-Century England," *Past & Present* 107 (May 1985): 144–167.

101. [Anon.], *The Life and Reigne of King Charles, Or the Pseudo Martyr Discovered* (London, 1651), unpaginated preface.

102. [Anon.], *Pseudo-Martyr Discovered*, 209.

103. John Donne, *Pseudo-martyr: Wherein out of certaine propositions and gradations, this conclusion is evicted, That those which are of the Romane religion in this kingdome, may and ought to take the Oath of allegiance* (London, 1610), 134–135.

104. William Cecil, *The Execution of Justice in England* [1583], in *The Execution of Justice in England and A True, Sincere, and Modest Defense of English Catholics*, ed. Robert Kingdon (Ithaca, NY: Cornell University Press, 1965), 7.

105. Susannah Brietz Monta, *Martyrdom and Literature in Early Modern England* (Cambridge: Cambridge University Press, 2005), 135.

106. Donne *Pseudo-martyr*, E recto.

107. John Milton, *Eikonoklastes*, in *Complete Prose Works of John Milton*, ed. Don Wolfe (New Haven, CT: Yale University Press, 1962), 3:342–343. On the publishing history, see Merritt Y. Hughes, "Introduction," 3: 147ff. On the work as a response to the aesthetics of the *Eikon*, see Stephen N. Zwicker, *Lines of Authority: Politics and English Literary Culture, 1649–1689* (Ithaca, NY: Cornell University Press, 1993), chap. 2. For Milton's view of kingship as idolatry, see Nelson, *Hebrew Republic*, 45ff.

108. Milton, *Eikonoklastes*, 3:346, 3:359, 3:360, 3:585, 3:584–585.

109. Milton, *Tenure of Kings and Magistrates*, in *Prose Works*, 3:254.

110. Milton *Tenure of Kings and Magistrates*, 3:197, 235 (on anointment), 3:237 (on sovereign justice); Milton, *Eikonoklastes*, 3:586 ("charme against Law").

111. Milton, *Tenure of Kings and Magistrates*, 3:221.

112. Milton, *Tenure of Kings and Magistrates*, 3:204, 3:361.

113. Milton, *Eikonoklastes*, 3: 601.

114. Milton, *Tenure of Kings and Magistrates*, 3:213. Milton's translation of Seneca, *Hercules Furens*, Act 4, lines 922–924. For other uses of the phrase, see John Canne, *The Golden Rule, or Justice Advanced* (London, 1649), 36; [Anon.], *The Resolver Continued, or Satisfaction to Some Scruples about Putting the Late King to Death* (London, 1649), title page epigraph; [Anon.], *Tyrants and Protectors Set Forth in their Colors* (London, 1654), 22.

115. Milton, *Tenure of Kings and Magistrates*, 3:586, 596. See also *Pseudo-Martyr Charles*, 214: "How shall Almighty God be satisfied for so much blood spilt throughout three Kingdoms, whose wrath cannot be appeased, neither the Land be cleansed, untill epiation be made for the bloud of one man, by the shedding of his blood which was the murtherer?"

116. Dig 15.1.§9; quoted in Alexander Murray, *Suicide in the Middle Ages* (Oxford: Oxford University Press, 1998), 2:179.

117. Thomas Hobbes, *Leviathan*, ed. Noel Malcolm (Oxford: Clarendon Press, 2012), 2:282.

118. On the genesis of *Leviathan*, see Jeffrey R. Collins, *Allegiance of Thomas Hobbes* (Oxford: Oxford University Press, 2005), 117ff.

119. Hobbes, *Leviathan*, 2:508. He does address the general issue of regicide as well in chap. 18 (2:270).

120. Hobbes quoted in Noel Malcolm, "Hobbes's Science of Politics and His Theory of Science," *Aspects of Hobbes* (Oxford: Oxford University Press, 2002), 148.

121. Hobbes, *Leviathan*, 2:16, 262.

122. Hobbes, *Leviathan*, 3:760–762.

123. Hobbes, *Leviathan*, 3:938, here also citing Luke 10.42. For Hobbes and theology, see my "Thomas Hobbes, DD: Theology, Orthodoxy, and History," *Journal of Modern History* 88 (June 2016): 249–274.

124. Hobbes, *Leviathan*, 2:198. It is not so much that Hobbes "cannot comprehend sacrifice"—he understands it perfectly fine—but he wants it to be *forbidden*; see Paul Kahn, *Putting Liberalism in Its Place* (Princeton, NJ: Princeton University Press, 2005), 63.

125. Hobbes, *On the Citizen*, ed. and trans. Richard Tuck (Cambridge: Cambridge University Press, 1998), 27.

126. Hobbes, *Leviathan*, 2:200.

127. See Richard Tuck, *Natural Rights Theories: Their Origin and Development* (Cambridge: Cambridge University Press, 1979), 49, 54, for the opposing sides.

128. Tuck, *Natural Rights Theories*, 56.

129. Dig 15.1.§9; Murray, *Suicide in the Middle Ages*, 2:179.

130. Murray, *Suicide in the Middle Ages*, 2:179 (Ulpian), 2:240 (natural inclination), 2:107 (Augustine).

131. Michael MacDonald and Terence R. Murphy, *Sleepless Souls: Suicide in Early Modern England* (Oxford: Clarendon Press, 1990), 61.

132. Grotius quoted in Tuck, *Natural Rights Theories*, 70–71.

133. Hugo Grotius, *De jure belli ac pacis*, trans. Francis W. Kelsey (Oxford: Clarendon Press, 1925), 2: 579 (II.25.iii). For the distinction between attributive and expletive justice, see Grotius, *De jure belli ac pacis*, 1:36–37 (I.1.viii). For discussion in relation to Grotius's *Defensio fidei*, see Jeremy Seth Geddert, *Hugo Grotius and the Modern Theology of Freedom: Transcending Natural Rights* (New York: Routledge, 2017), chap. 8.

134. Hobbes, *Leviathan*, 2:222. For fine-grained discussion of these passages, see Kinch Hoekstra, "Hobbes and the Fool," *Political Theory* 25 (Oct. 1997): 620–654.

135. Hobbes, *Leviathan*, 2:222.

136. Hobbes, *Leviathan*, 3:789 (Latin ed.).

137. Hobbes, *Leviathan*, 3:786–788.

138. Hobbes, *Leviathan*, 2:202.

139. Hobbes, *Leviathan*, 3:784–786.

140. Hobbes, *Leviathan*, 2:570, 2:176–178.

141. Hobbes, *Leviathan*, 3:1034.

142. Hobbes, *Leviathan*, 2:568, 570, quoting 1 Sam. 15.23.

143. William Lucy, *An answer to Mr. Hobbs his Leviathan with observations, censures, and confutations of divers errours, beginning at the seventeenth chapter of that book* (London: Edward Man, 1673), 184.

144. Edward, Earl of Clarendon, *A brief view and survey of the dangerous and pernicious errors to church and state, in Mr. Hobbes's book, entitled Leviathan*, 2nd ed. (Oxford: At the Theater, 1676), 255, 252.

145. Hobbes, *Leviathan*, 2:502 (conscience); 2:510 (spiritual kingdom).

146. Hobbes, *Leviathan*, 3:766.

147. John Locke, *Two Treatises on Government* and *A Letter on Toleration*, ed. Ian Shapiro (New Haven, CT: Yale University Press, 2003), 150; see also p. 8.

148. See Nelson, *Hebrew Republic*, chap. 1.

149. Christopher Clark, "When Culture Meets Power: The Prussian Coronation of 1701," in *Cultures of Power in Europe during the Long Eighteenth Century*, ed. Hamish Scott (Cambridge: Cambridge University Press, 2007), 27. See also Barbara Stollberg-Rilinger, *The Emperor's Old Clothes: Constitutional Language and the Symbolic Language of the Holy Roman Empire* (New York: Berghahn, 2015) esp. chap. 3.; Barbara Stollberg-Rilinger, "*Honores regii:* Die Königswürde im zeremoniellen Zeichensystem der Frühen Neuzeit," in *Dreihundert Jahre Preussische Königskrönung. Eine Tagungsdokumentation*, ed. Johannes Kunisch (Berlin, 2002), 1–26. Thanks to Dror Wahrman's *The Throne of the Great Mogul in Dresden: The Ultimate Artwork of the Baroque* (New Haven, CT: Yale University Press, 2023), 229 fn.25 for these references.

150. Quoted in Andrew Lacey, "The Office for King Charles the Martyr in the Book of Common Prayer, 1662–1685," *Journal of Ecclesiastical History* 53 (July 2002): 523.

151. James Daly, *Sir Robert Filmer and English Political Thought* (Toronto: University of Toronto Press, 1970), chap 3.

152. Filmer was unoriginal in many things: see Johann Sommerville, "Absolutism and Royalism," in *Cambridge History of Political Thought, 1450–1700*, ed. J. H. Burns and Mark Goldie (Cambridge: Cambridge University Press, 1991), 358–360.

153. Gerald Straka, "The Final Phase of Divine Right Theory in England, 1688–1702," *English Historical Review* 77 (Oct. 1962): 638–658; Sherlock quoted p. 647.

154. Generally, see Yann Lignereux, *Les rois imaginaires. Une histoire visuelle de la monarchie de Charles VIII à Louis XIV* (Rennes: Presses universitaires de Rennes, 2016), chap. 6. On the chaos and conflict of the late reign of Louis XIV, and more generally, the breakdown of divine kingship altogether, see Arnaud Orain, *La politique du merveilleux: Une autre histoire du Système de Law (1695–1795)* (Paris: Fayard, 2018), chap. 1.

155. Jacques-Benigne Bossuet, *Politics Drawn from the Very Words of Holy Scripture* (Cambridge: Cambridge University Press, 1990), 58–59, inter alia. See also Emile Perreau-Saussine, "French Catholic Political Thought from the Deconfessionalization of the State to the Recognition of Religious Freedom," in *Religious and the Political Imagination*, ed. Ira Katznelson and Gareth Stedman Jones (Cambridge: Cambridge University Press, 2010), 152.

156. On the end of the royal touch, see Marc Bloch, *The Royal Touch*, trans. J. E. Anderson (New York: Dorset Press, 1961), chap. 6.

157. Bossuet, *Politics*, 33. Italics mine.

Chapter 8: The Anthropology of the Atonement

1. For a beautiful exploration of this, see Erich Auerbach, "Figura," in *Scenes from the Drama of European Literature* (Minneapolis: University of Minnesota Press, 1984), 11–76.

2. Damian quote in Rachel Fulton, *From Judgment to Passion: Devotion to Christ and the Virgin Mary, 800–1200* (New York: Columbia University Press, 2002), 105.

3. Anselm, *Cur deus homo*, in *Basic Writings*, trans. S. N. Deane (La Salle, IL: Open Court, 1962), 261–262. On Anselm, see Fulton, *Judgment to Passion*, 177ff.

4. Anselm, *Cur deus homo*, 279.

5. Martin Luther, *A Commentary on St. Paul's Epistle to the Galatians*, trans. Philip F. Watson (London: James Clarke & Co., 1953), 269.

6. L. W. Grensted, *A Short History of the Doctrine of the Atonement* (Manchester: Manchester University Press, 1920), 205; see also 208ff. for Melanchthon.

7. John Calvin, *Institutes of the Christian Religion*, trans. Ford Lewis Battles (Louisville, KY: Westminster John Knox Press, 1960), 509 (II.16.5).

8. Calvin, *Institutes*, 511 (II.16.6).

9. Calvin, *Institutes*, 501 (II.15.6); see Richard A. Muller, *After Calvin: Studies in the Development of a Theological Tradition* (Oxford: Oxford University Press, 2003), 14, on the offices for Calvin and reformed christology more generally.

10. William Perkins, *The Golden Chain: or, The Description of Theologie Containing the Order of the Causes of Salutation and Damnation, according to Gods Word* ([Cambridge], 1600), 30.

11. Jaroslav Pelikan, *The Christian Tradition: A History of the Development of Doctrine. Reformation of Church and Dogma, 1300–1700* (Chicago: University of Chicago Press, 1971), 4:360.

12. Faustus Socinus, *Praelectiones theologicae*, in *Opera Omnia* (Irenopolis [Amsterdam], 1656), 1:537, 1:538.

13. See, e.g., his remarks in "Epistola F.S. qua excellentissimi cuiusdam viris literis respondet," in *Opera*, 1:490.

14. On Socinus's biography, see Zbigniew Ogonowski, "Faustus Socinus, 1539–1604," in Jill Raitt, ed., *Shapers of Religious Traditions in Germany, Switzerland, and Poland, 1560–1600* (New Haven, CT: Yale University Press, 1981); Earl Wilbur, *A History of Unitarianism: Socinianism and Its Antecedents* (Boston: Beacon Press, 1945), esp. chap. 29–30.

15. William Robert Godfrey, "Tensions Within International Calvinism: The Debate on the Atonement at the Synod of Dort, 1618–1619" (PhD. diss., Stanford University, 1974), 91.

16. On Ochino's ambivalent views of the atonement, see Mark Taplin, *The Italian Reformers and the Zurich Church, c. 1540–1620* (Aldershot: Ashgate, 2003), 118f.

17. George Hunston Williams, *The Radical Reformation* (Kirksville, MO: Truman State University Press, 2000), 822, 379; Taplin, *Italian Reformers*, on Ochino; on Denck, see Morwena Ludlow, "Why Was Hans Denck Thought to Be a Universalist?" *Journal of Ecclesiastical History* 55.2 (April 2004): 263.

18. Williams, *Radical Reformation*, 948.

19. Faustus Socinus, *De Jesu Christi servatore*, in *Opera*, 2:186, 2:188.

20. Socinus, *Praelectiones*, in *Opera*, 1:586.

21. For more expansive discussions of the theology, see Alan W. Gomes, "*De Jesu Christ servatore:* Faustus Socinus on the Satisfaction of Christ," *Westminster Theological Journal* 55 (1993): 209–231; Alan W. Gomes, "*De Jesu Christo Servatore*, Part III: Historical Introduction, Translation, and Critical Notes" (PhD diss., Fuller Theological Seminary, 1990); John Godbey, "A Study of Faustus Socinus' *De Jesu Christo Servatore*" (PhD diss., University of Chicago, 1968).

22. Socinus, *De Jesu Christo Servatore*, in *Opera*, 2:148. The reference is to Hebrews 9.15: "those who are called may receive the promised eternal inheritance, since a death has occurred which redeems them [ἀπολύτρωσιν] from the transgressions under the first covenant."

23. Socinus, *Praelectiones*, in *Opera*, 1:566.

24. Socinus, *De Jesu Christo Servatore*, 2:160.

25. "Inanis figura" or "inanem quandam umbram," e.g., Socinus, *De Jesu Christo Servatore*, 2: 159, 160.

26. See Ludwig Diestel, "Die socinianische Anschauung vom Alten Testamente in ihrer geschichtlichen und theologischen Bedeutung," *Jahrbücher für deutscher Theologie* 7 (1862): 764–765.

27. Socinus, *Praelectiones*, in *Opera*, 1:583.

28. See Kestutis Daugirdas, "The Biblical Hermeneutics of Socinians and Remonstrants in the Seventeenth Century," in *Arminius, Arminianism, and Europe: Jacob Arminius (1559/60–1609)* (Leiden: Brill, 2009), 89–113; and more generally, Kestutis Daugirdas, *Die Anfänge des Sozinianismus: Genese und Eindringen des historisch-ethischen Religionsmodells in den universitären Diskurs der Evangelischen in Europa* (Göttingen: Vandenhoeck und Ruprecht, 2016). Also Sarah Mortimer, *Reason and Religion in the English Revolution: The Challenge of Socinianism* (Cambridge: Cambridge University Press, 2010), esp. chap. 1.

29. Socinus, *De Jesu Christo Servatore*, in *Opera*, 2:158. See also the *Lectiones sacrae*, in *Opera*, 1:293.

30. Diestel, "Die socinianische Anschauung," 752.

31. Socinus, *Lectiones sacrae*, 1: 287.

32. Diestel, "Die socinianische Anschauung," 738.

33. The earliest version of this epitaph I have been able to locate is in the heresy-hunter Francois Pluquet's *Dictionnaires des hérésies, des erreurs, et des schismes* (Paris, 1762), 2: 581 (s.v. "Socinianisme"). From there it was recycled in Joshua Toulmin, *Memoirs of the Life, Character, Sentiments, and Writings of Faustus Socinus* (London, 1777), 12, and has since become part of the Socinus legend. See also Earl Morse Wilbur, "The Grave and Monument of Faustus Socinus at Luslawice," *Proceedings of the Unitarian Historical Society* 4.2 (1936): 25–42.

34. See Wilbur, *A History of Unitarianism*.

35. Editions in 1616, 1625, 1654, 1698. Later editions add two additional disputations. On the practice of professors authoring the dissertations of their respondents, see Ku-Ming (Kevin) Chang, "From Oral Disputation to Written Text: The Transformation of the Dissertation in Early Modern Europe," *History of Universities* 19.2 (2004): 150ff.

36. Wolfgang Franzius, *Schola Sacrificiorum Patriarchalium Sacra*, 2nd ed. (Wittenberg, 1625), preface, a3recto.

37. Franzius, *Schola*, a2verso.

38. See Franzius, *Schola*, Dissertation X, §9–15, 94–95 (on the Protoevangelium).

39. But also see Kirsten MacFarlane, *Biblical Scholarship in an Age of Controversy: The Polemical World of Hugh Broughton (1549–1612)* (Oxford: Oxford University Press, 2021), esp. chap. 2, for a very learned discussion of the challenge of Daniel's weeks in late sixteenth century chronology more broadly.

40. Joseph Scaliger, *Opus de emendatione temporum*, 2nd ed. (Leiden: Plantin, 1598), 567–68. See Anthony Grafton, *Joseph Scaliger: A Study in the History of Classical Scholarship* 2 vols. (Oxford: Clarendon Press, 1983–1993), 2:312, 318.

41. See, e.g., Anthony Grafton and Joanna Weinberg, *"I have always loved the Holy Tongue": Isaac Casaubon, the Jews, and a Forgotten Chapter in Renaissance Scholarship* (Cambridge, MA: Harvard University Press, 2011); esp. 214–230; Carl Philipp Emanuel Nothaft, "A Sixteenth-Century Debate on the Jewish Calendar: Jacob Christmann and Joseph Justus Scaliger," *Jewish Quarterly Review* 103.1 (Winter 2013): 47–73.

42. Franzius, *Schola*, Dissertation X, §18, §19, §60.

43. Franzius, *Schola*, Dissertation II, §2.

44. Franzius, *Schola*, Dissertation IX, § 14–17, 31, 47, 50–51.

45. See Th. Wotschke, "Wittenberg und die Unitarier Polens. II," *Archiv für Reformationsgeschichte* 15.57–58 (1918): 72, 68–69.

46. Martin Schmeissel and Klaus Birnstiel, "Gelehrtenkultur und antitrinitärische Häresie an der Nürnberger Akademie zu Altdorf," *Daphnis* 39.2 (2010): 245. On the spread of Socinianism more generally, see Daugirdas, *Die Anfänge des Sozinianismus*.

47. See Wilbur, *History of Unitarianism*, I:525, fn. 54.

48. Johann Adam Schertzer, *Collegii anti-sociniani* (Leipzig, 1684).

49. James [Jacob] Arminius, *Examination of a Treatise, concerning the Order and Mode of Predestination and the Amplitude of Divine Grace by William Perkins*, in *The Works of James Arminius*, trans. James Nichols (Auburn: Derby and Miller, 1853), 3: 347, italics mine. On Arminian Christology, see Richard Muller, "The Christological Problem in the Thought of Jacobus Arminius," *Nederlands archief voor kerkgeschiedenis* 68.2 (1988): 145–163. In general, see Philip Benedict, *Christ's Churches Purely Reformed: A Social History of Calvinism* (New Haven, CT: Yale University Press, 2002), 305ff.

50. "The Remonstrance, or The Arminian Articles," in *Creed and Confessions of Faith in the Christian Tradition*, ed. Jaroslav Pelikan and Valerie Hotchkiss (New Haven, CT: Yale University Press, 2003), 2: 549, italics mine; "Canons of the Synod of Dort," in *Creed and Confessions*, 2:580–581, italics mine. More generally, see Godfrey, "Tensions Within International Calvinism."

51. Henk Nellen, *Hugo Grotius: A Lifelong Struggle for Peace in Church and State, 1583–1645* (Leiden: Brill, 2015), 147; for the Vorstius affair more generally, see Daugirdas, *Die Anfänge des Socinianismus*, 398ff. Also, Jan Rohls, "Der Fall Vorstius," in *Religiöser Nonkonformismus und frühneuzeitliche Gelehrtenkultur*, ed. Friedrich Vollhardt (Berlin: Akademie Verlag, 2014), 179–198.

52. See Nellen, *Hugo Grotius*, 171ff.

53. For the complex controversial and publishing history of Grotius's work, and a fascinating investigation of Grotius's sources, see Edwin Rabbie, "Introduction," to Hugo Grotius, *Defensio fidei catholicae de satisfactione Christti adversus Faustum Socinum Senensem*, trans. Hotze Mulder (Assen/Maastricht: Van Gorcum, 1990), 1–63. See also see Hans W. Blom, "Grotius and Socinianism," in *Socinianism and Arminianism: Antitrinitarians, Calvinists, and Cultural Exchange in Seventeenth-Century Europe*, ed. Martin Mulsow and Jan Rohls (Leiden: Brill, 2005), esp. 121–122.

54. Vossius quoted in Edwin Rabbie's introduction to Grotius, *Defensio fidei*, 18–19.

55. More generally on this, see Debora Kuller Shuger, *The Renaissance Bible: Scholarship, Sacrifice, and Subjectivity* (Berkeley: University of California Press, 1995), chap. 2, and my "Sacrifice Before the Secular," *Representations* 105 (Winter 2008): 12–36.

56. Grotius, *Defensio fidei*, 135, 139, 135.

57. Generally, Benjamin Straumann, *Roman Law in the State of Nature: The Classical Foundations of Hugo Grotius' Natural Law* (Cambridge: Cambridge University Press, 2015).

58. Grotius, *Defensio fidei*, 137. The reference is to Digest 28.5.42.

59. Grotius, *Defensio fidei*, 143; Shuger, *Renaissance Bible*, 58.

60. Grotius, *Defensio fidei*, 157.

61. Grotius, *Defensio fidei*, 183.

62. Alan Watson, trans., *The Digest of Justinian* (Philadelphia: University of Pennsylvania Press, 1985), vol. 4, 46.3.52.

63. Watson, *The Digest*, 46.3.58.

64. Watson, *The Digest*, 20.6.6. On satisfaction, see Reinhard Zimmermann, *The Law of Obligations: Roman Foundations of the Civilian Tradition* (Oxford: Clarendon Paperbacks, 1996), 222f.

65. Grotius, *Defensio fidei*, 193.

66. Grotius, *Defensio fidei*, 226, 167–169.

67. Grotius, *Defensio fidei*, 247, 263–265.

68. Grotius, *Defensio fidei*, 257, 263.

69. Grotius, *Defensio fidei*, 259, 277.

70. On Grotius's work *De veritate religionis christianae* and its debts to Socinus, see Jan-Paul Heering, *Hugo Grotius as Apologist for the Christian Religion: A Study of his Work* De veritate religionis Christianae, 1640, trans. J. C. Grayson (Leiden: Brill, 2003), 118–120. For Grotius's personal connections to Socinian sympathizers in later years, see Nellen, *Hugo Grotius*, 529ff.

71. Jaroslav Pelikan, *The Christian Tradition: A History of the Development of Doctrine* (Chicago: University of Chicago Press, 1986), 4:360.

72. Martin Luther, *Epistle to the Galatians*, 269

73. Grotius, *Defensio fidei*, 169.

74. Grotius, *Defensio fidei*, 277.

75. Grotius, *Defensio fidei*, 277.

76. Shuger, *Renaissance Bible*, 70–71.

77. [Santes Pagnino], *Biblia* ([Lyons], 1528).

78. Moses Aberbach and Bernard Grossfeld, trans., *Targum Onkelos to Genesis* (New York: Ktav Publishing, 1982), 40.

79. Franzius, *Schola*, Dissertation III, §3, 4, 9.

80. On the early interest in Hebraic learning among medieval Christians, see Beryl Smalley, *The Study of the Bible in the Middle Ages* (Oxford: Basil Blackwell, 1983).

81. Generally on polyglots, see Alastair Hamilton, "In Search of the Most Perfect Text: Early Modern Printed Polyglot Bibles from Alcalá (1510–1520) to Brian Walton (1654–1658)," in *New Cambridge History of the Bible*, vol. 3, ed. Euan Cameron (Cambridge: Cambridge University Press, 2016), 143–147.

82. For a beautiful overview and a capacious bibliography, see Theodor Dunkelgrün, "The Christian Study of Judaism in Early Modern Europe," in *The Cambridge History of Judaism*, vol. 7, *The Early Modern World, 1500–1815*, ed. Jonathan Karp and Adam Sutcliffe (Cambridge: Cambridge University Press, 2017), 316–348. Also essential: Allison P. Coudert and Jeffrey S. Shoulson, *Hebraica Veritas? Christian Hebraists and the Study of Judaism in Early Modern Europe* (Philadelphia: University of Pennsylvania Press, 2004); Stephen Burnett, *Christian Hebraism in the Reformation Era (1500–1660): Authors, Books, and the Transmission of Learning* (Leiden: Brill, 2012); Scott Mandelbrote and Joanna Weinburg, *Jewish Books and Their Readers: Aspects of the Intellectual Life of Christians and Jews in Early Modern Europe* (Leiden: Brill, 2016); and MacFarlane, *Biblical Scholarship.*

83. Adrian Wilson and Joyce Lancaster Wilson, *A Medieval Mirror:* Speculum humanae salvationis *1324–1500* (Berkeley: University of California Press, 1985), 149.

84. William Owtram, *De sacrificiis libri duo; quorum altero explicantur omnia judaeorum nonnulla gentium profanarum sacrificia; altero sacrificium Christi utroque Ecclesiae Catholicae his de rebus Sententia contra Faustum Socinum eiusque Sectatores defenditur* (London: T. Roycroft, 1677), 22. Also, William Outram, *Two Dissertations on Sacrifices*, trans. John Allen (London, 1817), 34. Translations here are from the latter, with my silent amendments, and paginations from both in the form English/Latin.

85. Outram, *Two Dissertations*, 4–5/a2recto.

86. Benito Arias Montano, "Ariel, sive de templi fabrica, et structura," *Antiquitatum Iudaicarum libri ix* (Leiden, 1593), 86. On imaginative projects like this more generally, see my "Temple and Tabernacle: The Place of Religion in Early Modern Europe," in *The Making of Knowledge in Early Modern Europe: Practices, Objects, and Texts, 1400–1800*, ed. Pamela Smith and Benjamin Schmidt (Chicago: University of Chicago Press, 2008), 248–272.

87. Maurice Simon, trans., "Middoth" in *The Babylonian Talmud*, ed. I. Epstein (London: Soncino Press, 1935–1952), vol. 6. These Jewish sources got Montano in trouble with the papacy: see B. Rekers, *Benito Arias Montano (1527–1598)* (London: Warburg Institute, 1972), 49f; *Philip II and the Escorial: Technology and the Representation of Architecture* (Providence, RI: Brown University Press, 1990), 55; Helen Rosenau, *Vision of the Temple: The Image of the Temple of Jerusalem in Judaism and Christianity* (London: Oresko, 1979), 94.

88. Thomas Fuller, *Pisgah-sight of Palestine* (London, 1650), 355–408.

89. [Samuel Lee], *Orbis Miraculum, or the Temple of Solomon* (London, 1659), b recto, 11, 9. On Lee, see Theodore Hornberger, "Samuel Lee (1625–1691), a Clerical Channel for the Flow of New Ideas to Seventeenth-Century New England," *Osiris* 1 (1936): 341–355.

90. [Lee], *Orbis Miraculum*, 15, 166, 212, 191.

91. [Lee], *Orbis Miraculum*, 323, 332, 347–348, 166.

92. John Lightfoot, *The Temple Service As It Stood in the Days of our Saviour* (London, 1649), 66. For a modern version, see Seth D. Kunin, *God's Place in the World: Sacred Space and Sacred Place in Judaism* (London: Cassell, 1998), 25.

93. Lightfoot, *The Temple Service*, 69, 70–71.

94. Owtram, *Two Dissertations*, 39/27, 40/28.

95. See, e.g., Aiden Francis Cottrell-Boyce, "Judaizing and Singularity in England, 1618–1667" (PhD diss., Gonville and Caius College, University of Cambridge, 2018); David R. Como, *Blown by the Spirit: Puritanism and the Emergence of an Antinomian Underground in Pre-Civil-War England* (Oxford: Oxford University Press, 2004), 381.

96. Nicholas Tyacke, "Puritanism, Arminianism, and Counter-Revolution," in *Reformation to Revolution: Politics and Religion in Early Modern England*, ed. Margot Todd (London: Routledge, 1995), 63. See also Kenneth Fincham and Nicholas Tyacke, *Altars Restored: The Changing Face of English Religious Worship* (Oxford: Oxford University Press, 2007), and Julian Davies, *The Caroline Captivity of the Church: Charles I and the Remoulding of Anglicanism, 1625–1641* (Oxford: Clarendon Press, 1992).

97. Owtram, *Two Dissertations*, 8/2.

98. For a brief introduction to Maimonides, see Joel L. Kraemer, "Moses Maimonides: An Intellectual Portrait," in *The Cambridge Companion to Maimonides*, ed. Kenneth Seeskin (Cambridge: Cambridge University Press, 2006), 10–57.

99. Constantin l'Empereur, "Epistola dedicatoria," *Talmudis Babylonici Codex Middoth, sive, de mensuris Templi* (Leiden, 1630), *2recto-verso.

100. Constantin l'Empereur, "Epistola dedicatoria," *3verso. On l'Empereur, see van Rooden, *Theology, Biblical Scholarship, and Rabbinical Studies in the Seventeenth Century: Constantijn L'Empereur (1591–1648), Professor of Hebrew and Theology at Leiden* (Leiden: Brill, 1989).

101. See Jacob Dienstag, "Christian Translators of Maimonides' *Mishneh Torah*," in *Salo Wittmayer Baron Jubilee Volume* (Jerusalem: American Academy for Jewish Research, 1974), I, 287–309. More generally, see Aaron Katchen, *Christian Hebraists and Dutch Rabbis: Seventeenth-Century Apologetics and the Study of Maimonides' Mishneh Torah* (Cambridge, MA: Harvard University Press, 1984).

102. See, e.g., the remarkable *Biblia Americana* of Cotton Mather, which will extend to 10 volumes when the edition is complete; Reiner Smolinski et al., eds., *Biblia Americana: America's First Bible Commentary: A Synoptic Commentary on the Old and New Testaments* (Tübingen: Mohr Siebeck, 2010–). Maimonides is cited throughout.

103. Katchen, *Christian Hebraists*, 2–3; see also Wolfgang Kluxen, "Literargeschichtliches zum lateinischen Moses Maimonides," *Recherches de théologie ancienne et médiévale 21* (Jan.–June 1954): 23–50.

104. For Grotius's use of the *Guide*, see A. W. Rosenberg and H. S. Lake, "Hugo Grotius as Hebraist," *Studia Rosenthaliana* 12 (July 1978): 85ff.

105. Francisco de Vitoria, "On Dietary Laws," in *Political Writings*, ed. Anthony Pagden (Cambridge: Cambridge University Press, 1991), 215.

106. Robert Bellarmine, "De sacrificio missae," in *De Controversiis* (Venice, 1599), 3:774.

107. Franzius, *Schola*, Dissertation II, §87.

108. Grotius, *Annotationes ad vetus Testamentum*, in *Opera omnia theologica* (London, 1679), 1: 6 (note to Genesis 4.3).

109. Moses Maimonides, *The Guide for the Perplexed*, trans. Shlomo Pines (Chicago: University of Chicago, 1963), 507 (III.26), 518 (III.29).

110. See Fausto Parente, "Spencer, Maimonides, and the History of Religion," in *History of Scholarship: A Selection of Papers from the Seminar on the History of Scholarship Held Annually at the Warburg Institute*, ed. C. R. Ligota and J.-L. Quantin (Oxford: Oxford University Press, 2006), 285–286. See also Jonathan Elukin, "Maimonides and the Rise and Fall of the Sabians: Explaining Mosaic Laws and the Limits of Biblical Scholarship," *Journal of the History of Ideas* 63 (October 2002): 619–637.

111. Maimonides, *Guide*, 519, 518 (III.29); 521 (III.29), 526 (III.32).

112. Amos Funkenstein, *Theology and the Scientific Imagination from the Middle Ages to the Seventeenth Century* (Princeton, NJ: Princeton University Press, 1986), 213–214; Stephen D. Benin, *The Footprints of God: Divine Accommodation in Jewish and Christian Thought* (Albany: SUNY Press, 1993), 142.

113. Augustine quoted in Funkenstein, *Theology*, 223.

114. Benin, *Footprints*, 181–185.

115. Benin, *Footprints*, 189, 190.

116. To my knowledge, there has not yet been a thorough examination of Socinus's views of accommodation, but it is a powerful theme for him. See, eg., *Lectiones sacra*, in *Opera*, 1:292.

117. Maimonides, *Guide*, III.26, p. 509.

118. Maimonides, *Guide*, 581 (III.46), 582 (III.46); 582, 586 (III.46).

119. Maimonides, *Guide*, III.32, p. 530.

120. Maimonides, *Guide*, III.50, p. 615.

121. Maimonides, *Guide*, III.50, p. 615.

122. Owtram, *Two Dissertations*, 121–22/108.

123. Owtram, *Two Dissertations*, 25/13, 121–22/108, 122/108.

124. Owtram, *Two Dissertations*, 29/17, 215/201.

125. On Spencer, see Jan Assmann, *Moses the Egyptian: The Memory of Egypt in Western Monotheism* (Cambridge, MA: Harvard University Press, 1997), chap. 3; Dmitri Levitin, "John Spencer's *De Legibus Hebraeorum* (1683–85) and 'Enlightened' Sacred History: A New Interpretation," *Journal of the Warburg and Courtauld Institutes* 76 (2013): 49–92; Parente, "Spencer, Maimonides"; Daniel Stolzenberg, "John Spencer and the Perils of Sacred Philology," *Past & Present* 214 (Feb. 2012): 129–163; and my "Sacred and Profane: Idolatry, Antiquarianism, and the Polemics of Distinction in the Seventeenth Century," *Past and Present* 192 (August 2006): 37–66.

126. William Robertson Smith, *Lectures on the Religion of the Semites* (London: Adam and Charles Black, 1894), vi.

127. Assmann, *Moses the Egyptian*, 56. See also Guy Stroumsa, *A New Science: The Discovery of Religion in the Age of Reason* (Cambridge, MA: Harvard University Press, 2010).

128. Stolzenberg, "John Spencer," 147.

129. Spencer quoted in Levitin, "Spencer and Sacred History," 62.

130. John Spencer, *De legibus Hebraeorum ritualibus and earum rationibus libri tres* (Cambridge, 1685), 639.

131. Spencer, *De legibus*, 650.

132. John Tillotson, "Of the Great Duties of Natural Religion," in *Several Discourses* (London: Chiswell, 1697), 32–33, 40, 5.

133. Spencer, *De legibus*, 670.

134. John Tillotson, "Sermon II. Preached on the Feast of the Annunciation, 1691," in *Sixteen Sermons, Preached on Several Occasions* (London, 1696), 49.

135. Levitin, "John Spencer's *De Legibus Hebraeorum*," 64.

136. Spencer, *De legibus*, 179, 185.

137. Spencer, *De legibus*, 187, 186.

138. John Tillotson, "Sermon II," 52–54.

139. [Charles Leslie], *The Charge of Socinianism Against Dr. Tillotson Considered* (Edinburgh, 1695), 5, 4, 6.

140. Gilbert Burnet, *Four Discourses Delivered to the Clergy of the Dioceses of Sarum* (London, 1694), 44.

141. More generally on the trinitarian controversies of the 1690s, see John Redwood, *Reason, Ridicule, and Religion: The Age of Enlightenment in England, 1660–1750* (Cambridge, MA: Harvard University Press, 1972), chap. 7; the issue of convocation, see Mark Goldie, "The Nonjurors, Episcopacy, and the Origins of the Convocation Controversy," in *Ideology and Conspiracy: Aspects of Jacobitism, 1689–1759*, ed. Eveline Cruickshanks (Edinburgh: John Donald, 1982); on Burnet specifically, see Martin Greig, "The Reasonableness of Chrisitanity? Gilbert Burnet and the Trinitarian Controversy of the 1690s," *Journal of Ecclesiastical History* 44.4 (Oct. 1993): 631–651.

142. Charles Blount, *Great is Diana of the Ephesians: Or, the Original of Idolatry Together with the Politick Institution of the Gentile Sacrifices* (London, 1680), 3.

More generally, see J.A.I. Champion, *The Pillars of Priestcraft Shaken: The Church of England and Its Enemies, 1660–1730* (Cambridge: Cambridge University Press, 1992).

143. Blount, *Diana*, 39.

144. Blount, *Diana*, 37.

145. [Leslie], *Charge of Socinianism*, 25.

146. See Maimonides, *Guide*, 515 (III.29).

147. On La Peyrère's life, see Richard Popkin, "The Life of Isaac La Peyrère," in *Isaac La Peyrère (1596–1676): His Life, Work, and Influence* (Leiden: Brill, 1987), 5–25.

148. [Isaac La Peyrère], *A Theological System Upon that Presupposition that Men Were Before Adam* (London, 1655), 122–123.

149. [Isaac La Peyrère], *A Theological System*, 150–152 (Cain and Abel), 217 (Melchizedek).

Part IV: Sacrifice ad saeculum

1. Erich Auerbach, "Figura," in *Scenes from the Drama of European Literature* (Minneapolis: University of Minnesota Press, 1984), 42.

2. See, e.g., Jonathan Sheehan, *The Enlightenment Bible: Translation, Scholarship, Culture* (Princeton, NJ: Princeton University Press, 2005); more recently, "Religion and the Divine: The Encyclopedia's God," in *The Cultural History of Ideas in the Age of Enlightenment*, ed. Jack R. Censer (London: Bloomsbury Press, 2023), 121–136. Also Martin Gierl, *Pietismus und Aufklärung: Theologische Polemik und die Kommunikationsreform der Wissenschaft am Endes des 17. Jahrhunderts* (Göttingen: Vandenhoeck & Ruprecht, 1997).

3. Amos Funkenstein, *Theology and the Scientific Imagination from the Middle Ages to the Seventeenth Century* (Princeton, NJ: Princeton University Press, 1986), 3.

Chapter 9: The Enlightenment

1. Giambattista Vico, *The New Science of Giambattista Vico*, trans. Thomas Goddard Bergin and Max Harold Fisch (Ithaca, NY: Cornell University Press, 1968), 85.

2. Benedict Spinoza, *Tractatus Theologico-Politicus* in *The Collected Works of Spinoza*, ed. and trans. Edwin Curley (Princeton, NJ: Princeton University Press, 2016), 2: 277–278. Hereafter *TTP*.

3. Spinoza, *TTP*, 280, 267, 277, 267–268, 270, 328. On doctrinal minimalism, see Henk Nellen, "Minimal Faith and Irenic Ideals in Seventeenth-Century Scholarly Circles: Hugo Grotius as a Guardian of Isaac Casaubon's Legacy," *Church History and Religious Culture* 94 (2014): 444–478; G.H.M. Posthumus Meyes, introduction to Hugo Grotius, *Meletius, sive, de iis quae inter Christianos conveniunt* (Leiden: Brill, 1988), esp. 22–40.

4. Jonathan Israel, *Radical Enlightenment* (Oxford: Oxford University Press, 2001), 163.

5. On some of Spinoza's links to earlier humanist biblical criticism, see Anthony Grafton, "Spinoza's Hermeneutics: Some Heretical Thoughts," in *Scriptural Authority and Biblical Criticism in the Dutch Golden Age: God's Word Questioned*, ed.Dirk van Miert et al. (Oxford: Oxford University Press, 2017), 178–196.

6. Grafton, "Spinoza," 97, 116, 120, 124.

7. See, e.g., Spinoza, *TTP*, 66 (superstition), 123, 139 (ceremony).

8. Gottfried Arnold, *Unpartheyische Kirchen- und-Ketzer Historie*, 2nd ed. (Frankfurt am Main, 1700), 33, 38, 39, 57.

9. Arnold, *Unpartheyische*, 50, 107, 78, 105, 106–107.

10. Arnold, *Unpartheyische*, 141.

11. On Jansenism, see Dale van Kley, *Jansenism and the Expulsion of the Jesuits from France* (New Haven, CT: Yale University Press, 1975); Robert Kreiser, *Miracles, Convulsions, and Ecclesiastical Politics in Eighteenth-Century Paris* (Princeton, NJ: Princeton University Press, 1978).

12. For an elegant exploration of this world, see Timothy Wright, "Hidden Lives: Asceticism and Interiority in the Late Reformation, 1650–1745" (PhD diss., UC Berkeley, 2018). See also Patricia Ward, *Experimental Theology in America: Madame Guyon, Fénelon, and Their Readers* (Waco, TX: Baylor University Press, 2009). More broadly, see W. R. Ward, *The Protestant Evangelical Awakening* (Cambridge: Cambridge University Press, 1992); Martin Brecht, ed., *Geschichte es Pietismus*, 2 vols. (Göttingen: Vandenhoek & Ruprecht, 1993); Douglas Shantz, ed., *A Companion to German Pietism* (Leiden: Brill, 2015).

13. Gichtel quoted in Wright, "Hidden Lives," 51.

14. Ward, *Protestant Evangelical Awakening*, 48.

15. Marsay quoted in Wright, "Hidden Lives," 56.

16. Marsay quoted in Wright, "Hidden Lives," 68–69, 85.

17. Craig D. Atwood, "Understanding Zinzendorf's Blood and Wound Theology," *Journal of Moravian History* 1 (2006): 36; On Zinzendorf and Dippel, see Bernhard Becker, *Zinzendorf und sein Christentum: im Verhältnis zum kirchlichen und religiösen Leben seiner Zeit* (Leipzig: Jansa, 1900), 268–281.

18. Atwood, "Zinzendorf's 'Litany of the Wounds,'" *Lutheran Quarterly* 11 (1997): 207, 204.

19. Wesley cited in Joanna Cruickshank, "'Appear as Crucified for Me': Sights, Suffering, and Spiritual Transformation in the Hymns of Charles Wesley," *Journal of Religious History* 30 (October 2006): 315.

20. William Cowper, "Praise for the Fountain Opened," *Complete Poetical Works*, ed. H. S. Milford (London: Oxford University Press, 1913), 442.

21. Phyllis Mack, *Heart Religion in the British Enlightenment: Gender and Emotion in Early Methodism* (Cambridge: Cambridge University Press, 1992). On Wesley's improvisations with regard to the "doctrine" of the Atonement, see W. Andrew Tooley, "Reinventing Redemption: The Methodist Doctrine of Atonement in the Long Nineteenth Century" (PhD thesis, University of Stirling, 2013), esp. pp. 24–34.

22. On the *agape*, see Andrew McGowan, *Ascetic Eucharists: Food and Drink in Early Christian Ritual Meals* (Oxford: Clarendon Press, 1999).

23. David B. Eller, "The Recovery of the Love Feast in German Pietism," in *Confessionalism and Pietism: Religious Reform in Early Modern Europe*, ed. Fred van Lieburg (Mainz: Philipp von Zabern, 2006), 11–30 (quoted at 15). See also Wright, "Hidden Lives," 125, 141.

24. Jonathan Sheehan, *The Enlightenment Bible* (Princeton, NJ: Princeton University Press, 2005), 60.

25. Wesley quoted in Sheehan, *Enlightenment Bible*, 94.

26. The full catalogue is reprinted in: Dietrich Blaufuß und Friedrich Niewöhner, *Gottfried Arnold (1666–1714)* (Wiesbaden: Harrassowitz, 1995), 337–410.

27. On universal atonement, see Tooley, "Reinventing Redemption."

28. Wesley quoted in Isabel Rivers, *Reason, Grace, and Sentiment: A Study in the Language of Religion and Ethics in England, 1660–1780* (Cambridge: Cambridge University Press, 2000), 1:225.

29. See Sheehan, *Enlightenment Bible*, chap. 2.

30. More generally on this, see Jean Louis Quantin, *The Church of England and Christian Antiquity: The Construction of a Confessional Identity in the 17th Century* (Oxford: Oxford University Press, 2009). On Daillé, see pp. 228–238.

31. John Toland, *Nazarenus: Or, Jewish, Gentile, and Mahometan Christianity . . . Also, the Original Plan of Christianity occasionally explain'd* (London, 1718). On Toland, see Justin Champion, *Republican Learning: John Toland and the Crisis of Christian Culture, 1696–1722* (Manchester: Manchester University Press, 2003).

32. Matthew Tindal, *Christianity as Old as Creation* (London, 1730), 163; for the freethinkers and patristics, see Quantin, *Church of England and Christian Antiquity*, 408–410.

33. Matthew Hale, *The Primitive Origination of Mankind, Considered and Examined according to the Light of Nature* (London, 1677), 168. More generally, see Jonathan Sheehan, "Sacred and Profane: Idolatry, Antiquarianism, and the Polemics of Distinction in the Seventeenth Century," *Past and Present* 192 (Aug. 2006): 35–66.

34. William Lucy, *Observations, Censures, and Confutations of Notorious Errours in Mr. Hobbes, his Leviathan, and other his Bookes* (London, 1663), 85.

35. Spenser quoted in Peter Harrison, *'Religion' and the Religions in the English Enlightenment* (Cambridge: Cambridge University Press, 1990), 103.

36. Lucy, *Observations*, 85.

37. Hobbes, *Leviathan*, ed. Noel Malcolm (Oxford: Clarendon Press, 2012), I: 164, 170.

38. La Peyrère, *A Theological System*, 90.

39. Spinoza, *TTP*, 66.

40. John Edwards, *A Compleat History or Survey of all the Dispensations and Methods of Religion* (London, 1699), 251.

41. Blount, *Great is Diana*, 15. On the *Traité des trois imposteurs*, see also Winfried Schröder, *Ursprünge des Atheismus: Untersuchungen zur Metaphysik- und Religionskritik des 17. und 18. Jahrhunderts* (Stuttgart: Frommann-Holzboog, 1998), 452–464. Also Georges Minois, *The Atheists Bible: The Most Dangerous Book that Never Existed*, trans. Lys Ann Weiss (Chicago: University of Chicago Press, 2012).

42. John Toland, *Letters to Serena* (London, 1704), 130.

43. Pierre Bayle, *Dictionnaire historique et critique*, 5th ed. (Amsterdam, 1740), s.v. "Abel"; Horace, *Satires*, in *Satires, Epistles, and Ars Poetica*, trans. H. Rushton Fairclough (Cambridge, MA: Harvard University Press, 1026), I.3 lines 107–108.

44. Girolamo Imbruglia, "The Idea of Religion and Sacrifice from Grotius to Diderot's *Encyclopédie*," *History of European Ideas* 47.5 (2021): 689.

45. To witness an eighteenth-century cleric trying unsuccessfully to figure this out, see Arthur Andrew Sykes's effort to supply a "rational ground for this way of worship"; *Essay on the Nature, Design, and Origin of Sacrifices* (London, 1748), vii.

46. Dirk van Miert, "Structuring the History of Knowledge in an Age of Transition: The Göttingen *Geschichte* between *Historia Literaria* and the Rise of the Disciplines," *History of Humanities* 2 (Fall 2017): 405. See also Martin Gierl, "Historia literaria: Wissenschaft, Wissensordnung, und Polemik im 18. Jahrhundert," in *Historia literaria: Neuordnung des Wissens im 17. und 18. Jahrhundert*, ed. Frank Grunert and Friedrich Vollhardt (Berlin: Akademie Verlag, 2007), 113–128.

47. See Martin Mulsow and Helmut Zedelmaier, eds., *Skepsis, Providenz, Polyhistorie: Jakob Friedrich Reimann* (1668–1743) (Tübingen: Max Niemeyer Verlag, 1998); Martin Mulsow et al, eds., *Christoph August Heumann* (1681–1764): *Gelehrte Praxis zwischen christlichem Humanismus und Aufklärung* (Stuttgart: Franz Steiner Verlag, 2017).

48. Johann Albrecht Fabricius, *Bibliographia antiquaria* (Hamburg, 1713), chap. XI ("De sacrificiis, precibus, concionibus aliisque sacris, disciplinis, & ceremoniis, Judaeorum, Ethnicorum, & Christianorum").

49. Wolfgang Franzius, *Commentarius in Leviticum* (Leipzig, 1696).

50. [Johann Heinrich Zedler], *Grosses Vollständiges Universal Lexikon aller Wissenschaften und Künste* (Halle and Leipzig: Johann Heinrich Zedler, 1732–1754), s.v. "Opffer."

51. [Johann Heinrich Zedler], *Universal Lexikon*, s.v. "Opffer der Aussätzigen."

52. [Johann Heinrich Zedler], *Universal Lexikon*, s.v. "Opffer-Geräthe," translating from [Louis Jobert], *La Sciences des Medailles* (Amsterdam, 1693).

53. [Johann Heinrich Zedler], *Universal Lexikon*, s.v. "Opffer der Heyden"; "Opffer-Mahlzeiten."

54. [Johann Heinrich Zedler], *Universal Lexikon*, s.v. "Opffer-Messer," s.v. "Altar."

55. Ephraim Chambers, *Cyclopaedia: Or, a Universal Dictionary of Arts and Sciences* (London, 1728), vol. 2, s.v. "sacrifice."

56. Chambers, *Cyclopaedia*, vol. 2, s.v. "sacrifice."

57. Chambers, *Cyclopaedia*, vol. 2., s.v. "oblation."

58. Chambers, *Cyclopaedia*, vol. 2., s.v. "oblation"; vol. 1, s.v. "carnivorous."

59. [Denis Diderot and Jean D'Alembert, eds.], *Encyclopédie ou Dictionnaire Raisonné des Sciences, des Arts, et des Métiers* (Paris, 1751–1772), s.v., "Encyclopédie," 5:642.

60. [Diderot and D'Alembert], *Encyclopédie*, s.v. "Hostie," 8:318f.

61. [Diderot and D'Alembert], *Encyclopédie*, s.v. "Victime humaine," 17:240, 242.

62. [Diderot and D'Alembert], *Encyclopédie*, s. v. "Anthopophages," 1:498.

63. As Girolomo Imbruglia suggests, their principal author—the chevalier Louis de Jaucourt—seems to have imagined sacrifice in three phases, from an early voluntary sacrifice expressive of internal piety, to the establishment of public and political cults of sacrifice, to a final explosion of superstitious violence. See Imbruglia, "The Idea of Religion and Sacrifice," 691–693.

64. [Diderot and D'Alembert], *Encyclopédie*, "Sacrifice de Abel," 14: 478–480. Salomon Gessner, *Der Tod Abels* (Zürich, 1758) was translated into French (1760) and English (1763), with many later reprint editions into the nineteenth century.

65. Richard Yeo, "A Solution to the Multitude of Books: Ephraim Chambers's *Cyclopaedia* (1728) as 'the Best Book in the Universe,'" *Journal of the History of Ideas* 64 (Jan. 2003): 61–72.

66. Blandine Barret-Kriegel, *Les Académies de l'histoire* (Paris: Presses Universitaires de France, 1988), 98.

67. Bernard de Montfaucon, *Antiquité expliquée et representée en figures*, 2nd ed. (Paris, 1722), 1:xiii; 1: vi, xiv

68. Montfaucon, *Antiquité expliquée*, 2.1: plate LXXXV.

69. Montfaucon, *Antiquité expliquée*, 2.1: 8, 129, 144.

70. Montfaucon, *Antiquité expliquée*, 2.1: 147–48, plates LXV–LXVI, LXVIII; 2.1: 151, 154.

71. Antony van Dale, "De Origine ac Ritibus Sacri Tauroboli," in *Dissertationes IX. Antiquitatibus quin et Marmoribus cum Romanis, tum potissimum Graecis, illustrandis inervientes* (Amsterdam, 1702), 1–2.

72. Montfaucon, *Antiquité expliquée*, 2.1, 170, 171, repeating Van Dale.

73. Voltaire, *Henriade: An Epick Poem* (London, 1732), 100–101.

74. [Diderot and D'Alembert], *Encyclopédie*, s.v. "fanatisme," 6:393.

75. [Diderot and D'Alembert], *Encyclopédie*, 6:395.

76. David Hume, *A Natural History of Religion*, ed. A. Wayne Colver (Oxford: Clarendon Press, 1976), 26, 28, 31. For Hume in France, and polytheism more generally, see Chantal Grell, *Le Dix-huitième siècle et l'antiquité en France, 1680–1789* (Oxford: Voltaire Foundation, 2008), 2: 936–951.

77. Hume, *Natural History*, 61 fn. *j*.

78. Paul Sadrin, *Nicolas-Antoine Boulanger (1722–1759), ou, Avant nous le déluge* (Oxford: Voltaire Foundation, 1986), 135.

79. Reviewer for *Gazette Littéraire de l'Europe* quoted in Sadrin, *Boulanger*, 133.

80. Paul Henry Thiry d'Holbach, *Le Christianisme dévoilé, ou examen des principes et des effets de la réligionne Chrétienne* (A Londres, 1766), 42.

81. Nicolas-Antoine Boulanger, *L'Antiquité dévoilée par ses usages* (Amsterdam, 1766), 4, 5.

82. Anton M. Matytsin, "Enlightenment and Erudition: Writing Cultural History at the Académie des inscriptions," *Modern Intellectual History* 19 (June 2022): 339.

83. Boulanger, *Antiquité dévoilée*, 9, 10, 62, 58.

84. Boulanger, *Antiquité dévoilée*, 332, 59, 60, 332 (also see p. 43), 45, 46, 333.

85. Boulanger, *Antiquité dévoilée*, 6. For the epigram, see Vergil, *Aeneid*, in *Opera*, ed. R.A.B. Mynors (Oxford: Clarendon, 1969), II, line 97, p. 130.

86. Goethe, "Skizzen zu einer Schilderung Winckelmanns," in *Winckelmanns kleine Schriften zur Geschichte der Kunst des Altertums*, ed. Hermann Uhde-Bernays (Leipzig: Insel, 1913), 13.

87. Johann Joachim Winckelmann, *Gedanken über die Nachahmung der Griechischen Werke in der Malerey und Bildhauerkunst*, 2nd ed. (Dresden and Leipzig, 1756), 5. The frontispiece was an image by Adam Friedrich Oeser. On this sacrifice of Iphigenia, see H. Fullwider, "'The Sacrifice of Iphigenia' in French and German Art Criticism, 1755–1757," *Zeitschrift für Kunstgeschichte* 52.4 (1989): 539–549.

88. Gotthold Lessing, *Laocöon: An Essay on the Limits of Painting and Poetry*, trans. Edward Allen McCormick (Baltimore, MD: Johns Hopkins University Press, 1962), 16.

89. Johann Joachim Winckelmann, *History of the Art of Antiquity*, trans. Harry Francis Mallgrave (Los Angeles: Getty Research Institute, 2006), 199.

90. Alex Potts, *Flesh and the Ideal: Winckelmann and the Origins of Art History* (New Haven, CT: Yale University Press, 1994), 164.

91. Louis Arthur Ruprecht, Jr., "Curating the Profane: Johann Joachim Winckelmann, Neoclassical Art Historian and First Curator of a Public Profane Museum," *Journal of the American Academy of Religion* 90 (March 2022): 176–217.

92. Henry Hatfield, *Aesthetic Paganism in German Literature: From Winckelmann to the Death of Goethe* (Cambridge, MA: Harvard University Press, 1964). More generally, see Peter Gay, *The Enlightenment: An Interpretation. The Rise of Modern Paganism* (New York: Knopf, 1966).

93. Suzanne Marchand, *Down from Olympus: Archaeology and Philhellenism in Germany, 1750–1970* (Princeton, NJ: Princeton University Press, 1996), 9.

94. Friedrich Schiller, "Die Götter Griechenlands," lines 89–94, 97–98. in *Sämtliche Werke*, ed. Albert Meier (Munich: Carl Hanser, 2011), 1:166.

95. Schiller, "Die Götter Griechenlands," 1:166 (lines 103–104).

96. Dorothea von Mücke, "Der Wechsel der Treue-Zeichen: Opfer und Gabe in Goethe's *Die Braut von Corinth*," in *Die Gabe des Gedichts: Goethes Lyrik im Wechsel der Töne*, ed. Gerhard Neumann and David Wellbery (Berlin: Rombach Verlag, 2008), 165.

97. Goethe, "Die Braut von Korinth," lines 57–63, in *Goethes Werke*, ed. Erich Trunz (Hamburg: Christian Wegner, 1964), 1:269.

98. Goethe, "Die Braut von Korinth," 1:269 (line 51).

99. Guy Stroumsa, *A New Science: The Discovery of Religion in the Age of Reason* (Cambridge, MA: Harvard University Press, 2010).

100. More generally, see Lee Eldridge Huddleston, *Origins of the American Indians: European Concepts, 1492–1729* (Austin: University of Texas Press, 1967). Also Joan-Pau Rubiés, "Comparing Cultures in the Early Modern World: Hierarchies, Genealogies, and the Idea of European Modernity," in *Regimes of Comparatism: Frameworks of Comparison in History, Religion, and Anthropology*, ed. Renaud Gagné et al. (Leiden: Brill, 2019), 116–176.

101. Quoted in Colin Kidd, *Forging of Races: Race and Scripture in the Protestant Atlantic World, 1600–2000* (Cambridge: Cambridge University Press, 2006), 65.

102. Jacques Revel, "The Uses of Comparison: Religions in the Early Eighteenth Century," in *Bernard Picart and the First Global Vision of Religion*, ed. Lynn Hunt, Margaret Jacob, and Wijnand Mijnhardt (Los Angeles: Getty Research Institute, 2010), 341.

103. Joseph-François Lafitau, *Moeurs des sauvages ameriquains, comparée aux moeurs des premier temps* (Paris, 1724), 1:93. There is a very useful modern translation (*Customs of the American Indians Compared with the Customs of the Previous Times* [Toronto: Champlain Society, 1974], here 1:110). Translations here are from the latter, with some silent corrections of my own. All citations will henceforth include page references to both (French/English).

104. Lafitau, *Customs*, 1:121/199; 1:128–129/103–104.

105. Lafitau, *Customs*, 151/116.

106. Lafitau, *Customs*, 178/132. Italics mine.

107. Lafitau, *Customs*, 194/141; 242/167; 271–295/183–195. On the fragility of this project, see Andreas Motsch, *Lafitau et l'émergence du discours ethnographique* (Sillery, Quebec: Septentrion, 2001).

108. Lafitau, *Customs*, 267/180, 48/54.

109. Margaret Hodgen, *Early Anthropology in the Sixteenth and Seventeenth Centuries* (Philadelphia: University of Pennsylvania Press, 1964), 346. On la Crèquiniére, see Rubiés, "Comparing Cultures," 154ff.

110. [Anon.], *Dictionarium sacrum seu Religiosum. A Dictionary of All Religions Ancient and Modern* (London, 1704), unpaginated preface.

111. On Picart and Bernard's religious formations, and more generally on the volume, see Lynn Hunt, Margaret Jacob, and Wijnand Mijnhardt, *The Book that Changed Europe: Picart and Bernard's Religious Ceremonies of the World* (Cambridge, MA: Harvard University Press, 2010). Also see Hunt, Jacob, and Mijnhardt, eds., *Bernard Picart and the First Global Vision of Religion.*

112. On the later reception, see Tomoko Masuzawa, "Striating Differences: From 'Ceremonies and Customs' to World Religions," *Republics of Letters* 3 (April 2014): 1–25.

113. [Jean Frederic Bernard], "Dissertation sur le culte religieux," in *Cérémonies et coutumes religieuses de tous les peuples du monde* (Amsterdam, 1723), 1:iv.

114. [Bernard], *Cérémonies et coutumes religieuses des peuples idolatres* (Amsterdam, 1723), 1.1:15 (in the "Dissertation on the Peoples of the Americas"; the volume numbering restarts when they reach the idolatrous religions).

115. [Bernard], "Dissertation," 1:xiii. See also Bernard, *Cérémonies et coutumes religieuses des peuples idolatres*, 1.1:12 for a statement about this.

116. [Bernard], "Dissertation," 1:iv., 1:iv.

117. Hunt et al., *Book that Changed Europe*, 123.

118. [Bernard], "Dissertation," 1:iv, vi, viii, xiii.

119. Johann Lomeier, *De veterum gentilium lustrationibus syntagma* (Utrecht: Franciscus Halma, 1681), 3.

120. [Bernard], "Dissertation," 1:xvii fn. See also 1.xvii, xl.

121. [Bernard], "Dissertation," 1:xix, xxviii.

122. See, e.g., [Bernard], "Dissertation," 1:v, ix, xi, etc. Indeed, the work was passionately anti-Catholic, its final volume an erudite comparison of Catholic ceremonies with those of ancient paganism; for the discussions of the Catholic Mass, see especially [Bernard], *Cérémonies*, 8: 46–73.

123. [Bernard], *Cérémonies*, 1.1:147, 156.

124. [Bernard], *Cérémonies*, 1.1:15.

125. For various intepreations of Vico, see Joseph Mali, *The Rehabilitation of Myth: Vico's 'New Science'* (Cambridge: Cambridge University Press, 1992); Mark Lilla, *G.B. Vico: The Making of an Anti-Modern* (Cambridge, MA: Harvard University Press, 1993); Jonathan Israel, *Enlightenment Contested: Philosophy, Modernity, and the Emancipation of Man, 1670–1752* (Oxford: Oxford University Press, 2006), chap. 20; and John Robertson, *The Case for Enlightenment: Scotland and Naples, 1680–1760* (New York: Cambridge University Press, 2005), chap. 5.

126. Vico, *The First New Science*, ed. and trans. Leon Pompa (Cambridge: Cambridge University Press, 2002), 9. The comment might have been directed at Pierre Bayle, whose *Various Thoughts on the Occasion of a Comet* (1681) had imagined and defended the virtues of a "society of atheists." See Bayle, *Various Thoughts on the Occasion of a Comet*, trans. Robert C. Bartlett (Albany: State University of New York Press, 2000), §172, p. 212.

127. Vico, *New Science*, 29.

128. Vico, *New Science*, 67, 105, 106, 99, 100.

129. Vico, *New Science*, 173.

130. Vico, *New Science*, 174, 175.

131. Vico, *New Science*, 7, 8, 9, 10, 4.

132. Vico, *New Science*, 63

133. Vico, *New Science*, 85–86

134. Joan-Pau Rubiés, "From Christian Apologetics to Deism: Libertine Readings of Hinduism, 1650–1730," in *God in the Enlightenment*, ed. William J. Bulman and Robert G. Ingram (New York: Oxford University Press, 2016), 107–135.

135. On evangelicalism see, e.g., Boyd Hilton, *The Age of Atonement: The Influence of Evangelicalism on Social and Economic Thought, 1795–1865* (Oxford: Oxford University Press, 1991).

Chapter 10: The Deaths of Cato

1. Rousseau, *A Discourse of Political Economy*, in *Collected Writings*, ed. Roger D. Masters and Christoper Kelley, trans. Judith R. Bush et al. (Hanover, NH: Dartmouth College Press, 2010), 3:151.

2. See Helmut Walser Smith, *Germany: A Nation in Its Time* (New York: Liveright, 2020), 91; see also Helmut Walser Smith, "Same-Sex Male Love and Patriotic Sacrifice: On the Death of Ewald von Kleist, 1759," *German History* 34.3 (Sept. 2016): 402–418.

3. Ewald von Kleist, *Cissides und Paches in drey Gesängen* (Berlin, 1759), 36, 48, 56.

4. *Briefe Friedrich des Großen, in deutscher Übersetzung*, trans Friedrich v. Oppeln-Bronikowski and Eberhard König (Berlin: Reimar Hobbing, 1914), 2:53.

5. Reinhardt Koselleck, *Critique and Crisis: Enlightenment and the Pathogenesis of Modern Society* (Cambridge, MA: MIT Press, 1988), 39.

6. Koselleck, *Critique and Crisis*, 39, italics mine.

7. Koselleck, *Critique and Crisis*, 59.

8. See Daniel Gordon, *Citizens Without Sovereignty: Equality and Sociability in French Thought, 1670–1789* (Princeton, NJ: Princeton University Press, 1994)

9. G. J. Barker-Benfield, *The Culture of Sensibility: Sex and Society in Eighteenth-Century Britain* (Chicago: University of Chicago Press, 1992), xviii, xix.

10. On Shaftesbury, see Lawrence Klein, *Shaftesbury and the Culture of Politeness: Moral Discourse and Cultural Politics in Early Eighteenth-Century England* (Cambridge: Cambridge University Press, 1994).

11. Anthony Ashley Cooper, *Inquiry Concerning Virtue*, in *Characteristics of Men, Manners, Opinions, Times* (Cambridge: Cambridge University Press, 1999), 192. Italics mine.

12. Cooper, *Miscellany*, in *Characteristics*, 400.

13. Cooper, *Miscellany*, 400 n.10.

14. Cooper, *Miscellany*, 401.

15. James Hankins, *Virtue Politics: Soulcraft and Statecraft in Renaissance Florence* (Cambridge, MA: Harvard University Press, 2019), 38. On humanist republicanism, see esp. chapter 3.

16. James Hankins, "Exclusivist Republicanism and the Non-Monarchical Republic," *Political Theory* 38 (August 2020): 452–482; also see Eric Nelson, *The Hebrew Republic: Jewish Sources and the Transformation of European Political Thought* (Cambridge, MA: Harvard University Press, 2010).

17. See Alan Craig Huston, *Algernon Sydney and the Republican Heritage in England and France* (Princeton, NJ: Princeton University Press, 1991), chap. 4.

18. See Klein, *Shaftesbury*, 148.

19. Horace, *Odes*, trans. Niall Rudd (Cambridge, MA: Harvard University Press, 2004), 3.2.13, p. 145.

20. Livy, *Ab urbe condita* (Cambridge, MA: Harvard University Press, 1988), 10.28.13.

21. Machiavelli, *Discourses on Livy*, trans. Harvey C. Mansfield and Nathan Tarcov (Chicago: University of Chicago Press, 1996), 211 (3.1).

22. Cooper, *Miscellany*, 399.

23. Cooper, *Sensus communis*, in *Characteristics*, 48.

24. Cooper, *Sensus communis*, 52.

25. Cooper, *Miscellany*, 353.

26. Frederic M. Litto, "Addison's Cato in the Colonies," *William and Mary Quarterly* 23 (Jul 1966): 435.

27. Johnson, quoted in Litto, "Cato in the Colonies," 432.

28. Julie Ellison, *Cato's Tears and the Making of Anglo-American Emotion* (Chicago: University of Chicago Press, 1999).

29. Alexander Pope, prologue to Joseph Addison, *Cato a Tragedy* (The Hague, 1713), a2r-v.

30. Addison, *Cato*, 16.

31. Addison, *Cato*, 61.

32. Addison, *Cato*, 62. Italics mine.

33. Addison, *Cato*, 70.

34. Addison, *Cato*, 65.

35. Litto, "Cato in the Colonies," 445, 446.

36. Franco Venturi, *Utopia and Reform in the Enlightenment* (Cambridge: Cambridge University Press, 1971), 70, italics mine.

37. Venturi, *Utopia*, 71.

38. J.G.A. Pocock, *The Machiavellian Moment: Florentine Political Thought and the Atlantic Republican Tradition* (Princeton, NJ: Princeton University Press, 1975), 464.

39. John Trenchard and Thomas Gordon, *Cato's Letters. Or, Essays on Liberty, Civil and Religious, and Other Important Subjects*, ed. Ronald Hamowy (Indianapolis, IN: Liberty Fund, 1995), 1:42.

40. Bernard Mandeville, *The Fable of the Bees, or Private Vices, Publick Benefits* (Indianapolis, IN: Liberty Classics, 1988), 2:48.

41. Trenchard and Gordon, *Cato's Letters*, 1:45.

42. Trenchard and Gordon, *Cato's Letters*, 1:119.

43. Trenchard and Gordon, *Cato's Letters*, 1:203.

44. Pocock, *Machiavellian Moment*, 469.

45. See David Bell, *The Cult of the Nation in France: Inventing Nationalism, 1680–1800* (Cambridge, MA: Harvard University Press, 2001), chap. 2.

46. Marisa Linton, *The Politics of Virtue in Enlightenment France* (New York: Palgrave, 2001), 14. More generally, see Alexis de Tocqueville, *The Old Regime and the French Revolution* (New York: Random House, 1983).

47. [Diderot], *Principes de la philosophie morale, ou Essai de M. S*** sur le merite e la vertu* (Amsterdam, 1745), 174, 189.

48. [Claude Helvétius], *De l'esprit* (Paris, 1758), 73. More generally on Helvétius, see David Wooton, "Helvétius: From Radical Enlightenment to Revolution," *Political Theory* 28 (June 2000): 307–336.

49. [Helvétius], *De l'esprit*, 53.

50. [Diderot], *Principes*, 241–242.

51. [Diderot], *Principes*, 243.

52. Diderot, "*Éloge de Richardson*," in *Oeuvres Esthétique de Diderot*, ed. Paul Vernière (Paris: Garnier Frères, 1965), 31.

53. See Margaret Cohen, *The Sentimental Education of the Novel* (Princeton, NJ: Princeton University Press, 2018), esp. chap. 1.

54. Jean-Jacques Rousseau, *Julie, or the New Heloise*, in *Collected Writings*, trans. Philip Stewart and Jean Vaché (Hanover, NH: Dartmouth College Press, 2010), 6:97.

55. Rousseau, *Julie, or the New Heloise*, 6:255.

56. On editions, see Robert Darnton, "Readers Respond to Rousseau: The Fabrication of Romantic Sensitivity," in *The Great Cat Massacre and Other Episodes in French Cultural History* (New York: Basic Books, 1984), 242.

57. Rousseau, *Julie, or the New Heloise*, 6:314, 313, 322.

58. Montesquieu, "Dissertation on Roman Politics in Religion," in *Montesquieu: Discourses, Dissertations, and Dialogues on Politics, Science, and Religion*, ed. David Wallace Carrithers and Philip Stewart (Cambridge: Cambridge University Press, 2020), 72, 60.

59. Montesquieu, *The Spirit of the Laws*, trans. and ed. Anne M. Cohler et al. (Cambridge: Cambridge University Press, 1989), xi.

60. Montesquieu, *Spirit of the Laws*, 310.

61. Montesquieu, *Spirit of the Laws*, 317, 10, 325, xli.

62. Montesquieu, *Spirit of the Laws*, xli, 43.

63. Montesquieu, *Spirit of the Laws*, 43, 25, 69, 23.

64. Montesquieu, *Spirit of the Laws*, 468, 472, 459. On Montesquieu and religion, see Rebecca E. Kingston, "Montesquieu on Religion and the Question of Toleration," in *Montesquieu's Science of Politics: Essays on the* Spirit of the Laws, ed. David W. Carrithers, Michael A. Mosher, and Paul A. Rahe (Lanham, MD: Rowman & Littlefield, 2001), 375–408.

65. Interpreters have discovered in him anything from the monarchist to the liberal republican. For an overview, see Annelie de Dijn, "Was Montesquieu a Liberal Republican?" *Review of Politics* 76 (2014): 21–41.

66. Montesquieu, *Spirit of the Laws*, 529.

67. Montesquieu, *Considerations sur les causes de la grandeur des Romains, et de leur decadence* (Paris, 1734), 131.

68. David Bates, *States of War: Enlightenment Origins of the Political* (New York: Columbia University Press, 2012), 137.

69. Gabrielle Radica, "Rousseau," translated by Philip Stewart, in *A Montesquieu Dictionary* [online], directed by Catherine Volpilhac-Auger, ENS Lyon, September 2013. Available online at https://dictionnaire-montesquieu.ens-lyon.fr/en/article/dem-1377669928-en/en. See also, J. Kent Wright, "Rousseau and Montesquieu," in *Thinking with Rousseau: From Machiavelli to Schmitt*, ed. Helena Rosenblatt and Paul Schweigert (Cambridge: Cambridge University Press, 2017), 63.

70. Robert Bellah, "Civil Religion in America," reprinted in *The Religious Situation in America: 1968*, ed. Donald R. Cutler (Boston: Beacon Press, 1968). For a bibliographic survey of the field after twenty years, see James A. Mathisen, "Twenty Years after Bellah: Whatever Happened to American Civil Religion?" *Sociological Analysis* 50.2 (July 1989): 129–146.

71. Ronald Beiner, *Civil Religion: A Dialogue in the History of Political Philosophy* (Cambridge: Cambridge University Press, 2011), 1. See also Richard Tuck, "The Civil Religion of Thomas Hobbes," in *Political Discourse in Early Modern Britain*, ed. Nicholas Phillipson and Quentin Skinner (Cambridge: Cambridge University Press, 1993), 120–138; Mark Silk, "Numa Pompilius and the Idea of Civil Religion in the West," *Journal of the American Academy of Religion* 72 (December 2004): 863–896.

72. See, e.g., Hobbes, *Leviathan*, ed. Noel Malcolm (Oxford: Clarendon Press, 2012), chap. 17.

73. John Locke, *Two Treatises on Government*, ed. Ian Shapiro (New Haven, CT: Yale University Press, 2003), 138.

74. On the plasticity of this term, see Keith Baker, "Enlightenment and the Institution of Society: Notes for a Conceptual History," in *Civil Society: History and Possibilities*, ed. Sudipta Kaviraj and Sunil Khilnani (Cambridge: Cambridge University Press, 2001), 84–104.

75. Samuel Johnson, *A Dictionary of the English Language*, 2nd ed. (London, 1755–56), vol I, s.v. "civil." Italics mine.

76. [Diderot and D'Alembert], *Encyclopédie*, vol. 15 (1765), s.v. "société civile."

77. Johnson, vol. I, s. v. "civil"; [Diderot and D'Alembert], *Encyclopédie*, vol. 3 (1753), s.v. "civilité, politesse, affabilité."

78. John Milton, *Paradise Lost*, ed. Gordon Teskey (New York: Norton, 2005), 291 (12.230–32).

79. [Diderot and D'Alembert], *Encyclopédie*, s.v. "Société (Morale)," 15:256.

80. *Encyclopédie*, s.v. "Société (Morale)," quoted in Baker, "Institution of Society," 90. Italics mine.

81. Machiavelli, *Discourses*, 35 (1.11).

82. Rousseau, "Economie ou Oeconomie (Morale & Politique)," in [Diderot and D'Alembert], *Encyclopédie*, 5:339. For Montesquieu on the general will, see *Spirit of the Laws*, book XI, chap 6.

83. Rousseau, "Economie," 5:340.

84. Rousseau, "Economie," 5:341.

85. Alexandre Deleyre, "Fanatisme," in [Diderot and D'Alembert], *Encyclopédie*, 6: 401. Zev Trachtenberg, "Civic Fanaticism and the Dynamics of Pity," *Rousseau and l'infâme: Religion, Toleration, and Fanaticism in the Age of Enlightenment*, ed. J. T. Scott (Leiden: Brill, 2009), 204.

86. Rousseau, "Economie," 5:342.

87. Jean-Jacques Rousseau, *The Social Contract*, in *The Collected Writings of Rousseau*, ed. Roger D. Masters and Christopher Kelly, trans. Judith R. Bush et al. (Hanover, NH: University Press of New England, 1994), 4:139, 4:142.

88. Rousseau, *Social Contract*, in *Collected Writings*, 4: 150.

89. Rousseau, *Social Contract*, in *Collected Writings*, 4:151.

90. Rousseau, "Political Fragments," in *Collected Writings*, 4:58.

91. Rousseau, "Geneva MS," in *Collected Writings*, 4:117. See Ghislain Waterlot, *Rousseau: religion et politique* (Paris: Presses Universitaires de France, 2004), 5; Michaël Culoma, *La religion civile de Rousseau à Robespierre* (Paris: Harmattan, 2010), 33.

92. Rousseau, "Geneva MS," in *Collected Writings*, 4:104.

93. Culoma, *La religion civile*, 32.

94. Rousseau, *Social Contract*, in *Collected Writings*, 4:219, 220.

95. Rousseau, *Social Contract*, 4:222–223. Italics mine.

96. Rousseau, *Julie, or the New Heloise*, 6:97.

97. Rousseau, *Social Contract*, 4:217–218.

98. Culoma, *La religion civile*, 41, 37.

99. The literature on nationalism and religion is enormous, from its postwar beginnings with works by people like Carleton Hayes (*Nationalism: A Religion* [New York: Macmillan, 1960]) and Jacob Talmon (*Political Messianism: The Romantic Phase* [London: Secker and Warburg, 1960]), through to classics like Ernst Gellner's *Nations and Nationalism* (Oxford: Blackwell, 1983) to a more recent explosion of work on Christian nationalism in early twenty-first century America.

100. Rousseau, *Social Contract*, 4:216.

101. Nicolas Boulanger, "Political Economy," in *Encyclopedic Liberty*, ed. Henry C. Clark (Indianapolis, IN: Liberty Foundation, 2016), 402, 405.

102. Boulanger, "Political Economy," 406, 405, 408, 411.

103. Boulanger, "Political Economy," 413.

104. Boulanger, "Political Economy," 431, 436.

105. Boulanger, "Political Economy," 438.

106. Boulanger, "Political Economy," 438.

107. Boulanger, "Political Economy," 443, 440.

108. Ernst Kantorowicz, *The King's Two Bodies* (Princeton, NJ: Princeton University Press, 1957), 87.

109. Boulanger, "Political Economy," 442, 443, 444, 443. On Boulanger's monarchism, see Annelien de Dijn, "The Politics of Enlightenment: From Peter Gay to Jonathan Israel," *Historical Journal* 55.3 (2012): 785–805.

110. Charles Simon Favart, *Soliman second: Comédie en trois actes* (Paris, 1762), 34.

111. Bell, *Cult of the Nation;* also Edmond Dziembowski, *Un nouveau patriotisme français, 1750–1770: La France face à la puissance anglaise à l'époque de la guerre de*

Sept Ans (Oxford: Voltaire Foundation, 2014), 356–7 (on citizens); 359 (on patriotic zeal).

112. Rossel quoted in Bell, *Cult of the Nation*, 62; Rossel, *Histoire du patriotisme François, ou nouvelle histoire de France* (Paris, 1769)

113. Bell, *Cult of the Nation*, 78–85 (on Jumonville), 87–88 (on state involvement).

114. On the *Siege*, see Dziembowski, *Un nouveau patriotisme*, 472–486.

115. Dziembowski, *Un nouveau patriotisme*, 473.

116. Pierre-Laurent de Belloy, *Le siège de Calais* (Paris, 1765), 63.

117. Quoted in Bell, *Cult of the Nation*, 63.

118. Pierre Réstat, "Citoyen-Sujet, Civisme," in Rolf Reichert and Eberhard Schmitt, *Handbuch politisch-sozialer Grundbegriffe in Frankreich, 1680–1820* (Munich: R. Oldenbourg Verlag, 1988), 9:83.

119. Jay Smith, *Nobility Reimagined: The Patriotic Nation in Eighteenth-Century France* (Ithaca, NY: Cornell University Press, 2005), 41. On Boulainvilliers, see also Nannerl O. Keohane, *Philosophy and the State in France: The Renaissance to the Enlightenment* (Princeton, NJ: Princeton University Press, 1980), 346–350; and more generally, Harold A. Ellis, *Boulainvilliers and the French Monarchy: Aristocratic Politics in Early Eighteenth-Century France* (Ithaca, NY: Cornell University Press, 1988). Beyond France, one could look to the Viscount Bolingbroke and his ideal of the "patriot king." See, e.g., Pocock, *Machiavellian Moment*, 478–486; Isaac Kramnick, *Bolingbroke and His Circle: The Politics of Nostalgia in the Age of Walpole* (Ithaca, NY: Cornell University Press, 1968); but *pace* Kramnick, see David Armitage, "A Patriot for Whom? The Afterlives of Bolingbroke's Patriot King," *Journal of British Studies* 36 (October 1997): 397–418.

120. Teodora Shek Brnardić, "Modality of Enlightened Monarchical Patriotism in the Mid-Eighteenth Century Hapsburg Monarchy," in *Whose Love of Which Country?: Composite States, National Histories, and Patriotic Discourse in Early Modern East Central Europe* (Leiden: Brill, 2010), 631.

121. Eva Piirimäe, "Dying for the Fatherland: Thomas Abbt's Theory of Aesthetic Patriotism," *History of European Ideas* 35.2 (2009): 199.

122. Simon Grote, *The Emergence of Modern Aesthetic Theory: Religion and Morality in Enlightenment Germany and Scotland* (Cambridge: Cambridge University Press, 2017), 240.

123. Quoted in Piirimäe, "Dying for the Fatherland," 202.

124. Thomas Abbt, "Vom Tode für das Vaterland," in *Bibliothek der Geschichte und Politik: Aufklärung und Kriegserfahrung*, ed. Johannes Kunisch (Frankfurt: Suhrkamp, 1996), 614–15.

125. Abbt, "Vom Tode," 611, 600.

126. Benjamin Redekop, *Enlightenment and Community: Lessing, Abbt, Herder, and the Quest for a German Public* (Montreal: McGill-Queen's University Press, 2000), 142. Moses Mendelssohn, review of Abbt, *Briefe die neuste Literatur betreffend* 11 (1761): 43.

127. Abbt, "Vom Tode," 621.

128. *Briefe Friedrich des Großen*, 2:53.

129. Quoted in Piirimäe, "Dying for the Fatherland," 205.

130. Abbt, "Vom Tode," 621.

131. Smith, *Germany*, 93–94, quotation on p. 94.

132. [Johann Gleim], *Preussische Kriegslieder in den Feldzügen 1756 und 1757 von einem Grenadier* (Amsterdam, 1771), 5, 13–14.

133. Klopstock, "Kriegslied, zur Nachahmung des alten Liedes von der Chevy-Chase Jagd," in *The German Classics from the Fourth to the Nineteenth Centuries*, ed. Max Müller (Oxford: Clarendon, 1906), 2:36–37.

134. Abbt, "Vom Tode," 649.

135. Abbt, "Vom Tode," 628.

136. Redekop, *Enlightenment and Community*, 128, see also 138.

137. Abbt, "Vom Tode," 631.

138. Abbt, "Vom Tode," 617.

139. Eckhart Hellmuth, "Die 'Wiedergeburt' Friedrich des Großen and der 'Tod fürs Vaterland': Zum patriotischen Selbstverständnis in Preußen in der zweiten Hälfte des 18. Jahrhunderts," *Aufklärung* 10.2 (1998): 27, 31, 38.

140. More generally on the end of the Seven Years' War and the discontent that followed, see Fred Anderson, *Crucible of War: The Seven Years' War and the Fate of Empire in British North America, 1754–1766* (New York: Knopf, 2000), esp. chapters 66, 69–70.

141. Holger Hoock, *Scars of Independence: America's Violent Birth* (New York: Crown, 2017), 17, 29.

142. Sarah J. Purcell, *Sealed with Blood: War, Sacrifice, and Memory in Revolutionary America* (Philadelphia: University of Pennsylvania Press, 2010), 36.

143. Thomas Brockaway, *America Saved, or Divine Glory displayed* (Hartford, 1784), 19–20.

144. Brockaway, *America Saved*, 22, 23.

145. More generally, see Purcell, *Sealed with Blood*, chap. 2.

146. These short remarks hardly do justice to the ways that sacrifice threaded through the early American project, a deep treatment of which is outside both my own competence and the scope of this book. Minimally, such a treatment would have to explore the violence of conquest, the complex relations with indigenous Americans, and the institution of of chattel slavery. For an important beginning, see Susan Juster, *Sacred Violence in Early America* (Philadelphia: University of Pennsylvania Press, 2018). On the citizenship question, see Douglas Bradburn, *The Citizenship Revolution: Politics and the Creation of the American Union, 1774–1804* (Charlottesville: University of Virginia Press, 2009), and the classic work of James H. Kettner, *The Development of American Citizenship, 1608–1870* (Chapel Hill: University of North Carolina Press, 1978).

147. [Henry St. John, Viscount Bolingbroke], *The Idea of a Patriot King: With Respect to the Constitution of Great Britain* (London, 1740).

148. Louis-Antoine-Léon Saint Just, 13 November 1793, in *Regicide and Revolution: Speeches at the Trial of Louis XVI*, ed. Michael Walzer, trans. Marian Rothstein (Cambridge: Cambridge University Press 1974), 124.

149. Accessed June 2023 at the Avalon Project: https://avalon.law.yale.edu/18th_century/rightsof.asp. On the centrality of the Declaration to the revolutionary

project, see Marcel Gauchet, *La Révolution des droits de l'homme* (Paris: Gallimard, 1989).

150. Peter Sahlins, *Unnaturally French: Foreign Citizens in the Old Regime and After* (Ithaca, NY: Cornell University Press, 2004), 216, 272 (on the 1791 constitution). On citizenship more broadly in the Revolution, see esp. Renée Waldinger et al., eds., *The French Revolution and the Meaning of Citizenship* (Westport, CT: Greenwood Press, 1993) and Raymonde Monnier, *Citoyen et citoyenneté sous la Révolution française* (Paris: Société des études robespierriestes, 2006). On citizenship more broadly, see J.G.A. Pocock, "The Ideal of Citizenship Since Classical Times," in *Theorizing Citizenship*, ed. Ronald Beiner (Albany: SUNY Press, 1994).

151. On the tribunals and the importance of penal law to the revolutionary project, see Carla Hesse's important study, *The People's Justice* (Princeton, NJ: Princeton University Press, forthcoming). My gratitude to her for sharing the manuscript in advance of publication.

152. See especially Hesse, *People's Justice,* chap. 1 on the re-invention of legal institutions in the early Revolution.

153. 1791 Constitution, Title III, chap. 2, accessed at: https://www.conseil-constitutionnel.fr/les-constitutions-dans-l-histoire/constitution-de-1791. Italics mine.

154. Walzer and Rothstein, *Regicide and Revolution*, 112.

155. See, e.g., the Girondin Jean-Baptiste Maihle, writing on 7 November 1792, in Walzer and Rothstein, *Regicide and Revolution*, 97.

156. Saint Just, in Walzer and Rothstein, *Regicide and Revolution*, 121, 125, 123, 124, 122; Robespierre, in *Regicide and Revolution*, 133.

157. Walzer and Rothstein, *Regicide and Revolution*, 104.

158. Robespierre, in Walzer and Rothstein, *Regicide and Revolution*, 132.

159. [Louis-Marie Prudhomme], *Révolutions de Paris, Dédiées à la nation* (Paris, 1793), 15:204. On Prudhomme, see Joseph Zizek, "'Plume de Fer': Louis-Marie Prudhomme Writes the French Revolution," *French Historical Studies* 26 (Fall 2003): 619–660.

160. [Louis-Marie Prudhomme], *Révolutions*, 15:205.

161. [Louis-Marie Prudhomme], *Révolutions*, 15:206, 213.

162. On the revolutionary tribunals as tools of political pedagogy, see Hesse, *People's Justice*, esp. chapters 5 and 8.

163. See, e.g., Patrice Higonnet, *Goodness Beyond Virtue: Jacobins During the French Revolution* (Cambridge, MA: Harvard University Press, 1998), esp. 134–136.

164. Saint Just, speech of 27 December 1792, in Walzer and Rothstein, *Regicide and Revolution*, 167.

165. Saint Just, speech of 27 December 1792, 171.

166. Saint Just, speech of 27 December 1792, 171; Rousseau cited in Carol Blum, *Rousseau and the Republic of Virtue: The Language of Politics in the French Revolution* (Ithaca, NY: Cornell University Press, 1986), 178.

167. Robespierre, 28 December 1792, in Walzer and Rothstein, *Regicide and Revolution*, 179.

168. See Blum, *Rousseau and the Republic of Virtue*, 179; Mona Ozouf, "Public Spirit," in *A Critical Dictionary of the French Revolution*, ed. François Furet and Mona Ozouf, trans. Arthur Goldhammer (Cambridge, MA: Harvard University Press, 1989), 771–779.

169. Mona Ozouf, *Festivals and the French Revolution*, trans. Alan Sheridan (Cambridge, MA: Harvard University Press, 1988), 84.

170. See Jonathan Smyth, *Robespierre and the Festival of the Supreme Being: The Search for Republican Morality* (Manchester: Manchester University Press, 2016), 50–72.

171. Maximilien Robespierre, *Recuil d'hymnes républicains qui ont paru à la occasion de la Fête à l'Être supréme* (Paris, [1793]), 5–6.

172. Robert Simon, "David's Martyr-Portrait of Le Peletier de Saint-Fargeau and the Conundrums of Revolutionary Representation," *Art History* 14.4 (Dec. 1991): 463, 465.

173. Robespiere, quoted in David Andress, "Living the Revolutionary Melodrama: Robespierre's Sensibility and the Construction of Political Commitment in the French Revolution," *Representations* 114 (Spring 2011): 121.

174. Maximilien Robespierre, *Œuvres de Maximilien Robespierre* (Paris: Société des études Robespierristes, 1912–2007), 10:556.

175. See Ronald Schechter, "Terror, Vengeance, and Martyrdom in the French Revolution," in Dominic Janes and Alex Houen, *Martyrdom and Terrorism: Pre-Modern to Contemporary Perspectives* (Oxford: Oxford University Press, 2014), 157–160, 162, 173.

176. Schechter, "Terror, Vengeance," 170, 153, 177.

177. On the manes in Roman antiquity, see Charles King, "The Roman *Manes*: The Dead as Gods," in *Rethinking Ghosts in World Religions*, ed. Mu-Chou Poo (Leiden: Brill, 2009), here, 111; also Charles King, *The Ancient Roman Afterlife:* Di Manes, *Belief, and the Cult of the Dead* (Austin: University of Texas Press, 2009).

178. Joseph de Maistre, *Considerations on France*, ed. and trans. Richard A. Lebrun (Cambridge: Cambridge University Press, 1994), 13.

179. Joseph de Maistre, quoting Johann Jung Stilling, in *St. Petersburg Dialogues*, trans. Richard A. Lebrun (Montreal: McGill-Queen's University Press, 1993), 336, 371.

180. Jesse Goldhammer, *The Headless Republic: Sacrificial Violence in Modern French Thought* (Ithaca, NY: Cornell University Press, 2005), 58, 57, 61. For another version of this, see Ivan Strenski, *Contesting Sacrifice: Religion, Nationalism, and Social Thought in France* (Chicago: University of Chicago Press, 2002), 28–36.

181. Lynn Hunt, *The Family Romance of the French Revolution* (Berkeley: University of California Press, 1992), 9–10.

182. Hunt, *Family Romance*, 10.

183. Goldhammer, *Headless Republic*, 57.

184. Thus, for example, Hunt's quotation is a pastiche taken from over 13 pages of description. This has not stopped it from circulating widely as a definitive version of Prudhomme's views: see, e.g., Susan Dunn, *The Deaths of Louis XVI: Regicide and the French Political Imagination* (Princeton, NJ: Princeton University Press, 1994), 19; Eli Sagan, *Citizens and Cannibals: The French Revolution, The Struggle for Modernity, and the Origins of Ideological Terror* (Lanham, MD: Rowman & Littlefield, 2001), 346; Camil Francisc Roman, "Liminality, the Execution of Louis XVI, and

the Rise of the Terror in the French Revolution," in *Breaking Boundaries: Varieties of Liminality*, ed. Agnes Horvath et al. (New York: Berghan, 2015), 152.

185. Ozouf, *Festivals*, 282; Maistre, *Considerations*, 82 fn.5; Strenski, *Contesting Sacrifice*, 27; Hans Blumenberg, *The Legitimacy of the Modern Age* (Cambridge, MA: MIT Press, 1985), 113.

Chapter 11: The Heteronomy of the Secular

1. T. S. Eliot, "Little Giddings," in *Collected Poems: 1909–1962* (New York: Harcourt, 1963), 205.

2. Igor Stravinsky and Robert Craft, *Expositions and Developments* (Berkeley: University of California Press, 1962), 140; see also Richard Taruskin, *Stravinsky and the Russian Traditions: A Biography of the Works Through Mavra* (Berkeley: University of California Press, 1996), 1:862.

3. Taruskin, *Stravinsky*, 1:864.

4. Andrey Levinson, quoted in Taruskin, *Stravinsky*, 2:1012.

5. Levinson, quoted in Taruskin, *Stravinsky*, 2:1013.

6. Sigmund Freud, *Totem and Taboo*, in *The Standard Edition of the Complete Psychological Works of Sigmund Freud*, ed. James Strachey et al. (London: Hogarth Press, 1955), 13:146.

7. Freud, *Totem and Taboo*, 13:150–151.

8. Freud, *Future of an Illusion*, in *Standard Edition*, 21:17, 18.

9. See, e.g., Joseph M. Levine, *The Battle of the Books: History and Literature in the Augustan Age* (Ithaca, NY: Cornell University Press, 1991); Dan Edelstein, *The Enlightenment: A Genealogy* (Chicago: University of Chicago Press, 2010).

10. My thinking here is especially indebted to the work of literary scholars Victoria Kahn and Daniel Weidner. For the metaphor of *spolia*, see Weidner, *Rhetorik der Säkularisierung: Über eine Denkfigur der Moderne* (Frankfurt: Campus Verlag, 2024), 195. More generally, see Kahn, *The Trouble with Literature* (Oxford: Oxford University Press, 2020).

11. Here I found very useful Edward Said's framing in "On Repetition," *The World, the Text, and the Critic* (Cambridge, MA: Harvard University Press, 1983), 111–125.

12. Voltaire, "Abraham," in *Dictionnaire philosophique*, in *Oeuvres completes de Voltaire* (Paris: Dupont, 1823), 36:66.

13. [Anon.], *Letters, viz . . . That God was not the First Institutor of Sacrifices* (London, 1737), 48.

14. See Ronald Green, "Kant," in *Interpreting Abraham: Journeys to Moriah*, ed. Bradley Beach and Matthew T. Powell (Minneapolis, MN: Fortress Press, 2014), 87–100.

15. Immanuel Kant, *The Conflict of the Faculties*, in *Religion and Rational Theology*, ed. and trans. Allen W. Wood (Cambridge: Cambridge University Press, 1996), 283. See also *Religion within the Bounds of Mere Reason*, in *Religion and Rational Theology*, 124.

16. Green, "Kant," 90.

17. There is a robust discussion of whether and how sacrifice functions in Kant's broader ethics: see, e.g., Paolo Diego Bubbio, *Sacrifice in the Post-Kantian Tradition:*

Perspectivism, Intersubjectivity, and Recognition (Albany: State University of New York Press, 2014), here esp. 27–28. Also Sidney Axinn, *Sacrifice and Value: A Kantian Interpretation* (Lanham, MD: Lexington, 2010).

18. Theodosius quoted in Isabel Speyart von Woerden, "The Iconography of the Sacrifice of Abraham," *Vigiliae Christianae* 15.4 (December 1961): 229, fn.42.

19. Martin Luther, *Lectures on Genesis, Chapters 21–25*, in *Works*, ed. Jaroslav Pelikan (Saint Louis, MO: Concordia, 1964), 4:118.

20. Georg Wilhelm Friedrich Hegel, "The Tübingen Essay," in *Three Essays, 1793–1795*, ed. and trans. Peter Fuss and John Dobbins (Notre Dame, IN: University of Notre Dame Press, 1984), 53. On the Tübingen essay, see Thomas Lewis, *Religion, Modernity, and Politics in Hegel* (Oxford: Oxford University Press, 2011), 25–44.

21. See Paolo Bubbio, "Sacrifice in Hegel's *Phenomenology of Spirit*," *British Journal for the History of Philosophy* 20.4 (July 2012): 797–815. Also my "In the Christian Archives: Sacrifice, the Higher Criticism, and the History of Religion," *Modern Intellectual History* 19 (December 2022): 1208–1226.

22. G.W.F. Hegel, *Phenomenology of Spirit*, trans. A. V. Miller (Oxford: Oxford University Press, 1977), 49, 114.

23. Hegel, *Phenomenology*, 137–138.

24. Hegel, *Phenomenology*, 432.

25. G.W.F. Hegel, *Lectures on the Philosophy of Religion. Volume I. Introduction in the Concept of Religion*, ed. Peter C. Hodgson, trans. R. F. Brown et al. (Berkeley: University of California Press, 1984), 353.

26. Hegel, *Phenomenology*, 432, 434.

27. On this process, see Terry Pinkard, *Hegel's Phenomenology: The Sociality of Reason* (Cambridge: Cambridge University Press, 1994), 239.

28. Hegel, *Phenomenology*, 492.

29. Jeremy Bentham, *An Introduction to the Principles of Morals and Legislation*, ed. J. H. Burns and H.L.A. Hart (London: Athlone Press, 1970), 285, 284. First edition, 1789.

30. John Stuart Mill, *Utilitarianism* (London: Parker, Son, and Bourn, 1863), 24. Italics mine.

31. See, e.g., Charles Darwin, *The Descent of Man* (1871; reprint, Princeton, NJ: Princeton University Press, 1981), 70, 163 (on "survival of the fittest").

32. Benjamin Kidd, *Social Evolution* (New York: Macmillan, 1894), 125. Westermarck quoted in Susan L. Mizruchi, *The Science of Sacrifice: American Literature and Modern Social Theory* (Princeton, NJ: Princeton University Press, 1998), 259. On Kidd, see Mizruchi, *Science of Sacrifice*, 241–242.

33. See, e.g., William MacAskill, *What We Owe to the Future* (New York: Basic Books, 2022). My thanks to Jacob Sheehan for discussions of EA.

34. Søren Kierkegaard, *Fear and Trembling*, trans. Howard V. Hong and Edna H. Hong (Princeton, NJ: Princeton University Press, 1983), 39.

35. Kierkegaard, *Fear and Trembling*, 37.

36. Kierkegaard, *Fear and Trembling*, 74.

37. Kierkegaard, *Fear and Trembling*, 61 (on tragic heroes, see 57–59).

38. Kierkegaard, *Fear and Trembling*, 55.

39. Jesse Goldhammer, *The Headless Republic: Sacrificial Violence in Modern French Thought* (Ithaca, NY: Cornell University Press, 2005), 119.

40. Alan Sokel, introduction to *Visions of Excess: Selected Writings, 1927–1939* (Minneapolis: University of Minnesota Press, 1985), xi, xx.

41. Bataille, "Sacrifices," in Sokel, *Visions of Excess*, 132.

42. More generally, see my *The Enlightenment Bible: Translation, Scholarship, Culture* (Princeton, NJ: Princeton University Press, 2005).

43. Voltaire, "Abraham," *Dictionnaire philosophique*, in *Oeuvres completes*, 36:67; Voltaire quoted in Marco Piazza, *Voltaire Against the Jews, or the Limits of Toleration* (Cham, Switzerland: Springer, 2022), 96.

44. See Anders Gerdmar, *Roots of Theological Anti-Semitism: German Biblical Interpretation and the Jews, from Herder and Semler to Kittel and Bultmann* (Leiden: Brill, 2009), 44–46.

45. Adam Sutcliffe, *Judaism and Enlightenment* (New York: Cambridge University Press, 2003), 5. More generally, see David Nirenberg, *Anti-Judaism: The Western Tradition* (New York: Norton, 2013).

46. Jan Rohls, "Historical, Cultural and Philosophical Aspects of the Nineteenth Century with Special Regard to Biblical Interpretation," in *Hebrew Bible/Old Testament: The History of Its Interpretation*, ed. Magne Saebø (Göttingen: Vandenhoeck & Ruprecht, 2013), 3.1:41.

47. Friedrich Schleiermacher, *Kurze Darstellung des theologischen Studiums* (Berlin: Realschulbuchhandlung, 1811), 33–34.

48. Johann Gottfried Eichhorn, *Einleitung ins Alte Testament* (Leipzig, 1787), 1: vi. See also Thomas Römer, "'Higher Criticism': The Historical and Literary-critical Approach with Special Reference to the Pentateuch," in *Hebrew Bible/Old Testament: The History of Its Interpretation*, ed. Magne Saebø, vol. 3/1 (Göttingen, 2013), 393–423.

49. Eichhorn, *Einleitung*, 1: iii, iv, 15, 22, 21.

50. On de Wette, see John Rogerson, *W. M. L. de Wette, Founder of Modern Biblical Criticism* (Sheffield: Sheffield Academic Press, 1992) and *Old Testament Criticism in the Nineteenth Century: England and Germany* (London: SPCK, 1994); also Thomas Römer, "'Higher Criticism': The Historical and Literary-critical Approach–with Special Reference to the Pentateuch," in Saebø, ed., *Hebrew Bible/Old Testament*, 393–423.

51. Wilhelm de Wette, *Beiträge zur Einleitung in das Alte Testament* (Halle, 1806), 4, 6.

52. De Wette, *Beiträge*, 53.

53. De Wette, *Beiträge*, 4–5.

54. De Wette, *Beiträge*, 255.

55. Rogerson, *Old Testament Criticism*, 43.

56. Suzanne Marchand, *German Orientalism in the Age of Empire: Religion, Race, and Scholarship* (Cambridge: Cambridge University Press, 2009), 106.

57. More broadly, and for bibliographies, see the collection of essays in *Hebrew Bible/Old Testament*, ed. Magne Saebø, vol. 3.1.

58. Julius Wellhausen, *Prolegomena zur Geschichte Israels* (Berlin, 1883), 4, 65–66, 72, 74, 75, 79, 81. All citations will be to this text, technically the second edition of the *Geschichte Israels* (1878), though published with a new title.

59. Wellhausen, *Prolegomena*, 3, 4.

60. Wellhausen, *Prolegomena*, 58, 61. For Wellhausen, Jeremiah was a pre-exilic prophet.

61. Wellhausen, *Prolegomena*, 62, 105, 106.

62. Wellhausen, *Prolegomena*, 422, 427, emphasis added.

63. Here, see my "In the Christian Archives," esp. 1220–1221.

64. Mizruchi, *Science of Sacrifice*, 42; on Nietzsche as a reader of Wellhausen, see Andreas Urs Sommer, *Kommentar zu Nietzsches Der Antichrist, Ecce Homo, Dionysos-Dithyramben, und Nietzsche contra Wagner* (Berlin and Boston: De Gruyter, 2013), 129–136.

65. Friedrich Nietzsche, *Twilight of the Idols and the Anti-Christ*, trans. R. J. Hollingdale (London: Penguin, 2003), 150 (§26), 146 (§24).

66. Nietzsche, *Twilight*, 165–66 (§41).

67. On the ironies of philology, Nietzschean and otherwise, see Henning Trüper, *Orientalism, Philology, and the Illegibility of the Modern World* (London: Bloomsbury, 2020), chap. 1.

68. Schleiermacher quoted in Sheehan, *Enlightenment Bible*, 235.

69. W.M.L. de Wette, "Über den Verfall der protestantischen Kirche in Deutschland," in *Reformations Almanach für Luthers Verehrer auf das evangelische Jubeljahr 1817*, ed. Friedrich Keyser (Erfurt: Keyser, 1817), 332.

70. On the history, see Susannah Heschel, *Abraham Geiger and the Jewish Jesus* (Chicago: University of Chicago Press, 1998). For some of the current debates, see the many works of Daniel Boyarin, esp. *A Radical Jew: Paul and the Politics of Identity* (Berkeley: University of California Press, 1994) and *Border Lines: The Partition of Judaeo-Christianity* (Philadelphia: University of Pennsylvania Press, 2004).

71. Voltaire, "Abraham," in *Dictionnaire philosophique* in *Oeuvres completes*, 36:67.

72. Georg Friedrich Daumer, *Sabbath, Moloch, und Tabu: Eine historisch-theologische Andeutung* (Nuremberg: Bauer and Raspe, 1839); *Feuer- und Molochdienst der alten Hebräer* (Braunschweig: Otto, 1842); *Die Geheimnisse der christlichen Alterthums* (Hamburg: Hoffmann and Campe, 1847), 2 vols. On Daumer, see Paul Lawrence Rose, *German Question/Jewish Question: Revolutionary Antisemitism from Kant to Wagner* (Princeton, NJ: Princeton University Press, 1990), 255–257; Scott Spector, *Violent Sensations: Sex, Crime and Utopia in Vienna and Berlin, 1860–1914* (Chicago: University of Chicago Press, 2016), 229–231.

73. Friedrich Ghillany, *Die Menschenopfer der alten Hebräer* (Nuremberg: Johann Leonhard Schrag, 1842), see, e.g., 4, 63, 145 (Vatke), 263.

74. On the long history of the blood libel, see Magda Teter, *Blood Libel: On the Trail of an Antisemitic Myth* (Cambridge, MA: Harvard University Press, 2020).

75. Daumer, *Feuer- und Molochdienst*, 76. On the Damascus affair, Daumer, and Ghillany, see Jonathan Frankel, *The Damascus Affair: "Ritual Murder," Politics, and the Jews in 1840* (Cambridge: Cambridge University Press, 1997), 412–415.

76. G. Fr. Daumer, in *Ausgewählte Briefe von und an Ludwig Feuerbach*, ed. Wilhelm Colin (Leipzig: Otto Wigand, 1904), 2:98 (letter 132). On the Purim accusations, see Elliott Horowitz, *Reckless Rites: Purim and the Legacy of Jewish Violence* (Princeton, NJ: Princeton University Press, 2018), 218–221.

77. Daumer to Feuerbach, in *Briefe*, 2: 96. On Christian blood cults, see Daumer, *Die Geheimnisse des christlichen Alterthums*.

78. Ludwig Feuerbach, *Das Wesen des Christenthums* (Leipzig: Otto Wigand, 1841), 372, 369.

79. Michel-Rolph Trouillot, "Anthropology and the Savage Slot: The Poetics and Politics of Otherness," in *Trouillot Remixed: The Michel-Rolph Trouillot Reader*, ed. Yarimar Bonilla et al. (Durham, NC: Duke University Press, 2021), 53–84.

80. There is a vast literature here. On the German case, see Karl-Heinz Kohl, "Ethnology and the Ambiguity of German Colonialism," in *Bérose: Encyclopédie Internationale des histoires de l'anthropologie* (Paris, 2019) (https://www.berose.fr/article1773.html), and Andrew Zimmerman, *Anthropology and Antihumanism in Imperial Germany* (Chicago: University of Chicago Press, 2001). More generally see George W. Stocking, Jr., *Victorian Anthropology* (New York: Free Press, 1987) and *After Tylor: British Social Anthropology 1888–1951* (Madison: University of Wisconsin Press, 1995).

81. Bernard and Picart, *Cérémonies et coutumes religieuses de tous les peuples du monde* (Amsterdam, 1723), 2.1: 24–25. Along these lines, it is remarkable how *little* early moderns paid attention to the largest ongoing sacrificial feast in the world, the festival of *Eid-al Ada*, the Muslim feast honoring Abraham's sacrifice. Bernard and Picart devote almost no attention to this rite in their volume on Islam (see brief mentions at 5:259, 260).

82. On the nineteenth-century *sati* debates, see Lata Mani, *Contentious Traditions: The Debate on* Sati *in Colonial India* (Berkeley: University of California Press, 1998). On *sati* as a practice, see Catherine Weinberger-Thomas, *Ashes of Immortality: Widow-Burning in India* (Chicago: University of Chicago Press, 1999).

83. Article in the *Friend of India* missionary journal, reprinted in Andrea Major, ed., *Sati: A Historical Anthology* (New Delhi: Oxford University Press, 2007), see esp. 89.

84. On hookswinging, see Nicholas B. Dirks, "The Policing of Tradition: Colonialism and Anthropology in Southern India," *Comparative Studies in Society and History* 39 (Jan. 1997): 182–221; on Jagannath, see Ujaan Ghosh, "Chariots of the Gods," *History of Religions* 58 (Aug. 2018): 64–88. My thanks to Abhishek Kaicker for these references and broader suggestions.

85. The intimacy of colonialism, Christianity, and the nineteenth-century human sciences is by now well known. What would seem even more important at this point would be to coordinate this with a "ground-up" account of the colonized, one that treated their traditions as I have tried to treat Christianity, namely as themselves richly varied and historically dynamic. On the first issue, however, i.e., Jean Comaroff and John L. Comaroff, *Of Revelation and Revolution: Christianity, Colonialism, and Consciousness in South Africa* (Chicago: University of Chicago Press, 1991); Tomoko Masuzawa, *The Invention of World Religion, or, How European Universalism Was Preserved in the Language of Pluralism* (Chicago: University of Chicago Press, 2005); Talal Asad, *Genealogies of Religion: Discipline and Reasons of Power in Christianity and Islam* (Baltimore, MD: Johns Hopkins University Press, 1993); S. N. Balagangadhara, *'The Heathen in His Blindness . . .': Asia, the West, and the Dynamic of Religion* (Leiden: Brill, 1994).

86. Tylor quoted in Stocking, *Victorian Anthropology*, 192.

87. Edward Tylor, *Primitive Culture: Researches into the Development of Mythology, Philosophy, Religion, Art, and Custom* (London: John Murray, 1871), 2:109.

88. Tylor, *Primitive Culture*, 2:109, 2:341.

89. Tylor, *Primitive Culture*, 2:347, 350.

90. Tylor, *Primitive Culture*, 2:356.

91. See Tylor, *Primitive Culture*, 2:359 for self-abnegation.

92. Anthony Symondson, Richard J. Helmstadter, and Bernard Lightman, eds., *Victorian Faith in Crisis: Essays on Continuity and Change in Nineteenth-Century Religious Belief* (London: Macmillan, 1990).

93. William Robertson Smith, "Sacrifice," in *Encyclopedia Britannica*, 9th ed. (Edinburgh: Adam and Charles Black, 1886), 133, 134.

94. William Robertson Smith, *Lectures on the Religion of the Semites* (New York: Dutton, 1889), 234, 236, 247.

95. For an extended argument along these lines, see Robert Yelle, "From Sovereignty to Solidarity: Some Transformations in the Politics of Sacrifice from the Reformation to Robertson Smith," *History of Religions* 58 (Feb. 2019): 319–346.

96. Henry Sumner Maine, *Ancient Law, Its Connection with the Early History of Society, and Its Relation to Modern Ideas* ([1861]; London: John Murray, 1870), 131.

97. Numa Denis Fustel de Coulanges, *The Ancient City: A Study on the Religion, Laws, and Institutions of Greece and Rome* (Boston: Lee and Shepherd, 1874), 177.

98. Robert Alun Jones, *The Secret of the Totem: Religion and Society from McLennan to Freud* (Ithaca, NY: Cornell University Press, 2005), 45ff.

99. John McClellan, "The Worship of Plants and Animals," *Fortnightly Review* (London: Chapman and Hall, 1869), 6:408, and 7:213.

100. For Robertson Smith on the totem generally, see Jones, *The Secret of the Totem*, chap. 2.

101. Robertson Smith, *Lectures*, 212, 260.

102. Robertson Smith, *Lectures*, 260.

103. Robertson Smith, "Sacrifice," 1135.

104. Robert Ackerman, *J. G. Frazer: His Life and Work* (Cambridge: Cambridge University Press, 1987), 62, 57 (quotation).

105. J. G. Frazer, *The Golden Bough: A Study in Magic and Religion*, 2nd ed. (London: Macmillan, 1900), 1:2, 1:3, 1:7.

106. Maine, *Ancient Law*, 10, 6.

107. Maine, *Ancient Law*, 16.

108. Theodor Mommsen, *Römische Staatsrecht* (Leipzig: S. Hirzel, 1877), 2.1:12.

109. Frazer, *Golden Bough*, 1:7, 1:8.

110. Frazer, *Golden Bough*, 2:33, 34, 33, 46, 49.

111. Frazer, *Golden Bough*, 3:139, 140–141.

112. Tylor, *Primitive Culture*, 2:31.

113. Tylor, *Primitive Culture*, 38, 110, 365, 400 (quotation).

114. Frazer, *Golden Bough*, 3:40.

115. Henri Huber and Marcel Mauss, *Sacrifice: Its Nature and Functions* (Chicago: University of Chicago Press, 1964), 101. The essay was first published in volume 2 of Durkheim's journal *L'Ánnee sociologique* (1897/98).

116. Huber and Mauss, *Sacrifice*, chap. 1.

117. Huber and Mauss, *Sacrifice*, 97, 99.

118. Huber and Mauss, *Sacrifice*, 102.

119. On Durkheim as a reader of Robertson Smith, see Robert Alun Jones, "Robertson Smith, Durkheim, and Sacrifice: An Historical Context for *The Elementary*

Forms of the Religious Life," *Journal of the History of the Behavioral Sciences* 17 (1981): 184–205.

120. Émile Durkheim, *The Elementary Forms of the Religious Life*, trans. Karen E. Fields (New York: Free Press, 1995), 208, 209, 211, 213.

121. Durkheim, *Elementary Forms*, 342, 351, 352.

122. Robertson Smith, *Lectures*, 240.

123. Sigmund Freud, *Moses and Monotheism* in *Standard Edition*, 23:86.

124. James Joyce, *Ulysses*, ed. Hans Walter Gabler et al. (New York: Vintage, 1986).

125. Jan Assmann, *Moses the Egyptian: The Memory of Egypt in Western Monotheism* (Cambridge, MA: Harvard University Press, 1997), 1.

126. G. Spencer Brown, *Laws of Form* (New York: E. P. Dutton, 1972), xxix. First edition, 1969.

127. Nancy Levene, *Powers of Distinction: On Religion and Modernity* (Chicago: University of Chicago Press, 2017), 9, 8, 7.

128. Levene, *Powers*, 51.

129. Talal Asad, *Genealogies of Religion*, 13.

130. Paul Kahn, *Sacred Violence: Torture, Terror, Sovereignty* (Ann Arbor: University of Michigan Press, 2007), 173.

131. For some useful work in these areas, see: Jean Bethke Elstain, "Sovereignty, Identity, Sacrifice," *Social Research* 58 (Fall 1991): 545–564; William Pietz, "The Spirit of Civilization: Blood Sacrifice and Monetary Debt," *RES: Anthropology and Aesthetics* 28 (Autumn 1995): 23–38; Mizruchi, *The Science of Sacrifice*; Drew Gilpin Faust, *This Republic of Suffering: Death and the American Civil War* (New York: Knopf, 2008); Alex Houen and Jan-Melissa Schramm, eds., *Sacrifice and Modern War Literature: The Battle of Waterloo to the War on Terror* (Oxford: Oxford University Press, 2018); Jake Dyble, "General Average, Human Jettison, and the Status of Slaves in Early Modern Europe," *Historical Journal* 65 (2022): 1197–1220.

132. Kahn, *Sacred Violence*, 241.

133. See Paul Kahn, *Putting Liberalism in Its Place* (Princeton, NJ: Princeton University Press, 2005), esp. chap. 2. De Maistre already made a similar argument in the early nineteenth century (see "Elucidation on Sacrifices," p. 371). But see also, e.g., Juan Donoso Cortés, *Ensayo sobre el catolocismo, el liberalismo, y el socialismo* (Madrid: La Publicidad, 1851); Giorgo Agamben, *Homo Sacer: Sovereign Power and Bare Life* (Stanford, CA: Stanford University Press, 1995); Terry Eagleton, *Radical Sacrifice* (New Haven, CT: Yale University Press, 2018).

134. John Milton, *Paradise Lost*, 5.859–860.

135. T. S. Eliot, "Little Giddings," 205. I have learned much about Eliot from Katherine Booska.

136. T. S. Eliot, "Little Giddings," 206.

INDEX

Page numbers in *italics* denote figures.

A NOTE ON THE TYPE

THIS BOOK has been composed in Miller, a Scotch Roman typeface designed by Matthew Carter and first released by Font Bureau in 1997. It resembles Monticello, the typeface developed for The Papers of Thomas Jefferson in the 1940s by C. H. Griffith and P. J. Conkwright and reinterpreted in digital form by Carter in 2003.

Pleasant Jefferson ("P. J.") Conkwright (1905–1986) was Typographer at Princeton University Press from 1939 to 1970. He was an acclaimed book designer and AIGA Medalist.